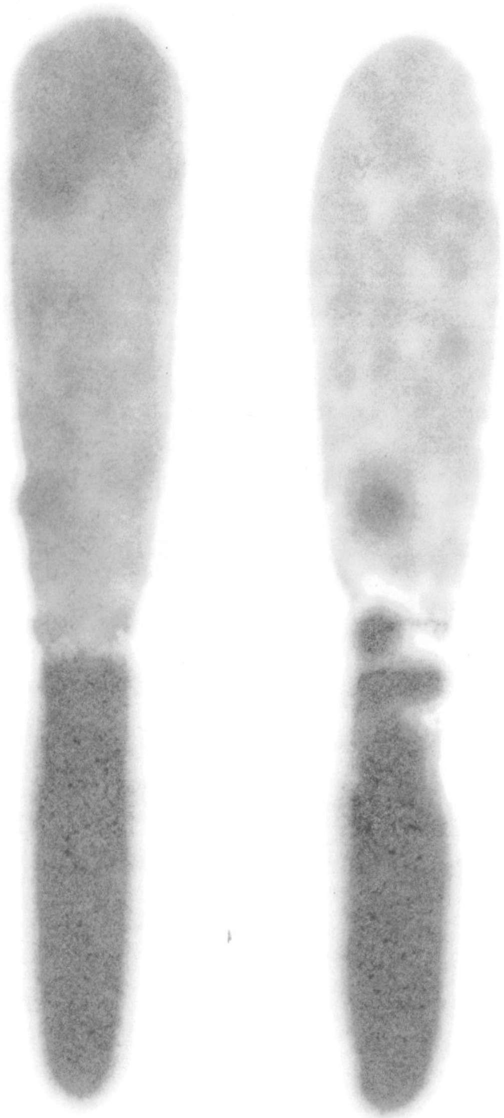

Investment Analysis and Securities Markets

INVESTMENT ANALYSIS AND SECURITIES MARKETS

Morris Mendelson
&
Sidney Robbins

Basic Books, Inc., Publishers
New York

Library of Congress Cataloging in Publication Data

Mendelson, Morris.
Investment analysis and securities markets.

Bibliography: p.
Includes index.
1. Investment analysis. 2. Securities.
I. Robbins, Sidney M., joint author. II. Title.
HG4539.M37 332.6′7 75-36776
ISBN 0-465-03594-9

Printed in the United States of America
Designed by Vincent Torre
76 77 78 79 80 10 9 8 7 6 5 4 3 2 1

To the Mendelson children

Jacqueline and Bruce

and the Robbins children

Seth, Lois, Joan, Kim, and Mark

CONTENTS

Part Four

ANALYZING FIXED-INCOME SECURITIES

Part Five

ALTERNATIVE INVESTMENT METHODS AND TECHNIQUES

PREFACE

It is to be expected that the authors of a textbook want to provide something that other books in the same area do not. In our case, there are several somethings.

We give more attention than is common to the securities markets. Institutional money managers now work closely with their traders to implement investment decisions. The procedures followed not only affect particular transactions but also could influence the general market and the price obtained by individual investors. It is imperative, therefore, to understand the economic and legal developments that are pressing toward a major restructuring of the markets.

Accounting occupies a comparatively important niche in our presentation. Both the SEC and the accounting regulatory bodies give weight to accounting disclosures that are helpful to investment decisions. It is desirable that the analyst be able to interpret this information and to make allowances for the financial implications of differences in the accounting policies pursued by corporations.

In recognition of the enhanced stature of options as a result of their being listed on exchanges, we have included a chapter on how options are traded and the strategies that have been formulated for their use.

Theoretical developments of recent vintage have contributed a good deal to a better understanding of the securities markets. We devote two chapters, specifically, to these developments and, in general, have endeavored to incorporate the ideas into applied investment practices. The outcome, we hope, is a text that provides the background of theory, institutional description, and analytic techniques requisite for operating in the modern investment world.

We consider it a privilege to use this preface as a medium to thank those who contributed in some particular way to the writing of our book.

Leon Levy, chairman of Oppenheimer & Co., Inc. and president of the Oppenheimer mutual funds, made available to us the rich talents of the Oppenheimer organization, an acknowledged industry leader in research and execution capacity. Bernard Garil, vice-president of Oppenheimer & Co., Inc. and assistant to the managing partner, read the entire text and made numerous insightful suggestions. Robert Galli, secretary of the Oppenheimer mutual funds, critically reviewed the chapter on investment companies.

In other areas, we were also fortunate in being able to consult with leading specialists, including various members of the New York and American Stock Exchanges and Fred Siesel of Weeden & Co. Professor Walter Werner, Columbia University School of Law, advised in the legal area. The chapter on *Protecting Investors* is largely based on an address given by Robert H. Mundheim, Fred Carr Professor of Financial Institutions and Law, University of Pennsylvania Law School. James R. Longstreet, Professor of Finance, University of South Florida, helped in the chapters on taxation and technical analysis. Carl Nelson, George O. May Professor of Financial Accounting, Graduate School of Business, Columbia University; Carl Bastable, Professor of Accounting, Graduate School of Business, Columbia University; and Lewis Jordan, Professor of Accounting and Assistant Dean of the Graduate School of Business Administration, Fordham University, counseled in the preparation of the accounting chapters. Edward W. Brennen, Associate Professor of Accounting, Wharton School, University of Pennsylvania, provided advice on the taxation chapter. Daniel Rie, Assistant Professor of Finance, also of the Wharton School, and Martin J. Whitman, president of M. J. Whitman, Inc., helped to clarify a number of points. The discussion on interest on interest (see pp. 434-440) draws upon *Inside the Yield Book*, a pioneering study in this field; we therefore would like to acknowledge our intellectual debt to its authors, Sidney Horner and Dr. Martin L. Leibowitz. Richard Carrigan, a partner of the Tortoise Fund, and Kurt Hiebaum, option arbitrageur at Drexel Burnham & Co., gave guidance in the option chapter. Maryrose Miller, reference librarian, Watson Library of Business and Economics, Columbia University, used her extensive knowledge of source material to comment on the chapter on sources of information. Bert Tyler of Gelberg & Tyler Associates generously provided programming assistance.

We were fortunate to receive permission from the Institute of Chartered Financial Analysts to use or adapt questions and problems prepared for the Chartered Financial Analyst Candidate Study and Examination Program.

In the course of the book's preparation, various research assistants provided help in the development of the analytic sections. Among them are: Jose Esejo, now an assistant professor at Duke University; Salvator P. Kami Twegasira, a Ph.D. candidate at Columbia University; and Esther Yip, now assistant product manager at Union Carbide. As is invariably the case, the secretarial pressures were acute. In this regard, special mention is made of Adlinna Liang, now a student at the Graduate School of Business, Columbia University, and Kim Robbins, now a student at New York Medical College. Neither quailed when the going got really rough.

Investment Analysis
and
Securities Markets

INTRODUCTION

What Is Securities Management?

A LOGICAL QUESTION

"Why don't experts in securities management use their knowledge to get rich themselves, instead of giving advice to other people?"

Mr. Jones wants to learn how the securities markets operate, and how he should invest his money; since he is just beginning the study of this field, his question seems logical to him. The "expert," he reasons, must have special skills in buying and selling securities; why, then, does he waste his time advising others when he could make a fortune for himself by practicing in the securities markets what he preaches to his clients?

THE ANSWER

Mr. Jones's question is not a new one; it reflects a common misunderstanding of investment problems. It is based on the implicit assumption that, as in the physical sciences, certain principles exist in the securities field that if applied correctly will produce consistent results. The facts prove otherwise.

Securities analysis is primarily concerned with gauging the effects that future developments will have on the operations of business firms and the reactions of the investment community to these outcomes. The efforts of the analyst, therefore, are directed to probing the future. Thus, he or she deals with uncertainties rather than with unchanging relations.

More than 50 years ago, a distinguished economist, Frank Knight, set in motion a major analytic trend by his study of risk, which he defined as measurable uncertainty.[1] In the securities field, Knight's theories paved the way for the modern notion that the role of the analyst is to value a security in the light of this element of risk. Much of the analyst's effort, therefore, is devoted to evaluating relative return against relative risk, so that the investor can select a course of action best suited to his or her needs.

Uncertainty implies a wide range of possible outcomes, a meaning that is conveyed in the concept of variability. Later in the book we shall discuss the statistical devices that have been used to measure risk. For the present, it is sufficient to know that variability has become a widely accepted surrogate term for risk.

The effect of this emphasis on risk is seen in the changing attitudes of analysts as the economic scene has changed. During the great bull market of the 1960s, the stress was on performance, and analysts leaned toward the selection of risky securities that were likely to outperform the market average. Following the devastating market experience of 1973 their perspective shifted; by mid-1974 the flag of conservatism was flying high. Reflecting this investment metamorphosis, echoes of an ancient term once more were heard in the canyons of Wall Street—preservation of capital.[2]

Securities analysis may be viewed as an intellectual discipline that provides individuals and institutions with the quantitative standards for selecting securities that meet their investment objectives. Over the years, this means that the emphasis on security types varies with the nature of the economic environment and the financial condition of the investor. Sometimes the assumption of risk will be in the foreground; under different circumstances, it will be relegated to the rear. In any event, the techniques of securities analysis are not so foolproof that their application in a world of uncertainty affords any assurance that even a risk-assuming investor will get rich. Nevertheless, securities are selected for their monetary returns, and therefore the question of getting rich cannot be dismissed entirely.

GETTING RICH

There are a number of ways to make a fortune. Probably the most common is sheer luck. The senior partner in a major investment firm, for example, likes to tell about the beginnings of his fortune. In the spring of 1942 he entered the U.S. Army. As a bachelor, he had no family responsibilities and decided to convert all his assets to common stock. Since he was risking his life, he reasoned, he might as well risk his money. If he was killed, the outcome of his transactions would be of no consequence; if he lived and lost heavily, his relief at surviving would more than compensate for his financial losses; if he survived and his stock prices were higher, he would be doubly fortunate. Five years later he was not only discharged as a colonel but also found that the value of his purchases had risen enormously. As he puts it, "I made more money while away from Wall Street than I had ever made before." Consider also how Dame Luck smiled on those in 1960 who bought the stock of Ling-Altec Electronics Inc. (then a modest-sized specialty company and not yet the giant conglomerate Ling-Temco-Vought) and held it for the next half-dozen years, or who bought Xerox, which had just produced its first desk-sized copying machine. More than analytic skill was necessary to predict in that early year the vast changes ahead for both these companies.

Some people have made large fortunes by having access to investment opportunities that were not available to the general public. If Mr. Jones is a scientist and invents a product which he correctly anticipates will have a substantial market, he can organize a firm, incorporate it, and eventually sell it to a larger firm or to the public. This kind of opportunity may not do many others besides Mr. Jones much good. Regardless of how astute an investor may be, he cannot purchase a security until it is publicly offered.[3] When the security becomes generally available, most of the profits may already have been realized, although, as we shall see later, this is not necessarily the case.

In his delightful book *The Money Game*, "Adam Smith" refers to this method as the "marvel of market capitalization of public ownership." He tells the story of Max Palevsky, a longtime graduate student in philosophy, who, fatigued by his academic exercises, moved to industry in the developing field of computers. After acquiring some modest experience with several companies, he obtained $920,000 from a venture-capital firm, invested $80,000 of his own, and started Scientific Data Systems, specializing in small computers. Within a relatively short period, the company began to make some money. A portion of the stock was sold to the public, and the market capitalized the company's earnings at a figure that produced a paper value of $50 million. That, according to Smith, made Max Palevsky's original investment of $80,000 worth somewhat less than $10 million; by the time Smith's book was written, the figure had leaped to about $50 million.[4]

A third road to riches that Mr. Jones might take is making highly risky investments. Some people would call it speculation. To take a classic case, in 1942 the Tri-Continental warrants seemed to have little intrinsic value and were selling at only 3 cents apiece. (See pp. 613-616 for a discussion of warrants.) At that time, the possibility of their achieving any real worth seemed remote. A bold speculator, however, might have been attracted by the fact that their duration was perpetual. After all, much can happen when time is open-ended. Had he then decided to buy $1,000 of the warrants, he would have been worth $1.5 million in 1965 as a result of this single purchase.

If thousands of Mr. Joneses took the speculative road, the average Mr. Jones would make out quite well, much better in fact than the typical investor. A few of the Mr. Joneses would achieve spectacular results, but for others the results would be disastrous. There is no way of knowing in advance which Mr. Jones one is likely to be. The riskier the road, the higher the earnings that may be expected but the greater the likelihood of catastrophe. If there were a scientific means of choosing securities that would yield exceptionally high returns without commensurate risk, the demand for those securities would be so great that their prices would rise high enough to make the expected rate of return no better than on other securities of comparable risk.

THE MAJOR PURPOSES OF SECURITIES MANAGEMENT

The function of securities analysis is not to determine which stock will generate a fortune. It is to provide assurance to the investor that the securities purchased will yield a return at least equal to that of any other investment of comparable risk. Since the market does not accurately price all securities at all times, the careful analyst in the course of screening will periodically encounter securities that the market has undervalued. Superior analysis should bring a higher than average rate of return, although not necessarily a spectacular one. A gifted analyst will do better than the market by avoiding overpriced securities. However, as more analysts examine securities, the possibility that many securities will remain substantially underpriced for any significant length of time becomes increasingly slim. This fact not only augments the competitive pressures of the securities market but also suggests that the margin of superiority a good analyst can hope to achieve at any given time may not be very great.

The management of securities does not end with the evaluation of individual securities. Mr. Jones will find that he has more issues to choose from than he can possibly put into his portfolio. Having screened his investment possibilities, he is still faced with the problem of picking an appropriate combination of securities, even though they all have rates of return that are commensurate with their risk or better. He could choose among them either by picking those with the highest rates of return or by simply tossing a dart at the list. If he selects those with the highest returns, he may find himself with a package or portfolio of securities that is too risky for his tastes. He cannot select randomly because, as will be shown later, even if all the stocks from which he is choosing are equally risky, alternative bundles of securities will not, in general, be equally risky.

From this discussion, we may conclude that the principal functions of securities management are (1) the evaluation of securities and (2) portfolio selection.

Evaluation of Securities

There are two fundamental tasks in securities evaluation. The first is to gauge the expected future cash receipts that the security will provide. In some cases, the schedule of receipts is specified in the security contract. If, for example, Mr. Jones buys a corporate bond with an 8 percent coupon, the certificate he receives will specify the date at which the corporation will pay him the face amount of the issue and will frequently have attached to it a string of coupons, each bearing a semiannual date when he will be entitled to receive $40 for each $1,000 bond that he holds. If the bond is in registered rather than bearer form, the issuer will simply send Mr. Jones a check for the amount of interest due. With bearer bonds, the issuer does not know the owner of its securities at any particular time; hence the need for coupons. Although the ease of transferability of bearer bonds has made them popular, there is a trend toward the registered form because their smaller size (absence of coupons) makes handling more convenient, interest is paid directly, and the holder has greater protection in the event of loss.

Not all securities contracts specify future receipts. If Mr. Jones buys a share of IBM stock, he will find that the company need not redeem the security at any time and that he is not entitled to any prescribed amount at fixed intervals. Instead, he will receive a pro rata share of the total dividends the board of directors decides are in the best interest of the company to distribute. In certain years, the boards of some companies may even decide to pay no dividends at all.

The second basic task is to determine the present value of the future income stream. This means discounting (reducing) each future year's dollar receipts obtained from the security by the rate of return the investor considers appropriate.

It is idle to speculate about which task is the more important. They are both equally vital. Various methods have been employed to combine them into an estimated valuation for a stock. Depending upon the training and sophistication of the investor, these methods can be relatively simple or quite complicated, as we shall discuss later.

As a small investor, Mr. Jones may choose to short-cut the various calculations required to determine a stock's fundamental values. Thus, he may say to himself that the price of a stock is a reflection of the market's anticipation of the entire future income stream accruing to the stock. In quantitative terms, this relationship may be determined by taking the ratio of the current market price to current earnings; it is therefore known, not unsurprisingly, as the *price/earnings (p/e) ratio.* This line of reasoning leads Mr. Jones to a useful truism. Since the price of a stock is neither more nor less than the earnings per share multiplied by its p/e ratio, he can gauge next year's price by making reasonable estimates of next year's earnings and p/e ratio. The rate of return to be realized by investing for the coming year then consists of the dividend he will receive plus the indicated incremental value of the stock. If Mr. Jones divides this figure by the price that he has to pay for the stock now, he has his expected rate of return.

Ms. Howard, a securities analyst, probably would be more meticulous than Mr. Jones in making forecasts of earnings and p/e ratios. Of course, if she wants to retain her client, she will probably refrain from pointing out to Mr. Jones that he is engaging in double-talk. If the current price of a stock is the present value of all future dividends, the value of the stock one year hence is the present value of all future dividends one year from now. The value of the stock today, therefore, is the present value of this year's dividends plus the present value of the estimated stock price one year hence. This latter figure turns out to be nothing more than the present value of a stream of dividends beginning one year hence. Confining ourselves, for the moment, to determining the present value, we may note that there is no single rate that Ms. Howard can apply for all securities. The rate which indicates whether a bond is worth buying is either the minimum rate that her client finds personally acceptable for an issue at that level of risk, or the rate that can be earned on alternative investments of the same quality, whichever is higher. A client of Ms. Howard may desire more than 8 percent on a good quality bond. He may be willing to accept 8 percent when nothing better is available, but there is hardly any reason for him to do so if he can buy a bond of comparable quality which will yield 9 percent. If, on the other hand, the best available yield is 7.75 percent, he may well decide that he does not want to invest in any bond at all.

Although it may be hard for Ms. Howard's client to zero in on what he would consider his minimal acceptable rate of return, this difficulty is minor in comparison with the problem that she faces in trying to determine the amounts that will be received at various future dates from the securities under consideration. For bonds, as we have noted, this forecast is relatively simple, but for stocks it is anything but easy. The future dividends a particular company is likely to pay are the outcome of a multitude of factors. Initially, they depend on the earnings the company realizes and on the proportion the company chooses to distribute. The earnings available for dividends, in turn, will depend on such things as the product mix the firm is capable of producing, the demand for various goods in the product mix, the cost of producing this particular mix, and the tax rates prevailing at the time. Both the demand for and the cost of the goods in a particular product mix will, in turn, depend on the general health of the economy. If there is little unemployment, the demand is likely to be quite healthy, but if there is great pressure on the economy's resources, rising costs may eliminate substantial parts of the profit margin. Another important consideration is whether the product or product mix in question is for final consumption or for intermediate utilization by producers. If the former, Ms. Howard will have to consider the demographic factors; if the latter, she will have to consider the demand for the products into which the company's goods and services become embedded.

Ms. Howard may well decide to advise Mr. Jones that he forgo trying to outguess the market in gauging a particular company's fortunes in the distant future, that he make life a lot simpler by not attempting to determine when the market will correct the way in which it values a security, and that he confine his efforts to finding the securities of companies whose next year's earnings are apparently underestimated by the market. But she knows that all this sounds easier than it really is. There still remains the very real problem of producing a good estimate of both next year's earnings and next year's p/e ratio. She knows that the p/e ratio is variable, and that even if investors generally make no fundamental reevaluation of the security, it will nevertheless fluctuate within a limited range. Accordingly, she will have to devise some method by which to determine the expected value of the p/e ratio.

The problems of determining next year's earnings and p/e ratio will be dealt with at greater length in the discussion of the analysis of common stocks. Here we want to make one further distinction between the roles of Mr. Jones and Ms. Howard in evaluating securities. Mr. Jones is typically concerned with whether he should buy stock *A* or *B* or bond *C* or *D*. His approach can be more simplistic than Ms. Howard's, for she has the additional responsibility of determining the relationship between a corporation's various policy decisions and the value of its outstanding securities. She knows that to understand the significance of a firm's dividend policy, she must return to fundamentals and treat a security as a claim against the stream of receipts. This means investigating the impact of the firm's policy on the receipt stream, with respect to both its expected overall value and its probable variability from year to year. Thus, the fact that we accept the short-cut method of securities evaluation does not mean that we denigrate, in any way, the importance of a thorough understanding of the analysis of fundamental values.

Portfolio Selection

Let us assume that through his own or Ms. Howard's analysis, Mr. Jones has determined the values of the stocks he is interested in. His next major problem is to put these issues into a portfolio that permits him to realize his investment objectives as closely as possible. Before we go any further, however, it must be pointed out that although we are referring to an individual investor, the same basic principles also apply to the institutional investor. Indeed, with the rapid growth of institutional investment in recent years, the portfolio selection phase of securities management has assumed increased importance.

In choosing securities for a portfolio, the investor must first establish an investment program. To formulate such a program he must set forth his objectives, the types of securities to be used in attaining these objectives, and the principles that will govern their purchase and sale. To carry out this program he may rely on market forecasts in determining the course of his transactions and in deciding how his portfolio should be apportioned between high-grade and speculative issues. He may base his own forecasts on analyses of underlying economic conditions and on an evaluation of the status of the market itself.

Correct timing is so difficult that automatic devices have been developed to govern transactions. These "formula plans" vary in details, but in general they provide for calculation of an average security level, suggest purchase of new issues as the market recedes from this average, and indicate sale as prices tend to exceed it. Although use of these plans has dwindled considerably, the principle they embody—seeking automatic rules to adjust the defensive and aggressive elements of the portfolio—still has significance.

Mr. Jones (or the institutional investment manager) presumably now knows the profit potential and risks associated with each stock, as well as the policies that underly the distribution of funds into the portfolio's defensive and aggressive portions. The defensive segment probably will be devoted to high-grade bonds, the aggressive segment to stocks. Or, as with certain types of institutional investors, *all* the funds may be characteristically held in equities, although the character of these stocks may vary with market expectations. Under any circumstances, in view of the indeterminate future, the investor is likely to refrain from absolute maximization of return in order to reduce risk. (For a discussion of risk and uncertainty see Chapters 9 and 10.) Thus, even though a single stock appears to have the greatest potential for market appreciation, the investor probably will want to introduce diversification into the portfolio to reduce the element of uncertainty or curtail the possibility of serious loss.

In recent years, many researchers have tried to develop scientific ways of selecting stocks for inclusion in portfolios. Thus far, their studies have followed two principal lines. The first approach relies on statistical techniques to develop a system permitting the formulation of portfolios that provide the maximum return at a given level of risk or the minimum risk at a specified rate of return. Once the investor has specified his trade-off between risk and return, the system indicates the distribution of funds among various securities. The second approach uses computer simulation to develop behavioral rules that result in the selection of stocks to achieve specified goals.[5] A portfolio formulated according to such rules resembles one that might be developed by the investment manager—only the process is swifter and more efficient.

TECHNIQUES OF SECURITIES MANAGEMENT

The major purposes of securities management have already been listed. To attain these goals, the investor must master certain fundamental techniques: (1) compiling statistical data; (2) identifying economic trends; (3) recognizing characteristics of securities; (4) using valuation procedures; and (5) managing investment portfolios. An individual investor will gradually become skilled in these techniques by applying analytic procedures to the selection and management of his or her own securities.

Compiling Statistical Data

An investor cannot make decisions without knowing the pertinent facts. The facts that Mr. Jones should know concern his personal needs, the business outlook, a particular industry's prospects, the financial characteristics of companies, and the features of specific securities.

In recent years the volume of available information has been increasing. The various securities acts compel corporations to issue large amounts of historical and current financial data. Organized stock exchanges have formulated detailed reporting requirements. Government agencies publish a wealth of economic statistics. Trade associations and private organizations, such as F. W. Dodge, contribute interesting and useful material in special fields. To facilitate business analysis, government and private institutions distribute publications that summarize economic activities in chart form. Considerable financial data is now available on computer tape.

Without this extensive source material, Mr. Jones would be severely handicapped; he would have to spend most of his time laboriously searching out isolated facts. Since this information has been compiled and is accessible to him, he can now use his time to uncover interesting relationships; successful decisions are often the direct result of obtaining data as soon as it appears and thereby reaching conclusions in advance of the general public.

Mr. Jones's initial responsibilities, then, are to ascertain what data is available and to develop a system for reviewing it logically. He must constantly keep his information up-to-date, so that his decisions can be in keeping with current conditions. These requirements may surprise him, since he has probably believed that buying securities meant simply turning over funds to a stockbroker or investment counselor and then reaping the benefits of the expert's "superior wisdom." But, as we shall see later, no investor can evade the task of keeping well informed about his or her own investments.

Identifying Economic Trends

Economic forecasting is an indispensable part of business operations. Capital expansions, inventory accumulations, and investment policies all depend on the accuracy of management's estimates of industrial prospects. Because forecasting is so important, considerable effort has been spent on developing effective techniques. Extravagant claims are sometimes made for the accuracy of favorite methods. Mr. Jones's own investment analyses will eventually enable him to judge both the limitations and the strengths of the various procedures.

Recognizing Characteristics of Securities

If Mr. Jones wants to buy a new car, he either knows or takes pains to learn about differences in the price, maintenance cost, performance, and numerous other features of the various types of automobiles now on the market. His choice may come down to a Chevrolet or a Ford; if he is seeking the advantages offered by such lower-priced cars, he will long since have eliminated a Cadillac. He should choose his securities in the same way. If he wants a volatile issue that will move with the market, he should be knowledgeable enough to avoid purchasing a conservative stock with characteristically lethargic market movements. Mr. Jones must be able to recognize the types of securities he wants, just as he should know the characteristics of the car he buys.

Securities represent values. These values can usually be assessed. For instance, depending on the price, certain stocks may immediately be labeled as suitable for conservative investors. Stocks showing the opposite characteristics are more suitable for the investor who wants market volatility. Mr. Jones must first become skilled in recognizing the salient characteristics of various kinds of securities; later, of course, he must also learn how to identify the most desirable issues among comparable types.

Risk taking and mental health. Perhaps Mr. Jones has heard that an investor should buy risky securities only as long as he sleeps soundly. He should heed this statement, which was made by a person with an understanding of human nature. When Mr. Jones buys high-risk securities for high returns, he can expect his returns in the form of capital gains. Buying securities primarily for capital gains is a specialized operation. Because it involves potential losses as well as profits, Mr. Jones should limit his transactions. Severe financial setbacks may cause mental turmoil far outweighing any possible benefits. To be an aggressive speculator, therefore, he must be a certain kind of person.

He must be stable enough to sustain the emotional impact of a heavy market loss. Psychological adjustment to the possibility of loss is important; Mr. Jones must not overestimate his own endurance. It is easy for him to say that he will take his losses in stride; he will find that accepting the actual event is another matter.

He must be financially able to assume losses without neglecting his personal and family responsibilities. He probably occupies a position in his community that entails a certain standard of living—and growing family interests increase the need for money. He would be foolhardy to endanger his family's well-being and his community status for the sake of quick profits in the securities markets. Does this seem to overemphasize the risks of excessive speculation? Overemphasis is hardly possible when we recall the disastrous experiences of people who bought, with borrowed money, larger amounts of highly speculative securities than they could afford.

Moreover, if Mr. Jones is like most investors, he prefers to avoid rather than to assume risks. The New York City financing episode illustrates the prevalence of this characteristic. In late 1975 it was hit or miss whether or not the city would be able to meet its maturing debts. The specter of default drove to substantial discounts the prices of its bonds, as well as those of its agencies, and the Municipal Assistance Corporation, created to buttress the city's tottering credit base. Individuals and institutions were thus confronted with an intriguing question, the answer to which dictated the correct investment strategy to pursue.

Would the Empire City of the United States renege on its obligations? It was inconceivable that federal and local legislators would permit this eventuality to take place, with its dismal implications to the nation's capital markets. Would New York be able to extricate itself from its financial morass by paying its debts, tightening financial controls, and observing accounting proprieties? Such a major financial rejuvenation seemed impossible. The inconceivable vs. the impossible—which would follow?

Given this choice, a risk assumer would dismiss the possibility of default and aggressively purchase city securities at their depressed levels; a risk avoider would be frightened by the prospects of default and seek safer investment outlets. The answer of most investors was given in trading interest, as activity in city and related issues dwindled, while investors flocked to buy the new short-term, relatively high-yielding, risk-free notes that the U.S. Treasury was offering at that time.

"Bucking" the trend. Rising markets generate waves of optimism that leave misleading rumors and "tips" in their wake. It is essential to Mr. Jones's success that he avoid the deadly habit of following the market. Indeed, should he become a successful speculator, he probably will find himself often "bucking" the majority. He must have imagination to recognize profit potentialities in situations that others may observe but not understand; the perception to see the most effective course of action; the ability to evaluate his chances of success; and, finally, the firmness to act swiftly and aggressively when he has made his decision. Speculation plays an important role in the growth of a capitalistic society; the successful speculator is usually well endowed with the aforementioned capabilities.

Using Valuation Procedures

In addition to assessing the general characteristics of a security, Mr. Jones will assign it some value which he will compare with the market price. Its gain potential then will be largely gauged by the relation of the calculated value to the actual price. To reach his valuation figure, Mr. Jones will employ financial statement analysis to gain some insights into the character of the company and to forecast its earnings. He will rely on market analysis to reach some understanding of prevailing and anticipated capitalization rates. His final valuation will involve integrating his earnings and capitalization estimates in some way. For this purpose, as we have indicated previously, Mr. Jones may use relatively simple techniques, while Ms. Howard prefers sophisticated methods.

Managing Investment Portfolios

Managing a portfolio requires a considerable expenditure of time and a knowledge of investment principles. Having set up his portfolio, Mr. Jones must formulate a system that assures constant surveillance of all the securities he has selected. He must be able to recognize the kinds of changing conditions that affect specific issues, and he must make periodic reviews of his holdings. Finally, he must take appropriate action when events call for positive measures; if he uses a formula plan to govern recurring purchases and sales, he will find its check on price movements particularly valuable.

If Mr. Jones does not have enough time or knowledge, he should seek outside advice. Perhaps a combination of his own judgment and the periodic assistance of bankers, brokers, or consultants will prove best for his purposes.

THE ROLE OF THE SECURITIES ANALYST

Without the skills we have just described, Mr. Jones would not be able to buy and sell securities in a logical fashion and would be completely dependent on the judgment of others. Through study and experience he can acquire these talents. However, whether he is only a beginner or already understands the field fairly well, he will find the services of a securities analyst helpful.

By the term *securities analyst* we refer to a relatively small group of individuals, connected with investment banking firms, stock brokerage houses, or institutional investors (such as life insurance companies, or investment advisory organizations), who devote their full time to evaluating the prospects of corporations and the securities they issue. Analysts often prepare detailed statistical studies that can help Mr. Jones to ascertain the outlook for particular industries and companies. The analysts' specialized knowledge, their familiarity with financial practices, and the first-hand information they obtain from contact with corporations are valuable to individual investors like Mr. Jones.

At present there are no formal requirements for securities analysts such as exist for certified public accountants, physicians, and attorneys. But there is a movement to raise standards in the field. Spearheading this drive is the Institute of Chartered Financial Analysts, which was formed by the Financial Analysts Federation in 1959. The institute awards the professional designation chartered financial analyst (CFA) to persons who have met the standards established by the institute for the professional practice of financial analysis. To obtain the designation, a candidate must fulfill prescribed requirements of education, experience, and written examinations. The body of knowledge considered relevant for a securities analyst undergoes constant development. In 1974 the major topics included were economics, accounting, quantitative techniques, analysis of fixed-income securities, analysis of equity securities, portfolio management, and legal and ethical standards.

In addition to providing useful information and making recommendations, securities analysts have been instrumental in bringing about better corporate financial policies. Ms. Howard, for example, achieves this through various activities in which she characteristically engages. She attends annual meetings, visits plants, and discusses problems with corporation executives throughout the country. When a corporation adopts measures that she believes are contrary to the best interests of the stockholders she represents, she is in a position to call the matter to management's attention. Because Ms. Howard is a specialist in corporate problems and may exert an important influence on the decisions of a number of stockholders, management is more likely to act on her suggestions than on those offered by individual stockholders like Mr. Jones.

As an individual stockholder, Mr. Jones cannot usually dispute the policies of boards of directors. In most instances, management can use its advantages (large financial resources, stock control, high-pressure public-relations facilities) to prevent a recalcitrant minority from enlisting Mr. Jones's support against management's decisions or policies. The securities analyst may be able to redress the balance in these disputes, since the many stockholders whom Ms. Howard serves have confidence in her judgment. Thus, if there is a disagreement between the management and the stockholders of a corporation in which he is interested, Mr. Jones may ask the advice of the securities analyst in the stock brokerage firm with which he deals.

Helping to improve management policies has now become a recognized function of the securities analyst. The results of these efforts may not be immediately apparent in the price of an issue, but better management-stockholder relations do have a beneficial influence on market values; the improvements are indirectly reflected in more favorable dividend policies, increased stock marketability, and sounder accounting practices.

SOME SHIBBOLETHS

Several current "fictions" about investment strategy must be disposed of before we go any further.

"Only the Quality of the Issuer Is Important"

This particular fiction generally is expressed in the belief that if the issuer is a risky firm, the security also is risky; and if the issuer is a solid enterprise, the security is safe. But this is a generalization that cannot bear close scrutiny. The securities of an extremely speculative firm may be so drastically underpriced (although, as we have already mentioned, such securities are becoming harder to find) that the downside risk is negligible. Conversely, a blue chip may be so outrageously overpriced that the possibility of a loss is very real. Thus, the character of a security is only one side of the analytic coin; the other side is the issue's price. In order to determine its attractiveness, both sides of the coin must be considered.

An example will illustrate this principle. In April 1974, A. G. Becker & Co.[6] regarded Polaroid unfavorably because its near-term earnings prospects were drab and the potential competitive threat of Eastman Kodak's entering the instant camera field had been magnified greatly. Nevertheless, Becker removed the stock from its sale list because the decline in stocks in the market had "carried PRD below its minimum downside target ($65-70)."[7]

"The Form of the Security Establishes Its Quality"

A bond is a contractual obligation. A corporation will therefore make every effort to meet principal and interest requirements, since failure to do so could lead to bankruptcy. There is no such pressure to pay dividends on a common stock. Accordingly, the bond form ordinarily is considered more conservative than a stock.

However, when a corporation is in a relatively weak position, it may have difficulty in meeting its fixed requirements, even though it desires to do so. Thus, the common stock of a very strong corporation in a particular period may prove more stable than the bonds of a less financially secure enterprise. As an illustration, contrast Cleveland Electric Illuminating common stock, which during the first half of 1975 fluctuated between 28⅜ and 23⅜ (or about 21 percent of the lower figure), with the Chicago, Milwaukee, St. Paul & Pacific Railroad (now controlled by the Chicago Milwaukee Corporation) 4½/2019, which moved between 34 and 23, a range of about 57 percent.

A strong corporation undoubtedly will meet required payments, but the price of its bonds will decline as interest rates rise. Even in this case, therefore, form is no protection against market changes. In the first ten months of 1967, for example, interest rates rose sharply. Reflecting this condition, long-term U.S. government bond prices declined over 10 percent, while the Standard & Poor's Industrial Average rose almost 16 percent in the same period. Accordingly, in evaluating a security, one must consider not only the quality of the issuer and the price of the issue but also, the general outlook in the capital and money markets.

"Intrinsic Value Is Everything"

We have stressed the need to establish intrinsic valuations in selecting securities. Nevertheless, it is important to recognize that profits may sometimes be achieved by evaluating the indicated attitudes of investors relative to the prevailing economic climate, thereby temporarily ignoring some basic tenets of securities analysis. In pointing out this characteristic of the securities markets, we are not recommending that investment policy be pointed in this direction. Quite the contrary. The dangers inherent in this approach suggest that, if tried at all, it should be used only by speculators capable of assuming such risks.

In the context of the securities markets, our analyst, Ms. Howard, knows that prices are the outcome of decisions taken by buyers and sellers of stock. She is aware of the fact that there is a sort of financial haute couture and that, over the years, securities—like women's dresses—have experienced certain style changes. Prior to World War I, for example, railroads were in strong favor. Between 1914 and 1923 the general position of industrial common stocks improved substantially; in the bull market that followed, blue chip stocks gained popularity, while speculative interest centered on new issues like those of public-utility holding companies. During the depression of the 1930s, many stocks were driven to very low levels; in the subsequent expansion, more attention was paid to fundamentals, including dividend record and asset valuations. Starting in the 1950s the growth stocks came into vogue.[8] In 1972 and 1973 there appeared a "two-tier market," the upper tier consisting of well-established growth stocks selling at high p/e multiples, the lower tier of stocks of companies that tended to sell at low ratios, presumably because they were not favored by the big institutional investors. In 1974 this distinction became blurred as the institutions extended their interests over a broader range of securities; declining prices in the first half of the year brought income-producing issues into the limelight.

Interspersed during these periods were several intervals in which "hot issues" (newly offered speculative issues that attract heavy demand and often rise to a quick premium) came to the forefront. One such interval was in 1967. Ms. Howard might have surveyed the scene at that time and recognized how the new technology had caught the public fancy. She might have reasoned that many observers, like herself, would note the attraction to the average investor of companies engaged in scientific fields such as aerospace or computers and would be tempted to speculate on this influence. As an acute analyst, she would have known the potential effect of sharp movements of stock prices on the average investor. During the late 1960s, the managers of small speculative investment companies often traded on the basis of what they thought the average investor would do rather than on the basis of fundamental corporate values. Average investors themselves tended to become increasingly aggressive, since more and more of them were from a generation which had never lived through the throes of a severe business contraction. Moreover, they placed great confidence in the ability of the planners of the "new economics" to use fiscal and monetary tools to ward off the impact of business depressions.

Because of this average-opinion syndrome, many science-oriented stocks of small companies with limited capitalization sold at large premiums immediately after their offering in the sizzling new-issue market of 1967. In August 1967, for example, Wang Laboratories (which designs, manufactures, and sells a line of electronic desktop calculators and computers) offered 240,000 shares at $12.50 each; the issue closed its first day of trading in the over-the-counter market at 40 bid, 40¼ asked. In the following month, Graphic Sciences offered 401,000 shares at $10 each; the company was too new to have any sales or earnings, but inclusion among its officers of two former employees of Xerox and its glamorous (but little understood) product, a "graphic transceiver," were sufficient to drive the closing price of the stock on the day of the offering to 29½ bid, 30½ asked. So it was with a whole series of new offerings during that period.

Ms. Howard would also have known that many of these companies probably could not survive and that in a number of instances the premium would be short-lived.[9] Nevertheless, she would have recognized that considerable profits probably could be made by individuals willing to speculate on the average opinion prevalent in the market at that time. Moreover, the risks involved could have been modified to some extent by buying a diversified list of such issues and disposing of them promptly.

As a general principle, securities analysts prefer to buy stocks that appear undervalued in the light of their earnings potential and fundamental characteristics. Nevertheless, Ms. Howard has an important personal issue to resolve. Should she avoid calling to the attention of at least her more speculative-minded clients the profit possibilities resident in the hot-issue market because the basis of fundamental analysis is lacking? Or should she mention these issues as well as the attendant risks, assuming that her responsibility is to point out the various avenues open to her clients and leave to them the determination of the route they will take? In the actual world of the securities markets, distinctions often arise between the theory and reality of obtaining market gains.

"Only an Investor's Needs Should Determine the Portfolio"

Another fiction that should be laid to rest is that Mr. Jones should design his portfolio solely in the light of his *needs.* Mr. Smith and Mr. Jones may find themselves in exactly the same economic circumstance. They may have the same income, net worth, family size, and health. Their jobs may be equally secure. Their personalities, however, need not be the same. One may be venturesome and the other timid. If so, they should not have similar portfolios. We can set ourselves up as moral arbiters and say that the poor people should not gamble, but the legitimacy of our judgment would be questionable. What is unfortunate is that investors sometimes take risks they would never dream of taking if they were fully aware of the true nature of their investment. In a rising market, some investors delude themselves into thinking they cannot lose.

This is not to say that an investor's portfolio is completely independent of personal needs. An individual's willingness to take risks will generally depend upon needs. The carefree bachelor who bought penny stocks with abandon may, when he has a wife and children and must be prepared for major household contingencies, switch to well-priced blue chips. The timid bachelor who started with blue chips in the first place may choose to abandon stock purchases entirely. Every investor faced with a choice between two securities of different risks has to answer the question of whether the greater return is sufficient to warrant undertaking the greater risk. If Mr. Jones asks himself that question seriously, he will have to make a mental comparison between the benefits of a fortunate investment and the penalties associated with an unsuccessful one. Only he can make that judgment for himself.

LIMITATIONS OF SECURITIES MANAGEMENT

The study of securities analysis and portfolio management will never tell Mr. Jones what a security is worth. It does give him an insight into what input is required for his analysis and tells him how to make logical decisions based on that input. Essentially it provides the analyst with decision rules. The output of Mr. Jones's analysis can be no better than the input.

There are two kinds of input involved in any particular analysis. First, there are the prognostications, which are inevitable whenever one takes a line of action with a future payoff. While the discipline of securities analysis can help in making such prognostications, the outcome is always in doubt. Second, there are the facts on which the prognostications are based. Unfortunately, the facts are not very hard. To be sure, many of them come from the corporation's annual reports and other announcements. Although these reports are now likely to be "audited" by an independent accounting firm, a careful review of the auditors' statements will disclose that the accountants purport to certify nothing more than that the figures are derived on a consistent basis in accordance with generally acceptable accounting principles. An examination of accounting methodology, however, may reveal that, at many points in the preparation of a report, choices must be made between different acceptable accounting conventions.

Within certain limits, accountants can report varying levels of earnings that do not conflict with acceptable accounting rules. The blind acceptance of reported figures can lead to totally unwarranted prognostications and disastrous investment decisions. A study of securities analysis can alert the investor to the pitfalls of accounting reports, but in the final analysis there is no substitute for the care and intelligence of the investor.

In this introduction, concerned with the scope of the field, we introduced Mr. Jones, an investor, and Ms. Howard, a securities analyst, in order to distinguish their respective roles. As we have mentioned, however, even the investor who turns over a portfolio to an outside adviser should have some awareness of the securities field, if only to work with the adviser and to judge the effectiveness of the advice. In the chapters that follow, we no longer call on either Mr. Jones or Ms. Howard; instead, we provide a discussion of the general principles, concepts, and analytic techniques employed in the management of securities.

ROAD MAP OF THE BOOK

Before embarking on our tour of the field of securities analysis, let us take an advance look at the major roads and where they will take us.

We start with the investment setting. Securities transactions are executed in markets that are partly self-regulated and partly regulated by the Securities and Exchange Commission (SEC). These markets are experiencing galvanic changes that will greatly alter their appearance during the next few years. In order to obtain the most efficient execution of orders at the minimum cost, the investor must understand how these markets operate at present and what new elements are being introduced. An awareness of the regulatory apparatus will help the investor to know how much confidence he can place in the professional participants and to understand their responsibilities and his own rights.

This background is only part of the information the investor should have. The other part covers a package of materials the investor needs for the analytic process. Securities provide various forms of income that are measured in different ways. Unless the investor appreciates these differences, and how they are affected by taxes, difficulty will be experienced in developing a financial program, which must be formulated in the light of an individual's own needs and personality. Consideration will also be given to the role of savings, which may affect the securities that the investor is willing to include in his or her own portfolio. These portfolio securities will be selected by analytic principles that, in turn, depend upon both the information that is available and the factors affecting the securities' prices.

After covering the background material, we pursue the analytic roads that lead to the selection of securities, starting with the analysis of common stock. A discussion of the nature of this instrument paves the way for an exposition of current methods for incorporating risk into the evaluation of securities. From this point the road becomes narrower, as the analysis focuses on various specific issues bearing upon the intrinsic worth of a stock. Included is a review of how accounting permissiveness, within generally accepted accounting principles, affects financial statements, and of the implications of this accounting flexibility for investment analysis. Evaluating a company's financial statements and the qualities of the company itself leads us to the development of analytic procedures for forecasting earnings, dividends, and a reasonable price range within which its stock may be bought and sold.

Thereafter, the analytic road traverses the area of fixed-income securities. Attention initially is given to the nature of bonds and to some strategies that have been developed for trading in these instruments. Subsequently, we examine the methods for analyzing the obligations of corporations, the U.S. government, state and local governments, and preferred stock. Because of the high interest rates that have recently prevailed, this area has assumed special importance.

Our tour of the field of securities analysis finally leads to an exploration of alternative investment routes. These other areas include investment companies, privileged securities (such as convertible issues), and stock options, which have gained popularity because of the new formal methods that have been created for trading these instruments. Lastly, consideration is given to technical analysis, which involves forecasting prices through their prior configurations. This alternative analytic technique has been severely criticized in the academic literature, but it is still followed by some practitioners.

Part One

THE INVESTMENT SETTING

In Part One an institutional picture is provided of how the securities markets work. Separate chapters are devoted to the current status of the markets, their evolving structure, and the regulatory framework that exists to protect the investor. Throughout the discussion, account is taken of the major legislative changes that occurred in 1975 and their implications for the development of the markets.

CHAPTER 1

Operations of the Securities Markets

One way of dividing the securities markets is to distinguish between *primary markets,* where stocks and bonds are initially sold, and *secondary markets,* where they are traded. Public offerings of corporate issues ordinarily are handled by investment banking intermediaries who purchase the securities from the issuing company, either by negotiation or competitive bidding, and thereafter sell them, through an underwriting syndicate, to individual and institutional investors. Once the securities have been issued and registered in accordance with Securities and Exchange Commission requirements, they are eligible for public trading, which may occur in a registered exchange, in the over-the-counter markets, or in the so-called third or fourth markets (see pp. 48-51 for a discussion of third and fourth markets).

All these markets are being buffeted by the forces of change. Once-powerful ramparts, such as the minimum-commission schedule, already have been pierced, and other bulwarks will topple before a stabilized structure is restored.

After four years of close investigation of the competitive, statutory, and economic issues facing the securities industry, Congress enacted the Securities Acts Amendments of 1975. Primarily, the measure directs the SEC to facilitate the establishment of a national market system. Since this objective requires a reorientation in the basic method of conducting business, Congress has for the first time involved itself with such operational concepts as "securities information processors," "clearing agency," "transfer agent," "market maker," and "quotations." This is a quantum jump from the original Securities Exchange Act, passed in 1934, in which Congress was reluctant to cross the regulatory threshold that separated the character of trading from actual trading methods. Reflecting the concern of the lawmakers that they may have bitten too deeply into an explosive bullet, the measure provides several "fail-safe" provisions that permit the restoration of former conditions.

The new law does a number of other things. It clarifies the relations of the SEC to the agencies it supervises, broadens the meaning of stock exchange membership, creates a new regulatory body in the municipal field, requires institutional investment managers to disclose their securities holdings and transactions, moves to prohibit stock exchange members from effecting transactions for affiliated accounts, liberalizes the fiduciary responsibilities of investment advisers, and facilitates the ability of management companies to sell investment advisory contracts.

In view of the major legal and structural adjustments that have occurred, it is difficult to describe the operations of the trading markets because methods in vogue now may be discarded or altered in the process of transition. The pace will be slow, because strongly entrenched interests are at stake and they yield ground sluggishly. Accordingly, our discussion is divided into two chapters: this chapter presents the operations of the major elements of the trading markets as they take place today; included are the modifications that have already occurred as a result of the 1975 legislation and the rules of the applicable regulatory bodies. Still more changes, however, are in store. In order to anticipate them and the problems they may generate, it is necessary to understand the forces that have been at work. The next chapter, therefore, provides an evaluation of the principal issues that have created the push toward a new central market.

THE CONCEPT OF SELF-REGULATION

Out of the legal struggles preceding passage of the Securities Exchange Act of 1934 emerged the notion of self-regulation, which is the major legislative principle underlying the SEC's role in carrying out the functions of the securities acts. Following this principle, the primary responsibility for insuring that the exchanges meet their public role rests with the exchanges themselves; the SEC intercedes only when necessary. To William O. Douglas, then chairman of the SEC, the relationship seemed like that of father and daughter—the father relies on his daughter's own scruples to preserve her honor, but he is prepared to use his protective shotgun should the need arise.

When the Exchange Act was introduced, self-regulation was thought to apply primarily to the commission and the exchanges. Extending the principle to the over-the-counter (OTC) market was an afterthought incorporated into the Exchange Act by Section 15A, the so-called Maloney Act (1938), named after its sponsor, Francis Maloney of Connecticut. This section permits any qualified association of broker-dealers to register under the act. Self-regulation under the Maloney Act followed the structure established in the Exchange Act, but with improvements emanating from the additional experience in this area of administration.

In drafting the Securities Acts Amendments of 1975, the legislators took a long look at the concept of self-regulation and came away with some important new principles. First, they apparently sought to modify the dominant consideration given to the exchanges under the 1934 act; the new legislation provides for equal treatment with the other self-regulatory bodies. Thus, the revised Section 19—which, in essence, lays down the new self-regulatory relationship—is titled "Registration, Responsibilities, and Oversight of Self-Regulatory Organizations." A self-regulatory organization, in turn, is defined in Section 3 as any national securities exchange, registered securities association, or registered clearing agency. Second, the rule-making authority and responsibilities of the different self-regulatory organizations are defined similarly. As a result, SEC's relationship to the National Association of Securities Dealers, Inc. (NASD), the only self-regulatory national securities association registered with the SEC, no longer differs from its relationships with the exchanges. Third, the roles of the SEC and of the self-regulatory organizations in administering their rule-making powers are clarified. The net effect is to deprive the organizations of much of their autonomy, despite the legislators' repeated assertions regarding the desirability of self-regulation.

In the 1975 law, the rule-making authority of the self-regulatory organizations is defined primarily in terms of objectives rather than subject matter. Many of these objectives are positive, clarifying in the sections applicable to the exchanges and to the registered securities associations what the rules must do; for example, they must be aimed at preventing fraudulent and manipulative acts. The objectives are also expressed negatively; the rules ordinarily must not impose any burden on competition.

Abandoned is the former 19(b) listing of the specific areas where the SEC could request an exchange to alter its rules. Instead, the new procedures call for any self-regulatory organization proposing a rule change to file with the SEC a concise statement of its purpose. Interested persons would then have the opportunity of participating in the review process. Proposed rules affecting the public interest must be approved by the commission prior to adoption or disapproved after an opportunity is afforded for public hearings. To gain approval the rules must meet the requirements of the act. Under certain circumstances the commission may summarily put into effect a proposed rule change, but it must institute the prescribed procedure promptly thereafter. In the event of disapproval, reasons must be given. Besides its review authority over the rules introduced by a self-regulatory organization, the commission may bring about an amendment of such rules by following the basic procedures specified in the Administrative Procedure Act (1946).

In the course of its deliberations, Congress showed concern over the possible abuse of power. Thus, in addition to following the Administrative Procedure Act, the commission is required to provide all interested parties with an opportunity to present their views, to keep a transcript of oral presentations, and to publish a statement of its reasons for taking action. Moreover, the new legislation safeguards the interests of members of self-regulatory organizations. The rules of such organizations must provide a fair procedure for disciplinary measures against a member, for denial of membership, barring a person from being associated with a member, or limiting the access of a person to the services offered by a member.[1] An organization that takes any such action must first file with the SEC, which, on its own initiative or at the request of the aggrieved person, may review the case.

To enhance the scope of SEC oversight, its options for dealing with self-regulatory shortcomings were increased. These options include suspending, deregistering, censuring, and limiting the activities of a self-regulatory organization. Such action may be taken if the organization fails to enforce compliance with its own rules, the Exchange Act, or SEC regulations. The commission also can suspend or expel any member from a self-regulatory organization; suspend or bar any person from being associated with a member; or remove from office or censure any officer or director of a self-regulatory organization.

The Exchange Act has always conferred upon the SEC certain direct powers. In order to facilitate the establishment and regulation of a national market system, the new amendments make it clear that these powers extend to processors of market information, operations of a composite tape and composite quotation system, and all market-making activities. (See p. 46 for a definition of "market-making.")

REGISTERED EXCHANGES

A securities exchange must be registered with the SEC as a national exchange unless its limited number of transactions make it exempt. Since the dissolution of the Richmond Stock Exchange in April 1972, the Honolulu Stock Exchange is the only exchange exempt from registration. Once registered, an exchange falls within the purview of the SEC, which has issued extensive regulations to fulfill its responsibilities under the Securities Exchange Act of 1934. On June 30, 1974, the following 13 exchanges were registered:

American Stock Exchange, Inc.
Board of Trade of the City of Chicago (its securities market is now closed, but the board has not withdrawn its registration)
Boston Stock Exchange
Chicago Board Options Exchange, Inc.
Cincinnati Stock Exchange
Detroit Stock Exchange
Intermountain Stock Exchange
Midwest Stock Exchange, Inc.
National Stock Exchange (registration now withdrawn)
New York Stock Exchange, Inc.
Pacific Stock Exchange, Inc.
PBW Stock Exchange, Inc.
Spokane Stock Exchange

There are about 1,500 common stocks listed on the New York Stock Exchange, 1,300 on the American Stock Exchange (AMEX), and 350 traded solely on one or more regional exchanges. Securities listed on the NYSE are not traded on the AMEX, partly because of that exchange's policy but also for legal reasons. The bulk of AMEX members are members of the NYSE, whose constitution requires the suspension or expulsion of any member connected with another exchange in New York City which permits dealings in any securities handled in the NYSE.[2] This provision has its antecedents in the hectic events of the nineteenth century, when the NYSE was struggling to ward off the challenges of other exchanges seeking to establish a trading niche in New York.

For a period of time in 1973 the détente between the two exchanges appeared threatened, as the AMEX indicated an interest in continuing to trade securities that shifted their listings to the NYSE, and the NYSE contemplated relaxing standards for trading warrants now largely concentrated on the AMEX. As volume expanded, however, both sides, at least for the time being, dropped these ideas. Periods of shrinking volume have created pressures on the two exchanges to merge at least some of their activities in order to cut costs. The Securities Industry Association (SIA), a trade group, has urged some form of combination to eliminate duplicate costs for companies by uniting all but the exchanges' trading floors. Although both exchanges have appointed committees to explore the merger idea, neither seems very enthusiastic about such a prospect.

In February 1971 the NYSE abandoned its status as a voluntary association and incorporated under the New York Not-for-Profit Corporation Law. Thereafter, the AMEX incorporated under the same law, while the Midwest Stock Exchange and the Philadelphia-Baltimore-Washington Stock Exchange incorporated under the Delaware General Corporation Law; at the time of its incorporation, the Philadelphia-Baltimore-Washington Exchange changed its name to the PBW Stock Exchange. The Chicago Board Options Exchange and the Pacific Stock Exchange are also incorporated.

NEW YORK STOCK EXCHANGE

From its inception, on May 17, 1792, under the famous buttonwood tree, to the passage of the Securities Exchange Act in 1934, the NYSE was run largely like a private club for the welfare of its members. However, the Exchange Act brought the NYSE under the blanket of Section 6, which, as revised, requires the commission to determine that the exchange and its members are in compliance with the provisions of the act and the exchange's own rules.

Under the 1975 measure, the scope of SEC authority over an exchange's rules has been broadened and clarified. As enumerated in an unchanged Section 10 and a revised Section 11, the commission, without going through the regulatory process, may continue to enact rules of its own in certain vital areas. Included are the operations of specialists and odd-lot dealers and the use of short sales, stop-loss orders, and manipulative or deceptive practices. Additionally, authority has been given the commission to regulate transactions of members on or off an exchange as well as transactions of nonmembers on an exchange. Section 8 has been amended by authorizing the commission to promulgate rules governing the lending by brokers and dealers of securities carried for the account of their customers. Previously, the Exchange Act covered the hypothecation but not lending of securities. Finally, the commission has been given the broad mandate of developing rules to create a national market system.

Development of Its Organization

After passage of the Exchange Act, the SEC sought a reorganization of the NYSE to provide more efficient management. The exchange responded by appointing an independent committee, headed by Carle C. Conway, then chairman of the board of directors of the Continental Can Company. In

January 1938 the Conway Committee submitted its report, which included far-reaching recommendations for converting the government of the exchange from a largely private affair to a more modern form. Following the furor created by suspension of the firm of Richard Whitney & Co. and by the expulsion of Whitney, who had been president of the exchange, the principal recommendations of the Conway Committee were adopted.

Despite the improvements effected at that time, the policy of private-club management continued to cast shadows on the exchange, while the overview exercised by the SEC proved relatively modest. In 1961 the commission, through a specially created group, undertook a major investigation of the securities markets. Out of the recommendations of this so-called Special Study of Securities Markets came the Securities Acts Amendments of 1964, which, among other things, provided for raising the standards of self-regulation. In the decade that followed, the exchange introduced a number of major face-lifting modifications of its own. As a result, partly under the prodding of the SEC and partly through its own initiative, the administrative organization of the exchange today has an aura of objectivity and efficiency that is a far cry from the cozy atmosphere of the Whitney era. In recognition of its own higher level of surveillance, as well as that of the SEC, the exchange has preferred to describe the relationship as "cooperative regulation."[3]

Top policymaking authority in the exchange rests in a board of directors chaired by the institution's full-time, paid chief executive. Apart from its chairman, the board includes directors representing the securities industry and the public. In August 1975 the NYSE membership voted a proposal, which required SEC approval, to raise the industry representation from 10 to 14 (including 5 floor members), while leaving the public representation at 10. The only requirement for public representation on an exchange's board of directors in the 1975 law is that at least one member must not be from the securities industry. In their discussion of the new measure, however, the conferees made it clear that this modest requirement did not suggest that an exchange should reduce the number of outside directors it may now have. A recommendation made by some observers that an exchange be required to appropriate funds for use by the public representatives was omitted from the final version, although it originally appeared in the House bill.

Reporting to the chairman and chief executive officer is a hierarchy of vice-presidents heading different phases of the exchange's operations. At present, the exchange's supervisory program covers a wide range to insure that its members conduct their activities in accordance with appropriate standards. Included are reviews of the financial condition of member firms; a "stock-watch" program to detect unusual price fluctuations; and supervision of selling practices, market letters, and advertising methods. In cooperation with the AMEX and NASD, the NYSE, in early 1972, launched a new uniform reporting operation in which computers process information overnight to detect such things as compliance with the minimum amount of capital a firm must maintain relative to its borrowings. As part of its regulatory program, the exchange undertakes disciplinary actions as required. These may range from minor penalties to fines, suspensions, or expulsions of member firms.

Membership of the NYSE

The Exchange Act originally defined a "member" only for an exchange. The definition included those who could effect a transaction without someone else acting as a broker, without payment of a commission, or with payment at a rate below that charged the general public. In a national system of competitive rates, this definition is largely outmoded. For one thing, institutions might be permitted to effect transactions on exchanges without someone else acting as a broker. Then again, the introduction of negotiated rates renders obsolete the notion of commissions charged to the general public. Accordingly, the revised act now states that a member is a person who has agreed to be regulated by a national securities exchange or a registered securities association, which, in turn, has agreed to effect compliance with its rules as well as with the Exchange Act.

Once membership is defined, a critical issue is the extent to which an exchange should have the authority to impose limitations. Contending that exchanges historically have been able to maintain their dominance in the marketplace through the maintenance of such limitations, the drafters of the House legislation originally provided for "open membership." This concept was dropped in the final version, which gives an exchange the authority to adopt restrictions, subject to certain qualifications. For one thing, its rules must permit any registered broker or dealer to become a member unless he or she cannot meet certain standards of conduct, financial responsibility, or competency. Broker-dealer affiliates of institutions, including foreign institutions, cannot be excluded from membership, but banks may not become members because they are specifically omitted from the act's definition of broker-dealers. Then again, an exchange cannot decrease the number of members or the number permitted to effect floor transactions below the levels in effect on May 1, 1975, or the date of its registration, whichever is later. Finally, in accordance with the commission's authority to amend any rule of a national securities exchange, the SEC may require an exchange to increase (but not decrease) the number of its members or the number permitted on the floor, or to remove any limitations entirely.

The equity of the NYSE is held by 1,366 members, each of whom owns a "seat," a term that has its roots in the early period of the exchange's history, when the president called securities to the seated members. Because active membership bears certain responsibilities, admission of new members falls within the control of the board of directors. The number of members has been fixed since 1933; therefore, a qualified new member must buy his seat from an existing member. Its price, like that of any commodity, depends on the prevailing demand and supply. The highest sale price was $515,000, in late 1968 and early 1969; the lowest was $17,000, in 1942. Members are entitled to appear on the trading floor of the exchange, although not all of them exercise this privilege.

A member may combine with other individuals to form a partnership or corporation that does business with the public as a member organization. The number of such organizations has been declining steadily, from 681 in 1961 to 508 at the close of 1974, about equally divided between partnerships and corporations. In 1970 the exchange permitted member corporations to sell stock publicly; by the close of 1973, 17 were publicly owned. Allied members (described in the act as persons associated with members) usually are either partners, officers, or directors of member organizations. While subject to most of the same rules and regulations as the members, allied members may not do business on the trading floor.

The different kinds of active members include floor brokers, specialists, independent (or "two-dollar") brokers, registered traders, and odd-lot dealers. These perform different functions, as discussed below.

Floor brokers. About half the members serve as floor brokers, executing customers' orders to buy or sell securities. In the ordinary channels of communication, a customer gives his order to a representative of a member firm who transmits it for execution to a floor broker. Many firms have more than one floor broker to permit the simultaneous handling of orders in different areas of the exchange floor.

Specialists. Approximately one-quarter of the members are specialists, organized into about 70 firms. Specialists concentrate on particular stocks at a trading post. In fulfilling his responsibilities on the exchange floor, the specialist serves both as a broker-agent, buying and selling for others, and as a dealer, buying or selling for his own account.

Customers often submit orders to purchase a stock below the prevailing price or to sell above it. When a firm's floor broker receives an order of this sort, he can hardly be expected to dally at the post where the stock is traded waiting for it to reach the designated price. If he did so, he would miss the opportunities to execute the market orders of other customers that could be completed promptly at different posts. Thus, the orders that cannot be currently handled are left with the specialist, who enters them in his "book" on the basis of price and time priorities. A typical page from such a book, for the $50 price range, is shown in Figure 1-1.

FIGURE 1-1

Page from a Specialist's Book

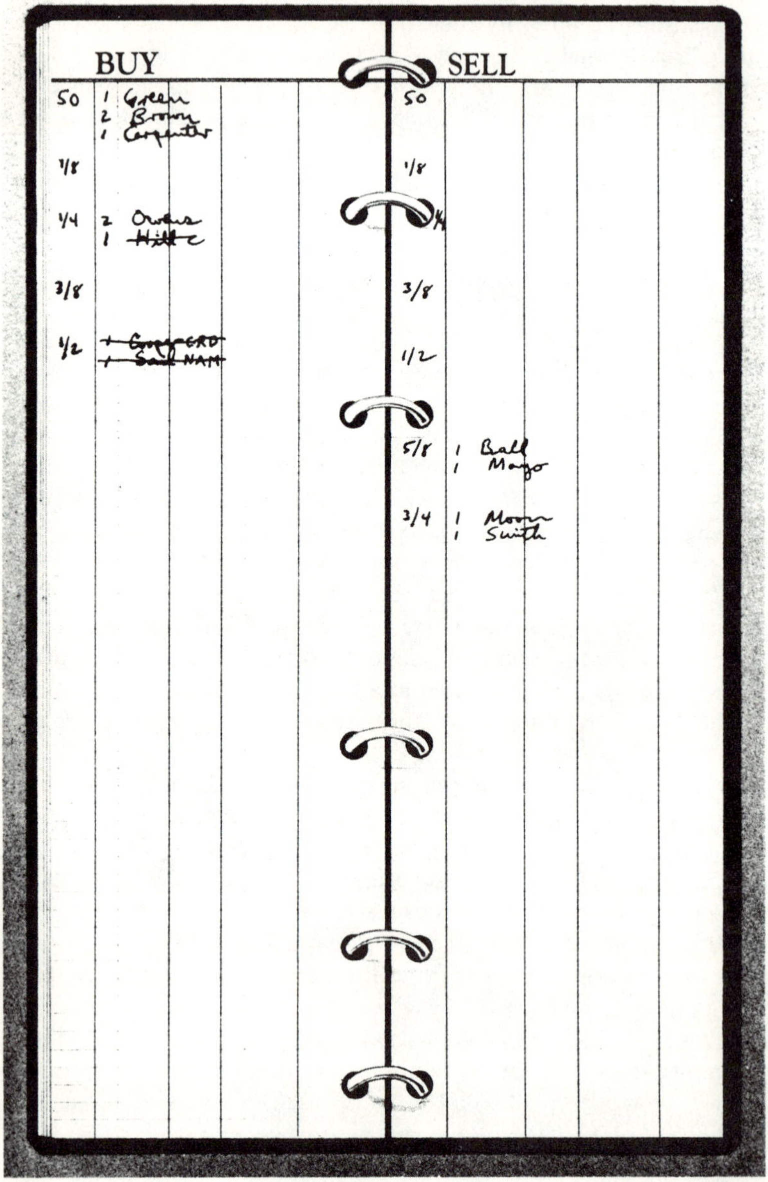

SOURCE: Reprinted from ***The Specialist***, published by the New York Stock Exchange, Inc., 1975.

The buy orders are arranged in ascending order from 50, the lowest level in the range, to 50½, the highest level at which a buy order has been submitted; the sell orders move in the opposite direction, starting with the highest level at which an order has been entered and ending with the lowest. Both the number of shares desired and the name of the requesting broker are also shown. Completed transactions are simply crossed out. In the illustrated page, for example, the buy orders at 50½ have been executed and the names of the selling brokers are indicated; the buy order for 100 shares at 50¼ has been canceled, as indicated by the absence of a selling broker's name. After these changes, the quotation of the stock is 50¼-50⅝, representing the highest bid and lowest offer in the specialist's book.

In his dealer's role, the specialist is expected to maintain a fair and orderly market in the stocks assigned to him. The Exchange Act originally contained a negative obligation that the specialist "... shall restrict his dealings so far as practicable to those reasonably necessary to permit him to maintain a fair and orderly market." This provision created confusion and was dropped in the new amendments. Indeed, the possibility of an automated central market raises a further possibility that the specialist's role might be confined to that of dealing on his own account, stripped of his capacity to act as a broker's broker.

The specialist serves to maintain a fair and orderly market by purchasing or selling shares for his own account when there is a wide disparity between the prevailing bid and offer prices. Let us assume, for example, that a stock's current quotation is 50-51 and that the last sale was 51. Deciding that this gap is too wide, the specialist might enter his own bid at 50½, thereby obtaining a more favorable price than would have been available without his intervention; better price continuity also would be maintained, since the variation from the last sale now would be a half point rather than a full point. (That might have been the case without the participation of the specialist.) Under somewhat different circumstances—say, if the last sale had been 50—the specialist might feel that the buying interest is stronger and therefore submit an offer at 50¼, hoping to achieve better market movements by this play.

The responsibility of maintaining orderly markets is important. To do so, a specialist keeps an inventory of stocks. He may also have to *sell short,* which means selling shares that he does not own. Because he is at the focal point of trading, the specialist also plays an important role in arranging the opening prices of stocks, seeking to balance the buy and sell orders available so that maximum executions are obtained in a manner that maintains price continuity.

The emergence of institutional trading in large blocks has diminished the key role of the specialist, but he still is a vital cog in the overall exchange machinery. Accordingly, it is important that qualified personnel are appointed. At present, allocation is made by a floor committee, most of whose members work on the trading floor. The committee determines which specialists should be assigned new stocks and, on the infrequent occasions when a change is considered desirable because of poor performance, it decides who should be the new recipient. Registration of specialists began in the mid-1930s, when the practice was authorized by the Exchange Act. Before 1934, member firms could choose stocks for specialization, and competition continued for a short time after the Exchange Act was passed. Gradually, however, competition disappeared, as the stronger firms eliminated the weaker ones. Recently, the NYSE has been considering a system of competing specialists.

Various tests have been employed to gauge the performance of the specialist in maintaining a fair and orderly market. The *participation rate,* for example, is calculated by dividing specialists' purchases and sales for their own accounts by all reported purchases and sales. The *stabilization rate* indicates the extent to which the specialist made purchases at prices below or sales at prices above the last different price. A third measure of performance is *price continuity,* which shows the percentage of transactions in a stock at the same price as the preceding one or at a variation of not more than ¼. In 1974 the participation rate for specialists in the NYSE was 13.4 percent, the stabilization rate was 91.1 percent, and price continuity was 97.8 percent. In order to insure that specialists are financially able to fulfill their responsibilities, the exchange also imposes certain capital requirements.

Despite these efforts to provide for high performance quality, the current specialist system has been attacked in various quarters. Critics have charged that specialization is a closed system which excludes competition; that many specialists are inadequately capitalized; that the tests do not properly measure performance; and that the specialists' earnings are too high because they function both as brokers, receiving commissions from other members, and as dealers. Reflecting these criticisms, the exchange has been reevaluating both its method of assigning stocks to specialists and its techniques for measuring their performance.[4] In its reevaluations, the exchange has developed new measures of continuity, depth, and spread; formulated standards for these measures based on regression analysis between the measures and several variables representing characteristics of the stocks; and experimented with gauging the performance of the specialists by comparing the measures applicable to their stocks with the standard measures.

The future of the specialist in the developing central market system is uncertain. For this reason, the SEC has been given various powers to adjust the specialist's role as circumstances warrant. Thus, the commission may permit the specialist to continue the dual roles of broker and dealer, or it may adopt rules to limit the specialist to either role. Additionally, the commission may require the specialist to reveal the orders in the book to all members of the exchange.

Independent brokers ("two-dollar" brokers). More than 100 brokers service commission houses that have no members on the exchange floor or assist houses whose floor members are too busy to handle their own transactions. Dubbed "two-dollar" brokers because they once received that amount for each 100-share lot of stock executed, these independent brokers continued to receive a fixed rate for a period of time during the era of negotiated commissions. Effective May 1, 1976, exchange rules cannot fix any minimum commissions for floor brokerage. In recent years the independent brokers have sometimes been of special help in the handling of large orders.

Registered traders. Approximately 75 members buy and sell for their own accounts. Declining to follow the recommendation of the Special Study of Securities Markets that registered traders be abolished,[5] the SEC in June 1964 adopted a rule that limits their activities. Both the NYSE and the AMEX thereafter issued implementing regulations.

In the original Exchange Act the commission was specifically accorded authority to regulate floor trading. The term, as such, does not appear in the revised law, which covers this area in the same section as institutional membership. This approach was criticized by the SEC because of the possible confusion that might be created. Presumably, however, the commission retains its full powers to regulate floor trading and members' trading for their own accounts.

Odd-lot dealers. Except for certain inactive and very high priced stocks, the unit of trading on the NYSE is a "*round lot*" that consists of 100 shares. An order to buy or sell a lesser number of shares is known as an *odd lot.* Through the Securities Industry Automation Corporation (SIAC), a jointly owned subsidiary of the NYSE and the AMEX, the odd-lot automation programs of both exchanges are being consolidated into a single order-switching operation that links the member organizations to the odd-lot systems of both exchanges. Most of odd-lot transactions in the NYSE are handled by Carlisle DeCoppett & Co., which receives a differential that is added (in the case of a purchase) or subtracted (in the case of a sale) from the price of the net round-lot transactions. That firm, in turn, trades round lots to offset the long or short positions that it acquires in the course of buying or selling odd lots. In 1972 the NYSE adopted a uniform ⅛ point per share differential for most stocks purchased or sold in odd lots. In the fall of 1975, the NYSE permitted the differential to be determined competitively, although Carlisle retained it. Merrill Lynch is undertaking a plan to trade odd lots without a differential; when proposed, the plan was not approved by the NYSE, but it has SEC support. This program involves matching buy and sell orders, where possible, and making up any imbalance from the firm's own inventory. The outcome to the odd-lot investor could be a better or inferior price, depending on the pattern of round-lot transactions.

Executing a Transaction

On the floor of the exchange, an investor has the protection of an auction market. Thus, a broker who has a sell order cannot simply match it with the buy order of another customer. Any lower prices submitted by the specialist or by a competing customer of another firm will displace the offer of the first broker's selling customer. The sell orders also will be matched against the highest bids that have been submitted. The essence of an auction market is this displacement process, which assures executions at the best prevailing bids and offers.

The NYSE auction market has two distinctive characteristics. First, it is continuous: the completion of one auction may be followed by the immediate start of another in the same stock. This method contrasts with the "call" market which existed in the early days of the exchange's history and still takes place in some foreign markets; in the typical call market, the auction of each security occurs as its name is called during a designated time period. Second, the auction is of a two-way sort: buyers competing by raising their bids, sellers by lowering their offers.

For those occasions when the regular auction market cannot absorb a block of stock within a reasonable time and at a reasonable price or prices, the exchange has devised special methods. The most important of these is the secondary distribution, which ordinarily involves a distribution after trading hours, through a selling group or syndicate, at a fixed price that does not exceed the last sale price on the floor. Another method is the exchange acquisition or distribution, whereby the necessary orders are accumulated and then crossed with the original order in the auction market on the exchange floor between the current bid-and-asked quotation. In a special bid or offer, the terms are printed on the tape to invite participation outside the auction market. Lastly, the specialists may be allowed to effect a negotiation outside the regular auction.

These special methods are intended to facilitate large transactions, but they are not widely used. Essentially, the trading mechanism is geared to handle orders of relatively modest size, and a round lot of 100 shares remains the basic unit of trading. But as institutions have become more important factors in the market, large transactions have grown increasingly significant. For example, in 1974 a total of 23,000 large blocks (defined as those involving 10,000 shares or more) were traded, representing 549.4 million shares, or 15.6 percent of reported volume. This compared with 2,171 large blocks in 1965 (when the NYSE first began publishing these statistics), representing somewhat over 48 million shares and only 3.1 percent of reported volume. (1973 and 1974 block transactions represented the only two declines since 1965.) Because the special methods could not cope with the pressures created by these large-scale demands, the members of the exchange developed their own system for dealing in them. Therefore executing ordinary-sized and big block trades must be distinguished.

The Ordinary-Sized Transaction

Let us assume that Mr. Smith in Seattle has decided to sell 200 shares of U.S. Steel. He goes to the brokerage firm where he has an account and asks his registered representative to ascertain the quotation for the stock. Through a terminal on his desk, the representative has instant access to a computer center that receives current information from the exchange's Market Data System. Integrated into this system are a number of optical card-readers strategically distributed among the trading posts to provide full automated reporting of stock transactions to the computer. By this means, information on transactions is transmitted to thousands of stock tickers and other display devices throughout the world and a variety of statistical information is made available to the brokers. Interrogating the system, the registered representative informs Mr. Smith that the current quotation is "54 to a quarter," meaning that the highest prevailing bid is $54 and the lowest prevailing offer is $54.25. (In order to ascertain the number of shares bid and offered, a call would have to be placed directly to the firm's floor broker.)

Mr. Smith instructs the registered representative to sell 200 shares at the market price. The representative, in turn, wires the order to the New York office, where it is phoned to the firm's member on the exchange floor. He, in turn, hurries to the booth, commonly called the post, where U.S. Steel is traded. There are 23 posts, each representing the trading center for a particular group of stocks. At the specialist's post, brokers interested in the stock are clustered, and the following dialogue takes place.

Floor broker 1: "How's Steel?"

Specialist: "Four bid, offered at a quarter." (The specialist or a broker in the specialist's book is willing to buy the stock at $54 and to sell it at $54.25; since some time has elapsed, the quotation could have changed.)

Floor broker 1: "Two hundred at four and an eighth." (The broker could have sold the stock at the highest prevailing bid of $54, but he wants to get the best possible price for his firm's customer, so he submits an offer that is below the lowest prevailing offer but still above the highest bid. In the parlance of the exchange, the number of shares precedes the price in an offer to sell, as in the illustration. The price comes first in a bid to buy: for example, "Four and an eighth for 200.")

Floor broker 2: "I'll take 200 at four and an eighth." (Indicative of the trading skill of floor broker 1, he has managed to attract another broker with an order to buy 200 shares of U.S. Steel.)

In this illustration, the auction process has permitted a transaction to be arranged without the intervention of a dealer. Had no broker been willing to buy the stock that Mr. Smith wanted to sell, the specialist probably would have submitted a bid for his own account as a dealer.

After this verbal agreement has been consummated, the two brokers exchange their firms' names and, through their phone clerks, report the transaction to their home offices for processing and notification to the customer. In the meantime, an exchange employee notes the stock's symbol, the number of shares involved, and the price on a special card that is placed in the optical reader for transmission to the Market Data System computer.

The last stage in this saga of a transaction is the exchange of securities and funds, arranged through the facilities of a clearing corporation. Clearing members report their transactions to the corporation, where they are compared; a list is prepared for each broker showing, for each security, the broker's purchases and sales for which matches have been found.

The broker must deliver net amounts sold to the clearing corporation, and he looks to the clearing corporation for delivery of net purchases. If the broker cannot deliver the required number of shares, he owes them to the clearing corporation, not to another brokerage house. Similarly, if brokers fail to deliver enough shares to the clearing corporation—so that the corporation, in turn, cannot complete deliveries to the buying brokers—the buying brokers continue to look to the clearing corporation for ultimate delivery, not to the brokers who failed to deliver. Most shares are transferred from one broker to another by appropriate entries in the records of shares on deposit with the Depository Trust Co., in which most NYSE member firms keep certificates placed in their custody by their customers. Brokers also keep cash balances with the clearing corporation; cash settlements are made by simple debits or credits to these accounts.

This system of clearing is known as the *continuous net settlement system.* It was originally developed by the Pacific Clearing Corp. and has now been generally adopted by all clearing corporations in the United States. As the following chapter indicates, these corporations are being integrated into a national clearing system that will reduce certificate deliveries and cut expenses.

In the absence of an agreement to the contrary, the settlement customarily occurs on the fifth business day following the date of the contract. A cash sale calls for delivery on the same day; such transactions are common on the last days of the year, in order to establish capital losses for tax purposes. A seller's option gives the seller the right to deliver the securities at any time within a specified period, ranging from not less than 6 business days to not more than 60. If the securities are not delivered as required, the recipient broker may "buy them in," as provided by the rules of the exchange.

Block Transactions

The implementation of an institution's decision to purchase or sell securities is a complex task involving a close working relationship between the institution's trader and the trader at an institutional brokerage house. Several factors are involved in the institution's choice of a broker-dealer. In addition to the overall expertise of the firm in handling such orders, the institution will consider whether the firm has done any research on the particular situation, whether the firm has recently traded any other large blocks of the same security, and whether the firm has recently expressed an interest in buying or selling the security on either its own or another customer's behalf.

After the firm has been chosen, the most effective means of implementing the purchase or sale must be determined. Should the brokerage house participate in transactions that are occurring on the floor, or should it be aggressive and initiate transactions? Should the brokerage house use its own communications facilities to contact potential parties on the other side? If a decision is made to participate in floor transactions, a working order will be handled by the firm's own floor broker either independently or in conjunction with the specialist. Restrictions might be placed on the price of the order. In addition, the amount of securities to be purchased or sold might be limited to a given percentage of the volume being transacted on the exchange floor. Such an acquisition or disposition program can continue for a number of days or even weeks. Often, however, the existence of such an order comes to the attention of an institution with the opposite intention, and the two parties can then be brought together to complete a cross of the stock.

To attract purchases it is usually necessary to offer some price concession from the last sale, but the selling institution ordinarily has its own limit as to how low it is willing to go. With these factors of supply and demand at various price levels in mind, the institutional brokerage house attempts to find buyers for the entire block within the price constraints set by the seller. Generally, if the broker is unsuccessful in finding buyers for all of the shares, he will either *position* that portion of the block which remains (that is, purchase it for the brokerage house's own account) or go back to the seller with a request that a lower price be accepted. While putting the block together, the institutional brokerage house is in continuous contact with its brokers on the floor of the NYSE and the regional exchanges, in order to determine whether there are any buyers available from these sources. Included among potential buyers would generally be the specialist in the stock.

After buying interest has been found for the entire block, the broker will check with all participants to see that they are satisfied with the terms; if they are, the block will be sent to the floor for execution. If the trade is to be done at a discount from the last sale, NYSE rules require that the specialist substitute his own bid for any public bid on the book and that he then buy 100 shares for his own account at the bid price. All other public orders on the book at that price (and at every interval down to the block price) will then be executed at the same price as the block. After the execution, the institutional brokerage house notifies all the buyers and sellers of the prices they have received or paid. The orders are then confirmed in writing for settlement on the fifth business day following the date of execution.

When it is ready to execute a block, the institutional brokerage house may choose to bring the block to a regional exchange rather than to the NYSE. The reasons for doing so have varied over time. They have included avoiding a print on the NYSE tape,* recapturing commissions, and avoiding New York State taxes. In addition, the brokerage house may wish to avoid surrendering part of the block to the specialist and his book, or it may believe that the regional exchange provides a better market.

Securities Traded

The gateway for trading on the NYSE is the listing standard, which has been evolving ever since, more than 100 years ago, the exchange issued its first requirement—that it be informed of all stock issued and valid for trading. At present, the rules are quite stringent, designed to attract companies of financial substance which have sufficient shares outstanding for adequate liquidity. To attract companies of this sort, the listing criteria set minimum standards for size, earning power, shares publicly held, number of round-lot shareholders, and aggregate market value. If these standards become seriously abridged in the case of an already listed security, the exchange may suspend trading or delist the shares.

Once a company has listed its shares, the NYSE imposes certain other requirements. The company must issue an annual report with certified financial statements and must allow common stockholders the right to vote for directors. The exchange has also encouraged listed companies to adopt good financial reporting practices. In a white paper on corporate disclosure, it recommended, among other things, corporate audit committees, a minimum

*With the inauguration of a consolidated tape in June 1975, such avoidance is no longer possible.

of three "outside" directors (at least two outside directors are required for newly listed companies), distribution of quarterly reports, and experimental changes in the form of the annual report.[6] In general, the listing standards of the other exchanges cover similar areas but are less exacting than those of the NYSE. For example, the average NYSE issue has approximately six times as many shares outstanding as the average AMEX issue, and the aggregate of all NYSE issues is approximately 16 times as great as the aggregate market value of all AMEX issues.[7] Nevertheless, there are a number of stocks listed on the AMEX or, for that matter, traded over-the-counter that meet NYSE standards.

The original Securities Exchange Act permitted an exchange to obtain unlisted trading privileges in a stock at its own request until 1936. Through this means, the stock could be traded on the exchange even though the company did not go through the listing procedures. Since this provision was temporary, the SEC was directed to study the subject further. Following the SEC's recommendations, Congress adopted an amendment to the Exchange Act intended to allow each type of market to develop according to its "natural genius." The amendment provided three ways of conducting unlisted trading, the most important of which was that the commission was empowered to extend such trading privileges to any security listed on any other national securities exchange. At first, the SEC insisted that to obtain permission for unlisted trading of a security, an exchange had to establish that adequate distribution and trading interest existed in its vicinity. But gradually this restriction was relaxed, and it became relatively simple to obtain trading privileges in any security listed on another exchange. Predominantly, this has meant unlisted trading in NYSE shares on the regional exchanges.

The 1975 amendments extend the authority of the SEC to define securities suitable for trading in the national market system and to allow an exchange to initiate trading in securities not listed on an exchange. Thus, unlisted trading in over-the-counter securities has become possible. To guide the commission in considering applications for unlisted trading privileges, the new measure establishes certain standards, including public trading activity in the security, the impact of the extension on existing markets for the security and on competition, and the progress that has been made toward development of a national market system. This extension of authority reflects the underlying theory that once such a system is functioning, stocks should attract the type of market warranted by their trading characteristics. Thus, stocks with sufficient investor interest would gravitate to markets where auction trading predominated, while less active issues would move to markets where the participation of dealers, buying and selling for their own accounts, was necessary. In these circumstances it was believed undesirable for corporate management to be able to limit the markets in which a security may be traded by deciding not to list it on an exchange.

REGIONAL EXCHANGES

The ten registered and one unregistered stock exchanges located outside New York City are loosely described as regional exchanges. By and large, they emerged to help finance the developing needs of different regions of the country. Without modern means of communication, these needs had to be satisfied through local investors, who found transactions with distant parties difficult. As New York City rose to prominence as the nation's commercial and money-market center, the NYSE outdistanced the regional exchanges, which nevertheless played a part in financing the growth of their localities.

The regional exchanges attained their peak of importance in the late 1920s, as hectic interest in the securities markets encouraged a greatly enlarged number of issuers to seek listings on the local exchanges. A change occurred in 1929, when the collapse of the securities markets led to a severe reduction in the number of previously listed stocks. Moreover, the regulation of listed securities embodied in the Exchange Act (plus various technological advances) encouraged interest in over-the-counter trading. Meanwhile, at the opposite end of the market spectrum, issuers tended to skip the seasoning period at the regionals and seek direct listing in New York.

As the number of solely traded securities waned, the regionals found a new source of vigor in the increased trading of securities on more than one exchange, particularly the NYSE, a practice known as *multiple trading*. This practice was encouraged by the lenient attitude of the SEC toward granting unlisted trading privileges. Additionally, the number of *dual members*—that is, regional members who also hold seats in the principal New York exchanges—increased noticeably.

The rise of multiple trading and dual members set the stage for the major modern development: competition for trading in NYSE listed securities. Sometimes this competition encouraged questionable practices that, in turn, led to pressure for change or regulation. For example, at one time a sole member that had to pay full NYSE commissions might direct an order to a dual member on the principal exchange as a basis for reciprocal commission business forwarded to it by the dual member; the inducement for this practice was eased in 1972, when, at the insistence of the SEC, the NYSE rules were amended to allow up to a 40 percent discount for nonmember broker-dealers. Then again, institutions at one time engaged in the practice of directing a broker-dealer to "give up" a part of the commission charges to other broker-dealers who provided some services to the institution; this practice encouraged directing business to the regional exchanges, which had relatively lenient "give up" rules. Under pressure by the SEC, the NYSE prohibited customer-directed "give ups", while the NASD adopted an "antireciprocal" rule prohibiting the use of portfolio executions by investment companies to reward broker-dealers who sell the investment company's shares.

These various factors contributed to a revival of activity in the regionals which, as indicated in Table 1-1, transacted in 1973 about 12 percent of both the market value and the number of shares traded on all registered exchanges.

TABLE 1-1

Dollar and Share Volume of Stocks Traded on Registered Exchanges, 1973

EXCHANGE	DOLLAR VALUE (IN THOUSANDS)	PERCENTAGE OF TOTAL*	SHARE VOLUME (IN THOUSANDS)	PERCENTAGE OF TOTAL*
American	$ 10,269,776	5.77	734,499	12.83
Boston	1,792,908	1.01	42,171	.74
Chicago Board of Trade	0	0	0	0
Cincinnati	118,849	.07	2,838	.05
Detroit	380,532	.21	10,676	.19
Intermountain	996	—	2,262	.04
Midwest	8,131,114	4.57	240,415	4.20
National	23,896	.01	7,462	.13
New York	146,450,834	82.33	4,336,581	75.77
Pacific	6,315,636	3.55	206,234	3.60
PBW	4,386,341	2.47	126,991	2.22
Spokane	6,685	—	13,031	.23
Total	$177,877,567	99.99	5,723,160	100.00

*Percentages do not add up to 100 because of rounding of data.

SOURCE: Dollar and share volume data from Securities and Exchange Commission, *Annual Report*, 1974, p. 158; percentages calculated by the authors.

Of the regional exchanges, the Midwest (which represents a merger of four prior exchanges) and the Pacific (representing a merger of the San Francisco and Los Angeles exchanges) are consistently the biggest. Next is the PBW, which was formed by the merger of the Philadelphia, Baltimore, and Washington exchanges and which also absorbed the Pittsburgh Stock Exchange at the close of 1969. The Boston Exchange, which at one time ranked with the principal regionals, has lagged behind in recent years.

THE OVER-THE-COUNTER MARKET

Perhaps the *over-the-counter* (OTC) *market* may be defined in a negative manner as representing transactions in securities outside the stock exchanges. There is no defined physical location to this market. Purchases and sales are effected through the facilities of a large number of brokerage firms of varying sizes; these keep in touch with each other through an intricate network of private wires, telephone lines, and most recently an electronic quotation system. Most of these firms are not members of any registered exchange. Their dealings, as well as the OTC transactions of the member firms, are subject to the rules of the NASD.

The 1964 amendments to the Securities Exchange Act ended the once lax regulatory aspect of the OTC market by requiring a registered securities association to establish appropriate standards for its members and by subjecting the relatively big companies with securities traded in the OTC market to periodic reporting requirements, proxy regulations, and insider trading rules similar to those applicable to listed companies.

OTC Trading

Approximately 20,000 securities are traded solely in the OTC market. Activity ordinarily revolves around the *market maker*, who serves as a wholesale dealer, indicating a willingness to buy or sell by maintaining quotations on both sides of the market. Market making may range from the sporadic activities of individual dealers to continuous competition among 30 or more dealers in the large, active issues. Unlike the specialist, the OTC market maker does not have the formal responsibility of keeping a fair and orderly market, but competition does put pressure on him to maintain reasonable pricing standards in the stocks for which he holds himself responsible. Thus, without having any legal responsibility to do so, the market maker, by assuming the risk of taking long and short positions, contributes marketability to a security. The 1975 law specifically authorizes the SEC to prescribe standards for OTC market makers.

A broker-dealer who is not a primary market maker and has no inventory in a particular stock may engage in a so-called riskless transaction. He does so by serving as a middleman between his customer and another broker-dealer, buying from one and selling to the other, as the case may be.

An investor who wishes to buy or sell an OTC issue ordinarily will deal with a firm that does a retail business. Such a firm generally executes standard-size transactions at the bid or offer of the market maker, who, in turn, adjusts his quotations in the light of his own inventory, the competition, and his judgment of market conditions. The firm doing business with the public may be a retailer or an integrated firm that engages in both retail and wholesale activities.

Transactions in the OTC market generally are conducted on a net basis—that is, there is no commission charge, but the price of the security includes a markup imposed by the dealer. The size of the markup is determined by such things as the type of firm, the size of the transaction, the state of the market, and the general relationship of the customer to the firm. Also important is the policy of the NASD, which maintains control over the relationship between the markup and the prevailing price of the security. Commissions on agency transactions in the OTC market during the period of fixed commissions tended to follow practices in the listed market. The investor is free to dictate that the transaction should be conducted on a net or commission basis, but if nothing is specified, the broker may use the method he prefers.

National Association of Securities Dealers Automated Quotation (NASDAQ) System

NASDAQ was introduced on February 8, 1971, by the NASD. It is a computerized system which enables price quotations to be displayed on a real-time basis on cathode ray terminals located in subscribers' offices.

The service operates on three levels. Level I, intended primarily for use by registered representatives, provides a current "representative bid and asked" quotation. The "representative bid" is the median bid of all market makers maintaining a quotation in that issue; the "representative asked" is determined by adding the median spread between the bid and asked quotations of all market makers to the median bid. Level II supplies the actual bid and asked quotations of all registered market makers. Level III furnishes the Level II information and allows the user to key in his own bid and asked quotations.

Any security, listed or not, which is eligible for SEC registration, has at least two market makers, and meets NASD "listing" requirements may be included in NASDAQ. To enter a quotation, a dealer must register as a market maker in that security, meet minimum capital requirements, and stand ready to execute a trade for at least one normal unit of trading (ordinarily 100 shares) at the price he or she is currently quoting.

OTC stocks that are not in NASDAQ may be quoted in the so-called "pink sheets" published daily by the National Quotation Bureau. Any broker who has paid the requisite fee can indicate an interest in receiving either bids or offers without being on both sides of the market. Because the "pink sheets" are published documents, the quotations tend to be out-of-date, and therefore a broker technically is required to make at least three inquiries in order to get the best price. For the great bulk of stocks in which there is trading interest, NASDAQ has supplanted the "pink sheets."

In 1975, NASDAQ was furnishing the quotations of more than 390 market makers in about 2,600 securities to 570 subscribers with approximately 1,160 terminals. In addition, NASDAQ provided representative quotations to registered representatives on 27,500 terminals. The NASD requires NASDAQ market makers to report their trading activity at the end of each day. Volume in the NASDAQ system for 1973 was 1.6 billion shares, a little more than twice the AMEX share volume and about 30 percent of that of the NYSE. NASDAQ trading volume reflects the number of shares bought and sold by market makers plus their net inventory changes.

At present, NASDAQ is a pricing system, and a subscriber still has to communicate directly with the market maker to complete the transaction. As a quotation system it has been criticized because of the shallowness of its quotations. Some market makers desert the system in periods of difficulty; others are opportunistic, "skimming the cream" for a short period, then adding to stock volatility when profit opportunities disappear. The NASD has been seeking to upgrade the system by tightening "listing" requirements, strengthening the role of the market makers, and including the number of shares in the quotation. Also, the NASD has been studying a plan, called automatic execution, that would permit shares to be bought and sold directly.

THIRD MARKET

The term *third market* refers to OTC trading in securities listed on an exchange by nonmembers of that exchange; by far the most important segment is in NYSE-listed stocks. From 1965, when the SEC first began collecting reports on these transactions, until 1972 volume increased steadily (see Figure 1-2). In 1972 the ratio of third-market volume to NYSE volume on a share basis was 7.3 percent, and 8.5 percent on a dollar basis; in 1965, the share ratio was 2.7 percent, the dollar ratio 3.4 percent. In 1973 the ratio dropped to 5.8 percent and 7.0 percent, the first decline since 1966. The share ratio continued the decline in 1974, reaching a level of 5.3 percent, while the dollar ratio stabilized at 7.0 percent. In part, the shrinkages may reflect a falloff in the proportion of NYSE volume done by institutions during this period. Because of differences in the methods of calculating volume in the two markets, these ratios of third-market to NYSE volume may be somewhat understated. In the first two months of consolidated tape experience, when NYSE and third-market volume were calculated on the same basis, the share ratio was almost 7 percent. At times, OTC trading in particular stocks has exceeded that on the NYSE.

At the heart of the third market is a small group of firms that are actively engaged as principals in buying and selling exchange securities and that serve as market makers in these securities. Their business is done with professionals, including commercial banks, insurance companies, investment

FIGURE 1-2

Third-Market Volume in NYSE Stocks

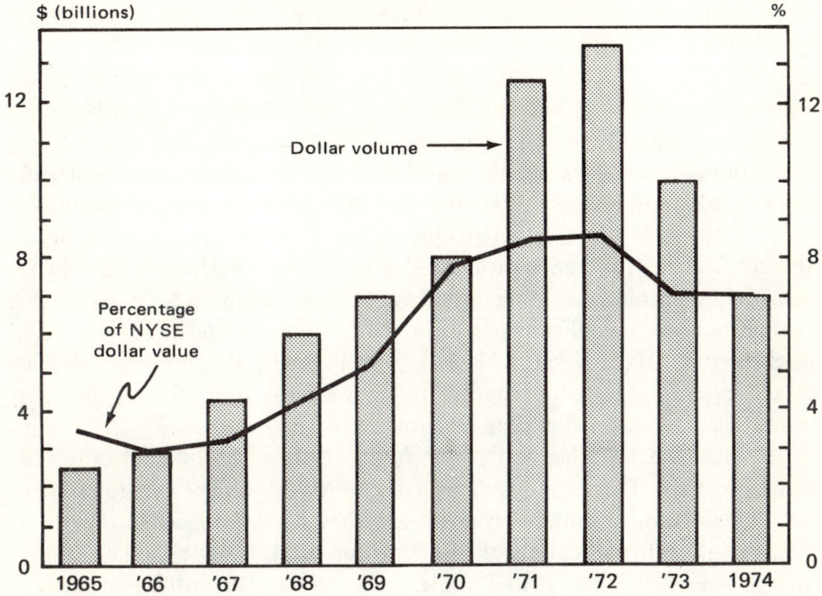

SOURCE: Securities and Exchange Commission, ***Annual Report***, 1974, p. 160; updated to include 1974 figures, taken from New York Stock Exchange, ***1975 Fact Book***, p. 16.

companies, pension funds, and brokers. Individual investors have access to the third market through brokers and commercial banks. Although the principal portion of the business of the third-market firms is in big orders, the bulk of their trades is in small orders. For example, in the fourth quarter of 1973, about 25 percent of the share volume of Weeden & Co. (the leading third-market firm) was in trades below 1,000 shares (including about 2.5 percent in odd lots), while approximately 88 percent of the firm's transactions was in trades falling in that size range. Through doing business with third-market firms, institutions hope to obtain a better price, reduce costs, or complete the transaction in a shorter period of time than by going to the exchange where the security is listed. Third-market firms may also make markets in unlisted securities.

Indicative of the nature of the business of third-market firms was the reaction of Weeden & Co. to New York City's program, effective as of August 1975, of raising the stock-transfer tax by 25 percent and imposing a new levy of 25 cents per $1,000 bond on both buyers and sellers. Unlike the typical broker, who acts for a client, Weeden is a dealer, trading from its own inventory at the best possible prices it can obtain. Thus, while a broker can transmit the tax cost to customers, Weeden, as a dealer, cannot; since the firm owns the securities, it pays the tax directly. Accordingly, the new measures imposed a formidable burden upon Weeden, leading the firm to plan a move of its stock- and bond-trading and trade-supported operations to New Jersey to reduce its tax cost.

This field is highly competitive, and institutions will both shop and negotiate to obtain the best possible terms. Prices depend on such factors as the dealer's inventory, his judgment of the market, his desire to be competitive, and the size of the trade involved. The third-market dealer has more freedom to operate than the exchange specialist, who is limited by NYSE Rule 113, which, among other things, prohibits his accepting orders directly from institutional customers. On the other hand, the specialist enjoys monopoly control of his book. Another NYSE limitation is Rule 394, which establishes a procedural program for member firms that desire to trade listed stocks in the OTC market. This rule gained considerable notoriety because of the pressure exerted primarily by third-market firms for its abandonment. (All the registered exchanges have such a rule.)

Under the 1975 legislation, the future of these rules is subject to SEC determinations. The commission is empowered to review the rules of all self-regulatory organizations to make sure they do not restrain competition. Responding to this direction, the SEC, within 90 days after the law's enactment, forwarded a letter to Congress, contending that off-board rules of exchanges–notably the NYSE's Rule 394–impose burdens on competition. Subsequently, in December 1975, the commission adopted Rule 19C-1, which provides that after March 31, 1976, an exchange may not restrict its members from executing an order off board as agent where a third-market firm or off-board block trader is involved. Until January 2, 1977, the rule permits an exchange to require its members to clear the book on such transactions. Although the commission did not prohibit exchanges from continuing to prevent members from doing principal transactions off the floor, the commission indicated that it would reconsider that decision no later than March 1, 1977.

FOURTH MARKET

The *fourth market* ordinarily is defined to encompass direct securities transactions between institutional investors that occur outside of normal brokerage channels. Historically, such transactions have permitted two institutions with heavy concentrations in single stocks to obtain some diversification by swapping some of their holdings. A typical example was the arrangement between the Ford Foundation and the Rockefeller Foundation to exchange the common stocks of the Ford Motor Co. and Standard Oil of New Jersey with each other. Eventually, some individuals entered into the business of bringing together parties that could profitably deal with each other in this manner. The most dramatic step was the appearance of Instinet, which is now the only fully automated communications system executing transactions in securities. (A licensee operates in England under the name of Arïel.)

The Instinet system places a computer terminal (a television screen with keyboard) in the trading department of each of its subscribers, almost all of which are major institutional investors.[8] By each terminal is a compact unit that prints confirmations and records of orders instantaneously, as they are sent or received. A private, leased telephone circuit links each subscriber's terminal to a large-scale computer. Subscribers enter their bids or offers into the system, showing the name and amount of the stock, the desired price, and any time limit on the bid or offer they may wish to set. They may indicate that this information is to be broadcast, in which case it will appear automatically on the screens of all other Instinet subscribers. Or they may enter an order only in the "book," where it will be seen only by subscribers who interrogate the system specifically about that security.

A trader who enters an order matching another order already in the "book" instantly receives a confirmation of a purchase or sale. If he enters an order which is not matched in the "book," he may attract another bid or counteroffer, which he can then negotiate to a trade. In either case, he receives his confirmation instantly, as does the trader on the other side. The system also simultaneously generates all the information necessary for the prompt settlement of the transaction through an escrow bank. All the negotiating information leading to the final trade is preserved in the system. Although Instinet has grown slowly, there is considerable logic to its method of bringing institutions together.

The charges for executing transactions through fourth-market firms typically have been below commission rates. Immediately after the advent of competitive rates, activity in the fourth market rose sharply; presumably because the pension-reform legislation and the introduction of competitive fees highlighted the fiduciary responsibility of obtaining best execution at the lowest price.[9] It is not clear, however, what the long-term effect will be.

THE BOND MARKET

There are about 2,200 bond issues on the NYSE, representing the debt of U.S. and foreign corporations, the U.S. government, New York City, international banks and foreign governments. Because bonds are traded in large amounts and have special characteristics, the rules of the NYSE ordinarily permit transactions to be executed off the floor even though the issue is listed. Accordingly, bonds are handled primarily in the OTC market, where, it will be remembered, dealers buffer the imbalances in the flow of orders by positioning the securities for which they make a market.

The actual buying and selling of securities are carried on by traders associated with dealer firms or with large institutions. An institutional trader becomes familiar with the dealers who make markets in the securities in which the institution is interested. By keeping close ties, the institutional trader can gauge whether the dealer is long or short, and the side of the market in which the dealer is likely to be aggressive.

An institution may have direct communications lines to the active dealers; the number of lines depends on its size. On the other hand, individual investors place orders with brokers, who transmit them to their traders for execution. The trader probably will explore the market and obtain several quotations before actually effecting a purchase or sale.

Dealer banks play an important role in the market for bonds of the U.S. government and federal agencies and for general obligations of state and local governments. In the case of U.S. government bonds, the Federal Reserve Bank of New York, which is the fiscal agent for the U.S. government and the Federal Reserve System, recognizes certain "primary dealers." By agreeing to abide by certain rules, such a dealer becomes entitled to a private line between the reserve bank's trading desk and its own. Without this direct line, which may be withdrawn if its performance is considered unsatisfactory, a dealer would be severely handicapped.

With respect to the primary market, the methods of distributing the different types of bonds have certain distinctive features. Corporate securities, whether bonds or stocks, are initially sold in much the same way. In the typical negotiated transaction, one or more investment bankers are selected to manage and develop the issue, help obtain SEC registration, arrange the offering price, and assemble a buying group. The managers also form a selling syndicate to market the issue. The issuer may invite investment bankers to form a syndicate to bid competitively for the offering.

Municipal obligations are also marketed through investment bankers, including, in this case, a number of major commercial banks; the bonds ordinarily are sold by competitive bidding, and they do not require SEC registration. U.S. government issues, on the other hand, are characteristically offered through the Federal Reserve System instead of being underwritten by investment bankers.

PLACING AN ORDER IN THE SECURITIES MARKETS

Before actually engaging in any securities transactions, the investor must open either a cash or a margin account with a brokerage firm. A *cash account* requires full payment for each security bought, while a *margin account* enables the investor to obtain a loan from the broker to meet part of the purchase cost of a security. After the account is opened, the investor may place various types of orders, depending on his or her objectives and assessment of the market.

Margin Buying

When an investor buys stock on credit, he buys "on margin."[10] The *margin* is the amount of cash he has to provide. In lieu of cash, he may deposit eligible securities with a loan value equivalent to the margin required. Under the Securities Exchange Act, the Board of Governors of the Federal Reserve System sets the fraction of the price that the investor must initially provide. In October 1934, when the board first acted under this authority, it established a requirement of 45 percent. Since that date, the rate has ranged between a low of 40 percent, established November 1, 1937, and a high of 100 percent, imposed January 21, 1946. Originally, OTC securities were not eligible for margin, but in July 1969 the Board of Governors set criteria for a list of such stocks that could be bought on credit. In June 1974 these criteria, governing the number of stockholders and the market value of outstanding securities, were eased somewhat.

Maintenance of continued margin requirements is subject to the jurisdiction of the exchange where the issue is traded, although individual brokers may provide higher requirements. For the purpose of computing the maintenance margin, a fall in the price of a stock is considered as totally absorbed by the investor, so that his equity in the security shrinks as its price falls. His *equity* is the difference between the market value of the security and the amount borrowed, which, in turn, is called the *debit balance.* Thus, assume an individual purchases 200 shares of a stock selling at 30 and turns $4,500 over to his broker. Disregarding commissions, his equity is $4,500; his debit balance is $1,500; and his margin is 75 percent, which may be defined as the ratio of his equity to market value.

Margin purchases enhance the profit potential of a commitment. Taking the previous example, if the price of the stock doubled to 60, the customer could sell his 200 shares for $12,000. After reimbursing his broker, he would have $10,500 left—a profit of 133 percent on his original investment, not counting costs. On the other hand, margin accounts may be severely affected in declining markets.

The broker always makes certain that his loan is well protected, and he will promptly issue a call for additional margin if he believes his position is endangered. Let us assume now that the maintenance margin requirement established by the broker is 25 percent, which is the minimum level required by the NYSE. If the market price of the security purchased recedes to 10, the total value of the investor's commitment amounts to $2,000. The debit balance still is $1,500, leaving an equity of $500 and a margin of 25 percent. Any drop below 10 in the price of the issue will be followed by a margin call. If the buyer does not immediately deposit additional cash or eligible securities, his account may be sold out; this means that the broker will liquidate sufficient stock to bring the customer's equity up to the minimum margin requirement.

If the equity in an account drops below the current initial margin requirements of the Federal Reserve but is above the minimum maintenance requirements, the account is restricted. This means that cash held in a special miscellaneous account may be withdrawn, provided the account does not become undermargined as a result. The special miscellaneous account is used to hold excess-margin funds derived from such sources as price appreciation, dividends, and the proceeds of sales. When there is no special miscellaneous account, various provisions govern both the withdrawal of funds and the substitution of securities.

In opening a margin account, a customer also signs a securities loan form which gives the broker the authority to pledge or lend securities carried in the account. All brokers hold margined securities in their own name, also known as "street name." (A cash-account customer may want stock to be held in "street name" to facilitate trading.) Dividends are credited to the account, and the customer may tell the broker how to vote the stock or may sell it at his own discretion.

Selling Short

Businessmen may make profits as a result of price advances or declines, provided that they are astute enough to predict the direction of the movements. If price rises are expected, inventories may be accumulated with a view to subsequent disposal at higher levels. If price shrinkages are foreseen, the businessman often seeks the largest possible volume of sales at current levels for future delivery. If the prediction proves correct and prices fall substantially, inventories can be accumulated at a subsequent date, to be converted into finished products for delivery when the market level rises again.

Similar processes occur in the securities markets. If a trader expects prices to rise in the future, he purchases securities at current levels and keeps them in his inventory (portfolio) until he can dispose of them at higher levels. However, if he expects the market to fall, he attempts to sell the largest possible volume of issues at existing prices. He does not own the "products" that he sells, but neither does the businessman who accepts orders that he cannot fill at present.

The principal distinction between the two types of transactions is that the trader in securities must make immediate delivery against his sale, whereas the businessman may make delivery in the future. The trader is therefore compelled to borrow the issues that he must deliver against the sales he makes at existing prices. The process whereby an individual sells a security that he does not own but has borrowed in order to make delivery is called a *short sale.*

The Securities and Exchange Commission has formulated an official definition of the short sale. According to this definition, a short sale is any sale of a security which the dealer does not own, or any sale which is carried out through delivery of a security borrowed by, or for the account of, the seller. These two conditions are separable. If an individual sells an issue he does not own, the transaction is necessarily a short sale. The seller may, however, own the security, but if he effects delivery by borrowing, the transaction is also defined by the SEC as a short sale. This kind of short sale might occur when an individual sells an issue that he owns but keeps too far from the place of sale to permit appropriate delivery; such a transaction is known as "selling against the box."

Borrowing the stock. Let us now assume that, anticipating a market decline, an investor directs his broker to sell 100 shares of General Electric short at 49 on the NYSE. At the appropriate time the order is forwarded to the floor of the stock exchange. After the sale is completed, the broker must deliver 100 shares of General Electric to the purchaser. Since the investor does not have the stock, his broker must either purchase the necessary number of shares or borrow them for him.

It is unlikely that immediate repurchase of General Electric would be profitable; therefore, a loan will probably have to be made. Machinery for facilitating such arrangements exists on the floor of the exchange. In addition, the investor's broker himself may have stock that he can lend, or he may be able to borrow the stock directly from other brokers or from certain nonbrokerage sources.

In return for the loan, the borrowing broker turns over to the lender a sum of money equal to the current market price of the issue—$4,900 in the present transaction. The result of this procedure is that the investor's broker obtains the stock necessary to effect delivery of the shares sold; the lender receives cash, which he may use in the course of his business.

Terms of the loan. Typically, a loan for a short sale is made "flat." The borrower of the securities neither pays interest on the securities he borrows nor receives interest on the money he leaves with the lending broker. However, if the demand for borrowed stock is very high relative to the number of shares available for loans, the borrower may have to pay a premium to the lender for the use of the stock.

Marking to the market. Under the rules of the Board of Governors, lending and borrowing brokers in a short sale are entitled to equalize the market value of the securities borrowed and the funds advanced for the loan.

Thus, if General Electric advances in value by 3 points after the investor's broker borrows the stock, the lender may forward a written request (called a "mark to the market") to the investor's broker for $300. Exchanges of this sort may occur several times during the course of a single short-sale transaction. Settlements may be made directly or through clearing facilities.

Alternatively, the borrower may simply be required to pay the lender the interest on the difference between the "mark to the market" value and the deposit originally made.

Treatment of dividends and rights. During the time that the short seller's broker borrows the 100 shares of General Electric, the company may distribute to its shareholders cash dividends, stock dividends, or rights that enable the holders to buy the company's shares for a specified short period at a discount. If the General Electric stock has been transferred to the name of the purchaser or his agent, neither the short seller nor his broker receives these distributions. The lending broker must, however, credit them to his client's account after the issue sells ex-payments. (The ex-date is the first date at which the buyer of a stock is not entitled to receive a dividend or rights that have been announced.) Accordingly, the short seller's broker is required to provide the lending broker with the cash dividends, stock dividends, or rights declared by the company during the period of the security loan. The broker, in turn, charges the short seller's account for the value of these payments.

"Covering" the short sale. A week has passed since the investor originally sold the 100 shares of General Electric short. The stock has declined to a level of 40. The investor now decides to "cover his position" and asks his broker to purchase 100 shares at the market.

The broker promptly buys the stock at 40. He delivers the 100 shares to the lending broker, who returns the money advanced to him (presumably $4,000 since $900 has been previously returned through marking to the market). The short seller's broker credits his account with this sum, less commissions, taxes, SEC registration fee, and any other charges, such as premiums and dividends. In the case of normal-sized, round-lot orders, these basic costs usually do not exceed 2-3 percent of the market value of the securities sold. The broker also debits the investor's account with the $4,000 required to purchase the stock. The difference of $900, less the cost of the transaction, represents the short seller's profit.

If the stock rises instead of declines, and if the short seller finds it necessary to cover his transaction, the procedure is the same. This time, though, he incurs a loss equal to the difference between the net price of the short sale and the purchase price, plus costs.

Regulating the prices of short sales. The SEC regulates the price at which a short sale may be made. These restrictions are designed to prevent speculative raids on securities, which drive prices down. To this end, the commission has ruled that a short sale may not be made below the price of the last regular-way sale. (Stockbrokers call a transaction made below the price of the last regular-way sale a "down tick.") The short sale may be made at the price of the last regular-way sale if this price is above the previous different regular-way price (a "zero-plus tick"). If the last price of a stock was 60, for example, a short sale could not be made at 59⅞ under any circumstances. It could be made at 60 if the price before the stock sold at this level was a regular-way sale at 59⅞ or less.

These regulations make it necessary for a member with a short-sale order first to ascertain the prices of the last regular-way sale and of the previous different regular-way sale, regardless of when these transactions occurred. "Plus" or "minus" indicators on the trading posts of the exchange supply this information.

Economic implications of short selling. Short selling in the securities markets has been bitterly criticized. It has been claimed that these transactions foster an unhealthy speculative urge and that they accentuate price fluctuations.

Yet the short sale has definite advantages for the economy. After a long market advance, speculators may sell short in expectation of a decline. This process places a blanket on the rising movement, tending to limit what might have developed into an unhealthy boom. If the market declines severely, short sellers begin to cover their positions, and this necessitates new purchases. The resulting buy orders (short covering) serve as a brake on skidding securities prices and tend to stabilize the fluctuations. On the technical side, short selling is a great help to specialists and dealers because it enables them to meet buy orders even though they do not have the stock in inventory.

Short selling also permits arbitrage operations between two markets. If the same securities sell at different prices on two different exchanges, arbitrageurs immediately begin to purchase the lower-priced shares and sell the higher-priced ones short. This process brings the prices of the securities in the different markets into line.

The short sale is one of the integral techniques of trading. As illustrated above, it can be a stabilizing rather than a disturbing influence on market prices. Since most of the dangers of speculative abuses have been eliminated through the supervision of the SEC and the self-regulatory agencies, the abolition of short selling, as now regulated, is undesirable.

Types of Orders

In order to obtain the price desired, the investor may submit various types of orders. The most common are market and limit orders and the stop-loss order.

Market and limit orders. An order may be made "at the market" or "at a limit." Market orders are those to be executed at the best price available. When such orders are presented at the specialist's post on an exchange, they are executed as quickly as possible. If a market order is to buy, the specialist may match the order with the best available on his book; he will usually do so if the result is not an excessive change in price from the last execution. Alternatively, he may sell on his own account at a better price than can be obtained from the book. The rules of the exchanges do not permit a specialist to execute an order on his own account if the book contains one at an equal or better price.

A limit order is one to trade at a specified price or better. For example, a limit order to sell at $50 authorizes a broker to sell the stock at $50 per share, or more whenever he can. Unless otherwise noted, both types of orders are good until canceled (abbreviated as GTC).

Stop-loss order. A stop-loss order generally is an order to purchase or sell a security at the market after a designated price is reached or passed.

For example, let us assume that at a time when Allied Stores common is selling at 29, an owner of the stock places the following stop-loss order: "Sell 100 ALS [the symbol for Allied Stores] 28 Long Stop GTC." Thereafter, Allied Stores sells at $28\frac{1}{2}$, $28\frac{3}{8}$, $28\frac{1}{4}$, $28\frac{1}{4}$, $28\frac{1}{8}$, 28, $27\frac{7}{8}$, $27\frac{7}{8}$, $27\frac{3}{8}$, $27\frac{5}{8}$. The price established in the order is 28. Our definition states that the order becomes a market order as soon as the price of the stock reaches this limit. At that time, the broker must sell the issue as soon as possible, as in any other market order. In the price sequence shown above, he would probably execute the order at $27\frac{7}{8}$. This is below the desired minimum level, but the investor is saved a further loss as the issue continues its decline.

The important principle of the stop-loss order is that it does not guarantee execution at any specific level. It merely converts a limit order to a market order after the limit is reached or passed.

Under normal conditions, a stop-loss order can usually be completed at approximately the price indicated, since price movements tend to be continuous. In volatile markets, however, changes may be abrupt, and the execution price of a stop-loss order may differ substantially from the level specified in the order.

SUMMARY

The major legislative principle underlying the SEC's role in implementing the various securities acts is self-regulation. Thus, primary responsibility for insuring that the exchanges meet their public role rests with the exchanges themselves, and the commission intercedes only when necessary. Under the Securities Acts Amendments of 1975 this concept is clarified, the role of the SEC is strengthened, and the SEC's relationships with all the self-regulatory organizations are made comparable.

On June 30, 1974, there were 13 exchanges registered with the SEC, of which the New York Stock Exchange was by far the dominant, with the American Stock Exchange second. Because of the NYSE's prominence, its operations have largely set the pace for the industry, although in specific areas the regional exchanges have had an impact. Originally run much like a social club, the NYSE, largely under the prodding of Congress and the SEC, has been developing an efficient and more objectively run organization, with public representation on its Board of Directors. According to the 1975 legislation, the rules of an exchange must permit any registered broker or dealer to become a member, unless he cannot meet certain standards of conduct, financial responsibility, or competency. Subject to this broad requirement, an exchange is given some authority to limit the number of members.

There are various categories of exchange membership; among these the specialist is particularly important, because he has a delegated responsibility to maintain fair and orderly markets.

On the floor of the exchange, an investor has the protection of an auction market, which is intended to ensure that executions will be obtained on that exchange at the best prevailing bids and offers. The growth of institutional trading has made it difficult for the regular auction market to absorb large blocks of stock within a reasonable period of time and at reasonable prices. Accordingly, a new form of block trading has developed, wherein an institution desiring to purchase or sell a large block of securities works out the transaction directly with a brokerage house. In such a relationship, the broker may have to position—that is, purchase for its own account—a portion of the block.

Competing with the major New York exchanges are the regional exchanges; a "third market," representing over-the-counter transactions in listed securities; and a "fourth market," representing direct transactions between large buyers and sellers without a broker intermediary. Besides the listed stocks, a great many other securities are handled in the OTC market, where trading is done largely through dealers under the self-regulatory supervision of the National Association of Securities Dealers. That organization has helped develop an automated quotation system, NASDAQ, which has improved considerably the reporting of quotations in the OTC market.

Various categories of orders for buying or selling securities may be placed in the exchange and OTC markets. Important types of transactions are margin buying and short selling.

CHAPTER

The Evolving Structure of the Stock Market

As the decade of the 1960s drew to a close, a confluence of short-term and long-term forces generated great difficulties for the United States stock market in general and for the New York Stock Exchange in particular. Congress, the Department of Justice, different segments of the securities industry, and even the Treasury Department became embroiled in extensive hearings and investigations concerning the industry. Different bills reflected differing intentions: to produce a central market, to strengthen the regulatory hand of the Securities and Exchange Commission, to develop a national clearing system, to eliminate fixed commissions, to clarify the role of institutions, and so forth. Some industry leaders even suggested creation of a new superagency to regulate the industry.

DIFFICULTIES UNDERLYING SECURITIES MARKETS DEVELOPMENT

Although negotiated commissions have been adopted and the Securities Acts Amendments passed, the shape of things to come is not yet clear, and both the commission and the industry view the future with uneasiness. To evaluate the influence of the new amendments and the related operating rules as they emerge, we must first assess the problems that led to the reform efforts.

Institutionalization of the Market

Possibly the most important development in the postwar period has been the gradual domination of the stock market by institutions. There have always been institutional investors, but they showed a dramatic growth during the 1960s, a growth accentuated by a shift in portfolio investment policy toward common stock. Between 1960 and 1971 the equity holdings of private, noninsured pension funds rose by over 500 percent, and state and local retirement funds by over 2,800 percent. Even mutual funds, whose portfolios had always been predominantly in equities, increased their holdings by over 300 percent.

Institutional trading now overshadows the market. At the end of 1974 the selected institutions covered by NYSE studies held one-third of NYSE-listed stocks, and they accounted for over half the exchange's dollar volume during the year. Figure 2-1, showing relative turnover rates, block trading, and contribution to New York Stock Exchange volume, reveals dramatically the importance of institutions in these areas.

The expanding role of institutions in the securities markets has had several important consequences, including a shift in the site of much trading from the floor of the exchange to the third market and the regional exchanges, the erosion of the minimum commission rate system, and the development of special trading patterns. As might be expected, the increased significance of the institutions attracted congressional attention. Senator Lloyd M. Bentsen, Jr., head of a subcommittee on financial markets which has contemplated the idea of limiting institutional holdings, has warned that "a great deal of American capitalism will be dead if institutional concentration in a few 'religion' stocks eliminates the ability of U.S. markets to provide capital for thousands of other corporations."[1] A Senate study of corporate ownership, released in January 1974, highlighted the substantial percentage of individual stocks held by individual commercial banks and recommended that all holders of 1 percent or more of a company's stock be required to report their interest quarterly to the Library of Congress for publication.[2]

The 1975 measure takes a big stride toward disclosure of institutional transactions. It requires institutional investment managers who exercise investment discretion over accounts holding at least $100 million market value of equity securities (as defined) to file reports of their holdings with the SEC, which could lower the threshold amount to $10 million. The reporting

FIGURE 2-1

Characteristics of Trading on the NYSE

Turnover Rates

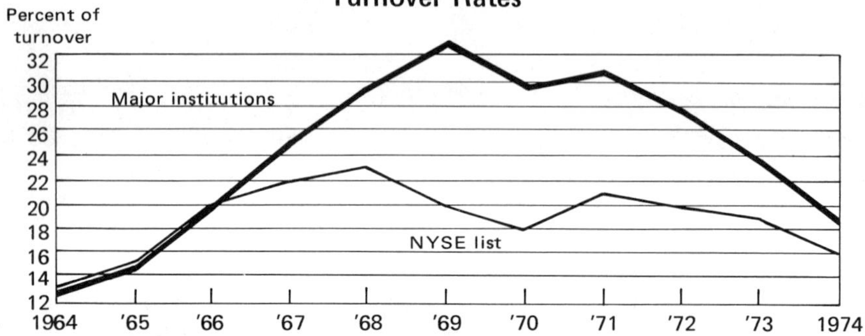

SOURCE: New York Stock Exchange.

Block Trading
As a Percentage of NYSE Reported Volume

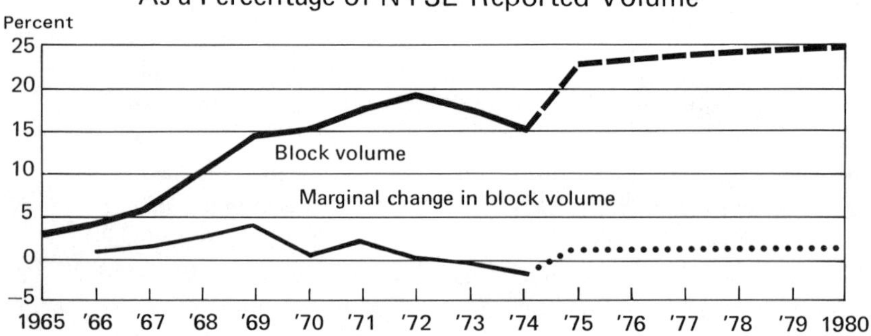

SOURCE: New York Stock Exchange.

Sources of NYSE Volume

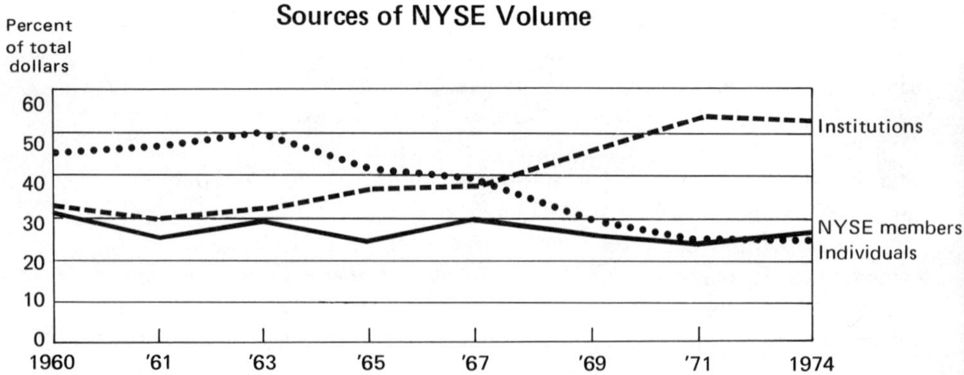

SOURCE: New York Stock Exchange.

period cannot be more than a year or less than a quarter, as prescribed by the commission. Authority is also given to the commission to require additional data, such as the voting power of the investment managers and the details of transactions involving at least $500,000. The commission is required to tabulate the information and make it available to the public at a reasonable fee.

Fragmentation of the Market

NYSE spokesmen have complained that the relatively liberal rules of the regional exchanges and the latitude permitted third-market dealers have attracted institutional business. As a result, the exchange market has been fragmented. These spokesmen have therefore recommended that their competitors be subjected to equal regulation. They assert that the public is hurt because the efficiency of the auction system is impaired by the dissipation of orders to different channels. Even the trades brought to the floor often might be worked out "upstairs" in the offices of the brokerage houses.

The announcement by Merrill Lynch of its plan (described on p. 37) to initiate trading in odd lots, therefore, sent a tremor throughout the exchange members of the financial community. The exchange is considering new rules, and other firms are planning odd-lot market making. This action in turn could lead some stock exchange firms to make their own off-floor markets in all orders for listed securities. As a result, dealer markets, where firms trade from their own inventories, would become more important.

Fragmentation not only means less business to the NYSE but also causes the floor to become a poorer market. There was and is a real possibility that this deterioration will accelerate. Worsening of the floor as a market and the improvement of other markets would give institutions more reason to execute orders elsewhere. To avert this possibility, the NYSE has sought legislative or SEC sanction to require securities that meet specified standards to trade on the floor. Such a provision is bitterly opposed by the third-market firms, since it would mean the end of their activities.[3]

Congress acted to ensure that the new central market would not result in a curtailment of depth and liquidity by the scattering of transactions. Among other things, the commission was empowered to:

(1) Create subsystems for particular types of securities with unique trading characteristics;
(2) Designate those securities qualified for trading in the national market system;
(3) Ensure equal regulation of all markets for qualified securities and of all exchange members, brokers, and dealers effecting transactions in such securities;

(4) Prohibit brokers and dealers from effecting transactions in listed securities except on a national securities exchange, if the commission finds that such transactions adversely affect the quality of the market; and
(5) Develop standards governing market makers and prohibit a dealer from acting as a broker in a security.

These are vast powers. They enable the commission to steer a careful course that could involve retracing its steps as it moves toward the goal of a central market. Meanwhile, the commission has given evidence that it will watch developments closely. Thus, in June 1975 it adopted Rule 17a-20, which, among other things, requires SEC notification of an intention to resign a membership interest in a national securities exchange.

New Trading Patterns

While the NYSE developed substantially to meet the needs of individual investors, other sectors of the market, especially the block positioners, thrived by responding to the needs of institutional trading. This type of business requires a considerable amount of capital and a willingness to risk it. That willingness, in turn, depends upon the ability of the trader to determine what other blocks of a given stock might appear on the market and who might be interested in accumulating a position.

Some specialists are capable of handling large orders as well as a block positioner can. Others are less proficient, either because their capital is inadequate or because they are reluctant to commit their capital to risky positions. Institutional traders soon learned that using these less qualified specialists meant poor executions, and they arranged their transactions off the floor even if the block finally crossed on the floor. Sometimes, to avoid the participation of a specialist, the block was brought to a regional exchange.[4] As a result of the inroads of block positioners, even able specialists found that they were not seeing all the orders, and they began to fear that the appearance of an unexpected block would depress the price of the stock in which they had a position. This situation added to the difficulty of making a good market.

Various studies indicate that institutional portfolio managers display diversity of judgment in their transactions and probably contribute to market liquidity.[5] Accepting this notion, the Treasury Department securities report points to the "success" of communications systems such as Instinet or AutEx, which facilitate direct institutional transactions, as additional evidence that institutions buy and sell to and from each other.[6] Still, parallelism does occur, consciously or otherwise, and could have an enormous influence on the market for individual stocks. In specific instances, moreover, an unusually large, careless, or hurried operation could lead to trading imbalances and severe market pressures. Thus, institutions appear to exert a mixed influence, usually swapping with each other but often moving strongly on one side of the market.[7] This condition has created new patterns in which enhanced overall liquidity is marked by abrupt trading squalls.

Commission Rates

The commission rate problem has been extremely controversial in the securities field. Broadly speaking it falls into two parts. The first, generally described as rate structure, refers to the segments included in building a rate schedule. Separate segments, for example, might be assigned to the major functions of clearance and execution, as well as to such ancillary services as research and custodianship. The second part of the problem is establishing, within a given structure, the level of charges to be imposed.

Traditionally, structural differences have only been recognized in the commission schedule for members. In this case, the NYSE rate has provided for separating the segments for executing and clearing, executing only, and clearing only. Member firms without the capacity to execute transactions on the floor or to handle the related movement of paper channel their exchange orders through other member firms that possess these facilities. For these services, the deficient firm, acting on behalf of its customer, pays an execution and clearance commission that varies with the price of the stock and was substantially below that paid nonmembers. Similarly, the prescribed intermember rate was given to the specialist and "two-dollar" broker for the services they rendered. The nonmember schedule, on the other hand, was built upon a uniform foundation underlying all the functional segments.

An important issue in rate making is the degree to which the cost of the services included in the rate package should be "unbundled," with separate charges imposed for each segment. Some argue that investors should be given their choice of the services they want and are willing to pay for. Those who prefer the traditional arrangement contend that unbundling would result in a deterioration of services and be against the public interest. A related issue is the extent to which, within any given structure, preferential rates should be allowed certain classes of investors. Do professionals deserve special treatment when they bring business to the exchange floor without any direct benefit to themselves? Of course, professionals may receive a return through reciprocal arrangements. For a number of years, various regional exchanges allowed NASD-member dealers who were not members a discount from full commission rates. The NYSE resisted this practice until March 1972 when, under pressure from the SEC, it granted a 40 percent discount to qualified nonmember broker-dealers.

Under the umbrella of the Exchange Act, the exchanges, essentially led by the NYSE, determined the level of commissions by requiring minimum charges, without drawing antitrust condemnation. For a number of years, the NYSE schedule specified commissions on a round lot of 100 shares for each price at which a stock may sell. In this arrangement, the commission on an order for 20,000 shares was 200 times that for a single round lot. Since costs did not rise in a commensurate manner, there was considerable "fat" in the commission dollar, and institutions resorted to a variety of devices to subvert the NYSE minimum commission rate system. To alleviate this condition, the NYSE was forced in December 1968 to allow discounts on transactions in excess of 1,000 shares.

Continued pressure thereafter first forced the abandonment of fixed rates on the part of an order in excess of $500,000 and, subsequently, on the part in excess of $300,000. In September 1973 the SEC announced that it would not seek any further breakpoint reductions but would require the termination of fixed commission rates after April 30, 1975. However, on April 1, 1974, the SEC no longer permitted exchanges to fix commissions on orders of less than $2,000, leading brokerage firms to create a variety of plans for the small investor.

The impending termination of fixed commissions invoked sharply differing reactions. The NYSE and much of the industry foresaw dismal outcomes. Under competitive rates, they reasoned, member firms would be encouraged to desert the exchange. As nonmembers they would be free to make markets in any listed stock they desired and could cross orders off the floor. Furthermore, they would still have access to exchanges simply by paying a small amount of floor brokerage to have orders executed. As these dealer markets proliferated "upstairs," the role of the specialist would diminish, member firms would lose their incentive to bear the costs and regulatory responsibilities required by the exchanges, and the exodus from the exchanges would be accelerated. Thus, the demise of the auction market as practiced on the exchanges, a market generally considered to be in the public interest, loomed as a real possibility.[8] On the other hand, supporters of termination believed that it would lead to a sounder and more competitive industry by finally putting a halt to the evasions that characterized the fixed-rate system, eliminating inefficient firms, and reducing the cost of brokerage.[9]

In early 1975 the SEC issued Rule 19b-3, which officially mandates the elimination of fixed public commission rates on exchange transactions (fixed intermember rates were permitted for an additional year). Chary about doomsday prophecies, however, the commission shortly thereafter announced a program to collect information concerning various industry trends, including revenues, market activity, commission rates paid by individual and institutional customers, and the distribution of trading among the various marketplaces.[10]

The 1975 Securities Acts Amendments affirm the ending of fixed rates by stating that no national securities exchange may impose such a schedule after the measure's enactment (an extension for intermember rates was allowed until May 1, 1976). Like the SEC, however, Congress was uneasy about what might happen and therefore provided for a backward slide. Until November 1, 1976, the commission could issue a rule permitting a national securities exchange to fix rates. Subsequent to that date, the commission could still allow fixed rates, but only after finding that they are reasonable in relation to costs and do not interfere with competition. The commission would also have to publish the standards employed in adjudging the reasonableness of the rates.

It will be some time, running through cycles of high and low volume, before the full implications of negotiated rates can be assessed. After these rates were introduced, so-called "execution boutiques," offering no services but charging minimal amounts, made their appearance. The established firms announced various plans, including discounts on limited-service orders, reduced rates for in-and-out trades, special investor packages (including, in one case, a discount on auto rentals), and unbundled transactions providing separate charges for certain services (which required special SEC clearance). Overshadowing these "feelers" was the evidence of rate slashes, as firms sought under competitive pressure to hold and attract insitutional business. On easy-to-execute orders, these cuts ran as high as 40-70 percent of the abandoned fixed-fee schedule.

To some extent, rate reductions also stemmed from a change in the method of handling transactions. During the period of fixed rates, the NYSE required the determination of commissions on the basis of orders executed on the same day, in the same stock, for the same customer, and on the same side of the transaction (buy or sell). As a result, if an institution submitted a substantial sell order that had to be broken up into smaller lots for execution over a period of time, commissions were calculated for each lot and were therefore substantially higher than if they had been set for the entire transaction. After the advent of negotiated rates, this requirement was no longer applicable, and many institutional customers insisted on the establishment of commissions on the entire order, even if it had to be executed over a period of time.

A factor working toward limiting the rate cuts is a 1975 amendment to section 28 of the Exchange Act. This new provision represents that it is not necessarily a breach of fiduciary duty for an investment adviser to pay a higher commission for effecting a securities transaction than might be charged by another broker or dealer. To obtain this leeway, the investment adviser must determine in good faith that the charge was reasonable in relation to the value of brokerage or research services provided. Presumably, therefore, a higher commission could be paid either for difficult executions and such related functions as clearance, settlement, and custody; or for advice or analyses concerning such things as industries, securities, economic factors, portfolio strategy, and investment performance.

Congressional reports on the new legislation indicate that reasonableness does not mean that the investment adivser must be able to show specific benefits to particular accounts. Rather, reasonableness is to be interpreted in the light of benefits to the execution of transactions or to the investment adviser's general responsibilities over the accounts on which discretion is exercised. Moreover, "paying up" may be done only for services done by the executing brokerage firm. Presumably, therefore, an institution may not pay one broker for services rendered by another—a form of the "give-up."

This new section 28(e) of the Exchange Act eases the burden of investment advisers in the execution of their fiduciary responsibilities over the accounts they administer. Nevertheless, the underlying uncertainty remains of how an institution, if legally pressed, could demonstrate that it is receiving the extra benefits for the higher rates it is paying.

Institutional Membership

The minimum-commission rate system contributed to the fragmentation of the markets and to the drive for a central market. It also abetted institutional interest in stock exchange membership. In part, this interest arose because of the desire of the financial institutions and brokerage firms to diversify. By acquiring a broker-dealer affiliate that did a public business, for example, an insurance company or investment adviser would not only broaden its own activity but would also provide a new source of capital to the broker-dealer.

In part, also, the interest reflected a desire to reduce the costs of brokerage. Thus, the institution might acquire a so-called "shell broker"—that is, a broker who became a member of a regional exchange solely to get back some of the brokerage commissions paid by the parent to other brokers. At times, this recapture was effected through a circuitous route whereby the affiliate referred its parent's order to a dual member who executed the transaction on the NYSE, then directed a predetermined amount of commissions on unrelated transactions to the affiliate, which finally rebated part or all of the commissions to the parent.

A related development also encouraged institutional interest in exchange membership: the expansion of a number of brokerage firms into the management of large pools of money, such as the portfolios of pension funds. Such firms could earn a fee on the managed accounts and receive a substantial portion of the commissions they generated. Because they received these commissions, they were often able to charge lower advisory fees to their clients. This competition from exchange-member firms created pressure on the financial institutions to reduce costs to their clients, and one way of doing this was by obtaining their own exchange memberships.

The various exchanges responded to this institutional flirtation with exchange membership in several ways. The NYSE and American Stock Exchange adopted rules that denied membership to any person or entity whose so-called parent was not also engaged in the securities business. Some exchanges opened their membership without any requirement that it be employed for public purposes. Still other exchanges adopted rules that fell somewhere in between these extremes. Eventually, impelled in part by this diversity, the commission, in January 1973, adopted Rule 19b-2 in a long release which is particularly important because it spells out the commission's philosophy on the public nature of securities exchanges and its rule-making authority to implement this philosophy.[11]

In essence, SEC Rule 19b-2 required each exchange to adopt rules specifying that the principal purpose of membership is the conduct of a public securities business. This purpose was considered fulfilled if at least 80 percent of the volume of a member's securities transactions on all registered exchanges was effected for nonaffiliated accounts or contributed to the liquidity of markets (as do the transactions of a stock exchange specialist in an assigned security).

The commission did not have much opportunity to gain experience with this rule because the 1975 law acted to sever the relations between brokers and affiliated accounts. While the new amendments give the commission some flexibility in permitting or prohibiting transactions, the conferees specifically cautioned the commission that any action to limit exchange membership to firms with an 80-20 business mix, as was attempted in Rule 19b-2, would violate both the letter and the spirit of the law.[12]

As written, the new measure makes it unlawful for any member of a national securities exchange to effect transactions on that exchange for its own account, the account of an associated person, or an account that permits the exercise of investment discretion. Exceptions are provided for market makers and odd-lot dealers; for certain types of transactions, such as stabilizing transactions effected to facilitate the distribution of a security; for dealings with affiliated individual accounts; and for transactions for a member's own account, provided that the member is in the securities business and the transaction is effected in compliance with SEC rules.

Congress recognized the possibility that the statutory limitation on self-dealings in exchange markets could lead members who depend on brokerage business from managed accounts to leave the exchange. Accordingly, the law gives the commission the authority to extend the ban to any broker or dealer effecting transactions either on or off an exchange. The possibility was also envisioned that exchange members could channel their affiliated business into the third market to escape the prohibition. Should this result prove detrimental to the market, the commission is also empowered to extend the ban to members' transactions off the exchange.

The statutory prohibition on the combination of brokerage and money management does not apply for three years to firms that were members on May 1, 1975. Presumably, this grace period provides the opportunity for adjustment to the changed conditions, which may involve a host of reciprocal arrangements that will be hard to police. The statutory ban will prevent affiliated accounts from receiving special benefits, such as low commission rates, that were sometimes given them under the prior arrangement.

Defining an Appropriate Securities Role for Banks

The laws that circumscribe the participation of banks in the securities field were written a number of years ago. The Banking Act of 1933 (Glass-Steagall Act) is an omnibus measure which, among other things, separates commercial from investment banking and prevents a bank from buying stock for its own account. Certain leeways, however, are allowed. Thus, U.S. Treasury bonds and the general obligations of a state or its political subdivisions are specifically exempted from the underwriting ban. The banks may also engage in securities transactions as agents for their customers. Moreover, the various securities laws are relatively generous to the banks, which are specifically excluded from the definition of "investment adviser" by the Investment Advisers Act and from the definition of "broker" or "dealer" by the Securities Exchange Act.

These basic laws were framed in an atmosphere of restraint in which the primary concern was to prevent the self-dealing and bank failures that had occurred in the past. In the ensuing years, important changes have occurred both in philosophy and method of operation. After the economic growth of the 1960s and the appearance during that decade of huge economic units in different fields of enterprise, competition has become the prevailing doctrine of the 1970s. Guided by this principle, legislators have tended to look with some favor on the desire of the banks to underwrite revenue bonds and to penetrate the securities industry.

The legal path, however, is not clear. In 1971, for example, the Supreme Court supported the contention of the Investment Company Institute (ICI), the national association for mutual funds, that the First National City Bank's program for collective investment of a managed agency account, approved by the comptroller of currency, was in violation of the Glass-Steagall Act.[13] This decision was only a temporary setback. The banks expanded their securities services in various ways: they developed dividend reinvestment plans; devised automatic services for deducting monthly specified amounts from clients' accounts and investing them in a list of stocks supplied by the bank; introduced voluntary investment plans for monthly purchases of securities selected by a customer from a list compiled by a participating broker-dealer; inaugurated "mini-account" services which provide individual portfolio management to investors with as little as $10,000; and developed investment advisory programs for investment companies, generally closed-end (see Chapter 23).

The SEC has viewed with some concern the banks' inroads into the securities industry. The commission has indicated that legislation might be necessary to clarify its jurisdiction over these new services, since participating investors might not be receiving adequate regulatory attention. As a guide to an appropriate course of action, the commission instituted an inquiry to obtain public comments on the subject.[14]

The new amendments take cognizance of this problem by directing the commission to study the extent to which banks maintain accounts on behalf of public customers for buying and selling securities, and whether their exclusion from the Exchange Act's definitions of "broker" and "dealer" is consistent with the purposes of the act. Included in the study would be an evaluation of the adequacy of the regulations of the securities activities of banks. The commission is not authorized, however, to study or to make recommendations concerning whether these activities should remain permissible under the Banking Act of 1933. It should be noted, however, that the provision in the 1975 act prohibiting member trading on a national exchange for affiliated accounts will prevent banks from executing trust account trades on an exchange through an affiliated brokerage firm, even if the Glass-Steagall Act were changed to permit banks to operate affiliated brokerage firms. It is unlikely that the Glass-Steagall Act would make a specific exemption for banks.

Foreign Access to U.S. Securities Markets

Gross foreign activity in U.S. equities has mounted sharply over the past decade, from the $4-7 billion range in the early 1960s to an annual average of more than $20 billion since 1968, with a peak of $26.4 billion in 1972. It is estimated that aggregate commissions from foreign activity, after allowing for commission rate changes, probably increased about 400 percent during this period. The allure of this business undoubtedly contributed to the interest displayed by foreign financial institutions in obtaining direct access to the U.S. securities markets through membership on an exchange or through other kinds of domestic operations.

Further abetting this interest have been the dollar devaluations, the basic economic strength of the United States, and the dominant position occupied by the U.S. capital markets. At the close of 1974, foreign investment in U.S. securities firms, including NYSE nonmembers, amounted to about \$250 million, more than all the money raised by firms through public offerings. Rather than establishing a new subsidiary, foreign investors have tended in recent years to purchase a minority share in existing firms. Typical illustrations are Belgium's Banque Lambert's interest in William D. Witter & Co.; Milan's Banca Commerciale Italiana's interest in Lehman Brothers and Model Roland, since merged into Shields; Zurich's Credit Suisse Bank's interest in White, Weld; and Warburg-Paribus's interest in A. G. Becker.[15]

Additionally, some foreign broker-dealers apparently thought it desirable to join one of the regional exchanges which allowed foreign members. In the long run, costs could probably be reduced by this means. Then again, the U.S. markets tower above their foreign counterparts. In 1972, for example, the total value of shares bought amounted to \$160 billion on the NYSE, \$20 billion on the AMEX, and \$204 billion on all U.S. exchanges. These levels compare with \$75 billion on the Tokyo Exchange, \$60 billion on the London Exchange, and about \$25 billion on all the other major European exchanges combined. Accordingly, some foreign broker-dealers may feel that there is an element of prestige derived from association with an American exchange that helps them in competing for investment banking business and in winning invitations to participate in underwriting distributions.[16] In January 1973 there were 37 foreign firms (not counting Canadian), including a number of banks, that were identified with U.S. brokerage affiliates.

The Securities Exchange Act allows foreign entities to establish brokerage subsidiaries in the United States, provided they meet the same capital and competency requirements that apply to American brokerage houses. Within this framework, the exchanges have adopted various provisions of their own. Under the constitution and rules of the NYSE, foreign membership, except for Canadian firms, is not allowed, nor may a member organization have a foreign person or entity as a parent. The basis for the definition of a parent is control, which is presumed to exist when there is ownership of more than 25 percent of voting stock. Moreover, foreign persons (except Canadians) as a group may not control more than 45 percent of the total debt plus equity of a member organization. The American, Cincinnati, and Detroit stock exchanges generally prohibit foreign memberships entirely, while the Boston, Midwest, Pacific, and PBW exchanges allow foreign broker-dealers to become members, provided they meet the same qualifications as are required of a U.S. brokerage firm. The NASD freely admits foreign securities firms as members if they meet the same requirements that pertain to U.S. applicants.[17] By and large, most other countries have more restrictive rules and practices toward foreign broker-dealers than the United States does. These restrictions may not be permissible under the Securities Acts Amendments of 1975; therefore changes will probably be made in the legal scene when an overall policy is established.

The question of foreign access to the U.S. securities markets has become a prominent issue not only because of the expanding volume of business from abroad and the entry of overseas firms into U.S. markets but also because of a growing awareness by the industry of the desirability of developing uniform national guidelines. In this sense, the question of foreign access to the U.S. securities markets is an aspect of the government's general concern with foreign investors obtaining major interests in U.S. firms. This concern was reflected in the SEC proposal in August 1975 to obtain information about who really owns American corporations. Reflecting the importance of the foreign access issue, specifically, the SEC instituted a study of the matter in early 1974. On the positive side is a general feeling that foreign access provides a desirable stimulus to capital flows, strengthens international ties, and cements the worldwide stature of the U.S. markets. A liberal policy on foreign entrance might also add to market liquidity and would be compatible with the current predilection for opening the doors to competition. On the negative side are the inroads that foreign firms might make into the business of U.S. securities firms, already reeling under severe financial strains, and uncertainty as to the effects of foreign entry into markets that are already undergoing considerable change.

If access is permitted, the NYSE has indicated its belief that there should be mutual nondiscrimination and full adherence to U.S. national policies and laws. Such a requirement would bring the foreign banks in the United States under the Glass-Steagall Act. Thus, they would presumably have to separate their commercial and investment banking business, a contingency they are not likely to find palatable. Furthermore, since foreign banks themselves are often heavily involved in the securities business, sometimes trading for their own accounts, sometimes for affiliated accounts, and sometimes for the public, admitting U.S. brokerage affiliates of foreign banks raises some very nasty problems regarding the enforceability of the 1975 act's prohibition of trading for affiliated accounts. Foreign secrecy laws may even prohibit any sort of inspection of books. As is true of so many aspects of the international area, thorny and sensitive problems have to be resolved before a national policy can be formulated.

TOWARD A CENTRAL MARKET

Out of the turmoil that beset the securities markets in the 1960s and early 1970s, a general agreement arose that change was necessary. The SEC was concerned that trading barriers prevented the markets from serving the best interests of the investor; the NYSE saw fragmentation as a threat to its dominance; the regionals wanted freedom to build local satrapies; and third-market dealers complained about rules that limited their ability to trade with NYSE members. Eventually, these conflicting views coalesced into two divergent concepts, both issued, oddly enough, under the same banner of a "central market."

Meaning of a Central Market

In its letter transmitting the *Institutional Investor Study Report* to Congress, the SEC gave a diffuse character to its notion of a central market, stating: "In summary, our objective is to see a strong central market system created to which all investors have access, in which all qualified broker-dealers and existing market institutions may participate in accordance with their respective capabilities, and which is controlled not only by appropriate regulation but also by the forces of competition."[18] About a year later, William McChesney Martin, Jr., the first paid president of the NYSE, longtime chairman of the Board of Governors of the Federal Reserve System, and a highly respected figure in financial circles, delivered a report to the NYSE in which he presented a much different notion of the central market. His view embodied a single source for the trading of each eligible stock: "To serve the interests of the public and the nation, as well as the interests of the securities industry itself, a national exchange system must be developed to provide a single, national auction market for each security qualified for listing."[19]

In two succeeding major reports, the SEC put some flesh on the skeleton of its initial idea. Its statement on the future structure of the securities markets stressed the importance of communications and rules: "The term 'central market system' refers to a system of communications by which the various elements of the marketplace, be they exchanges or over-the-counter markets, are tied together. It also includes a set of rules governing the relationships which will prevail among market participants."[20] The statement further indicated that various committees would be appointed to study components of the problem. After these committees submitted their recommendations the SEC published another policy statement, which became known as the white paper on market structure.[21] It established some functional principles as the basis for further action.

A crucial issue in the conceptual development of the central market was the place of the third market. It occupied a significant spot in the original SEC proposal but was eliminated in the NYSE plan. The 1975 amendments fully accept the competitive role of the third market and, as mentioned previously, even direct the commission to take steps to eliminate any anticompetitive aspects that it discovers in exchange rules. However, the commission is given considerable authority to deal with any serious disruptions in the exchange markets caused by trading in the third market. The SEC can impose affirmative marketmaking obligations on third-market dealers; prevent a securities firm from dealing as principal in a security; and finally, as a last resort, prohibit all trading of listed securities in the third market if it finds that the orderliness of the exchange market has been affected and that the exchange has no anticompetitive rules.

Difficulties of Implementation

The central market is intended to allow investors to buy or sell shares at the then best possible price wherever a stock may be traded. The heart of the system is a set of communications linkages consisting of a real-time composite last-sale reporting mechanism, a composite quotation arrangement for displaying the bids and offers of all qualified market makers in listed securities, and a central repository for limit orders. The regulatory structure governing operations of the network is designed to maintain the integrity of the communications linkages; to ensure that the competing market makers within the system maintain fair and orderly markets; and to make certain that the system maintains the best auction features of the exchange market. There is little question that the technical equipment to produce such a system is available or can be developed, but progress has been slow because of disputes among the interested parties and because of genuine uncertainty regarding the specifics of the new rules.

For example, to establish a consolidated tape, the SEC adopted a rule requiring the exchanges and the NASD to file plans specifying how the necessary information would be disseminated. The New York, American, and various regional exchanges, as well as the NASD, filed a joint plan, but even at this stage compromises had to be reached on such matters as criteria for listing, hours of operation, and the distribution of authority. Eventually, the commission approved a plan designed to provide in one system the latest sale price, volume, and source of transaction. The tape consists of two data streams. One called tape A, started June 16, 1975, shows trades in NYSE stocks on all markets including the NYSE, regional exchanges, the third market, and Instinet. Tape B will show trades in AMEX and selected sole regional issues.

Even more troublesome is the problem of developing a composite quotation system, another integral component of the central market. Initially, following its earlier procedure, the SEC proposed a rule designed to force the exchanges or the NASD to formulate a comprehensive plan for a quotation system. When this proposal ran into snags, the commission substituted a new strategy to develop a system for issuing quotations. In this approach, the exchanges were instructed to change their rules restricting access to quotation systems to permit their more widespread purchase. Thus, anyone with a legitimate interest in securities would be able to receive the latest bid and asked price of any listed stock from any exchange through an information retrieval system, thereby providing for a nationwide scheme of distributing competitive quotations.

The idea that a composite quotation system should evolve through the free interplay of its participants, rather than through a prescribed formula, reflects the philosophic underpinning of the new amendments. The House version had directed the commission to establish a national structure and even prescribed its basic elements, including a transactional reporting system, a composite quotation system, and a system of rules and regulations designed to provide fair competition among the participants. The Senate bill, which prevailed on this question, omitted such specifications. Rather, it directed the commission to facilitate the creation of a system in accordance with enumerated congressional objectives. Thus, the thrust of the new measure is to rely upon competitive forces, freed by removing unnecessary restrictions, to bring about the national market system. Nevertheless, the regulatory authority of the commission, which remains in the background, is to be moved to the forefront if competition proves insufficient.

To implement this clear philosophic commitment to competition, the powers of the commission over the self-regulatory agencies have been strengthened. A new Section 11A extends this authority over securities information processors by requiring their registration with the commission, which grants or denies approval based upon such standards as performance capability and financial condition. The commission is empowered to review and take steps to correct any impediments imposed by a securities processor on access to its services. The commission may also censure a processor, limit its activities, suspend it for a period up to 12 months, or revoke its registration.

In addition to enacting certain "fail-safe" provisions, Congress reflected its concern over the implementation of a central market system in a series of organizational and reporting requirements:

(1) The commission is authorized to create advisory committees and to employ outside experts to help create a national market system.
(2) The commission is required to establish a National Market Advisory Board of 15 members, geographically dispersed. Members are appointed for two five-year terms; the majority are to be associated with brokers and dealers, with the remainder representing the public. The board is given a broad mandate to provide its views and to make recommendations on the development of a central market system. Specifically included is a review of self-regulation and of

the desirability of establishing a new self-regulatory organization to administer the national market system.

(3) The commission is authorized to conduct studies and make recommendations to the Congress from time to time as to the possible need for modifications of self-regulation.

(4) The commission, agencies, and self-regulatory organizations are required to submit annual reports to Congress concerning their central market-related activities. The items to be included in the commission's report, enumerated in detail, cover such areas as the self-regulatory organizations, clearance systems, elimination of the physical movement of certificates, the effect of the absence of fixed commissions, and the viability of small brokers and dealers. More generally, the report must assess the progress toward establishment of a national market system.

Basic Trading Rules

To protect the auction market, the SEC white paper proposed two basic trading rules. One, called the *auction trading rule*, provides price priority protection for all public orders throughout the system. Thus, a broker desiring to execute an order may approach any specialist, who, in turn, will have to check all markets to provide the best possible price before executing the order. Similarly, any existing public order in the system would have priority over a negotiated transaction that had been "crossed" (that is, arranged by a broker for the buyer or buyers and by a broker for the seller or sellers, with the broker often the same in both cases) if the public order was entered at a better price.

The second pillar of the SEC's central market system, the *public preference rule*, prevents any member of the system from participating as a principal in any system transaction unless his purchase price is higher or his sale price lower than any public bid or offer recorded in the system. According to this proposal if a market maker offering a stock at 40 receives a bid to buy at the same price, he must nevertheless match the bid with a public sell order at 40, even if his own order was entered into the system first. This rule may result in excessively wide margins or discourage the participation of market makers by forcing them to hold positions too long.

In the 1975 amendments, Congress clearly indicated an intent to preserve the auction market, and the legislators specifically gave the SEC authority to implement the trading rules it had proposed in the 1973 white paper. The law permits a member of a national securities exchange to trade for its own account, but only in accordance with SEC rules, which at a minimum must provide that such orders yield priority, parity, and precedence to public orders. The authority given the commission to require disclosure to all exchange members of orders placed with the specialist helps achieve these conditions. Since dealers in the third market fall within the province of SEC rules, their orders presumably would also be made subject to the public priority and precedence principles.

Executing an Order

Shifting from present operating methods to the fully automated methods of the future may require the installation of highly complex electronic equipment. Involved are various organizational devices that employ a bewildering number of acronyms. The Securities Industry Automation Corporation (SIAC), formed in July 1972 to consolidate the automation planning and operations of the New York and American stock exchanges, is the processor of the new consolidated tape. SIAC has described the Central Exchange Network Trading and Unified Reporting system (CENTAUR), which, in turn, was based on the work of the AMEX Computerized Order Display and Execution system (AMCODE). As envisioned, CENTAUR would contain the elements that could be incorporated into the future central market system. Current work focuses on the parts rather than on the whole.

When all this gadgetry is finally installed, a broker will have access to terminals that permit checking the status of all the markets where a particular security is being traded. The order may electronically be routed to the "best market," or, in the case of limit orders, to a consolidated book that will also be kept electronically. Through the computer system the trade is arranged, verified, and "locked in" for instantaneous transmission to the member firms involved, the consolidated ticker, and the clearing system.[22]

Clearing the Order

Clearing the order is the climax of a securities transaction. It involves a comparison of both sides (to ensure agreement on price and number of shares) and final settlement by delivery of certificates and receipt of payment. At one time, the "daily balance order" method was employed, whereby the clearinghouse merely served as a conduit for brokers to settle trades with each other. The current method, spearheaded by the regional exchanges, adopted by the National Clearing Corporation (NCC), which is operated by the NASD for clearing OTC trades, and finally accepted by the NYSE and AMEX in the latter part of 1974, is called *continuous net settlement*. Under this method, the brokerage firm deals directly with the clearinghouse which stands on either side of every transaction. If a firm "fails" to deliver stock on the settlement day, the clearinghouse records the stock's market value and the firm is required to mark to the market daily, thereby eliminating the risk of price fluctuation. A major advantage of this procedure is that a broker need make only one delivery of securities daily. It is planned that SIAC will provide the processing of a clearing entity for the NYSE, AMEX, and NASD.

Despite the improvement in clearing methodology, the use of a certificate remains cumbersome. To immobilize this instrument, the NYSE developed the Central Certificate Service (CCS) to keep certificates on deposit and transfer them through computerized bookkeeping entries. To extend this system to the brokerage and banking communities, CCS was converted in May 1973 into the Depository Trust Co. (DTC), a limited-purpose trust company chartered by the New York State Banking Department and a member of the Federal Reserve System. Regional depository facilities provide deposit information to the DTC system, which interfaces with the major clearing corporations throughout the country.

The DTC holds stock certificates for some 230 brokerage firms, 22 banks, and six other stock markets' clearinghouses and depositories.[23] When the depository was initially opened to commercial banks some years ago, they were promised the opportunity of buying into the system. In the fall of 1975 the NYSE fulfilled this promise by offering about 40 percent of the stock to the banks, the AMEX, the NASD, and the PBW and Midwest exchanges.

The NYSE, the AMEX, the major regional exchanges, and the NASD have been working on the development of a national clearance and depository system. Eventually, these national systems will be integrated into a single automated system, so that executed trades would be cleared and settled electronically without the use of certificates. However, many operational and legal hurdles—and the opposition of vested interests—will have to be overcome before this goal is attained.

The 1975 amendments recognize the importance of linking all clearance and settlement facilities and the development of uniform standards and procedures in this area. Accordingly, the new law directs the commission to facilitate the establishment of such a national system. Toward this end, authority to regulate, coordinate, and direct operations of all participants in the securities handling process is centralized in the commission. In general, the commission has rule-making and policy oversight responsibility for all clearing agencies and transfer agents. To the extent that these agencies are banks, however, primary responsibility for the conduct of examinations rests with the appropriate bank regulatory authority. Similarly, the establishment of record-keeping and reporting requirements for bank transfer agents rests primarily with the banking authority. Provision is made for coordination between the commission and the banking authorities in the allocation of their respective responsibilities.

The Antitrust Threat

Following an extensive discussion of the regulatory and competitive aspects of the securities industry in the SEC's Special Study of Securities

Markets, authorized by Congress in 1961 and completed in August 1963, and the decision of the U.S. Supreme Court in *Silver* v. *New York Stock Exchange*, which was decided a few months earlier, the attention of the Antitrust Division of the Justice Department was directed toward the practices of the NYSE. This interest was sharpened by a subsequent rash of private antitrust suits and threats of suits. By and large, the contested areas included the minimum commission schedule, the rules limiting the freedom of members to trade off an exchange, and membership restrictions.

The basic position of the exchanges before 1963 was that antitrust laws did not apply to them, primarily because exchange functions are regulated by the Exchange Act. The opposite viewpoint, offered by the Department of Justice, was that antitrust immunity could not be justified for practices that restrict competition. The legal doctrine, developed since 1963, under the facts of Silver, was that antitrust immunity could be implied only to the extent necessary to permit the Exchange Act to work. However, in an important brokerage fee decision handed down in 1975, the Supreme Court held that the Securities Exchange Act was intended by Congress to leave the supervision of reasonable commission rates to the SEC.[24] Since a basic objective of the 1975 amendments is the elimination of undesirable burdens on competition, the commission seems to have the touchy job of reconciling antitrust principles with the regulatory scheme of the securities laws in areas other than commission rates. With respect to commissions, the issue has been set aside by the ending of fixed rates in May 1975.

A major innovation of the 1975 amendments is a provision for judicial review in federal appeals courts of SEC rules adopted pursuant to various provisions of the act, principally relating to the self-regulatory bodies and the national market system. Previously, the review of rules of administrative agencies, including those of the SEC, was provided for in the district courts under the Administrative Procedure Act. Prior to 1971, the SEC even took the position that when it permitted the exchanges to increase commission rates, its action was not a final order that could be appealed under the Exchange Act.

In expanding the scope of direct judicial review of SEC decisions, Congress indicated that it was aware of the potential conflict with collateral antitrust attacks on actions by self-regulatory organizations. Thus, a self-regulatory rule, after approval by the SEC, may be reviewed in a court of appeals to determine whether it imposes a burden on competition which is neither necessary nor appropriate in furtherance of the purposes of the Exchange Act. The same rule, however, could be challenged in a federal district court under the antitrust laws, where a somewhat different standard might be applied.

In discussing this area, the legislators appeared confident that the courts could avoid actual conflicts by flexible use of existing precedents. They also indicated, however, that they would watch closely the implementation of the statutory provisions by the courts. If competitive and regulatory factors could not be adequately reconciled under current procedures, Congress would consider legislation on the subject.[25]

SECURITIES INDUSTRY

During the past decade the securities industry has gone through some brutal economic experiences. In the late 1960s there was the so-called "paperwork crisis." As trading volume grew during these years, the firms found themselves inadequately staffed and had to hire inexperienced personnel. Too few clerks, inadequately trained, could not cope with the workload, and effective record keeping collapsed. Firms that sought to fill the clerical gap by introducing computers also experienced difficulties, because it was not easy to adapt the new technology to the processing of securities. A highly publicized barometer of the operational problems of that period was the increased use of the designation "fails to deliver," representing securities that could not be delivered on settlement date. Many firms incurred financial burdens as they provided funds to selling customers but were not reimbursed by the buyers, who delayed payment because they had not received their securities.

By 1970 the operating efficiency of the brokers began to improve, but a new critical problem appeared. Volume subsided in the face of rising costs, driven upward by inflationary pressures. Coincidentally, declining securities prices produced heavy losses in the investment portfolios of brokerage firms and shrunk capital represented by securities. In many cases, subordinated lenders and limited partners withdrew from the firms, adding to capital shortages at the very time that more abundant supplies were required to meet the needs of institutional clients and to diversify activities. Recognizing the financial plight of its members, the NYSE in March 1970 permitted public ownership of member firms; the following year, the NASD issued regulations that enabled its members to underwrite the public offerings of their own securities or to use independent underwriters. As stock prices continued their slide, however, only a handful of firms were able to avail themselves of this financing avenue.

The bulk of a broker-dealer's revenue comes from securities commissions and trading activities, as indicated in Figure 2-2. Against this inflow, the principal expenditures are for clerical and administrative employees and for registered representatives. While firms can cut costs during periods of economic drought, as they did in the early 1970s, such practices expose them

FIGURE 2-2

Securities Industry Dollar: 1973

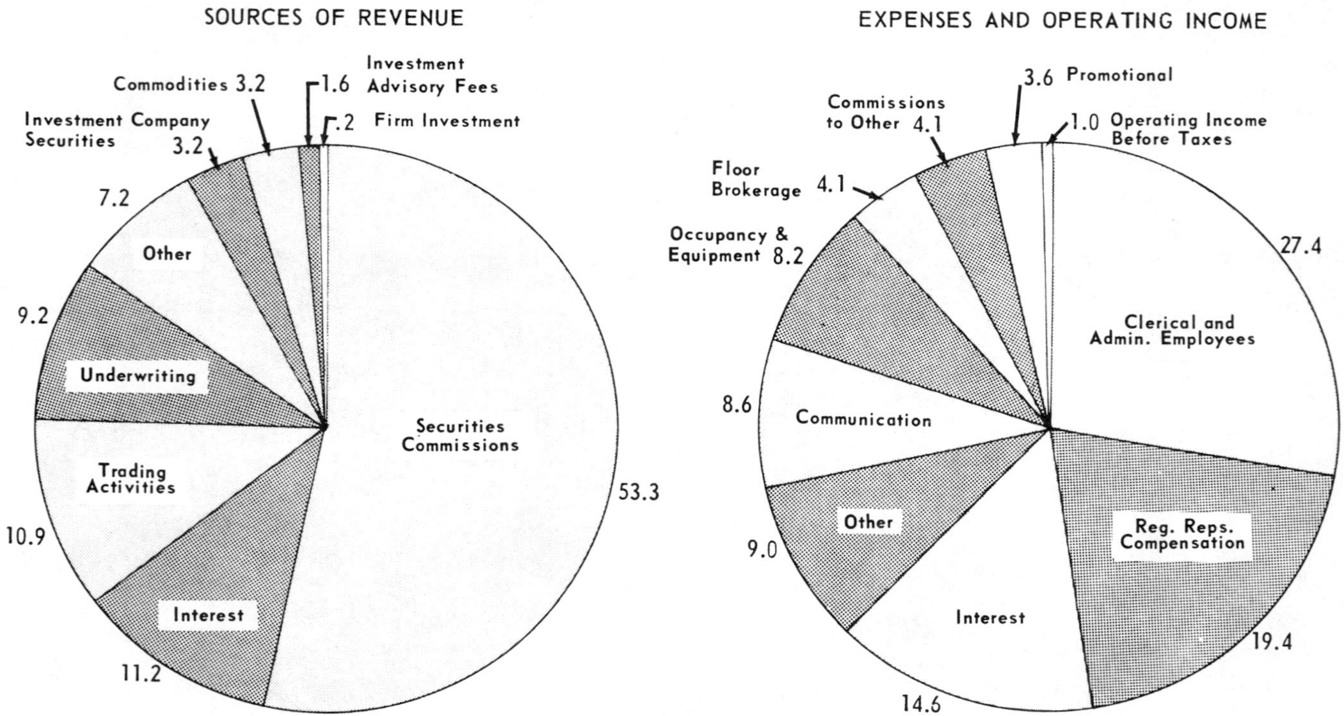

SOURCE: Securities and Exchange Commission, *Annual Report*, 1974, p. 145.

to potential operational difficulties should an upturn ensue. Moreover, the inception of negotiated rates, as well as the increasing pressure exerted by the entrance of other financial institutions into the securities area, places a cloud of uncertainty over this whole sector of business. Accordingly, the large firms have been seeking diversification by broadening their securities functions and by moving into other fields, such as real estate, insurance, leasing, and specialized ventures. To facilitate the diversification process, several firms have formed holding companies that own separate subsidiaries, one of which is the securities brokerage unit.

The difficulties of the 1970s have also caused a severe contraction in the number of securities firms through mergers, takeovers, and liquidations. As shown in Figure 2-3, about 4,000 broker-dealers were registered with the SEC on June 30, 1974, a decline of some 1,200 since 1970. Caution is also revealed in the reluctance to open new branches and the considerable

FIGURE 2-3

Broker-Dealer Registrations
As of End of Fiscal Years, 1965-1974

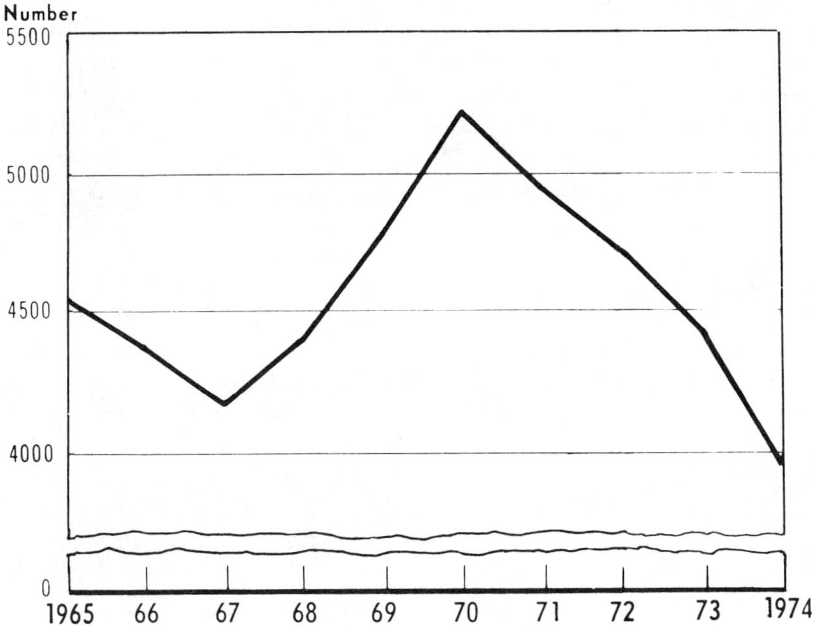

SOURCE: Securities and Exchange Commission, *Annual Report*, 1974, p. 147.

shrinkage that has occurred in the exchange community from 165,000 personnel in 1969 to about 123,000 in 1974.

Over the long run, as regulatory requirements raise the standards for entry into the business and as competition places increased pressure upon profits, this tendency is likely to continue. To survive in the future, firms may take two divergent paths. Some firms will probably seek to extend their diversification activities while other enterprises will strip their functions to offer a bone-hard core of commission business or a limited but highly personalized service. For example, in July 1975 Coleman & Co., which had been regarded as a leading firm in providing institutional research services, announced that it would abandon this area. Instead, the firm indicated it would concentrate on offering deep brokerage-rate discounts to financial institutions.

In its sweeping reconstruction of the Exchange Act, Congress did not overlook the financial problems encountered by brokers in recent years. Accordingly, it specifically assigned the SEC authority to devise rules to safeguard the financial responsibility of brokers and dealers. Included in this area are the custody and use of customers' securities and the carrying and use of customers' deposits (credit balances). Congress further specified that the rules should require the maintenance of reserves against credit balances and the establishment of minimum financial requirements for all brokers and dealers. In developing these rules, the commission is empowered to classify brokers and dealers and to prescribe the different requirements for different firms. It may also prescribe the form, content, and principles governing the preparation of financial statements filed under the Exchange Act. Aside from these provisions, which are designed to ensure the financial credibility of brokerage firms, the commission may adopt standards of operational capability, including provisions for training, experience, competence, and other qualifications.

In June 1975 the SEC adopted uniform net-capital requirements for all brokerage firms, as well as for nonbank dealers in municipal securities, a category brought within the commission's fold by the 1975 amendments.[26] The rule, launched some 2½ years earlier in a different form, provides for the maintenance of a maximum 1:15 ratio of net capital to aggregate indebtedness. An alternative approach, of particular interest to large firms, is to maintain a minimum financial reserve tied to the amount of money owed by customers. Special capital requirements are provided for market makers, firms writing options not listed on an exchange, and firms that sell only mutual fund shares. These requirements are all part of the U.S. government's campaign to improve the financial stability of the industry. Underlying all these developments is the persistent uncertainty of volume fluctuations, which could drastically change the industry's profitability—up or down.

SUMMARY

Despite the extensive studies preceding enactment of the Securities Acts Amendments of 1975, Congress felt sufficient uncertainty about their effects on the securities industry to include "fail-safe" provisions; these enable the SEC to retrace its steps if serious disruptions occur.

Among the difficulties in the postwar period which led to the reform efforts, probably the most important was the gradual domination of the stock market by institutions. This expanding institutional role has had several important consequences, including a shift in the site of much trading from the floor of the NYSE to the third market and the regional exchanges. As business drifted away, the NYSE invoked the red flag of fragmentation, which it contended led to poorer markets; other observers of market developments, however, asserted that the shift represented the effects of competition and led to better markets.

Under the umbrella of the Exchange Act, the exchanges, essentially led by the NYSE, determined the level of commissions by requiring minimum charges for a number of years. The levels established resulted in considerable "fat" in the commission dollar, and institutions resorted to a variety of devices to subvert the NYSE minimum commission rate system. Continued pressure from the SEC, the Department of Justice, and Congress eventually resulted in the demise of fixed commissions. In early 1975 the SEC issued a termination rule that was subsequently affirmed in the new legislation. The immediate reaction to the advent of competitive commissions was a rate war. While it is still too early to judge the long-term effects, there are signs that stable relations will develop as institutions recognize the continuing need to deal with brokerage firms capable of providing good executions and satisfactory research. The 1975 law provides that it is not necessarily a breach of fiduciary duty for an investment adviser to pay a higher commission for effecting a securities transaction than might be charged by another broker or dealer.

The minimum commission system also abetted interest by the institutions in stock exchange membership. The exchanges adopted varying rules to deal with this institutional flirtation. The SEC sought to resolve these conflicts with a new rule that was soon superseded by the 1975 legislation. This measure permits institutional membership, but it makes unlawful the combination of brokerage and money management after a three-year period. Other issues still to be resolved are the role of the commercial banks in the securities markets and the degree to which foreign firms should have access to the markets.

Out of the turmoil that beset the securities business rose the movement toward a central market. Two concepts of a central market gained prominence. One, sponsored by the NYSE, envisioned a market where stock trading would be concentrated in a single source; the other stressed competition. Supported by the SEC and Congress, the drive is toward the competitive model, with the central market conceived as a system of communications linkages among the participants, including clearing and settlement facilities. The SEC is empowered to take the lead in developing such a system, which would include a financially sound securities industry.

CHAPTER 3

Investor Protection

Regulation must be geared to objective criteria. The constant refrain in the securities acts has been the public interest and the protection of investors; the Securities Acts Amendments of 1975 add fair competition. Since the U.S. securities markets are lively, it is to be expected that the regulatory review will be restless, constantly seeking to aid the public interest, protect the investor, and (now) insure fair competition. Sometimes these efforts improve the traditional regulatory paths; sometimes they carve out new ones. Highlighting these efforts has been the thrust for improved disclosure, raising the responsibilities of professional participants, strengthening restrictions on insider trading, eliminating anticompetitive provisions, and reforming stock market practices.

SIGNIFICANT AREAS OF ACTIVITY

The primary thrust of federal securities regulation is disclosure. A substantial portion of regulatory energy in the last few years has been devoted to rethinking how best to implement the disclosure principle, so that the most relevant information is broadly available for both the professional analyst and

This chapter is based on an address by Robert H. Mundheim to the Instituts für Kapitalmärkforscung, University of Frankfurt. With Professor Mundheim's permission, this address was updated and expanded by the authors, who therefore assume all responsibility for errors.

the ordinary investor. Perhaps the most interesting recent disclosure debate centered on whether the inclusion of earnings projections should be permitted or required in prospectuses or other documents filed with the Securities and Exchange Commission. Although the SEC traditionally took the position that it would be improper to include them, after intensive hearings in 1972 the commission indicated its intention to integrate projections into the disclosure system.[1]

In addition to improving disclosure to investors, regulatory attention has also focused on attempts to expand the professional responsibilities of brokers, dealers, and others who advise the investing public about the purchase and sale of securities.[2] These efforts include a reexamination of many of the conflicts of interest which have traditionally been permitted to exist.[3] For example, as indicated previously, the 1975 amendments provide that a money manager, such as an investment adviser for a mutual fund or a broker-adviser of a pension fund, may not, with prescribed allowances and exceptions, execute portfolio transactions on behalf of the customer-advisee.

There have also been rapid developments in extending and making more effective the prohibitions relating to trading on inside information. Improvements in the monitoring of trading activity make it hard for large-scale insider trading to take place unnoticed. Moreover, there is a tendency to expand the class of persons to whom insider trading prohibitions apply. The prohibitions apply not only to management of the corporation whose stock is traded, but also to investors who receive information from or confirm information with persons who occupy a traditional insider position. Indeed, there have been suggestions that "insider" restrictions may apply to any person who possesses material nonpublic information, regardless of the source from which the information was obtained. Further, the doctrine has been extended beyond prohibiting trading on information about events and circumstances which affect a company's assets or earning power; trading on information relating solely to the market for the company's securities is now also prohibited.[4]

Finally, the U.S. trading markets are undergoing major changes, largely in response to the demands placed on existing market arrangements by the rapid growth of institutional investment. The changes reflect the introduction of much more efficient communications systems. The overall effort is toward the development of the central market concept.

The appropriate regulation of the U.S. securities business and the operation of the trading markets have been the subject of intensive congressional concern over the last few years. Public hearings in both the Senate and the House of Representatives have resulted in multivolume studies of the securities industry. The Securities Acts Amendments of 1975 cover not only the basic considerations discussed earlier, but also certain important organizational questions, such as stock exchange disciplinary actions, the rules of the self-regulatory agencies, and the authority of the SEC. In this chapter we provide an overview of the sources of regulation which affect the U.S. markets.

THE NATURE OF GOVERNMENT

Economists assert that the major function of the securities markets is the allocation of capital to those users who will apply it most profitably. The efficient performance of the allocative function in turn requires rapid dissemination of relevant information about all the companies whose stocks are traded, so that pricing decisions can be informed ones. The emphasis of U.S. securities regulation on disclosure has already been mentioned. Considerations of allocational efficiency also make it necessary to prevent fraud and manipulation in the trading markets, so that pricing decisions will not be distorted by extraneous factors.

Effective stock markets also encourage a flow of funds into the equity market. An active secondary market in equities tends to lower the cost of capital and expands the financing options open to corporations. This function of the securities markets requires regulation to promote confidence, so that the public will be prepared to see its capital committed to equities.

U.S. regulation of insider trading, for example, serves both the disclosure and the confidence-building function of regulation. By preventing an insider from trading while in possession of material, nonpublic information, the law removes any incentive to delay the disclosure of corporate news. In addition, such regulation, if vigorously enforced, helps promote feelings of fairness, since market participants will believe that particular investors do not have an unfair edge over others. Insider trading prohibitions were applied[5] to institutional investors who sold Douglas Aircraft securities on the basis of nonpublic information about a sharp decline in Douglas's earnings which they learned or confirmed as a consequence of their relationship to the brokerage firm Merrill Lynch, Pierce, Fenner & Smith, the underwriter of a projected Douglas debenture issue. The SEC stressed the unfairness of these large investors obtaining advantages over other investors in Douglas stock, finding that, in its opinion, the institutional investors had violated the law.

The Douglas Aircraft case underscores an additional point about U.S. regulatory philosophy. It assumes that the individual investor should be encouraged to participate actively and directly in the equities markets. Individual investors have been playing a decreasing role in U.S. trading markets in the past few years. In the United States, where concentration of power is an overriding concern, this decline is viewed warily, because the presence of many decision makers in the market is believed to ensure a healthy dispersion of power. In addition, it is believed that a market reflecting the choices of diverse decision makers will be more liquid and more stable. The desire to preserve small broker-dealers is one reflection of this aspect of American regulatory philosophy.

Such a philosophy has its costs. Encouraging substantial numbers of individuals to invest in securities presupposes a willingness to tolerate active merchandising of securities. Active merchandising in turn creates opportunities for abuse, leading to calls for regulatory safeguards; this may help explain why the United States has a much more elaborate regulatory structure than other countries. The regulatory structure is costly. It may also encourage monopolistic practices.

Corporate Law

In the United States, both corporate law and securities regulation are possible sources of investor protection. Corporate law generally defines the respective roles of shareholders and managers. Although the definitions of these roles might be expected to provide a major source of shareholder protection, this has not been the case. To understand why requires an appreciation of three facts. First, corporate law is state law. Each state (as well as the District of Columbia) has its own corporation statute. Second, there are revenue advantages to a state in having a corporation organized under its laws. Third, U.S. conflicts-of-law principles provide that the corporate law in the state of incorporation governs with respect to the internal affairs of the corporation, including such issues as the duties of management and the rights of shareholders.

These circumstances explain why a relatively small state, Delaware, is the most popular state of incorporation for the major NYSE-listed corporations. Delaware occupies that position not because it is a leading commercial center but because it has a corporate law which gives management broad freedom to act and restricts the areas in which shareholders can or must act. The competition to be the domicile of major corporations tends to produce legislation that meets management's needs, not legislation that reflects a sensitivity to the protection of investor interests.

The shareholder protection vacuum left by state corporate law has been filled, to a substantial extent, by federal securities regulation, in particular by the proxy and antifraud rules. However, a growing number of commentators have been unhappy about this patchwork development and have called for a federal corporate law to govern national corporations.[6]

Such a law might establish greater scope for shareholder initiatives, set standards of management responsibility to broadly defined interests in the corporation (including, for example, consumer interests), and give these interests the right to sue if responsibilities were not met. It might also mandate the creation of boards of directors representing the spectrum of interests to which the corporation is conceived to be responsible.

Although these calls for reform have stirred academic interest, there does not seem to be much chance of such legislative passage in the next few years. Thus, the major source of shareholder protection will continue to be federal securities law.[7]

Federal Securities Laws

Federal securities regulation consists of seven basic statutes passed by Congress. One, the Securities Act of 1933, deals with the issuance of securities. The second, the Securities Exchange Act of 1934, regulates the trading markets in securities and provides the basis for regulating broker-dealers. It also contains periodic disclosure requirements and provisions governing insider trading and proxies for companies whose shares are listed on an exchange or have $1 million in total assets and a class of equity securities held by 500 or more persons. A third statute, the Investment Company Act of 1940, regulates investment companies. A companion statute, the Investment Advisers Act of 1940, governs the conduct of persons who provide investment advice for compensation. The Public Utility Holding Company Act of 1935, no longer very important in the regulatory scheme, and the Trust Indenture Act of 1939, which seeks to raise the standards for corporate bond trustees, round out the basic statutes at present. A recent addition to the federal securities laws, the Securities Investor Protection Act of 1970, which is described at the close of this chapter, provides protection against certain losses to customers of brokerage firms which are liquidated under the act. As discussed previously, major amendments to the 1934 Exchange Act give the SEC sufficient authority over markets, firms, securities, and the processors of market information to create the desired central system. The SEC has also proposed a bill to extend its authority over investment advisers.

Since questions about securities law are rarely politically exciting, it is difficult to get Congress to enact needed legislative changes, particularly when a change impacts unfavorably on a particular economic interest group. Fortunately, Federal securities legislation tends to be broadly framed, thus leaving substantial discretion to the administrative body, the SEC, which is charged with implementing the legislation. For example, the Exchange Act grants the commission the power to adopt such proxy rules as it deems "necessary or appropriate in the public interest or for the protection of investors." It is hard to conceive of a much broader grant of power. The latitude for growth through administrative action helps explain why U.S. securities regulation has been able to adapt to meet new challenges.

SECURITIES AND EXCHANGE COMMISSION

The Securities and Exchange Commission is an independent, bipartisan, quasi-judicial agency of the U.S. government. It is composed of five commissioners appointed by the president of the United States with the consent of the Senate. Bipartisanship requires that no more than three commissioners may be from any particular party. The commissioners are appointed for five years (or for the unexpired portion of a five-year term, when a commissioner resigns prior to the end of his term) and may be removed only for cause. However, their independence is somewhat limited because each year the agency's budget must be approved by the White House and passed by Congress.

The commissioners are supported by a staff of roughly 1,800. The staff includes lawyers, accountants, financial analysts, engineers, examiners, and clerical and administrative personnel. Although most of the staff works in Washington, there are also 17 regional and branch offices located throughout the United States. Many SEC staffers are career employees. However, there is a significant flow of people between private law practice or the securities business and the SEC. This flow helps the SEC to remain current on the business it regulates and to take a realistic view of the impact of its regulatory activities. Recently, cross-fertilization between the SEC, private practice, and the industry has been formalized through limited-term SEC fellowships.

There is no need to spell out here the various formal ways in which the SEC acts to administer the federal securities laws.[8] However, the extraordinary degree to which the SEC is willing to work with practitioners and others on an informal basis should be emphasized. For example, the staff informally reviews registration and proxy statements and through "comment letters" raises questions and suggests the need for clarification or additional information. The staff also responds to inquiries as to whether it would recommend SEC enforcement action if a described course of conduct were followed. These responses are known as "no action" letters.[9] The commissioners and staff also participate in a host of programs designed to educate lawyers and members of the affected industries about the operations of the securities laws. For example, a program called "The SEC Speaks," featuring short presentations by SEC staffers, followed by a series of questions from a panel of private practitioners, has annually drawn over 1,000 listeners to Washington, D.C. Since 1970 the Practicing Law Institute has held an Annual Institute on Securities Regulation in New York City to review major regulatory developments. In this program, practitioners or academics make the presentations, but high SEC staff officials actively participate in the give-and-take of panel discussions.[10]

This stress on the SEC's relations with the legal community reflects the reality of the commission's operations. By and large, at least until the last few years, the commission has kept out of the economic area. Responsibility for prescribing margin regulations, which takes credit conditions into account and therefore has important economic overtones, is given to the Board of Governors of the Federal Reserve System by Section 7 of the Exchange Act. While the SEC's *Institutional Investor Study*, undertaken several years ago, sought to evaluate the role and influence of institutional investors in the securities markets, the corps of economists who conducted it was largely recruited from outside the commission and left after the study was completed. In recent years, the commission has taken an active role in the setting of commission rates and their eventual abolition, as well as in the development of a central market. Its own staff of economists, however, remains small, and much of their effort is devoted to collection of statistics on the securities markets and the economy.

STOCK EXCHANGE REGULATION

Although governmental regulation is the major source of investor protection in the United States, self-regulation also plays a substantial role. The Securities Exchange Act of 1934 provides that a stock exchange may be organized as a marketplace only if it has rules for disciplining its members for conduct inconsistent with just and equitable principles of trade. In other words, an exchange must function as a self-regulatory organization.

Indeed, a number of cases hold that failure by the exchange to police its rules carefully may result in civil liability to any person harmed thereby.[11] Exchange self-regulation operates in several areas. A stock exchange has responsibilities involving the financial responsibility, competence, and integrity of its members. For example, the NYSE imposes net capital requirements on its members and limits their permitted aggregate indebtedness to net capital ratios. It also administers examinations for principals and employees of member firms.

Exchanges define and police compliance with proper trading practice. A case in point is the NYSE stock-watch program, to identify unusual stock price movements which may require investigation. The exchanges have also developed professional standards of conduct for their members. In addition, the corporate disclosure requirements of the major stock exchanges go beyond existing legal obligations in requiring listed companies to make prompt disclosure of material information.

Exchanges have been interested in policing the quality of the companies whose stocks are traded in their markets. Not only must an NYSE company have demonstrated earning power; the exchange is also prepared, to some extent, to impose good business and financial practices on its listed companies. Thus, an NYSE-listed company may not issue nonvoting common stock and must get shareholder approval for the granting of stock options to directors, officers, or employees.

Exchanges have also engaged in economic self-regulation; practices include limiting the number of memberships and denying direct access to exchange facilities to certain classes of persons (for example, to foreign brokers). The Securities Acts Amendments of 1975 struck down some of these self-regulatory practices, such as imposing minimum commission rates and denying membership to financial institutions. Competition for business between exchanges has been a dynamic force in stimulating a reconsideration of the regulatory justification for certain restrictive economic practices. Moreover, the movement toward a central market has resulted in legislation to eliminate regulatory disparities.

Exchange regulation is imposed through a board of directors and implemented by large professional staffs. Since the directors serve on a part-time basis, the quality of the staff to a large extent determines the quality of the regulatory effort. Exchange budgets for staff have grown substantially over the past decade.

Self-Regulation: An Appraisal

Has stock exchange self-regulation been successful? The answer depends on the context in which the process is examined. For example, the self-regulatory bodies seem to do a creditable job in dealing with specific fraudulent acts and infractions of fairly clearly defined proscriptions. They have been less successful in providing economic regulation in the public interest and in implementing kinds of regulation which run counter to significant economic interests of substantial segments of the brokerage community. For example, the self-regulatory authorities failed to force brokerage firms to build up and maintain back-office operations commensurate with their rapidly increasing retail activities. As noted earlier, back-office problems contributed significantly to the financial failure of many brokerage firms in the late 1960s. Moreover, the exchanges did not show much initiative in coping with the question of the commission rate structure.

Effective self-regulation seems to depend on the power of the SEC to act in the event that the self-regulatory authorities do not meet their responsibilities. Although the increase in the number and improvement in the quality of public representatives on self-regulatory bodies were stimulated by a desire to strengthen self-regulation, the presence of a vigorous, governmental backup seems necessary to accomplish some of the unpleasant tasks of regulation. SEC oversight responsibilities were strengthened by the 1975 legislation.

REGULATION BY PRIVATE LITIGATION

Regulation by public bodies like the SEC and by quasi-public bodies like the stock exchanges is supplemented by civil suits brought by private litigants who claim to have been harmed by conduct allegedly violating the federal securities laws, the rules promulgated thereunder, or, in certain cases, the rules of the self-regulatory organizations. Private actions have been helpful in establishing the reach of the antifraud rules (particularly Rule 10b-5) and in defining standards of professional responsibility for broker-dealers.

Feasibility

How does private enforcement of federal securities regulation work? In effect, individual attorneys, acting on behalf of a private client, can function as entrepreneurs in the business of enforcing the law against those who have violated it. This is possible for a number of reasons. First, each party in litigation normally pays his own counsel's fees whether he wins or loses. Second, a party is free to negotiate a contingent fee arrangement with his counsel. Third and most important, the class action device permits the lawyer to bring an action not only on behalf of the specific client who came to his office but also on behalf of a large number of similarly situated clients whom he has never seen and whose names he does not know. Suppose a company sells 1 million shares of stock at $10 per share on the basis of an allegedly false and misleading prospectus. After the prospectus has been corrected, the stock is worth $8 per share. If the client who came to the lawyer's office bought 300 shares of this stock in the distribution, his damages would be $600 at maximum—hardly enough to pay the lawyer's fee. But if the lawyer can sue on behalf of all purchasers in the distribution, there is a potential recovery of $2 million. A contingent fee of 20 percent of that amount amply rewards the lawyer for his work and risk.[12]

It is true that this technique of law enforcement provides opportunities for abuse.[13] Some years ago, for example, an independent investor named Eisen sought to recover $70 damages through alleged overcharges on the execution of odd-lot transactions. In view of the complexity of the case and the small amount involved, lawyers were not interested in taking it unless Eisen became representative of the class of odd-lot traders in the NYSE. In this case, there could be several million persons and huge amounts involved. The Court of Appeals for the Second Circuit decided that the case failed as a class action because of its unmanageability on that basis and because of the enormous difficulty of giving notice to the multitude of shareholders falling within the class. In discussing the case, Judge Harold R. Medina noted that the class action was a useful tool for the administration of justice but that some responsible attorneys consider many such actions as "legalized blackmail."[14]

Despite opportunities for abuse, the possibility of private action has helped alert people to their responsibilities. For example, a suit against a leading Philadelphia investment banking firm, which had underwritten securities in a bowling enterprise that ultimately went bankrupt, effectively reminded all investment bankers of their obligations carefully to investigate companies whose securities they are offering to the public.[15] It seems that the suit did prompt a thorough review by investment banking firms and others similarly occupied.[16]

Role of the Securities Bar

Another important source of regulatory input comes from the securities bar itself. Regulation works well if the people affected are persuaded that, on the whole, the regulatory requirements are proper and beneficial.

Lawyers play a major role in shaping business transactions and drafting documents. (Their role in these areas is much larger than the role played by lawyers in any other country.) Thus, they educate clients in the requirements of the federal securities laws and serve as an integral part of the process of compliance. The flow of ex-SEC staff members into private practice and the constant interaction between the bar associations and SEC staff and commissioners promote a sympathetic respect for and an understanding of the purposes the federal securities laws seek to achieve. In addition, the bar works with the SEC, through bar association committees, to solve regulatory problems, including the drafting of SEC rules. The major effort of the American Law Institute to recodify the federal securities laws has enlisted the active cooperation of SEC officials, members of the practicing bar, and academics specializing in the area. A substantial majority of the consultants and advisers for the Federal Securities Code project, as well as its reporter, Professor Louis Loss, have served either as commissioners or as staff members of the SEC.

Antitrust Laws

Securing disclosure and preventing fraud have been the traditional goals of federal securities laws. However, in recent times, regulatory attention has begun to focus more sharply on economic issues, such as the rate structures of stock exchanges and distribution schemes for mutual funds; the antitrust laws play a major role in resolving such issues. Securities regulation has often been restrictive. Stock exchange rules have commanded members to deal with nonmembers at a minimum or fixed price, to trade in a specified place, and to refuse membership to certain classes of persons. At one time or another, the SEC has acquiesced in the adoption of many of these rules.

Roughly ten years ago, ruling on a private suit,[17] the U.S. Supreme Court stated that restrictive regulatory practices were justified only to the extent that they were necessary to make the regulatory scheme work. That standard requires the articulation and examination of the reasons why certain restrictions are thought necessary to achieve desired regulatory ends. Such examination has taken place primarily in private actions attacking specific restrictive practices, but these suits have also goaded the SEC into taking a more active and questioning role. To a large extent, this antitrust attack spearheaded the drive for competitive commission rates in the United States.

PROTECTING THE INVESTOR'S SECURITIES AND FUNDS

As a result of the operating and financial difficulties that the securities industry experienced from 1968 to 1970, a number of firms, including some of the industry's largest, were forced into liquidation, and many others were eliminated through mergers. Through the activity of the NYSE trust fund and the transfer of accounts to stronger firms, hundreds of thousands of customers were saved from major loss. In these rescue efforts the industry expended some $130 million.[18]

The potential loss to investors was too great, however, to rely upon voluntary methods of protection, particularly since the trust fund might have been exhausted and nonmembers were not covered anyway. Accordingly,

Congress enacted the Securities Investor Protection Act of 1970, creating the Securities Investor Protection Corporation (SIPC). This agency provides insurance for customer accounts of all registered broker-dealers, with a maximum limit of $50,000 for each customer, of which $20,000 may be in cash. The insurance program was originally funded by assessing the firms 0.5 percent of their gross revenues from the securities business until the fund reached $150 million; then assessments could fall to 0.25 percent until all lines of credit were phased out. If, at any time, the fund fell below $100 million, the 0.5 percent assessment would be reinstated.

If the funds accumulated by the assessments and lines of bank credit prove insufficient, the SEC can borrow up to $1 billion from the Treasury and advance these funds to the corporation. According to the legislation, the existing self-regulatory organizations must continue to inspect their members for compliance with "financial responsibility" rules and make such reports as the corporation may require. After passage of the SIPC legislation, the NYSE announced the termination of its voluntary customer assistance program and indicated its intention to phase out the special trust fund.

The SIPC insurance program is cumbersome. The starting point is an SEC request for the agency to liquidate a troubled firm. SIPC then asks the court to appoint a trustee, who, in turn, engages an accounting firm to audit the brokerage house's books to ascertain its holdings of customers' cash and securities. After the audit, SIPC forwards claims forms to all customers, who have 60 days to enter their claims. Following verification of the claims, the fully paid certificates in customers' names are returned to their owners, and the remaining assets are placed in a pool so that customers may establish claims against them up to the specified insurance lines. Amounts beyond the insurance limits are grouped with the claims of the general creditors.[19]

Liquidation of small houses has generally taken several months, but as much as a year may be required for a large firm. Meanwhile, the customers' funds and securities are tied up. Large amounts, of course, are not covered by any insurance. During the uncertainties of the early 1970s, account protection became a major issue. The large, well-capitalized firms were able to obtain additional protection (in some cases as much as $450,000) from several insurance companies, but smaller firms, even those in a solid financial position, experienced difficulty because of their small capitalization. Consequently, the smaller firms were placed at a competitive disadvantage.

In view of these difficulties, the SIPC requested Congress to increase the coverage of firms' individual accounts from $50,000 to $125,000. Moreover, a brokerage industry task force also issued a report in which it recommended major revisions in the act to "streamline the administration of a liquidation proceeding."[20]

Included in the SIPC legislation was a provision requiring the SEC to investigate unsafe and unsound practices in the industry. In its study, submitted to Congress, the SEC recommended that Congress extend the commission's regulatory oversight in the following areas: securities processing, rule-making authority of the self-regulatory organizations, enforcement of the rules of the self-regulatory organizations, and the administration of disciplinary proceedings conducted by the self-regulatory organizations.[21] A number of these proposals were included in the new central market legislation.

Following the enactment of SIPC, both the NYSE and the SEC took various steps to ensure the financial responsibility of broker-dealers. Toward this end, the NYSE lowered the maximum permissible *net capital ratio* (the ratio of aggregate indebtedness to net capital), raised the minimum net capital requirements, and improved the quality of member capital by placing limits on its withdrawal. The SEC also strengthened its net capital rules, established a formal procedure for brokers to keep track of securities held by them and not in their possession, and adopted rules providing for more disclosure to customers of brokers' financial condition. Of importance is the rule, authorized in the SIPC legislation and announced by the SEC in November 1972, providing for the maintenance of basic reserves against customers' deposits or free credit balances, and for standards to govern the physical possession or control of customers' fully paid and excess margin securities.[22]

An analysis by the SIPC indicates that the principal causes of broker failures include poorly kept books, possible fraud, dealing in highly speculative securities, excessive costs and inadequate financial controls, and insufficient knowledge of the securities business. In 1973 almost 25 percent of all failures were for the final reason. These facts suggest the need for prospective brokers to furnish fuller background information when they apply for SEC or NASD registration.[23] The broker-dealer registration requirements under the 1975 amendments, including the authority of the SEC to require standards of training and competence, may meet this need.

SUMMARY

Traditionally, the underlying thrust of the securities acts has been to safeguard the public interest and to provide for investor protection primarily through regulation. The Securities Acts Amendments of 1975 elevated competition to a legislative objective.

U.S. regulatory philosophy encourages the active participation of individual investors in the equities markets to ensure a healthy dispersion of power. The rapid dissemination of relevant information and the prevention of fraud and manipulation permit effective pricing decisions that, in turn, enable the securities markets to perform their major function of allocating capital efficiently. The regulation of insider trading helps promote feelings of fairness because market participants can believe that particular investors will not have an unfair edge over others.

Regulation is achieved in various ways. In the area of government, the primary role has been played at the federal level, through seven basic statutes. These laws are broadly framed, leaving substantial discretion to the administrative body, the SEC, which is charged with implementing the legislation.

Although governmental regulation is the major source of investor protection, self-regulation by the exchanges themselves has also been of some importance. Self-regulation has involved monitoring the financial integrity of members, maintaining effective trading practices, and policing the quality of the companies whose stocks are traded in the markets.

Less usual sources of protection for the investor in equity securities include civil suits brought by private litigants, the role of the securities bar, and the application of antitrust laws. While subordinated to the basic regulatory functions of government and the self-regulatory bodies, these other sources provide useful supplementary services.

As a result of the operating and financial difficulties that the securities industry experienced between 1968 and 1970, a number of firms, including some of the industry's largest, were forced into liquidation, and many others were eliminated through mergers. The potential loss to investors was too great to rely on voluntary methods of protection. Accordingly, Congress enacted the Securities Investor Protection Act of 1970, which created the Securities Investor Protection Corp. to provide insurance for customer accounts.

Part Two

THE APPROACH TO INVESTMENT

In this part we add to the background material that the investor must understand before actually buying and selling securities. Chapter 4 explores some important concepts of income measurement that enter into financial planning. The next two chapters focus on the programs of individual investors. Chapter 5 assesses the role of savings and investment, including a comparison of the major savings sources. Chapter 6 analyzes how current tax legislation may affect the individual's investment policies. Chapter 7 classifies and provides a broad view of the major resources the investor may draw upon for information about the industries and companies in which he or she may be interested. In evaluating the factors that influence the prices of securities, the last section, Chapter 8, sets the stage for the formal analytic process.

CHAPTER 4

Income from Securities

An owner of a security may obtain three principal types of income. If he is a stockholder, he may receive dividends; if he is a bondholder, he may receive interest; and whether he is a stockholder or a bondholder, he may incur a capital gain or loss (negative income) amounting to the difference between the purchase and sale prices of a security. Each of these sources requires special consideration.

DIVIDENDS

The board of directors of a corporation is responsible for establishing the policy governing payment of dividends. Decisions are reached at regular or special meetings and issued as soon as they are made. It is customary for the board to announce dividends well in advance of the payment date.

The announcement specifies the amount of dividends, the date payment will be made, and when the stockholder's name must be recorded on the books of the corporation in order to receive payment. This date is generally about two weeks prior to payment; it is established to permit corporate management to ascertain which stockholders are entitled to payments. Because of the rapid turnover of holders on the books of a large corporation, it would be impossible to determine to whom dividends should be paid without such lead time.

Common Stock Policy

The common-stock dividend-paying policies of corporations vary. A few firms have attempted to maintain uniform payments, but eventually even most of these have found it desirable to introduce changes. For example, American Telephone & Telegraph kept its historic $9.00 annual payment for some 35 years, but in 1959 the company finally split its stock three-for-one and paid an annual amount equivalent to $9.45 on the former basis. In 1964 the stock was split once more, this time two-for-one. By 1975 the company was on an indicated annual rate of $3.40 per share, amounting to $20.40 on the old stock. Companies ordinarily distribute quarterly, but there are departures from this practice. For example, Downey Savings & Loan Association pays annually, and Materials Research pays semiannually; Downey is listed on both the AMEX and the Pacific Stock Exchange, while Materials Research is listed on the AMEX.[1]

Some corporations make disbursements irregularly, depending on conditions at the time of payment. Others combine the regular and irregular payment plans by keeping regular payments but distributing extra dividends whenever possible. If a corporation is in a position to make a large disbursement but does not believe the payment is likely to be repeated, it may declare a special dividend. Finally, stock dividends, representing the distribution of additional stock to existing stockholders, usually on a fractional basis, may be used to permit dividend payments without incurring cash outlays.

In the investment-company field, several funds offer an ingenious dividend scheme providing a choice to investors of either dividend income or capital gains. For example, the Gemini Fund, Inc., a closed-end investment company, has two types of stock outstanding: one, called income shares, entitles holders to at least $0.56 cumulative dividends annually, plus an extra dividend payable on the first payment date following the close of the fiscal year; the other, called capital shares, does not entitle holders to dividends until the income shares have been redeemed in full, after which the capital shareholder receives all dividends and distributions on the fund shares.

The investor should become familiar with the dividend policies of the corporations in which he or she is interested. This information will help the investor gauge the amount and regularity of the payments likely to be received.

The Ex-Dividend Date and Its Effect on Stock Prices

We have observed that a typical dividend announcement includes the date when the payment will be made and the date by which the stockholders must be listed on the corporation's books in order to receive payment. In theory, the price of the stock reflects the expected dividend; therefore, on the day on which purchase of the issue no longer includes the announced dividend (called the *ex-date*), the price should decline by exactly the amount of the distribution.[2]

Subsequently, if no other factor has affected the issue's price, it should rise each day until the next ex-date. In practice, many factors determine the price of a security; thus, the price may actually rise on the ex-date if the favorable forces are strong enough to offset the drop caused by the dividend payment. In this case, the price advance is presumably lessened by the amount of the distribution.

Securities exchanges are responsible for determining when issues become ex-dividend. The New York Stock Exchange has ruled that all transactions in a stock except those for "cash" sell ex-dividend on the fourth business day preceding the record date fixed by the corporation. "Cash" transactions become ex-dividend on the business day following the record date. The exchange may make special arrangements when desirable.

Due-bills. Due-bills are instruments showing the transfer of title to a dividend received by the seller of a security but belonging to the buyer. When a security is sold before its ex-date but delivery is made too late to enable the buyer to obtain transfer in time to become a holder of record, the seller is paid the dividend because his name appears on the corporation's books on the record date. When this happens, the seller must deliver to the buyer, within five days after the record date, a due-bill equivalent to the amount of the dividend. These bills are ordinarily redeemable on the date the dividend is paid. In the case of a cash dividend, the seller delivers a due-bill check; this is a due-bill in the form of a check payable on the date of payment of the cash dividend.

Restrictions on dividend payments. Although the directors of a corporation may authorize dividend payments, they do not have complete freedom in this respect. Limitations may be imposed by state law, federal regulations, or the company's certificate of incorporation and trust indenture, which contains a detailed description of the terms of a corporate bond. State-imposed restrictions are designed to protect both creditors and stockholders against dissipation of capital in the form of dividends. Regulations in corporate charters and trust indentures, and rules imposed by the federal agencies, including the Securities and Exchange Commission, tend to be more stringent. These rules seek to ensure corporate financial stability and the maintenance of a sound capital structure.

Provisions that curb the freedom of management to pay dividends may be of great importance to the investor studying a corporation's prospects. Despite the availability of earnings and the willingness of management to make distributions, payments may have to be withheld or kept low until a statutory, charter, or indenture restriction is met. Consequently, if there is any doubt of a corporation's legal ability to make disbursements, the investor must check these restrictions.[3] For example, in 1972, Sprague Electric reported consolidated earnings of $1,526,260 and retained earnings of $12,182,265. The company, however, paid no dividends. According to its loan agreements, cash dividends of the parent company are restricted to the consolidated net income earned after December 31, 1966, plus $5,000,000 and the proceeds from issue or sale of capital stock after that date, less cash dividends paid after December 31, 1966. On December 31, 1973, consolidated retained earnings were deficient by $1,200,000 of the minimum amount required to permit cash dividend payments. The investor must also consider the possibility that management may not want to pay liberal dividends because it needs funds for plant expansion, strengthening working capital, or other reasons. Thus, profits in 1974 enabled Sprague to free $9,600,000 of consolidated retained earnings from dividend restrictions. The company, however, paid no dividends, possibly because, as indicated in its annual report, profitable operations, at least during the first six months of 1975, were highly unlikely.

Pressures for dividend payments. Corporate management is also exposed to pressures for the adoption of liberal dividend policies. These pressures arise partly from a desire to cultivate the goodwill of stockholders. (Dividend checks are probably the chief public relations vehicle of management.) Legal requirements may constitute another type of pressure.

Ordinarily the courts are reluctant to interfere with management in the matter of paying dividends. However, since 1913, when the federal personal income tax became a permanent part of our financial environment, Congress has been trying, through the threat of punitive taxes, to prevent corporations from unnecessarily accumulating earnings.[4]

The current Section 531 tax on accumulated earnings applies primarily to cases in which closely held corporations retain income in order to prevent payment of taxes by stockholders. This policy does not usually obtain in corporations with widely held stock, although the tax has occasionally been levied on such firms.[5] At present, therefore, tax pressures are not an important inducement for corporations with publicly held securities to distribute large portions of their earnings as dividends.

Alternative methods of taxation have been suggested which would obviate a punitive tax on accumulated earnings. Until a new solution is provided, some form of surtax on accumulated earnings is likely to remain in the law. The vigor with which it is enforced will probably depend on prevailing political conditions and the need for additional federal revenue. The present Section 531 tax paves the way for more severe government methods of compelling corporations to adopt liberal dividend policies.

Is the Dividend Payment the Decision Variable?

The dividend pattern of a corporation cannot be fully appreciated unless one realizes that the dividend is a mirror image of retention policy. In this matter a corporation really has only one degree of freedom. It can decide how much it wants to retain for reinvestment and distribute the remainder as dividends, or it can decide how much it wants to disburse as dividends and keep the rest for reinvestment. After one of the decisions is made the other automatically falls into place and does not call for independent consideration. It is not wholly clear which decision is the conscious one and which the residual.

Corporate management probably bases its dividend policy on three important premises.[6] The first is that stockholders are interested in stable dividends. The second—perhaps reflecting the first—is that dividends should be a relatively stable fraction of basic earnings. This relationship between dividends and earnings is known as the *payout ratio* and its relative consistency over periods of time suggests that there is a target payout figure. The third is that when management finds that the actual ratio differs from the target ratio, it does not attempt to close the gap in one bold step. The procedure for determining the appropriate dividend seems to be one of comparing the target rate with the last dividend and considering the advisability of effecting modifications. The dividend for each period is not established de novo.

A variety of factors inhibit a firm from completely adjusting the actual dividend rate to the target. The two most important considerations presumably are the confidence that management has in the reliability of its reported earnings and, even if accounting results are believed to be accurate, the uncertainty as to whether the reported figure represents a true or normal level, since earnings contain a random element. By making partial adjustments, management gives itself time to evaluate the changing fortunes of the firm and to determine the extent to which the increments to earnings are the reflections of underlying trends rather than transitory phenomena. The reaction time of the corporation, in turn, may be influenced by such factors as the variability of earnings, the liquidity of the corporation, and the rate of growth.

While the reaction times of corporations differ, each corporation's dividend policy will reflect management's judgment of the true level of earnings. In the annual report, management may make an optimistic forecast of the earnings trend, but stockholders are justified in expecting action to back this forecast. The evidence that management is not just whistling in the dark is its willingness to commit itself to a dividend commensurate with the earnings trend it is asking the shareholders to anticipate.

In a number of instances, an indicated shift in dividend policy can provide useful corroboratory evidence. Thus, on an adjusted basis, AT&T's dividend payments were increased gradually every few years from 1963 to 1974, a period that witnessed a comparable rise in the corporation's earnings. Similarly, distributions of the American Electric Power Co. were lifted regularly in the 1960s, paralleling gains in earnings. National Distillers & Chemical Corp., a diversified enterprise in the fields of chemicals, metals, plastics, and beverages, maintained its dividends unchanged between 1960 and 1964, as earnings stabilized; the dividend increase of 1965 then ushered in a period when earnings were at a generally higher level. In the same vein, Homestake Mining Co., producing gold, lead, and zinc, reduced its dividends in 1967 and held it at this lower level until 1972, reflecting an abrupt initial decline in earnings, followed by relative stability. Then, in 1972, higher gold prices caused an upward earnings spurt, which was confirmed by a sharp dividend increase in 1973.

BOND INTEREST

Bond interest represents a fixed liability of a corporation. The rights of the bondholders in the event of default on an interest payment depend on the terms of the bond and of the trust indenture. These instruments generally permit bondholders not only to bring suit for interest payments but also to take steps to accelerate the maturity of the debt.

Corporations usually attempt to maintain interest payments even when dividend distributions have been halted. The rate of return on bonds, therefore, tends to be lower than that available on the common and preferred stocks of comparable corporations. In order to avoid fixed interest charges, corporations wishing to issue bonds sometimes create instruments called income bonds. (For a discussion of income bonds, see pp. 476-478.) During periods when interest rates are unusually high or when investors emphasize growth, the return from dividends may be less than that on bonds, presumably because of the expectation that this differential will be more than offset by capital gains.

CAPITAL GAINS

Capital gains are measured by the difference between the cost and the sale prices of a security, less the expenses of making the purchase and sale. These gains may be substantial, but the uncertainty associated with them is greater than that associated with a dividend. In the case of common stock, the shareholder is "entitled" to a pro rata share of the earnings of the corporation. The portion which is not distributed in the form of dividends is reinvested and—at least in theory—shows up in the value of the share. If the market's expectation of a company's future earnings and its evaluation of the risk associated with that corporation in particular and with conditions in general did not change, the price of the share would indeed reflect retained earnings. However, the market either continuously or sporadically reevaluates both the corporation and the economic environment. As a consequence, the year-to-year rise in the price of the stock usually will be quite different from the per share increment in retained earnings.

At one time, a neat distinction was drawn between realized and unrealized capital gains. When a security which has appreciated in value is liquidated, the gain is *realized*; as long as the security remains in a portfolio, the gain is *unrealized*. When markets are ebullient, investors tend to become more interested in capital gains than in dividends. Such a shift suggests that both may be considered as income. An important difference is that income in the form of a capital gain is not taxed until realized and, when realized, is taxed at a rate lower than that applicable to dividends.[7]

The logic of considering an unrealized capital gain as income may be illustrated by the following example. If it is argued that the gain should not be counted as income until realized, it is then equally logical to maintain that the wealth of an investor is not affected by unrealized capital gains. Suppose that an investor liquidated all of his wealth (a total of $300,000) and invested the entire amount in 10,000 shares of stock at $30 a share. Several years later, another inherits a net amount of $550,000, which he uses to buy the same stock at $55 per share. Both investors now own 10,000 shares of the same stock, worth $550,000. It is absurd to say that one is wealthier than the other. It is equally absurd to say that the first investor is really only worth $300,000 because that is the price he paid for the stock. But if he originally was worth $300,000 and today is worth $550,000, the increment must have come from income. Aside from bequests, income is by definition the only source of added wealth.

The principal objection to viewing an unrealized capital gain as income is that it is relatively ephemeral and could vanish just as easily as it appears. That is true. But if an unrealized capital gain is eliminated by a subsequent fall in the price of the stock, or is converted to a loss (realized or unrealized), its disappearance does not mean that the investor did not have income in the first place.

INCOME MEASUREMENTS

Having discussed the different types of income to be derived from securities, we now consider the tools available for measuring such income. There are four principal devices: (1) the dollar return; (2) the stated rate of return; (3) the annual rate of return; and (4) the yield to maturity.

These measures may be known by various names. Each device involves a different type of calculation and has its own special uses. The investor should be familiar with all of them.

Dollar Return

The *dollar return* is the amount of money that the corporation pays yearly on each share of stock or on each bond outstanding. To determine the total cash income from a particular security, the investor multiplies the dollar return by the total number of bonds or shares of stock that he holds in the corporation. For example, if in a particular year a corporation paid $0.90 on each share of common stock, the total cash income for an investor holding 100 shares of the issue would be $90.00.

Stated Rate of Return

The *stated rate of return*, which applies only to bonds and preferred stocks, is the stipulated rate of payment. It is ordinarily expressed as a percentage of the par value of preferred stock or of the principal value of bonds.

Corporations sometimes state directly the dollar return of a preferred stock. This is done when the issue has no par value or, occasionally, when the par value is very low. A company's certificate of incorporation assigns a par or stated value to the stock or indicates that it has no par value; the designation appears on the stock certificate. The product of the number of shares outstanding and the par or stated value per share determines the amount of capital stock in the balance sheet. Par value has no analytic significance.

More often, the investor must calculate the dollar return of a preferred stock by multiplying the stated rate by the par value of the issue. For example, the par value of Reynolds Metals Co. 4.75 percent Series A preferred is $50; the dollar return is $2.375 per share.

In the case of most bond issues, the stated rate may be converted to the dollar return simply by multiplying by $1,000. Thus, the stated rate on the Consolidated Edison's 5s due in 1990 is 5 percent; the dollar return is $50.

Annual Rate of Return

Neither the stated rate nor the dollar return considers the price of a security. But if two corporations pay the same dividends on their stock or the same interest on their bonds, it is obvious that the lower-priced issue affords a better return. In order to measure this relative return, therefore, the investor must take the price into account by expressing the dollar amount received as a percentage of the price of the issue. This figure is variously called the *annual rate of return, current rate of return,* or *current yield.*

Thus, in mid-1975, Reynolds Metals 4.75 percent preferred stock was selling at about 37; its annual rate of return, therefore, was 6.42 percent (\$2.375 ÷ \$37.00). At that time the Con Ed 5s/1990 were selling at about 52; their annual rate of return was 9.62 percent (\$50 ÷ \$520.00).

Tables are available which show the annual rates of return for various dollar amounts and bond coupon and price relationships. The calculation, however, is very simple. With the advent of mini-calculators, therefore, the tables are not much used.

Yield to Maturity

A corporation is required to pay the principal amount of its bonds at maturity; otherwise, if the issue is callable, it may elect to pay the redemption price at a designated time before the bond matures. The redemption price which the corporation pays if it exercises the call option ordinarily is above the principal due at maturity. If an investor purchases a bond at a level higher than the price at which the issue eventually matures or is redeemed (referred to as a *premium*), he must provide for this difference over the life of the bond. Conversely, if he buys at a level below the eventual maturity or redemption price (called a *discount*), he eventually receives a sum that includes the differential. A potential capital decrease or increase may be realized if the bond is sold before maturity at a price different from the purchase price.

In determining the return an investor can expect from a bond he will hold until it is redeemed, the stated return must be adjusted by the positive or negative differential that will be realized when the issue is paid. The net yield, adjusted in this way, is called the *yield to maturity.* If the investor bought the bond at a premium, the yield to maturity will be less than the stated return, unless the bond is expected to be redeemed at a call date and the redemption premium is greater than the premium paid; but if the bond is bought at a discount, the yield to maturity will be higher than the stated return.

The true yield, or the yield to maturity, can be defined as the discount rate which equates the present value of all future receipts to be obtained from holding a security to the present price of that security. In formula terms, the yield is the value of r which satisfies the equation

$$P = \sum_{t=1}^{T} R_t/(1+r)^t$$

where P stands for the price of the security and R_t for the cash receipts in period t. If this term is summed over all values of t up to the point where T approaches infinity, the formula is applicable to both stocks as well as bonds. If the bond matures or is called at the end of n years, the value R_t for all values of t greater than n is simply zero. R_n is the final receipt and can be decomposed into the last interest and redemption payments.

The concept applied to stocks. In the case of stocks, the cash receipts should theoretically be taken over an infinite period. It is easy to see, however, that this process is not necessary. Suppose the investor intends to hold the stock for $T < \infty$ years. Consider all terms from period $T + 1$ on. The present value of the sum of these terms can be written as

$$\sum_{j=1}^{\infty} \frac{R_{T+j}}{(1+r)^{T+j}}$$

where R_{T+j} represents the cash receipts in period $T + j$. In this formula the denominator can be decomposed into $(1+r)^T \times (1+r)^j$. Since that is the case, $1/(1+r)^T$ can be factored out of the sum, so that it reads:

$$\frac{1}{(1+r)^T} \sum_{j=1}^{\infty} \frac{R_{T+j}}{(1+r)^j}.$$

An examination of the term $\sum_{j=1}^{\infty} R_{T+j}/(1+r)^j$ indicates that it is equal to P_T, the expected ex-dividend price at time T. This is the present value of all dividends to be received from that date forward. If P_T is substituted for this term, we may write $P_T/(1+r)^T$, which represents the present value of the price at which we could expect to liquidate the stock at time T. It follows that the yield on a share of common stock for any given investor's horizon is the rate which equates the present value of all dividends to be received between now and time T and the present value of the price of the stock at which we anticipate liquidating in time T. This last term is the parallel to the redemption value of the bond. The major difference between this term and the redemption value is that the redemption value, except for the possibility of default, is known at the time the investment is considered, whereas the anticipated liquidation value of the stock must be estimated.

By formulating the problem in this manner, we are able to point out in still another way the logic of including capital gains in income. Let $T = 1$. According to the formula we have just described

$$P_0 = R_1/(1 + r) + P_1/(1 + r).$$

Multiplying both sides by $1 + r$ and dividing both sides by P_0, we have

$$1 + r = R_1/P_0 + P_1/P_0.$$

P_1 may be decomposed into $P_0 + \Delta P$, where ΔP represents the capital gain (or loss). Substituting that, we may then write

$$1 + r = R_1/P_0 + P_0/P_0 + \Delta P/P_0.$$

Canceling the one from both sides of the equation, and collecting the terms on the right hand side over the common denominator, we have

$$r = (R_1 + \Delta P)/P_0,$$

which may be larger or smaller than the dividend yield R_1/P_0, depending upon whether ΔP is greater or less than 0. The combination of dividend return and capital gain or loss on a stock may be called its total yield. Thus, in 1972, Pepsico and B. F. Goodrich declared dividends of $1 a share on their common stocks. An investor who bought Pepsico on December 31, 1971 at 70¼ obtained a current yield of 1.42 percent, while the purchaser of B. F. Goodrich on the same day at 28⅜ received a current return of 3.52 percent on the basis of the same $1 dividend. One year later, on December 29, 1972, the price of Pepsico had risen to 87⅛ making its total yield 25.44 percent for the period, while B. F. Goodrich was selling at 28¼ leaving its yield substantially unchanged.

The concept applied to bonds. The determination of the yield on a common stock requires gauging both the dividends that will be received and the capital gain or loss that will be incurred. This type of estimate is eliminated in the case of a bond, where interest payment is fixed and the maturity value is $1,000 or the redemption price.

As may be observed from the previous discussion, the variables needed to calculate the mathematical value of a bond are its maturity or redemption price, the specified interest rate, the yield to maturity or first call date, the number of years until redemption or maturity, and the frequency of interest disbursements. When these factors are known, the value of the bond is found to consist of the sum of two elements. The first is the present value of the price at date of final payment (maturity or redemption), with the yield to that date used as the discount factor. The second is the present value of an annuity comprising the interest payments discounted at the rate of yield to the date of final payment. If a formula is developed that embodies these two factors, the price of a bond at any given yield to maturity may be ascertained. Conversely, if the price is given, the yield can be determined.

If the yield is calculated by means of the bond-price formula, trial and error substitutions must be employed. This procedure is cumbersome; although the formula is of interest to students concerned with the mathematics of finance, the investor will probably never use it. Whenever the yield to maturity must be calculated, the investor undoubtedly will employ either the approximate method, involving certain arithmetical computations, or bond tables, if they are available. Moreover, relatively sophisticated mini-calculators are now available that permit ready calculation of present values and bond yields.

Using the approximate method, the investor divides the net annual income he will receive over the life of the bond by the average amount of money he will have invested during this period. If he buys the bond at a premium, his net annual income equals the dollar return less the average annual amount required to eliminate the premium by maturity. Similarly, if he purchases a bond at a discount, the net income is equal to the dollar return plus the average annual accumulation required to reach the principal value by maturity. The average amount of money invested during the life of the bond is the average of the issue's purchase price plus the maturity or call value, whichever is chosen.

The formula for determining the yield to maturity by the approximate method may be expressed as follows:

$$\text{Yield to maturity} \cong \frac{\text{Annual dollar return} \begin{array}{c} + \text{ annual accumulation} \\ \text{or} \\ - \text{ annual amortization} \end{array}}{(\text{Current market price} + \text{maturity or redemption value}) \div 2}.$$

To illustrate the approximate method, let us apply it to the determination of the yield to maturity for a bond selling at a premium and for one selling at a discount.

Let us first consider the Mack Truck $5\frac{1}{8}$s, due April 1, 1981, selling at \$802.50 on October 1, 1973. The annual dollar return is \$51.125; the life of the bond is $7\frac{1}{2}$ years; the discount is \$197.50; the average annual accumulation is \$197.50 divided by $7\frac{1}{2}$, or \$26.33; and the maturity value is \$1,000. Substituting the appropriate figures in the formula, we find:

$$\text{Yield to maturity} \cong \frac{\$51.125 + \$26.33}{(\$802.50 + \$1{,}000.00) \div 2} = \frac{\$77.455}{\$901.25} = 8.59 \text{ percent.}$$

Now let us consider Dow Chemical 8.9s, due November 1, 2000, priced at about \$1,090 on November 1, 1973. The life of the bond is 27 years; the premium is \$90; the average annual amortization is \$90 divided by 27, or \$3.33; and the maturity value is \$1,000. Substituting in the formula we obtain the following results:

$$\text{Yield to maturity} \cong \frac{\$89.00 - \$3.33}{(\$1{,}090 + \$1{,}000) \div 2} = \frac{\$85.67}{\$1{,}045} = 8.20 \text{ percent.}$$

This method is simple and sufficiently accurate to determine the relative yields of bonds for analytic purposes. Dealers and brokers commonly employ tables of bond yields to determine the actual purchase price of securities.

To give some idea of the implications of these two methods, let us consider the following example: Assume that two bonds, one bearing a 5 percent coupon and one with a 6 percent coupon, both have 20 years remaining to maturity and afford the same yield to maturity. If the 5 percent coupon bond is selling at par, the investor will find that he has to pay about 113 for the 6 percent bond. He may regard the implications of this relationship by means of either the basic or the approximation formula. In the first case, he may consider the coupon of 6 percent as providing a repayment of principal of roughly 1 percent a year. A quick check of an annuity table will show that the present value of an annuity of one dollar discounted at 5 percent for 20 years is very close to the premium paid. In the approximation formula, the annual rate of return of a 6 percent bond at the average redemption price of \$1,065 $\left(\text{that is, } \frac{\$1{,}130 + \$1{,}000}{2}\right)$ is about 5.6 percent. Reducing this by the amortized rate of 0.6 percent $\left(\frac{\$130 \div 20}{\$1{,}065}\right)$ provides a yield to maturity of 5 percent.

The investor must be careful about interpreting yields on discount bonds when the maturity is close at hand. During periods of low interest rates, a deep discount on an early maturing obligation probably would imply doubt about the company's ability to pay the principal when due. Such an issue might be attractive as a speculation on the possibility of payment, but it could not be purchased for yield. On the other hand, during periods of high interest rates such as prevailed in the early 1970s, many low coupon bonds sold at substantial discounts even when maturity was close at hand.

Bond tables. Bond tables generally contain separate pages for different coupon rates. A horizontal column near the top of each page shows varying numbers of years to maturity; a left-hand vertical column contains either prices or yields. If prices are shown in the left vertical column, the main body of the page reveals, for designated coupons, the different yields that correspond to these prices and the appropriate maturities. If yields are shown in the left vertical column, the main body of the page contains prices corresponding to these yields and maturities. The ranges of coupon rates, prices, and yields differ, depending on the tables used.

Underlying the construction of bond tables are two assumptions: that the bonds are held to maturity and are paid at par, and, ordinarily, that interest is disbursed semiannually. Special tables or adjustments are required for bonds not fitting this description.

Bond tables may be used to determine the price of a bond when the yield is known and the yield of a bond when the price is known. The procedure for finding the yield to maturity is as follows:

(1) Establish the factors required for the calculation—the coupon rate, the number of years and months to maturity, and the price of the bond.
(2) Turn to the section in the bond tables that contains the appropriate coupon rate.
(3) Select the column with the designated maturity date.
(4) Select the row in the column with the appropriate price.
(5) Read from the table the yield corresponding to the designated maturity and price.

If the yield to maturity is known and the price of the bond is wanted, a similar procedure is followed. The major difference is that the row containing the designated yield is selected, and the price corresponding to this yield and the appropriate maturity are read from the table.

Use of the bond tables for determining yields may be clarified by an illustration. For this purpose, let us use the sample page of bond tables shown in Figure 4-1 to calculate the yield of the Dow Chemical 8.9s, due November 1, 2000, determined previously by the approximate method. Since the coupon rate is 8.9 percent, we must refer to the page containing this rate. The bond has 27 years to run to maturity, and therefore we glance down this column until we reach the figure 109.90 (representing a price of $1,099.00; the table figure is multiplied by 10 to get the actual price). The bond's price of $1,090 falls between the figures 109.90, corresponding to a yield of 8.00 percent and 108.72 (price of $1,087.20), corresponding to a yield of 8.10 percent. We must therefore interpolate to find the yield corresponding to the bond price of $1,090. For this purpose, we calculate the percentage that $9.00 (the difference between the $1,099 in the table and the $1,090 price of the bond) is of $11.80 (the difference between the table prices of $1,099.00 and $1,087.20). This figure, 76.3 percent ($9.00 ÷ $11.80), is applied to the yield differential of .10 percent (8.10 percent − 8.00 percent) between the yields at the two table prices. The result, .08 percent, is added to the 8.00

FIGURE 4-1

Page from Table of Bond Values

MAN BROTHERS HIGH YIELD TABLES SEMI-ANNUAL INTEREST PAYMENTS INTEREST RATE 8.900

.D	23 YRS EVEN	24 YRS EVEN	25 YRS EVEN	26 YRS EVEN	27 YRS EVEN	28 YRS EVEN	29 YRS EVEN	30 YRS EVEN	31 YRS EVEN	32 YRS EVEN	33 YRS EVEN	34 YRS EVEN
00	152.95	154.16	155.31	156.40	157.44	158.43	159.37	160.27	161.13	161.94	162.71	163.45
10	151.11	152.26	153.35	154.39	155.38	156.32	157.21	158.06	158.87	159.64	160.37	161.06
20	149.31	150.40	151.44	152.42	153.36	154.25	155.10	155.90	156.66	157.39	158.08	158.73
30	147.53	148.57	149.56	150.49	151.38	152.22	153.02	153.78	154.50	155.19	155.84	156.45
40	145.79	146.77	147.71	148.60	149.44	150.24	150.99	151.71	152.39	153.03	153.65	154.23
50	144.07	145.01	145.90	146.74	147.53	148.29	149.00	149.68	150.32	150.93	151.50	152.05
60	142.38	143.27	144.11	144.91	145.66	146.38	147.05	147.69	148.29	148.86	149.41	149.92
70	140.73	141.57	142.37	143.12	143.83	144.50	145.14	145.74	146.31	146.85	147.35	147.83
80	139.10	139.90	140.65	141.36	142.03	142.67	143.27	143.83	144.37	144.87	145.35	145.80
90	137.50	138.25	138.96	139.64	140.27	140.87	141.43	141.96	142.46	142.94	143.38	143.81
00	135.92	136.64	137.31	137.94	138.54	139.10	139.63	140.13	140.60	141.04	141.46	141.86
10	134.38	135.05	135.68	136.28	136.84	137.37	137.87	138.33	138.78	139.19	139.58	139.95
20	132.86	133.49	134.09	134.65	135.17	135.67	136.14	136.57	136.99	137.38	137.74	138.09
30	131.36	131.96	132.52	133.04	133.54	134.00	134.44	134.85	135.24	135.60	135.94	136.26
40	129.89	130.45	130.98	131.47	131.93	132.37	132.78	133.16	133.52	133.86	134.18	134.48
50	128.44	128.97	129.46	129.92	130.36	130.76	131.15	131.50	131.84	132.16	132.45	132.73
60	127.02	127.51	127.98	128.41	128.81	129.19	129.55	129.88	130.19	130.49	130.76	131.02
70	125.62	126.08	126.51	126.92	127.29	127.65	127.98	128.29	128.58	128.85	129.10	129.34
80	124.25	124.68	125.08	125.45	125.81	126.13	126.44	126.73	127.00	127.25	127.48	127.70
90	122.90	123.30	123.67	124.02	124.34	124.65	124.93	125.20	125.45	125.68	125.90	126.10
00	121.57	121.94	122.28	122.61	122.91	123.19	123.45	123.70	123.93	124.14	124.34	124.53
10	120.26	120.60	120.92	121.22	121.50	121.76	122.00	122.23	122.44	122.63	122.82	122.99
20	118.97	119.29	119.58	119.86	120.11	120.35	120.58	120.78	120.98	121.16	121.32	121.48
30	117.70	118.00	118.27	118.52	118.76	118.97	119.18	119.37	119.54	119.71	119.86	120.00
40	116.46	116.73	116.97	117.21	117.42	117.62	117.81	117.98	118.14	118.29	118.43	118.56
50	115.23	115.48	115.70	115.91	116.11	116.29	116.46	116.62	116.76	116.90	117.02	117.14
60	114.03	114.25	114.46	114.65	114.82	114.99	115.14	115.28	115.41	115.53	115.65	115.75
70	112.84	113.04	113.23	113.40	113.56	113.71	113.84	113.97	114.09	114.20	114.30	114.39
80	111.68	111.85	112.02	112.17	112.32	112.45	112.57	112.68	112.79	112.88	112.97	113.06
90	110.53	110.69	110.83	110.97	111.10	111.21	111.32	111.42	111.51	111.60	111.68	111.75
00	109.40	109.54	109.67	109.79	109.90	110.00	110.09	110.18	110.26	110.34	110.40	110.47
10	108.29	108.41	108.52	108.62	108.72	108.81	108.89	108.96	109.03	109.10	109.16	109.21
20	107.19	107.30	107.39	107.48	107.56	107.64	107.71	107.77	107.83	107.88	107.93	107.98
30	106.12	106.20	106.28	106.36	106.42	106.49	106.55	106.60	106.65	106.69	106.74	106.77
40	105.06	105.13	105.19	105.25	105.31	105.36	105.40	105.45	105.49	105.52	105.56	105.59
50	104.01	104.07	104.12	104.17	104.21	104.25	104.28	104.32	104.35	104.38	104.40	104.43
60	102.99	103.03	103.06	103.10	103.13	103.16	103.18	103.21	103.23	103.25	103.27	103.29
70	101.97	102.00	102.03	102.05	102.07	102.09	102.10	102.12	102.13	102.15	102.16	102.17
80	100.98	100.99	101.00	101.02	101.03	101.03	101.04	101.05	101.06	101.06	101.07	101.08
90	100.00	100.00	100.00	100.00	100.00	100.00	100.00	100.00	100.00	100.00	100.00	100.00
00	99.04	99.02	99.01	99.00	98.99	98.98	98.98	98.97	98.96	98.96	98.95	98.94
10	98.09	98.06	98.04	98.02	98.00	97.98	97.97	97.95	97.94	97.93	97.92	97.91
20	97.15	97.12	97.08	97.05	97.03	97.00	96.98	96.96	96.94	96.92	96.91	96.89
30	96.23	96.18	96.14	96.10	96.07	96.04	96.01	95.98	95.96	95.93	95.91	95.89
40	95.32	95.27	95.22	95.17	95.13	95.09	95.05	95.02	94.99	94.96	94.94	94.92
50	94.43	94.37	94.30	94.25	94.20	94.15	94.11	94.07	94.04	94.01	93.98	93.95
60	93.55	93.48	93.41	93.35	93.29	93.24	93.19	93.15	93.11	93.07	93.04	93.01
70	92.69	92.60	92.53	92.46	92.39	92.33	92.28	92.23	92.19	92.15	92.11	92.08
80	91.83	91.74	91.66	91.58	91.51	91.45	91.39	91.34	91.29	91.25	91.21	91.17
90	90.99	90.89	90.80	90.72	90.64	90.57	90.51	90.46	90.40	90.36	90.32	90.28
00	90.17	90.06	89.96	89.87	89.79	89.72	89.65	89.59	89.53	89.48	89.44	89.40
10	89.35	89.24	89.13	89.04	88.95	88.87	88.80	88.74	88.68	88.63	88.58	88.54
20	88.55	88.43	88.31	88.21	88.12	88.04	87.97	87.90	87.84	87.78	87.73	87.69
30	87.76	87.63	87.51	87.41	87.31	87.22	87.15	87.08	87.01	86.95	86.90	86.85
40	86.98	86.84	86.72	86.61	86.51	86.42	86.34	86.27	86.20	86.14	86.09	86.04
50	86.21	86.07	85.94	85.83	85.72	85.63	85.55	85.47	85.40	85.34	85.28	85.23
60	85.45	85.31	85.17	85.06	84.95	84.85	84.76	84.69	84.61	84.55	84.49	84.44
70	84.71	84.56	84.42	84.30	84.19	84.09	84.00	83.92	83.84	83.78	83.72	83.66
80	83.97	83.82	83.68	83.55	83.44	83.33	83.24	83.16	83.08	83.01	82.95	82.90
90	83.25	83.09	82.94	82.81	82.70	82.59	82.50	82.41	82.33	82.27	82.20	82.15
00	82.54	82.37	82.22	82.09	81.97	81.86	81.76	81.68	81.60	81.53	81.47	81.41
10	81.83	81.66	81.51	81.37	81.25	81.14	81.04	80.96	80.88	80.81	80.74	80.68
20	81.14	80.97	80.81	80.67	80.55	80.44	80.34	80.25	80.16	80.09	80.03	79.97
30	80.46	80.28	80.12	79.98	79.85	79.74	79.64	79.55	79.46	79.39	79.33	79.27
40	79.78	79.60	79.44	79.30	79.17	79.05	78.95	78.86	78.78	78.70	78.64	78.58

SOURCE: Lehman Brothers, ***High Yield Tables***, p. 469. Reprinted with permission.

percent yield corresponding to the price of $1,099 to obtain the yield at a price of $1,090 since the lower the price, the higher the yield. Thus, the yield of 8.08 percent, determined from the bond table, differs by only 12 basis points from that of 8.20 percent obtained by the approximate method. (There are 100 basis points to one percentage point of yield.)

Determining the yield for callable bonds. Bonds may contain call features that permit their redemption prior to maturity at either par or a designated premium. If the bonds are callable at par, the yield to the first call date is calculated on the basis of the number of years to that date. If the bonds are callable at a premium, an adjustment is necessary. Bond tables often contain special provisions for this purpose.

In calculating the yields afforded by callable bonds, it is the conservative practice for investors to make the following assumptions:

(1) When the bonds are selling at a premium and are callable at par, the yield should be calculated to the first call date.
(2) When a premium bond is callable above par, the yield should be calculated to maturity and to the first call date; the lower figure is used.
(3) When bonds are selling at a discount, the yield should always be calculated to maturity, whether or not the issue is callable at par or at a premium.

Determining the yield for sinking fund bonds. When the bond indenture, stipulating the bond's terms, carries a provision for a sinking fund, a certain portion of the bonds will be returned on each of the designated dates. A *sinking fund* is the periodic appropriation of cash to purchase or redeem bonds. Typically, certificates are chosen for redemption randomly, or the bonds are bought in the open market. The actual holding period for an investor, therefore, may be any one of several, all with equal probability. Under such circumstances, it is advisable to compute the yield to the "average" maturity, on the assumption of regular calls.

The determination of the average maturity of a bond is not difficult. Consider a $20,000 bond maturing in ten years, with sinking fund payments of $4,000 per bond beginning at the end of the sixth year. The payments are to be equal and the debt is to be wiped out by maturity. Payments at the end of each period can be represented by the following schedule:

PERIOD	PAYMENT
1	$ 0
2	0
3	0

PERIOD	PAYMENT
4	0
5	0
6	4,000
7	4,000
8	4,000
9	4,000
10	4,000
Total	$20,000

The first step is to calculate the total dollar-years the bonds are outstanding, as follows:

AMOUNT RETIRED		YEARS OUTSTANDING	DOLLAR-YEARS
$4,000	X	6	$ 24,000
4,000	X	7	28,000
4,000	X	8	32,000
4,000	X	9	36,000
4,000	X	10	40,000
Total			$160,000

If we divide the total dollar-years outstanding by the total amount of the bonds ($20,000), the result is the average length of time, in this case eight years, each dollar was outstanding. As long as the sinking fund payments are equal in size and exhaust the outstanding debt, the calculation of the average maturity can be considerably simplified. In computing total dollar-years outstanding, if we factor out the common term the average maturity can be written as: $4,000 (6 + 7 + 8 + 9 + 10)/$20,000. The quantity in parentheses is a sum of integers. As any elementary algebra book will indicate, the formula for such a sum is $n(I + L)/2$, where n is the number of terms in the sum, I is the initial integer, and L is the final integer. The average maturity can therefore be written as $4,000 × 5 (6 + 10) ÷ 2/$20,000.

In this particular formula, the product to the left of the parenthesis must equal the denominator of the fraction. This relationship arises from the fact that the denominator of the fraction is the total issue and the left coefficient of the numerator is the product of the annual sinking fund payment times the number of payments required to exhaust the total debt. Thus, to find the average maturity of a sinking fund bond with equal payments that exhaust the total issue, simply add the year when the first payment is to be made to the year when the bond matures and divide by two.

SUMMARY

The holder of a security may receive income from it in the form of dividends, interest, and capital gains or losses (negative income).

In determining its dividend policy, a corporation may either decide how much it wants to retain for reinvestment and distribute the remainder or it can determine how much to disburse as dividends and keep the rest for investment. The relative stability of dividends and the erratic behavior of retention suggest that the payment decision is the calculated one. As a result, changes in the level of distributions provide some indication of management's judgment as to the future of earnings. This relationship must be used with caution, however, because there are both various external pressures and restrictions on the amount of payments. The securities exchanges have developed various rules governing procedures for the payment and receipt of dividends.

Corporations try to maintain interest disbursements on their bonds because failure to pay could lead to bankruptcy. Accordingly, this source of income is relatively secure. Capital gains, on the other hand, are an important, but uncertain source of income.

Different tools are used to measure these types of income. The dollar return is the amount of money that the corporation pays yearly on each share of stock or on each bond outstanding. The stated rate of return applies only to bonds and preferred stock; it is the stipulated rate of payment. The annual rate of return expresses the dollar amount received as a percentage of the price of the issue. The yield to maturity applies primarily to bonds; basically it represents the stated rate of return adjusted by the positive or negative differential that is presumed will be received on maturity if the issue is bought at a discount or premium.

Mathematically, the yield to maturity of a bond can be defined as the discount rate, which equates the present value of all future coupon payments plus the principal payment at maturity to the present price of the bond. Conceptually, a parallel can be made with stocks. In this sense, the yield on a share of common stock is the rate which equates the present value of all dividends to be received between now and the time of sale plus the present value at which it is anticipated the stock will be liquidated.

Typically, bond yields are determined by reference to tables. These yields may also be approximated arithmetically and calculated by relatively sophisticated small, electronic calculators. Special adjustments may be necessary for callable bonds and to take into account the possibility of redemption by sinking fund.

These different yield measurements are widely used in evaluating the attraction of a security relative to its risk.

CHAPTER 5

Savings and Investment

A nation's output is derived from expenditures for human and physical resources. In the lexicon of the economist, therefore, income and output are two sides of the same coin; when appropriately defined, their dollar values are equal. If consumption is subtracted from both income and output, the residuals must be equal. On the income side, this remainder is called savings; on the output side, it is called investment. Thus, savings occurs when only a portion of the income stream is consumed, with the rest deferred in order to permit future consumption on a grander scale or at a more opportune time. Investment, in turn, represents the accumulation of capital goods.

For purposes of financial planning, it is commonplace to give further shades of meaning to these terms. Ordinarily, the funds derived from deferred consumption are placed in capital goods through the use of financial instruments. Thus, a public utility may obtain funds to buy generating equipment by issuing securities; these may be bought directly by individuals or indirectly through financial intermediaries with funds deposited by individuals. The process of acquiring financial instruments, whether issued by corporations or by financial intermediaries, is generally described as investing.

The acquisition of a financial asset which pays off in the future, called investment, is subject to varying degrees of risk. When, at one extreme, the operation embodies a minimum of market risk, it may be described as saving; at the opposite extreme, when the risk of market fluctuations is high, it may be called speculation. As one moves along the investment spectrum, increased risks tend to be associated with expectations of increased rates of return. But in the case of nonmarketable savings, the risk of market fluctuation is eliminated entirely.

REPOSITORIES FOR SAVINGS

For certain activities it is important to know the *dollar amount* that is available at any time. For example, people ordinarily recognize the desirability of setting aside funds to meet a possible emergency, such as a serious illness, that may require substantial expenditures beyond the scope of current income and insurance. Then again, most people desire to acquire some expensive durable goods, such as an automobile or a home, that necessitate heavy initial disbursements. For this purpose, they may have to accumulate a certain amount of funds over time to meet the required outlays.

Retirement is an important consideration. Nine out of ten workers in the United States are earning protection under Social Security. For over a dozen years, self-employed persons have been able to put aside tax-free a portion of their income (the portion was liberalized for 1974 income) in Treasury-approved retirement plans. For the first time, starting in 1975, employees not covered by private pension plans have been permitted to segregate up to 15 percent of their income tax-free, up to a $1,500 maximum, to finance their retirement. People generally want to know at least the minimum amount that will be available in future years. Over the years, Social Security benefits have been raised, and as a result of legislation enacted in 1972, benefits increase automatically as the cost of living goes up. Nevertheless, at any specific time, an individual can ascertain the minimum benefits to which he or she would be entitled under specified circumstances. Similarly, a large portion of individuals' tax-protected appropriations tends to be placed in sources that permit the determination of future dollar amounts with considerable assurance.

In financial planning, after provision is made for current consumption needs, the next segment of personal income ordinarily is set aside to satisfy purposes, such as those described above, for which the individual must feel confident that the dollar amounts will still be available when needed. Such funds are usually put in savings sources where market uncertainties are minimized. The principal savings sources are furnished by the U.S. government, thrift institutions, life insurance companies, and mutual funds. In evaluating these sources, the individual should consider rate differentials, safety, liquidity, and limitations on placement of funds. Convenience may also be a factor.

U.S. Government Securities

The federal government issues many kinds of securities. Those sold in the open market vary in price, ordinarily afford relatively low yields after taxes, and are subject to some restrictions with respect to units of trading for certain issues. Nevertheless, as interest rates soared in the late 1960s and early 1970s, individuals manifested increasing interest in federal obligations.

U.S. savings bonds are common repositories for the savings of individuals. Their popularity is attributable to various factors. As obligations of the federal government they represent the highest-grade security that can be purchased; they are not subject to market fluctuations and may readily be converted to cash; the restrictions on the amount a family can purchase are modest; and different issues are available to meet the needs of different investors.

During periods of advancing interest rates, the government has attempted to keep savings bonds competitive by adjusting their price redemption schedule. An inevitable lag occurs, however, before such modifications are introduced. In these circumstances, the return on savings bonds has tended to lag behind that available on marketable obligations. Another drawback of savings bonds is that their return may be reduced substantially if the bonds are redeemed before maturity. Furthermore, savings bonds are not transferable and may not be hypothecated as collateral for loans. Offsetting advantages include optional deferment of income taxes on savings bonds purchased at a discount and the fact that bondholders need take no action to enjoy the maturity extensions that the government has regularly provided.

Traditionally, commercial banks were the big purchasers of Treasury bills, representing short-term, marketable U.S. government obligations sold at a discount. As corporations became more sophisticated in the ways of the money market, they found this security a useful vehicle for investment of temporarily excess funds. Eventually, individuals too became interested in Treasury bills, as their rates rose above those available from conventional thrift accounts and the government reduced the minimum amount required for purchase.

Individuals have also begun to buy Treasury notes, marketable U.S. government obligations, which have longer maturities and, ordinarily, somewhat higher yields than the bills. For example, in early August 1974 the Treasury sold a new issue of six-year notes bearing interest of 9 percent, the highest rate since the Civil War era. At that time, the Treasury's latest series of 13-week bills afforded a yield of about 8 percent, and the companion 26-week issue about 8.5 percent. The new Treasury notes, which were available in denominations as low as $1,000, appealed to small investors and competed vigorously with the variable-interest notes that various financial institutions had begun offering, also to attract the funds of individual investors. While the variable-interest notes paid a somewhat higher rate, this advantage tended to be offset by the fact that interest income from Treasury obligations is exempt from state and local taxation. For New York State residents reporting taxable income between $28,000 and $32,000, that bite comes close to 15 percent.[1] The importance attached to tax savings is an indication of the increased sophistication with which individuals take rate of return differentials into account. Somewhat over a year later, the Treasury sold several series of relatively high yielding, short-term notes that once more attracted individual investors, thereby draining funds from the thrift institutions.

Thrift Institutions

The principal thrift institutions are the mutual savings banks, savings and loan associations, and credit unions. Although they differ in various organizational and regulatory respects, these distinctions ordinarily are not important to the average investor. The savings departments of commercial banks may also be considered as possible attractions for investors.

Federal deposit interest rate ceilings were initially applied to commercial banks by the Banking Act of 1933, but for three decades these ceilings were not significant in banking competition. In 1966, however, a "credit crunch" ensued, and rates reached postwar highs. Investors responded to rate differentials by shifting funds among the competing sources. To give regulatory authorities greater control over this situation, the Interest Rate Adjustment Act (1966) was adopted. This act subjected the rates paid by the savings banks and savings and loan associations to federal control for the first time.

Thereafter, various regulatory changes allowed the institutions to offer certificate accounts that were more competitive with open-market instruments. In general, these certificates afforded higher rates than passbooks but required minimum amounts and specified retention periods. A short-lived experiment with the elimination of rate ceilings on certificates was abandoned, as a rash of so-called "wild card" certificates led to unprecedented rate wars.

At present, federal regulations apply interest rate ceilings on consumer-type savings and time deposits in all insured institutions, with ceilings on deposits in thrift institutions 25 basis points higher than for commercial banks. Ceilings range from 5 percent to 7.50 percent for commercial banks and from 5.25 percent to 7.75 percent for thrift institutions.[2] Starting in mid-1973, substantial deposit withdrawals (disintermediation) once more occurred at these institutions, as individuals sought the higher returns available from open-market instruments. Consequently, the thrift institutions tried to obtain a relaxation of the limits imposed by the regulatory agencies on the rates they could pay. As interest rates subsequently declined and funds flowed back, this pressure was eased.

To make themselves more competitive with commercial banks, the thrift institutions have tried to extend their powers. They have sought, for example, authority to provide some sort of check-writing services, lend to consumers, write variable mortgages, and create different types of accounts. Congress has been studying the advisability of granting the thrift institutions expanded lending and checking powers as well as changing or eliminating interest rate ceilings and differentials.

Commercial banks. Although not usually included with thrift institutions, most commercial banks do accept savings accounts. Because of their large holdings of government bonds and their conservative lending policies, the commercial banks as a group have great financial strength. Nevertheless, it is prudent to restrict deposits in any one bank to the amount covered by the Federal Deposit Insurance Corporation (FDIC); this amount is now $40,000 per person. (Individuals may legally deposit larger sums, and the major institutions usually have no special restrictions of their own.) Interest on savings deposits in commercial banks is regulated by the Board of Governors of the Federal Reserve System, the FDIC, or state authorities, depending on the type of bank. To a large degree, therefore, the competitive attractions of these institutions depend on the regulatory judgment of a government agency, principally the Board of Governors. Within this framework, the banks have offered different types of deposit accounts and interest-compounding terms. They have also created special savings accounts providing somewhat higher rates of interest to those who hold their deposits for specified periods of time; in the highly competitive atmosphere that prevailed in 1973, some banks even offered accounts that had both adjustable interest rates and an indicated rate floor. For large investors, banks issue marketable certificates of deposit that are exempt from interest rate ceilings. Since November 1975, they may offer passbook savings accounts to corporations.

In July 1974, Citicorp, the parent concern of the First National City Bank, displayed some financial derring-do by offering an innovative security. Citicorp guaranteed a 9.70 percent return through May 1975, compared with the bank's posted rate of about 9.25 percent for large-denomination certificates of deposit with a similar maturity; thereafter, the issue bore a rate that was 1 percentage point above the interest equivalent of the average weekly discount rates for three-month Treasury bills. The "floating-rate notes," as they were called, matured in 1989 but were repayable semiannually at par commencing June 1, 1976, at the option of the holder. These terms were modestly different from those originally announced because of pressure exerted by the Federal Reserve Board. Shortly after Citicorp's announcement, various other financial institutions, including Chase Manhattan, Continental Illinois, Mellon National, Crocker National, and the New York Bank for Savings, as well as Standard Oil of Indiana, followed a similar financing route. Declining interest rates, however, lessened the attractiveness of these instruments.

Mutual savings banks. Mutual savings banks usually have conservative investment policies, and deposits are insured by either the Federal Deposit Insurance Corporation or state insurance programs. Interest rates, which are under governmental regulation, have generally been held in line with those of the savings and loan associations and have been permitted to be somewhat above those of the savings departments of the commercial banks. Of the 17 states in which the mutual savings banks operate, 11 do not restrict the amount of funds a person may place in one bank; the others have limitations that vary from state to state. Individual institutions may also establish their own provisions governing maximum deposits.

A floating-rate note issued by the New York Bank for Savings is of particular interest because it provides some indication of the cost of liquidity in the mid-1970's. Previously, Citicorp had created continuing liquidity for its issue by enabling holders, at their own option, to obtain redemption semiannually beginning June 1, 1976; the New York Bank for Savings, on the other hand, simply permitted redemption of the notes by the bank on and after September 1, 1981, and provided for payment on maturity on December 1, 1981. In general, to offset the reduced liquidity of its notes, the bank provided an initial guaranteed rate of 10 percent (compared with Citicorp's 9.70 percent) and established its floating segment 1.25 percentage points above the U.S. Treasury bill rate (compared with Citicorp's 1 percentage point).

While there were other differences between the notes of the two institutions, the 10 vs. 9.70 percent initial fixed rate and the 1.25 vs. 1 point floating margin over the bill rate were clear rate-of-return tidbits. The New York Bank for Savings apparently believed them necessary to compensate for the absence of a continuing redemption privilege at the holder's option. The savings bank was unable to provide the continuing redemption privilege because it falls under the jurisdiction of the Federal Deposit Insurance Corporation, which frowned on this policy, while commercial bank holding companies are subject to SEC jurisdiction.

Savings and loan associations. Because savings and loan associations hold considerable investments in home mortgages, it is difficult to evaluate their financial status. This uncertainty makes it important for individuals to confine their commitments to institutions that are members of the Federal Savings and Loan Insurance Corporation, a federal agency that insures individual accounts to $40,000. The associations make payments, called interest, under the provisions of the Housing and Urban Development Act of 1968. These rates are regulated by the Federal Home Loan Bank. There is generally no maximum limitation on the amount a person may place with an association, but individual institutions may adopt their own restrictions. Associations are formed under either state or federal law.

Credit unions. Closely knit groups—for example, employees of a company or members of a fraternal society—are the usual sponsors of credit unions. In recent years, however, regulatory authorities have accepted a looser interpretation of the underlying relationship. In the case of the Wisconsin State Central Credit Union, for example, the common bond is only that the members live in the same state.

Deposits in federally chartered credit unions, which represent about half those in the country, are insured up to $40,000 per account; some 15 percent of the state-chartered institutions are also covered by federal insurance. The National Credit Union Administration, a federal agency, regulates the federally chartered credit unions, while the state institutions are regulated by local agencies. To help ensure liquidity, the U.S. Central Credit Union was formed; this institution obtains its funds from contributions by individual credit unions and, in turn, funnels funds back through central state or regional credit unions.

The individual credit unions are owned by their depositors, who hold shares in proportion to their savings. Dividends have been paid regularly on deposits at rates which range between 5 and 7 percent, somewhat below those of other thrift institutions. Primarily active in the consumer lending field, the credit unions have sought to extend their activities aggressively and have been growing at a relatively rapid rate.[3]

Life Insurance

The huge resources and conservative investment practices of life insurance companies reasonably guarantee their ability to discharge their contractual obligations. The companies sell policies designed not only to protect dependent persons in case of the death of the insured but also to provide a means of savings. Dividend payments to policyholders are low. To obtain the full benefits of a policy, an individual must hold it to maturity; he receives only designated cash surrender values if he liquidates prior to the prescribed termination date. Among the great virtues of the life insurance policy as a source of savings income are its convenience, the individual's obligation to conform to the savings program, and possible tax advantages.

There are three principal types of life insurance: (1) term; (2) whole life, also called ordinary life; and (3) endowment life. In addition, life insurance companies write annuity contracts which do not include provisions for life insurance. These contracts are predicated on life expectancy and may provide a life annuity, with or without a guaranty for a specified number of years should the annuitant die before his annuity payments are equal to the cost of the contract. The savings and protection aspects of the different life insurance contracts vary.

Term. Term life insurance is furnished under a contract whereby the insurance company agrees to pay a stipulated amount if the individual dies within a designated period of time. If the individual lives beyond the stated term, the policy expires and the beneficiaries receive nothing. The term periods vary, ranging over intervals of five, ten, or 20 years; or the period may end at a designated age, such as 65. These periods are often renewable at the option of the insured. The rates on term insurance are very low in the early years of life but mount rapidly as the individual ages. Because no savings are involved, this policy is the cheapest way of protecting beneficiaries against the death of the insured.

Whole life. A whole life policy provides protection for the entire life of the insured, who may elect to pay premiums continuously during the entire period of the contract; if the dividends are left with the company, the policy may be paid up prior to death. When the individual dies, his beneficiaries receive the amount of the insurance. A portion of the premium payments represents reserves, which are really savings by the individual; this feature provides the policy with gradually increasing cash surrender values. The costs of the policy over a lifetime compare favorably with those of term insurance because the savings are small and must accrue for a lifetime to equal the policy's face value. Continuous whole life policies are generally taken by persons who seek protection for life under a more permanent plan than that provided by term insurance.

Limited payment life is a form of whole life insurance. Under the limited payment plan, the premium payments are limited to a specified period, usually 20 or 30 years. After this period, no further payments are required, but the insurance coverage remains in force until the death of the insured. Regardless of when this occurs, the beneficiaries receive the full amount of the insurance. The premium payment period may be shortened if the dividends disbursed by the insurance company are accumulated with the company. The savings on this policy are greater than in continuous whole life insurance. Consequently, the cash surrender value is also greater.

Individuals use limited payment life insurance when their ability to pay is limited to a certain period, or when they want to avoid the continued burden of payments for life. They may also use this form of insurance if the need to protect their beneficiaries is likely to have expired by the time the policy is paid up. At the end of the period, the full cash surrender value of the policy is available for use by the insured.

Endowment. In an endowment contract the insurance company agrees to pay the amount of insurance in the event of death and also contracts to make stipulated payments if the insured is alive at a designated date. The savings feature predominates, so the overall premium is high. As in most whole life policies, payments are leveled; this means that the insured is charged the same rate throughout the contract. As a result, the portion of the premium representing insurance is initially large. In later years, this part shrinks and the savings segment grows, until at maturity only the savings aspect exists. Endowments are used to provide guaranteed savings for old age or to finance some expected future event, such as the education of a child.

Annuities. In a regular annuity the insurance company agrees to pay the insured a definite income, starting at a particular date. Annuities contracts may be of three principal types: (1) a life annuity, in which the company guarantees payment only during the life of the annuitant; (2) a life-and-years-certain annuity, in which payment is guaranteed for life, but if the annuitant dies before a specified date, the company also guarantees payment for the prescribed period to the beneficiary; and (3) a refund annuity, in which the company guarantees payment for the life of the annuitant, but if he dies before the company has paid a sum equivalent to the cost of his contract, the company also guarantees to pay the amount to the beneficiary, either in installments or in a lump sum. In these contracts the savings feature is most prominent because no life protection provisions are involved.

Choosing insurance. The insurance companies have adapted their programs to meet individual requirements. The standards of selecting insurance salesmen have been raised, and many of them receive specialized training; hence, more life insurance salesmen are now able to provide the individual with worthwhile advice about different contracts. Highly trained salesmen may even help in the programming of complete estates.

However, the suitability of insurance policies to individual needs is primarily a personal affair. A successful investor can probably better the return received on the savings portion of an insurance policy without assuming serious market risks. For such an investor the most satisfactory type of policy is one that provides only protection to beneficiaries at his death. Other individuals may not be capable of managing their own savings or investment programs; for them, the savings features of life insurance policies may offer more protection.

Mutual Funds

Entrustment of savings to mutual funds can be either sporadic or systematic. (See Chapter 23 for a detailed discussion of investment companies.) To compete in this area, some insurance companies have developed funds, while the mutual savings banks sell a fund of their own. The insurance companies have also introduced programs in which a portion of the individual premium is placed in a common-stock fund.

In the initial years of their development, the mutual funds appealed primarily to small investors, but now they also attract the attention of wealthy individuals, especially those who do not have the time to manage their personal portfolios. Certain municipal investment trust funds concentrate their portfolios in municipal bonds and in obligations of certain U.S. territories or possessions. As a result, the interest they pay investors is tax-exempt and, as an extra inducement, may be paid monthly.

In the early 1970s, as interest rates rose and the stock market sagged, a category of mutual funds was created to appeal to investors who preferred to remain aloof from equities until the outlook clarified. These funds concentrate their investments in liquid instruments, such as commercial paper, large-denomination certificates of deposit, and Treasury bills.

TRENDS IN INSTITUTIONAL INVESTMENT

The savings-investment nexus that we described previously has provided the basis for financing the enormous growth in the tangible wealth of the United States. In the initial stages of this development, investors often were able to provide the funds for expansion from their own savings. As industrial activity became more complex and financing needs much greater, the identity between saver and investor tended to break down. Enterprises, increasingly taking the corporate form, issued securities to obtain the necessary funds from outside their own resources. Just as some entrepreneurs sought external financing, however, others found that their savings exceeded their own requirements, and it became profitable for these net savers to lend their surplus funds to the deficit group. Initially, such transfers could be effected directly; over time, however, financial institutions, operating through developing financial markets, became increasingly important as intermediaries, relieving fund users and savers of the burden of finding each other directly. Indicative of this dual trend—the growth of external financing and the rise of the financial intermediary—is the fact that between 1900 and 1968 the value of paper claims measured against the nation's stock of real assets grew from 65 to 130 percent.[4]

Just as the creation of financial assets enabled investors to own tangibles indirectly, the appearance of financial institutions enabled the investor to own the securities of issuing corporations indirectly. But financial institutions provide other benefits. Through their investment skills they can combine return and risk more efficiently than the less-skilled individual investor; through their economies of scale they can hold down both investment management and operating costs. As a result, over the long run the financial institutions have tended both to reduce the borrowing cost of the issuer and to raise the return to the lender relative to the risks involved. Financial institutions have also transformed the nature of investment by buying corporate securities with differing risks and maturities and then making available to savers their own securities, which may better suit the savers' needs. Moreover, the institutions have moderate transaction costs and, through their ability to assemble diversified portfolios, they can acquire securities that in themselves might be risky but which, in conjunction with other holdings, contribute to portfolio stability.[5]

An institution's investment policies reflect its primary functions. Thus, early maturing securities are important to commercial banks because of the short-term nature of their liabilities, while long maturities are more suitable to life insurance companies that can both predict and space their liabilities over long periods of time. The heavy involvement of savings and loan associations with mortgages leaves them little opportunity for investments in securities. On the other hand, mutual funds and pension funds are heavy buyers of securities because that is their primary means of obtaining a return for their constituents. Most institutional investors have experienced difficulty in finding suitable outlets for their greatly enlarged resources; the pressure to expand their investment portfolios has grown accordingly. Meanwhile, issuers have come to offer a variety of securities to meet their own financing requirements and have provided greatly increased information about their own activities. To cope with these two developments, institutional investors have strengthened their own staffs of securities experts or have turned to outside advisers who assemble such staffs. As analytic competition grows keener, the discovery of undervalued securities becomes more difficult.

The present tendency toward liberalizing institutional portfolio restrictions will probably continue. Indeed, the current phenomenon might be described as the homogenization of financial institutions. As portfolio restrictions are removed, there will be a growing tendency for financial institutions to pursue the same types of portfolio policies. By and large, the institutions are likely to be more conservative than an individual managing his or her own investments would be.

Thus, the National Bureau of Economic Research, in its part of the *Institutional Investor Study*, found that individuals have held around 70 percent of outstanding corporate securities since the late 1950s, even though they were net sellers during much of this period. According to the bureau, this fact suggests that the securities held by individuals have appreciated more rapidly than those retained by institutions. This conclusion, in turn, indicates that individuals have held relatively much larger amounts of risky securities, subject to wide price swings, than did the institutions, which often favor the better known, listed stocks.[6] While individuals appear to have withdrawn from the market as a result of the high interest rates available in fixed-interest instruments and the considerable uncertainties that have prevailed in recent years, their return is likely when conditions change.

Within this framework of comparative conservatism, however, considerable variation may exist. As Figure 5-1 indicates, there is a sharp disparity between the size of the institutions and their holdings of corporate stocks. Among the mutual funds, particularly, are companies that stress aggressive policies. Moreover, the performance cult that tended to emerge in the 1960s had a liberalizing effect on the policies of most institutions.

The Securities Acts Amendments of 1975 require institutional investment managers of substantial portfolios to file disclosure reports with the SEC, which must tabulate the information and make it available to the public. Such a policy is likely further to broaden the range of securities bought and to raise portfolio turnover rates.

More flexible portfolio requirements increase the responsibility of the institutions' executives to adjust investment policies to meet changing economic conditions; this highlights the importance of sound securities management. Although more lenient standards permit institutions to augment their income, this greater freedom also exposes them to the danger of serious asset shrinkages in the event of a sharp business downturn.

Given our progress in economic planning, however, there may be an equal danger of becoming overly sensitive to the possibility of a serious slump. Clearly the millennium has not arrived in controlling economic fluctuations. The ability to make fine-tune adjustments is limited, and the experience of the 1970s reveals that much still has to be learned if we are to cope with the hazards of inflation and unemployment. But even if sharp reactions do occasionally recur, the consequences to financial institutions need not necessarily be disastrous if their overall policies are sound. Liberalization of institutional portfolios may create certain investment risks, but undue restrictions limit potential benefits. In the long run, optimum results depend upon the successful judgment of individual managers operating in a sufficiently free environment to provide adequate room for choice.

FIGURE 5-1

Distribution of Financial Assets and Corporate Equities among Selected Institutions

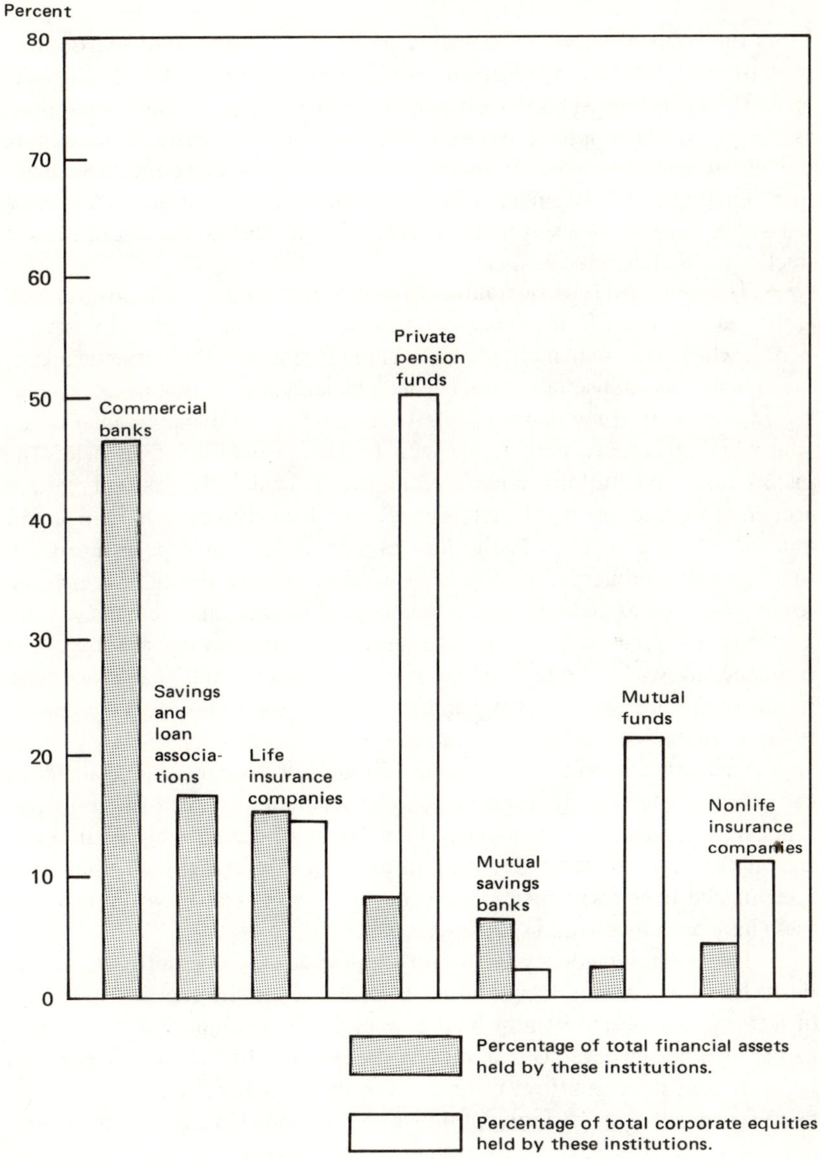

SOURCE: Data from Federal Reserve Board, ***Flow of Funds Accounts 1965-1973*** (September 1974): 32, 34-36, 42 (1974 Supplement).

SUMMARY

From the point of view of financial planning, any acquisition of an asset that pays off in the future is subject to varying degrees of risk. At one extreme, when the operation embodies a minimum of market risk, it may be described as saving; at the opposite extreme, when the risk of market fluctuation is high, it may be called speculation. As one moves along the investment spectrum, increased risks tend to be associated with expectations of increased rates of return. In the case of nonmarketable investments, the risk of market fluctuation is eliminated entirely.

The principal savings sources are furnished by the U.S. government, thrift institutions, life insurance companies, and mutual funds. U.S. savings bonds, which are nonmarketable, are common repositories for the savings of individuals. As individuals have become increasingly conscious of rate of return, however, they have manifested interest in the marketable issues, which afford considerable choice with respect to maturity and yield. The major thrift institutions include commercial banks that accept savings accounts, mutual savings banks, savings and loan associations, and credit unions. All these types of institutions have some form of deposit insurance; they compete primarily on the basis of interest rates (most of which are regulated), type of account, and convenience. Life insurance companies offer a variety of policies that combine protection and savings features. The open-end investment companies have created special funds that invest only in short-term, high-grade instruments in order to attract investors who desire to avoid the risk of market fluctuations.

Financial institutions, operating through developing capital markets, have become increasingly important as intermediaries between the users and suppliers of funds. As a result, they have expanded considerably both in size and in the scope of their activities. In the course of this growth, they have accumulated huge reservoirs of money beyond their operating needs; much of these have been invested in securities.

The present tendency is toward the liberalization of portfolio restrictions. Furthermore, the move toward increased disclosure exposes the results of institutional investors to the hard glare of public opinion. As a result, most of the institutions have become more aggressive. Continued wide divergences in investment policies reflect differences in the nature of the institution and, more specifically, the differing outlooks of their individual money managers.

CHAPTER 6

Tax Considerations in Investment Planning for Individuals

Most securities generate two kinds of incremental wealth: periodic cash distributions and/or increments in the market value of the securities. In the case of stock, periodic cash distributions take the form of dividend payments. In the case of bonds, the cash receipts take the form of interest payments. During a tax year, however, the investor may find that not only has he or she received cash dividends and/or interest, but the value of the securities themselves has appreciated or depreciated. The real incremental wealth of investors depends on after-tax receipts plus appreciation or minus depreciation in value. Investment planning thus must give careful consideration to the amount and timing of tax payments.

The tax liability incurred by an investor is affected by the cash dividends and interest received. Accrual of value per se is not taxable. The Internal Revenue Service (IRS) does not recognize value appreciation as taxable unless the appreciation has been "realized." Typically, this means that appreciation is not taxable until the securities have been sold. Proceeds from sales are then compared with the original costs of the securities or, more accurately, with their tax bases. For one reason or another, the tax basis of a security may not be quite equal to its original cost.

In this chapter we shall examine separately the tax implications of the dividend and interest receipts and the tax implication of the realization of appreciation (capital gains). When we consider the latter, we shall discuss some of the considerations that lead to differences between the tax basis and the original cost of an investment.

TAXES OF INVESTMENT INCOME

Constructive Receipt of Income

Suppose a corporation mails a check for interest to a bondholder at 4 P.M. on December 31 of year t. That check will not be received until some day in year $t + 1$. Is that income to the recipient in year t or $t + 1$? Change the case slightly. Assume that the bondholder has a bearer bond with coupon cashable on December 31, but that he does not redeem until the next business day. (See p. 414 for a description of bearer bonds and interest coupons.) To what year will the IRS attribute that income? Finally, suppose that a savings bank does not post in its passbooks until after January 1 of $t + 1$ the interest earned on accounts in year t. Does a saver count the interest as income in year t or $t + 1$?

To appreciate the differences between these situations, we must recognize the doctrine of *constructively received income*. Under that doctrine, income is received when ownership is established, regardless of when the income recipient gets it. The bondholder in our first illustration cannot go to the corporation on the last business day (or any earlier day) of year t and claim his interest. In fact, he cannot establish his right to ownership until he receives the check. That receipt will not take place until year $t + 1$, and so the interest is considered income in year $t + 1$. (The corporation, incidentally, is permitted to treat the interest payment as an expense for the year in which the check was issued.) On the other hand, the holder of the bearer bond could cash his coupons on December 31 of year t, if the banks were open on that day. Thus, the value of the coupons is considered income in year t, regardless of whether the investor does in fact cash them. He can if he wishes, and that determines the fact that he received the income in year t. However, if December 31 was a bank holiday, the investor could not cash the coupon until after January 1, in year $t + 1$. Under those circumstances, the income is taxable in year $t + 1$. In the third case, the saver can go to the bank on December 31 of year t, or on the last business day of that year, and withdraw all his money, including the interest that has accrued during year t. The fact that he does not choose to claim the interest in year t, or that the bank has not yet posted it, does not alter the fact that the interest is effectively or, more technically, *constructively* his.

If an investor owns a savings bond that is redeemable, he has somewhat greater flexibility. In general, the increment in value represented by the difference between the price paid for the bond and its redemption value is considered interest. A taxpayer who is on a cash basis, however, need not report the increase in redemption value of his bonds as it occurs. He may instead elect to include that amount in gross income for federal income tax purposes in the taxable year of final maturity or actual redemption, whether that takes place before or after final maturity. He may also decide in any year to begin reporting this income annually. On the other hand, an owner who chooses to report the increase in redemption value each year as it accrues must continue to do so, unless he obtains permission from the IRS to change to a different reporting method.

Tax Exemption

The interest on a bond issued by a state or any of its instrumentalities (including cities, counties, school districts, authorities, and so forth) is generally exempt from federal income taxes and may be exempt from state income taxes and state intangible personal property taxes. The exception to the tax exemption relates to the so-called *industrial revenue bonds*. These are bonds typically issued by state or local governments to provide facilities that would encourage corporations to stay in or move into the area. Prior to the 1969 revisions of the Internal Revenue Code, all such bonds were tax-free, but since then the exemption has become more restrictive. Today, if the bond is issued to finance the construction of pollution control plants or equipment, the privilege still obtains. The interest on industrial bonds issued for other purposes is taxable unless the issue is for less than $5 million.

Most states have income taxes.[1] The interest on bonds issued by the government of one state is not exempt from the income taxes of other states. However, such interest is usually exempt from the income tax of the state in which the bond originated. (See pp. 513-518 for a further discussion of the tax-exemption aspects of municipal securities.) U.S. government bonds are subject to federal income taxes but are free of all state income taxes.

Cash Dividends

Cash distributions to stockholders may represent a distribution of income, a return of capital, a capital gain, or some combination of these components. Capital gains distributions are typically made by investment companies and are discussed under a separate heading.

A cash distribution is a return of capital if the corporation pays dividends in excess of its cumulative retained earnings. Such an excess may result from the use of accelerated depreciation for tax but not for financial purposes. Under these circumstances, taxable income for a growing company will be less than net income reported to stockholders. Then, if the company has a high payout ratio, the dividend may actually exceed the aftertax income reported to the IRS; the excess is deducted from retained earnings on the balance sheet filed with the IRS. If this continues for long, eventually all retained earnings may be wiped out. A portion of the annual dividend will then have to be charged against capital on the IRS balance sheet. That portion is considered a return of capital to the investor rather than income, and hence is not subject to tax. Such returns of capital reduce the tax basis of the investor's stock. Returns of capital often occur for public utilities, not only because they have large annual capital expenditures and high payout ratios but also because they capitalize a portion of their interest expense (include the interest with the value of the capital asset), based on the amount of plant under construction during the year, in stockholders reports but not in tax reports.[2] As a result, the cash dividends paid by public utilities have often been greater than the aftertax income reported to the IRS. Investors can obtain lists of companies whose cash dividends are likely to be tax-sheltered from financial services or their own brokers.

Cash distributions from income are what the investor typically thinks of as dividends. Under current federal legislation, the first $100 of such payments by domestic corporations may be excluded from taxable income. Married persons filing joint returns may each claim the $100 exclusion, but one spouse cannot claim the unused exclusion of the other. Investment company dividends are not eligible for the exclusion unless the investment company identifies the amount that is qualified for this purpose. This designation is required because the investment company may have in its portfolio the securities of foreign corporations, real estate investment trusts, or other corporations whose dividends are not subject to exclusion.

Stock Dividends

Most stock dividends involve distribution of additional common stock to existing owners. Stock dividends greater than 25 percent are construed to be stock splits and ordinarily are charged against capital surplus at par or stated value, while the capital stock account is correspondingly increased. Stock dividends of less than 25 percent are equated to regular dividends for accounting purposes. The market value of the distribution is charged against retained earnings; since the market value per share is likely to be above par or stated value, the capital stock and capital surplus accounts are correspondingly increased. The ratio of the stock dividend distribution to the number of shares held by the individual often results in fractional shares. In this event, the corporation usually provides the investor with the opportunity to buy or sell enough fractional shares to round his holdings to whole shares. The difference in the accounting treatment of stock dividends does not necessarily reflect a difference in their tax treatment.

For some time, neither the laws nor the court decisions governing the tax status of stock dividends have been clear. Stock dividends of the kind described above generally do not alter the basic position of the stockholder in the corporation; other kinds may change the stockholder's interest. Usually, the first class of stock dividends is nontaxable, but a dividend may have to be scrutinized carefully to determine whether it belongs in the first or second category under the terms of the Internal Revenue Code.

Prior to 1954, stock dividends were tax-free. Legislation in that year taxed the so-called bail-out, a simple device by which a corporation sometimes tried to distribute its earnings tax-free. It would issue preferred shares to its common stockholders, who would then sell the preferred to institutions. Subsequently, the issuing corporation would repurchase the preferred, possibly through a sinking fund or whenever the corporation thought such a step desirable. The net effect was that the stockholders received cash and the ultimate capitalization was no different from what it would have been if the company had paid a cash dividend.

To prevent the issuance of preferred as a means of tax avoidance, the 1954 code defined, in Section 306, stock dividends whose sales proceeds would be treated as taxable income. Such stock dividends became known as Section 306 stock. If the stock is passed on without being sold, the part of the proceeds equal to the original distribution is treated as ordinary income when the shares are subsequently sold. Because of this, Section 306 stock is said to be "tainted." Sometimes preferred stock received as consideration in a merger is classified as 306 stock. The taint is removed by selling the shares and paying the tax.

The Tax Reform Act of 1969 designates some stock dividends as taxable at the time of the distribution. These dividends are defined in Section 305, which now includes some dividends that were formerly included in Section 306. While this differentiation reduces the range of Section 306, it does not eliminate its applicability, since distributions under both sections are taxable as ordinary income. The difference lies in the dating of the tax liability. Roughly speaking, the distinguishing feature of the 305 stock is that the common stockholders do not all receive the same dividend. Thus, if stockholders can choose between a stock dividend and a property or cash dividend, the stock is likely to be considered 305 stock. Similarly, if there are two classes of stock—one entitled to stock dividends, the other entitled to cash dividends—the stock dividend will be 305 stock. Sometimes the stockholder is not even the recipient of a distribution. For example, if there are convertible preferred shares outstanding and the conversion ratio is increased, the holders of the convertible may be treated as having received a taxable distribution. In effect, holders of convertible preferred are entitled to a certain number of shares of common stock; this defines their proportionate interest in the company. A change in the conversion ratio entitling them to more stock increases their proportionate interest. Aside from Section 305 and Section 306 distributions, stock dividends generally are not considered income for tax purposes.

A capital gain or loss may occur when all or any portion of an investment in stock is sold. To determine the extent of the gain or loss, the holder must adjust the original per share cost of the stock to reflect the effect of any stock dividends. When a nontaxable dividend represents common stock paid to holders of common stock, the adjusted cost basis is calculated by dividing the cost of the old shares by the total number of old and new shares combined. When a nontaxable dividend is in preferred stock distributed to holders of common shares, the adjustment is more complicated, requiring an allocation between the old and the new stock.[3] In either case, the holding period for tax purposes is measured from the date of acquisition of the old issue.

Before leaving this subject, we must caution the reader that our purpose is to provide a broad picture of the tax status of stock dividends. The subject is very involved, and the subtleties are not discussed here.

Taxation of Stock Rights

Issuance of stock rights creates no income. However, when the recipient exercises or sells them, he may incur a tax liability, depending on whether the rights are considered taxable or nontaxable. As a general rule, the value of stock rights does not have to be included in taxable income. Nevertheless, there are exceptions, similar to those discussed earlier in relation to stock dividends.

If a stockholder sells taxable rights, the proceeds are taxed as ordinary income.[4] If the stockholder exercises taxable rights, the tax cost basis of the stock acquired is the subscription price plus the amount of taxable income recognized on the receipt of the rights. The holding period for the shares acquired is calculated from the date the rights are exercised to the eventual sale of the stock. Both the cost basis and the holding period of the old shares are unchanged.

The recipient of nontaxable stock rights must apportion the cost basis of his or her stock between the original shares and the rights if the fair market value of the rights is 15 percent or more of the value of the stock.[5] These independent, apportioned values then become the basis for calculating capital gains or losses if the stock or rights are sold. The holding period in either event is measured from the date the old shares were acquired. Typically, the value of stock rights is less than 15 percent of the market value of the stock, and the stockholder has the option of assigning a value of zero to the rights or allocating a portion of the cost basis of the original shares, as outlined in footnote 5. The election to allocate costs between the rights and the original shares must be made in a statement attached to the shareholder's return for the year in which the rights are received. The option to allocate may not be taken if the rights are allowed to lapse without being exercised or sold.

If the investor exercises nontaxable rights, the cost basis for the shares acquired will be the subscription price plus the cost allocated to the rights, divided by the number of shares acquired by exercising the rights. The holding period for the stock acquired by exercising rights begins with the date on which the rights are exercised.

Finally, the recipient of stock rights does not obtain a deductible loss if the rights are allowed to expire without sale or exercise. However, a purchaser of rights may claim a loss if he does not exercise or sell them prior to expiration.

CAPITAL GAINS

The Internal Revenue Code makes special provisions for earned income and preference income. Earned income is ordinarily from wages, salaries, and personal services. It is subject to a maximum tax rate of 50 percent. Preference income is income, such as capital gains, which is taxed at less than normal rates. If the amount of preference income exceeds certain limits, the excess is subject to a 10 percent surcharge. Because of the way in which the tax bill is calculated, the presence of a large preference income may reduce the amount of income that is protected by the maximum tax rate of 50 percent. The income that loses this protection may be taxed at marginal rates as high as 70 percent.

For tax purposes, capital gains are realized increments in the value of assets; a share of stock bought for $100 and subsequently sold for $110 produces a $10 capital gain. If the stock is held *more than* six months, the gain is considered long-term; otherwise, it is short-term. Generally, short-term gains are treated as ordinary income. For taxpayers with a marginal tax bracket of less than 50 percent, half of the excess of 50 percent of net long-term capital gains over net short-term losses is included in taxable income.[6] Alternatively, the taxpayer may simply pay 25 percent of the excess of net long-term gains (long-term gains minus long-term losses) over net short-term losses (short-term losses minus short-term gains), if that method is advantageous. The first method always yields a lower tax when the investor's top tax rate (marginal tax rate) is less than 50 percent.[7]

Short-term losses, current or carried forward, may be offset against short-term gains, net long-term gains, and ordinary income, in that order. If short-term gains and net long-term gains are not large enough to offset all the short-term losses, only up to $1,000 of the remaining net short-term losses may be offset against ordinary income in any tax year, but the losses can be carried forward indefinitely. Long-term capital losses must be offset against long-term capital gains, net short-term gains, and ordinary income, in that order. The maximum reduction of ordinary income by short- and long-term capital losses combined is $1,000. While only 50 cents of ordinary income may be offset by one dollar of net long-term capital losses, a full dollar of net short-term gains may be offset. Unused net long-term capital losses may be carried forward to future tax years indefinitely.

The application of rules governing the taxation of large capital gains to determine the tax liability can be cumbersome because of the convoluted steps involved. As he dutifully moves from line to line, an investor preparing his own return probably feels, at times, like a rat blindly wandering through a maze—and the feeling is justified.

Three factors increase the tax bill disproportionately when capital gains are large:

(1) Only the first $50,000 of capital gains is subject to the 50 percent ceiling on marginal rates.
(2) Large capital gains may bring into play a 10 percent surcharge on preference income if preference income becomes large enough.
(3) The specialized treatment of preference income may have an impact on the taxes paid on earned income. As a result, the incremental tax burden from large reported capital gains may raise the marginal tax rate on these gains to even more than 35 percent.

Rational investment planning requires careful consideration of tax implications. Accordingly, when large accounts are involved, consultation with a tax accountant or tax lawyer well before the end of the taxable year is usually desirable.

Considerations Affecting the Capital Gains Tax

Timing. As noted, capital gains may be either long- or short-term. In general, the investor is better off keeping gains long-term and losses short. Certain principles may be helpful in determining when to take these gains and losses.

First, if there are only a few days to wait in order to extend the holding period long enough to convert what would be short-term capital gains into long-term gains, and if the sale of stock which has appreciated in value is not contemplated because its price is expected to fall immediately, the investor may reduce the capital gains tax by 50 percent or more by extending the holding period past the six-month dividing line between short- and long-term gains.

Conversely, if a stock has experienced losses and is not expected to rebound, the investor should be careful not to let the holding period go beyond six months.

Second, it may be possible to postpone the tax on gains by one year or to make a loss applicable to the following year through the timing of sales. For income tax purposes, transactions are recognized on the settlement date rather than the transaction date. Since settlements are normally five trading days after the transaction date, it is possible to execute a sale near the end of the year—for example, on December 27—and have the capital gains or losses fall in the following calendar year. Thus, postponing the realization of a capital gain for a few days—say, from December 22 to December 27—may delay the tax payment on the capital gain by 12 months.

Similarly, it may be worthwhile to delay recognizing a short-term loss until the following year if the investor has recognized large long-term capital gains in the current one. If net short-term losses can be used to offset ordinary income, each dollar of net losses so used reduces taxable income by a full dollar. If the net short-term losses offset net long-term gains, each dollar of net losses so used reduces taxable income by only 50 cents. As a consequence, it is usually advantageous to take net long-term gains and net short-term losses in separate years.

Wash Sales

An investor cannot establish a tax-deductible loss by selling a security and immediately reinvesting in the same stock or bond either shortly before or after the sale. The investor must allow more than 30 days to elapse between the sale and repurchase of a security for a tax-deductible loss to be established. There are no such time restrictions on transactions that result in taxable gains.

A *wash sale* is defined as a sale or other disposition of a security at a loss accompanied by purchase of a substantially identical security during a period beginning 30 days before the date of sale and ending 30 days after that date—a total period of 61 days. When a loss is disallowed for tax purposes as being a wash sale, the tax basis of the securities acquired in the transaction will be their acquisition price plus the loss that was disallowed.

Investors seeking to establish deductible losses for tax purposes while retaining their investment position in a company or an industry may adopt a variety of alternative strategies. If they feel that the security's market price is near its low and is likely to begin to appreciate, they may "double-up" on their investment in the security, purchasing additional shares with the intention of selling the old (high-cost shares) 31 days later. If an investor is not optimistic about the short-run price performance but wants to retain a long-run position, he may "step out" temporarily by selling his securities to establish his tax loss, then repurchase the same number of shares 31 days later.

While the definition of a wash sale is stated in terms of "substantially identical securities," the IRS interpretation is quite favorable to investors. Even bonds of the same issuer, differing only in their maturity dates and coupon rates, have been exempt from the category "substantially similar," and there is apparently no question about "tax swaps" involving common stock of companies in the same industry.

Lock-in Effect of Capital Gains Tax

The capital gains tax is unique in that the timing of the tax payment is almost entirely within the control of the taxpayer. As long as an investor postpones realizing a capital gain via sale, the capital gains tax can be delayed. If the capital gains are not realized during the investor's life, the tax payment has been effectively avoided, since after the investor's death the tax base for the estate steps up to the fair market value, without any taxable capital gains recognition.

If an investor postpones realizing capital gains for a period of years but does sell prior to his or her death, the delay in triggering the capital gains tax payment can be considered the equivalent of an interest-free loan. However, the value of that loan to an investor, plus the value of minimizing the tax burden on the investor's estate, may still be less than the income potential of alternative investments.

The psychological impact of voluntarily triggering a tax payment may lead investors to keep securities that have unrealized capital gains, even though retention is not a rational investment decision. To the extent that investors refuse to sell holdings in order to postpone the capital gains tax, without reference to the investment merits of the securities, they have become "locked in" by inertia and not by the tax.

Rationally, investors should always be willing to realize their capital gains and pay the capital gains tax if alternative investments are sufficiently more attractive than the securities they hold. If the proceeds from the sale of a security, less the transaction cost and the capital gains tax, can be reinvested in an alternative instrument that, in the investor's opinion, offers greater value in the long run than the securities sold, failure to trigger the capital gains tax is irrational. The proper comparison should be the discounted present value of the dividends and the net terminal value of the securities held, versus the discounted present value of the dividends and the net terminal value of the investment that could be acquired with the net proceeds from the sale of the securities.

For example, assume an investor in the 40 percent marginal tax bracket owns 100 shares of XYZ Co. common stock, purchased at $20 per share, and that XYZ common is currently trading at a price of $100 a share. The investor has a substantial unrealized capital gain and feels the natural inclination to postpone the tax payment. However, it is quite possible that, in the investor's opinion, the future performance of XYZ may be substantially poorer than alternative common stock in the same risk class.

If the investor sells the holdings of XYZ, a capital gains tax payment of $1,600 will be triggered. The realized gain will be $8,000, which will be subject to a 20 percent tax, since the investor is in the 40 percent marginal tax bracket. The net proceeds from the sale (ignoring transaction costs) amount to $8,400, which will be available for investment elsewhere. The proper procedure is to compare the investment performance of XYZ, currently worth $10,000, with the anticipated performance of the best alternative investment (ALT), given the time horizon of the investor. To simplify the comparison we assume XYZ and ALT have comparable risk. If that were not the case, allowance for risk would have to be made. Assume that the investor's best estimate of future performance of the two securities can be summarized as indicated in the Table 6-1:

TABLE 6-1

Comparing Estimates of Future Stock Performance

	XYZ	*ALT*
Current market value	$10,000.00	$ 8,400.00
Number of shares	100.00	200.00
Expected dividends per share	4.20	2.25
Total annual dividends	420.00	450.00
Estimated price per share in five years	130.00	60.00
Market value in five years	13,000.00	12,000.00
Tax basis	2,000.00	8,400.00
Unrealized capital gain	11,000.00	3,600.00
Capital gains tax	2,200.00	720.00
Net realizable value, fifth year	10,800.00	11,280.00

Under these circumstances, despite the fact that the immediate sale of XYZ common results in the payment of a $1,600 capital gains tax, the investor should sell the holdings of XYZ. The net proceeds, even though they are only 84 percent of the current market value, can be reinvested to produce a higher current income ($450 vs. $420) and a higher expected realizable value ($11,280 vs. $10,800) at the time horizon five years hence.

If the capital gains tax payment is expressed as a percentage of the current market value, there is a 16 percent immediate loss of market value as a result of triggering the capital gains tax in this example. However, if alternative investments offer a dividend yield that is equal to or greater than the dividend yield on the current holdings divided by one minus the investor's tax bite percentage, there will be no loss of current investment income. In our example, the dividend yield on XYZ was 4.2 percent. The break-even dividend yield for alternative investment would have to be 5 percent (4.2 ÷ 0.84) in order to preserve the same amount of dividend income. The dividend yield on ALT is 5.4 percent.

Any investor whose goal is to maximize economic well-being, as opposed to simply minimizing tax payment, should always be willing to consider selling securities that have unrealized capital gains. It is always possible that the benefits obtained by postponing the payment of taxes may be less than the opportunities foregone in alternative investments.

TAX SHELTERS

An important distinction should be made between tax evasion and tax avoidance. Tax evasion results from the overstatement of expenses and/or the understatement of revenues as defined in the tax laws. Tax avoidance is the utilization of the provisions of the law which permit taxpayers to reduce current income or increase current expense. The cynic might define tax avoidance as legalized evasion. Tax shelters form a subclass of devices for tax avoidance.

Tax shelters can be divided into three (not mutually exclusive) types: (1) those which make it possible to expense nonexisting costs, such as depletion; (2) those which make it possible to convert income into long-term capital gains and so have the income taxed at lower rates; and (3) those which permit the postponement of income. By definition, the second category always involves the third.

The majority of the tax shelters available to investors can also be broadly classified into three general categories: (1) extractive operations, particularly those of an exploratory nature; (2) farm enterprises, such as cattle breeding and feedlot operations; and (3) real estate projects. Each has its advantages and disadvantages, and most shelters require some specialized knowledge if risks are to be held within reasonable limits.

Frequently, the discussion of tax shelters places primary emphasis on the availability of tax-deductible losses, but it is important to remember that the primary purpose of investing is to generate positive aftertax cash flow, not a simple increase in tax deductions.

Tax shelters have come under attack in recent years. There has been considerable pressure to change the provisions of the tax code that make such shelters possible or, alternatively, to limit the amount of income that escapes taxation. In addition, many tax shelters have proved to be unprofitable because the economic venture was basically unsound. The SEC has been considering changes in its regulations that would require more disclosure. That alone would probably curb the enthusiasm of many promoters of tax shelters.

While few, if any, investments can be made without giving full consideration to all the tax implications, no investment should be based solely on its tax advantages. An investor trying to maximize his or her own economic well-being should focus on the aftertax cash flows that an investment will produce. This inevitably requires a forecast of the future performance of the investment based on the time horizon of the investor.

SUMMARY

Since not all returns on investments are taxed equally, the relevant consideration is the aftertax return. Generally, the periodic receipts of cash from investments are treated as ordinary income in the tax period in which they are received. A major exception to this rule is the interest received on the issues of state and local governments and authorities. Because the realized appreciation in the value of investments is generally taxed at half the rate applicable to ordinary income, investments with appreciation potential are attractive to individual investors, especially to individuals in high tax brackets. Individuals in very high tax brackets may actively seek tax shelters—that is, investments for which the law provides especially favorable tax treatment.

CHAPTER

Sources of Information

People sometimes talk of having a "feel" for a security. Nevertheless, the belief that certain investors have a special financial intuition probably is not true, and it would be foolhardy to conduct transactions in securities on any such basis. The commonsense explanation is that a serious student of the subject can acquire, through experience, the ability to analyze investment information rapidly and accurately. In order to undertake these analyses he must have the necessary data, and for this he must know how and where to get the data he needs.

INVESTMENT INFORMATION

Published financial information is available in quantity. Each investor must find for himself the material he needs and must keep himself informed about financial matters. If he does not develop effective methods of obtaining data, he may find himself reviewing seemingly endless reports when he might more profitably be analyzing securities. The knack of selecting pertinent material from the plethora of published information is more important than wide and indiscriminate reading.

Sources of Information

The major sources of investment data are reports issued by corporations, Securities and Exchange Commission filings, exchange listing applications, trade publications, plant visits, and various financial services and publications.

Reports Issued by Corporations

Corporations outline their financial position through published reports, which may be issued annually or on some interim basis. They constitute an accessible and extremely important source of basic information.

Annual reports. All publicly held companies prepare some sort of annual statement as a matter of policy. Corporations with securities listed on a national securities exchange, as well as a number of large corporations with issues traded in the over-the-counter markets, are required to publish annual reports. (The Securities Acts Amendments of 1964 extend the periodic reporting for listed companies to OTC corporations that meet minimum tests of gross assets and number of shareholders.) During the early period of American corporate development, these reports were dull and contained little information. More recently, corporate management has become aware of a report's public relations potential and often devotes considerable effort to the production of attractively designed and informative publications. Reports are also available in microfiche form. Moreover, public libraries often keep elaborate files of annual reports, and the corporations themselves will usually forward copies to individuals on request. Many companies now disclose reports summarizing the discussions at annual meetings.

In addition to a detailed balance sheet, income statement, and an analysis of the sources and applications of funds, the modern report includes a discussion of the current operations of the company, a description of the products most recently developed or sold, some corporate financial statistics, historical comparisons of data, and a statement concerning expected conditions. By comparing reports over a period of years, the investor may trace the financial development of a corporation and appraise its progress, the ability of its management to realize announced plans, and the major problems confronting the enterprise. In reading these studies, he must make allowance for tendencies on the part of management to gloss over difficulties and to make roseate forecasts of future operations.

The character of the report may at least suggest something about the character of the company's management. For example, during the heyday of Litton Industries, some stockholders may have been impressed by a management that could issue a handsomely illustrated, glossy book boldly entitled *The Era of Opportunity*, with chapter headings that read "Opportunity and Space," "Opportunity in the Sea," "Opportunity and the

Atmosphere," "Opportunity on Earth," and "The Business of Opportunity." But this book, with 38 pages of rhapsodic text and a detailed index, but only seven pages of financial information (including footnotes), posed as the company's annual report in 1963. The contrast between considerable verbiage and relatively little financial information undoubtedly aroused suspicion in the minds of some analysts about the policies of the company and suggested a cautious attitude toward the stock well before its staggering drop from a high of 104¼ in 1967 to a low of 2⅞ in 1974.

It is imperative that the investor understand the accounting policies underlying the financial statements in a company's annual report. To help in this respect, Opinion no. 22 of the Accounting Principles Board requires companies to provide an integrated summary of accounting policies. This account, together with the footnotes to the financial statements, represents an extremely important segment of the annual report. Typical areas that are covered include the principles of consolidation; translation of foreign currencies and a statement of foreign operations; the valuation of different categories of assets; depreciation, depletion, and amortization; research and development; the investment credit; retirement plans; the handling of investments in affiliated companies; litigation; a breakdown of outstanding debt; contingent liabilities; income taxes; pensions; leases; extraordinary items; and changes in accounting policies. This information may be quite extensive—in Boise Cascade's 1972 annual report, the notes to the financial statements, including a summary of significant accounting policies, covered 14 pages of a 52-page report; in an extreme case, the footnotes to the 1974 annual report of the International Controls Corp., a manufacturing and engineering company that had been involved in the financial manipulations of Robert L. Vesco and Investors Overseas Services (IOS), ran to 19 out of 32 pages.

Also of importance is the independent accountant's report. Ordinarily, it is confined to one or two bland paragraphs incorporating the "boiler-plate" observations that the financial statements ". . . present fairly the consolidated financial position [of the company] . . . in conformity with generally accepted accounting principles consistently applied during the period." In August 1975 the American Institute of Certified Public Accountants issued two auditing pronouncements, one of which was concerned with the meaning of the certification that a company's financial statements are presented "fairly." In this "Statement on Auditing Standards," the position was taken that "fair" should be gauged within the framework of generally accepted principles rather than on subjective or commonsense standards, thereby suggesting that continued emphasis would be placed on technical criteria.

If there is a special problem, however, the auditing firm will qualify its report particularly in view of the recent tendency of the courts to apply stern standards in evaluating its performance. Lewis Gilbert, the well-known representative of stockholders' interests, has posed a warning in dramatic style: "Beware the three-paragraph audit." A classic illustration of this precept was the extra paragraph in the report by Price Waterhouse & Co., the independent public accountants, of Roosevelt Field, Inc., at that time a 71 percent-controlled subsidiary of Webb & Knapp, Inc. Appearing in the company's 1960 annual report was a paragraph raising a question ". . . as to whether or not principles of accounting applicable to a going concern should continue to be followed with respect to carrying values of assets and deferred charges." Shortly thereafter, the Webb & Knapp system went into bankruptcy. For an elaboration of a qualification, the auditor is likely to refer to an appropriate footnote related to the financial statements. In effect, therefore, the report and footnotes represent an integrated segment providing analytic comments on the financial status of the company.

If the financial problem leading to the qualifications is sufficiently serious, the auditor, as in the Roosevelt Field case, may hoist the red flag of questionable "going concern" value. In the case of Planet Oil and Mineral Corporation, for example, there were two such serious problems: unprofitable operations and the uncertainty of obtaining future financing. These circumstances were observed in the auditor's report to the 1973 financial statement:

> The Company has sustained operating losses during the past five years and continuation as a going concern is dependent upon its ability to achieve future profitable operations and to obtain additional financing. As discussed in note 2, the Company does not plan to sell its investment in the shares of Physics International Company until such time as favorable market conditions occur.... While management expects that the proceeds from disposition of certain of its assets, including the Physics shares, and additional financing, or other financial arrangements, will permit the Company to conduct its ranching and other operations, there is no present assurance that it will be able to do so or that the financial position of the Company will improve in the foreseeable future.

The financial well-being of Marlboro Enterprises, Inc., another "going concern" case, rested upon the willingness of Mitsubishi International Corporation, which owns 27.7 percent of Marlboro's shares, to provide financial support to the latter firm. The auditor's report to Marlboro's 1973 annual report reflected this fact:

> During the current year the Company sustained substantial operating losses, which resulted in deficiencies in both working capital and total capital as at December 31, 1973. The Company's future economic

> viability is, in effect, totally dependent upon its ability to receive the continued financial support of Mitsubishi International Corporation (Note 4) and the resumption of profitable operations.

Another typical problem is the uncertainty of developing sufficient business from a new activity to cover locked-in prior costs. Thus, the auditor's report to the 1973 annual report of Optical Systems Corp. stated:

> As explained in Note 2, at December 1, 1973, the Company had an investment of $5,174,904 in unrecovered development costs, $1,798,920 in property and equipment, and $556,869 in patent costs. Realization of these amounts is subject to the Company's ability to develop a successful commercial market for its products and services.

Similarly, the 1973 statement of Western Union observed:

> As discussed more fully in Note K, recoverability of certain start-up costs is dependent upon the ability of a subsidiary to achieve and maintain a satisfactory level of operations.

The subsidiary in question was GiftAmerica, Inc., which had been recently established as a new, nationwide gift service.

In the case of Ecological Assistance Corp., the financial problem producing the qualification was the company's uncertain ability to utilize, through licensing arrangements, assets no longer needed for operations that had been terminated.

> Subsequent to January 31, 1974, the Company ceased manufacturing and marketing its solid waste compactor product line, which will be produced and marketed in the future through licenses. Two such licensing agreements have been entered into and are subject to the approval of the stockholders. Realization of the principal assets of the Company, as discussed in Note 2, is dependent upon the Company's ability to enter into sufficient licensing agreements and the success of future operations of such licensees.

When the outlook is sufficiently uncertain, the auditor may be reluctant to express an opinion and therefore will issue a disclaimer. For example, in the 1973 annual report, the certification of Crown Corporation was unusually long. It discussed the difficulty of evaluating the statements of a financial subsidiary and the heavy burden of funding the maturities of long-term debt for the next five years. The report then concluded with a refusal to express an opinion.

> Because the possible effects on the financial statements which may result from matters set forth in the second paragraph could have a material impact on the results of operations of Crown Corporation and subsidiary companies for the years ended December 31, 1973 and 1972, we express no opinion on the results of their operations and changes in their financial position.

In the case of Airlift International, Inc., Price Waterhouse first expressed concern about "going concern" values in its 1971 audit:

> The financial statements examined by us have been prepared in conformity with principles of accounting applicable to a going concern.... However, ... the stockholder's deficit and the excess of liabilities over tangible assets at June 30, 1971, raise a question as to whether or not such principles should continue to be followed.

The auditor then concluded:

> Because of the possible material effect on the financial statements of [these] uncertainties . . . we do not express any opinion on the abovementioned financial statements.

As a result of its difficulties, the company proposed a recapitalization plan that was completed about a year later.

A combination of declining business and auditors' apprehensions about possible lawsuits led to a substantial increase in qualified opinions in 1974 reports. The managing partner of one major accounting firm estimated that his firm was writing qualifications at three times the 1973 rate, often for companies whose reports had never been qualified previously. Real estate lenders and builders, particularly, were receiving qualified opinions because of the liquidity problems the industry was experiencing. Qualifications were typically given for uncertainties involving such matters as the recovery of undepreciated assets or deferred costs, the outcome of a lawsuit, the permanence of "temporary" rate increases allowed public utilities, and the future market action of investments carried at original cost that is above market value. While "disclaimed" opinions also were on the rise, it was expected that they would decline in 1975 because audit rules adopted in the fall of 1974 discouraged their use.[1]

Because they are so important, both the footnotes and the auditor's report should be clearly visible in the company's annual report. Lewis Gilbert suggests another useful adage: "The less readable the footnotes, the more likely are impending financial difficulties." Thus, the 1972 annual report of

Mobile America Inc. contained 11 footnotes set forth in hard-to-read, small type. The auditor's report, in turn, cautioned that

> . . . continuation [of the Company] as a going concern is dependent upon obtaining additional financing since estimated future cash requirements are in excess of amounts available under present financing agreements.

Traditionally, the auditor's report applies to the financial statements of a company. In what may be a milestone for the accounting profession, Coopers & Lybrand, a major accounting firm, has offered its clients an extended audit that also covers the historical data covered in the "president's letter" and other usually unaudited portions of annual reports. The extension, however, does not include earnings or sales forecasts because they do not contain past data. In 1974 the Aluminum Company of America (ALCOA) availed itself of this service. The auditor's report for that year, therefore, contained a third paragraph—this time of a constructive nature. It stated:

> In addition, we have read the financial information included in the Financial highlights on page 1 and in the Twenty-year Summary under the captions, "Earnings," "Financial position" and "Share data" on pages 18 and 19 of this annual report, have compared it to data taken from the audited financial statements, subjected it to audit procedures, and verified its mathematical accuracy. In our opinion, such data is fairly stated in relation to the audited financial statements taken as a whole.

The SEC has indicated that an annual report is potentially the most effective medium for transmitting readable and understandable information to investors, while Form 10-K (an annual report to the SEC, discussed later in the chapter) may be better suited to securities analysts. Nevertheless, noting that its rule revisions have resulted in considerable improvement in the 10-Ks, the commission has extended considerably the disclosure requirements of the annual reports. Thus, companies must now include the following information in their annual reports:

(1) Audited financial statements for the last two fiscal years;
(2) A reconciliation of any material differences between the financial statements in the 10-K and the annual report;
(3) A summary of operations for the last five fiscal years, including management's discussion and analysis of the summary;
(4) A brief description of the business done by the company in the last fiscal year;

(5) A breakdown of the company's revenue and income by lines-of-business for the past five fiscal years.
(6) Specific information about the company's directors and executive officers; and
(7) The principal trading markets for each class of the company's voting securities and a two-year summary by quarters of price ranges and dividend payments.

Despite the commission's vigorous action, there is some question about its authority over company annual reports. In October 1972 the National Committee for an Effective Congress and Public Citizen, Inc., petitioned the commission to require the disclosure, in proxy solicitation materials or in annual reports, of information required to be filed with Congress under the Federal Election Campaign Act of 1971, generally concerned with amounts paid by corporations for political campaign purposes. The commission refused to require corporations to provide this information in their annual reports on the ground that its authority to prescribe the content of the reports is limited and has been exercised only with respect to the inclusion of certified financial statements and the avoidance of misleading statements.[2]

Interim reports. The emphasis on disclosure is also reflected in the increasing number of companies that provide quarterly reports to their shareholders. While the New York Stock Exchange requires that corporations with listed securities publish quarterly statements, the large over-the-counter companies also tend to follow this practice. Despite the fact that the quarterly report of sales and earnings may have an important effect on the market price of a company's stock, there is no requirement for an independent audit of such reports. Both the SEC and the American Institute of Certified Public Accountants (AICPA) have issued proposals that would give outside auditors an enlarged role in the preparation and checking of interim statements. The AICPA proposal provides for "limited reviews" at the request of a company's board of directors, while the SEC prefers mandatory compliance and full public disclosure.

Special reports. A number of companies issue postmeeting reports, specialized magazines, and statistical supplements. This information, particularly the statistical supplements, may provide insights into the company's operations. However, a shareholder may not receive all this information routinely and will have to write to the company to be placed on its mailing list. (The 1974 annual report of Archer Daniels Midland Co. had an odd twist—the financial information was a supplement to a report, 11 inches square, containing a series of large, handsome photographs of foods incorporating the company's products.)

Very few industrial corporations publish regular monthly financial statements, although a number of companies send out monthly data covering sales, deliveries, and unfilled orders. Railroads, which are subject to Interstate Commerce Commission requirements, publish operations reports that cover the preceding month and the year to date. Many public utilities issue monthly earnings reports.

SEC Filings

Corporations must file information with various federal and state regulatory agencies. Of these, the most important, and the one with which the investor is likely to have the most acquaintance, is the SEC. The commission administers various measures that give it considerable authority over corporations that issue public securities. Acting under this authority, the commission has imposed on the corporations a number of requirements that effectively make available to investors a substantial body of information.

Basic registration statement. Under the Securities Act of 1933, disclosure is obtained primarily through the registration statement that must be filed by those engaged in a public distribution, including issuers, underwriters for issuers, and persons in a control relationship to an issuer. A schedule of the act calls for a substantial amount of material to be incorporated into the registration statement, including information on the issuer, its capitalization, its officers and directors, the purpose of the financing, the terms of the underwriting, financial statements, and a number of legal agreements. A prospectus, which represents the first part of the statement, is distributed publicly and contains the financial and other information relevant to investors. The second part of the statement has material of a technical nature, such as marketing arrangements, and various legal exhibits. The registration statement is available for examination at the offices of the SEC or may be obtained from the commission, in whole or in part, by paying a fee to cover the costs of photocopying.

Under the SEC's Regulation A, companies with offerings not exceeding $500,000 are exempt from registration. These companies need only file a limited amount of information and furnish an offering circular containing such information; moreover, their financial statements need not be certified. This reporting gap primarily affects the small investor, who is likely to be attracted to issues of this type, and presents a problem to the SEC, which is reluctant to impose an undue reporting burden on small companies.

Prospectus. The prospectus represents the primary sales literature of a corporation involved in an original public offering. With certain exceptions, it must accompany or precede all such securities sold in interstate commerce. This statutory requirement is buttressed by an SEC expectation that broker-dealers participating in an underwriting will distribute a preliminary prospectus to buyers at least 48 hours before confirmations are mailed.

Although it is much more accessible than the registration statement, its chief drawback is that there is no provision for keeping distributed documents up-to-date. Moreover, the prospectus may be complex and difficult for the average investor to understand. The SEC and interested financial officials have for some time been seeking ways to make the prospectus simpler and more readable.[3] The commission is also seeking to provide prospective investors with a reasonably complete account of major uncertainties.

As a step in this direction, the commission now requires that a reporting company provide near the front of the prospectus a summary of its business, plan of operation, material risks associated with the offering, and basic financial information. Figure 7-1 shows just how far this statement of risks may go. The company, Modular Computer Systems, Inc., a designer and manufacturer of computer systems primarily for measurement and communications applications, offered 500,000 shares of common stock in the latter part of 1973.

The statement clearly puts a prospective investor on notice regarding the company's limited history of earnings, accumulated deficit, and reliance on technical personnel who might prove difficult to recruit, as well as the concentration of business, the keen competition in the industry, and the unappealing fact that no dividend payments are in sight. It also refers to the fact that a substantial number of formerly restricted shares might come to the market under the SEC's Rule 144, permitting such sales under specified conditions. This listing of negative factors inserted at the beginning of the prospectus undoubtedly hobbles the underwriter's ability to sell shares and reflects the SEC's concern that investors be provided with full disclosure about an issuer's condition.

In order to provide the basis of disclosure to purchasers of securities in the immediate after-market, the Securities Act of 1933 provides that, except for unsolicited brokerage transactions, a prospectus must also be delivered in every transaction involving a registered security by any dealer, whether or not he participated in the original offering, during a 40-day period subsequent to the start of the offering. The Securities Acts Amendments of 1964 extend this period to 90 days for transactions in a security where no prior public offering has occurred, with the commission having the power to shorten the period.

Periodic reports. As a prerequisite to listing, the Securities Exchange Act of 1934 provides that corporations must file with both the applicable exchange and the commission a registration statement somewhat similar to that required for registration of new issues under the Securities Act of 1933. The information for listed companies, as well as for large over-the-counter companies, is kept current in various ways.

Changes in control, the acquisition or disposition of assets, changes in the amount of outstanding securities, and legal proceedings are typical of the

FIGURE 7-1

Risks Listed in the Preliminary Prospectus of Modular Computer Systems, Inc.

INTRODUCTORY STATEMENT

Risks

The following factors should be carefully considered by potential investors:

1. *Limited History of Earnings and Accumulated Deficit.* Although the Company had net come before extraordinary item of $100,372 and $292,432 for the year ended December 29, 1 and the six months ended June 29, 1973, respectively, it had substantial losses in the two p fiscal years, which were the first two years of its operations, and as of June 29, 1973 had an accu lated earnings deficit of $1,281,150 (see "Financial Statements").

2. *Competition.* The computer industry is characterized by intense competition and rapid te nological change (see "Business—Competition").

3. *Key Personnel.* The Company and the development of its products depend upon the availabi of an adequate number of highly skilled technical personnel. The loss of several highly quali personnel over a short period of time could have an adverse effect on the Company (see "Busines Employees" and "Management").

4. *Customer Concentration.* For the year ended December 29, 1972 and the six months en June 29, 1973, the Company's largest customer accounted for approximately 18% and 19 respectively, of sales. During both such periods, the Company's next five largest customers a group accounted for approximately 32% of sales. It has been the Company's experience tha large percentage of its sales in any particular period has been attributable to a few custom although the identity of its largest customers has changed periodically. The Company expects t type of customer concentration to continue into the foreseeable future (see "Business—Sales a Marketing").

5. *Possible Sales Under Rule 144 and Registration Rights.* From the Company's inception date, the Company effected several private placements which have resulted in 1,925,040 shares Common Stock outstanding which are "restricted securities" as defined in Rule 144 ("Rule 14 promulgated under the Securities Act of 1933, as amended (the "Act") and are not publ tradable without registration under the Act or compliance with one of the limited exempti from registration under the Act. The Company has also issued in private placements a note debentures which are convertible into an aggregate of 225,548 shares of Common Stock, which also restricted securities as defined in Rule 144. In addition to other exemptions which may available to the holders of the foregoing restricted securities, Rule 144 permits the sale un certain circumstances of limited amounts of restricted securities owned at least two years by e holder thereof. Although the Rule 144 exemption will not be available to the holders of restric shares of the Common Stock for a period of 90 days following the effective date of this Prospec there can be no assurance that a substantial number of restricted shares of Common Stock will be sold in the public market pursuant to Rule 144 following such 90-day period or pursuant some other exemption following the public offering.

In these private placements, the Company granted to the purchasers registration rights wh enable such purchasers to resell such securities in compliance with the Act. These rights gener allow the purchasers to add their securities to certain registration statements which may be fi by the Company and, under certain circumstances, to require the Company to file a registrat statement at the request of the purchasers. Registration rights applicable to this offering have be waived. Nevertheless, the existence of such rights in the future may impair the Company's abi to raise equity capital.

6. *Dividends.* The Company has not paid any cash dividends and does not intend to pay ca dividends in the foreseeable future (see "Dividends").

Source: *Preliminary Prospectus of Modular Computer Systems, Inc.*, Fall 1973.

kinds of events that must be reported on the SEC's Form 8-K. The deadline for filing is the tenth day of the month following that in which the change occurred. The commission also requires companies to explain changes in auditors and large write-offs or other charges.

Form 10-K is an annual report that must be filed within 90 days after the close of each fiscal year. This form may be the most important source of current information concerning a company. The financial statements it contains are governed by SEC Regulation S-X, which calls for information on leases, funded debt, stock options, inventories, and depreciation that may not appear in comparable detail in the company's annual reports. To ensure that investors have sufficient data to evaluate the liquid position of companies, the SEC, after much study, in 1973 issued a series of revisions to Regulation S-X. These called for disclosure in financial statements of information on short-term interest rates, compensating balances, unused confirmed lines of credit, and commercial paper.[4]

Form 10-K also requires the breakdown of both sales and earnings by major lines of business; companies with sales greater than $50 million must report any product line contributing 10 percent or more to total volume or pretax profits, while smaller companies must report product lines contributing 15 percent or more. In addition, the 10-K calls for a description of a company's principal products, markets, and methods of distribution, as well as a description of any material changes and developments in the company's business during the fiscal year. It also requires the company to report on nine specific topics, including expenditures on research and development, the dollar volume of order backlogs, competitive conditions, and degree of reliance on a small number of customers.

If the SEC permits voluntary inclusion of forecasts in its filings—a major departure from prior policy—it will probably provide guidelines to ensure that projections, whether filed or not, meet certain standards. It is likely that a company issuing forecasts outside of filings, to securities analysts and others, would have to report such projections to the commission.[5] An important reason for the protracted hesitation of the SEC to issue a rule is apprehension that companies would provide less information in order to avoid a statement that could be construed as a forecast and therefore require filing.

The 10-K forms are available at the SEC's Washington and regional offices and at the NYSE for its listed companies. Through arrangements with the SEC, one private firm also furnishes them in microfiche, while another firm issues permanently bound volumes. Some registered companies now include 10-K forms in their annual report mailings to shareholders. Outboard Marine Corporation, for example, states that "the financial section of the 1974 Annual Report is identical in all material aspects with the Form 10-K which will be filed with the Securities and Exchange Commission." Other companies are now required by the SEC to state in their reports that copies of the 10-Ks may be obtained on request without cost, although a charge may be imposed for particular exhibits.

Sometimes a company's annual reports and 10-K forms are very similar, but often substantial differences occur. Accordingly, an investor who desires to make a careful study of a company must check its 10-Ks. For example, Consolidated Edison indicated in its 1973 report that adjusted earnings amounted to $2.79 per share and tersely observed that "the dividend remained at $1.80." Yet, shortly thereafter, the company shocked the investment community by omitting a quarterly payment. Part of the reason for this drastic step was a poor cash flow caused by sluggish customer payments. The only reference in the annual report to the company's deteriorating collection systems, however, was this laconic observation: "Provisions are made for uncollectible accounts by charges to other operations which for the years 1973 and 1972 amounted to $28,819,000 and $16,605,000 respectively." Contrast that statement with the following graphic account in the 10-K of the increasingly serious problem the company was encountering with slow payments and badly overage receivables:

> During the period January 1, 1968 to December 31, 1972, accounts receivable from electric and gas customers increased from $98,900,000 to $227,300,000, and at July 31, 1973 were $267,700,000. . . . The Company estimates that a substantial portion of this increase is attributable to deteriorating customer payment patterns. A measure of this deterioration is the age of accounts receivable. The collectibility of a receivable tends to decrease with age, resulting in higher credit losses.[6] As of July 31, 1973, $34,500,000 (or approximately 20%) of retail (residential, religious and small commercial) electric and gas receivables were over six months old, as compared to $2,200,000 (or approximately 5%) as of November 30, 1967. . . ."

An explanation of this sort in the annual report might have alerted more investors to the company's cash-flow problem and helped them anticipate the dividend reduction.

Quarterly reporting to the SEC is required through Form 10-Q. In keeping with the general trend in the industry, there is pressure for full disclosure in these reports as well. For example, in its filing with the SEC for the first quarter of 1973, Avis failed to report gains from vehicle sales. Accordingly, the company's subsequent disclosure to securities analysts that some 65 percent of the company's first-quarter pretax profits came from sales of used vehicles created a stir and probably contributed to the sharp decline the stock experienced. Apparently, concerned by this reaction, the company in its second-quarter report resumed publication of a footnote, which had appeared in its 1972 filings, showing the gains from car sales.[7] Additionally, the SEC has commented on the need for companies to comply in the 10-Q reports with developments affecting accounting principles and to reflect all adjustments necessary for a fair statement of results for the period. While the commission eventually may require an auditor's statement for the quarterly report, it could achieve this result indirectly by providing that audited year-end financial statements carry data on sales and profits at intermediate stages during the year.[8]

In September 1975 the SEC adopted regulations that did require companies whose stocks are listed on an exchange and OTC companies whose stocks (NASDAQ) are subject to Federal Reserve Board credit regulations (all told, an estimated 3,800 companies) to include quarterly data in a footnote to their 10-K annual reports. Although the footnote appears in the audited portion of the annual report, it may be labeled "unaudited." The footnote provides data for each quarter in the two most recent fiscal years, including net sales, gross profits, income before extraordinary items, the cumulative effect of any accounting changes, net income, and earnings per share. It must also describe "unusual" or "infrequently occurring" items in any quarter.

In addition, the regulations require that all publicly held companies that file with the SEC (estimated at about 10,000 companies) must expand their 10-Q reports. Under these rules, a company must now provide quarterly a balance sheet, a full income statement, and a statement of the source and application of corporate funds. The company must also include a "narrative analysis" explaining any important quarter-to-quarter changes in revenue or expense items.

Accountants have tended to oppose the expanded interim requirements on the grounds that they could increase the exposure of auditing firms to lawsuits. Additionally, the critics contend that the interim data could mislead stockholders because the data are overly sensitive to random and short-term influences. On the other hand, the SEC believes that the quarterly information is necessary to keep stockholders adequately informed about emerging trends in corporate affairs. From the investors' viewpoint, the data are undoubtedly useful, so long as they are appropriately reported. Moreover, the likelihood is that many companies will begin to include the same information in their reports to shareholders.

Disclosure for uncertainty. The importance of uncertainty in the evaluation process is reflected in the willingness of the SEC to discard traditional accounting practices in order to present information that will be helpful to understand reported financial statements. Indicative of this attitude is its encouragement of estimates in certain instances. For example, in November 1974 the commission amended Rule 5-02.3 of Regulation S-X, governing the accounting for financial statements, to provide that corporations state the amounts of accounts receivable expected to be collected after one year under different conditions; the commission also amended Rule 5-02.6 to provide, among other things, estimates arising from costs of long-term contracts. (See p. 260 for further discussion of disclosure relative to long-term contracts.)

About a month later, the SEC issued a statement indicating that registrants have the responsibility for specifically disclosing in their financial statements any new important uncertainties affecting their business. In these circumstances, the commission points out, "It is not sufficient to assume that the numbers shown in conventional fashion on the face of the financial statements will adequately inform investors. . . . In such cases, registrants must consider the need for substantial and specific disclosure of such uncertainties, and, in extreme cases, the need for deviation from the conventional reporting model."[9]

Illustrative of "substantial uncertainties" where the outcome could importantly affect a company's success or failure is a major aircraft project. In this case accounting for the present would require an estimate of the total number of units to be sold over the life of the project and the length of time that would be required to complete the sale. Disclosure of the sensitivity of results could be done in various ways, such as modifying appropriate captions in the face of the statement; providing substantial footnotes to illustrate results under alternative assumptions; or revising the basic format of the conventional financial statement to reveal a range of outcomes.

Proxies. The Exchange Act and its amendments authorize the SEC to prescribe rules governing the solicitation of proxies by listed and major over-the-counter companies. Among other things, information must be provided about the persons on whose behalf the proxies are being solicited. If a question of control is involved, the names and interests of all parties to the contest must be disclosed. In specified instances financial statements are required, and if the proxy pertains to a meeting at which directors are to be elected, the shareholders must be provided with an annual report containing appropriate financial statements.

Insider trading. The Exchange Act imposes various checks to prevent corporate officials from using insider information to their own advantage. The commission's famous Rule 10b-5, adopted under the Exchange Act, limits the ability of insiders to act on the basis of the information at their disposal. Also of interest to investors is the provision of Section 16 that each officer, director, and beneficial owner of more than 10 percent of any class of stock of a listed or large over-the-counter corporation must file with the SEC and the exchange an initial statement of his holdings and must thereafter make monthly reports of changes in these holdings. However, this information has not proved very useful as an indicator of insiders' investment policies, because of the delay in making it available to the public. By the time an outsider learns of a shift in an insider's holdings, the insider may have effected a reverse transaction. The information has proved helpful in legal actions because it permits an outsider to compare the public statements of corporate officials concerning a company's outlook with their actual transactions in its shares.

Analysts can often anticipate the results of developments affecting a corporation; therefore, the eventual reporting of this information may not have a serious effect on the price of the stock. It is difficult, however, to know what insiders are doing before the formal release of this information. Accordingly, the reporting of insider transactions may aggravate the pressure on the price of a stock exerted by the actual selling. For example, besides the slowing of Avon Products' growth rate in mid-1973, another factor that adversely affected the price of the stock was the release of SEC insider reports showing substantial selling by officers and directors. These reports demonstrated that in the first eight months of 1973, the Avon insiders had sold $10 million of the company's stock on the open market.[10]

Investment companies. The Investment Company Act of 1940 requires, among other things, investment companies to register with the commission and to disclose information on financial conditions and investment policies. Thereafter, the companies report annually on Form N-1R, including the diversification of assets, underwriting commitments, asset coverage of senior securities, portfolio turnover rates, and information regarding directors and officers. In Part II of the form, nonpublic classification may be requested on such matters as transactions with affiliated persons.

Listing Applications

Every corporation desiring to list securities in the New York Stock Exchange must file a listing application. The information given in this application enables the exchange to gauge the suitability of a security for public trading and helps investors to evaluate the issue. If the security is already listed and the application is required to establish the distribution of an additional amount or to cover a change in its terms, an abbreviated form may be used.

Listing applications follow a uniform outline, although the data included may vary among industries and companies. Much of this material, covering a company's background, properties, capitalization, and financial record, appears in the published financial manuals. Some of the information, however, is less common, such as that dealing with the company's business and financial policies. The company pays for printing 450 copies, which the exchange distributes on request.

Trade Publications

Various publications specialize in reporting and analyzing news developments of particular industries. Some of these journals are technical; others contain information of interest to investors. These useful periodicals help the investor to keep abreast of the economic and technological progress of an industry, to learn about the new products and activities of individual companies, and to obtain economic data concerning the industry as a whole. Trade publications are indispensable for industry studies. Some of this material may be obtained from libraries, stockbrokers, and business organizations.[11]

Financial Services

The most convenient sources of information on individual corporations are the publications of the financial services. There are two principal services: Moody's Investors Service, controlled by Dun & Bradstreet, and the Standard & Poor's Corp., controlled by McGraw-Hill. These firms provide an abundance of information concerning specific issues, individual corporations, and major U.S. industries. Starting with its 1975 basic manuals, Moody's inaugurated a fee for companies that desire "expanded coverage." The information for companies that do not accept this plan is kept to a bare minimum. In the latter part of 1975, Standard & Poor's also asked companies to pay an annual fee for inclusion in their records. The publications of the services are of various types.

Basic corporation records. These annual volumes present the historical background, principal developments, and financial records of the major corporations with securities outstanding. The basic manuals are augmented by current supplements. These media are the most extensively used source of financial information about a corporation and its securities.[12]

Records of dividends, called securities, and new issues. Separate volumes are generally provided for this purpose; the material is kept up-to-date by means of loose-leaf supplements. Investors and analysts use this information to obtain such data as latest dividend payments, payable dates, ex-dividend dates, and redemption dates and serial numbers of called securities.

Stock and bond reports. Succinct descriptions of the background and current position of leading corporations with publicly outstanding securities are summarized in card form. This information is revised periodically and filed in separate loose-leaf binders for listed stocks, unlisted stocks, and active bonds. An opinion is included on the corporation's prospects and the investment or speculative merits of its securities. Figures 7-2 and 7-2a show a typical report for the Carnation Co., prepared by Standard & Poor's. To illustrate how current the reports are kept, this one, dated August 7, 1975, shows under the heading "Recent Developments" sales for the first quarter of 1975. The appraisal of the stock and the summary information provided are useful primarily to suggest issues that warrant further investigation. The investor eventually may find that his conclusions differ from those of the service.

Stock and bond summaries. These are pocket-sized, soft-cover booklets, issued at least monthly. The stock summaries provide the names, prices, earnings, income return, capitalization, financial status, and ratings of securities. The information covers all stocks listed or traded on the New York Stock Exchange and the American Stock Exchange, as well as important local stocks traded in other major exchanges and in the over-the-counter markets. The bond summaries give similar information for a number of listed and unlisted bonds.

Typical pages from Standard & Poor's guides are shown in Figures 7-3, 7-3a, and 7-4. These summary booklets are very useful in making quick comparisons. For example, one might wonder why, based on the data shown, Eli Lilly common stock on April 1975 sold at a p/e ratio of 27, compared to a p/e ratio of 9 for Liggett & Myers stock. Or one might question the 8.05 percent yield to maturity in September 1973 of the A-rated Alabama Gas 7¼s/94, compared with the 8.65 percent yield of the Addressograph-Multigraph 9⅜s/95, also rated A at that time. This latter comparison is of particular interest because the discrepancy was actually observed in the October 1973 booklet. Either the Addressograph-Multigraph issue was relatively undervalued or the company's prospects suggested a lowering of the rating. In fact, the latter situation materialized. As a result of Addressograph-Multigraph's deteriorating financial condition, Standard & Poor's lowered its rating to BBB in May 1974 and to BB in April 1975. Consequently, the 60-basis-point spread in 1973 between the two bonds widened to 323 basis points by May 1975.

Industry surveys. In these studies, major U.S. industries of the country are analyzed, pertinent statistics are presented, and brief comments are made on the leading corporations. The information is kept current through periodic revision, and the separate reports are bound in loose-leaf volumes.

Miscellaneous publications. The financial services also issue economic and business statistics, records of per share earnings, earnings forecasts, weekly stock and bond letters, a register of directors and executives, daily flash reports, a review of fixed-income securities, a transportation service, and regular surveys on investment policy. Individual assistance is usually rendered on a fee basis. Each service does not necessarily cover all these phases, and one may emphasize a particular field more strongly than another.

Computer tapes. The most important innovation in financial research in recent years has been the introduction of computer tapes that provide data banks as well as analytic results. The Compustat tapes, introduced by Standard & Poor's, contain detailed balance-sheet and income statement

FIGURE 7-2

Standard & Poor's Report

CMK

Carnation Co.

7454

Stock—	Price Aug. 1'75	[2]P-E Ratio	Dividend	Yield
COMMON	74	17	[1]$1.20	1.6%

APPRAISAL: This major producer and marketer of dairy-based products has expanded its product line through internal development and acquisitions. Earnings have been in an unbroken uptrend since 1953. A flow of new products and upgrading and expansion of production facilities suggest a continuation of the growth pattern.

THE COMPANY'S POSITION

Carnation produces a wide variety of dairy and dairy-based products, tomato and tomato-based products, other packaged convenience foods, similar lines for the food service industry, pet foods, animal feeds, and miscellaneous items. The company also maintains extensive facilities abroad; net income from these operations contributed 23% of the 1974 total.

Dairy and dairy-based products accounted for 44% of 1974 sales. The company is the leading factor in the evaporated milk market and, though industry sales have declined in recent years, Carnation expanded its share of the market. Other products include Carnation Instant Nonfat Dry Milk, Instant Breakfast, Slender (a diet product), Carnation Hot Cocoa Mix, fresh milk, ice cream, cottage cheese, yogurt, and cream. Carnation also operates 20 ice cream restaurants.

Other food and grocery products (38%) consist of Contadina tomatoes, tomato paste and other tomato-based lines, Coffee-Mate (a non-dairy creamer), pet foods marketed under the Friskies, Mighty Dog and Buffet labels, Spreadables sandwich spread, and canned fruits, canned meat-based prepared foods, cereals, and prepared potato products.

The company also makes a variety of miscellaneous products (18%), which include tinplate and aluminum cans for internal use and sale to others; eggs and turkeys; and animal feed products, including poultry, dairy and beef cattle, horse, calf and specialty feeds.

Through Herff Jones, the company makes class rings, yearbooks, graduation stationery, caps and gowns, and scholastic aids. Carnation also has interests in animal genetics through Genetics, Inc., and in the tooling industry through Dayton Reliable Tool & Manufacturing.

Employees: 21,700. Shareholders: 8,-045.

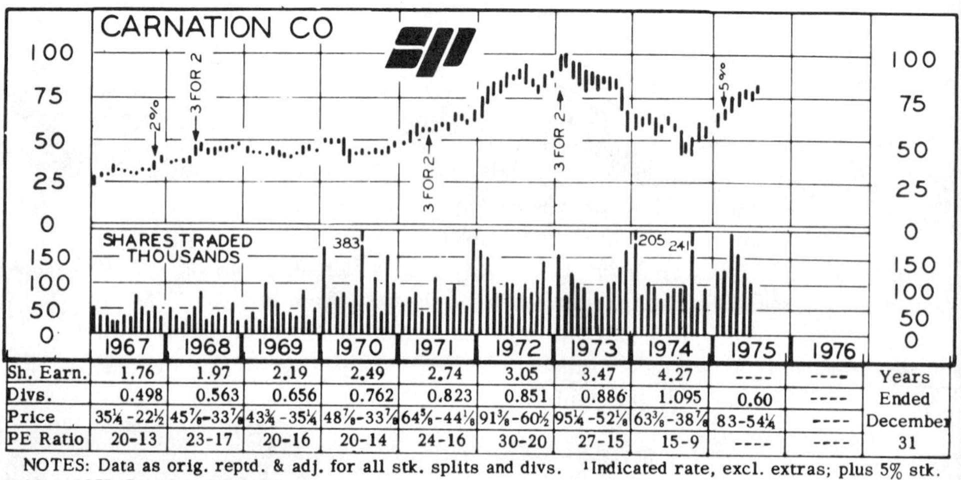

	1967	1968	1969	1970	1971	1972	1973	1974	1975	1976	
Sh. Earn.	1.76	1.97	2.19	2.49	2.74	3.05	3.47	4.27	----	----	Years
Divs.	0.498	0.563	0.656	0.762	0.823	0.851	0.886	1.095	0.60	----	Ended
Price	35¼-22½	45⅞-33⅞	43¾-35¼	48⅞-33⅞	64⅝-44⅛	91⅜-60½	95¼-52⅛	63⅜-38⅞	83-54¼	----	December
PE Ratio	20-13	23-17	20-16	20-14	24-16	30-20	27-15	15-9	----	----	31

NOTES: Data as orig. reptd. & adj. for all stk. splits and divs. [1]Indicated rate, excl. extras; plus 5% stk. in Mar. 1975. Based on latest 12 mos. earnings.

STANDARD A.S.E. STOCK REPORTS **STANDARD & POOR'S CORP.**

Published at Ephrata, Pa. Editorial & Executive Offices, 345 Hudson St., New York, N.Y. 10014

Vol. 10, No. 63 Thursday, August 7, 1975 Sec. 8

CARNATION COMPANY

EARNINGS AND BALANCE SHEET POSITION (Million $)

YEAR ENDED DEC	OPER REVS	% OPER INC OF REVS	OPER INCOME	DEPR & AMORT	NET BEFORE TAXES	NET INCOME	-COMMON SHARE DATA ($)- PRIMARY EARNGS	CASH DIVS	BOOK VALUE
1974	1886.8	10.0	188.29	27.25	160.47	79.66	4.27	1.095	24.56
1973	1472.2	10.4	152.90	22.96	130.41	64.87	3.47	0.886	22.02
1972	1249.3	10.6	131.89	20.77	109.32	55.85	3.05	0.851	19.66
1971	1148.2	10.6	121.90	18.93	100.97	50.24	2.74	0.823	17.47
1970	1053.4	10.5	110.36	17.27	92.83	45.88	2.48	0.762	15.56
1969	964.4	10.5	101.69	14.50	85.92	39.57	2.19	0.656	14.15
1968	929.9	10.1	94.07	13.29	77.80	35.54	1.97	0.564	12.66
1967	879.2	8.9	77.99	10.87	64.42	31.77	1.76	0.498	11.30
1966	812.9	8.2	66.69	9.50	56.17	28.03	1.55	0.470	10.07
1965	539.9	7.9	42.70	5.96	35.78	20.48	1.17	0.415	8.81

DEC	GROSS PROP	CAPITAL EXPEND	CASH ITEMS	RECEIV-ABLES	INVEN-TORIES	--CURRENT--- ASSETS	LIABS	NET WORKG CAP	CUR RATIO ASSETS TO LIABS	LONG TERM DEBT	RET ON COMMON EQUITY
1974	425.3	60.6(1)	96.7	188.7	383.5	677.6	276.3	401.3	2.5-1	163.1	18.3%
1973	378.9	30.5	114.0	150.6	242.2	515.2	187.9	327.3	2.7-1	115.2	16.8%
1972	343.2	24.9	120.8	115.6	184.7	426.0	152.4	273.6	2.8-1	91.4	16.4%
1971	322.5	36.3	91.6	98.2	173.5	367.2	129.6	237.6	2.8-1	96.7	16.6%
1970	306.5	34.2	67.1	89.0	158.5	319.9	130.7	189.2	2.4-1	74.6	17.0%

NOTE(S): DATA AS ORIG. REPTD. AND ADJ. FOR STK. SPLITS AND DIVS. EX PRIOR TO 04/10/75.
1)NET OF CUR. YR. RETIREMENT.

RECENT DEVELOPMENTS

Sales for 1974 rose 28.2% from those of 1973. The gain reflected the inclusion of purchased acquisitions during the year, growth in volume of certain established products, particularly canned tomatoes and Mighty Dog dog foods, price increases, and to some extent foreign currency translations. Margins, however, came under some pressure from higher costs of agricultural products, other ingredients and packaging, and from the inflationary impact on other production costs. Operating income advanced 23.1%. An increase in other income was offset by a rise in non-operating charges (a 45% boost in interest expense was attributable to debt sold in May, 1974, and increased borrowings by the international operation), and pretax income rose 23.2%. After taxes at 50.3%, against 50.1%, net income advanced 22.8%.

Largely reflecting higher prices, sales for the 1975 first quarter were up 13.5%, year to year. Margins widened and operating income rose 18.0%. Pretax income increased 13.5%. After taxes at 48.7%, against 49.4%, and minority interest, net income advanced 16.5%.

DIVIDEND DATA

Payments in the past 12 months were:

Amt. of Divd. $	Date Decl.	Ex-Divd. Date	Payment Date
0.27.......	Aug. 16	Aug. 22	Sep. 16'74
0.27.......	Nov. 22	Nov. 27	Dec. 16'74
0.10 Ext.	Nov. 22	Nov. 27	Dec. 16'74
5% Stk. ..	Nov. 22	Feb. 25	Mar.24'75
0.30.......	Feb. 21	Feb. 25	Mar.15'75
0.30.......	May 14	May 23	Jun. 16'75

CAPITALIZATION

LONG TERM DEBT: $163,146,666, incl. $25 million of 4% sub. debs., due 1988, conv. into com. at $104.05 a sh.

MINORITY INTEREST: $3,115,704.

COMMON STOCK: 18,603,776 shs. ($2 par); some 50% controlled by the Stuart family.

SALES (Million $)

Quarter:	1975	1974	[2]1973	1972
Mar........	508.1	447.7	353.5	306.1
Jun.........		445.7	335.9	292.6
Sep.........		491.6	375.3	324.6
Dec.		501.8	407.5	326.0

[1]COMMON SHARE EARNINGS ($)

Quarter:	1975	1974	[2]1973	1972
Mar........	1.11	0.95	0.83	0.73
Jun.........		0.99	0.82	0.62
Sep.........		1.10	0.86	0.83
Dec.		1.23	0.96	0.87

[1]Adj. for 3-for-1 split in 1972, and 5% stk. in 1975. [2]Incl. Herff Jones.

INCORPORATED in Del. in 1920. OFFICE—5045 Wilshire Blvd., Los Angeles, Calif. 90036. TEL—213-931-1911. CHRMN & CHIEF EXEC—H. E. Olson. PRES—D. L. Stuart. SECY—G. E. Sperling Jr. VP-TREAS—C. G. Todd. DIRS—H. C. Arnest, N. Barker Jr., T. F. Crull, A. H. Gordon, R. D. Kummel, F. G. Larkin Jr., H. L. Lucas Jr., W. D. Mertz, G. R. Mitchell, D. A. Moore, C. A. Nelson, H. E. Olson, D. L. Stuart, R. F. Stuart, C. G. Todd. TRANSFER AGENT & REGISTRAR—Company's office.

SOURCE: Standard & Poor's Corporation, *A.S.E. Stock Reports* 10 (August 7, 1975). The material provided in the report was up to date at the time of its publication; later reports reflected subsequent developments. Reprinted by permission of Standard & Poor's Corporation.

FIGURE 7-3

Standard & Poor's Stock Guide

STANDARD & POOR'S CORPORATION

INDEX	Ticker Symbol	STOCKS NAME OF ISSUE (Call Price of Pfd. Stocks)	Market	Earns &Div Rank-ing	Par Val.	Inst. Hold Cos	Inst. Hold Shs. (000)	PRINCIPAL BUSINESS	PRICE RANGE 1960-73 High	1960-73 Low	1974 High	1974 Low	1975 High	1975 Low	Apr. Sales in 100s	April, 1975 Last Sale Or Bid High	Low	Last	% Div. Yield	P-E Ratio
1	LNX	Lenox, Inc.	NYS	A—	1¼	13	327	Fine china,jewelry,candles	45⅝	3¼	27⅝	10	21	11¾	2453	21	16	19	3.8	10
2	LSLV	Leonard Silver Int'l	OTC	NR	1¢	...	...	Mfr & dstr giftware	18⅝	5	6	2¾	4½	3¾	77	4½	3¾	4¼ B	...	4
3	LES	Leslie Fay	ASE	B+	1	4	197	Women's dresses, sportswear	19⅜	1¾	6⅛	3⅛	5⅛	3⅜	322	4¾	4	4⅜	s7.3	4
4	LE	Leslie Salt	PS	B	10	...	...	Salts, spices: sp food prods	150	21	40¼	19½	40	36	5	40	38	38	3.2	7
5	LFB	Leverage Fd Boston Cap	NYS,PB	...	1	2	18	Diversified closed-end,Cap:	15	6⅝	8¾	3½	6⅞	4⅛	250	6⅞	6	6⅝	...	..
6	Pr	$0.75 cm Inc Shrs (13.725 in '82)	NYS	...	1	8	119	cap gains: Inc: inv income	15	9⅞	13½	9⅞	12½	11	121	12⅛	11¼	12	†9.4	..
7	LVI	Levi Strauss & Co	NYS,MW,PS	NR	1	6	551	Apparel: jeans, slacks, shorts	63⅜	12½	22⅜	12⅛	27½	13	2254	27½	23½	27¼	1.8	8
8	LSHP	Levingston Shipbldg	OTC	B	2	1	52	Builds offshore drilling rigs	24	1⅛	15⅞	7½	18	14¾	317	16⅝	15¾	16⅝ B	†2.7	3
9	LEV	Levitz Furniture	NYS,Bo,MW,PB,PS	B	10¢	11	125	Retail home furn. chain	60½	1¼	5½	1½	4⅝	1¾	6344	4⅜	3¼	3⅞	...	17
10	LEW	Lewis Business Forms	ASE	B+	1	...	...	Form & data processing cards	14⅞	2⅜	8	3⅞	8	5¼	203	8	7¼	8	†3.6	4
11	LEXC	Lexitron Corp	OTC	NR	20¢	1	30	Videotype electr typewriter	15⅜	6	11¾	2½	5¾	3	371	5½	4½	5B	...	d
12	LFE	LFE Corp	NYS,Bo,PB	B—	1	3	114	Traffic controls: hydraulic eq	70½	3	4⅞	2	4½	2¼	401	4½	3¾	4¼	...	7
13	Pr	$0.50 cm Cv A Pfd (10)vtg	NYS	B	No	...	...	pumps,electro-mech devices	9⅞	5	5½	4	5½	4⅛	9	5⅜	5	5B	10.0	..
14	LOF	Libbey-Owens-Ford	NYS,Bo,De,MW,PB	B+	5	47	467	Auto glass for GM: bldg glass	70½	23¾	32⅜	12½	22¼	13⅞	3126	19⅜	15½	16¼	4.9	9
15	Pr	$4.75 cm Cv A Pfd ([54]103¾)vtg	NYS	A	No	19	55	hose fluid-carrying applic	107¾	58⅜	67¾	46	55½	48½	75	54⅛	51½	52¾ B	9.0	..
16	LJ	Libby,McNeill/Libby	NYS,Bo,MW,PB,PS	B—	1	2	20	Large diversified food packer	19⅛	4⅛	6¾	3⅜	5⅞	3¾	430	5½	4⅝	5	...	5
17	LIBRF	Liberian Iron Ore Ltd	OTC,TS	NR	No	...	...	Hldg co: jt w/Liberian gvt	21	8½	11⅝	9⅜	13½	9¾	91	13½	10	13½ B	11.9	3
18	LC	Liberty Corp	NYS	...	2	10	454	Insurance hldg: TV: R.E.	28¼	7	15⅝	7⅛	11½	7⅛	272	10¼	9⅝	9⅞	4.1	5
19	LBY	Liberty Fabrics Of N Y	ASE	B—	1	...	...	Knitted lace: nettings	28⅜	1⅛	3¼	1¼	4⅜	1¾	84	3¾	2¾	2⅞	...	3
20	LIBH	Liberty Homes	OTC	B—	1	...	...	Mfr of mobile homes	25¾	⅞	2½	¾	2⅞	⅞	556	2⅞	1⅞	2B	...	..
21	LLC	Liberty Loan	NYS	C	1	6	134	Personal loan bus: fin instal-	41⅝	7	15⅜	1⅜	5¼	1¾	283	3½	3	3	...	d
22	Pr	$1.25 cm Cv Pref (25)1/5vote	NYS	NR	25	9	84.4	ment sales: insur subsids	26⅛	12	16	3½	6½	4	30	6¼	5¾	5¾	...	..
23	LIBN	Liberty Nat'l Corp	OTC	...	10	10	95	Bank hldg: Oklahoma City	42¾	18⅞	38	24	30½	24⅜	13	30½	24⅜	29B	5.5	6
24	LNAT	Liberty Natl Life Ins	OTC	...	2	34	1563	Ordinary & industrial life	37⅜	11⅛	38⅛	17¾	30¾	24⅜	3895	27	24⅜	24¾ B	2.4	12
25	LIGA	Life Insur Co Ga	OTC	...	2½	11	148	Life,accident,health insur	42	9	18¼	11⅜	17⅞	12⅞	368	17⅞	16¾	16¾ B	4.1	6
26	LINV	Life Investors	OTC	...	1	9	388	Life,health,title insurance	31⅝	3⅞	12½	3¼	5½	3¾	2249	5¼	3¾	4½ B	1.8	5
27	LM	Liggett & Myers	NYS,Bo,Ci,De,MW,PB	A—	1	31	494	Tobacco prdts,liquor,pet	74¼	27¼	32¾	24⅛	31⅝	25⅝	980	30⅜	27¾	29¾	8.4	9
28	Pr	7% cm Pfd (NC) vtg	NYS([10])	A	100	15	24	food,cereals,watch bands	164½	89	99¾	72	88	74	6	82½	80½	80½ B	8.7	..
29	Pr A	$5.25 cm Cv Pref ([58]109)vtg	NYS	BBB	1	...	...		165	70¾	77	58½	70	60	2	69¼	67	67B	7.8	..
30	LOL	Lightolier, Inc	ASE	B	1	4	90	Light'g fixtures,port lamps	27¾	2⅝	4¾	1⅞	5⅛	2¾	80	4⅝	3¾	4½	...	4
31	LCFS	Lil'Champ Food Stores	OTC	NR	10¢	...	...	Convenience stores,Florida	12¼	5	8	4½	6⅛	4½	62	5¾	5¼	5¼ B	...	5
32	LLA	Lilli Ann	ASE,PS	B	No	...	...	Women's high-fashion apparel	23¼	3⅝	6	3½	5	3⅝	46	5	4⅜	4⅝ B	4.8	5
33	LLY	Lilly (Eli) & Co	NYS,Bo,MW	A+	62½¢	221	3839	Ethical drugs:agri chem,cosm	92½	7⅝	82¾	55¾	79¾	57½	9205	71¾	65¾	70	1.6	27
34	LIN.A	Lily Lynn Cl A	ASE	B—	1	...	...	Mfr of women's apparel	30¼	⅞	3¼	⅝	1⅞	⅞	74	1¾	1¼	1⅝	...	5
35	LIMT	Limited Stores	OTC	NR	No	...	...	Women's apparel stores	24¼	1 1/16	13¾	4¾	13¼	6	288	13¼	8¾	13¼ B	0.6	10
36	LINB	LIN Broadcasting	OTC	B	2	9	346	Radio & TV stations	32½	3¼	6¾	2	7	2⅝	1376	7	5½	6⅜ B	...	7
37	LAC	Lincoln American	ASE	...	1	4	263	Insur-life,prop-liab:constr	31⅜	1⅜	2¾	1⅛	2⅝	1¼	373	2⅝	1⅝	2⅜	...	9
38	LFBK	Lincoln First Bank	OTC	...	10	8	32	Multiple bank hldg:Roch,NY	51½	20⅛	27	14½	19⅜	15½	420	19⅜	17¼	19⅜ B	9.7	6
39	LNC	Lincoln Nat'l	NYS,MW	...	2½	96	2252	Insur hldg:life, accident	48¾	19¼	43½	19	33½	24	2729	31⅜	27⅛	29	5.5	9
40	Pr	$3.00 cm Cv A Pfd (80)vtg	NYS,MW	...	No	18	101	& health: title insurance	97½	60½	87⅜	38½	66	49	174	63	54	56	5.4	..
41	LND	Lincoln Nat'l Dir P Fd	NYS	...	1	6	13	Closed end non-div mgt inv	25⅜	17	21¾	12¾	18½	13½	187	17½	16⅛	17	†10.3	..
42	LTEL	Lincoln Tel & Tel	OTC	A—	6¼	4	91	Telep sv in Nebraska, CATV	49	15⅞	28	18⅜	23½	18½	75	23½	23	23B	7.0	7
43	LNDL	Lindal Cedar Homes	OTC	NR	1	1	1	Pre-cut cedar homes	42	1¼	3½	⅝	1⅜	¾	106	1¼	¾	1B	...	d
44	LIND	Lindberg Corp	OTC	B	2½	...	...	Heat treating of metals	7⅞	2½	6¼	4¼	9	4⅞	260	9	6⅛	8⅜ B	†7.2	4
45	LIO	Lionel Corp	NYS,Bo,De,MW,PB,PS	B—	2½	2	3	Retail toys,leisure gds:mfg	35⅞	2	3	1	2⅛	1⅛	435	1⅞	1⅝	1⅝	...	d

Uniform Footnote Explanations—See Page 1. Other: [51]®$1.11,'74. [52]□$19.33,'71. [53]△$0.09,'74. [54]To 12-31-75, scale to $100 in'79. [55]®$1.02,'74. [56]®$2.16,'74. [57]Accum on Pfd. [58]®$3.27,'74. [59]To 1-24-76, then $108,scale to $100 in'84. [60]®$0.83,'74. [61]®$3.18,'74.

COMMON AND PREFERRED STOCKS

INDEX	Some Divs. Ea. Yr. Since	DIVIDENDS: Latest Payment: Per $	Latest Payment: Date	Ex. Div.	$ So Far 1975	Total Ind. Rate	$ Paid 1974	FINANCIAL POSITION: Mil-$ Cash & Equiv.	Mil-$ Curr. Assets	Mil-$ Curr. Liabs.	Balance Sheet Date	CAPITALIZATION: Long Term Debt Mil-$	Shs. 000: Pfd.	Shs. 000: Com.	End	$ Per Shr—EARNINGS—$ Per Shr: Years 1970	1971	1972	1973	1974	Last 12 Mos.	INTERIM EARNINGS OR REMARKS: Period	$—Per Share—$ 1974	1975	INDEX
1◆	1958	Q0.18	3-28-75	3-3	0.18	0.72	0.63	4.70	63.6	20.1	12-31-74	15.2	...	3786	Dc	1.25	1.36	1.77	2.27	1.84	1.86	3 Mo Mar	0.19	0.21	1
2	.....	None Paid			....	Nil	....	0.58	12.9	8.62	12-31-74	....	...	648	Dc	0.64	0.71	0.86	1.04	[51]1.15	1.15				2
3◆	1962	5%Stk	4-30-75	3-21	s0.152	0.32	s0.297	2.75	55.6	27.5	4-30-74	15.4	...	3281	Ap	0.88	1.00	△1.09	1.36	ʃ1.09	1.08	9 Mo Jan	0.82	0.81	3
4	1974	Q0.30	5-12-75	4-22	0.45	1.20	0.15	1.87	11.8	4.77	12-31-74	9.13	...	368	Dc	△d2.14	[52]□1.83	•1.96	•4.31	ʃ•5.81	5.24	3 Mo Mar	•0.64	1.21	4
5	.....	None Paid			....	Nil	....	Net Asset Val $9.56			4-25-75	....	1992	1992	Dc	§13.75	§16.37	§18.26	§10.94	§5.40	....				5
6	1967	†0.56¾	4-30-75	4-3	†0.75½	1.13	†1.04	...	...	...		....	1992	...	Dc	0.91	0.95	0.97	1.04	1.13	....				6
7	1935	Q0.12	4-1-75	3-4	0.24	0.48	0.48	11.0	394.	195.	2-23-75	77.5	...	10880	Nv	1.92	1.86	2.30	1.09	3.20	3.33	3 Mo Feb	0.35	0.48	7
8	1974	0.10	5-1-75	4-15	0.20	0.45	†0.45	3.44	19.9	10.1	12-31-74	1.80	...	889	Je	△1.52	0.89	d2.45	0.72	4.93	5.96	6 Mo Dec△	1.35	2.38	8
9◆	.....	None Paid			....	Nil	....	6.62	112.	52.3	1-31-75	11.6	...	16955	Ja	0.29	0.57	0.72	0.51	0.23	0.23				9
10◆	1966	0.048	4-1-75	3-10	†0.144	0.29	0.162	2.46	14.1	4.94	10-31-74	2.16	...	1435	Oc	0.51	0.48	0.59	△0.80	[53]△1.91	2.01	3 Mo Jan	0.26	0.36	10
11	.....	None Since Public			....	Nil	....	1.41	11.3	1.90	12-31-74	6.05	...	2949	Dc	§d0.12	d0.65	d1.00	d0.55	d0.27	d0.27				11
12	.....	None Paid			....	Nil	....	1.53	33.8	11.4	4-26-74	16.2	166	1973	Ap	△0.50	△d0.27	□d1.27	•△0.05	•0.50	0.61	9 Mo Jan	•0.32	•0.43	12
13	1970	S 0.25	4-1-75	3-4	0.25	0.50	0.50	Conv into 0.5 shrs common				....	166	...	Ap	6.14	d2.63	d14.63	1.13	6.40	....				13
14	1933	Q0.20	6-14-75	5-12	0.60	0.80	2.20	15.5	296.	121.	12-31-74	79.7	1096	11012	Dc	1.45	3.97	4.22	5.15	2.40	1.85	3 Mo Mar	0.53	d0.02	14
15	1968	Q1.18¾	6-10-75	5-12	2.37½	4.75	4.75	Conv into 1.5 shrs common				....	1096	...	Dc	15.18	35.60	40.52	54.13	28.92	....				15
16	.....	1%Stk	9-1-67	8-8	....	Nil	....	10.2	224.	94.4	6-30-74	61.0	24	9722	Je	△d1.58	△0.04	△d0.19	△0.45	[55]•1.08	1.05	9 Mo Mar	•0.83	0.80	16
17	1965	t0.40	5-22-75	5-2	t0.80	1.60	t1.45	2.03	3.23	2.03	12-31-73	....	...	3955	Dc	1.81	□1.55	2.07	□2.17	P3.38	5.12	3 Mo Mar	0.94	2.68	17
18	1941	Q0.10	6-30-75	6-6	0.20	0.40	0.35	Equity per shr $16.60			12-31-74	42.6	282	6762	Dc	1.16	1.58	△1.92	△2.30	[56]□2.24	2.17	3 Mo Mar	□0.52	□0.45	18
19◆	.....	5%Stk	3-13-70	2-6	....	Nil	....	0.59	6.47	1.94	12-28-74	1.82	27	591	Dc	d1.59	•0.24	d1.79	0.17	•▲1.04	1.04				19
20◆	.....	None Paid			....	Nil	....	0.62	6.77	1.68	12-31-74	1.58	...	4500	Dc	0.60	0.71	0.39	d0.20	0.11	0.02	3 Mo Mar	0.01	d0.08	20
21	1935	0.10	1-1-74	12-7	....	[57]Nil	0.10	42.6	552.	312.	12-31-73	175.	951	2664	Dc	1.03	•1.01	•△1.12	d1.12	d5.90	d5.90				21
22	1968	0.312	4-1-74	3-8	....	Nil	0.62½	Conv into 0.78125 shr to 7-1-78				....	610	...	Dc	4.96	4.88	5.27	d2.70	d19.40	....	Accum $1.25 to 4-1-75			22
23◆	1935	Q0.40	4-15-75	3-26	0.80	1.60	1.60	Book Value $41.75			12-31-74	15.0	...	826	Dc	□3.50	△3.25	△3.64	□4.69	△5.10	5.27	3 Mo Mar	△1.19	△1.36	23
24◆	1933	Q0.15	5-6-75	4-23	0.30	0.60	0.47	Equity per shr $16.11			12-31-73	....	...	19938	Dc	1.24	1.53	1.66	□1.90	□2.03	2.04	3 Mo Mar	△0.34	□0.35	24
25◆	1934	Q0.17	3-12-75	2-24	0.17	0.68	0.58	Equity per shr $21.62			12-31-74	....	...	6000	Dc	k1.23	1.94	△2.25	△2.68	□2.90	2.90				25
26◆	1974	S 0.04	11-14-75	10-17	0.08	0.08	0.06	Book Value $7.48			12-31-74	17.9	101	5631	Dc	•0.47	•0.60	•0.91	•1.15	□1.00	0.88	3 Mo Mar	0.30	□0.18	26
27	1912	Q0.62½	6-2-75	5-9	1.25	2.50	2.50	7.42	388.	134.	12-31-74	119.	234	8172	Dc	□3.56	4.22	△3.49	3.39	[58]3.30	3.30	3 Mo Mar	1.02	1.02	27
28	1912	Q1.75	4-1-75	3-10	3.50	7.00	7.00	...	...	...		....	115	...	Dc	253.1	304.2	260.9	255.1	247.7	....				28
29	1969	Q1.31¼	5-1-75	4-7	2.62½	5.25	5.25	Conv into 2.3 shrs common				....	119	...	Dc	174.2	236.9	219.8	238.1	232.6	....				29
30	.....	0.07½	6-1-71	5-7	....	Nil	....	0.85	31.8	12.0	5-31-74	10.2	...	1342	My	□1.36	△d0.72	0.71	0.77	1.06	1.14	9 Mo Feb	0.74	0.82	30
31	.....	None Since Public			....	Nil	....	0.54	1.89	1.28	4-27-74	1.12	...	609	Ap	....	....	§0.84	0.51	0.88	0.96	9 Mo Jan	0.61	0.69	31
32◆	1973	A0.22	6-15-74	5-24	....	0.22	0.22	1.32	7.93	1.13	12-31-73	0.37	13	629	Dc	0.63	0.57	0.80	0.86	....	0.89	9 Mo Sep△	0.73	0.76	32
33◆	1885	Q0.27½	6-10-75	5-12	0.55	1.10	0.97	263.	850.	390.	12-31-74	5.57	...	69038	Dc	1.40	1.48	1.85	2.26	2.59	2.60	3 Mo Mar	0.84	0.85	33
34	.....	0.12½	12-31-65	12-10	....	Nil	....	0.80	15.7	8.89	11-30-74	4.54	...	1529	Nv	•0.60	□0.37	□0.52	0.67	ʃ0.33	0.34	3 Mo Mar	0.01	0.02	34
35◆	1970	0.02	3-25-75	3-12	0.02	0.08	0.02	3.84	6.84	3.78	2-1-75	★5.27	...	1334	Jl	0.11	0.20	0.35	0.72	1.15	1.36	6 Mo Jan	0.68	0.89	35
36	.....	h....	1-7-69	12-23	....	Nil	....	0.90	4.68	5.60	12-31-73	21.4	...	2297	Dc	•0.27	□0.78	•0.94	ʃ•1.07	[60]P0.95	0.96	3 Mo Mar	0.12	0.13	36
37	.....	0.07½	2-24-70	2-2	....	Nil	....	Equity per shr $6.06			2-28-74	7.76	17	5192	Fb	•△0.09	△d0.72	□0.22	•0.21	....	0.26	9 Mo Nov△	•0.11	•△0.16	37
38	1963	Q0.47	5-1-75	4-15	0.94	1.88	1.88	Book Value $39.56			12-31-74	65.3	2007	3217	Dc	□4.38	△3.67	□3.91	□3.49	[61]□3.26	3.40	3 Mo Mar	□0.79	△0.93	38
39◆	1920	Q0.40	5-1-75	4-4	0.80	1.60	1.40	Equity shr $38.07			12-31-74	2.40	1645	20531	Dc	△2.49	△3.02	△3.51	△3.90	□3.19	3.19				39
40	1965	Q0.75	6-5-75	5-9	1.50	3.00	3.00	Conv into 2 shrs common				....	1645	...	Dc	24.63	29.59	37.67	41.87	46.26	....				40
41	1973	0.14½	6-3-75	4-28	†0.88½	1.75½	1.70	Net Asset Val $18.48			3-31-75	....	...	2428	Dc	....	....	§23.10	§22.26	§17.92	....				41
42	1937	Q0.40	4-10-75	3-24	0.80	1.60	1.60	0.47	6.48	25.7	12-31-74	45.8	125	1452	Dc	△2.08	3.03	3.13	3.13	3.38	3.38				42
43	.....	None Paid			....	Nil	....	0.96	6.59	5.93	12-31-73	4.80	...	605	Dc	0.50	0.80	0.84	d0.72	Pd4.08	d4.05	3 Mo Mar	d0.97	d0.94	43
44◆	1956	Q0.12½	6-2-75	5-5	0.25	0.60	0.47½	1.49	5.48	2.99	12-31-74	3.08	...	1141	Dc	□0.27	0.25	0.65	1.42	2.05	2.21	3 Mo Mar	0.48	0.64	44
45	.....	0.20	9-30-58	9-16	....	Nil	....	2.82	39.3	24.6	12-31-74	11.0	...	5155	Dc	□0.08	•0.23	•△0.33	•0.33	0.17	d0.05	3 Mo Mar	d0.15	d0.37	45

◆ **Stock Splits & Divs By Line Reference Index** [1]2-for-1,'70:adj to 2%,'72. [3]3-for-2,'71:Adj to 5%,'75. [9]2-for-1,'71:3-for-1,'72. [10]4-for-3,'74:5-for-4,'75. [19]Adj to 5%, '70. [20]3-for-2,'71. [23]10%,'73. [24]4-for-3,'73. [25]50%,'73. [26]3-for-2,'72. [32]10%,'71,'72. [33]2-for-1,'71. [35]2-for-1,'71,'72:adj for 3%,'71. [39]2-for-1,'72. [44]2-for-1,'75.

SOURCE: Standard & Poor's Corporation, *Stock Guide* (March 1975): 128-129. Reprinted by permission.

FIGURE 7-4

Standard & Poor's Bond Guide

STANDARD & POOR'S CORPORATION

Title-Industry Code & Co. Finances (In Italics) / Exchange ↓ Individual Issue Statistics	*Ind* / Interest Dates	*Chgs. 1972* / S&P Quality Rating	Eligible ↓	*Times Earn. 1973* / Bond Form	*Times Earn. 1974* / Legality (C t, M a, N H, N J, N Y)	*Yr. End*	*Cash & Eqv* / Redemption Provisions: Refund Earliest/Other	*Current Assets (Million $)* / Call Price For S.F.	*Current Liabs (Million $)*	*Date* / Call Price Regular	*L. Term Debt (Mil $)* / Out-st'd'g (Mil $)	*Debt % Prop* / Underwriter Firm	Underwriter Year	*Interim Times Earn. Period* / Price Range 1960-73 High	1960-73 Low	*Interim Times Earn. 1974* / Price Range 1974 High	*Interim Times Earn. 1975* / 1974 Low	1975 High	1975 Low	Mo. End Price Sale(s) or Bid	Curr Yield	Yield to Mat.
Abbott Laboratories	*21a*	*5.20*		*4.34*	*3.20*	*Dc*	*N/A*	*583*	*267*	*3-75*	*208*	*74.0*		*3 Mo Mar*		*5.20*	*3.23*					
• SF Deb 6¼s '93	Jj15	AA-	X	R	- - - - -		[1]102.88	100		±103.74	21.1	G1	'68	103½	78¾	87⅝	73⅛	82⅝	80½	s81⅝	7.66	8.26
• SF Deb 7⅝s '96	Ms	AA-	X	R	- √- - -		[2]103.56	[3]100		±105.696	60.0	L4	'71	106	96	92	80	95	86½	s85	8.97	9.27
• SF Deb 9.20s '99	aO15	AA-	X	R	- √- - -		[4]104.60	[4]100		±109.20	100	G2	'74	....	....	103¼	99½	104⅜	99½	A100	9.20	9.20
Abex Corp[5]	*55*	*4.58*		*5.29*	*4.49*	*Dc*	*5.17*	*215*	*98.5*	*12-74*	*44.7*	*46.4*										
• Deb 8¾s '77	jD	A	X	R	- - - - -		....	....		[6]100	25.0	S1	'70	107½	99	104	92½	102½	96	s100¾	8.68	8.37
Acme Steel Co.	*66b*	***Now Interlake., Inc.: See***																				
SF Deb 4⅞s '77	Jd	BBB+	X	CR	- - - - -		....	100		±100½	5.22	B7	'57	102½	72	90	82	91	87½	90¼	5.40	11.19
Addressograph-Multigr	*48a*	*3.11*		*1.37*	*1.02*	*Jl*	*5.99*	*318*	*169*	*7-74*	*87.6*	*100*										
• SF Deb 9⅜s '95	Jd30	BB	Y	R	- - - √-		[7]104.675	[3]100		±107.025	60.0	S7	'70	114	99¾	106⅜	60	75	53½	72	13.02	13.44
Aerojet-General	*2*	***Now General Tire & Rubber, see***																				
SF Deb 5¼s '81	Mn	....	X	CR	- - - - -		....	100		±101⅜	[8]7.01	K2	'61	104	59	83	73	86	70	81½	6.44	9.55
[9]***Akron,Cant.&Youngs***	*54*	*1.23*		*3.91*	*....*	*Dc*	*0.61*	*2.76*	*3.21*	*12-73*	*4.85*	*27.3*		*12 Mo Dec'74*		*4.01*	*6.58*					
ConMtgeA 4s '88	aO	BB	Y	CR	- - - - -		....	100		100	0.99	Reorg	'44	88	30	46	41	47	42	46	8.70	12.47
ConMtgeB 4½s '88	aO	BB	Y	CR	- - - - -		....	100		100	1.35	Reorg	'44	89½	30	50½	45	50	46¾	49	9.18	12.52
Akzona,Inc	*68b*	*3.74*		*4.33*	*4.64*	*Dc*	*13.0*	*249*	*83.9*	*3-75*	*★177*	*42.9*										
• Deb 7½s '97	Fa15	A	X	R	- - - - -		[10]103¾	[11]100		±106⅜	60.0	M5	'72	100¼	94½	100¼	100¼	75½	75	79	9.49	9.87
Alabama Bancorporation	*10*	*1.64*		*1.36*	*1.27*	*Dc*					*56.3*			*6 Mo Jun*		*1.30*	*1.32*					
• [12]Flt'g Rate Nts [13]10½s '99	[14]mS	N/R	X	R	- - √- -		Z100	....		[4]100	30.0	F2	'74	....	....	104	100	104½	100	s100¼	10.47	....
Alabama Gas Corp	*73b*	*2.17*		*2.40*	*1.53*	*Sp*	*2.43*	*11.3*	*12.0*	*9-74*	*40.3*	*45.7*		*12 Mo Jun*		*1.80*	*2.58*					
1st E 5⅛s '84	fA	A	X	CR	√- √√√		....	±100.54		±102.07	2.49	H2	'59	106	69⅛	78⅝	66	73⅝	68⅝	69⅞	7.33	10.39
1st F 7¼s '94	Fa	A	X	R	√- √√√		....	100		107¼	9.74	W5	'69	101¾	82¾	90¼	70½	81⅛	73⅝	75⅜	9.62	10.25
1st G 8¾s '96	Jj	A	X	R	√- √√√		[6]109¾	[6]100		109¾	16.0	W5	'71	108½	100	102½	80¼	92⅜	84¼	85⅜	10.25	10.50
[15]***Alabama Power Co.***[15]	*72a*	*2.16*		*2.35*	*1.89*	*Dc*	*9.73*	*160*	*335*	*6-75*	*1050*	*46.3*		*12 Mo Jun*		*2.14*	*1.88*					
1st 3¼s '77	aO	A-	X	CR	√√√√√		....	100		100	10.0	F2	'47	89⅝	68	86	81⅞	89	85⅛	88⅛	3.69	9.69
1st 3⅜s '78	jD	A-	X	CR	√√√√√		....	±100⅝		±101⅛	10.3	H2	'48	90⅜	66⅝	82½	76⅝	83⅞	80⅛	82⅝	4.08	9.75
1st 3¼s '81	mS	A-	X	CR	√√√√√		....	±100⅝		±101⅜	15.0	M9	'51	87⅜	58⅜	73	64½	72⅛	68⅛	70½	4.61	9.89
1st 3⅜s '82	Ao	A-	X	CR	√√√√√		....	±100.90		±101.19	12.0	B7	'52	88⅜	59	72	62⅝	70⅝	66⅝	68⅝	4.92	9.99
1st 4⅛s '83	Mn	A-	X	CR	√√√√√		....	±100.85		±101¼	11.9	U2	'53	98	63⅛	74⅛	63¾	71¼	66⅝	68⅝	6.01	10.10
• 1st 3⅛s '84	Ms	A-	X	CR	√√√√√		....	±100.59		±101.24	17.0	M9	'54	81½	56⅛	63⅛	59½	62⅝	59½	60⅝	5.15	10.15
1st 3½s '85	Jd	A-	X	CR	√√√√√		....	±101.10		±101.69	15.0	B7	'55	88½	55⅛	65⅝	54¼	62⅜	57½	59⅜	5.89	10.16
1st 3½s '86	Ms	A-	X	CR	√√√√√		....	±101.38		±102.01	13.7	U2	'56	88	52¾	64⅛	52½	60¾	55¾	57½	6.09	10.18
1st 4⅝s '87	Mn	A-	X	CR	√√√√√		....	±100.88		±102.33	14.5	M9	'57	104¼	62⅜	71⅛	57⅞	66¼	60⅝	62⅜	7.41	10.22
1st 3⅞s '88	Jj	A-	X	CR	√√√√√		....	±100.26		±101.79	23.0	L4	'58	92¾	54⅜	64¼	51⅜	59¾	54⅜	56	6.92	10.23
1st 4⅞s '89	Mn	A-	X	CR	√√√√√		....	±100.26		±102.37	20.0	M9	'59	107⅞	62½	71	56½	65⅜	59½	61	7.99	10.23
1st 5s '90	Ao	A-	X	CR	√√√√√		....	±100.21		±102.57	6.96	B7	'60	105½	63¼	71¼	56⅜	65¼	59¼	60¾	8.23	10.24
1st 4½s '91	Ms	A-	X	CR	√√√√√		....	±101.15		±103.19	13.0	E1	'61	102	58¼	66	51⅝	60¼	54⅜	55⅞	8.05	10.24
1st 4⅜s '92	Jd	A-	X	CR	√√√√√		....	100		±102.35	17.0	B7	'62	100½	56	63¾	49⅜	58	52⅛	53⅜	8.20	10.26
1st 4⅜s '93	Mn	A-	X	CR	√√√√√		....	±100.07		±102.62	16.0	L4	'63	100⅜	55⅜	63	48½	57	51⅛	52½	8.33	10.24
1st 4⅝s '94	Mn	A-	X	CR	√√√√√		....	±100.95		±103.63	29.0	F2	'64	102¼	57⅛	64⅝	49⅝	58¼	52¼	53⅝	8.62	10.24
1st 4⅞s '95	mS	A-	X	CR	√√√√√		....	±100.71		±103.69	40.0	B7	'65	102¾	58⅜	66¼	50¾	59½	53⅜	54⅝	8.92	10.25
1st 6¼s '96	aO	A-	X	CR	√√√√√		....	101.18		105¼	29.4	B7	'66	106½	71¾	79⅝	61½	71½	64⅜	65¾	9.51	10.24
1st 6½s '97	aO	A-	X	CR	√√√√√		....	100		104.71	28.0	L4	'67	100	73½	82	63⅛	73⅜	66	67½	9.63	10.24

Uniform Footnote Explanations—See Page 1. Other: [1]From 1978. [2]From 1981. [3]From 1977. [4]From 1984. [5]Subsid of Illinois Cent Ind. [6]From 1976. [7]From 1980. [8]$0.8m called 8/1/75. [9]Contr by Norfolk & West'n. [10]From 1982. [11]From 1983. [12]Repayable from 9/1/76. [13]Thru8/31/75then same or 1%over Treas.Bill Rate. [14]From 3/1/76at 1%over Treas.Bill rate or by co. [15]Subsid of Southern Co.

information, as well as a broad range of other financial and marketing statistics. The service covers approximately 2,700 listed and over-the-counter industrial companies (plus certain major groups of nonindustrials) on an annual and quarterly basis, about 850 OTC industrials on an annual basis, 150 utilities on an annual and quarterly basis, and 110 banks on an annual and quarterly basis. There are also 450 Canadian industrial companies on an annual basis. For most companies, the information is available for at least ten years and 20 quarters and, in some cases, for as many as 20 years and 40 quarters. The tapes are updated weekly. Through frequent personal visits with clients, assistance is provided in the interpretation and utilization of the product.

Compustat, which is now operated by a subsidiary, Investors Management Sciences, Inc., will provide a tape that can be converted for use in any of the major computer systems now in operation; remote access is also available through time-sharing systems. Investors Management Sciences also provides other services under the designations Comparative Analysis, Financial Dynamics, Financial Data Scan, Financial Analyzer, and Financial Summary. Although there are gaps in the data for the testing of analytic techniques, the Compustat tapes are an invaluable source of information and permit analyses of specific companies.

Various industrial firms and brokerage houses offer computer services, including a number of already prepared programs. Tapes from other sources cater to macroeconomic studies. For example, the National Bureau of Economic Research provides a data bank of national income and product accounts, as well as other aggregate time series for the United States since the end of World War II. Included in these other series are data on economic indicators, banks, the labor force, federal finance, and business and manufacturing. The Federal Reserve has a tape of various FTC *Quarterly Financial Report* balance-sheet and income statement variables for 24 industry classifications. Most series start as early as 1947.

Other Services

There are a number of other services. Perhaps the best known of these is the *Value Line Investment Survey*, which, in July 1975, provided basic information on 1,630 stocks that are subject to regular review. In addition to these analyses, the survey contains data on estimated yields, appreciation potential, the ranking of industrial groups based on expected performance, and selected other topics. Some services provide general investment guidance, while others specialize in different areas, such as growth stocks, new issues, OTC securities, technical analysis, convertibles, and mutual funds. Wiesenberger Services, Inc., publishes an annual manual on investment companies, with quarterly updates called "Management Results"; a subsidiary, Vickers

Associates, Inc., publishes loose-leaf volumes showing portfolio changes of investment companies, insurance companies, and college endowments. After a federal ruling required all national banks with equity holdings of $75 million or more to make detailed disclosure of their trust portfolio transactions and holdings as of the final quarter of 1974, Vickers issued a new loose-leaf guide on bank trust portfolios, covering approximately 185 national banks.

Plant Visits

Many corporations with publicly outstanding securities have recognized the desirability of maintaining good relations with analysts and securities holders. For this reason, management not only permits but also often encourages personal tours of its plants. Further attesting to this concern about the attitude of investors is the policy, now often followed, of having top-level executives appear at annual meetings to provide firsthand accounts of company operations. In addition, management has shown a willingness to answer the inquiries of stockholders, to visit the offices of investment institutions to discuss company financial affairs, and to attend meetings of financial analysts throughout the country. Stockbrokers, investment counselors, and financial services, in turn, have become increasingly active in sending members of their staffs on plant surveys.

The entire relationship between corporate management and the general public, including securities analysts, has been clouded by two landmark cases of the 1960s. In the first, a group of Texas Gulf Sulphur officers and directors was found guilty of having violated the securities laws by failing to make prompt and adequate disclosure about minerals discovery. In the second, an administrative action against the giant Merrill Lynch securities firm, a number of its officers and salesmen, and various investment companies, the SEC claimed that the firm had transmitted inside information to the investment companies relative to the 1966 earnings of Douglas Aircraft; Merrill Lynch presumably had access to this information because it was Douglas's underwriter. Both cases concerned the alleged wrongful use of information: to buy stocks before the public disclosure of favorable news, in the case of Texas Gulf Sulphur; to have customers sell stock before the public disclosure of unfavorable news, in the case of Merrill Lynch. The two cases enabled the SEC to broaden its Rule 10b-5, which prohibits insiders from taking advantage of nonpublic information.

A 1974 decision by a U.S. district court may open a Pandora's box of new uncertainties. This case involves a civil suit against Shearson, Hammill & Co. (merged into Hayden Stone), the investment banker for Tidal Marine International Corp. The plaintiff had bought Tidal Marine stock through Shearson, Hammill, which, the plaintiff contended, knew about the firm's impending financial difficulties through the investment banking association.

In its decision, the court stated that Shearson, Hammill should have either promptly disclosed the adverse information or, if bound by judiciary ties from revealing it, should have abstained from handling orders in Tidal Marine stock. Thus, Shearson, Hammill has been charged with wrongdoing because it failed to use inside information and permitted its retail customers to buy the stock. If this decision is upheld, it could generate costly conflict-of-interest suits against securities firms that serve both as investment banker and as broker or dealer in the same securities.[13]

As a result of these developments and subsequent similar cases, corporations have become more cautious in their dealings with securities analysts. A good deal of legal maneuvering still must occur before there is any genuine clarification. The SEC has promised guidelines to help corporate officials cope with these uncertainties but is experiencing difficulty in preparing them.

Government Publications

The various departments and agencies of the U.S. government publish an enormous quantity of information on a multitude of subjects. A practical means of finding one's way through this labyrinth of data is to use the *Monthly Catalog of United States Government Publications*, issued by the superintendent of documents. Each issue contains detailed indexes, and an annual cumulative index appears in the December issue. An item may be found in the index under subject title or under the name of the government agency issuing the publication. Each item refers to an entry number (rather than a page number) in the *Monthly Catalog.*

The investor may encounter a number of major government publications in the course of his studies.[14] From the financial point of view, he may be interested in the reports issued by the U.S. Treasury Department, in the *Federal Reserve Bulletin*, published by the Board of Governors, and in the bulletins of the 12 reserve banks. He will find the extensive data prepared by the regulatory agencies indispensable to a study of the industries over which the commissions have jurisdiction. If he is thinking of buying municipal securities, he will find helpful statistics in Census Bureau publications on the finances of city and state government finances. The Department of Commerce publishes various industry reports, as well as an annual volume, *U.S. Industrial Outlook*, which provides an analysis of future trends.

The Securities and Exchange Commission merits special comment. The agency issues announcements and releases concerning its own rules, as well as reports pertaining to the operations of the securities markets and the transactions of corporate "insiders" and stock exchange members. The weekly *Statistical Bulletin* contains information on round-lot and odd-lot volumes on stock exchanges, OTC volume in selected securities, securities registrations and offerings, net changes in corporate securities outstanding, working capital of U.S. corporations, assets of noninsured pension funds, and 8-K reports. Formal opinions, available in bound form, are published on problems brought to the attention of the commission in connection with its administration of the Securities Acts. These opinions contain the conclusions of the commissioners, together with the details of each case and the theoretical justification for each decision. The opinions often include exhaustive analyses of the financial positions and prospects of the corporations involved. It is desirable to keep abreast of the SEC's thinking, since the commission's actions may significantly affect the market value of securities. Important for this purpose is the *SEC Docket*, a weekly compilation of announcements, releases, rules, and opinions. In addition, the commission issues a daily news digest and a monthly summary of insider transactions. Of interest also are the commission's annual reports and special studies.

The basic books and journals issued by various agencies of government reduce the investor's need to refer to diverse publications for data. These publications are compilations of statistics on different economic activities covering a long period of time. Of outstanding importance are the monthly *Survey of Current Business*, with weekly supplements, and the *Statistical Abstract of the United States*, published annually by the Bureau of the Census.

Of help in economic forecasting is *Business Conditions Digest*, issued monthly by the Commerce Department. The information is patterned after that developed by the National Bureau of Economic Research in its business cycle studies. Included in the *Digest* are the well-known leading, coincident, and lagging indicators of the National Bureau. Also provided is a large body of other information covering the gross national product and its components, key economic indicators such as prices and wages, diffusion indexes, and analytic ratios. The insights contained in the *Annual Economic Review* of the President's Council of Economic Advisers are useful in forecasting economic trends; the council also publishes the monthly *Economic Indicators.*

The Federal Trade Commission publishes the *Quarterly Financial Report for Manufacturing, Mining and Trade Corporations.* This report contains income statements and balance sheets for all manufacturing corporations, classified by industry as well as asset size. The information provides a useful benchmark against which to compare individual companies in the same industry or of comparable size. Starting with the fourth quarter of 1974, the commission began to publish aggregate financial data for corporations in mining, retail trade, and wholesale trade.

Business and Financial Publications

Various publications concentrate on business and financial information. These include newspapers, financial periodicals, business periodicals, scholarly journals, and bulletins issued by large commercial banks. Many of these documents are indexed in the *Business Periodicals Index*, the *Public Affairs Information Service*, and *The F & S Index of Corporations and Industries.* For information on a particular business subject, the investor should find the appropriate topic heading in these indexes.[15]

The important weekly (or semiweekly) publications that concentrate on financial developments are the *Commercial and Financial Chronicle* (includes a Monday statistical issue and a Thursday issue containing articles and the texts or summaries of speeches and reports on financial subjects), the *Money Manager*, *Investment Dealer's Digest*, *Barron's National Business and Financial Weekly*, *Wall Street Transcript*, and *M/G Financial Weekly*. Others issued less often include *Forbes* (semimonthly, plus an annual report on American industry), *Finance* (monthly), *Euromoney* (monthly), *Institutional Investor* (monthly), *Journal of Portfolio Management* (quarterly), *Bankers Magazine* (quarterly), and *Options Letter* (biweekly).

The Financial Analysts Federation publishes the *Financial Analysts Journal*, a professional journal for securities analysts. In the academic area, the American Finance Association issues the *Journal of Finance*, and the Financial Management Association issues *Financial Management*. The *Journal of Financial and Quantitative Analysis* has a strong mathematical orientation.

Publications that are more concerned with general business are *Business Week, Dun's Review, Fortune, Nation's Business,* the Conference Board's *Record*, and, for foreign news, the *Economist* and *Business International.* Many banks also produce reports that cover both business and financial conditions. The reports of the First National City Bank of New York, the Morgan Guaranty Trust Company, and the Chase Manhattan Bank are frequently cited. A well-known journal issued under academic auspices is the *Harvard Business Review*, while the *Columbia Journal of World Business* concentrates on the international area.

Economic Research Organizations

Several research institutions devote their efforts to the study of economic problems. These organizations are financed through private donations and the sale of their publications. The following is a list of some of the important examples.

Brookings Institution. Brookings sponsors investigations in the field of economics and national and international affairs. Its studies are published as pamphlets and books which are timely and of interest to the investor. It also publishes a journal, *Economic Activity*.

Committee for Economic Development. The committee, formed in 1942 by a group of businessmen, sponsors research studies on important problems affecting government, business, and labor. Its reports are well balanced and readable.

National Bureau of Economic Research. The bureau is the most important of the private organizations devoted to economic research. Its contributions concerning business cycles, capital formation, and national income are outstanding. Many of the studies are presented in a technical fashion and are not suitable for the average investor.

The Conference Board. The board's various publications, ranging from weekly to annual and including special reports, are addressed primarily to the businessman. They include elaborate studies of special problems, as well as brief comments on current affairs.

Twentieth Century Fund. The fund, founded in 1919 by the late Edward A. Filene, originally disbursed grants to outside organizations. Since 1938 it has conducted its own studies in the fields of economic research and public education. The board has made several excellent comprehensive surveys of the securities markets.

National Planning Association. This is an independent, private, nonprofit organization that conducts research and formulates policy in the public interest. The association, founded in the early 1930s to bring together the activities of diverse social groups, issues a number of reports and studies designed to help policymakers and planners in the government and private sector.

Brokers' Reports

The investor will be interested in the recurring and special reports issued by the statistical staffs of commission brokers. The value of such reports may be modified by the need to publish studies frequently, the pressure for decisions on subjects not readily analyzable, and the fact that it is difficult for a commission broker to adopt an extreme market position. Thus, although the reports contain statistics and recommendations of interest to the investor their quality varies considerably. Accordingly, the investor should evaluate the information carefully and make independent checks before taking any direct action.

A variety of reports are offered by different firms. Included are market letters, news wires, research publications containing in-depth data on industries and companies, regularly issued magazines, and basic data on individual securities. Also available are investment seminars, special meetings, computerized evaluations of portfolios, and measurement services for portfolios. During the era of fixed commissions, much of this material was offered free. Now, however, the general practice is to impose charges that vary with the reports or services received. It is also common for firms to distinguish between reports that will be generally furnished and those given primarily to institutions for commission business. Two services of the latter type are *Quality of Earnings Report*, now issued by Wiesenberger, which provides a continuing assessment of corporate financial accounting, and *Datagraphs*, a "relative strength service" published by William P. O'Neil, which provides weekly comparisons of different types of market movements.

Business Charts

A simple and effective way of observing the development of current trends in business and financial data is through the *Federal Reserve Monthly Chart Book on Financial and Business Statistics.* These charts are the most important graphs prepared by the statistical division of the Board of Governors for use by the Federal Reserve Board. Also available are historical supplements to the basic charts, showing fluctuations of the constituent series for previous years. The investor will find the *Federal Reserve Monthly Chart Book* helpful in maintaining perspective on changing economic conditions.

Other government agencies issue chart series that sometimes stress special activities. The Bureau of the Budget prepares charts relating to the president's annual budget message. In May 1948 the Council of Economic Advisers inaugurated *Economic Indicators*, a monthly publication that contains basic charts and tables covering the nation's economic status.[16] In addition, private organizations publish chart books; for example, the Conference Board publishes *Road Maps of Industry.*

Reports on Securities Developments

Various services issue reports covering issues and developments affecting the securities business. These include the *Securities Regulation and Law Report*, published weekly by Bureau of National Affairs; the *Review of Securities Regulation*, published monthly by Standard & Poor's; and the *Securities Regulation and Transfer Report*, published monthly by Management Reports, Inc., a research affiliate of the *Banking Law Journal.* Designed primarily for attorneys, these reports stress SEC regulations and court cases. They also cover financial and accounting matters, however, and are useful as guides to the changing regulatory climate. Similarly, the *Securities Regulation Law Journal*, issued quarterly by Warren, Gorham & Lamont, Inc., is intended primarily for lawyers, but contains useful information on the securities markets in general.

Obsolete Securities

Investors sometimes find themselves in possession of securities representing corporations whose records are not contained in the standard statistical services. The status of these companies should always be investigated. They may have been dissolved or reorganized, or their charters may have been forfeited. In such cases, it is useful for tax purposes to know that the issue has no value. The investor may even discover that a security formerly believed worthless actually has some salvage value or may be exchanged for the issues of a going concern.

The status of obsolete and little-known securities may be checked in the Robert D. Fisher *Manual of Valuable and Worthless Securities.* The manual contains information on many corporations that is not readily found in other sources. In addition, the publisher of the manual, R. M. Smythe & Company, maintains a service that provides subscribers with data on issues of doubtful value.

NEWS AND THE SECURITIES MARKETS

The flow of economic and political information influences the value of securities. Likewise, information on securities affects economic and political conditions. Without the means of disseminating news–wire services, radios, private telephone and teletype systems, and every other modern means of communication–the national securities market would shrivel into a series of small local institutions.

The sensitivity of securities prices to news events generates tremendous competition to obtain information as rapidly as possible. For this reason, most large investment houses maintain private news wires. Analysts and securities advisers constantly use their personal contacts with business and government officials to try to anticipate the reported information.

Instantaneous Information

Two kinds of information are instantaneously available. However, as shall be seen shortly, the word "instantaneous" can have two interpretations. Instantaneous news comes over a ticker, through which news items are flashed to all outlets. Through the ticker service, known as the "broad tape," information on dividends and other important corporate activities is first disseminated to the investing public. The two U.S. ticker systems are owned by Dow Jones & Co. and Reuters Economic Services.

The volume of trading in common stock may change drastically from one year to another, but it is generally estimated that present volume is in excess of 8 billion shares annually. Of this total, some 4 billion shares represent issues listed on the New York Stock Exchange and traded on that exchange; 1 billion are NYSE issues traded through regional exchanges or over-the-counter; and another 1 billion shares represent trading in issues listed on the American Stock Exchange and traded almost exclusively at that exchange. The remaining 2 billion shares represent trading in OTC stocks through the National Association of Securities Dealers Automated Quotation (NASDAQ) system, which displays quotations on a real-time basis on cathode ray tubes in subscribers' offices.[17]

Transactions in stocks traded on the two major exchanges appear promptly on the stock ticker, but NASDAQ at present is only a quotation system and does not report any transactions. The NASDAQ system, however, transmits daily statistical data on its securities to the wire services, which edit the material, based on criteria established by the NASD, for national NASDAQ OTC stock tables. This information, including representative bid and asked prices as well as volume data, appears in the nation's major newspapers.

The composite tape is a key element of the central market concept. Common and preferred stocks, warrants, and rights that meet NYSE or AMEX listing requirements are eligible for inclusion, whether they are registered or admitted to unlisted trading. Last sale prices are made available by means of a high-speed line, even if the tape is running late. A distinctive symbol is provided for transactions by broker-dealers who are not members of any exchange. The tape operates as long as any national securities exchange is open for business. There are two tapes: one contains price and volume data on NYSE stocks wherever traded, with the site identified; the other contains similar information on other stocks.

There is, however, another form of instantaneous information, combining the ticker's rapid transmission of news and financial information with an information retrieval capability. The development of the electronics industry has made it possible to place on the desks of brokers and dealers compact machines which put considerable material at the operator's disposal. By registering the symbol of the security in question and by depressing the appropriate buttons, a broker can obtain a considerable amount of information, such as the listing exchange; tick (direction of price movement); last, bid, asked, and opening prices; high and low price for the day and year; the previous trading session's closing price; latest yearly dividend rate; time since last sale; yield; earnings per share and p/e ratio; and exchange of last execution. In addition to providing these basic statistics, the system has been ingeniously designed to furnish special information to meet the user's needs. For example, a news service is offered; a display of the major market indexes is available; a quotation-type service shows simultaneously the 15 largest percentage advances and declines for the national marketplace; sequential trades are provided to indicate trends; block trades of any size specified may be continuously observed; the user may be alerted to indicated events when they occur; and interoffice information may be broadcast. Another service provides real-time data on a great number of different money-market instruments.

Much of this information is already stored in computers, and the information is instantaneous only in the sense that it is instantly retrieved. But since the memory bank of the computer is fed new data as changes occur, information on bid and asked prices, recent trading prices, and volume of trading may also be instantaneous in the same sense that ticker information is.

Newspapers

Despite this pressure for learning about events as soon as possible, the most consistent and comprehensive source of facts remains the newspaper. Advance information may permit traders to take advantage of flurries in prices and may sometimes help individuals to forecast market changes. Nevertheless, the factors affecting securities prices are usually more profound and persistent. Such basic information is best reported in the daily papers and ordinarily receives prompt analysis by editorial and feature writers.

There are two newspapers published weekly that are of special interest to those concerned with the securities markets. The *Wall Street Transcript* is one that is clearly intended for the professional analyst. It reproduces, among other things, the texts of material the editors consider important, such as talks by management representatives at securities analysts' societies, analyses by leading brokerage houses, and addresses by company officials at annual meetings. Media General Financial Services, Inc. (Richmond, Virginia), publishes the *M/G Financial Weekly*, which contains articles but more importantly, provides an elaborate compendium of statistics and charts on a large number of stocks. Media General also publishes the monthly *Industriscope*, showing financial data and ratios for a large number of stocks by industry groups and subgroups. A sample page is shown in Figure 7-5.

Reading the daily newspaper. In order to keep abreast of developments throughout the world that may affect his securities interests, the investor must read carefully a daily paper large enough to include adequate coverage of news events. Even though this paper may have a good financial section, he should read another daily paper that concentrates on financial news, such as the *Wall Street Journal.* By this means he will be able to follow developments both of general interest and of a more special nature, such as corporate earnings, dividend announcements, and annual meetings.

Newspaper reading habits are the product of personal taste and convenience. Whatever approach the investor uses, his chief aim is to foster an analytic attitude that enables him to relate the implications of a news story to economic developments and even to particular corporations.

011 – 023 Company and Market		Market Value: Price Per Share	Market Value: Shares Outstanding	Market Value: Market Value	Month's Trading: Dollar Volume	Month's Trading: Pct of Market Value	Last Annual Revenue	Last Annual Earnings	EPS: Last 12 Mos	EPS Fiscal Year: Last	EPS Fiscal Year: 1 Year Ago	EPS Fiscal Year: 2 Years Ago	EPS Fiscal Year: 3 Years Ago	EPS Fiscal Year: 4 Years Ago	EPS Latest Report: Last Year	EPS Latest Report: This Year	EPS Latest Report: Pct Change	5-Year Growth Rate	Price Chg: Last 52 Weeks	Price Chg: This Year	Price Chg: Last Month	P/E Ratio: At Last Close	P/E Ratio: 52 Weeks Ago	P/E Ratio: 5-Year Avg High	P/E Ratio: 5-Year Avg Low	Ratio of Price to Equity	Ratio of Price to Revenue	Ratio of Debt to Equity	Profit Margin	Return on Stock Equity	Dvd Yield	Beta Co-efficient: Up Mkts	Beta Co-efficient: Down Mkts	Liquidity Ratio
	-	$	000	$Mil	$Mil	%	$Mil	$Mil	$	$	$	$	$	$	$	$	%	%	%	%	%	-	-	-	-	-	-	-	%	%	%	-	-	$000
01 Aerospace																																		
011 Aerospace Industries																																		
Boeing Co	N	19⅛	21,689	414.8	11.7	2.83	2,409.0	30.4	2.07	1.40	1.04	1.02	.47	3.84	1.06	1.73	63n	0	-12	-24	-1	9.2	17.4	45.7	22.0	.48	.17	.58	1.3↑	3.5	2.1	2.74	1.52	266
Curtiss-Wright	N	18	8,707	156.7	11.4	7.25	247.4	4.8	.91	.56	.03	-.32	1.36	1.25	.27	.62	130n	-19	-42	-44	-21	19.8	NC	169.6	97.8	.94	.63	.02	1.9↑	2.9	.0	1.09	2.57	158
Curt-Wright A	N	23½	259	6.1	.1	2.03	247.4	4.8	30.68	18.49	.62	-2.81	23.72	22.37	9.48	21.67	129n	4	-43	-42	-13	.8	2.9	13.9	7.1	.04	.02	.02	1.9↑	2.9	.0	.19	2.97	2
Fairchild Ind	N	5¾	4,550	26.2	.6	2.36	233.7	6.2	-.06	1.19	1.28	1.24	1.24	-4.52	1.07	-.18	NE	38	-42	-40	-18	NE	7.8	13.2	6.8	.45	.11	.65	2.7↓	10.5	5.2	1.77	2.94	9
Gen Dynamics	N	25½	10,546	268.9	4.9	1.82	1,542.6	26.0	2.95	2.47	1.96	-.62	.24	2.83	1.08	1.56	44s	20	3	0	0	8.6	11.2	65.0	32.1	.74	.17	.36	1.7↑	7.2	.0	2.26	1.96	120
Grumman Corp	N	11¼	6,809	76.6	1.6	2.15	686.3	-70.0	-8.30	-8.65	-2.08	2.62	2.76	2.43	.79	1.14	44s	-57	-7	13	-4	NE	NE	15.5	8.4	1.14	.11	2.04	-10.2↑	NE	.0	2.03	.89	59
Lockheed Air	N	5⅝	11,359	63.9	1.3	2.06	2,479.4	13.0	1.09	1.15	1.02	-7.60	-2.90	3.64	.89	.83	-7n	NE	-44	-38	-10	5.2	9.6	15.1	8.7	.24	.03	2.86	.5↓	4.9	.0	3.10	1.51	37
McDonnell D	N	20⅛	37,672	758.1	8.8	1.16	2,757.2	111.7	3.31	2.82	2.10	2.45	3.06	2.49	1.38	1.87	36s	3	-25	-28	5	6.1	10.7	13.3	7.9	.91	.27	.18	4.1→	13.4	2.0b	3.69	1.73	166
Northrop Corp	N	19⅞	3,748	74.5	1.0	1.34	581.4	11.1	2.06	2.22	2.05	3.31	3.06	2.63	1.57	1.41	-10n	-8	-13	-14	7	9.6	NC	15.1	9.0	.51	.13	.48	1.9↓	7.3	5.0	1.56	2.41	17
Rockwell Int	N	30	28,711	861.3	7.4	.86	2,385.2	77.9	3.36	2.65	2.23	2.05	2.09	2.59	2.21	2.92	32n	6	-11	-7	-3	8.9	12.5	15.3	10.2	.83	.28	.34	3.3→	9.8	6.0	1.53	.73	434
Thermo Electron	O	48	834	40.0	.8	2.03	39.1	1.3	1.57	1.57	1.06	1.05	1.40	1.06	1.06	1.57	48f	14	-6	-2	9	30.6	48.1	97.1	43.1	1.95	1.02	.45	3.3↑	4.3	.0	NC	NC	23
Unit Aircraft	N	31⅛	12,122	377.3	11.7	3.09	2,034.7	50.6	4.56	3.91	2.26	3.54	4.00	4.80	3.03	3.68	21n	-3	-33	-30	-4	6.8	13.1	16.3	9.3	.71	.19	.42	2.5→	9.5	5.8	2.28	2.89	243
012 Aerospace Components																																		
AAR Corp	A	14½	1,255	18.2	.4	2.11	37.3	1.5	1.34	1.30	.80	.45	.31	.40	.32	.36	13q	41	-32	-42	-7	10.8	21.9	34.4	17.2	1.46	.49	.46	4.0↓	12.0	.2	2.88	2.87	5
Aerodex Inc	A	2	1,215	2.4	-	.80	14.6	-2.8	-1.77	-2.28	-2.05	-2.09	.63	1.70	-.33	.18	NE	-81	7	23	23	NE	NE	28.7	13.9	4.88	.17	G	-19.2↑	NE	.0	1.96	-.68	0
Aeronca Inc	A	1¾	1,441	2.5	.1	2.40	37.9	-1.9	-.57	-1.33	-5.06	1.06	1.01	.70	-.59	.17	NE	-77	-50	-44	-13	NE	NE	29.5	15.3	1.14	.07	3.95	-5.0↑	NE	.0	1.61	2.98	1
Aiken Indus	A	2⅞	2,631	7.6	-	.23	23.8	.7	.31	.20	.13	.08	.33	.14	.13	.24	85n	9	-12	0	15	9.3	16.3	93.8	29.6	.75	.32	.37	2.9↑	6.9	.0	2.31	1.39	0
Altamil Corp	A	6	1,690	10.1	.3	2.70	60.3	2.0	1.10	1.10	1.00	-.84	.49	.90	1.00	1.10	10f	55	-24	-16	0	5.5	7.9	21.5	10.7	.80	.17	.39	3.3↓	14.3	.0	2.47	1.40	5
Automatn Ind	N	3⅝	7,205	26.1	.6	2.21	201.0	4.7	.23	.56	.19	-.03	.77	.75	.41	.08	-80n	-22	-49	-53	-15	15.8	15.5	37.8	18.7	.46	.15	.25	2.3↓	7.2	.0	3.75	1.63	13
CCI Corp	N	2½	3,054	7.6	.1	1.54	105.1	.0	-.05	-.14	.14	-1.21	-1.81	.89	-.03	.06	NE	NE	-57	-41	-5	NE	82.1	42.1	23.9	.40	.07	1.50	.0↑	NE	.0	2.05	1.86	1
Conrac	N	18⅞	1,261	23.8	1.4	5.92	58.3	2.4	2.00	1.76	1.40	1.12	1.26	1.25	1.24	1.48	19e	11	-39	-38	-11	9.4	18.6	35.2	17.9	1.06	.41	.55	4.1→	10.7	3.2	3.39	2.17	21
Dynalectron	A	4¼	6,788	28.8	.5	1.85	95.7	.7	.21	.12	.26	.29	.25	.14	.10	.19	90n	-1	0	3	6	20.2	26.6	77.7	37.0	1.45	.28	.35	.7↑	3.8	.0	2.55	3.12	8
Genisco Tech	A	1¾	1,511	2.6	-	.47	8.2	.1	.12	.09	-1.76	.08	-.88	.35	.07	.10	43n	NE	NC	NC	0	14.6	NC	NC	NC	1.77	.32	.00	1.2↑	6.7	.0	.98	.90	0
Hexcel Corp	O	17¼	1,293	22.3	.3	1.32	32.3	1.5	1.48	1.26	1.01	.64	.58	1.11	.90	1.12	24n	13	-10	-25	-7	11.7	16.3	40.3	17.9	1.72	.62	.21	4.6→	12.8	2.8	-.11	-.32	13
Kaman Corp A	O	15½	985	15.3	.7	4.38	115.9	2.3	2.50	2.00	1.64	1.39	1.07	-2.84	1.46	1.96	34n	28	-13	-14	5	6.2	9.4	14.1	6.9	.48	.10	.74	2.0→	9.3	1.8	.49	1.06	19
Lundy Elec	A	3⅞	866	3.4	.1	2.43	17.3	.1	.17	.17	.59	-1.65	.02	.12	.59	.17	-71f	-48	-57	-52	-6	22.8	15.3	542.1	215.5	.88	.19	1.53	.6↓	13.2	.0	2.24	6.74	1
OEA Inc	A	5⅜	1,421	7.6	-	.15	10.6	1.2	.87	.84	.71	.75	.70	.46	.52	.55	6n	12	-28	-26	-4	6.2	8.2	11.8	6.8	1.00	.72	.00	11.3↑	15.8	1.9	1.92	1.11	1
Pneum Dyn	A	5¼	2,073	10.9	.3	2.84	279.4	-1.7	-.01	-.95	.49	1.09	1.54	.42	-.12	.82	NE	-26	31	27	8	NE	NE	36.9	18.2	.36	.04	.98	-.6↑	NE	.0	.72	1.98	.4
Raytheon Co	N	32¾	15,377	503.6	13.8	2.75	1,474.3	41.2	2.87	2.58	2.37	2.24	2.31	2.08	2.01	2.30	14n	6	7	-3	19	11.4	12.2	20.1	11.7	1.52	.35	.24	2.8↑	12.3	2.1	3.11	1.83	256
Rocket Research	O	3⅝	1,494	5.4	.1	1.68	11.4	-4.7	-2.38	-3.13	-.11	.27	.16	.07	-.50	.25	NE	-85	-22	0	-9	NE	NC	297.9	115.2	1.15	.48	.55	-41.2↑	NE	.0	-2.38	3.64	2
Rohr Industries	N	14⅝	4,079	59.7	1.4	2.35	373.2	6.4	1.42	1.42	1.12	1.07	2.62	2.51	1.12	1.42	27f	-15	-20	-35	-6	10.3	16.4	18.1	11.0	.73	.16	.51	1.7↓	7.8	6.2	-.27	2.15	34
Royal Ind	N	8½	5,073	43.1	1.5	3.49	155.6	5.7	1.36	1.11	.90	.52	.42	.74	.82	1.07	30n	21	-19	-25	-6	6.3	9.5	30.3	13.3	1.02	.28	.70	3.7↑	13.5	.0	2.40	2.75	30
RSC Indus	A	2⅛	3,458	7.3	.1	1.21	8.9	.2	.14	.07	.01	.15	.13	.07	.04	.11	175s	-6	-15	13	0	15.2	50.0	189.3	77.0	1.15	.83	.02	2.2↑	3.1	.0	2.29	.71	1
Sargent Indus	A	2⅞	3,909	11.2	.1	.88	70.6	-.6	-.17	-.19	.10	-.54	.30	.40	-.01	.01	NE	-44	-28	-26	-8	NE	NC	59.3	27.9	.74	.16	1.17	-.8↑	NE	.0	2.54	2.52	1
Sierracin Corp	A	12½	686	8.6	.4	4.85	10.4	.3	.59	.45	.44	.43	.34	1.01	.40	.54	35n	-6	-26	-20	14	21.2	27.7	66.3	26.5	1.68	.82	.08	2.9↑	5.9	.0	2.67	3.52	6
Simmonds Prec	N	4⅜	3,265	14.3	.2	1.28	35.3	1.2	.46	.36	.23	.08	.15	.91	.22	.32	45n	0	-8	-8	-8	9.5	19.0	88.8	31.8	.93	.40	.36	3.4↑	7.8	.0	3.04	1.70	3
SSP Indus	A	8½	929	7.9	.1	.85	24.2	1.3	1.53	1.36	1.05	.71	.87	.46	.62	.79	27s	27	-4	-27	-7	5.6	6.9	15.9	9.4	.94	.33	.23	5.4→	15.5	2.4b	1.79	.64	3
Sundstrand Cp	N	33¼	5,491	182.6	14.0	7.67	306.4	8.9	1.77	1.11	.32	1.01	1.97	2.82	.73	1.39	90n	-15	9	-1	25	18.8	30.9	44.8	24.9	1.29	.59	1.07	2.9↑	6.4	2.4	2.56	3.60	219
Thiokol Chem	N	14¼	5,822	83.0	2.0	2.40	253.9	10.0	2.04	1.66	1.16	.72	1.20	1.19	1.23	1.61	31n	13	-25	-30	4	7.0	12.3	17.1	9.6	.94	.34	.01	3.9↑	10.9	3.7	1.77	2.31	69
VSI Corp	N	20	2,979	59.6	.5	.81	108.9	7.1	2.38	2.23	1.66	1.01	1.77	1.70	.45	.60	33q	9	-13	-6	8	8.4	12.9	21.9	11.9	1.42	.55	.04	6.5→	16.9	2.6	1.67	1.03	16
Watkins Jhnsn	N	21⅝	3,022	65.4	3.7	5.59	45.6	3.8	1.44	1.27	1.09	.97	.66	1.10	.93	1.10	18n	11	-39	-41	-7	15.0	28.4	43.7	20.8	2.35	1.43	.00	8.3→	13.7	.0	1.79	6.07	58
Western Gear	O	7⅝	3,906	29.8	.3	1.00	96.9	-3.9	1.02	-1.01	-.93	.09	1.16	1.18	-1.18	.85	NE	-29	45	33	9	7.5	NE	72.1	31.7	1.14	.31	.41	-4.0↑	NE	.0	-1.11	-.50	9
Wyle Labs	A	4⅛	3,036	12.5	.3	2.61	93.0	.9	.43	.27	-.52	-.68	.32	.78	.11	.27	145s	-26	6	-3	27	9.6	NE	42.0	17.3	.68	.13	1.63	1.0↑	4.9	.0	2.60	1.22	3

SOURCE: Media General Financial Services, Inc., *Industriscope*. Reprinted by permission.

The financial section. Financial and business news has become so closely connected with the national scene that reference to the "financial section" of a newspaper is almost a misnomer. News items of predominantly financial import appear throughout the paper. Spectacular financial events, such as major stock developments, large-scale currency devaluations, and the federal and municipal budgetary problems, even crowd their way onto the front pages of national newspapers.

Nevertheless, most large papers segregate a designated number of pages, referred to as the financial section, for business and financial developments. In papers serving the largest cities this section may contain as many as ten pages, including several devoted solely to securities prices; in those serving small cities the section may be relatively insignificant. Embedded in the financial section are many items of a technical nature, such as securities prices, business indexes, and money-market statistics.[18]

AVERAGES AND INDEXES OF SECURITIES PRICES

To judge the movements of securities prices both averages and indexes are used. By and large, the averages are simple aggregates of the prices of comparable groups of securities, divided by the number of issues in each group and adjusted for comparability. Indexes relate the changes in the prices of similar groups of securities to a base year and weight each component security according to its importance. Averages and indexes have been calculated for U.S. government and state and local government bonds as well as for corporate securities. They have been calculated for broad composite groups of issues, for several ratings of bonds, and, in the case of corporate bonds and stocks, for the various major industry groups.

The measures are extensively used. Financial analysts and writers find them helpful for determining trends of securities prices. Market technicians employ them to observe market formations and to establish price support levels. Investors generally compare price fluctuations of particular issues with corresponding changes in the average or index; the reader should notice large discrepancies and attempt to ascertain the reasons for the more or less favorable showing of specific issues. These averages and indexes have a wide circulation in financial and business publications.

Dow-Jones Averages

Dow Jones & Co., publisher of the *Wall Street Journal*, issues various averages. The best known are its stock statistics, which cover a composite average of 65 stocks and separate averages of 30 industrial, 20 transportation, and 15 utility issues. These data are calculated hourly from 10 A.M. until 3 P.M. and at the close of each NYSE operating day. The original separation of rail and industrial figures dates back to 1896 and formed the basis of the well-known Dow Theory discussed in Chapter 26. As the importance of railroads declined and that of other means of travel rose, the rail average was converted to a transportation average. The utility series was introduced in 1929.

In order to keep the averages representative, both the number and the nature of the stocks included have been changed over the years. A difficulty is the problem of maintaining a continuous price series despite stock splits and dividends. At first, the price of each stock included was simply adjusted to take capitalization changes into account, but this procedure proved awkward and time-consuming. In 1928 Dow Jones altered the method of computation to its current basis.

In this technique the prices of the stocks are aggregated with no adjustment for splits or stock dividends, and the sum is divided by an equalizing figure to obtain the average. The equalizing figure is determined by dividing the adjusted average (calculated by offsetting the influence of capitalization changes) into the unadjusted aggregate of stock prices. To illustrate: Assume an average comprises four stocks selling at 20, 36, 40, and 20, respectively, after the first and third stocks have been split in half. The adjusted average, obtained by multiplying the split stocks by 2, is 44 $[(20(2) + 36 + 40(2) + 20) \div 4]$. This figure is divided into 116, the unadjusted aggregate of prices (20 + 36 + 40 + 20), to give an equalizing figure of 2.636. Thereafter, by dividing the equalizing figure into the unadjusted aggregate of prices, the adjusted averages are obtained. The same equalizing figure is used until further splits or stock dividends occur.[19]

Despite general reliance on the Dow-Jones averages, they have several serious shortcomings. First, they include the stocks of outstanding corporations and therefore do not truly reflect all listed issues, which include those of a number of companies with indifferent financial records. Second, the averages are not weighted. As a result, all issues have equal influence on the finally reported figure, regardless of the number of shares outstanding. Third, although use of the adjusting figure gives accurate results on the day a stock split occurs, over a period of time a slight distortion is created that becomes aggravated as the number of splits increases. Finally, the averages are not usually adjusted to take the issuance of rights into consideration.

Standard & Poor's Stock Price Index

In contrast with the Dow-Jones averages, those published by Standard & Poor's are both weighted and related to a base period. Standard & Poor's

Industrial Index is based on 425 stocks. Its railroad index includes 25 stocks, and its utility index 50 stocks. Standard & Poor's also publishes a 500-stock composite of these three, as well as a number of special industry stock price indexes.

In these indexes the price of each stock is multiplied by the number of shares outstanding. The aggregate market value of the issues in the index is then divided by the average of the aggregate during the years 1941-1943, and that ratio is in turn divided by 10. Because the index reflects the relative change in the total value of the stocks outstanding, it is unaffected by stock splits and dividends, and no adjustments have to be made for them. The 1941-1943 base was established in 1957, when the old index, based on 1935-1939 as 100, reached a level of approximately 370. (The new base was made equal to 10 rather than 100 by dividing by 10.) The starting level in 1957 was 47, which was very close to the average price ($45.23) of the common shares listed on the New York Stock Exchange at the time.

Exchange Indexes

Both the AMEX and NYSE developed indexes in mid-1966. The AMEX index was revised in 1973 so that the method of construction is essentially the same as the NYSE and the NASDAQ indexes. Like these two, the AMEX index relates the total market value of its securities on each trading day to a base year. The AMEX base is August 31, 1973, set at 100. The securities covered include common stocks, warrants, and ADRs (American Depository Receipts, representing foreign securities). Eight industrial and eight geographic subindexes are part of the index system.

The NYSE Common Stock Index is a composite of all the common stock issues listed on the exchange. The NYSE also publishes a finance index, a transportation index, a utility index, and an industrial index. Each time the composite index is calculated, the aggregate value of all the listed stocks is determined. This aggregate value is then related to a base market value (December 31, 1965) after making some necessary adjustments; the base was calculated so that it would have a value of 50, which closely approximated the average price of 53 on that date. The NYSE has indicated that it will attempt to keep the magnitude of the index closely related to the actual average price of listed stock. Like the AMEX index, the NYSE index is adjusted for new listings and delisted stocks. Both composite indexes are calculated every half hour. Announced changes are calculated from the previous day's close.

Over-the-Counter Stock Price Index

For many years, no over-the-counter index was calculated that was comparable to the indexes and averages available for listed securities. In response to persistent requests by investors for some means of following the performance of OTC issues, the National Quotation Bureau, in 1948, finally prepared an industrial stock index. This index is based on 35 stocks—those OTC issues that have substantial market values, a large number of holders, and suitable quotation records. The index is an average calculated like the Dow-Jones averages. Figures are issued as of the first, tenth, and twentieth of each month, and the series has been brought back to October 1938.

NASDAQ Over-the-Counter Indexes

With the introduction of NASDAQ, early in 1971, its indexes made their debut. NASDAQ not only generates a composite index for all the 2,000-plus stocks listed on the device but also generates six group indexes, covering industrials, banks, insurance companies, other financial institutions, transportation, and utilities. These indexes are designed to measure the aggregate market value of OTC domestic common stocks traded on the NASDAQ system. Neither the "Composite" index nor the "Other Finance" index includes mutual funds. The prices used in the computation of the value of each index are the median bids of market makers. The indexes are adjusted to eliminate the effect of capitalization changes and listing changes. Each stock in an index is represented by the aggregate value of the issue outstanding; the base (100) is the close of the market on February 8, 1971. The values of all indexes for that date were set at 100. When there are changes in the stock listed on NASDAQ, the base period market value is adjusted by the following calculation:

$$\text{Adjusted base period market value} = \frac{\text{Current market value after list change}}{\text{Current market value before list change}} \times \text{Previous base period market value.}$$

Once the adjusted base period market values have been computed, the current index is simply 100 times the ratio of the current market value to the adjusted base period market value. The indexes are continuously computed and distributed every five minutes. Hourly, daily, and weekly summaries are provided for the wire services.

SUMMARY

Because of the considerable amount of financial information issued, the investor could easily be inundated with material. Accordingly, it is important that the investor become familiar with the resources available in order to ascertain those most useful for his purposes.

Corporate reports represent an accessible and extremely important source of basic information concerning an enterprise. In addition to financial statements, the modern annual report includes a discussion of the current operations of a company, a description of the products most recently developed or sold, some historical statistics, and a statement concerning expected conditions. The auditor's report and the footnotes to the financial statements are of special interest in spotlighting problems the company may be facing. Because of the importance that it attributes to the annual report, the SEC has expanded considerably the disclosure required. Since interim reports are becoming increasingly popular, the SEC and the accounting profession have been trying to determine the degree to which these should be checked by outside auditors.

Corporations must file information with various federal and state regulatory agencies. Of these filings, the investor is likely to find those placed with the SEC the most important. A considerable amount of basic information appears in the registration statement which, under the Securities Act of 1933, must be filed in connection with public distributions. A prospectus, which represents the first part of the statement, contains information particularly relevant to investors and, with certain exceptions, must accompany or precede the actual sale of securities in interstate commerce. The SEC also requires various periodic reports, the most important being Form 10-K, which must be filed annually.

Among the most convenient sources of information are the financial services, principally Moody's Investors Service, controlled by Dun & Bradstreet, and Standard & Poor's, controlled by McGraw-Hill. In addition to their corporate manuals, these services issue a variety of publications that include basic statistics, financial analyses of individual companies, and summarized financial information. The most important innovation in financial research in recent years has been the introduction of computer tapes that provide data banks as well as analytic results. Foremost among these tape services is Compustat, which can provide tapes compatible with any of the major computer systems now in use, together with more specialized services.

Other sources of information are listing applications, trade publications, government reports, publications of economic research organizations, business and financial publications, and reports affecting the securities business generally. Brokers provide a variety of services that now may be subject to various charges as a result of the abolition of fixed commissions. Reading the daily newspapers is important if the investor is to keep abreast of information that may influence securities values directly or indirectly. Developments in electronics have extended the range of news and data available instantaneously through different devices.

To judge the movements of securities prices, both averages and indexes are used. Best known are the Dow-Jones averages, the Standard & Poor's price indexes, the New York Stock Exchange and the American Stock Exchange indexes, and the NASDAQ over-the-counter indexes.

CHAPTER

Factors Affecting Securities Prices

The securities markets comprise many thousands of securities representing a great number of corporations. At any one time, similar developments may affect these corporations in different ways. For example, a relaxation of military spending would adversely affect companies heavily dependent on the production of munitions but benefit those that stress civilian projects, particularly heavy construction, as funds moved to such areas as highways and hospitals. Rapidly advancing commodity prices tend to favor companies engaged in producing raw materials over those selling finished goods. A continuing important issue is the direction of interest rates; a decline in rates would help financial institutions (such as savings and loan associations) and industries dependent on the housing market, but it would be less favorable to short-term lenders, especially the commercial banks.

TYPES OF CHANGES IN SECURITIES PRICES

Commission brokers recognize that securities prices do not necessarily react in the same way to the same set of circumstances, as is evidenced by the variety of lists these brokers prepare. The investor need only name the type of security desired, and his broker will probably have a list available: stocks that will benefit by a commodity price rise or by a price decline, by a rise in short-term rates or a shrinkage, by a growth of the space program or a cutback, as well as by tax modifications or by changes in the international scene. Indeed, one of the authors recalls a list that played the odds both ways to come up with a winner; it contained securities that would be helped as well as those that would be hurt by either an extension or a diminution of international tensions.

These varying effects on corporations of similar economic conditions cause mixed reactions in the prices of securities, regardless of the general market trend. In 1973, for example, industrial production was generally declining, but the Standard & Poor's stock price averages for different groups, based on the first quarter, showed diverse movements even within the common area of heavy industry. Thus, the average for industrial machinery declined sharply in the second quarter, then rose rapidly during the rest of the year; the average for electrical equipment also declined sharply in the second quarter, then rose moderately in the third, but experienced a decline in the fourth; the average for steel dropped slightly in the second and third quarters and then showed a mild upward reversal in the fourth; and the average for metal fabrication shrank sharply in the second quarter, rose slightly in the third, and fell perceptibly in the fourth. These movements are shown in Figure 8-1. It is, of course, easier to explain such diverse movements after they occur than to anticipate them. Whatever the reasons, however, market declines may become indiscriminate, leaving in their wake underpriced issues that may be identified through careful analysis.

Innumerable factors—wars, floods, earthquakes, weather, inventions, elections, and many others—may strongly influence the price of a particular issue or the level of securities in general. It is impracticable to list all these interactions and to explain their implications for the securities markets. If the investor does not develop an orderly approach, however, he may find that his avenues of investigation are merely blind alleys. It is therefore desirable to reduce this host of possible considerations to a workable size, so that reasonable cause-and-effect sequences may be established. At the outset, a distinction must be drawn between two general types of changes: those that occur in high-grade, fixed-income securities and those that take place in all other issues. The factors affecting prime securities are discussed in chapter 18, which deals with bond analysis. In the present chapter we evaluate the sources of price changes in the second category.

PRICE CHANGES OF SECURITIES NOT OF HIGH GRADE

The fixed-income securities of corporations below the top grade and the common stock, rights, and warrants of most corporations are categorized as

FIGURE 8-1

Movement of Standard & Poor's Averages for Selected Industries

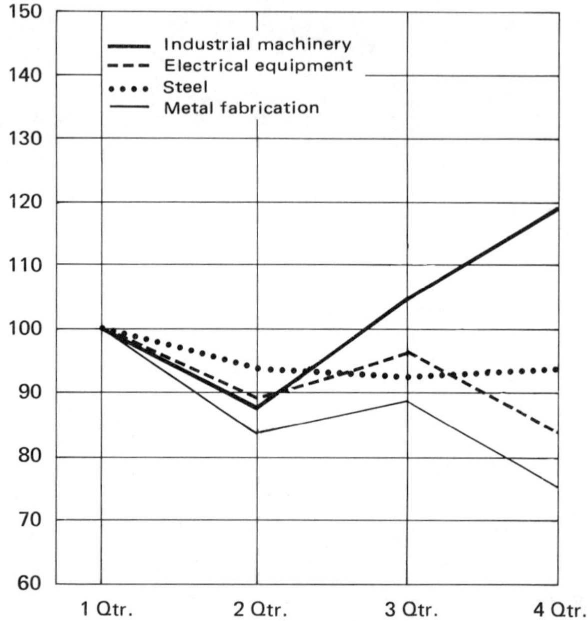

SOURCE: Based on Standard & Poor's ***Security Price Index Record***, 1974, pp. 40, 65, 69, 98.

"not of high grade." The stock could represent a strong corporation with a long-term dividend record, an enterprise on the verge of bankruptcy, or a firm already in reorganization. Thus, Avon Products, Inc. is an outstanding company and its stock generally is regarded as a sound issue, but when its price was driven to 140 during the growth mania of 1972 and sold at 64 times earnings, it properly could be considered speculative.[1] The 11⅛ certificates (due 1987) issued by Braniff Airways represent senior obligations, but because of the company's marginal financial condition the issue afforded a high return in mid-1975 and was clearly speculative in nature. On the other hand, the equipment trust certificates of the Chicago, Milwaukee, St. Paul & Pacific Railroad might be considered a high-grade, fixed-income security; as such, its price is not influenced by the same factors as the company's other bonds or stock, which are speculative.

Because of the vulnerability of non-high-grade issues to changing circumstances, their price fluctuations are susceptible to more complex forces than those which influence the price movements of prime obligations. As a consequence, the returns of non-high-grade securities vary widely both between different risk classes and within a given class. In this area, classification is extremely difficult and price relationships are constantly shifting.

Eventual Market Recognition of an Intrinsically Undervalued Issue

In the elegant world of theory, where there is such a thing as a perfect market, undervaluation does not exist, since securities are always correctly priced. But even in these ideal circumstances, a distinction could be drawn between market and business valuations. Thus, to the investor the price of a stock reflects his judgment of the company's future earnings based on the resources available to it, but to the businessman the price may also take into account the added opportunities the company may offer him, such as entering a new market, gaining access to a new technology, or obtaining another product line.

Some firms utilize their resources inefficiently. Tradition may prevent management from redirecting the firm's activity into a more profitable direction. For the typical investor, such knowledge by itself may not have great value. A major investor or expansion-oriented corporation, however, may visualize the possibility of gaining control and improving the effectiveness with which the resources of the target firm are utilized. The managerial skills of the buyer are thus used to change the stream accruing to the securities of the target firm; reflecting this development, the market value of the securities will rise. In this operation, the essential feature is the acquisition of control. For an investor who cannot influence the utilization of the firm's resources, the opportunity to benefit is much further removed, but he may hope to follow in the path of the control seeker.

In effect, the businessman, the major investor, and the typical investor all may have access to the same information, but the first two can use it to affect security values, while the typical investor cannot. Such an investor can, however, use his judgment to evaluate the actions of the major investor and the businessman. A related matter is the question of time, because the expected rate of return may be subject to considerable erosion if the change is on a distant horizon. Suppose, for example, that the security of firm A sells for \$1 and its intrinsic worth is \$2. If the investor has to wait only one year, he will realize a rate of return of 100 percent. However, if it is necessary to wait two years, the return falls to $\sqrt{(2/1)} - 1$ or about 41 percent; if he has to wait n years, the return is only $\sqrt[n]{(2/1)} - 1$. A five-year wait reduces the return to less than 15 percent.

If the market is less than perfect, as some economists believe, underpricing is a reality. Economists recognize that numerous factors affect the price of a security, including the current level of earnings, expectations of change, the desired rate of return, and the dividend payout rate. Given two securities where these variables are the same, therefore, the one that sells at a lower price may be considered undervalued compared with the other. The concept is a relative rather than an absolute one.

For the quantitative-minded investor who leans toward mathematical demonstrations, the following analysis might be of interest. Consider firms A and B, both of which earn the same amount, pay out the same fraction in dividends, and have identical investment opportunities. Let the p/e ratio of firm A be θ and that of firm B $\lambda\theta$, where $\lambda < 1$. If each firm earns \$1 per share in year t, the dividend per share D_t will be numerically equal to the payout ratio d, and the price of each firm's stock will be numerically equal to the p/e ratio. Thus in year t the dividend yield of the stock of firm A is d_t/θ and for B it is $d_t/\lambda\theta$. In year $t+1$ the earnings of either firm will be $E_t + (1-d)rE_t$, where r equals the rate of return on investment and E_t represents the earnings per share in year t. Under these circumstances the incremental value of A's stock will be $\theta(1-d)rE_t$, and the rate of growth in its price—that is, the percentage capital gain—will be $(1-d)r$. (Since θE_t is in the numerator and denominator, it is eliminated.) The total return to investors in firm A, k_a, is the sum of the dividend yield and the expected percentage capital gains, i.e., $k_a = d/\theta + (1-d)r$. The incremental earnings to firm B are the same $(1-d)rE_t$, and the rate of increase in the price of B's stock, if the undervaluation is not recognized, is $\lambda\theta(1-d)r/\lambda\theta$. Thus, $k_b = \mathrm{d}/\lambda\theta + (1-d)r$. It follows, therefore, that $k_b - k_a = d/\lambda\theta - d/\theta > 0$, since $\lambda\theta < \theta$.[2] This illustration simply shows that even if the p/e differential persists and other things remain the same, the return of the lower-priced issue will exceed the other's by the amount of its higher dividend yield.

Another possibility is that eventually other investors will recognize the undervaluation and take steps to correct it. So long as the market is less than perfect, therefore, this possibility provides the greatest opportunity for profit to the astute analyst. His job is to recognize that other investors have failed to gauge the price-influencing variables correctly and to buy the undervalued security on the assumption that this condition will eventually be detected. When the analyst is employed by a brokerage firm, he may help speed the detection process by calling the presumed undervaluation to the attention of his institutional clients. He may also benefit by having his firm become the direct recipient of commission business.

Effect of Psychological Factors on Securities Prices

The uncertain mass reaction of individuals to developments affecting the securities markets is one of the imponderables that handicap stock market forecasting. A mild market flurry caused by a spurt in business activity may generate a wave of buying enthusiasm that raises securities prices to boom levels. As an indication of this tendency, from January 1967 through December 1968 the American Stock Exchange Index more than doubled in the face of a business activity advance of about 10 percent. The starry-eyed optimism of buyers who believe that prices are heading indefinitely higher may produce substantial advances that are not justified by underlying financial considerations.

On the other hand, pervasive investor gloom, generated by economic or political uncertainties, could drive prices to levels that appear equally unjustified by standard financial tests. For example, in the fall of 1974 investors were uncertain whether double-digit inflation would continue or, if halted, would be replaced by a serious business recession. Investors were also depressed by U.S. political uncertainties emanating from the Watergate affair and its aftermath and by chaotic international conditions attributable to Arab oil policies and money flows. These psychological factors led investors to stay away from the equity market. As a consequence, prices declined sharply, leaving in their wake the common stocks of substantial companies with fine prior records; these stocks now sold at levels below their net working capital asset values and only several times above their earnings per share. As the official of one such firm dismally observed, the net liquid assets of his company could be sold at a profit to its common stockholders and still leave intact the company's factories, equipment, and excellent business reputation.

The occasionally irrational attitude of buyers was noted by John Maynard Keynes, who said that professional investors ". . . are concerned, not with what an investment is really worth to a man who buys it 'for keeps,' but with what the market will value it at, under the influence of mass psychology, three months or a year hence." He then likened professional investors to entrants in a newspaper competition in which the prize is awarded to the person who selects from a group of 100 photographs the six prettiest faces that most closely correspond to the average choice of the group of competitors. Thus, each competitor does not select the faces he regards as the prettiest or those that most people consider the prettiest; instead, he attempts to predict "what average opinion expects the average opinion to be."[3] Psychological factors motivating individuals to buy and sell securities are difficult to evaluate and make hazardous the role of a stock market prophet. They also, however, present opportunities for substantial profits and therefore cannot be ignored by the more adventuresome investor. Indeed, stemming from the Keynes analogy cited above, we have thought it appropriate to describe the following method of speculating on certain psychological phenomenon as the "pretty girl" approach.

During the past decade, a large number of offerings have come to the market for the first time, as closely held firms have gone public or new corporations have been formed. When these offerings had a psychological appeal because of such things as the glamorous business in which the issuer was engaged or the successful prior association of a member of management, the price of the new stock often rose to an immediate substantial premium. These stocks were characteristically called "hot issues." Substantial profits could be made by purchasing such an issue at the offering and disposing of it shortly thereafter, hopefully at a much higher level. There were substantial risks, since many of these companies had little merit and eventually went bankrupt.[4] In effect, the speculator was buying the stock not because of its intrinsic value but because he thought that other people, like himself, would believe that still others would be attracted by the nature of the company, and that this combined effect would drive its price up.

In accordance with the principles of disclosure, the Securities and Exchange Commission has required for some time that a company indicate in its prospectus the risky characteristics of a stock deemed particularly speculative. In mid-1973 the commission went a step further, adopting new disclosure rules designed, among other things, to "cool down" the hot-issue market, should it materialize once more. The additional disclosure requirements apply to the prospectuses of new issues of unseasoned companies. Required disclosures include such things as more "meaningful information concerning competition in the industry, additional information about the experience and background of management, and inclusion by first-time issuers without a three-year operating history of a plan of operation disclosing the disposition of the cash proceeds of the sale and how long they will satisfy the requirements of the company."[5]

Effects of Changing Expectations

More fundamentally, the changing mood of the investing public can affect the price of a stock by producing changes in the evaluating criteria. As a result, under buoyant conditions, expectations are likely to be for rapid growth and substantial market gains, leading to high current prices. When pessimism is prevalent, growth expectations become modest and prices tend to be depressed. The quantitative-minded investor may wish to consider the following example.

Let E_t, D_t, and P_t represent earnings, dividends, and stock price, respectively, in period t. Let b represent the payout ratio, and g the rate of growth of earnings. We may therefore write:

(1) $E_t = (1 + g)E_{t-1}$ and

(2) $D_t = bE_t$.

Substituting equation (1) into equation (2) we have:

(3) $D_t = b(1 + g)E_{t-1} = (1 + g)D_{t-1}$.

Clearly, dividends and earnings grow at the same rate, and g may be written to represent either. As a consequence, if we let k represent the rate of return on equity required by the market, using a well-known valuation model in the academic literature we may write:[6]

$$(4) \qquad P_t = D_t/(k - g).$$

Now, consider a stock with a \$2.00 dividend and an expected growth rate of 5 percent, on which investors require a 10 percent rate of return. We can see from equation (4) that investors will price the stock at \$40 in order to realize the required rate of return. If investors become pessimistic and foresee a rate of growth for the company of only 4 percent, the price of its stock from equation (4) will fall to $P_t = \$2.00/(.10 - .04) = \$33.33$. On the other hand, if investors become optimistic and expect a growth rate of 6 percent, they would be willing to pay \$50 for the stock to obtain the same return, since $\$2.00/(.10 - .06) = \$50$. In both cases, the required rate of return remains at 10 percent, but under conditions of pessimism the price drops, while when optimism prevails the price rises. The illustrations based on this model are not intended to show the actual level at which a stock will sell, but they do suggest the magnitude of price shifts that can follow changes in expectations.

Changes in Investor Composition

As the supply of and demand for securities change over time, different types of investors are attracted to the market. If the risk preferences of these new investors are not the same as those of investors already present, the required rate of return tends to shift. Accordingly, price relationships will change quite independently of any modification in earnings expectations.

Figure 8-2 portrays some of these effects. It compares the price fluctuations of the Standard & Poor's Composite Index of 500 industrial companies with three other market indexes which generally are considered to reflect speculative influences to a greater extent. During 1967 and 1968, when optimism was generally prevalent, individual investors, willing if not necessarily able to assume risks, were attracted to the market. These investors paid relatively high prices for the stocks of companies that had promising outlooks for special reasons, such as new product developments or merchandising methods. During this period, therefore, as indicated in the graph, the speculative market indexes sold at comparatively favorable levels.

The day of reckoning came gradually, as institutional investors grew more influential in the market. These investors for the most part shunned the youthful companies that might have promise; the markets in many of these stocks were too thin to permit purchases in the amounts required to fill

FIGURE 8-2

Comparison of Prices Fluctuation of Different Market Indexes, 1966-August 1975

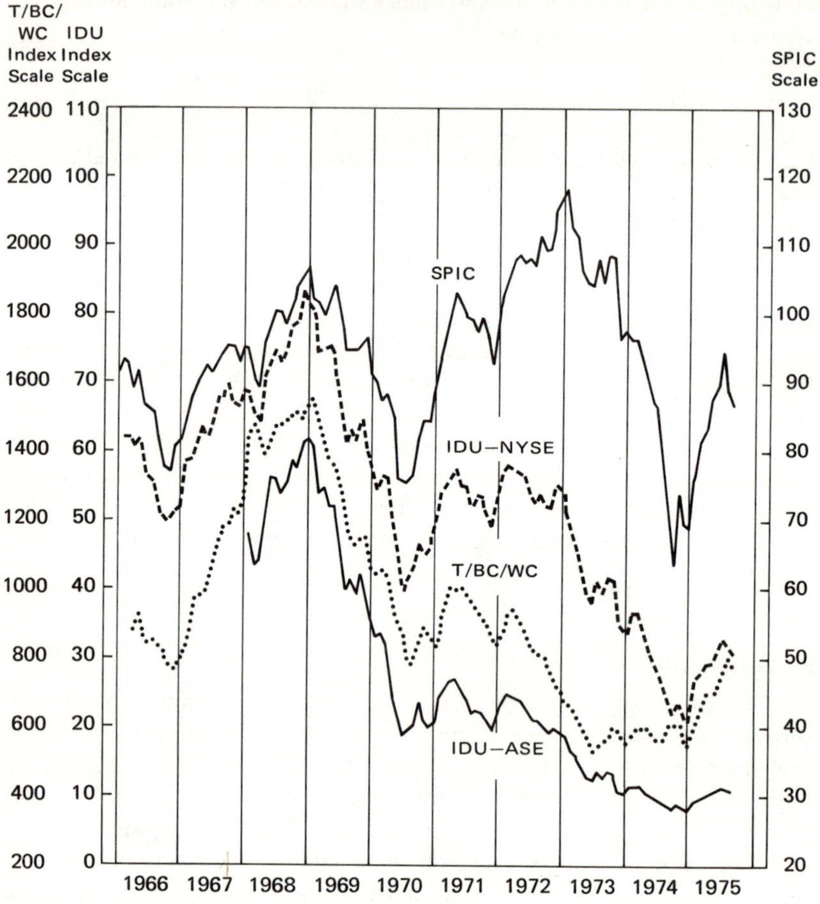

SPIC: ———— Standard & Poor's 500 Industrial Composite. This index is made up of 425 industrial securities and 75 utilities and rails, weighted for the shares outstanding in each security.

IDU-NYSE: - - - - - - - - Indicator Digest Unweighted Index of the New York Stock Exchange. This index is made up of a large majority of the securities on the NYSE, unweighted for shares outstanding.

IDU-ASE: ———— Indicator Digest Unweighted Index of the American Stock Exchange. Same as IDU-NYSE except applicable to a large majority of the securities traded on the American Stock Exchange.

T/BC/WC: .... Trendex Blue Chip White Chip Index. This index is constructed from the relationship between Standard & Poor's high-grade stock index and Standard & Poor's low-price index. This index is generally thought of as an indicator of the amount of speculation in the market.

SOURCE: Oppenheimer Management Corporation. Reprinted by permission.

institutional investment needs, and the restricted or spotty records of their companies did not appeal to the relatively conservative institutional buyers. Thus, purchasing power veered to the stocks of companies with demonstrated records. As a result, the Standard & Poor's Industrial Composite experienced the least precipitous drop during the 1969-1970 decline and then rose at a relatively rapid pace until 1973. Thereafter, all sectors participated in the severe downward movement that started earlier for the other indexes. The net result was that between December 1968 and December 1974, the Standard & Poor's Composite fell by about 35 percent, compared with declines ranging from 65 to 85 percent in the two Indicator Digest Unweighted indexes and the Trendex Index. The graph clearly reveals the disparities in the price movements of the different categories of stocks.

It is sometimes difficult to draw conclusions from presumed demand-supply illustrations. Thus, the growth of institutional demand has been compared with the small volume of net new equity flotations over the past two decades to suggest continued upward pressure on stock prices. Offsetting this relationship, however, has been net selling by individuals and the considerable growth of corporate retained earnings. In effect, earnings retention is the equivalent of a cash dividend followed by a compulsory subscription to stock. At least some of the sell-off by investors may be attributed to a sloughing off of unwanted accumulations of equity obtained through this implicit method of compulsory stock subscription. Thus, the supply of stock coming to the market may be augmented at any time by such secondary sales. Additionally, in some years, the volume of new common stock offerings has exceeded retirements by substantial amounts.

Influence of Business Conditions on Securities Prices

Securities prices are based on the potential earning power of corporations. This factor is influenced directly by economic conditions. As a result, fluctuations in the general level of non-high-grade securities largely reflect investor consensus concerning the economic outlook. Over a period of years, it is logical to expect a close relationship between business activity and changes in stock prices. This relationship is shown in Figure 8-3.

While there is general conformity between the curves of business activity and stock prices, divergent movements do occur. Between 1925 and 1929, for example, stock prices rose swiftly, while general economic conditions changed relatively little. Between the fall of 1940 and the spring of 1942—the uneasy years prior to and immediately after America's entrance into World War II—stock prices dropped precipitously in the face of a sharp and continued revival of economic activity. From the close of 1943 to the early part of 1946—the twilight period of World War II—stock prices boomed, whereas industrial activity slipped. Since that time there have been other

FIGURE 8-3

Dow-Jones Industrial Average and Federal Reserve Board Index of Industrial Production, 1925-1974

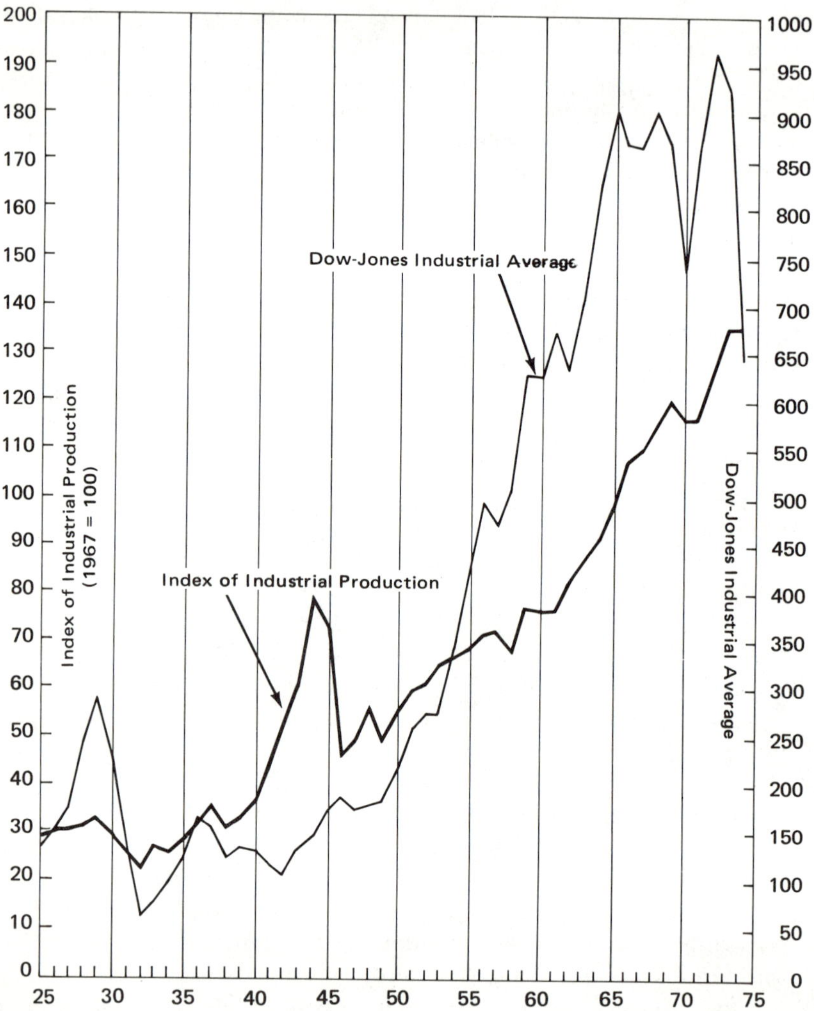

SOURCE: Data taken from Board of Governors of the Federal Reserve System, ***Federal Reserve Bulletin***, various issues, and Standard & Poor's Corp., ***Trade and Securities Statistics***, various issues.

sharp but relatively brief divergent movements, such as the short, swift decline in stock prices in the spring of 1962 in the face of a continued business upswing, the 1971 stock rise while business remained relatively stable, and the severe market drop in 1974 compared with a relatively modest decline in business.

In part, these distorted relations may probably be ascribed to the hasty reaction of investors to dramatic events. However, more fundamental economic factors also may be at play. For one thing, increased industrial activity may be accompanied by even more rapidly rising costs; these exert pressure on the future level of corporate profits, which is the relevant factor in the pricing equation. Then again, the stock market tends to lead business activity, although the length and magnitude of the divergences may vary.

Whatever may be the causes that prevent the synchronization of stock prices and economic activity, readjustments eventually occur, and the two series tend to follow similar patterns. This relationship, as well as the temporary periods of distortion, make it necessary for the investor to keep constantly abreast of changing economic conditions, so that he may formulate his own investment policy.

More particularly, he may shift his investment program in accordance with his expectations of business changes. For example, if he foresees an improvement in economic activity, he may prefer to buy cyclical stocks. On the other hand, should he expect more stable conditions and declining interest rates, he may lean toward fixed-income obligations or the issues of public utilities. Then again, the investor may examine the long-term upward trend of economic activity, the modest recessions of the post-World War II era (at least until recently), the lengthening periods of business boom, the more refined fiscal and monetary techniques now available to the economist, and conclude that the dangers of a serious depression are remote. He may therefore be willing to hold a portfolio composed primarily of stocks, on the theory that their long-term trend is upward and it is not worthwhile to worry about short-term movements. It probably took a bold heart, however, to maintain such a viewpoint in the 1974 period of pronounced market pessimism and the 1975 faltering business upturn.

Shocks

The major erratic changes in market level often come as a consequence of news developments that affect the psychology of the investor and therefore his attitude to the factors determining prices, which, as we have seen, essentially are based on expectations. In general, expectations are extrapolations of reactions to past events, weighted in accordance with the timing of the events, the extent to which they were anticipated, and the likelihood of their being repeated. Because it is extremely difficult to determine the allocation of weights by investors to particular events, it is often very hard to predict how the market will react to new developments.

Certain events that suggest a rise in corporate earnings may nevertheless have a traumatic effect on the public and therefore exert a negative influence on the market. The reason is that trauma produces uncertainty, which is tantamount to a reduction in the quality of the income streams associated with the various stocks. Thus, even though a dramatic event, such as the sudden threat of war, may raise the level of expected earnings, it may also increase uncertainty sufficiently to more than offset the benefits of improved earnings expectations.

The traumatic effect may be compounded if it increases risk aversion as well as uncertainty; investors will then require a higher rate of compensation for a given degree of risk. This explains why some major event with no obvious economic implications may nevertheless cause stock prices to recede. Thus, the assassination of President Kennedy did not provide any reason to expect a change in corporate earnings, but it did generate considerable bewilderment, and the resulting decline in stock prices far outlasted any fear for the stability of the government. On the other hand, economic implications may have been inferred from President Eisenhower's heart attack in 1955. The conservative business community probably feared the results of the upcoming presidential election if the president was not the Republican standard-bearer.

The market may eventually become immune to certain types of trauma. The reaction to the 1968 Soviet invasion of Czechoslovakia, for example, was mild by any standard. This may have been due, in part, to the fact that the news broke on a day that the stock exchange was closed; it may also have reflected relative investment inurement to the constant international tensions of that era. Thus, the changing military fortunes of the protracted Indochina conflict caused relatively modest stock market ripples, and the outbreak of war in the Middle East in October 1973 was initially ignored by the market.

"Growth" Stocks—the Results of Spectacular Expansion

The spectacular expansion of many corporations after the outbreak of World War II created keen investor interest in so-called "growth" stocks. Great profits were reaped by individuals with sufficient vision, luck, self-confidence, or a combination of these qualities to acquire the stock of a struggling enterprise just before it crossed the threshold into prosperity.

Through a series of impressive expansions, including acquisition of the important Reliance Insurance Co., the total income of Leasco Corp. rose 55 times between 1965 and 1968. In the enthusiasm engendered by the company's swift advance, the market price of the common stock experienced a spectacular 2,800 percent rise during this period. Similarly, the conglomerate boom in the late 1960s catapulted the price of Ling-Temco-Vought common stock from a low of 17¼ in 1965 to a high of 169½ in 1967. As demand boomed for mobile homes and travel trailers, the sales of Skyline Corporation expanded 19-fold between 1962 and 1972, and the price of its common stock rose from 10 to 70.

Because of the enormous profit potentials of "growth" companies, one of the enticing pastimes of the securities markets has been the effort to uncover securities of this type. A chance for expansion, even though remote, was used to justify poor earnings, restricted dividends, and operational inefficiencies. When the magic word "growth" was used to offset intrinsic weaknesses in a company's financial position, sharp market losses also resulted. Thus, on the basis of Ling-Temco-Vought's impressive prior record, much of it achieved through so-called "funny money" (for example, unconventional securities, warrants, etc.), the company was still cited as an attractive "growth" situation while the stock was selling close to its all-time high in mid-1968. In these recommendations, apparently, little weight was given to the company's complex capital structure. As the financial vulnerability of the company became more manifest, the price of the issue plummeted from its 1969 high of 97¾ in January to a low of 24⅛ in December of that year, a decline of about 75 percent in the face of only an 8 percent decline in the Standard and Poor's Industrial Index during the same period.

A long-term backward look may be helpful at this point. The automotive field, which perhaps more than any other group has reflected this country's advance to the position of the world's leading industrial nation, may be used to illustrate the mistaken notion that market gains necessarily follow purchase of the securities of even prominent companies in a rapidly expanding field. During the period of its initial great growth, many corporations struggled for a dominant role in the automobile industry. Thereafter, output came to be concentrated in the hands of a relatively small number of companies. A gradual weeding-out process occurred, resulting in the elimination of those units which could not withstand the severe competitive pressures generated within the industry.

Included among the automotive corporations that eventually disappeared were some formerly important organizations. In 1929, sales of the Franklin Manufacturing Co. were $26.1 million; the preferred stock sold at a high of 92, while the common stock reached a peak of 46¾. During the same year, the Marmon Motor Car Co. reported sales of $23.9 million, and the common stock hit a high of 104; the Auburn Automobile Co. had sales of $37.6 million, and the stock sold at 514; the Pierce-Arrow Motor Car Co. announced sales of $28 million, the 6 percent preferred stock sold as high as 87½, and common shares reached a level of 37⅞. None of these corporations is now operating.

The investor should adopt a cautious attitude toward the stocks of "growth" companies, since this description often obscures considerable risk and overpricing. Nevertheless, it is important to recognize that the acquisition of an interest in a youthful and dynamic industry offers unique opportunities for achieving great gains in the subsequent period of growth.

To appreciate the problem, one must recognize just what growth stocks are. They have been ordinarily characterized as issues of companies whose total earnings per share or total assets are increasing rapidly. Neither definition satisfactorily characterizes the growth stock. Total assets may be expanded rapidly by new financing, with little benefit accruing to the existing stockholders. Rapid growth of earnings per share can also be deceptive, for such growth is a function of two factors: the rate of return on new investment and the payout ratio. The latter determines how much of the stockholders' money is plowed back into the business, while the former provides the earnings that will flow from the reinvestment. It is the rate of return which is critical. Even a company with humdrum investment opportunities may have a substantial growth if it plows back enough of the stockholders' money.

In view of these limitations, a growth firm has been characterized in the academic literature as one whose return to equity investment exceeds the rate of discount the market applies to that firm's stock. If the market is fully aware of these investment opportunities, it presumably takes them into consideration in the pricing of the stock, which rises to the point where the subsequent rate of return will be quite ordinary. On the other hand, a substantial potential for capital gains obtains when the market fails to recognize that exceptionally favorable investment opportunities are available to the firm; the problem is to recognize when the market has, in fact, overlooked them. The possibility of making such a discovery is greater for the relatively obscure stocks, but a retarding influence is the reluctance of many institutional investors to include such secondary stocks in their portfolios.

EFFICIENT MARKET HYPOTHESES

Thus far, this chapter has been primarily concerned with unraveling the factors that bring about price changes. It is clearly difficult to classify these influences because they overlap and are interrelated. As investors reach different opinions regarding market prospects, some companies disappear from the scene and others enter. At any one time, therefore, a medley of factors work on the market, including economic judgments, market attitudes, individual expectations, risk-assuming characteristics, and psychological responses to special events.

Academicians have long been interested in the phenomenon of price changes in the securities markets. During the 1960s, this interest flowered into an explanatory theory, certain aspects of which (as we note later) have filtered into the real world of the practitioner. For the present, an overview of the major aspects of the theory—which differs in approach from the one described above—will serve to show the direction of the current academic thinking on the subject.[7]

Weak Form of the Theory

In its weak form, the efficient market hypothesis states that successive changes in the prices of stocks are largely unrelated and that prices therefore tend to move in a random fashion.[8] Various tests confirmed this hypotheses: there was a very low serial correlation coefficient between successive price changes of individual stocks; and successive runs of zero, positive or negative changes in the prices of stocks were about what might be expected of random series.[9] Cumulations of random numbers, when charted, produce configurations that strongly resemble those of stock prices.

Challenges were hurled at these demonstrations of randomness in stock prices by the introduction of so-called "filter rules." Critics of the theory argued that by "filtering" price changes through buy-and-sell rules, greater profits could be achieved than through a simple buy-and-hold strategy. A typical filter rule might provide for buying stocks after they have advanced by a designated percentage and then selling or "shorting" them after they declined by a designated percentage.[10] Countercriticisms of the filter tests, in turn, suggested their application was technically defective—for example, through the omission of transaction costs or questionable assumptions about ease of effecting purchases and sales. It was asserted that when adjustments are made to correct those deficiencies, the usefulness of the filter rule disappears.

The primary thrust of the random-walk criticism applies to "chartists" who tend to interpret future stock movements in the light of their prior configurations. The weight of evidence suggests that this approach, popularly known as technical market analysis, is not particularly valid. Nevertheless, it still attracts a popular following and therefore is discussed in Chapter 26.

Semistrong Form of the Theory

The semistrong form of the hypothesis states that prices promptly reflect all available information.[11] This hypothesis rests upon the assumption of an efficient market in which there are many rational participants, with full access to all information, freely and equally competing for securities. In these circumstances, it is held, competition will cause the prices of stocks to reflect their intrinsic worth. As a result, stock prices will rapidly respond to new information, which, in turn, occurs in a random way. Accordingly, prices, themselves, will move randomly.

The tests of the semistrong form were both less direct and less convincing than those applied to the weak form. In general, these tests measured price movements relative to the general market of stocks before and after some news event and found that the event had little effect, presumably because the news was already reflected in the prices of the stocks. For example, it was found that after stock splits there was very little change in the rates of return of those issues with dividend increases, but that declining rates were experienced by the split stocks of those companies with no subsequent dividend increase; the interpretation was that the informational implications of the split were already anticipated in the price of the stock. In another study, no relationship was found between the declines in the price of a stock as a result of secondary offerings and the size of the block offered; the inference drawn was that the declines were caused by the information implicit in the offerings, particularly since the declines were largest in those secondary offerings made by corporations or corporate officers. In still another test, it was concluded the informational content of earnings announcements was anticipated by the market, since the average rates of returns of the stocks that had earnings gains advanced in the year preceding the announcement, while the stocks with decreased earnings declined during this period.[12]

If the semistrong form of the hypothesis is correct, the prices of stocks reflect all the public information that can be obtained about them. Accordingly, there is no such thing as an undervalued security, since the current price is the best indication of its intrinsic value. In these circumstances, the return that an investor can expect to obtain is primarily dependent on the degree of risk he is willing to assume; the theory and implication of risk is discussed in the following chapter. There is little question that expected long-run return is related to risk. Sufficient evidence of price discrepancies among securities exists, however, to doubt that market price invariably represents intrinsic value; therefore, one need not give up the quest for undervalued securities. To the extent that there are such undervaluations, the theory would hold that they reflect market imperfections. From the point of view of the investor, the reason may be less important than the fact that profits still can be made by identifying undervalued securities, even though as markets become more rational the process of identification becomes more difficult.

Strong Form of the Theory

Going one step further, the strong form of the efficient market hypothesis asserts that the prices of stocks already take into account both what is known through public announcements and through access to extensive private analyses. Typical of these private analyses are those bought by institutional investors with commission dollars.

The tests of the strong form of the theory characteristically were based on the performance of mutual funds. Presumably, if the funds performed well, the reason could be ascribed to their access to unique analyses; if their performance was not superior, that would confirm the notion that the prices of stocks reflect all relevant information, whether obtainable through public sources or private analyses. The tests invariably found that the performance of individual funds was insignificantly different from that of unmanaged portfolios or randomly selected portfolios of comparable risk.[13]

Explanations of these results ordinarily point to the fact that the performance of the market really reflects the best judgments of fiercely competing portfolio managers. It is, therefore, logical that the performance of an individual fund would not differ much from a portfolio derived from the general market. One must bear in mind, however, that the bulk of institutional investments are in a fairly small segment of the stock market. It should hardly be surprising that such competition impacts information on prices too quickly to permit the portfolio returns to be affected. Furthermore, the managers operate under constraints so that their portfolios are not freely chosen and must make returns sufficient to pay the expenses and management fees. If the managers could not find underpriced securities, they would earn a return less than a random portfolio of equal risk. Finally recognizing an underpriced security may be a matter of skill, but finding one to recognize in the first place is a matter of luck, randomly distributed. It could be argued that the relative inability of managers to outperform randomly selected portfolios of equal risk means that the managers have not yet sufficiently cultivated their skills. One would therefore conclude that considerable effort should be made to improve the tools and techniques of securities analysis.[14]

SUMMARY

The vulnerability of non-high-grade securities to changing circumstances makes it difficult to segregate the factors affecting their price movements. Nevertheless, for purposes of analysis, some effort at classification is desirable.

The price of a security may rise because of eventual recognition that it has been undervalued. In a perfect market, such undervaluations would not occur; many economists believe that market imperfections may arise out of such things as differences in the analytic capacities of the participants or discrepancies in the flow of information. In these circumstances, undervaluations may be found, with consequent benefits for those who detect them.

Special events may generate an investor psychology that drives securities to unjustifiably high or low levels. Speculators have sought to benefit from this condition by purchases of so-called "hot issues." For the most part, these represent new offerings whose glamour has a psychological appeal but which have only modest economic values. Substantial profits have been made by purchasing such issues at the offering and disposing of them shortly thereafter at higher levels. In mid-1973 the SEC adopted new disclosure rules designed, among other things, to "cool down" the hot-issue market, should it materialize once more.

Shifting investor expectations regarding the growth of a company may affect the level at which its stock sells without modifying the investor's required rate of return.

As economic conditions change, investors with different risk preferences enter and exit the market. These investors are attracted by different types of securities; their subsequent purchases and sales alter existing price relationships accordingly.

Securities prices are based primarily on corporate potential earnings, which, in turn, are influenced directly by economic conditions. Over a period of years, therefore, there is a reasonably close correlation between business activity and the economic outlook, although important discrepancies occur.

Shocks often have a negative influence on the market. The reason is that trauma produces uncertainty, which is tantamount to a reduction in the quality of the income stream associated with the various stocks. Thus, even though a dramatic event, such as the sudden threat of war, may raise the level of expected earnings, it may also increase uncertainty enough to more than offset the benefits of improved earnings expectations.

The spectacular expansion of many corporations after the outbreak of World War II created keen investor interest in so-called "growth" stocks. Without doubt, the acquisition of an interest in a youthful and dynamic industry offers unique opportunities for achieving great gains in the subsequent period of growth. Nevertheless, the investor must adopt a cautious attitude toward such issues, since the term "growth" often obscures considerable risk and overpricing.

Academicians have long been interested in the phenomenon of price movements in the securities markets. This interest has flowered into an explanatory theory that does not require the classification of market forces. In its weakest form, the theory simply asserts that successive changes in the prices of stocks are largely unrelated and that prices therefore tend to move in a random fashion. A stronger form of the efficient market hypothesis asserts that prices instantaneously respond to new developments; because these occur in a random way, prices themselves move randomly. Going one step further, the strong form of the efficient market hypothesis asserts that the prices of stocks already take into account what is known both through public announcements and through extensive private analyses.

Part Three

ANALYZING COMMON STOCK

Assessing a value for common stock is the heart of securities analysis. As might be expected, therefore, this section is the longest in the book. It is introduced by a discussion of the characteristics of common stock, which provides the framework for developing an analytic theory. Much of this theory is devoted to the measurement of risk and how it affects the values of a security. These values, in turn, are largely based on future corporate earnings, from which dividends will be paid, and on the discount factor for capitalizing earnings. Earnings determination entails an understanding of the corporation's financial statements and of the accounting policies underlying their preparation. With this understanding as the backdrop, the final chapters in this section offer a step-by-step analysis of the elements entering into the forecast of prices and dividends and some of the basic considerations affecting the forecast.

CHAPTER 9

The Nature of Common Stock and a Theoretical Framework for Its Analysis

THE COMMON STOCKHOLDER

The scope of the common stockholder's rights is determined by the contract between him and the corporation. This contract is, in effect, embodied in applicable law and in a corporation's charter, bylaws, and stock certificates. In addition to the basic rights of sharing in the corporation's earnings and in its assets if it is dissolved, the common stockholder has the right to elect the corporate directors, vote on matters affecting his corporate interests, transfer his shares, and inspect the corporation's books; often, he also has the right to subscribe to new issues of stock. He may sacrifice any of these rights voluntarily, or the contract may embody modifications of them.

A stockholder's voting right is a potential threat to management. Rival groups may develop which, through the modern proxy system of balloting, could accumulate sufficient votes to oust incumbent directors. At one time, to relieve itself of this threat, management not uncommonly issued two classes of stock, classified A and B, alike in all respects except that only one class, which it controlled, had voting power.

Growing investor sophistication and government disapproval have curtailed this practice. The Public Utility Holding Company Act of 1935 endows the Securities and Exchange Commission with the power to require newly issued common stock of corporations subject to the act to carry voting privileges. The Bankruptcy Act forbids corporations to carry out reorganization plans that provide for issuance of nonvoting stocks. Since 1926 the New York Stock Exchange has refused to list common stocks that do not bestow on its holders the right to vote. Because of these influences, very few major corporations still have outstanding a class of nonvoting common stock.[1]

Through dividend payments the common stockholder shares in the profits of a corporation. Absence of a fixed rate means that a ceiling does not limit the size of possible disbursements. Offsetting this advantage is the fact that when business recedes, these distributions are the first to be eliminated. Moreover, among the holders of securities the common stockholder is the most vulnerable to complete elimination in the event of bankruptcy.

Thus, among the corporation's securities holders, the owner of common stock is the principal risk bearer.* On the positive side, there is no limit to the potential capital gain a stockholder can achieve, whereas the extent of the loss cannot be greater than the original investment. In some instances, holders of common stock have achieved substantial gains, the magnitude of which may be concealed by repeated splits. For example, at the beginning of 1951 a share of IBM stock cost $216; 20 years later, at the outset of 1971, it amounted to about $317. What this comparison fails to show is that if the investor had purchased one share of stock in 1951 and retained all the shares acquired from stock dividends and stock splits, he or she would have approximately 34½ shares at the beginning of 1971. As we have pointed out earlier and will discuss in detail later, the return to the stockholder is not simply the dividend but the dividend plus the capital gain.

Stock Certificate

A stock certificate is a written instrument signed by the proper officers of a corporation, acknowledging that the person named in the certificate is the owner of a stipulated number of shares of stock. It is the evidence of stock ownership and the physical instrument by which transfers are made, but it is not the stock itself. Most state laws prescribe the form of the certificate, generally requiring that it show the number, kind, and classes

*A dictionary definition of risk is the chance of loss. The major objective of this and the next chapter is to identify a method of *measuring* risk, but specification of a measurement is substantially a definition. In the interim we use the word in the dictionary sense.

of shares represented. The NYSE has established further requirements to prevent counterfeiting or errors.

Negotiability is an important legal concept that has many technical aspects outside the concern of this book. Essentially, it means that one who qualifies as a holder of an instrument in due course (that is, generally, one who takes in good faith and for value) may obtain better rights and title to it than the original owner. For example, a person who steals a check made out in good form, a typical negotiable instrument, does not obtain title to it, but if the check is negotiated a subsequent holder in due course may obtain good title. To be negotiable, an instrument by law must have certain characteristics, including an unconditional promise or order to pay a sum certain in money.

In general, stock certificates do not have the requisite characteristics; hence, they would not be negotiable under Article 3 (commercial paper) of the Uniform Commercial Code. However, Article 8 (investment securities) of the UCC treats these certificates as negotiable. Accordingly, title is transferable by delivery of the instrument after endorsement or assignment. Thus, persons who buy the certificate in good faith and for value acquire it free of prior deficiencies. This rule makes it important for owners to report the loss of a certificate promptly to the transfer agent or company. The transfer agent will stop the transfer of the certificate, and on receiving an affidavit of loss and a surety bond from the owner will issue a new certificate. The 1975 Securities Acts Amendments authorize the SEC to require all persons involved in the handling of securities transactions to report information about missing securities, authenticate securities used in certain financial transactions, and to be fingerprinted. The commission is also authorized to inquire into the handling of lost securities. It is expected that the commission will delegate some of the responsibilities to banking agencies.

The investor probably pays little attention to the stock certificate, but the securities industry has given much thought to its form, both to prevent tampering and to reduce costs. The traditional certificate has "corner pieces" in the upper right- and left-hand corners where the following legends appear: "Less than 100 Shares," "100 Shares," or "More than 100 Shares." For 100-share certificates, the number 100 is engraved in numeric form in the "share counter," which is located near the right "corner piece" and is engraved in alpha form in the "open throat" in the body of the instrument. For the other denominations, the numbers are typed in numeric form in the "share counter" and in alpha form in the "open throat." Except for the 100-share certificate, a punch panel is furnished (columns of numbers where the correct share amount is purchased by the transfer agent) to deter tampering with the certificate. This panel may be omitted from the "more than 100-share" certificate where the transfer agent may either perforate the number of shares or, more often, macerate it (the process of maceration penetrates the paper fibres of the certificate similar to a check-writer).

As a consequence of the growth of institutional trading and a substantial increase in volume, the exchange has been running a pilot program (available at the option of the issuer) that utilizes a single form certificate. Initiated in January 1972, this program utilizes a certificate with punch panels. The "corner piece," however, has a legend indicating some upper limitations, such as "Not More than 100,000 Shares." In such a case, the panel has a number of columns to permit punching the appropriate amount.

In April 1973 the exchange instituted another type of single certificate without a punch panel. This certificate lends itself to computer processing and so eliminates the need for manual handling. A blank certificate is provided in which the number of shares involved is typed. In addition, the computer has a special ribbon for printing the purchaser's name and the number of shares, so that the ink utilized by the computer's printer penetrates the fibres of the paper. Several other protective devices are also provided.

In the case of bonds, the standard amounts of $1,000, $5,000, or $10,000 (and occasionally larger amounts) may be engraved in the instrument. At the option of the issuer, a blank bond is also available where the information is typed and then macerated on the instrument.

The SEC has been concerned that persons whose securities are held in "street name" or nominee accounts for convenience, safety, or other personal reasons, receive information about the issuer of the securities in a timely manner. Accordingly, the commission has adopted regulations that impose obligations upon corporate issuers of securities and on registered brokers to facilitate the transmission of information to individuals holding securities in "street name" and to nominees. To obtain the cooperation of banks and trust companies, which are not subject to SEC jurisdiction, the commission has followed the policy of transmitting its proposals to the federal banking agencies.

Facilitating Transfers

Purchasers of stock may prefer to leave their certificates in the name of their broker or some other nominee, so as to facilitate delivery in the event of future sale. Certificates held in the broker's name are described as in "street name." The 1975 Amendments direct the SEC to study the practice of registering securities in "street name" to determine (1) whether such registration is consistent with the policies of the Exchange Act, and (2) whether steps can be taken to facilitate communications between corporations and their shareholders while retaining the benefits of "street name" registration. The commission is to report its preliminary findings to Congress within six months and its final recommendation within one year. The initial report indicated the commission is studying various alternatives.

Nominees for "street name" certificates may be individuals, partnerships, or corporations which hold title to the stock but are neither the real nor beneficial owners. The procedure of leaving the stock in street name or in the name of some nominee permits it to be sold without having to go through the transfer books. The corporation sends all communications to the person or organization whose name appears on the certificate and in the records of the transfer agent; dividends and other important notices are duly forwarded by the broker or other nominee to the real owner. Purchasers of stock may also permit the certificates to remain in the name of the original holder, leaving the endorsed certificates with the buying broker; this again facilitates transfer. When any important development is expected, such as declaration of dividends, there is a flurry of transfers to the names of the new owners.

The development of a large volume of trading in the late 1960s, and especially the advent of institutional trading, shed glaring light on the traditional transfer system.[2] In order to overcome the difficulties that arose, the NYSE, as described previously, developed a central depository share-transfer system designed to immobilize certificates. Current efforts are directed toward creating a national clearing system and, perhaps, eliminating the certificate completely. Thus, among other things, the new Section 17A of the Securities Acts Amendments of 1975, concerned with a national system for clearing securities, provides that the commission shall seek to end the physical movement of securities certificates in connection with the settlement of brokers' and dealers' transactions.

INCORPORATING RISK INTO THE ANALYSIS OF COMMON STOCK

Investments in common stock are considered risky to some degree. This riskiness affects the rate of return that investors of a stock *will consider satisfactory*, and that rate of return, together with the stock's expected earnings, will determine its value. The single-period rate of return on a security R_t is defined as $R_t = (P_t + D_t - P_{t-1})/P_{t-1}$, where P_t is the price at time t and D_t is the dividend (or interest) received in the period. This definition thus identifies the rate of return as the ratio of capital gains plus dividends to the initial price.

One technique of analysis is to seek those stocks that promise the highest rate of return in any given risk class. (A risk class may be viewed as those assets with roughly the same degree of risk, however that may be measured. For the moment it will suffice to consider a group of assets that has a given chance of loss riskier than a second group if the chance of loss on the assets in the second group is smaller.) An investor will still have to determine which risk classes should be represented in his or her portfolio. If the investor believes the market will move up, a shift may be made to more risky groups; if a general downturn is foreseen, conservative stocks, bonds, or even cash may be emphasized. Some major banks, seeking quantitative means of handling the huge sums under their management, structure portfolios into different risk categories. At one extreme, for example, a portfolio might be divided into 80 percent relatively riskless fixed-income securities and 20 percent risky stocks; at the opposite extreme, 80 percent could be in risky stocks and 20 percent in relatively riskless issues. The institution selects the portfolio structure desired and buys and sells securities to maintain or adjust the structure as market conditions change.

Risk has always occupied an important niche in the evaluation of securities. In recent years much effort has been expended in trying to understand and quantify this concept. The effort has largely involved the development of a theoretical framework that integrates risk into the analysis of stock. To appreciate the implications of the measure of risk that has emerged, it is desirable and necessary to have some understanding of this theoretical underpinning.

Accordingly, in the remainder of this chapter and in the following chapter we explore evolving financial theory. The going may not be easy. Much of this material involves the use of mathematics, which some students and investors find distasteful. We shall adhere with particular care to the policy followed throughout this book of showing only the most basic mathematical relationships.

The modern concept of risk, involving primarily the so-called capital-asset pricing model (a model which purports to explain how asset values are determined in a perfect market) has attracted considerable interest in both academic and business circles. The theoretical apparatus has some interesting implications for securities analysis; as scholars continue their work in the area, even more useful applications may be forthcoming. We shall have occasion to refer to the capital-asset pricing model later in the text.

THE CONCEPT OF RISK

Securities have two basic characteristics—return and risk. To a large extent, therefore, selecting securities involves a comparison of these two features and determining the appropriate trade-off. Investors ordinarily have a reasonably clear idea of return, but risk is a more involved concept. To understand it, we must fall back on another important notion, that of utility, which is a subjective quality arising out of individual needs and attitudes.

Utility

Assume that an individual expects to live for two more periods. Because of a unique illness, death is certain at the end of the second period, and the individual intends to leave no estate. All income and wealth, therefore, must be disposed of over the two periods. In exchange for this wealth and income the choice of a number of contracts is offered. The contracts are numbered, and contract j can be written as (c_{1j}, c_{2j}), where c_{ij} is the dollar amount of consumption in period i provided by the jth contract. Assume further that there exists a rule or function which we designate as $U(c_{1j}, c_{2j})$ that enables the individual to assign a number or index value to the option provided by contract j. The rule may be, for example,

$$(1)\quad U = a_1 c_{1j} + a_2 c_{1j}^2 + b_1 c_{2j} + b_2 c_{2j}^2,$$

so that the index value not only depends upon the dollar amounts of consumption in each period, but also upon the squares of those amounts.

The a's and b's may be interpreted as the weights given to the dollars spent and their squares in periods 1 and 2, respectively. $U(c_{1j}, c_{2j})$ and equation (1) are known as utility functions.

When any two options are offered, say $K_1 = (c_{11}, c_{21})$ and $K_2 = (c_{12}, c_{22})$, assume that the individual can state:

(a) K_1 preferred to K_2, or
(b) K_2 preferred to K_1, or
(c) no preference.

Confronted with three options, the individual can state:

(a) K_1 preferred to K_3, if K_1 preferred to K_2 and K_2 to K_3, or
(b) no preference between K_1 and K_3, if no preference between K_1 and K_2 and between K_2 and K_3.

A person with such tastes may be said to make choices *as if* he or she were maximizing some index such as U, which we have called a utility function.

Finally, if given the choice between K_1, K_2, and $\alpha K_1 + (1-\alpha)K_2$, i.e., $(\alpha c_{11} + (1-\alpha)c_{12}, \alpha c_{21} + (1-\alpha)c_{22})$, where $0 < \alpha < 1$, the individual always chooses the third option the utility function is said to be concave.[3] Such a utility function might resemble *EACBF* in Figure 9-1.

FIGURE 9-1

A Utility Function

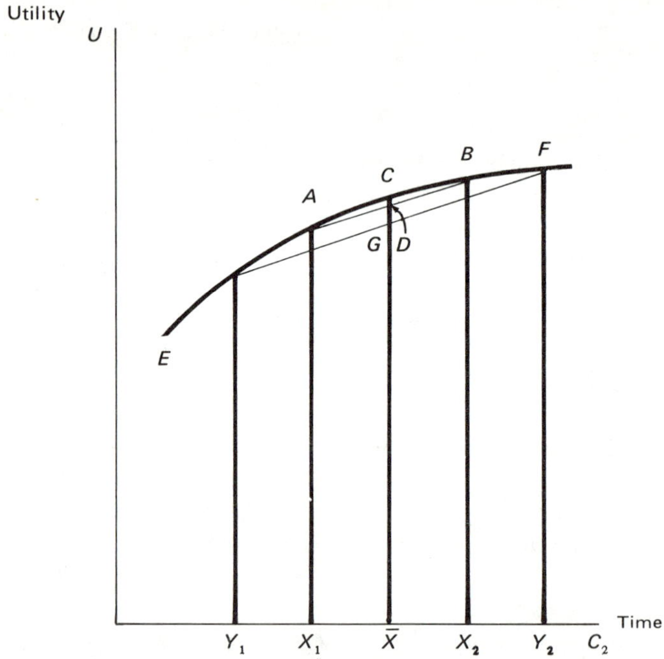

In the case under consideration, the utility for the individual in question depends on the amount of consumption in both periods. If the level of consumption in the first period is fixed, however, the utility function may be written in terms of consumption in the second period alone, $U(c_2)$, as in Figure 9-1. (In writing c_2 without a second subscript, we are substituting a variable for a quantity. In Figure 9-1, $U(c_{2j})$ would be represented by a point on *EACBF*.) In this chart utility (U) is measured along the vertical axis, and consumption in period two (c_2) along the horizontal axis. The curve is drawn concave with respect to the c_2 axis—that is, a straight line like *AB* joining any two points of *EACBF* lies wholly between the curve and the c_2 axis. As will be seen, this concavity is important in the chain of reasoning that is being developed.

How Dispersion Introduces Risk

Continuing with this example, let the individual's initial wealth and the market value of all income to be received in the two periods equal w_1. If, instead of buying contracts, the individual sets aside for spending c_1 in period 1, and invests the amount $h = w_1 - c_1$, earning income at rate of return r, $h(1 + r)$ will be available for spending in period 2. In accordance with our assumptions, this full amount is spent in the second period, so that $c_2 = h(1 + r)$. In this discussion both w_1 and c_1 are fixed amounts, and therefore the size of h is completely determined. If r represents a contract rate, there can be no uncertainty about the values of $h(1 + r)$ or c_2. When the individual is faced with only one possible outcome, there is no risk. The outcome may be unpleasant, but that is not necessarily risk.

Let us now change the conditions and introduce risk by providing for a multiplicity of possible returns. Let $\tilde{r}$ be a random variable.* The value of the investment and therefore of consumption in the second period is $\tilde{c}_2$. Furthermore, the probability distribution of the value of the investment and $\tilde{c}_2$ will be determined completely by the probability distribution of $\tilde{r}$.†

The significance of a multiplicity of possible rates of return can be seen by returning to Figure 9-1. There $\tilde{r}$ can have the values r_1 or r_2, and the individual's original investment,[4] h, can have one of two corresponding terminal values, X_1 or X_2. The curve *EACBF* traces out the utility index values, or simply the utility of the various possible levels of c_2. If $c_2 = X_1$, its utility is A—that is, $U(c_2) = A$. If $c_2 = X_2$, then $U(c_2) = B$. If the probability that the lower of the two rates of return (r_1) will prevail is α, and $(1 - \alpha)$ is the probability that r_2 will prevail, the expected utility of the original investment h is $D = \alpha A + (1 - \alpha)B$, a point on a straight line between A and B. Since the probability of X_1 occurring is α, the expected investment value is $\bar{X} = \alpha X_1 + (1 - \alpha)X_2$, and its utility is C. [Expected values of a variable X will be indicated by a bar, as above, or by the notation $E(X)$.] D will always be perpendicularly below C when the utility function is concave.[5]

*That is, a rule which assigns a value to every member of a set of events. Note that r will be unknown if there are no investments that mature at the end of the first period and the investment must be sold at that time at the prevailing market price. That price will depend on the market rates that are expected to prevail after the end of period 1. These rates are not known at the time the investment has to be made (the beginning of period 1). Once those rates are given, r will assume (or be "assigned") a specific value. A tilde (~) indicates that the variable is random.

†It is not necessary to "know" the probability distribution of outcomes in the sense that the probability distribution of withdrawing an ace from a deck of cards is "known." We seek a course of action which will yield the greatest satisfaction based on what we know and *believe*. The intelligent investor, in contrast with the fortuitous investor, determines this path in the light of available information. If the investor chooses between investments by tossing a coin and realizes a profit, he has been lucky but not smart. If an analyst recommends an investment on the basis of the best available information, but developments that could not have been anticipated play havoc with his choice, he has been unlucky but is not therefore less competent.

In the long run, the intelligent investor is presumably more likely to achieve good results than the one who depends on luck. The future involves the unknown. In most instances, investors have to base decisions on probability distributions they have guessed at and developed from knowledge and beliefs, rather than on distributions such as those associated with the mortality tables used by the insurance industry, which are based on a multitude of observations. While this difference may seem important, it is not as sharp as one might suppose.

To see the consequence of a greater dispersion of outcomes, let us now assume that the possible rates of return are more extreme and terminate in investment values of Y_1 and Y_2 instead of X_1 and X_2. We continue to assume, however, that the probability of the lower rate of return prevailing is α, and that the expected investment value is $\bar{X}$.[6] As a result, the utility of the expected investment value is still C but the expected utility of the investment[7] will be G on the straight line EF directly below D. In other words, $E[U(c_2)]$ decreases as the range of possible outcomes increases. Thus, the expected utility of the investment and of c_2 is a function not only of $E(c_2)$ but also of the dispersion of $\tilde{c}_2$. Indeed, it varies directly with the first (the expected return) and inversely with the second (the dispersion or spread). Because of this, maximizing expected utility is not the same as maximizing expected return.

If there were many possible outcomes, the investor could measure dispersion of returns by the standard deviation of returns. If the return was likely to be 10% ± 2%, where 2% was the standard deviation, we would be less uncertain of the outcome than if the return was likely to be 10% ± 4%. It is a short step from uncertainty to risk, and so the standard deviation of a portfolio's rate of return may be taken as a measure or surrogate of its risk.[8]

The discussion above has been based on planning for a single period. Comprehensive planning is inevitably multiperiod, with an obscure terminal point. The terminal point is obscure because the critical factor in determining the ultimate planning horizon is death, and the timing of that is uncertain indeed. Although utility theory does lend itself to multiperiod planning and can take death into consideration, the extended theory is highly complex. The simpler schema has nevertheless proved very useful, and we shall retain it.

MEASURING THE RISK OF SECURITIES

In exploring the alternatives of the individual in the earlier example, we saw that his level of consumption in the second period was dependent on the terminal value of his portfolio. That in turn was dependent on the rate of return he realized on his investment h. Therefore, the primary concern of the individual is with the return on his *total portfolio of assets*, on which his future level of consumption depends. It is the riskiness of the portfolio that generates the uncertainty regarding the level of consumption in period 2.

A portfolio, however, is simply a collection of assets. Logically, the risk of any particular asset in the portfolio should be measured by its contribution to the riskiness of the portfolio.[9] If we can measure this contribution, we will have a specific risk measure for stocks.

Portfolio Risk

The volatility of stock prices is a fact of life. Recognition of this volatility leads to uncertainty about what the price will be when it is necessary or desirable to liquidate the stock. Volatility and uncertainty are related, but they are not the same thing. Volatility involves a historical sequence of prices. Uncertainty and risk relate to the fact that at any moment in the future the stock may have any one (and only one) of several prices, and we are unable to specify which one.

As a practical matter, many writers assume that the future rates of return will have the same dispersion as the historical rates of return; they use the standard deviation of past rates of return as the measure of the standard deviation of the judgmental probability distribution.[10]

While the rate of return on a portfolio is simply the weighted average returns of the component stocks, the weighted average of the standard deviations of the returns on those stocks is not the standard deviation of the portfolio. The reason is that the deviations of the stocks' returns from their expected values may offset one another. As an illustration, consider two securities whose rates of return move in opposing patterns, as in lines *A* and *B* in Figure 9-2. An investor holding either security *A* or security *B* would be taking some risk, but one who held both would take none at all. (The return would be the average of the two.) Actually, stocks do not behave in this fashion, and showing fluctuations in the rates of return of two securities as mirror images of each other is a figment of the text writer's imagination.[11]

Effect of Diversification

Suppose an investor has a choice of stocks *A* or *B*, or a combination, *C*, of the two. As can be seen in Figure 9-3, the returns on all three investments have a fair amount of volatility, but *C*'s is obviously less than either *A*'s or *B*'s. Often the deviations of the returns on *A* and *B* will be in opposite directions, so that the deviation of the returns on the combination is dampened. If the deviations of the returns on *A* and *B* are positive half the time, the probability that both will be positive at the same time is only $\frac{1}{2} \times \frac{1}{2} = \frac{1}{4}$. In the case of three securities, the chance that some deviation will be offset is increased and, therefore, the probability that three securities will have simultaneous positive deviations is only $\frac{1}{2} \times \frac{1}{2} \times \frac{1}{2} = \frac{1}{8}$. Clearly, the dampening process continues as the number of securities combined is increased.

FIGURE 9-2

Returns on Inversely Correlated Investments

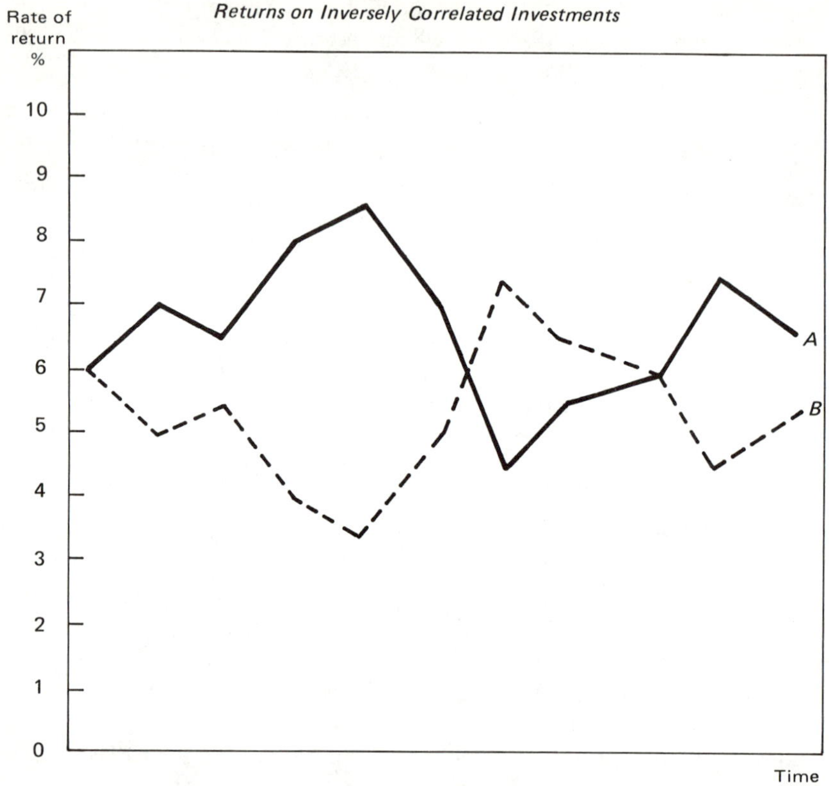

It can be shown that the risk, measured by the standard deviation of the returns of a portfolio, can be reduced almost to zero by sufficient diversification if the returns are independent. If the returns are correlated, however, the portfolio's standard deviation can only be reduced to the average covariance of the rates of returns of the stocks in the portfolio with each other. It has been estimated that as few as 16 stocks will eliminate 90 percent of the achievable reduction in variability.

To illustrate the differential impact of diversification when the returns of the securities are and are not correlated, we calculated the standard deviations of the rates of returns of General Motors (GM), Standard Oil (SN), and United Air Lines (UAL) for a ten-year period:

GM	26.2%
SN	23.7%
UAL	32.4%

If the returns of the three securities had been uncorrelated, the standard deviation of the return of a portfolio consisting of an equal invest-

FIGURE 9-3

Uncorrelated and Pooled Securities

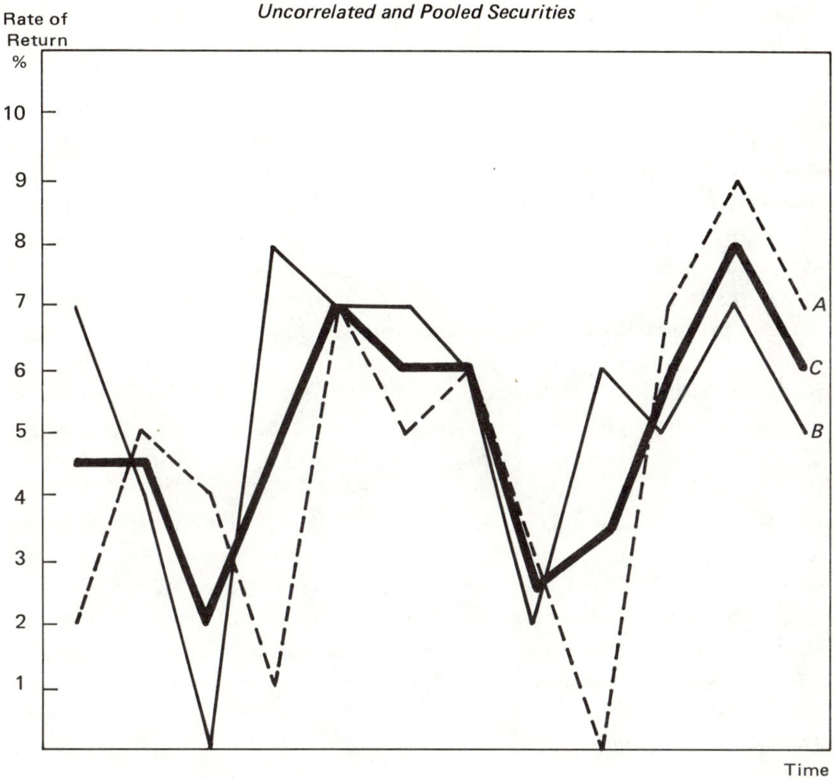

ment in each stock would have been 15.9 percent. Since, in fact, the returns were correlated, the standard deviation of the rate of return on the portfolio actually was 23.4 percent. It is worth noting that, in both cases, the portfolio's standard deviation is less than that of any of the three stocks that comprise it.

Security Risk

In our quest for a measure of the risk of a security, we have thus far shown that, up to a certain point, adding stocks to a portfolio reduces its risk. It is clear, therefore, that the standard deviation of a stock's rate of return does not measure its effect on the riskiness of a portfolio in which it is included. Thus, not all the risk represented by the standard deviation of the stock's rate of return is necessarily relevant. It appears that we need only concern ourselves with that part of the variability of a stock's rate of return which affects the risk of the portfolio—that is, the part which does not disappear when the stock is included in a portfolio. If we consider a portfolio consisting of a single stock, the risk of the portfolio is the standard deviation of the stock's rate of return. When a stock is joined by others, part of the risk represented by its standard deviation is diversified away. The part which remains contributes to the risk of the portfolio itself.

We shall focus now on the portion of risk that cannot be (or is not) diversified away when the stock is included in the portfolio of the investor's choice. It is customary to describe as *systematic* that portion of a security's risks that cannot be eliminated by diversification. The other portion, which is *unsystematic*, depends on factors unique to the company, such as possession of special technology or market domination. Through diversification, the unsystematic risk of a portfolio may be weaned away, leaving only the systematic or market-related risk. Since market movements are merely the averages of changes in the prices of all stocks, the return on a well-diversified portfolio is likely to move very closely with the market. The returns on specialized portfolios may move more or less independently of the market.

Our focus now is on systematic risk. We seek a device for measuring it; that device should be practical and reasonably comprehensible to the professional investor. Through some mathematical manipulations, analysts have reached a helpful conclusion that is formidable in appearance but relatively simple in concept. They have shown that the contribution of a security to the risk of a portfolio is the sum of the covariances of the rate of return of that security with the rates of return of every other security in the portfolio, weighted by the proportion of each of those securities to the entire portfolio divided by the standard deviation of the portfolio's rate of return. This amount can legitimately be interpreted as the risk of a security in the portfolio. In fact, it is never necessary to calculate the risk of a stock by this complicated formula because, as we show later, it turns out to be the equivalent, under certain circumstances, of another, much simpler measure that is in common use. The risk of the portfolio itself is nothing more than the weighted average of the risks of the securities (as just defined) in the portfolio, where the weights are again the proportions of the securities in the portfolio.

SUMMARY

Evaluating common stock is the heart of securities analysis. Every share represents a fractional claim of ownership. Most shares have privileges for voting on matters affecting the interests of the corporation. The precise rights of a share are defined in the applicable law, the corporation charter, the bylaws, and the stock certificates. Stockholders typically share in the profits of a corporation through dividend payments, which are paid when the board of directors declares them. Ownership today is ordinarily represented by a certificate which is a negotiable instrument. The certificate is a cumbersome device, and the need to deliver and transfer it when a stock is sold vastly complicates trading in common stock.

The return to a stockholder is not confined to the dividends received. The stock may appreciate or depreciate in value. Because the corporation is under no contractual obligation to declare any dividend and because the price of the stock will fluctuate with the fortunes of the company and the vagaries of the market, the annual increment in wealth accruing to the stockholder is quite uncertain, and investments in stock are quite risky. Risk has always been an important consideration in the evaluation of securities. It is therefore necessary to understand the modern concept of risk. That necessitates some understanding of the concept of utility.

If an individual can order options, and if the ordering is consistent in the sense that when *A* is preferred to *B* and *B* is preferred to *C*, then *A* is preferred to *C*, the individual can be said to make choices as if maximizing a utility index. If the utility curve (the graph of the utility index) is concave, as in Figure 9-1, and the individual is confronted with uncertainty (i.e., the possibility of one of several outcomes), then the expected utility of a portfolio will vary inversely with the degree of uncertainty (i.e., the dispersion of the possible outcomes). The degree of uncertainty of a portfolio can be expressed as the standard deviation of the rate of return of the portfolio. That standard deviation is related to the riskiness of the stocks included in the portfolio. For the evaluation of a stock, the relevant portion of the stock's total risk is the fraction of the total portfolio risk the stock contributes. The standard deviation of a stock's rate of return is not a measure of the stock's risk. When different stocks are combined in a portfolio, the standard deviation of the portfolio's return is less than the standard deviation of most of the stocks included in the portfolio.

CHAPTER 10

Introducing Beta into Securities Analysis

A REFERENCE PORTFOLIO

In the preceding chapter we saw that an individual with certain common kinds of tastes made choices as though he were maximizing a utility index. This means that, when confronted with uncertainty, the individual made choices as though he were maximizing expected utility rather than expected income or wealth. It can easily be seen in Figure 9-1 (p. 218) that if the expected value of the Y option were just slightly in excess of $\bar{X}$, its expected utility would still be less than that of the X option. The riskiness of a stock will affect the choices between two portfolios only to the extent that it affects the utility of the portfolio in which it is included. It affects the expected utility of a portfolio to the extent that the inclusion of the stock affects the return and the riskiness of the portfolio. Regardless of how risky the stock may be in isolation, if the investor includes it in a portfolio the only relevant risk of the stock is the contribution of that stock's risk to the portfolio risk.

Note, however, that we have developed a concept of relevant risk of a particular security in a *specific* portfolio. If an investor considers the same

FIGURE 10-1

Efficient Portfolios

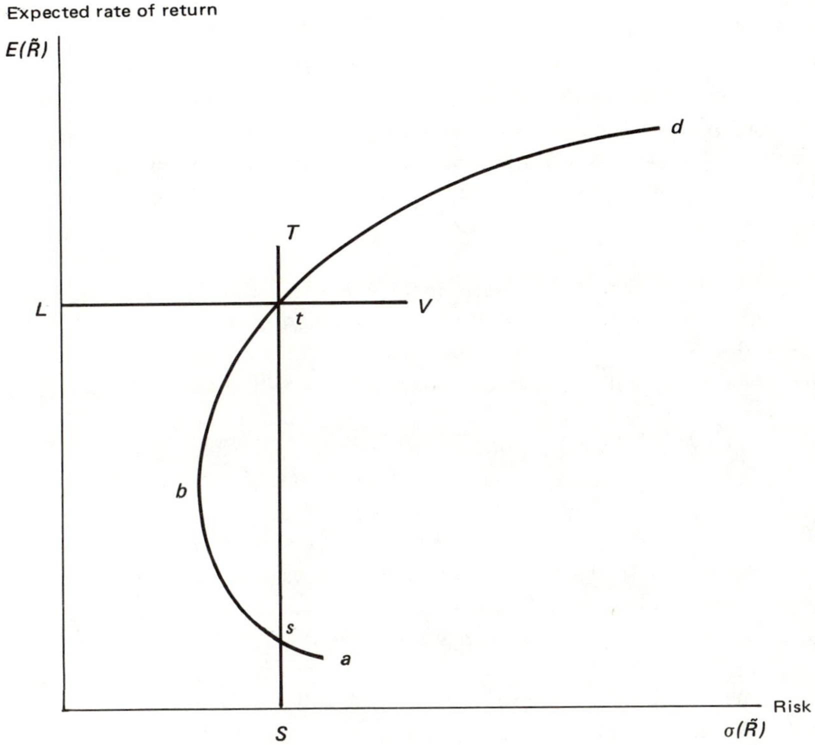

security in two different portfolios, he will derive two different figures for risk. It would be helpful if we could identify a portfolio that all investors can use as the reference point for determining the risk of an individual security. Fortunately, that can be done.

Efficient and Optimal Portfolios

The portfolio chosen as a reference portfolio for this purpose must be one that will maximize the investor's expected utility. It can be shown that finding such a portfolio is the equivalent of selecting a so-called efficient portfolio whose expected utility exceeds that of any other efficient portfolio. A portfolio is *efficient* if the standard deviation of its returns is less than that of any other portfolio with the same rate of return; and if its rate of return is greater than that of any other portfolio with the same standard deviation.

Consider Figure 10-1. Let the curve *asbtd* represent the left boundary of all portfolios that can be constructed from the universe of existing risky securities. The point at which a line parallel to the vertical axis is tangent to the *asbtd* curve has been labeled *b*.

Consider the vertical line *ST* that cuts the segment *ab* at *s* and the segment *bd* at *t*. The portfolio *t* has the same standard deviation as *s* but a higher rate of return. Portfolio *t* is said to "dominate" portfolio *s*, in that it offers a higher rate of return than *s* for the same risk exposure. All portfolios on the segment *ab* are dominated by portfolios on the segment *btd.* For any portfolio on *ab* there is one on *btd* which has a higher return for the same risk. Therefore, no portfolio on the segment *ab* can be considered efficient.

On the other hand, since the curve *abtd* represents the leftmost boundary of possible portfolios, the segment *btd* must represent efficient portfolios. On the line *ST* no portfolios above *t* are feasible. Therefore, *t* has the highest rate of return of all portfolios with standard deviation *S*. Similarly, if one draws a line *LtV*, portfolio *t* dominates all portfolios to the right of *t*, and no portfolio to the left of *t* is feasible. Therefore, *t* has the smallest standard deviation of all portfolios with expected rate of return *L*. Every point on the segment *btd* has that characteristic. The segment *btd* is therefore the efficient set–in other words, it represents the universe of efficient portfolios. This curve shows the relationship between the expected rates of return $E(\tilde{R})$ and the standard deviations $\sigma(\tilde{R})$ of efficient portfolios. The curve has two important properties: its slope is positive throughout its length, and it is concave with respect to the σ axis. It can be shown that this curve cannot have a scallop.

To find the efficient portfolio whose expected utility exceeds that of any other efficient portfolio, we juxtapose in Figure 10-2 the indifference curves I_1, I_2, and I_3 of individual *I* and a curve representing the efficient set of portfolios (*aeb*). An *indifference curve* traces the combinations of variables on the vertical and horizontal axes which will yield the investor the same utility. In this case, it represents the combinations of expected rates of return and standard deviations. Any point on one indifference curve vertically above a point on another indifference curve represents a higher rate of return with the same risk exposure. Therefore the higher curve signifies greater utility.

Investor *I* will clearly maximize his expected utility by choosing the portfolio that puts him on the highest indifference curve he can reach. In the diagram this is portfolio *e*. This portfolio is both optimal (because it gives him the highest utility) and efficient, since it is located on the efficient set. Since this is the portfolio that *I* would choose if he were a rational investor, he must consider the risk of particular securities in terms of their contribution to the risk of portfolio *e*. This is the reference portfolio for the investor, and it is unique.

FIGURE 10-2

Optimal Portfolio

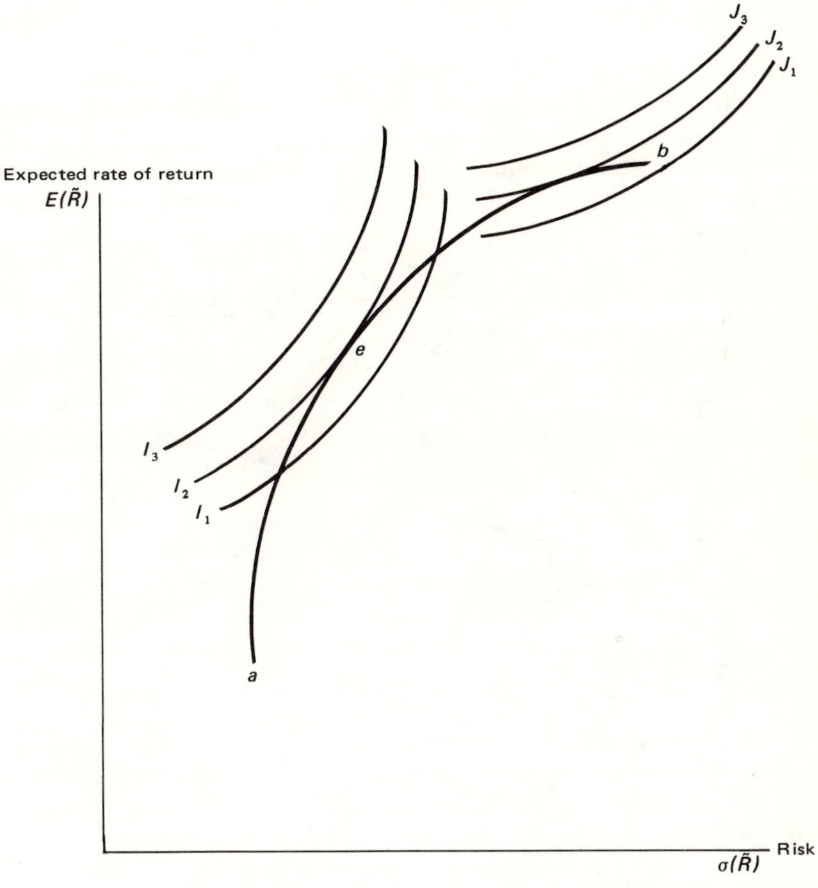

If all investors have the same subjective probability distributions for returns on assets, they are said to have *homogeneous expectations.* If their opinions of possible returns on assets differ, their expectations are said to be heterogeneous. If expectations are homogeneous, they will all have the same efficient set. However, the indifference curves of any two investors *I* and *J* will not be the same except by chance. Consequently, the two investors will not necessarily have the same reference portfolio and will not necessarily attribute the same risk to a given security. The contribution of that security to the riskiness of the two reference portfolios will not necessarily be the same. To be most useful, however, a measure of relevant risk should be investor-independent—that is, the same for all investors. Development of a *market measure of risk* is the next stage.

FIGURE 10-3

Optimal Portfolio with Risk-Free Assets

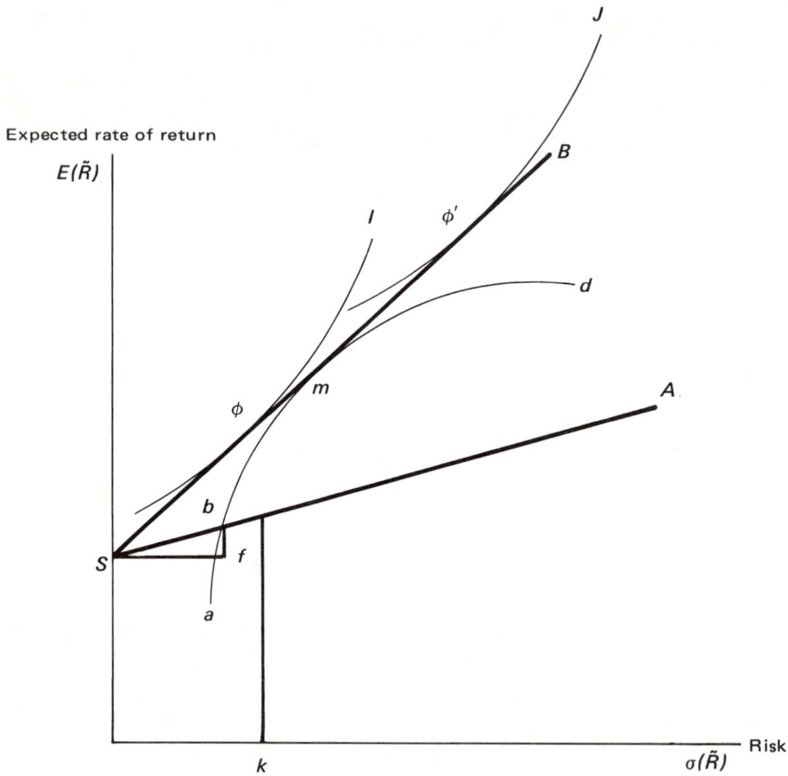

A MARKET MEASURE OF RISK

To develop a market measure of risk we must introduce three concepts successively: a risk-free asset, unlimited borrowing at the risk-free rate, and the assumption that all investors attribute the same probability distributions to the various securities outstanding (homogeneous expectations). Risk-free assets are those without any danger of default. U.S. Treasury securities typically are considered risk-free.

Risk-Free Asset

Consider an investor whose efficient set of risky securities is shown by the curve *abmd* in Figure 10-3. Now assume that there exists a risk-free asset with a rate of return *S*, identifying it as a safe or risk-free security. Finally, consider the straight line *Sb*, which intersects *abmd* at point *b*. Every point on this line represents a portfolio consisting of a combination of portfolio *b* and the safe asset. Similarly, the line *Sm*, which is tangent to the efficient set of risky securities at *m*, represents the various portfolios that can be made by combing portfolio *m* and the safe asset. Obviously, for every portfolio along *Sb*, there is a portfolio on *Sm* vertically above it, and therefore with a higher rate of return for the same risk exposure. The portfolios along *Sm* are better than those along *Sb*. Since *Sm* is tangent to the efficient set of risky securities, it is the highest line from *S* that the investor can reach. The portfolios along *Sm* therefore dominate the portfolios on any other line from *S* that connects with *abmd*.

Once we have a risk-free asset, such as a Treasury security, we have to distinguish between the efficient set of portfolios and the efficient set of portfolios *of risky securities.* Thus in our illustration, the introduction of a risk-free asset changes the efficient set of portfolios from *abmd* (the efficient set of portfolios of risky securities) to *Smd.*

Investor *I* will find that by moving along *Sm* a higher indifference curve can be reached than by moving along *abm*. Indeed, investor *I* will choose portfolio ϕ, which is a combination of *S* and *m*.

Effect of Ability to Borrow at the Risk-Free Rate

Now consider investor *J*, confronted with a set of portfolios of risky securities *abmd* and a risk-free asset *S*. Although we use the same Figure 10-3 to depict *J*'s options, we do not mean to imply that the options confronting *J* and *I* are the same. Quite the contrary. If their expectations are not homogeneous, their options will be different. We have not assumed homogeneity of expectations for the moment, and therefore the sets *abmd* observed by *I* and *J* may be different.

For investor *J* we postulate an additional market condition. Not only can *J* lend at the riskless rate *S* by buying risk-free assets, but he or she can also borrow without limit at that same rate. If *J* prefers a portfolio with risk greater than R_m, *J* can acquire one along the segment *md*. Alternatively, by investing all available funds in *m* and borrowing at rate *S* to hold more of portfolio *m*, *J* can obtain a portfolio along *mB.* All such portfolios will dominate those on *md* and on any line below *SB. J*'s efficient set is thus *SmB. J* will acquire portfolio ϕ', which is determined by the tangency of the indifference curve *J* and *SB*.

Effect of Homogeneous Expectations

Finally, if investors do indeed have homogeneous expectations, all investors will confront the same set, in this case *abmd*. If, in addition, investors can lend and borrow at the rate *S*, they will all confront the same efficient set *SB*. Differences in risk preferences will be reflected in differences in the location of indifference curves and their points of tangency with *SB*. However, all investors will have portfolios along *SB*, some of them combining portfolio *m* with risk-free assets, and some of them borrowing so that they can invest more than 100 percent of their funds in portfolio *m*. Some may even hold just the risk-free asset in their portfolio, and some just portfolio *m*,

The ratio of the investment in any risky security to the total investment in portfolio *m* must be equal to the ratio of the current market value of all the outstanding shares of that security to the total market value of all risky securities outstanding. Otherwise, when the desired portfolios of all investors were added together, the amounts of that stock demanded and outstanding would not be the same. If the amount wanted exceeded the number of shares outstanding, the price would be bid up, while if the amount wanted fell short of the number outstanding, the price would decline. In either case, relative yields would change, and a new efficient portfolio would evolve. The flux in prices would not cease until the demand for each security equaled its supply.

Since the safe asset is riskless, the risk of the whole portfolio is proportional to that of the risky component, the market portfolio. The impact of the riskiness of a given stock is solely the consequence of its impact on the risky component. Hence, *m* is the appropriate reference portfolio. Thus, with the additional assumptions of homogeneous expectations and borrowing and lending at the riskless rate, all holders of risky assets will have the same reference portfolio of risky securities, the market portfolio, for purposes of evaluating the riskiness of the component securities of their portfolios.

THE MEASURE OF RISK

In our earlier discussion, we described a measure of risk (see p. 224). We can now develop it. It is simple and usable. Our takeoff point is the interesting fact, established above, that the market portfolio may serve as a common reference portfolio for all investors. Our measure of risk is the contribution of a security to the riskiness of the market portfolio. It can be shown that

$$(1) \qquad E(\tilde{R}_i) = S + \left[\frac{E(\tilde{R}_m) - S}{\sigma(\tilde{R}_m)}\right]\left[\frac{cov\,(\tilde{R}_i, \tilde{R}_m)}{\sigma(\tilde{R}_m)}\right].$$

FIGURE 10-4

The Market Price of Risk

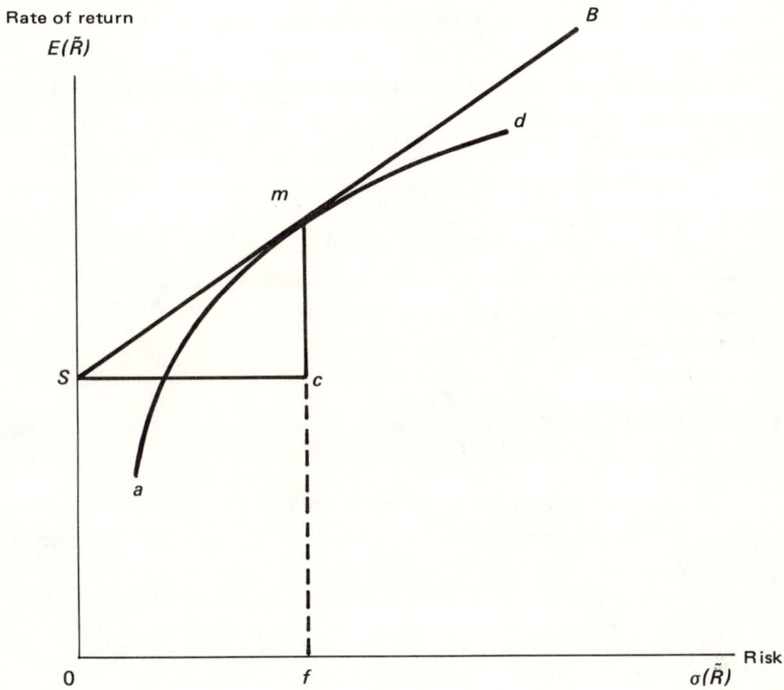

The meaning of this equation is quite straightforward. The first term on the right hand side of the equation (S) is the rate of return on a safe asset. The covariance term $\left[\frac{cov(\tilde{R}_i, \tilde{R}_m)}{\sigma(\tilde{R}_m)}\right]$ is equal to the contribution of security i to the risk of the market portfolio—that is, the risk of security i. The numerator of the coefficient

$$\left[\frac{E(\tilde{R}_m) - S}{\sigma(\tilde{R}_m)}\right]$$

is the excess of the expected market return over the return on a safe asset. It is clearly the risk premium (that is, the excess of the rate of return on a risky asset over the return of a safe asset) on the market portfolio. The denominator $\sigma(\tilde{R}_m)$ is the measure of the riskiness of the market portfolio. The ratio is thus the risk premium per unit of risk, or the market price of risk. Clearly, in Figure 10-4,

$E(\tilde{R}_m) - S = mc$ and
$\sigma(\tilde{R}_m) = Of = Sc;$

the ratio mc/Sc = the slope of SmB. The slope therefore measures the market price of risk.

It is convenient to have a simpler expression for that price. Hence we let $\lambda = \dfrac{E(\tilde{R}_m) - S}{\sigma(\tilde{R}_m)}$. Substituting λ into equation (1) above we have

$$(2) \qquad E(\tilde{R}_i) = S + \lambda \left[\frac{cov(\tilde{R}_i, \tilde{R}_m)}{\sigma(\tilde{R}_m)}\right].$$

λ has no subscript. It appears in the equation for every security. If the terms of (1) are rearranged, as in

$$(3) \qquad E(\tilde{R}_i) - S = \frac{\lambda\, cov(\tilde{R}_i, \tilde{R}_m)}{\sigma(\tilde{R}_m)},$$

we can see that the expected risk premium on security i, the left-hand side of equation (3), is the market price of risk λ times the risk of security i, $\dfrac{cov(\tilde{R}_i, \tilde{R}_m)}{\sigma(\tilde{R}_m)}$. Equations (1) and (2) thus say that the expected rate of return on security i equals the risk-free rate (S) plus a risk premium as shown above.

If the terms of equation (1) are rearranged to produce

$$(4) \quad E(\tilde{R}_i) - S = [E(\tilde{R}_m) - S]\frac{cov(\tilde{R}_i, \tilde{R}_m)}{\sigma(\tilde{R}_m)\,\sigma(\tilde{R}_m)} = [E(\tilde{R}_m) - S]\frac{cov(\tilde{R}_i, \tilde{R}_m)}{V(\tilde{R}_m)},$$

where $V(\tilde{R}_m)$, the variance of $\tilde{R}_m$, is the square of $\sigma(\tilde{R}_m)$, we can see that the risk premium on security i is the risk premium on the market portfolio multiplied by the ratio of the risk of security i to the risk of the market portfolio. This ratio is a widely used measure of risk and is known as beta (β). β measures the risk of a security or asset on a scale in which the risk of the market portfolio is 1, since $\dfrac{cov(\tilde{R}_m, \tilde{R}_m)}{V(\tilde{R}_m)} = \dfrac{V(\tilde{R}_m)}{V(\tilde{R}_m)} = 1.$

The risk premium on security i in equation (1)

$$\left[\frac{\{E(\tilde{R}_m) - S\}}{\sigma(\tilde{R}_m)}\right]\left[\frac{\{cov(\tilde{R}_i, \tilde{R}_m)\}}{\sigma(\tilde{R}_m)}\right]$$

and in equation (2) $\left[\lambda \dfrac{cov(\tilde{R}_i, \tilde{R}_m)}{\sigma(\tilde{R}_m)}\right]$ can be written as $\beta_i[E(\tilde{R}_m) - S]$.

Beta as a Measure of Volatility

In the present context, we have shown that the expected rate of return on an individual security is related to the expected rate of return on the market through β. Suppose an investor now asks what would be the effect on the rate of return of a particular security if the actual market return turned out to be different from the expected return? Would it be an appropriate answer to this question to state that the rate of return on the security is a linear function of the rate of return on the market? If so, we can write

$$(5) \qquad \tilde{R}_i = a_i + b_i\tilde{R}_m.$$

This relationship is known as the *characteristic line.* Besides the characteristic line, the literature often refers to the *capital market line*, a linear relationship between the return and risk (as measured by the standard deviation of returns) of efficient portfolios, and the *security market line*, a linear relationship between the expected rates of return on securities and their betas for a given expected rate of return on the market portfolio. These two concepts do not enter into the argument as we have developed it.

If the characteristic line is valid, any variation of the actual market return from the expected return will produce a corresponding variation of the stock's actual return from its expected return. Indeed, the variations are proportional. This may easily be shown in symbolic terms. For equation (5) to be true, it must follow that

$$(6) \qquad E(\tilde{R}_i) = a_i + b_iE(\tilde{R}_m).$$

By substituting β in equation (1) we can write

$$(7) \qquad E(\tilde{R}_i) = S + \beta_i[E(\tilde{R}_m) - S].$$

Rearranging the terms, we can see that

$$(8) \qquad E(\tilde{R}_i) = S(1 - \beta_i) + \beta_i[E(\tilde{R}_m)].$$

If the left-hand sides of equations (6) and (7) are the same, the right-hand sides must also be. Thus, if the characteristic line is valid, β_i must equal b_i, as indeed it does. If β_i equals b_i, it follows that $S(1 - \beta_i)$ equals a_i. Accordingly, we may substitute $S(1 - \beta_i)$ for a_i and β_i for b_i, respectively. Finally, by subtracting equation (8) from (5), we get

$$\tilde{R}_i - E(\tilde{R}_i) = \beta_i[\tilde{R}_m - E(\tilde{R}_m)],$$

since a_i and $S(1 - \beta_i)$ cancel out and β_i factors out.

Thus, variations of the actual market return from the expected market return will indeed produce proportional variations of a stock's actual return from its expected return. Since the proportionality factor is β, it may legitimately be interpreted as a volatility measure as well as a measure of risk.

Beta as a Measure of Systematic Risk

The return on common stocks is the sum of two components: one depends on the movements of the market, while the second is unique to the individual security. This is illustrated in Figure 10-5, which shows the characteristic line of security i tracing the relationship between its rate of return, R_i, and that of the market portfolio, R_m.

In this graph, each point represents an observation reflecting the rate of return of security i and the coincidental rate of return on the market portfolio m. The slope of the characteristic line is β_i. The higher the market return, the higher the return on security i. If all the observations (R_i, R_m) fell on the characteristic line, the return on security i would depend entirely

FIGURE 10-5

Characteristic Line of Portfolio or Security i

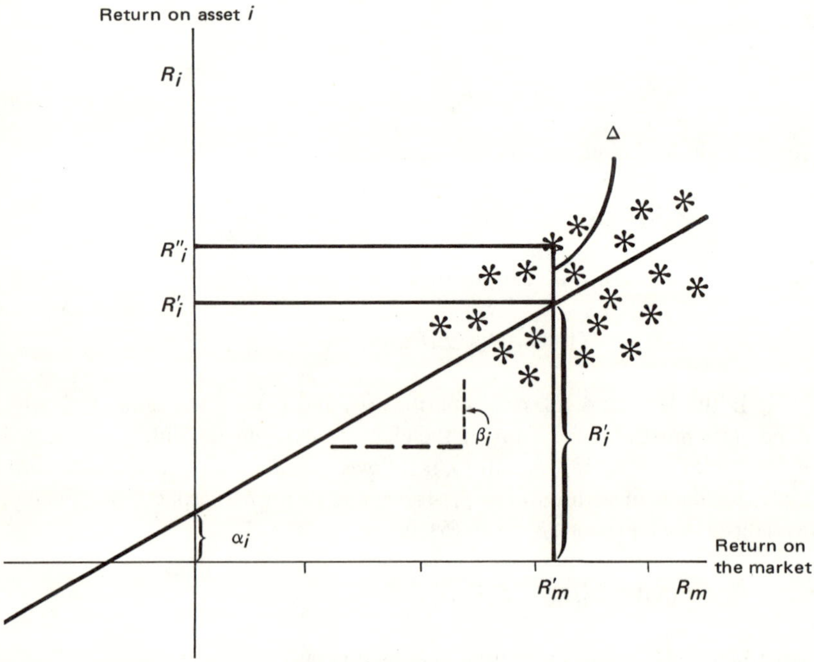

on β_i and the market. Ordinarily, however, the observations do not fall on the characteristic line. They cluster around it, as in Figure 10-5, because of the unique characteristics of the particular security. Thus, the return R_i'' is composed of two parts, one (R_i') determined by the characteristic line, and the other (Δ) determined by some special circumstances peculiar to the security. This extra amount, for example, might reflect such factors as the development of a special technology by the company or the introduction of a new, aggressive management.

On the average, the return on the market explains about 50 percent of the monthly variation in rates of return. The variation in securities returns attributable to unique factors may be reduced or even eliminated through diversification.

Measuring Beta

β may be measured simply by regressing R_i on R_m. A regression is a statistical tool for measuring the relationship between two or more sets of figures. As taught in basic statistics, if variable X is regressed on variable Y to derive the relationship $X = a + bY + \epsilon$ the formula for estimating b is $\frac{cov(X, Y)}{V(Y)}$. If R_i is regressed on the market return, R_m, the resulting relationship is $R_i = a_i + b_i R_m + \epsilon_i$. In this case, therefore, the estimate of b_i will be $cov(R_i, R_m)/V(R_m)$. (To preserve β and make the notation consistent, we substitute the Greek α for the Roman a, and write $R_i = \alpha_i + \beta_i R_m + \epsilon_i$.)

It can be shown that the β of our model, based on expected values, can be approximated by those obtained from regressions based on historical data. Typically, the return on a well-known index such as that of Standard & Poor's is taken as the return on the market for such regressions. In the academic writings on β, the so-called Fisher Index is often used instead of the Standard and Poor's Index. The Fisher Index, which assumes that an equal amount is invested in each stock, however, is not readily accessible. Generally, it is advisable to have at least 60 monthly observations; if too short a period is used, estimates of β tend to be erratic. It is then simple to fit a straight line to these observations and to use the slope of the line as the measure of β.

The justification for identifying regression βs with the βs of our model assumes that β is invariant over time—or, as the β-cult would say, it is assumed that β is stationary. In fact, while the βs for reasonably diversified portfolios do indeed seem to be stationary, the situation for individual stocks leaves something to be desired. One could bring additional information to bear and use more sophisticated statistical techniques, but it is not clear whether, for present purposes, the payoff warrants the extra complications.

Evaluation of Beta

The role of β in securities analysis has generated considerable controversy. It clearly is not a measure that can be used blindly. But once its shortcomings are appreciated, β can provide the analyst with useful insights into a stock and especially into a portfolio.

A basic assumption underlying the theory of β is that the securities market is in equilibrium and that the model as described correctly reflects the market. In these circumstances, the risk-adjusted premium (that is, the risk premium per unit of risk), which is found by dividing the β of a security into its risk premium, on all stocks should be the same. If a temporary aberration occurs and a stock is improperly priced, its risk-adjusted premium should either exceed or fall short of the market risk premium. As a result, an underpriced security should promptly attract demand, and an overpriced security should lead to attempted liquidations and short sales. According to the theory, prices should promptly adjust, and the opportunity for profits from dealing in incorrectly priced securities should be ephemeral.

Strict adherence to the implications of the capital asset pricing model, therefore, would lead to the conclusion that the search for underpriced securities is illusory. Such a rigid conclusion, however, is unjustified. For one thing, the predictive property of the model—in the final analysis the most important test—is faulty. We believe that there are opportunities for discovering underpriced securities open to alert investors who can evaluate better than their peers the financial factors affecting the prospects of a company.

Another shortcoming of β for securities analysis arises from the use of historical data in its determination. The time span covered by such data is rarely long enough to reflect long-run risks for any one company. For example, βs cannot anticipate such major factors as phantom products that can significantly influence the long-run outcome of an investment.

Despite these shortcomings, β is a useful tool of investment analysis, provided its limitations are recognized and it is used with discretion. The measure can help the investor in evaluating rates of return, developing an investment strategy, and measuring performance.

Evaluating rates of return. According to the capital asset pricing model, the risk premium per unit of risk on every stock and portfolio is equal to the risk premium of the market. When that equality does not hold, therefore, it follows that the security is mispriced. As an illustration, suppose that we are considering a stock with an expected return of 12 percent and that we gauge the market's expected return to be 10 percent. Is the stock an attractive investment? If its β is 1.8 and the yield on a one-year Treasury security, which we take to be the risk-free asset, is 6 percent, the stock's risk-adjusted risk premium will be (12% – 6%)/1.8 = 3.333%. The risk premium on the market, however, will be 10% – 6% = 4%. In these circumstances, the stock is not attractive.

Let us alter the conditions somewhat and now assume that the stock's expected rate of return is 15 percent. This would raise the risk-adjusted risk premium to 5 percent, which brings it above the market's risk premium of 4 percent. As a result, the stock may now be considered underpriced.

Objection might be raised to this procedure because of the defects of the market model. These defects do make questionable a comparison, such as that made above between a high β stock and the market for which $\beta = 1$. They would not invalidate, however, a comparison of two stocks with comparable (but not necessarily equal) βs. For example, it would be appropriate to compare the risk premiums of Abbott Laboratories and Allegheny Ludlum, both with value-line betas of 1.05 in November 1975 though they are in different industries. Similarly, the risk premium of Marriott Corp., with a β of 1.55, might be compared with the risk premium of McDonald Corp., with a β of 1.55. The βs of individual stocks depend upon both the period and method selected for their calculation. These βs, therefore, may vary. Nevertheless, at any one time, they provide an indication of the risk characteristics of the stocks.

A plausible procedure for determining the stocks whose risk-adjusted premiums may be compared is as follows:

(1) Arrange the stocks which might be included in the investor's portfolio in descending or ascending order of βs.
(2) Divide the range of βs into a reasonable number of intervals.
(3) Strike comparisons of stocks that are in the same intervals.
(4) Alternatively, strike comparisons of stocks that are bracketed by the interval distance.

A factor that may distort the price of a stock is the quality of its market. Appropriate pricing can be realized only if it is reasonably possible to move in and out of a stock. If a market is thin, even a small investor can be a price maker. For an institutional investor, the situation is much more difficult. The evidence that exists on the performance of markets is based on a random selection of widely traded stocks rather than on a random selection of all stocks. Thus, considerable speculative opportunities may exist for an astute securities analyst who is able to deal in stocks with thin markets.

Developing an investment strategy. At one time it was common practice to recommend shifting into defensive stocks when the market was expected to decline and into aggressive stocks when the market was expected to advance. β enables us to be more precise in carrying out this strategy. It provides us with a scale that makes possible a determination of the degree of defensiveness or aggressiveness that has been achieved.

In developing this strategy, the investor must keep an eye on the β value of the entire portfolio. The desired β levels can be achieved by changing the proportion of the risk-free assets in the portfolio, by shifting to stocks in the β range appropriate to market expectations, or by some combination of these two tactics.

Measuring performance. The performance of an investment adviser or institution may be evaluated by finding the risk-adjusted risk premium that was earned. To do so, it is necessary to define the portfolio in a way that facilitates analysis on some per unit basis, like the stock of a mutual fund. The relevant return to be tested, then, is that of a unit. For example, suppose an individual has committed $100,000 to an investment adviser for management. We might then consider that this sum had "purchased" 100 units of $1,000 each. Let us assume that another $11,000 is committed six months later, when the value of the original portfolio had risen to $110,000. As a result, each of the original units is now worth $1,100, affording an annualized rate of return of 20 percent. We may consider that the additional $11,000 "purchases" another 10 units at a net unit value of $1,100. Suppose further that at the end of the year the investment adviser delivers to the investor $5,500, and that the value of the total account remaining is $132,000 or $1,200 per unit. So, in the last six months of the year, the investor's return equaled $100 of capital appreciation per unit and $50 dividends per unit. This total amount represents an annualized rate of return $2 \times \frac{\$150}{\$1{,}100} = 2 \times 13.6\% = 27.2\%$. Thus, his net return for the year is $(1.10 \times 1.136) - 1.00$, or 25 percent.

If the investor had engaged the services of the same adviser for a long period of time, the investor could regress the periodic rate of return, as calculated above, against the return on the market to obtain the β of the portfolio. If the number of observations is not sufficiently large to warrant the calculation of a regression line, the investor may take the weighted average of the βs of the stocks of the portfolio; many of these βs are available in public sources. A procedure for evaluating the performance of investment companies is discussed in Chapter 23.

Some writers have observed that the intercept of the characteristic line, α_i as shown in Figure 10-5, has some performance significance. They contend that an investor may achieve superior performance by acquiring stocks with high αs. This is not entirely true.

Theoretically, as we have seen, the intercept α_i equals $S(1 - \beta_i)$. Therefore, the α of one stock may exceed that of another simply because the β of the first differs from that of the second. If the βs of two stocks are quite close, however, differences in αs could indicate differences in performance.

For example, Figure 10-6 shows the performance of two funds. Both have the same βs, but fund *A* has an α of +3, while that of fund *B* is −3. Because of its higher α, fund *A* provides a better return than fund *B*.

Because of the theoretical equality between α_i and $S(1 - \beta_i)$, we can compare $\alpha_i/(1 - \beta_i)$ with S, the risk-free rate. Any difference between the

FIGURE 10-6

Comparison of Alphas for Two Funds

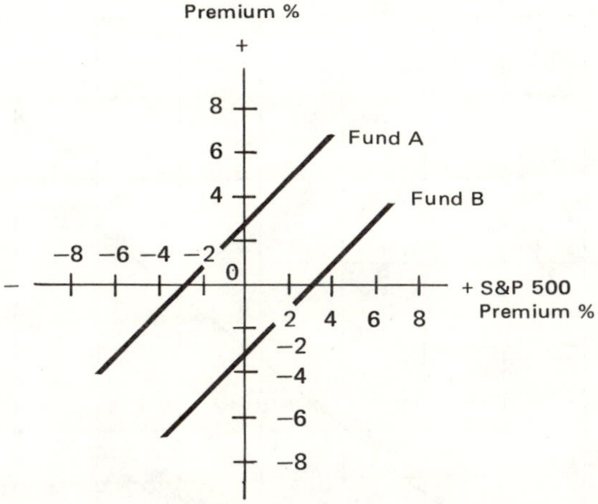

SOURCE: Becker Securities Corporation, ***Institutional Funds Evaluation Services Brochure***, 1973, p. 15. Reproduced with permission of Becker Securities Corporation.

two quantities would indicate deviations from standard performance. Unfortunately, there is a body of evidence that suggests that the model is not wholly satisfactory. Under the circumstances, it is difficult to infer anything about the performance of a stock from a comparison of α_i and $S(1 - \beta_i)$.

Portfolio Profile

A number of securities firms have embraced β, making available to clients the β values for a large number of stocks. They also determine the values of customers' portfolios and recommend adjustments that will either improve the return for the determined level of β or bring the portfolio's β to a level more consistent with the customer's investment objectives.

Becker Securities Corporation has done pioneering work in the field of performance measurement. It serves over 2,600 pension and profit-sharing plans throughout North America with an aggregate value of over $40 billion, ranging in size from $1 million to over $1.5 billion.

In order to permit a manager to understand the performance results of his portfolio, Becker prepares a number of exhibits. Included is a portfolio profile, as illustrated in Figures 10-7 and 10-7a. The graph (Figure 10-7) shows the portfolio's quarterly premium rate of return, which is the actual rate of return minus the risk-free rate (average 91-day Treasury bill rate). This rate is plotted against the premium on the Standard & Poor's 500 Index. The

FIGURE 10-7

Portfolio Profile: Total Equities

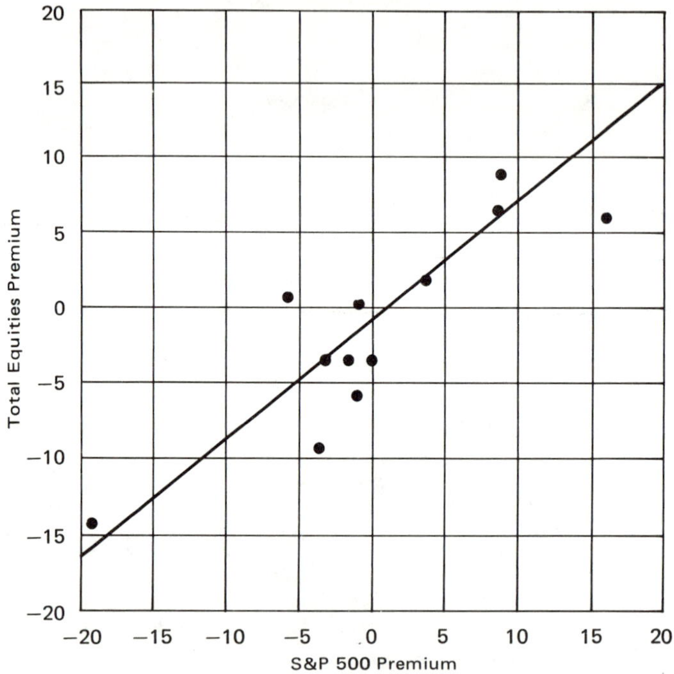

SOURCE: Becker Securities Corporation, ***Institutional Funds Evaluation Services Brochure***, 1973, p. 24. Reproduced with permission of Becker Securities Corporation.

slope of the line drawn through the coordinates of the portfolio and market premiums is β, which measures market sensitivity. The intercept, where the line crosses the vertical axis, is annualized from quarterly figures. Figure 10-7a summarizes the data in the graph and provides the actual estimates of both β and the intercept. The table also shows R^2, which is not plotted, and portrays the degree to which β and the intercept explain the relationship between the risk-adjusted returns of portfolio and the market.

FIGURE 10-7a

Portfolio Profile: Analysis of Data

Sensitivity (Beta)	0.69
Standard Error	0.12
Intercept-Annualized	−3.76
Standard Error	0.04
R-Squared	0.78

Year	Quarterly Premium	
	Your Fund	S&P 500
1970		
1	–	–
2	–	–
3	–	–
4	–	–
1971		
1	−4.74	−3.85
2	−14.35	−19.69
3	6.47	15.29
4	7.69	8.95
1972		
1	8.19	8.49
2	−3.73	−0.74
3	0.51	−1.89
4	2.60	3.45
1973		
1	−3.73	−3.12
2	−9.70	−4.55
3	1.26	−5.59
4	−5.59	−2.09

SOURCE: Becker Securities Corporation, *Institutional Funds Evaluation Services Brochure*, 1973, p. 24. Reproduced with permission of Becker Securities Corporation.

SUMMARY

The risk of a stock can be divided into systematic (or nondiversifiable) risk and nonsystematic (or diversifiable) risk. Only the nondiversifiable risk can command a premium rate of return in the market. To determine the nondiversifiable risk, we need to identify the relevant portfolio in which diversification has been attempted. In pursuit of that portfolio, the rational risk-averse investor chooses one that will maximize his or her utility (optimum portfolio) and one that will simultaneously give the maximum rate of return for the risk exposure (efficient portfolio). The set of efficient risky portfolios is concave on the $[E(R), \sigma(R)]$ plane.

If the investor can freely invest in a risk-free asset or borrow at the risk-free rate, the set of efficient portfolios is improved. The set now includes the portfolios along the tangent to the efficient set of *risky* securities that goes through the return on a safe asset. All investors will then hold portfolios that consist of the risk-free asset and the portfolio of risky securities represented by the point of tangency.

If all investors have the same outlook on securities, the optimal and efficient portfolio that everyone holds will include as its risky component a replica of the market portfolio. That portfolio is thus taken as the reference portfolio. The risk premium can be written as $\beta_i [E(R_m) - S]$, and β_i can be interpreted as a measure of the volatility of security *i*. This measure of risk premium is convenient because β_i can be measured by regressing R_i on R_m.

The basic assumptions of the capital asset pricing model do not strictly obtain. If they did, securities would always be priced correctly and there would be little point to securities analysis. Since certain major risks such as bankruptcy are rarely reflected in the statistics typically used to measure βs, they cannot reflect all the risk associated with securities. β is nevertheless a useful tool of analysis, particularly in evaluating rates of return, developing investment strategies, and measuring performance.

CHAPTER 11

Evaluating the Quality of a Company's Earnings: Revenues

Our venture into theory was intended to provide a means of understanding the importance of risk in the analysis of securities and the methods that have been formulated to measure it. This understanding paves the way for the development of an investment strategy which could follow different routes. But regardless of which route is taken, particular securities have to be selected. For this purpose, the rational investor will prefer those that will perform relatively well in any given risk category. To reach this decision, the investor needs some insights into the future prospects of the issuing corporation. We are now ready, therefore, to enter the pragmatic area of developing procedures that will enable the investor to gain such insights. The point of departure for this analysis is an appreciation of the accounting policies of the corporation that affect its reported earnings.

SOME BASIC CONSIDERATIONS

Recognition of the importance of a company's accounting policies in evaluating its securities has given prominence to the phrase "quality of earnings." In early 1975, for example, the stock of Minnesota Mining & Manufacturing, once an institutional favorite, was under continuing pressure, while the shares of other longtime favorites continued to advance smartly. One of the reasons for this relatively dispirited performance was a question raised about certain accounting policies revealed in a 3M prospectus issued in connection with a secondary offering at that time. In reviewing this situation, a *Wall Street Journal* columnist noted that " . . . some Street analysts consider [the policies discussed] a cause for concern over the quality of earnings. . . . "[1]

About twice a month, Arthur Wiesenberger & Co., the brokerage subsidiary of Wiesenberger, Inc., issues a report formerly published by Coenen & Co. that analyzes statements " . . . to eliminate the unforeseen investment risks produced by either inadequate disclosure or liberal accounting procedures." These reports are widely used by institutional investors, who ordinarily purchase them by directing commission business to the firm. The series title, appropriately enough, is the *Quality of Earnings Report.*

Thus, the term "quality of earnings" is really an assessment of accounting policy. "Good quality" implies that current revenues are not being reported in a manner that jeopardizes future revenues, nor are costs reported so as to benefit current profits at the expense of future profits. "Poor quality" implies just the opposite: accounting practices that inflate current revenues or curtail costs, postponing problems until some future day of reckoning.

Illustrative of this condition, among the factors depressing the price/earnings ratios of public utilities in 1974 was increasing investor recognition that in many cases reported earnings were made up of bookkeeping components that produced no cash flows. As a result, danger signals began to fly about the generous dividend payments that once were considered secure. Consolidated Edison, for example, reported earnings of $2.79 per share which presumably was ample protection for its $1.80 dividend payment. Of the $2.79 figure, however, $1.06 represented a change in the accounting for fuel costs, 82¢ represented an allowance for funds used during construction, and 66¢ represented capitalized overhead costs of construction. Without the benefit of these bookkeeping contributions, the company's earnings would have been a slim 25¢.

To help investors evaluate the quality of a company's earnings, accounting regulation has sought to introduce some degree of standardization into reporting practices and to require disclosures that allow the investor to gauge the effect on earnings of these practices. Thus, according to the SEC's 1973 annual report, its amendment to Guide 22, "Summary of Earnings," of the Guides for the Preparation of Registration Statements under the Securities Act of 1933 was intended to clarify the information so as "to enable investors to appraise the quality of earnings reported in the summary."

How Accounting is Regulated

Various legal bodies have some jurisdiction over accounting. Thus, state laws generally impose liabilities on a board of directors for improper payments, such as disbursing dividends out of capital and granting unlawful loans. The major stock exchanges maintain surveillance over the reporting practices of listed corporations to detect departures from generally accepted accounting practices, but the exchanges ordinarily do not determine what these practices should be. To a large extent, this responsibility has been left with the Securities and Exchange Commission and the accounting profession itself, although other regulatory agencies also play a part.

The Securities and Exchange Commission

The securities acts and amendments give the SEC much power over accounting matters. The commission has broad authority over prospectuses and the periodic reports filed with it, as well as over the form of financial statements and the methods to be followed in the preparation of accounts. The SEC's Regulation S-X governs the content of required reports and various other official releases on specific subjects. In general, the commission has recognized that the primary responsibility for the adequacy of the information filed rests with management and has tended to let the accounting profession develop its own principles. More recently, however, the commission has begun to exercise more leadership and to develop a philosophy of its own. Thus, the commission is carving out important new conceptual territory by distinguishing between information intended for the professional analyst and for the average investor and by requiring a determination of the impact of certain policies on reported net income.[2]

The commission also has been pursuing with renewed vigor its basic doctrine of disclosure. An important example of this effort is the adoption of revised guides for the preparation and filing of reports and registration statements.[3] These guides are not rules of the commission but represent policies and practices followed by the SEC's Division of Corporation Finance and, in this instance, the Office of the Chief Accountant in administering the disclosure requirements of the federal securities laws. The new guides require an explanation of the summaries of earnings and operations in registration statements and 10-K reports to enable investors to appraise the quality of earnings. Thus, whenever there are material changes in the amount and source of revenues and expenses, including tax expenses, or changes in accounting principles, methods, or applications that have a material effect on net income, an appropriate analysis and explanation is required. To enable investors to understand and evaluate material periodic changes in the various items of the summary of operations, a separate section is called for, entitled "Management's Discussion and Analysis of the Summary of Operations." This discussion is similar to a president's letter in an annual report to stockholders and is now required in company annual reports.

The Financial Accounting Standards Board

Accounting authority in the United States is exercised primarily by the American Institute of Certified Public Accountants (AICPA). Through the opinions issued by the AICPA's former chief policymaking arm, the Accounting Principles Board (APB), and by the APB's predecessor committee on accounting procedure, the institute helped mold the concept of "substantial authoritative support," which, in turn, forms the basis of "generally accepted accounting principles," the term used in audited corporate financial statements.

The APB, however, ran into hurdles that were not readily surmountable. When it did not promptly attempt to correct alleged abuses, the board was criticized because of its lack of vigor; but when it reacted promptly, it encountered a hornet's nest of opposing views. In the wake of a study by a panel headed by Francis M. Wheat, a former SEC commissioner, the institute adopted a new rule-making approach that is administered by the full-time Financial Accounting Standards Board (FASB). The former voluntary board has been replaced by one that has full-time paid members, and the administrative organization has been revamped to include representatives from various groups that have a major interest in financial reporting. In arriving at a rule, the FASB's decision-making process resembles that of the APB; first, it appoints an advisory panel of experts; next it distributes a memorandum outlining the issues for consideration; and then it conducts public hearings and provides a preliminary exposure draft of the proposed rule. Finally, a standard is adopted.

Other Agencies

Other governmental and private bodies also play a role, although less pervasive and influential, in affecting public financial statements. Thus, the regulatory agencies in the public utility, transportation, insurance, and banking fields have considerable authority, but it is directed to the specialized industries they supervise. The Cost Accounting Standards Board (CASB) was created as an agency of Congress by the Defense Production Act Amendments of 1970 to develop uniform cost-accounting practices applicable to the pricing, administration, and settlement of negotiated defense contracts. Federal procurement regulations have extended the standards to contracts of nondefense agencies. Because of the importance of governmental contracts, these standards have an influence on accounting policies generally. The National Association of Accountants (NAA), the representative body of industrial accountants, has formulated policy statements on accounting practices through its Management Accounting Practices Committee (MAP).

Still other organizations, more remotely related to accounting, may exercise an influence on financial statements. The Federal Trade Commission, for example, is involved in publishing aggregate line-of-business data on particular lines of business for manufacturing industries. The Financial Executives Institute, representing financial officers, and the Financial Analysts Federation, representing securities analysts, are active in reacting to proposals of the SEC and the FASB and in preparing studies that relate to accounting.

The Auditor

At one time, the auditor (independent public accountant) of a firm could follow relatively routine practices and provide the standard two-paragraph statement without much concern of incurring legal responsibility. In specific instances, he might also be encouraged to take a broad view regarding the conformance of the firm's practices with generally accepted accounting principles in order to maintain his affiliation. Stiffer attitudes in the courts toward the responsibilities of auditors, plus the frauds that have been made possible by lax reviews, have led to a change in both these positions. As a result, auditors are exerting a sterner influence on the accounting policies of the companies within their purview.

The SEC also has been vigorous in seeking to ensure both the auditor's independence and his willingness to meet his responsibilities. For one thing, as has been mentioned, the SEC now requires that a company explain any change that it has made in its auditors and afford the ousted auditor the opportunity to present an opposing point of view. All this information now appears in Form 8-K, which provides for the current reporting of certain events, such as capitalization changes, acquisitions, or management shifts; changes in auditors, as well as any related disagreements with management, must also be reported in proxy statements. Additionally, the SEC has taken an increasingly hard look at the standards employed by the profession to ascertain the independence of auditors selected to review a company's financial statements.

Accounting Flexibility

These circumstances all point toward greater uniformity in financial reporting. Even so, the reported results of a firm's operations still reflect the aims of management as well as the opinions of the accountant. The acceptable rules are sufficiently flexible to enable an accountant to make numerous decisions within a consistent accounting framework, each of which influences the reported income. Firms may use different accounting methods for internal management performance, payment of taxes, and reporting to the stockholders. Different managements dealing with the same set of facts may show strikingly different results to their shareholders.

Accounting flexibility aggravates the difficulty of using reported earnings as the basis of forecasting future results and of effecting comparisons with the figures of other companies. Yet effective securities analysis necessitates the making of such forecasts and comparisons. Thus, the investor must be able to appraise the quality of the reported earnings; for this purpose, in turn, he requires an understanding of the financial statements.

For the income statement, an accountant must determine both revenues and costs to measure a company's operating results in dollar terms. *Revenues* represent the inflow of dollars in the form of cash or receivables, for a specific accounting period, resulting from the sale of goods or services. When revenues extend over several periods, as in the case of long-term contracts for the sale of goods or services, a determination must be made as to which revenues should be attributed and allocated to a particular period.

Costs, which usually are measured at acquisition prices, are not synonymous with cash outlays in the current period. For one thing, costs may include write-offs, such as depreciation charges arising from outlays in prior periods, and may include only a portion of the outlays in the current period if the other portion is applicable to future revenues. Moreover, the value of inventory included in the cost of goods sold may have been built up with cash expenditures in prior years.

Net income or profit is the excess of recognized revenues over costs in the accounting period. Theoretically, costs should be matched with the revenues they produce. In any specific period, therefore, the amount of profit reported depends upon how this matching has been made.[4]

Once determined, profits accrue to the proprietors or stockholders of the firm, and any amount that is not withdrawn remains as an addition to the equity interest. Thus, the primary decisions confronting the accountant embrace both revenues and costs. The major areas of revenue that warrant attention are discussed in the present chapter, while the areas of cost are discussed in the following chapter.

TREATMENT OF SUBSIDIARY EARNINGS

A parent may elect to combine the assets, liabilities, revenues, and expenses of subsidiaries with its own corresponding items into consolidated financial statements.[5] While regulatory authorities require certain minimum percentage holdings in order for statements of a subsidiary to be included in the consolidated figures, in general the guidelines for consolidation are loose. If the parent elects to consolidate, it is possible that restrictions, such as those contained in bond indentures or arising from foreign-exchange controls, might limit the subsidiary's ability to tap retained earnings for distribution of dividends. Accordingly, whenever such limitations exist, both SEC requirements and accepted accounting principles call for the insertion of appropriate notes in financial statements; otherwise, the entire amount of retained earnings may be presumed to be unrestricted as to dividend distributions. These barriers to the payment of dividends may be serious. For example, Boise Cascade reported a substantial $133.7 million in retained earnings at the close of 1972, but under the terms of certain loan agreements this entire amount was restricted as to the payment of cash dividends on common stock. Thereafter, the company was able to negotiate amended or new loan agreements which restricted the payment of cash dividends on common stock to 15 percent of consolidated net income earned subsequent to December 31, 1972. The amount of retained earnings not restricted by these provisions at December 31, 1973, was approximately $11.5 million, compared with total retained earnings on that date of $271.5 million.[6] Since such negative covenants can limit the ability of a company to disburse dividends, it is important for the analyst to be aware of their presence and to evaluate their potential threat to future payments.

At one time, if the parent did not consolidate, it could "manage" the reported earnings by manipulating the "upstream" dividends or could shield its own statement from subsidiary deficits. To prevent abuses of this sort, the equity method of accounting is now required for investments in unconsolidated subsidiaries and for other investments where the investor may exercise a significant influence over the firm's operating and financial policies; this influence is presumed where a voting interest of 20 percent or more is held.[7] Under this method, the investor recognizes a share of earnings or losses in the period for which they are reported by the firm, rather than in the period when a dividend is declared. Similarly, the investor adjusts the carrying amount of the investment for its share of the earnings or losses and reduces its investment for dividends received.

In some instances, this requirement has had a perceptible influence on reported statements. For example, P. R. Mallory & Co. had previously carried its investments in unconsolidated subsidiaries and affiliates at cost and counted the dividends received from them in its consolidated net earnings. During 1971 the company's share of the net earnings of these companies was only $126,235, but they paid dividends of $553,880, which the parent included in its consolidated statement. After adoption of the equity method, net earnings for 1971 were reduced by $427,645, the equivalent of 11 cents per share, representing the difference between the dividends declared and the earnings of its unconsolidated subsidiaries and affiliates.[8] In the case of Kaiser Industries, the company's equity in the earnings of unconsolidated subsidiaries amounted to $52.7 million in 1973, compared with a loss from its consolidated operations of $3.6 million.[9] Indicative of the effect of the equity method, in 1974 Kaiser included in its consolidated statement a major subsidiary that had been previously unconsolidated and accounted for by the equity method. As a result of this change, Kaiser, in its 1974 report, restated the 1973 figures. The prior consolidated loss was eliminated, but net earnings remained the same. On the other hand, Phelps Dodge's share in equity basis investments represented a net loss of $9.1 million that was more than 10 percent of consolidated net income for 1972.

Since World War II, international markets have been broadening substantially, and American corporations have established an extensive system of subsidiaries throughout the world. Accordingly, to an increasing degree, these corporations are being confronted with accounting problems arising from the relationship with their foreign subsidiaries. Not only is the question of adopting suitable practices particularly important in the foreign area, where appropriately trained accountants may not be readily available, but also a determination must be made of the taxes to be paid and of how statements expressed in foreign currencies should be translated to a dollar basis for purpose of consolidation.

Incorporation of Foreign Earnings

While American parents generally prefer wholly owned subsidiaries, they often must be content with partial ownership because of policies of host foreign governments. These policies raise interesting questions about the reliability of overseas profits for purposes of financial reporting.[10]

The requirement for reporting the earnings of nonconsolidated subsidiaries on the equity method and the revised method of accounting for the taxation of foreign earnings have reduced some of the discrepancies in accounting practices.[11] While the common practice is to report on the equity basis, there still is much variation in how the taxation of foreign earnings is counted. In general, the current requirement is to presume that all undistributed earnings are transferred to the parent with an appropriate income tax accrued, unless there is sufficient evidence to show that the subsidiary has invested or will invest the undistributed earnings indefinitely or that the earnings will be remitted in a tax-free liquidation.

Within the framework of this requirement, a number of companies follow the practice of Crown Cork & Seal, which tersely observes that "no provision has been made for additional income taxes which could result from distribution of earnings of foreign subsidiaries since such earnings, for the most part, are permanently invested."[12] A further reason why Crown Cork & Seal does not provide additional taxes is that the incremental U.S. revenue taxes which would become payable upon distribution of unremitted foreign earnings would be offset by foreign tax credits.

A number of other companies, including Eastman Kodak, United Merchants & Manufacturers, and Pillsbury provide for the tax effects of that portion of foreign undistributed earnings that is not expected to be indefinitely reinvested. Black & Decker has the interesting policy of requiring subsidiaries as a group to remit dividends to the company in amounts which, net of foreign withholding taxes, equal approximately the same percentage of their aggregate earnings as current cash dividends to the company's stockholders bear to consolidated earnings, subject to certain of the foreign countries' exchange controls and to restrictions which affect withdrawals of undistributed earnings. Income taxes are provided on the estimated amount of planned remittances of subsidiaries' retained earnings.[13]

Opinion no. 23 of the Accounting Principles Board further provides that if circumstances change and it becomes apparent that some or all of the undistributed earnings of a subsidiary will be remitted but income taxes have not been recognized by the parent company, these taxes should accrue as an ordinary expense of the current period income taxes attributable to that remittance. Caterpillar Tractor, however, notes that if, for some reason not currently contemplated, the company found it necessary to pay out some of the undistributed foreign profits for which no tax has been provided, there are sufficient available credits to reduce substantially the amount of the tax otherwise due.[14]

The evaluation of the amount and quality of a company's foreign earnings is an important consideration to the investor now and will probably become even more important in future years, as the American multinational enterprise continues to spread its network of subsidiaries abroad. The degree to which data on foreign operations are available in reported statements varies, although the FASB is moving to minimum requirements as part of segment reporting.

United States regulatory authorities have evinced an awareness of the need to furnish this information to investors. It is likely that the SEC eventually will extend and tighten reporting requirements for the activities that a domestic parent conducts through its foreign subsidiaries. Part of the problem is that the accounting procedures of multinational enterprises have not kept pace with the growth of overseas activities. As a result, in the past a variety of accounting methods were used and there often was inadequate disclosure. In October 1975, the FASB issued a statement that established standards of financial accounting and reporting in this field.

Translating Statements of Foreign Subsidiaries to Dollars

There is a veritable mystique about the procedures for translating the statements of foreign subsidiaries into dollars for purposes of consolidation that makes it very difficult for management, let alone the stockholders, to understand the impact of such translation on a multinational corporation's financial position. For a long time, the most authoritative method was the current-noncurrent system proposed by the AICPA. By this method, current items in the balance sheet were translated at current rates, and long-term items at historical rates of exchange; operating items in the income statement were translated at an average rate for the period, while depreciation and amortization charges were translated at the rates in effect when the underlying assets were acquired.[15] However, the National Association of Accountants criticized use of this traditional breakdown of assets into current and noncurrent categories for purposes of determining an exchange rate, and the association has favored a distinction based upon physical and financial assets (monetary-nonmonetary method).[16] The current-rate method, which provides for translating all accounts at the current rate, is employed abroad but is not acknowledged as generally accepted in the United States. Another proposal, the temporal method, translates assets and liabilities in the same manner as the accounting basis to measure them. Under current accounting principles, the temporal and monetary-nonmonetary approaches produce similar results.[17] Methods that combine these concepts also have been suggested.[18]

After the translation date is selected, a decision still must be reached concerning the particular rate to use, a problem that is aggravated by an international policy of floating rates. At any one time, multiple rates may exist, reflecting not only market influences but also governmental regulations that apply different exchange rates to different transactions, such as dividend distributions, loan repayments, parent investment, payments for imports, and receipts for exports. For example, Kaiser used "the official rate of exchange"; Rohm and Haas "the parities established by the International Monetary Fund"; and Dayco "the official or free rates of exchange." H. H. Robertson translated "at fixed rates, which as to some countries are the central rates of exchange and as to others are the approximate current year-end rates." The FASB now requires that the exchange rate at which dividends are remitted should be used for translation purposes.

Regardless of what translation method or rate of exchange is employed, the procedure for determining the subsidiary's net income for consolidation purposes starts with the financial statements of the subsidiary expressed in its local currency (LC). On the closing balance sheet, varying rates are applied to different asset items, depending on the classification employed. It is common practice to carry equity at the historical rate and leave retained earnings or surplus as a floating figure equivalent to the amount necessary to bring the asset and liability segments of the balance sheet into line. The income statement is also translated into dollars by applying rates chosen in accordance with the method used. The net income figure, which is a measure of operating results in dollars, is combined with the determined change in retained earnings, which represents the difference between the balance sheet figures at the beginning and end of the year. If the operating figure is greater than the change in retained earnings, the difference is called an *unrealized exchange loss,* while if the operating figure is smaller the difference is called an *unrealized exchange gain*; these differences are caused by the translation process. The subsidiary may also incur a *realized exchange loss or gain* in liquidating a foreign obligation when there is an actual conversion of currencies at a different rate from that prevailing when the obligation was incurred; a subsidiary's realized losses or gains are generally included in its reported income, whereas the unrealized losses or gains are excluded and appear only in the consolidated statement.

An illustration will clarify these calculations. At the close of 1974, the subsidiary of an American multinational corporation reports its financial statements in units of local currency as indicated in Table 11-1. During 1974 the rate of exchange remained unchanged at LC6 = $1, but during 1975 the local currency gradually declined, and a devaluation at year-end brought the rate to LC10 = $1; the average rate during the year was LC8 = $1. In 1974 the subsidiary had an obligation of $1,000,000 that it carried on its books at the historical rate of LC6 = $1; this debt was paid in dollars at the close of 1975.

In terms of its local currency, the subsidiary shows a substantial operating profit of LC10,000,000, which, using an average exchange rate of 8-1 (except for depreciation), is equivalent to $833,333. To protect an operating profit against the inroads of currency deterioration, the multinational company ordinarily attempts to finance its overseas activities by borrowing locally as much as possible and holding down monetary assets. This procedure has not been followed by the subsidiary in the statements shown. In the first place, the subsidiary had a relatively large foreign obligation, on which it realized an internal exchange loss of LC4,000,000 when it acquired dollars to make payment at an exchange rate of 10-1 instead of the 6-1 rate that prevailed when the debt was incurred. Then again, the subsidiary has a heavy net monetary asset balance; as a result, it experienced a further substantial unrealized exchange loss of $4,516,666 in translating the local statement for purposes of consolidation. The net effect is that, on a dollar

TABLE 11-1

Translating Foreign-Currency into Dollar Statements

	LOCAL CURRENCY	EXCHANGE RATE*	DOLLARS
BALANCE SHEET	DECEMBER 31, 1974		
Cash	LC 30,000,000	6-1	$ 5,000,000
Accounts receivable	15,000,000	6-1	2,500,000
Inventory	20,000,000	6-1	3,333,333
Fixed assets	50,000,000	6-1	8,333,333
Total	LC115,000,000		$19,166,666
Accounts payable	LC 4,000,000	6-1	$ 666,666
Notes payable (in dollars)	6,000,000	6-1	1,000,000
Common stock	75,000,000	6-1	12,500,000
Retained earnings	30,000,000	6-1	5,000,000
Total	LC115,000,000		$19,166,666
INCOME STATEMENT	YEAR ENDING DECEMBER 31, 1975		
Sales	LC 50,000,000	8-1	$ 6,250,000
Cost of goods sold	20,000,000†	8-1	2,500,000
Gross profit	30,000,000		3,750,000
Depreciation	10,000,000	6-1	1,666,667
Selling and administration expenses	10,000,000	8-1	1,250,000
Operating profit	10,000,000		833,333
Realized exchange profit (loss)	(4,000,000)	—	— ‡
Taxes	2,000,000	8-1	250,000
Unrealized exchange loss	—		(4,516,666)
Net profit (loss)	LC 4,000,000		($ 3,933,333)
BALANCE SHEET	DECEMBER 31, 1975		
Cash	LC 38,000,000	10-1	$ 3,800,000
Accounts receivable	35,000,000	10-1	3,500,000
Inventory	20,000,000†	10-1†	2,000,000†
Fixed assets	40,000,000	6-1	6,666,667
Total	LC133,000,000		$15,966,667
Accounts payable	LC 24,000,000	10-1	$ 2,400,000
Common stock	75,000,000	6-1	12,500,000
Retained earnings	34,000,000		1,066,667
Total	LC133,000,000		$15,966,667

*Based on temporal method.

†The firm uses the LIFO method of measuring inventories. Since the inventory did not change during the year, the cost of goods sold reflects current-year costs and is translated at the average rate for the year. Inventory must be reported at the lower of cost or market. At cost, translated at the historical rate, the dollar value is $2,000,000. Accordingly, the lower figure is used.

‡Although there is a local currency exchange loss, no dollar loss is shown because the original dollar value of the notes payable was $1,000,000 and $1,000,000 was repaid.

basis, the net profit of LC4 million is reflected in a net loss of $3,933,333 as determined above.

When alternative translation methods could be used, companies were able to report exchange adjustments of different amounts under identical circumstances, depending on the method employed. In general, companies using the monetary-nonmonetary method and operating in countries whose currencies had weakened relative to the U.S. dollar were likely to fare better than companies using the current-noncurrent method. On the other hand, companies using the monetary-nonmonetary method may do less well if their operations are in countries whose currencies have strengthened in relation to the U.S. dollar.

The FASB has indicated its preference for the temporal method, which translates assets and liabilities carried at past, current, or future prices (expressed in foreign currency) in a manner that retains the accounting principles used to measure them in the foreign statements; that is, the attributes of the assets and liabilities measured are the same after translation as before.[19] Under present accounting procedures, the results of the temporal method and the monetary-nonmonetary method coincide. To show the effect of the method selected, Table 11-2 compares the results of the monetary-nonmonetary method and the once popular current-noncurrent method when the value of a foreign currency changes. (It shows the accounting sensitivity of currency translations.)

Companies A and B have the same balance sheets at the date of devaluation or revaluation. However, company A, using the monetary-nonmonetary method, has a net liability position of LC600 involving accounts susceptible to translation effects; company B, using the current-noncurrent method, has a net asset position of LC800 involving accounts susceptible to translation effects. The reason for this difference is that inventory is carried at acquisition rates and noncurrent debt at current rates under the monetary-nonmonetary method, whereas the opposite policies are followed under the current-noncurrent method. The effect is that company A's net liability position of LC600 produces a translation gain of $120 when its operations are in a country whose currency is devalued by 20 percent relative to the dollar. On the other hand, company B's net asset position of LC800 results in an exchange adjustment loss of $160 under similar conditions. If the local currency is revalued upward, however, the effects are reversed, and company A experiences an exchange adjustment loss of $120, while company B has a gain of $160.

In view of the trend toward internationalization, it is clearly imperative that the analyst assess the accounting implications of a company's operations. Using his knowledge of modern reporting practices, he can determine the foreign contribution to overall earnings, the parent company's policy with respect to drawing upon or reinvesting these earnings, the system's exposure

TABLE 11-2

Comparison of Monetary-Nonmonetary and Current-Noncurrent Methods

	BALANCE SHEET AT DEVALUATION OR REVALUATION DATE	ACCOUNTS TO BE ADJUSTED FOR THE RATE CHANGE	
		COMPANY A: MONETARY-NONMONETARY METHOD	COMPANY B: CURRENT-NONCURRENT METHOD
Cash and current receivables	LC 800	LC 800	LC800
Inventory	900	–	900
Fixed assets (net of depreciation)	700	–	–
Total assets	2,400		
Current payables	(900)	(900)	(900)
Noncurrent debt	(500)	(500)	–
Net worth	LC1,000		
Net position to be adjusted		LC(600)	LC800
		DEVALUATION OF FOREIGN CURRENCY	
U.S. $ equivalent before devaluation (LC1 = $1)		$ (600)	$ 800
U.S. $ equivalent after devaluation (LC1 = $.80)		(480)	640
Exchange adjustment—gain (loss)		$ 120	$ (160)
		REVALUATION OF FOREIGN CURRENCY	
U.S. $ equivalent before revaluation (LC1 = $1)		$ (600)	$ 800
U.S. $ equivalent after revaluation (LC1 = $1.20)		(720)	960
Exchange adjustment—gain (loss)		$ (120)	$ 160

SOURCE: Financial Accounting Standards Board, "An Analysis of Issues Related to Accounting for Foreign Currency Translation," discussion memorandum, February 21, 1974, pp. iv, vi.

to currency fluctuations, and management's indicated ability to deal with these fluctuations.

INFLUENCING THE FLOW OF REPORTED EARNINGS

Once revenues are created, questions still arise as to when and where they should be reflected in financial statements. The first question is concerned with timing, including the issue of leasing. The second is concerned principally with directing revenues to the current year's income or retained earnings and the identification of extraordinary items; the investment credit is a special case of influencing the reporting of revenues.

Timing the Reporting of Revenues

Ordinarily, revenues are reported in the period in which sales are made, goods delivered and accepted, facilities completed and accepted, or services rendered. If performance extends over a long period of time, however, proration may be appropriate as work progresses.[20] When a company is engaged in long-term construction—such as shipbuilding or the manufacture of large electronic equipment—sales, costs, and profits may be accrued on the basis of percentage of completion, rather than reported as complete units are shipped. In these circumstances, profits are recorded prior to completion of a contract, and estimated results are revised as work progresses.

Here again, different companies recognize revenues and costs under long-term contracts in different ways. For example, Babcock & Wilcox and Curtiss-Wright generally follow the percentage of completion method, whereas Chicago Bridge & Iron and Otis Elevator employ the completed contract method. Depending upon the route a company takes, the effect on income can be substantial. When, some years ago, Raytheon, in connection with certain contracts, shifted to reporting profits on the basis of percentage completion rather than units shipped, its net income was raised some 5 percent. For financial reporting purposes on certain long-term contracts, Westinghouse Electric bases its earnings on percentage of completion, but for tax purposes it reports on a completed contract basis. In 1973 the amount reported to shareholders was $22.2 million greater than was reported to the Internal Revenue Service; in 1972 the difference was $11.6 million. Noting this discrepancy, Coenen & Co. observed in its *Quality of Earnings Report* that "in our opinion, WX should provide an explanation to investors as to why the company does not choose to utilize the more conservative completed contract method of accounting for contracts in process."[21]

The percentage completion method may be abused by a company that deliberately seeks to show a good earnings face to its shareholders. In the National Student Marketing case, which garnered considerable publicity some years ago, the company used this method to report earnings on contracts for which eventual payment was questionable.[22] Recognizing the problem, the SEC has proposed that companies provide expanded disclosure about long-term contracts.

Another form of the revenue recognition issue arises when a company's sales are paid over several periods, in which case it may use either the installment or the accrual method of accounting. Under the installment method, federal income taxes are deferred until collection takes place; under the accrual method, taxes are charged against income concurrently. Accordingly, some companies prefer to defer their income tax by utilizing the installment method, thereby improving their cash flow, even though they report to stockholders on the accrual method. W. T. Grant, for example, has followed this policy.[23]

The amount of tax deferred can be substantial for a company that reports to the Internal Revenue Service on a completed contract or installment basis. Moreover, if there is no change in the income tax and the deferral is recurring, the result may be a permanent saving. Some people contend, therefore, that this saving constitutes, in effect, a perpetual interest-free loan. Even if the tax eventually is paid, its present value could be substantially reduced. Thus, for every dollar of deferred tax, a company that earns 10 percent need invest only 39 cents in order to generate enough funds to pay its tax bill of $1.00 ten years later; the other 41 cents provides additional earnings that eventually will result in new pretax income. Additionally, if the tax rate is expected to decline, the company has another reason for effecting deferrals.

The Problem of Leasing

The timing of the take-down of profits by the lessor creates a problem in leasing which has been a troublesome accounting issue that has been highlighted by the recent dramatic increase in leasing transactions. Over the past 25 years, the various accounting regulatory bodies have sought to clarify appropriate accounting procedures for leases,[24] including the recording of receivables by the lessor. Out of these extensive examinations, a concept of leasing has emerged that recognizes two basic types.

In one type, the lessor transfers to the lessee substantially all of the benefits and risks incident to ownership of the property. Such a transaction was described by the APB and the SEC as a financing lease. The FASB's 1975 Draft, which has drawn criticism, refers to this approach as a capital lease. In its economic implications, this leasing method resembles an installment purchase. Accordingly, the essence of the classification tests established to identify it rests upon the transfer of all or most of the ownership benefits and risks, such as that the lease term equals 75 percent or more of the estimated economic life of the property.

The FASB August 1975 Exposure Draft further distinguishes between capital leases that are equivalent to the sale of property with the price collectible over a period of time (sales-type leases) and capital leases that are in essence financing transactions (direct-financing leases). In both cases, the lessor records as receivables the minimum rentals during the lease term (reduced by operating expenses, such as maintenance, taxes, and insurance paid by the lessors) plus any bargain purchase option price (a provision allowing the lessee, at his option to purchase the leased property for a price that at the inception of the lease is expected to be substantially less than the fair value of the property at the date the option becomes exercisable). These receivables are subject to the same considerations as other assets in classifying them as current or noncurrent.

Under both methods, too, the gross receivables are reduced by an amount of unearned income that is amortized over the lease term in proportion to the remaining balance of the receivables. In the sales-type lease, the gross receivables are reduced to their present value using the lessee's incremental borrowing rate as the discount rate. Since this present value is considered the sales price, to the extent that it exceeds cost, a manufacturer's or dealer's profit is recognized at inception. In the case of the direct-financing lease, the gross receivables are reduced to the cost value of the property and therefore no immediate gain is taken into account. Unearned income for sales-type leases equals the difference between gross receivables and the present value of the receivables (the sales price); unearned income for direct-financing leases equals the difference between gross receivables and the cost of the property.

The second type of lease refers to those not meeting the tests of a capital lease and therefore classified as operating leases. The Exposure Draft provides for lessors including in fixed assets the cost of the leased property arising out of these leases and depreciating it over time in accordance with their normal policy. Rent is reported as income over the lease term as it becomes receivable. Depreciation of the leased property, maintenance, insurance and the cost of other services are included in the income statement as expenses. Separate information is also provided for leveraged leases. These involve three parties–a lessee who is contractually bound to fulfill his obligation under the lease; a long-term creditor (lender), who furnishes the major portion of the purchase price without recourse; and a lessor (the equity participant), who provides the remainder of the purchase price and acquires the asset.

These regulatory efforts are making available a considerable body of data on which to evaluate the financial status of lessors. Of particular importance is the distinction drawn between short- and long-term receivables arising out of capital leases, so that attention can be centered on the extent to which the lessor is dependent upon future arrangements. Of importance, too, is the provision for identifying unearned income arising out of capital leases and for including it in current income on a uniform basis. For ordinary leases, where the risks of ownership remain with the lessor, the analysis of the company's net investment in different kinds of property on lease or held for lease will throw additional light on the distribution of the company's business. The implications of the regulatory efforts to the lessee are discussed subsequently in the text (see pp. 444-445, 451-452, and 461-462).

Deflecting Revenues to Retained Earnings

Stockholders are primarily interested in a corporation's earnings capacity, which provides the basis for the eventual distribution of income. This capacity, in turn, is the outcome of all the corporation's activities over a period of years. As these activities become more diverse, it is often difficult to determine which may be considered routine and which extraordinary. Recognizing this problem some accountants favor an all-inclusive statement in which the reported net income takes into account all items, whether usual or not. Other accountants, contending that a distinction should be drawn between an enterprise's recurrent operations and those arising from unusual circumstances, favor the so-called current operating performance concept. Over the years, the tendency has been toward the all-inclusive statement.

In a series of opinions between 1947 and 1973, the APB established the principle of reflecting in the current period all items of profit and loss recognized during the period, but the board also provided for the segregation and separate reporting of extraordinary items.[25] The guidelines for determining extraordinary items were broad, however, leaving much to the discretion of the companies. As a result, the number of companies reporting extraordinary items increased substantially, and what was counted as extraordinary varied considerably. Eventually, therefore, the APB issued another opinion in which "extraordinary" was defined more restrictively, so that the event must now be both unusual and nonrecurring when judged in the light of the company's business. Moreover, the board created a new section of the income statement to show the effects of disposing of a segment of the business. The APB also required separate disclosure in income from continuing operations of material events that are either unusual or nonrecurring but which are neither extraordinary nor disposals of a segment of a business.[26]

In a sense, the new format of the income statement is a step toward simplification. Presumably, the reporting of extraordinary items will be reduced, and ordinarily a single net income figure will be shown. This figure, however, may now reflect unusual or nonrecurring events that must be assessed in evaluating the company's earnings outlook. Accordingly, it is more important than ever for the investor to examine the entire income statement, as well as the related footnotes, in order to ascertain the presence and understand the significance of such events.[27] As an illustration, in 1973, Pitney Bowes reported a loss of $1.76 per share, the first in the company's 54-year history. Examination of the income statement, however, revealed that of this, 41 cents was attributable to losses from a discontinued segment of the company's business, and $2.85 to the actual disposition of this segment of the business; a profit of $1.50 per share was incurred from continuing operations.[28]

Opinion no. 30 (par. 23) did at least one other thing. It asserted positively that "gains or losses from exchange or translation of foreign currencies, including those relating to major devaluations and revaluations" should not be treated as extraordinary items. It did not, however, end the controversy as to when these items should be included in income. Company practices have varied considerably. In its exposure draft on the subject, the Financial Accounting Standards Board examined the various reasons for justifying deferral and dismissed them all.[29] The board's subsequent statement requires that the results of translation (gains and losses) be reported in the income of the current period and not be deferred to the future.

In determining how unusual items should be handled, it is important to remember that a primary objective of the investor is the projection of earnings for the following year. Under these circumstances, giving undue weight to extraordinary income should be avoided, but their effect cannot be ignored. One method of handling the problem is to project operating earnings and then make separate estimates, necessarily subjective, of the expected value of nonrecurring earnings for the coming year. It does not seem reasonable for the market to capitalize nonrecurring earnings the same way it capitalizes operating earnings; the market does not expect repeat performance unless it has been given good reason to do so. Nor is it reasonable to suppose that the market ignores these extras. We can therefore hypothesize that reported or detected nonrecurring earnings influence stock prices through their effect on the expected value of these earnings. This value, in turn, may be obtained by identifying the total of extraordinary items and then capitalizing it at a higher rate (lower price/earnings ratio) than that used for the more normally achieved earnings.

Investment Credit

The Revenue Act of 1962 provided for an investment credit designed to encourage development of the nation's productive facilities. Under this act, the maximum credit was 7 percent for general business and 3 percent for certain public utilities, if the useful life of a qualifying piece of property was eight years or more. A limit was provided on the amount of credit that could be taken in any one year, and provision was made for carrying back any unused credit for three years and forward for five years.

The credit was rescinded in 1969, reinstated in 1971, and given an additional boost in the antirecession tax bill of 1975. Under that measure, the allowable write-off for business equipment was increased for the next two years to 10 percent from 7 percent for most businesses and to 10 percent from 4 percent for utilities. Certain other specialized benefits were also provided, including an additional 1 percent credit (to an 11 percent total) if an amount equal to 1 percent of the qualified investment is contributed to an Employees' Stock Ownership Plan (this was the first statutory enactment of a pet project of the Senate Finance Committee). The credit may be extended again.

After the original act was passed, virtually all companies reduced their taxes payable by the amount of the investment credit in the year during which the equipment was acquired. Disagreement arose, however, over the accounting periods during which the credit was to be included in the income statement. According to one viewpoint, the credit reflected a reduction in the cost of the property, and therefore the benefits to income had to be recognized over the productive life of the property. Another approach considered the credit to be a reduction in income taxes, which justified having the credit "flow through" the income statement in the year of acquisition.

To observe the effects of these two methods, assume that at the beginning of the taxable year a company acquires property at a cost of $10,000 with a depreciable life of ten years, employs a straight-line basis of depreciation, and pays an income tax of 50 percent. Under both methods, an annual income tax requirement of $5,000 is established.

Under both methods, also, the amount of taxes payable is reduced immediately by an investment credit of $1,000 (10 percent), but the methods differ as to when the credit should be reflected in the income statement. In the first case, with the credit apportioned over the life of the property, the net income after taxes would be $5,100 each year (assuming the same conditions); after ten years the full $1,000 credit would be reported as income. In the second case, when the credit "flows through" immediately to the income statement, reported earnings would be $6,000 in the year when the property is acquired but would be $5,000 in each subsequent year, until the property is written off (assuming unchanged conditions).

While Congress was considering restoration of the investment credit in 1971, the Accounting Principles Board proposed an opinion which would require accounting for the investment credit as a reduction of income tax expense over the periods in which the cost of the related property was charged to income. The possibility that the flow-through method might be barred created concern both among companies that wanted to reflect the benefit of the credit in reported income immediately and among U.S. Treasury officials, who felt that flow-through accounting was imperative to stimulate equipment purchases, thereby aiding the economy. As a result, the Revenue Act of 1971, which restored the credit, provides that no taxpayer be required to use any particular method of accounting for the credit; once a method is selected, however, it must be consistently followed, unless authority for a change is obtained from the Treasury Department. Congress thus took the extreme step of legislating an accounting requirement, despite the objections of the professional accounting associations and of other interested parties, such as the Financial Analysts Federation, which preferred uniformity in financial accounting.[30]

SUMMARY

The accounting policies that a firm follows have an important influence on its reported earnings. Within accepted principles, management has the leeway to effect substantial variations. As the SEC and the self-regulating accounting agencies require improved disclosure, analysts are better able to evaluate the quality of a company's earnings. If management elects approaches that buoy a company's earnings, the quality of the reported figures may be regarded as poor; if its choices produce conservative results, the quality of the earnings may be judged good. All other things being equal, the price/earnings ratios of companies known to have good quality earnings are likely to be higher than the ratios of companies whose reported earnings are of poor quality.

Various legal bodies have some overseeing responsibilities over accounting. Principal authority in the United States is exercised by the American Institute of Certified Public Accountants (AICPA), which created the Financial Accounting Standards Board (FASB), successor to the Accounting Principles Board (APB), to study accounting issues and provide guiding rules. While the Securities and Exchange Commission is given considerable authority by the securities acts and amendments, it has encouraged the accounting profession to generate its own principles; however, in recent years the commission has become active, particularly in the area of disclosure. Other agencies also play some type of supervisory or advisory role.

In assessing earnings, the relationships between a parent and its subsidiaries are important. If the parent elects to consolidate, restrictions such as those contained in bond indentures might limit the subsidiary's ability to tap retained earnings for distribution of dividends. If the parent does not consolidate, it must now recognize its share of earnings or losses of a subsidiary in the period for which they are reported. While this requirement has reduced some of the differences in the accounting of subsidiary earnings, important problems still exist with respect to the taxation of foreign earnings and the translation of these earnings into dollars.

Once revenues are created, questions arise as to when and where they should be reflected in financial statements. With respect to timing, companies may use discretion in reporting revenues, costs, and profits when a long-term contract is involved or when sales are paid over several periods. The timing of the take-down of profits has been a particularly troublesome problem in the case of leasing, where use of the device to avoid the reporting of debt in balance sheets has also been an issue. While the Financial Accounting Standards Board has been considering this area, the SEC now requires the disclosure in financial statements of the present value of all noncapitalized financing leases and the impact on net income if all such leases were capitalized.

With respect to where revenues should be reported, major concerns involve the practices of deflecting revenues to retained earnings rather than reported earnings for a period and of distinguishing between ordinary and extraordinary income. In a series of opinions, the Accounting Principles Board established the principle of reflecting in the current period all items of profit and loss during the period. It also has provided for the segregation and separate reporting of extraordinary items and has created guidelines for this purpose.

The Revenue Act of 1962 created an investment credit that was rescinded in 1969, reinstated in 1971, and given an additional boost in 1975. Virtually all companies reduce their taxes payable by the amount of the investment credit in the year when the equipment is acquired. Policies are split, however, on whether the reduction in income should "flow through" to the income statement in that year or should be recognized over the property's productive life.

CHAPTER 12

Evaluating the Quality of a Company's Earnings: Costs

In addition to having discretion over how revenues are shown, management may influence the reporting of costs. There are three major areas where control is exercised: valuing assets, obscuring costs, and allocating costs.

VALUATION OF ASSETS

Corporations have various kinds of assets, and their carrying values affect reported profits in different ways. Thus, the level of fixed assets is the point of departure for determining depreciation charges; the price of inventories constitutes the basis of profit margins; accounts receivable may be written down through bad-debt allowances; and certain intangible assets can be amortized over time.

Valuing Fixed Assets

The economic value of a fixed asset is the sum of the earnings it is expected to generate, discounted at an appropriate rate. If the accountant used such an unstable criterion, the carrying values of fixed assets would depend upon estimates that changed with prevailing circumstances. Instead, for purposes of income reporting, the accountant views fixed assets as prepaid costs to be written off over time on the basis of their original values.

From the investor's viewpoint, this procedure eliminates much of the uncertainty underlying the valuation of fixed assets. An element of managerial judgment may still enter the picture, however, because the total amount to be written off depends not only on its original cost but also on what the company will recover when the asset is scrapped. The accountant, of course, cannot wait to find out what will actually be recovered from the asset; therefore, he must provide a gauge for its salvage value beforehand. Storm Drilling & Marine, Inc., which preserves substantial cash flow through depreciation, allows 15 percent for salvage values on its offshore drilling and marine service equipment.[1]

While the accountant has some leeway in establishing the amount to be depreciated, he cannot arbitrarily determine the salvage value because of the overview exercised by the Internal Revenue Service. At times, the audit of a company's federal income tax returns may provide for salvage values that result in a lowering of the allowable depreciation charge, an increase in federal income taxes plus accrued interest, and corresponding credits and charges to retained earnings.

The convention of recording fixed assets at cost may result in seriously underestimating their current values during a prolonged period of inflation, such as has been occurring in the United States. In these circumstances, not only is the company's net worth understated, but the periodic depreciation charge allocated to income is also understated, thereby overstating income. Paying taxes on this overstated income reduces net cash from operations. Since World War II, companies have complained about this state of affairs. For example, in its 1969 annual report, Caterpillar Tractor pointed out that

> the generally accepted accounting principle followed with respect to buildings, machinery and equipment is the systematic allocation to each year's operations of a portion of the original cost of these facilities. The plant assets currently in use were acquired over many years at price levels which were lower than current price levels. The portion of the original cost of these assets allocated to each year and used in determining profit was, therefore, substantially lower than if a provision had been made on the basis of current replacement price levels.

Ordinarily the investor cannot count on the market's recognizing such an underdevaluation. To the extent that he desires to benefit by this condition, his primary hope probably rests on the possibility that some organization will initiate a take-over attempt. Acquisition-minded companies have sometimes sought old enterprises which have held their properties for long periods of time and therefore may be carrying them at a fraction of their present worth. The persistence of inflation in recent years, however, has finally persuaded the accounting profession to give serious consideration to showing the influence of inflation in reported information. The approach could be through either expressing financial statements in units of general purchasing power or reflecting changes in the current replacement values of goods held or obligations owed by an enterprise.[2]

General purchasing power represents the restatement of historical dollars, through use of a price-level index, to dollars in terms of current general purchasing power. In current replacement value accounting, on the other hand, in lieu of historical costs, there are substituted estimates of the cost to replace the assets as determined by appraisals or by prices applicable to the specific assets. The commission has been veering toward replacement cost data. In August 1975 it issued a proposal that would require publicly held companies to disclose in footnotes to their financial statements various items of information concerned with the effects of inflation. Included would be the current net replacement cost and the amount of depreciation, depletion, and amortization that would have been accrued if the company had figured them on the basis of current replacement cost. This information would be helpful in gauging the extent to which current depreciation is failing to keep pace with the rising price of capital goods. The commission recognized that compliance with the new rules would require considerable estimating. It is therefore weighing the advisability of labeling such accounting "unaudited" and requiring it only for companies of a designated minimum size.

Pricing Inventories

The physical volume of goods sold and the physical volume of goods produced or purchased are not necessarily the same, because sales may be derived from existing inventories or inventories may be augmented by producing more than is sold. Determination of the cost of goods sold (and therefore the operating profit) depends on which costs are associated with units sold, since purchases may have been made at different prices. Two principal methods are used for this purpose. In one, it is assumed that the oldest costs are drawn first from inventory (first in, first out, or *FIFO*), while in the other it is assumed that the most recent costs are assigned to units sold (last in, first out, or *LIFO*). Both of these methods have their physical analogues. In a liquid storage tank with an input valve at the top and an outlet at the bottom, the flow would literally be on a FIFO basis. (It should be noted that a firm using LIFO for pricing inventories is not representing that its goods physically move in and out, as is implied by FIFO.) On the other hand, in the case of a storage bin with a single opening for entry or egress, material would move on a LIFO basis. In another fairly common method, called average cost, the cost of goods sold is a weighted average of the beginning inventory and the additions that are subsequently made; this approach tends to result in an amount for the cost of goods that is somewhere between the LIFO and FIFO methods.

Until about the middle of 1974, the FIFO and average cost method of valuing inventories tended to be predominant. In both these methods, the inventories sold are valued at their older, cheaper prices, and costs tend to be understated. The profits are considered unrealistic, however, because they do not take into account the fact that the company will have to replenish inventories at higher prices. This differential–between the historical cost of an item and its replacement cost at the time it is sold–represents an "inventory profit" or "holding gain" that does not reflect an increase in economic earning power and is not normally repeatable unless prices continue to rise.

In determining its national accounts, the Department of Commerce distinguishes between profits arising out of production and distribution, which are considered part of the gross national product, and book-value gains resulting from higher prices, which are excluded from the gross national product. In the second quarter of 1974, inventory profits were estimated to be running at an annual rate of $37.3 billion, almost one-third of all pretax profits of nonfinancial corporations.[3]

The corporate users of the FIFO and average cost methods during this period were disturbed by the need to report high "paper" profits on which "hard cash" tax payments had to be made. Accordingly, in 1974, a host of companies announced that they were switching to the LIFO method. In some cases, the changeover had a substantial effect. For example, du Pont estimated that its shift to LIFO from the average cost system would reduce 1974 pretax earnings by about $300 million; pretax earnings in 1973 were about $1.04 billion.[4]

The SEC, in turn, became concerned that investors were not being adequately informed about the effects of inventory profits on corporate earnings. Consequently, it urged registrants "to disclose the extent to which reported profits are comprised of potentially unrepeatable and usually unsegregrated inventory profits," as well as to provide a discussion of the relationship between costs and profits.[5] According to the commission, it got very little response from this suggestion. The August 1975 proposal called for information on the effect of inflation on inventories. It would require publicly held companies to show the current replacement cost of inventories as well as the approximate cost of sales for the two most recent years, based on the current replacement cost of the goods and services sold.

The availability of such information would enhance the analyst's ability to evaluate the effects of a company's profits on its reported earnings, a problem that has generally been very troublesome.

There are also current disclosure requirements of the APB and the SEC that are concerned with the valuation of inventories. When a company changes to the LIFO method, it must disclose the effect on earnings in the period of change, in accordance with APB Opinion no. 20. When Crown Cork & Seal switched to LIFO accounting for all U.S. can, crown, and closure inventories, net income for 1974 was reduced by $7.2 million dollars (about 18 percent). If the LIFO method is used, SEC Rule 5.02 of Regulation S-X requires that the excess of replacement or current cost over the stated LIFO value should, if material, be indicated parenthetically or in a footnote to the financial statements. (Modification of this requirement has been under study.)

Valuing Accounts Receivables

Since some receivables are never collected, companies must take that fact into account. The common procedure is to provide an allowance for bad debts by charges against revenues, which are used to absorb the eventual losses the company sustains. Since the amount of this allowance is an estimate, the periodic charges to earnings depend to a large extent on managerial judgment.

Holders of large volumes of receivables, such as commercial banks, may write down outstanding accounts by a greater margin than the actual size of expected defaults and then report subsequent gains when the accounts are collected. A small number of companies do not provide allowances and simply write off receivables against earnings as they become worthless. When allowances for possible bad debts are reported, the typical ratio runs between 2 and 3 percent of net receivables, but substantial differences occur. For example, at the close of 1972, AMF Inc., engaged in the manufacture of leisure time and industrial products, reported an allowance for possible losses that was 11.5 percent of its net receivables (over 10 percent were due beyond one year). The bad debt allowance of its 50 percent-owned Japanese subsidiary, which had $118 million sales in 1972, constituted 27.7 percent of its net receivables (47 percent of which were due beyond one year).[6] The House of Vision had a bad debt ratio of 8.7 percent in 1974; Pitney Bowes, 5.7 percent; and Allied Chemical, 4.4 percent. In contrast to these relatively generous ratios, Bobbie Brooks had a ratio of 1.1 percent, while Briggs & Stratton, National Distillers, and Chemical Bank each had a sparse 0.8 percent. If the ratio is out of line, the analyst may check to determine whether the allowance makes provision for factors other than doubtful accounts; for example, the whopping 13.5 percent ratio of Hospital Affiliates, Inc. in 1974 makes allowance for contractual adjustments as well as for doubtful accounts.

Bad debt ratios that are over 3 percent or under 2 percent may be due to the characteristics of a particular industry, to the nature of the company's relationships with its customers, or to an effort on the part of management to influence reported profits. The analyst has the responsibility of determining which is the cause.

The SEC has been concerned about the unique risk and liquidity characteristics of both inventories and receivables arising out of long-term contracts. Accordingly, in November 1974 it issued Accounting Series Release no. 164 (revising Rule 5-02.3 and Rule 5.02-6 of Regulation S-X), which calls for registered corporations to segregate the long-term aspects of both these assets. Information is specifically required on long-term receivables whose ultimate realization is uncertain; registrants must include an estimate of the amount expected to be collected after one year.

This provision has thrown light on the relatively long-term receivables that companies have outstanding. For example, in its 1974 annual report, Wheelabrator-Frye showed net receivables of $54.8 million and, as a separate amount, $14.6 million of contracts in process to be billed. Included in the net receivables were $5.8 million of contract retainages, representing amounts billed but not paid by customers under long-term contracts. The company further indicated that it expected these retainages to be substantially collected in 1975 and that the contracts in process to be billed will be billed and collected in 1975.

Recognizing Intangibles

Business firms are going concerns with established clienteles and a great many ways of making money that are not reflected in bricks and mortar or any other type of tangible assets. For example, although there may be a considerable difference of opinion on the value of a particular patent, few will disagree that when the patented product is enjoying profitable sales, it has a value. The goodwill represented by a name like Coca-Cola undoubtedly brings in considerable business and is a real asset. Ordinarily, the money spent on research by a modern firm in order to remain technologically competitive is considered an expense of the period. Yet, since the fruition of this research may not be realized in the period in which the expenditures are made, there is merit to the argument that these outlays should be capitalized and shown as an asset to be amortized over time, rather than charged against current income. The Financial Accounting Standards Board, however, requires that research and development costs be charged to expenses as incurred, although it excludes research conducted for others under contractual arrangements.[7] The SEC has amended its rules to conform with this provision.

The inclusion of values for customer goodwill, patents, or capitalized research is not uncommon, but these values are clearly difficult to determine.

Just as difficult is the problem of ascertaining the speed at which these values are being consumed and, consequently, the appropriate annual amortization. In some industries, patents and goodwill are extremely important, and yet the various companies treat them quite differently.

The problem of intangibles became particularly acute in the recent merger waves. Accepted accounting principles permit reporting a merger either as a purchase or a pooling of interests.[8] In the latter case there is a presumed continuity of interest in the ownership of the two firms. The transaction is substantially a stock-for-stock exchange; from an accounting point of view, the financial statements are simply "combined" or added together. Under this concept, the acquired companies are considered to have been part of the new corporate system, and their operating results are included both in the current financial statements and in the figures restated for prior years. The net assets are recorded at values carried on the books of the acquired companies.

When a company is purchased, its earnings are included only from the date of acquisition. The acquired company's physical and financial assets are appraised, and any difference between the total of this value and the sum of assumed liabilities plus the price paid is attributed to goodwill. Therein lies the rub. If the goodwill is amortized over any reasonable length of time, it might seriously affect the reported earnings per share. Since many acquisitions are made in an attempt to portray a picture of ever-growing earnings per share, this requirement can prove self-defeating.

In order to avoid the restrictive influence on earnings of purchase accounting, many firms elected to combine by the pooling route. Reacting to this situation, the AICPA adopted certain guidelines which permit pooling only if the merger involves the exchange of common stock or its equivalent (other requirements must also be met); if any other securities or cash are used, the transaction has to be recorded as a purchase. Another major ruling applies to purchase accounting: any goodwill resulting from a merger must be amortized over a period of not more than 40 years.[9] An unpalatable aspect of this write-off is that it is not deductible for tax purposes. While a number of companies have opted to use the maximum allowable period of 40 years in their write-offs, variations do occur. For example, FMC amortizes the intangibles of acquired companies over periods not exceeding 20 years, and Central Soya employs a 15-year period. Still other companies, like Nabisco, follow the requirement of APB Opinion no. 17 that applies the maximum write-off period to assets acquired after October 31, 1970; these companies amortize that part of the excess which relates to 1971 or subsequent acquisitions, while asserting that the portion of the excess relating to assets acquired before that date represents continuing values and therefore need not be amortized.

OBSCURING COSTS

Corporate policies in different areas may affect the amount of costs reported. Two important areas are the use of reserves to absorb costs and compensation programs that affect the reporting of personnel costs.

Creation of Reserves

Management may "segregate" certain parts of the retained earnings segment. By doing so, it creates a dividend shield and informs the reader of certain contingencies. In no sense, however, will such segregation prevent the contingencies from happening or reduce the financial impact if they occur. At times, this practice has also been extended to the income statement, and special reserves have been charged against the current year's earnings. By this means, high-earnings years may be reduced and future losses absorbed into the reserve, thereby conveying an unrealistic picture of earnings.

International Telephone & Telegraph appears to have been a conspicuous follower of this policy. For example, in 1970 it changed the inventory policy of its Grinnell acquisition from LIFO to FIFO, thereby boosting ITT's pretax profits by $13.8 million. But net earnings took no proportionate leap because the company immediately blunted the impact of this change by establishing $9.2 million as a reserve against possible losses on Grinnell's "obsolete" inventory. This illustration reflects ITT's apparent policy of setting aside large reserves and spreading big profitable transactions in order to offset the positive impact of nonrecurring gains. Rather than showing large earnings jumps, ITT seems to have been more interested in consistent earnings increases.[10]

The weight of accounting opinion is against the use of reserves arbitrarily to reduce income or to shift income from one period to another for the purpose of creating a semblance of stability.[11] But, even more specifically, the FASB has issued a statement limiting the flexibility of companies to create reserves by charges to income in anticipation of future losses. In accordance with this statement, a company may not create a self-insurance reserve unless (1) at the date of the financial statement an asset has been impaired or a liability has been incurred; (2) one or more events are reasonably expected to occur that will confirm the loss; and (3) the amount of the loss can be reasonably estimated. Thus, risk of loss or damage by casualties not insured against may not be provided until they are clear.[12]

While the SEC has not played an active part in determining accounting policy for creating reserves, it has been concerned about the reporting of unusual items, as has been mentioned previously. In order to prevent the appearance of an unexpectedly large charge or credit to income or a material provision for losses, the commission in January 1973 issued Accounting Series Release no. 138. In it, the commission admonished registrants to make special efforts to recognize incipient problems that might lead to substantial charges and to identify them as early as possible. Disclosure should be made, for example, of the undepreciated cost of plant and equipment currently considered to be obsolete or of marginal utility. The commission also adopted various amendments to its supporting forms to provide increased information on unusual charges and credits to income.

Extracompensation Costs

A combination of social and moral pressures, competition, and tax advantages has led corporations to seek different ways of rewarding their personnel outside of salaries and wages. Two prominent methods are pensions and stock options. Both have accounting implications that may affect income. The FASB is seeking appropriate accounting standards for them.

Pension plans. When pension plans have been introduced, companies have treated past-service costs (payments required to cover eligible employees for services prior to the inception of the plan) differently. In the past, some companies charged them directly to retained earnings, while others charged them to income in the period when the plan was introduced. Now, however, both the American Institute of Certified Public Accountants and the Internal Revenue Service favor spreading the costs over the present and future years and counting an appropriate amount in pension expense. The majority of companies presently adhere to this practice. For example, Eastman Kodak includes in its pension expense amortization of prior service costs over periods ranging up to 30 years.[13] For other concerns, the amortization period is generally anywhere from 25 to 40 years.

After a plan has been in effect, a company may need to change its underlying base. When this is done, the company may be able to modify the required payments. Since those payments represent expenses of doing business, changes in their terms affect reported income. A new reference framework was introduced with congressional passage of the Employee Retirement Income Security Act of 1974 (ERISA). Among other things, the new law requires that companies accept full liability for all vested or guaranteed benefits, whether they are funded or not. While funding still may be continued over the next 25 to 40 years, financial liability is assumed immediately. Moreover, annual contributions to pension plans probably will have to be increased substantially to meet increased actual liabilities as a result of mandatory improvements in plan benefits. Disclosure requirements are provided and fiduciary responsibilities tightened.

Pension assets must now be related to market values rather than book values. This requirement will reduce actuarial assumptions during rising markets but will increase them during depressed conditions like those prevalent when the law was passed. It is likely that the legislation will impose enlarged costs on companies, will weaken capital structures because of the burden of increased legal liabilities, and will make plan administrators more cautious.

Stock options. Management has supported stock options as a means of attracting talented executives. To the extent that such options reduce the sizes of the salaries that might otherwise have to be paid, they are useful devices and probably helpful to the value of the stock. At the same time, options exert a depressing influence on a stock's price, since they are likely to be exercised as the market advances. Even if not exercised, they may have an adverse effect, since investors probably will give increasing attention to per share earnings on a fully diluted basis where options could have an important influence. The investor need not be disturbed if the amount of options is small relative to the outstanding stock; but if the proportion is large, he should regard the options as a negative factor that is likely to be a drag on potential market gains.

ALLOCATING COSTS

Management has some latitude in the treatment of costs that are applicable to different periods of time. Here the primary decision is determining the period to which they should be charged.

Depreciation

Every company owns numerous assets that render services over extended periods of time. The annual cost of each asset is prorated over its life span, in the form of depreciation, depletion, or amortization charges against income. There is no certain way of calculating these charges. Thus, the amount that appears on the income statement depends on such factors as tax considerations, personal judgments, and accounting practices. Two firms with similar assets may make substantially different charges in the same year. Since these differences are reflected in the tax bill and dividend payments, they affect the cash flow and therefore can be extremely important, particularly when the cost of money is high.

Depreciation may be a substantial portion of total costs. IBM, for example, assumes a rapid obsolescence and, therefore, a fairly short life for its lease equipment. As a result, its depreciation charges have characteristically exceeded its net earnings after taxes.

Most methods of depreciation are based on the principle that the decline of an asset's value is a function of time. The major methods employing this concept are the straight-line, the sum-of-the-years/digits, and the multiple declining balance. In straight-line depreciation, equal charges are allocated to successive periods of time. In the sum-of-the-years/digits method, the fraction of the value depreciated each year is equal to a ratio: the numerator is the number of remaining years to the life of the assets, and the denominator is the sum of the n digits, where n is the expected economic life of the asset. In the multiple declining balance method, the amount of depreciation charged each year is $1/n$th of x percent of the undepreciated balance; the Internal Revenue Code of 1954 permitted x to equal 200 percent on most new assets, and 150 percent on secondhand assets. The rapid write-off customarily is used until the remaining balance becomes quite small; then a switch is made to straight-line depreciation, in order to effect a full write-off.

In general, assets may be depreciated not to zero but to some final salvage-value figure. While the total amount of depreciation over an asset's life is the same regardless of the method used, the periodic allocation may differ sharply. The straight-line method provides smaller amounts and less of a tax shelter in the early years of the asset. The present value of taxes saved by reducing income through faster depreciation could be substantial in the other methods, with the value of the savings dependent on the cost of capital.

Another basic method of depreciation is related to units of production. In this method, depreciation costs are treated as a result of asset deterioration from continued output; charges are therefore established in relation to production. To determine a depreciation rate, the economic life of the asset is expressed in terms of units of activity. The ratio of the units consumed during the year to the total economic life of the asset is then applied to the asset's dollar cost (less salvage value) to obtain the depreciation charge for the period.

Corporations usually employ depreciation methods that are a function of time. Formerly, they tended to rely on the straight-line method, but the 1954 Internal Revenue Code permitted the use of the sum-of-the-years/digits and the multiple declining balance methods.

In order to obtain the benefits of early high depreciation charges, many companies use an accelerated method for tax purposes. At the same time, these companies may report on a straight-line basis to their stockholders in order to curtail the annual depreciation charges shown. In this case, the amount of taxes reported to stockholders will differ from that actually paid. Accepted accounting policy calls for recognizing this differential by an appropriate charge to the income statement, with a related credit to a deferred tax account in the balance sheet.[14] As an illustration, Scott Paper reports on a straight-line basis for financial accounting, but for income-tax purposes it uses accelerated methods. Primarily for this reason, $8.2 million of federal taxes were deferred in 1973, an amount that was almost twice as great as the federal taxes actually paid. As the company stated, "Using the larger depreciation expense on tax returns reduces current tax payments, thereby increasing working capital."[15]

The tax savings from deferring taxes has been likened to an interest-free loan from the government. On this basis, the amount shown as a deferred account in the balance sheet would represent the present value of what will eventually have to be repaid, rather than the amount of the savings. A growing company, however, may never have to make a repayment. Thus, in 1974 Scott Paper's tax relationship reversed that of 1972, as current federal charges of $11.6 million were about twice as great as the $5.5 million federal taxes deferred. But the company noted that "deferred taxes for 1974 and prior years . . . will not become payable under existing tax laws so long as the Company maintains its historical rate of capital expenditures."[16] If the tax savings truly represent a permanent interest-free loan or even one of a finite but extended duration, they are hardly distinguishable from a gift. Thus, some public utility commissions have at times refused to recognize a charge for deferred taxes, while others have permitted it but with only a trivial rate of return on the assets financed by this means. For this reason, some public utility companies have resisted using accelerated depreciation.

Although there is no requirement that a company use the same method of depreciation for all assets, once a selection is made for income tax purposes, that method must be used over the lifetime of a particular asset unless a convincing case can be made to the IRS for changing it; the sole exception permitted is the shift from the multiple declining to the straight-line method. The choice of depreciation method gives management some flexibility in determining the annual charge to income. Where management has discretion, it may desire to manage profits by gearing depreciation to economic conditions. Thus, it will use accelerated depreciation when earnings and tax rates are high and straight-line depreciation when earnings and tax payments are small. In the analysis of embryonic firms, changes in depreciation methods should be anticipated. New firms lose money in their early years, and they are permitted to carry these losses forward until they incur significant tax liabilities; accelerated depreciation would only depress earnings and consequently is avoided. When the firm becomes successful, the depreciation policy is likely to be changed.

Companies on an economic decline prefer straight-line depreciation because the accelerated methods would only aggravate the shrinkage of earnings. For example, in 1960 the former New York Central, faced with low profits, abandoned the rapid amortization of the costs of certain equipment and facilities. Similarly, the former Underwood Corp., which at one time was a thriving typewriter firm, found the going rough in the electronics field after

World War II. To paint the best possible picture, "the company took the lowest possible depreciation for tax purposes on its facilities, mortgaging the future."[17]

There may be reasons other than economic difficulties that cause a company to adopt straight-line depreciation for financial reporting; such a change may boost reported earnings or may better conform with industry practices. For example, effective January 1, 1972, Monsanto changed from the sum-of-the-years/digits method to the straight-line method of computing depreciation for financial statement purposes on domestic assets placed in service on or after that date; the change resulted in reduced depreciation charges of $5 million and an increase in net income of $2.6 million, or 8 cents a share for the year. National Cash Register adopted a similar shift applicable to the same period; it cut the estimated useful life of certain equipment and reduced its net loss for 1972 by 11 cents per share.[18]

Adequacy of Charges

Depreciation prevents a portion of the income stream from flowing toward stockholders. If the allowance is generous, management may have funds at hand to meet current operating requirements in times of adversity. If the depreciation allotment is lean, dividend distributions may represent, in part, a return of capital. Determining the appropriateness of the depreciation charge under present circumstances has become difficult. As long as the bulk of companies were using straight-line depreciation, there was at least a common basis of comparison. Even this degree of standardization is absent today, when various methods of depreciation are acceptable and may be applied to different assets.

The individual investor cannot indulge in the luxury of field trips, or must undertake them very sparingly. This limitation usually prevents him from evaluating depreciation requirements directly. Probably the best practical alternative is to measure the appropriateness of a corporation's charges by comparing them with those of other well-established enterprises in the same field. For this purpose, he may consider three aspects of the depreciation allowance.

First, he may obtain from the company's registration statement, prospectus, or listing statement an outline of the annual depreciation rates applied to the different categories of fixed assets. These rates are sometimes summarized in annual reports and financial manuals. The investor can then compare the rates with those used by other companies in the same field.

Second, he may study the ratio of the annual depreciation charges of a company to the value of its fixed depreciable assets, exclusive of accumulated depreciation. This ratio suggests the number of years used to write off capital equipment; as a rough measuring rod, the operating life of corporate property generally ranges from 10 to 20 years, depending on the specific assets. This figure assumes an average requirement of 5 to 10 percent for annual depreciation charges.

Third, the investor may compare the amount of annual depreciation charges with net sales during the year. This ratio must be used with great caution, since depreciation is largely a product of time and use, whereas sales are a function of many economic forces, such as demand, prices, and costs. There is, however, a certain degree of logic to the assumption that within the same industry there is some correlation between sales and depreciation. The ratio is particularly applicable to public utilities, where output is stable and production equipment largely uniform.

Depletion and Amortization

Closely akin to depreciation are depletion and amortization. Nevertheless, to evaluate their significance, the investor should recognize the distinction between them.

Depletion. Depletion is the decline in value of wasting assets, such as coal mines, metal ores, oil wells, and timber land; it arises from extraction of units of the original quantity. Unlike depreciable assets, which may be replaced, those subject to depletion become exhausted after the raw material is fully exploited.

For tax purposes, depletion represents an allowance for the loss of a capital value. Some form of this allowance has been provided since 1913, when the income tax was ratified as the 16th Amendment to the U.S. Constitution. In general, it enables oil and gas operators, as well as producers of more than 100 or more other minerals, to deduct in determining taxable income an amount equal to a specified percentage of their gross revenues from a producing property; this percentage is based on the relation of units produced to recoverable reserves.

After considerable controversy, Congress included in the Tax Reduction Act of 1975 a provision that repealed the percentage depletion for oil and gas production, with certain limited exceptions for "regulated natural gas." An exemption was allowed for "independent" companies, granting them a phased-down deduction starting at 22 percent for the first 2,000 barrels or 12 million cubic feet of average daily production. In 1984 the rate will stabilize at 15 percent, and the exemption will be 1,000 barrels or 6 million cubic feet a day.

Amortization. The term "amortization" refers to deterioration in the value of an asset owing to the passage of time. It may occur for many reasons. Advance payments made for a leasehold which runs for a specified period of years are treated as an asset that must be written off during the life of the lease. Improvements in leased property revert to the landlord when the lease expires and must be charged off prior to the expiration date. Similarly, intangible assets, such as patents and copyrights, have a limited legal and economic usefulness; this makes it necessary to absorb their value in measuring earnings. Earlier in the chapter, we discussed some of the policies of companies writing off goodwill that arises from purchase accounting.

Capitalizing Costs

The border line between capital outlays and expenses is not a clear one. Consequently, firms have much latitude with respect to determining whether certain outlays should be treated as an expense of the period or capitalized and written off over time. The treatment of large expenditures for plant maintenance or refurbishing is a case in point. Theoretically, the decision should be based on whether such expenditures materially increase the service life of an asset. Since this is often difficult to ascertain, some firms will increase the value of the buildings carried on their books, while others expense charges of similar magnitudes.

The decision to capitalize or expense is particularly important for industries that make heavy outlays for exploration, development, research, or marketing. In the aircraft industry, for example, where new program development costs may be very substantial, company practices have not been consistent. Oil and gas accounting has been a particularly thorny problem. Large and old companies in the industry tend to charge off immediately the costs of exploration and drilling that prove unsuccessful (e.g., dry hole costs). Nevertheless, the relatively new and small "independent" producers ordinarily capitalize these costs and write them off gradually against future revenue from production. Questions also arise concerning when—or if ever—"intangible" costs should be capitalized; furthermore, if capitalization is permitted, what should be allowed? (Intangible costs cover a broad spectrum, including expenditures for geological surveys and outlays for labor, fuel, power, and equipment rentals in drilling operations.) Although this issue has been under consideration by the FASB, impetus for action was provided by inclusion in an energy bill introduced in the House of Representatives in 1975 that requires the SEC to adopt rules creating uniform accounting practices for oil and gas concerns.

Technological pressures and the need for new markets have led companies to make substantial expenditures on engineering and marketing research. Although outlays for these purposes are made in one fiscal year, they clearly are applicable to the operations of future periods. For example, in 1974, Comsat incurred and capitalized $6.7 million in research and development costs; amortization of such costs for that year amounted to $7.4 million.[19] As mentioned previously, however, the FASB now requires that research and development costs be charged to expense when incurred. It also requires that these costs be disclosed in each period for which an income statement is presented.

Another area where capitalizing policies are important is the treatment of business development costs. For example, ITT has expended significant amounts each year in connection with the establishment of new plants, businesses, and products. These costs, which represent amounts invested to bring new activities into normal operation, have been included in "other assets" and amortized against related future income, generally over a three-to five-year period. The deferred costs are subject to immediate write-off in those instances where a profit potential is no longer probable.[20] This policy has afforded the company room for the exercise of judgment, particularly since the amounts involved are large. In the 1973 balance sheet, for example, deferred business development costs, after deducting applicable reserves, amounted to $47.8 million; in the income statement, $17.5 million was amortized for this purpose.

Public utilities commonly capitalize interest costs and allocate them to assets. As other companies began to adopt this practice, the SEC became concerned. The commission noted that the conventional accounting model applicable to companies other than public utilities has not traditionally treated the cost of capital as an asset. Accordingly, pending the issuance of standards by the FASB, the SEC stated that except for certain exempt companies, including public utilities, registered companies that have not previously disclosed a policy of capitalizing interest cost may not follow such a policy in the future.[21]

SUMMARY

Chapter 11 reviewed the major areas of revenue that may affect the quality of a company's reported earnings. Revenue, however, is only half the story. The other half is cost. Major areas for discretion in reporting involve valuing assets, obscuring costs, and allocating costs.

Assets to be valued include fixed assets, inventories, receivables, and intangibles. To determine the annual depreciation charge, fixed assets ordinarily are valued at cost, but management has some leeway in establishing the terminal salvage value. The undervaluation of fixed assets during periods of rapidly rising prices has contributed to the concern expressed about reporting the influence of inflation on financial statements. As a large number of companies have shifted from the FIFO to the LIFO method of pricing inventories, both the accounting profession and the SEC have moved to provide information on the effect of such a move on financial statements. Of importance in evaluating a company's accounts receivable is the bad debt allowance and the degree to which relatively long-term accounts are included; the SEC now requires information to be reported on the latter item. In recent years mergers have sometimes created goodwill, which must be amortized and therefore affects earnings. Accounting guidelines have been established to determine both the merger method that may be used and the length of time any resulting goodwill may be amortized.

The weight of accounting opinion is against the use of reserves arbitrarily to reduce income or to shift income from one period to another for the purpose of creating a semblance of stability. Moreover, the tendency is to limit the freedom of companies to create reserves in anticipation of future losses. The SEC has admonished companies to make special efforts to recognize incipient problems that might lead to unexpected large charges or credits to income or a material provision for losses. Both pension plans and stock options affect the reporting of income and have been subject to government and accounting regulation.

Depreciation probably is the principal cost that must be allocated over a period of time. The amounts involved often are large and subject to such influences as taxation, accounting practice, and personal judgment. To check the appropriateness of the depreciation charge, the investor may compare the reported rates with those used by other companies in the same field; study the ratio of the annual depreciation charge to the value of a company's fixed depreciable assets, exclusive of the accumulated depreciation; or compare the amount of annual depreciation charges with net sales during the year. Closely akin to depreciation are depletion and amortization, charges for which the investor also may have to develop independent judgments. While firms have latitude in determining which outlays should be treated as an expense of the period and which may be capitalized, increased regulation is tending to restrict the extent of the companies' discretion.

CHAPTER 1[illegible]

Analyzing the Income Statement

Having evaluated the quality of a company's earnings, the investor is ready to analyze the company's major sources of income. This step has become particularly important in recent years because of the appearance of conglomerates and the increasing tendency of companies to diversify into various areas of activity. At one time, it was difficult to obtain a breakdown of income sources, but over the past decade professional groups, the Securities and Exchange Commission, the New York Stock Exchange, and various congressional committees all have manifested interest in the development of segmented reporting.

Out of this investigatory ferment have emerged research studies by different groups and official pronouncements by the American Institute of Certified Public Accountants. The initial regulatory step was taken by the SEC, which, in 1969, issued requirements for line-of-business reporting in registration statements. At that time it required companies to include in their registration statements an indication of the relative importance of any class of products contributing 15 percent or more to gross revenues. In the following year, the commission extended these requirements to its 10-K forms and in 1974 to company annual reports. In general, the requirements now call for registrants engaged in more than one line of business to state for each of the last five fiscal years the approximate amount or percentage of total revenues and income (before taxes and extraordinary items) attributable to each line of business. This breakdown is required for each line of business that accounts for minimum designated percentages of revenues and income.

Additionally, the SEC requires the reporting of revenues in dollars or percentages by "class of similar products and services," which may be the same as line of business; the identification of individual significant customers; and the submission of information about the volume, profitability, and risks of foreign operations. The FASB's program brings such information into a company's financial statements and provides uniform standards.[1]

RATIO ANALYSIS

The most widely used method of analyzing a statement is through ratios intended to reveal the pertinent financial characteristics of a company. Techniques of ratio analysis are used in many fields. Credit managers have developed a series of ratios designed to appraise the borrowing capacity of clients; accountants use ratios in connection with cost investigations; and management relies heavily on ratio analysis to measure internal operating efficiency. The investor is primarily interested in using the income statement to gauge the earnings potential of an enterprise. To achieve this aim, he may adopt ratios used in other fields or, as he gains experience, formulate some useful ones of his own.

The major difficulty with ratio analysis is the underlying assumption that the two variables comprising the ratio are strictly proportional to each other. This may not be so. For example, one ratio frequently examined is that of cash to sales, yet theoretical economics has long suggested that cash should only increase with the square root of sales. Once again, even if the relationship is strictly linear, the assumption that the intercept (where the straight line crosses the y axis) is zero is often unwarranted. For example, consider the following relationship:

$$\text{Cash} = a + b\ (\text{Sales}).$$

Compare it with this relationship:

$$\text{Cash}/\text{Sales} = b.$$

It is not uncommon to assume that cash is a prescribed percentage of sales. For this relationship to be true, however, a (the intercept in the first relationship) must be equal to zero, a condition that is not likely to exist. Furthermore, the frequent use of industry averages as reference points assumes that the proper relationship does not depend on the size of the firm. A more flexible analytical device is regression analysis, a statistical tool which shows how a dependent variable is affected by specified independent variables. This technique enables the investor to modify the relationship between financial variables to discover those that are particularly significant.

In essence, this information is intended to provide the analyst with insights into factors that are subject to a company's direction. Unless the analyst is associated with a major institution, however, regression analysis may prove cumbersome and costly; additionally, the mere fact that relationships appear does not necessarily prove that they are meaningful. On the other hand, if the analyst confines himself to ratio analysis, he will find that the financial services have already supplied him with many reference points.[2] Because of its simplicity and convenience, therefore, ratio analysis can be beneficial when undertaken with discretion. Moreover, although ratios are relatively unsophisticated statistical measures, they can give realistic insights into a company's condition and draw attention to impending problems. For example, an analysis of 14 standard ratios for Penn Central in comparison with ten other railroads for the years 1968 and 1969 reveals that the results of the Penn Central were consistently poor and the trend was downhill.[3] The company entered into reorganization under the Federal Bankruptcy Act in June 1970.

If ratio analysis is employed indiscriminately, however, its applicability is impaired because of the danger of entanglement in a network of detail. To avoid this hazard, the investor need use only those ratios that are most helpful in gauging the character of the corporation and the value of its securities. Among the popular ratios for this purpose are the rate of earnings on invested capital, the operating ratio, and the rate of inventory and plant turnover. The investor may gauge the adequacy of these ratios by comparing them with industry averages and, more desirably, with the performance of similar enterprises.

Recent investigations have also shown that certain ratios are reasonably good surrogates for β.[4] Among the best of such ratios are average payout and earnings variability, where the latter is defined as the standard deviation of the ratio of earnings to the price at the beginning of the earnings period.

Earnings on Invested Capital

A businessman contemplating purchase of an operating enterprise is interested in the probable net return from his investment. Similarly, an individual contemplating purchase of a stock is usually concerned with the earnings of the issuing corporation as measured against its invested equity capital. This ratio is computed by dividing net income by net worth. Included in net worth are capital stock, retained earnings, and proprietary reserves. A high percentage indicates a profitable enterprise and successful management; a low percentage suggests unsatisfactory profits, inefficient management, or a weakening position.

The rate of return on capital may vary with both the size of the corporation and the industry in which it operates. Figures 13-1 and 13-1a

FIGURE 13-1

Annual Rates of Profit on Stockholders' Equity, by Size Group, 1964-1974 (after taxes)

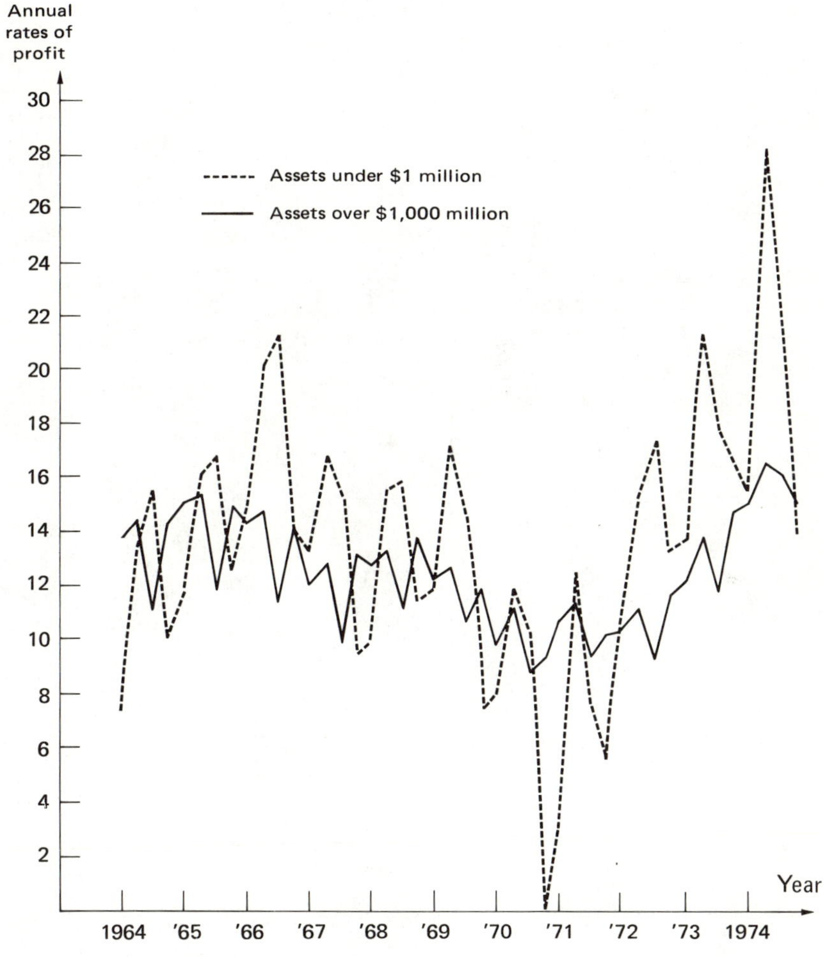

SOURCE: Data taken from Federal Trade Commission, ***Quarterly Financial Report for Manufacturing, Mining and Trade***, 1964-1974.

compare profit rates based on both these factors. The two curves in Figure 13-1 show fluctuations in returns of very large and very small corporations; the curves in Figure 13-1a reveal the variations in a typical cyclical and noncyclical industry (textiles and tobacco, respectively).

The most striking thing about the curves based upon size is the considerably wider range of the small-company returns, which move between

FIGURE 13-1a

Annual Rates of Profit on Stockholders' Equity, by Industry Type, 1964-1974 (after taxes)

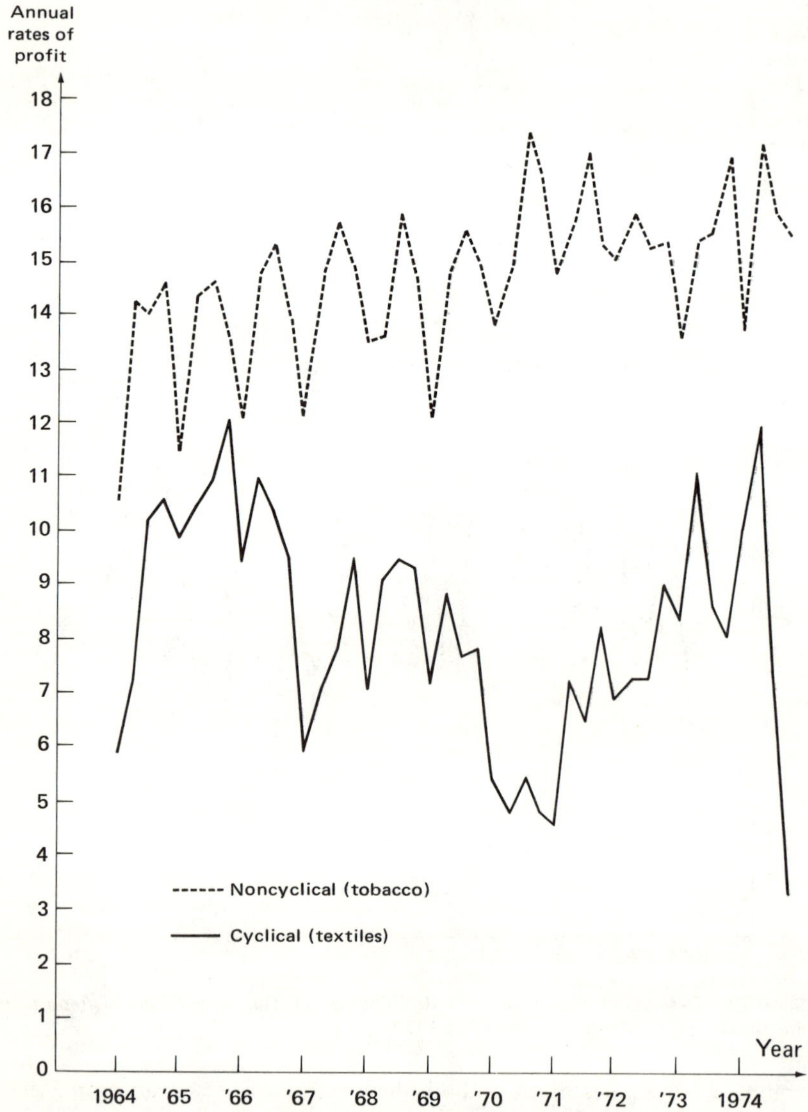

SOURCE: Data taken from Federal Trade Commission, ***Quarterly Financial Report for Manufacturing, Mining and Trade***, 1964-1974.

a low of 0.4 percent in the fourth quarter of 1970 and a high of 28.1 percent in the second quarter of 1974, compared with the big-company range of 8.8 percent (low) in the third quarter of 1970 and 16.5 percent (high) in the second quarter of 1974. Not only is the range of the small-company curve wider and the fluctuations sharper, but the timing of the movements often differs. The varying characteristics of the two curves suggest that, to a significant degree, changes in the economic environment do not have the same effects on big and small firms; these differences also indicate that, other things being equal, a commitment in a small firm is likely to be more speculative than one in a big enterprise.

In general, the range of the cyclical curve is somewhat greater than that of the noncyclical curve. Thus, the return on companies engaged in textiles (cyclical) varied between 3.3 and 12.0 percent; for tobacco (noncyclical), between 10.6 and 17.4 percent, a more limited range. Moreover, the textile curve shows a decided cyclical swing that does not appear in the tobacco curve. In general, however, it is becoming more difficult to distinguish between cyclical and noncyclical firms, as companies have characteristically diversified during the past decade.[5] Still, industry profits often show divergent movements. For example, Figure 13-2 shows profits before taxes as a percentage of equity for a number of different industries and identifies the years since 1962 when the returns were highest and lowest. Out of 20 industries covered, three reached their highs in 1965, eight in 1966, three in 1968, and six in 1973. Conversely, four hit their lows in 1962, three in 1963, one in 1965, seven in 1970, four in 1971, and one in 1972. Clearly, the investor has ample opportunity to distinguish among industries that will react differently under varying economic conditions.

It is commonplace to break down the rate of return figure into a measure of capital turnover and margin of profit. For this purpose, sales per unit of assets (sales/assets) may be used as a gauge of turnover, and earnings per unit of sales (earnings/sales) as a gauge of the profit margin. When these two ratios are multiplied, the sales item cancels and the rate of return is obtained. A low sales/assets ratio usually suggests a rigid cost structure because of the influence of the substantial fixed investment. In this ratio, assets are used because profits may come from assets financed by bonds. (See pp. 395-397 for a further discussion of turnover and profit margin.)

Operating Ratio

The operating ratio is a convenient gauge of a firm's efficiency. It is calculated by dividing total operating charges by total revenues. This concept is simple, but analysts do not agree on the composition of the ratio.

The traditional procedure is to count all charges except those of a financial nature, such as bond interest and special expenses clearly unrelated

FIGURE 13-2

Comparison of Profits Before Taxes as Percentage of Equity for 20 Industries, 1962-1973

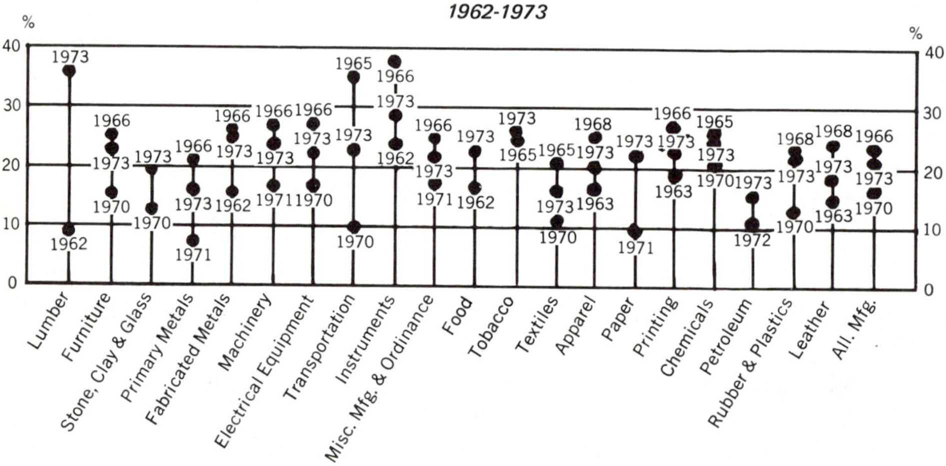

NOTE: Year on top is highest profit rate in 1962-1973 span. Year on bottom is lowest profit rate in 1962-1973 span. 1973 is shown separately if it is not either the high or the low rate.
SOURCE: Cost of Living Council, Federal Trade Commission.

SOURCE: *New York Times*, August 4, 1974, sec. 3, p. 1. © 1974 by the New York Times Company. Reprinted by permission.

to the operations of the company. If this practice is followed, the operating charges of a typical industrial company include four principal components: cost of goods sold; selling, general, and administrative expenses; maintenance and depreciation; and all taxes.

It may be preferable, however, to exclude income taxes from the calculations. In concept, they represent a sharing of profits with the government rather than an expense of operation. When taxes are light, their inclusion with operating expenses does not materially alter the ratio. But the massive sums many corporations now pay may obscure the significance of the other costs if they are grouped with taxes. To obtain a clearer picture of efficiency, it is therefore desirable to calculate the ratio without income taxes, thereby permitting a separate evaluation of the impact of taxes and costs of an operating character.

A portion of a company's operating expenses is fixed and will not change materially, regardless of sales fluctuations. During periods of declining business, sales are likely to shrink more rapidly than expenses, and this causes the operating ratio to rise. If the corporation cannot restore control over costs, profits may disappear. Given this condition, a low operating ratio is a favorable sign. It suggests the ability of a corporation to convert a relatively large portion of sales to profits, and it provides a buffer against a contracting volume of business.[6]

The investor must not assume that a low operating ratio is necessarily a measure of efficiency. It may be caused, for example, by a deliberate stinting of depreciation and maintenance charges, which could result in a severe deterioration of the productive capacity of an enterprise. Moreover, the characteristics of the industry in which a company is engaged affect its operating ratio.

For a better insight into the implications of this ratio, each of its major components may be compared with net sales. Determination of these subordinate ratios is sometimes difficult, because a detailed breakdown of expenses may not appear in published statements. The items listed under similar headings may also vary. Consequently, the investor must interpret these figures with caution. To obtain more complete information, he may find it desirable to check the SEC 10-K reports. These are available from the SEC or companies; often they are on microfiche at university libraries.

Inventory Turnover

The more rapidly a company can turn over its merchandise, the less the amount of capital that it must tie up in inventories and the lower the margin of profit at which it can sell its merchandise. Inventory turnover is calculated by dividing the cost of goods sold by the average value of inventory on the books of the corporation during the same period. In this case, cost of goods sold rather than sales is used in order to eliminate "markups," which are excluded from both cost of goods sold and inventory.

A high ratio suggests more efficient merchandising practices. Unfortunately, it can also mean an inadequate stock, foregone sales and profits, and alienation of customers. High ratios, therefore, warrant a careful examination of the company's liquidity to make sure that the low inventories relative to sales are indeed due to efficiency rather than financial stringency.

A low ratio, on the other hand, should be checked to see if it is caused by slipping sales or is the result of a calculated policy of building inventories. In the latter case, the company's reported profits are exposed to the effects of price changes, and its position must be gauged in the light of the investor's estimate of inflationary pressures.

Plant Turnover

The plant turnover ratio is calculated by dividing net sales by the depreciated value of a company's fixed operating assets. Its purpose is to show the productivity of each dollar invested in operating plant and equipment. A high ratio suggests management's ability to exploit its tangible assets; a low ratio indicates that the company has relatively large funds invested in capital assets that are not producing sufficient revenues in comparison with similar enterprises. However, a low ratio may also be caused by large expenditures on plant improvements, which may reduce costs and result in a lower operating ratio. It is therefore important to use the plant turnover ratio in conjunction with the other tests that have been described to ascertain the character of a company's operations.

TAXATION

Tax rates vary with economic circumstances, international conditions, and political expediencies. Changes in tax rates and policies may have serious and differing effects on the earnings of individual enterprises. To appraise the influence of taxation, the investor must be familiar with the prevailing tax structure and keep abreast of current developments that suggest future revisions.

The basic tax rate for large corporations is 48 percent, consisting of a so-called normal tax of 22 percent on all income, plus a surtax of 26 percent of all income over $25,000.[7] An important provision of U.S. tax law is the carry-back and carry-forward provision. Corporate operating losses can now be carried back three years and forward five. If company *A* incurred a loss in 1974, the income of 1971 may be reduced by that amount. If the 1974 loss exceeds the 1971 income, the remainder may be used to reduce 1972 income, 1973 income, and the income of any subsequent year through 1979. A company which has losses that can be carried back or forward may become an attractive acquisition target.

Finally, minority stockholders in closely held corporations should be aware of the fact that the tax laws give them some protection against niggardly dividend policies. Section 531 of the Internal Revenue Code incorporates penalties for undue retention of earnings. Although the primary purpose of this provision is to discourage corporations from retaining earnings so that the controlling stockholders can avoid taxes, this section may be made applicable to publicly held corporations. (See p. 106.)

In studying a corporation, the investor will probably find that its income tax liability influences his conclusions in several ways. First, he must make allowance for this factor in projections of future earnings. In considering possible tax changes, attention must be paid to alterations in both rates and types of levies.

Second, the investor will find it useful to consider the relation between a corporation's accounting and financial policies and its tax bill. Because taxes are imposed externally, there is a tendency to overlook the control that management may exert over the size of its payments. Yet various decisions, such as those dealing with types of securities issued, the acceptance or deferment of certain charges, and the investment of surplus funds, have a bearing on tax liabilities. Judging the correctness of tax decisions is not easy, since other factors may overshadow possible tax benefits. For example, despite the obvious tax advantages of bond financing over equity financing, the desire to avoid risk or the condition of the capital market might justify issuance of stock. In addition, the detailed accounting steps underlying determination of taxable income are often not apparent from published statements. It is not uncommon for corporations to maintain different books for shareholders and for the Internal Revenue Service. However, by examining the comments of corporate executives on tax issues, the size of payments in relation to earnings over a long period of time, and any special measures adopted to alleviate tax burdens, the investor may be able to assay the judgment of management on income tax matters. The tax bill of a corporation cannot be overlooked in judging the flexibility of its management or its prospects for future earnings.

Because companies may not report the same figures to the Internal Revenue Service and to the public, there is often a difference between the amount of recorded income tax and the amount computed by multiplying income before tax by the statutory federal income tax rate. Recognizing the desirability that investors understand the reason for such a discrepancy, the SEC included among the amendments to Regulation S-X adopted in late 1973 a requirement that registrants reconcile these two amounts. The additional light that this requirement throws on the tax policies of a corporation is indicated in Figure 13-3, which shows the reconciliation for Reynolds Metals of the $18.9 million tax expense the company actually reported in 1973, at an effective rate of 30 percent, and the approximately $30 million it would have reported had the statutory rate of 48 percent applied.

There were actually 22 percentage points, representing lower tax rates, but an offsetting 4-point payment was provided because of a prior year's earnings distribution by a consolidated foreign subsidiary. Of the 22-point differential between the reported and statutory tax rates, 6 percentage points were due to the lower rates incurred by nonconsolidated subsidiaries that presumably were located abroad. A potential tax therefore existed if the policy changes eliminated this disparity. A savings of 4 percentage points was obtained by using the nonconservative flow-through method of accounting for investment tax credits. Another 4 points came from income taxed at the lower capital gains rate, although this presumably nonrecurring transaction was not shown separately in reported earnings. Available special benefits in

FIGURE 13-3

Reconciliation of Reported Tax Expense and Indicated Tax Expense (at 48 percent Statutory Rate) for Reynolds Metals Co., 1973

	1973
Federal—current	$ 4,120,000
State	612,000
Foreign	10,386,000
Deferred	3,773,000
	$18,891,000

The deferred tax expense results from various timing differences (principally depreciation) between financial income and taxable income. Investment tax credits for 1973 and 1972 amounted to $2,400,000 and $1,900,000, respectively.

Total tax expense for 1973 of $18,891,000 reflects an effective rate of approximately 30%. The details of the differences between this rate and the U.S. Federal tax rate of 48% are as follows:

Equity in net income of unconsolidated subsidiaries and associated companies subject to less than 48% tax rate	6%
Investment tax credits	4
Income taxed at capital gains rate	4
Percentage depletion allowance	4
Western Hemisphere trade corporation deduction	4
Prior years earnings distribution by consolidated foreign subsidiary	(4)
	18%

The amount of undistributed earnings of subsidiaries not taxed, the remittance of which is expected to be indefinitely postponed, was immaterial after exclusion of unremitted earnings of domestic tax-consolidated subsidiaries and other earnings which, if remitted, will be in tax-free form.

SOURCE: Reynolds Metals Co., *Annual Report*, 1973, p. 29.

the tax law accounted for 8 additional percentage points. In view of the uncertain character of these benefits, some question existed as to the company's long-term ability to maintain its unusually low tax rate.

In 1973, Reynolds added to its deferred tax expense because of timing differences, principally depreciation, between financial and taxable income. Of interest, however, is the fact that in the prior year the company drew upon its deferred tax account, thereby reporting an indicated tax credit that enabled it to show net income for the year.

USE OF PER SHARE EARNINGS DATA IN EVALUATING COMMON STOCK

To study the common stock of a corporation, analysts express its earnings on a per share basis. They calculate this figure by dividing the corporation's net income, after deducting preferred dividends, by the weighted average number of common shares outstanding. In this case, as contrasted to that of fixed-income securities, it is logical to employ per share data. These statistics reflect the interest of each stockholder in the enterprise's residual earnings, which management can distribute at its own discretion.

Calculating Per Share Figures

Earnings per share is a major measure employed by the financial community in the evaluation of a stock. It is calculated by deducting preferred dividends from net income determined after subtracting all charges including taxes. This final net income figure is then divided by the appropriate number of common stock shares outstanding.

In financial analysis, earnings per share reveal past earning power expressed in terms of a share of stock, the basic unit of trading in the securities market. The historic data, in turn, are commonly employed as a starting base to forecast future earnings per share.

Some corporations, particularly those with substantial noncash charges such as depreciation, have contended that earnings per share do not accurately reflect their performance and have therefore provided the *cash flow per share.* This measure typically is calculated by adding the noncash charges to net income. The commission has frowned upon this practice. It has pointed out that "it is not clear that the simple omission of depreciation and other noncash charges deducted in the computation of net income provides an appropriate alternative of performance for any industry either in theory or in practice."[8]

To take care of cases where management believes that conventional income per share does not realistically reflect its operations, the commission suggests that management present an explanation of the reasons and a description of possible alternatives which might be used to measure results. The presentation of data in tabular form is acceptable. The commission makes clear, however, that per share data other than that relating to net income, net assets, and dividends should be avoided in reporting financial results.

Adjusting Per Share Figures

The earnings record used to analyze a common stock should cover a number of years. During this span of time, the corporation may change its capitalization several times to meet shifting economic conditions. These alterations could have an important effect on the earnings per share of common stock. In order to have a consistent series, the reported earnings per share must be adjusted to reflect certain of these capitalization revisions. As a general guideline in this area, the Accounting Principles Board provides in its Opinion No. 15 that earnings per share should be related to the capital structure existing during each of the periods, except for adjustments for stock dividends or splits. These modifications are probably the most common and are particularly pertinent because they affect the per share figures without influencing the amount of reported income. Thus, a corporation with 100,000 shares of stock outstanding could double this number by a 100 percent stock dividend or a two-for-one stock split. This capitalization change requires a 50 percent reduction in the pèr share earnings reported previously, but has no effect on income. A reverse split involves combining the number of shares outstanding, which must be offset by a proportionate increase in all previously reported earnings per share.

Eastman Kodak's 1963-1972 record illustrates the need to consider stock splits in comparing current with prior figures. On the basis of capitalization outstanding at the close of the year, Kodak reported earnings of $3.75 per share of common stock in 1963 and $3.39 in 1972. During this period, it split its stock two-for-one in both 1965 and 1968 and paid stock dividends of 5 percent in 1964. After adjustments for these changes, the 1963 earnings were 89 cents per share. Thus, earnings actually experienced a rise of some 280 percent between 1963 and 1972, rather than the fall of about 10 percent suggested by the reported data.

A stock dividend ordinarily provides for the issuance of a relatively small number of shares of new stock, while a stock split calls for a big change. For this reason, in a stock dividend the accounting charge offsetting the issuance of shares is to retained earnings at a value determined by the market price. Consequently, when the price of a stock is high, the drain on earnings may be severe, a factor that caused IBM to abandon its traditional stock dividend policy after 1959. On the other hand, in a stock split, the charge is to capital surplus at par value. The criterion generally employed by accountants to determine whether an announced dividend paid in stock should be treated as a stock dividend or split is 25 percent. A stock may also be split, of course, by reducing its par value.

There is less agreement on the type of adjustment, if any, that should be made with respect to a capitalization change involving the sale of stock. Yet, depending upon how the funds derived are employed, the effect upon per share earnings could be important. As an illustration, let us assume that a corporation has a basic income of \$3 million before income taxes and bond interest; the corporation has outstanding \$10 million of 8 percent bonds, convertible into common stock at \$10 per share, and 1 million shares of \$10 par value stock. In Table 13-1 we list various possible changes involving the sale of securities and show their effect on reported earnings.

Line 2 of the table illustrates the change resulting from the sale of common stock to replace a senior security. In this case, earnings reported prior to the transaction are increased by the amount of fixed charges saved, less the higher income taxes that would be incurred; the resulting figure is then divided by the larger number of shares of stock. Line 3 shows a refunding of a high-interest obligation with a low-interest obligation. Use of a lower-cost security increases earnings by the savings in interest payments, offset to some extent by the higher resulting income taxes. Sometimes the new security bears larger charges; this may occur during periods of rising interest rates or through the sale of a junior fixed-income security to replace a lower-cost senior issue, as in line 4.

Another type of capitalization change involves selling new securities for cash (lines 5, 6, 7). Expansion of the total outstanding capitalization causes an initial drag on earnings. Issuance of new senior obligations increases fixed charges, thereby curtailing net income; sale of common stock lowers earnings per share in proportion to the reduced equity of each stockholder in net income. In these transactions, however, the corporation acquires additional funds, which presumably augment its earning power. As a consequence, we show the impact on earnings both before and after the investment of the proceeds.

SEC Form 10 for general registration under the 1934 Exchange Act and Form 10-K for annual reporting both now require a five-year statement of operations, including earnings and dividends per share. The annual reports of corporations also contain a historical summary of operations, going back five (and sometimes ten) years and including per share earnings data. The financial services and investment houses calculate earnings per share each year and collect the data in series covering a number of years. In all these cases, adjustments are ordinarily made for major stock dividends and splits, but it is questionable to what extent other types of capitalization changes are taken into account. Yet, as seen in Table 13-1, these, too, can affect earnings

TABLE 13-1

Influence of Capitalization Changes on Reported Earnings of $3,000,000

ASSUMED CHANGES IN CAPITALIZATION	BOND INTEREST	PROFITS BEFORE INCOME TAXES	TAXES AT 50%	PREFERRED DIVIDENDS	NET INCOME AFTER INCOME TAXES AND SENIOR CHARGES	EARNINGS PER SHARE OF STOCK
(1) Initial statement of income	$ 800,000	$2,200,000	$1,100,000	—	$1,100,000	$1.10
(2) Sale of 1,000,000 common shares at $10 each, funds used to redeem $10,000,000 bonds	—	3,000,000	1,500,000	—	1,500,000	0.75
(3) Issuance of $10,000,000 refunding bonds at 6% to replace 8% bond issue	600,000	2,400,000	1,200,000	—	1,200,000	1.20
(4) Issuance of $10,000,000 of 9% preferred stock to replace 8% bond issue	—	3,000,000	1,500,000	$900,000	600,000	0.60
(5) Sale of 1,000,000 additional shares of common stock at $10 each						
Initially	800,000	2,200,000	1,100,000	—	1,100,000	0.55
After investment of proceeds*	800,000	3,700,000	1,850,000	—	1,850,000	0.925
(6) Issuance of $10,000,000 of 7% additional bonds						
Initially	1,500,000	1,500,000	750,000	—	750,000	0.75
After investment of proceeds*	1,500,000	3,000,000	1,500,000	—	1,500,000	1.50
(7) Issuance of $10,000,000 of 8% preferred stock						
Initially	800,000	2,200,000	1,100,000	800,000	300,000	0.30
After investment of proceeds*	800,000	3,700,000	1,850,000	800,000	1,050,000	1.05

*It is assumed that both capitalization and earnings before taxes increase by 50%.

materially. As a practical matter, the investor ordinarily will use the statistics already compiled in government records, company statements, and the reports of the services and investment houses. It probably is undesirable, however, for an investor to rely completely on prepared data; otherwise, when a security for which previous studies are not available must be evaluated, it may be difficult to calculate the historical series of per share earnings on which the analysis is based. For these reasons, we have reviewed in some detail the problems of developing a uniform record of earnings expressed on the basis of current capitalization. Current procedures also provide, as discussed below, for the calculation of per share earnings by treating certain securities in the capitalization as "common stock equivalents" or by treating earnings as "fully diluted."

"Primary" and "Fully Diluted" Earnings Per Share

In the late 1960s, convertible securities were used extensively in corporate acquisitions, and the volume of outstanding options and warrants grew significantly. The accounting profession and securities analysts became increasingly concerned with the significance of data on earnings per share when substantial potential dilution lurked in the background. The attitude of the accounting profession was crystalized in Accounting Principles Board Opinion no. 15, which was released in May 1969.

This opinion, which is important for the securities field, defines elaborate rules for computing earnings per share. Basically, a requirement is established for the publication of data on earnings per share on the face of the income statement; for companies with complex capital structures, a distinction is made between "primary" and "fully diluted" earnings per share. It is provided that the reporting of both these categories of earnings should be consistent with the income statement presentation called for by Opinion no. 9; this means showing earnings per share for income before extraordinary items, for net income, and preferably for the amount of the extraordinary items. The calculation of primary earnings per share is based on the outstanding common shares, plus securities that in substance are equivalent to common shares and have a dilutive effect.

Common stock equivalents include a company's options and warrants, as well as its convertible preferred stock and debentures that had cash yields less than two-thirds of the bank prime interest rate prevailing at the time the security was issued. However, when a convertible is classified as a common stock equivalent, outstanding securities that had been offered at earlier dates *with the same terms* are reclassified as common stock equivalents if they have not been so treated before. Similarly, subsequent issues with the same terms are treated as common stock equivalents even if the yield test of equivalence is not met when they are issued.

When cash payments accompany the exercise of options, warrants, and their equivalents, the assumption is made that the cash is used to repurchase stock at the average price that prevailed during the period. The amount of stock used in calculating earnings per share is increased by the amount issued and decreased by the amount theoretically repurchased. For the purpose of determining primary earnings per share, this calculation is done after the market price of the common stock obtainable has exceeded the exercise price for substantially all of three consecutive months, ending with the last month of the period to which the earnings per share relate. This adjustment technique is described as the *treasury-stock method*. If the number of shares of common stock obtainable upon exercise of outstanding options and warrants exceeds 20 percent of the total of common shares outstanding, a modification of the treasury-stock method is proposed. Under these circumstances, it is assumed that all the options and warrants have been exercised and the funds derived applied to the repurchase of up to 20 percent of the outstanding shares, in accordance with the treasury-stock method. The remaining funds are then used first to reduce any short- or long-term borrowing; any balance is assumed to be invested in U.S. government securities or commercial paper, with appropriate recognition of the income tax effect. Computation of earnings per share is based on the weighted average number of common shares and common share equivalents that are outstanding.

Fully diluted earnings per share are intended to show the prospective maximum potential dilution of current earnings per share. The calculation is based on total earnings, divided by the number of shares that would be outstanding if all convertible securities, options, warrants, and stock purchase contracts were exercised. In order to reflect maximum potential dilution, the market price at the close of the period reported is used in the case of options and warrants to determine the number of shares which would be assumed to be repurchased under the treasury-stock method. For this purpose, also, the common shares to be issued on exercise of the options or warrants are included from the beginning of the period or from the date of issuance of the options or warrants, if later.

In calculations of neither primary nor fully diluted earnings per share are contingent issues considered if their effect would be antidilutive—that is, if their inclusion would increase earnings per share or decrease the loss per share for the period. Whenever the exercise price of an option or warrant is above its market price, more stock would be retired under the treasury-stock method than would be issued, and the effect is antidilutive.

Table 13-2 illustrates the calculation of the weighted average number of shares outstanding for the purpose of determining primary and fully diluted earnings per share. This table makes the following assumptions:

(a) Market price of common stock:

	Low	High
First quarter	20	22
Second quarter	21	23
Third quarter	23	26 (at end of quarter)
Fourth quarter	27	33
Closing price for year	33	

(b) Common stock outstanding

Beginning of year	1,000,000 shares
Conversion of preferred during year	200,000 shares
Total outstanding at year-end	1,200,000 shares

(c) At the beginning of the third quarter, the company issued 200,000 shares at a premium of $3.00, 5% cumulative preferred stock ($50 par), convertible into common stock at $25 per share; 100,000 shares were converted during the year.

(d) The bank prime rate was 7.5% during the entire year.

(e) At the beginning of the year, the company issued options to buy 100,000 shares of common stock at $25 per share.

The Investor's Dilemma

These rules are not wholly satisfactory, although they do much to correct the inherent abuses of showing earnings per share figures that give no effect to potential dilution. The basic difficulty is that the circumstances prevailing at the time convertibles were issued are water over the dam. The major consideration for the stockholder is how much of the contingent obligation is likely to be issued. Absent impending bankruptcy, it is fairly safe to assume that convertibles of growing companies with fairly long remaining lives to maturity will eventually be converted. Whether conversion of early maturing privileges will take place is more difficult to determine. Much depends upon the relationship between the market and conversion prices. If the market price exceeds the conversion price, there is a presumption that conversion will take place. Even so, it can only be a presumption, since in some cases there may be market reversals before all conversions occur. Prior to Penn Central common's drop from over $80 to less than $10 per share, many of the outstanding warrants were exercisable, but these subsequently became worthless. Similarly, even if the conversion price is above the market price, conversion eventually may take place, since the market can improve

TABLE 13-2

Calculation of Weighted Average Number of Shares

COMMON STOCK	OUTSTANDING AND ISSUED
1,000,000 shares	Outstanding at the beginning of period.
50,000 shares	Average number of shares outstanding resulting from conversion of convertible preferred stock. Each preferred share was convertible into 2 shares of common. The conversion of 100,000 shares of preferred resulted in the issue of 200,000 shares of common. It is assumed that conversion occurs evenly between July 1 and December 31, so that the average amount outstanding between July 1 and year-end was 100,000 and between January 1 and year-end was 50,000.
(1) 1,050,000 shares	
	COMMON STOCK EQUIVALENTS
150,000 shares	The whole 200,000 shares of preferred stock represent common stock equivalents, since their yield at issuance was 4.72% ($2.50/ $53) which was less than two-thirds of the 7.5% bank prime rate (APB ¶ 33). Therefore, it is assumed that 400,000 common shares become outstanding on July 1, which, on a weighted basis, are equal to 200,000 shares, or 150,000 shares in addition to those created under primary earnings.
4,167 shares	The market price of the common stock was less than the exercise price of options during most of the first three quarters. Under the treasury-stock method no provision for exercise is made, since the result would be antidilutive. During the entire last quarter, however, the market price was above the exercise price, permitting the assumption of exercise. On this basis, $2,500,000 would be obtained ($25 × 100,000 shares). These funds could purchase 83,333 shares ($2 500,000 ÷ $30). On balance, 16,667 shares (100,000 − 83,333) would be issued and outstanding for one quarter (APB ¶ 36).
(2) 154,167 shares	
	FULLY DILUTED
20,075 shares	The $2,500,000 theoretically derived from exercise of the warrants is applied to purchase of common stock at the year-end price of $33, resulting in retirement of 75,758 shares ($2,500,000 ÷ $33) and a net issuance of 24,242 shares (100,000 − 75,758); in the calculation of dilution, it is assumed that they are outstanding for the full year. Since 4,167 shares have been counted as common stock equivalents under the treasury method, 20,075 *additional* shares are now included in the calculation (APB ¶ 42).
(3) 20,075 shares	
1,204,167 shares	Weighted average number of shares to calculate primary earnings per share: sum of (1) and (2).
1,224,242 shares	Weighted average number of shares to calculate fully diluted earnings per share: sum of (1), (2), and (3).

before the privilege expires. Indeed, most convertibles are issued with the conversion price in excess of market, but with the intent that conversion will occur.

The investor, however, need not make a yes-no decision with respect to conversion. The desired projection is *expected* earnings per share. The proper thing to do is to find the *expected* number of shares or claims against earnings. Thus, the investor may wish to attach a probability of eventual conversion to the residual securities. The company in question may have outstanding options on 50,000 shares, and a convertible issue which potentially can increase the number of shares by another 500,000. The analyst may think that there is only a 50-50 chance the debentures will be converted, but nine chances in ten the option will be exercised. Under these circumstances, the expected increment in shares outstanding will be 295,000 (50 percent of 500,000, plus 90 percent of 50,000). Such an approach might be used by an investor who is skeptical about the results provided by either primary or fully diluted earnings per share measurements and desires an expression of more realistic outcomes. On the other hand, it must be recognized that the market is likely to give considerable weight to the published data that follow the reporting principles of the American Institute of Certified Public Accountants and fall within the orbit of the audited statement.

The existence of a complex capital structure creates a dilemma for the investor, who cannot be sure of the eventual outcome of potential capitalization changes. The problem is aggravated when there are extraordinary gains or losses. For example, in 1969, G. W. Murphy Industries (merged into Baker Oil Tools) realized a capital gain from the sale of some operating properties. The reduction of earnings per share because of the assumption of conversion of senior securities and issuance of contingent shares apparently was more than offset by the additions to income as a result of eliminating the senior charges. The larger number of shares outstanding on the assumption of conversion, however, lowered the earnings per share for extraordinary items. Because of these relationships, interestingly enough, fully diluted earnings were antidilutive for income before extraordinary items and dilutive for net income.

Thus, it is desirable that the investor check the implications of the major components of earnings to make certain that he or she does not overlook any factors of significance. It is also important to know which figures are being used in the reports on a particular company. As a general rule, in the absence of evidence to the contrary, it is prudent to assume that all privileges will be exercised and that the more meaningful figure is represented by fully diluted earnings per share before extraordinary and other unusual charges. In the case of G. W. Murphy, however, the more conservative policy would have been to use primary earnings from continuing operations, particularly in view of the operating difficulties cited by the company in its report.

SUMMARY

A major reporting development has been the introduction of line-of-business information, which provides some insight into the relative contribution to sales and income of the different segments of a company's business. In exploring the factors affecting income, a flexible tool is regression analysis, which shows how a dependent variable is affected by specified independent variables. Because of the technical aspects of this approach, however, its application is limited. Accordingly, the most widely used method of analyzing the income statement is through ratios intended to reveal the pertinent financial characteristics of a company.

A basic ratio is the return on capital, which is computed by dividing net income by net worth. It is commonplace to break down the rate of return into a measure of assets turnover and margin of profit. For this purpose, sales are divided by assets to obtain a gauge of turnover, and earnings are divided by sales to measure the profit margin. When these two ratios are multiplied, the sales item cancels and the rate of return is obtained. In general, companies with substantial amounts of invested capital may be expected to have low capital turnovers and high profit margins, while companies in service industries are more likely to have high assets turnovers but low profit margins. (Invested capital is defined as assets.)

The operating ratio is a convenient reflection of a firm's overall efficiency. It is calculated by dividing total operating charges by total revenues. The more rapidly a company can turn over its merchandise, the less the amount of capital that it must tie up in inventories and the lower the margin of profit at which it can sell its merchandise. Inventory turnover is calculated by dividing the cost of goods sold by the average value of inventory on the books of the corporation during the same period. Plant turnover shows the productivity of each dollar invested in operating plant and equipment. This ratio is calculated by dividing net sales by the depreciated value of a company's fixed operating assets. In all cases, a low or high ratio gives some information about the company's operations, but it must be interpreted in conjunction with the nature of the company's costs and the characteristics of the industry in which it operates.

In studying a corporation, the investor probably will find that its income tax liability influences the analyst in two ways. First, allowance must be made for this factor in projections of future earnings. Second, the degree to which a company can keep its tax bill down is a consideration in judging the caliber of its management. The Internal Revenue Code affords management considerable leeway in making decisions that legitimately affect the amount of taxes paid. To help the investor assess the nature of the tax-reducing steps taken by management, the SEC now requires that a company reconcile the difference between the amount of recorded income taxes and the amount obtained through multiplying income before tax by the statutory federal income tax rate.

In order to analyze the earnings record of a company, the investor needs a consistent series, adjusted to reflect capitalization revisions. As a general guideline in this area, the Accounting Principles Board has provided that earnings per share should be related to the capital structure existing during each of the periods covered, except for adjustments for stock dividends or splits. Current procedures also provide for the calculation of "primary" and "fully diluted" earnings per share. Primary earnings are based on the outstanding common shares, plus securities that in substance are equivalent to common shares and have a dilutive effect. Fully diluted earnings per share are intended to show the prospective maximum potential dilution of current earnings per share.

CHAPTER 14

The Balance Sheet

The balance sheet summarizes the types and amounts of assets, liabilities, and capital of a company on a particular date. Changes may be the result of *income transactions* or *capital transactions.* Income transactions arise from the everyday operations of a business. They are directly reflected in the sales, expenses, and earnings figures of the income statement and are eventually translated into corresponding changes in the assets, liabilities, or capital accounts of the balance sheet. Capital transactions occur outside the regular business operation. They include sale or retirement of securities, purchase of equipment, and liquidation of a subsidiary. These activities may appear as changes in balance sheet accounts without any direct effect on the income statement. They may also affect net income; for example, in a 1975 statement, the FASB required changes in the value of equity securities carried as current assets to be reflected in net income.

COMPONENTS

The form of the balance sheet is standard and the composition of its major accounts is reasonably uniform. This section briefly describes these accounts, with particular attention to the major areas in which discrepancies may occur.

Asset Side

Current assets. These include cash, marketable securities, notes receivable, accounts receivable, and inventories. The major problems in this area are (1) counting assets as current that are not convertible to cash or its equivalent within one year; (2) classifying securities as marketable that have no ready market; (3) failure to reveal current assets that have been pledged for loans; (4) over-statement of accounts or notes receivable; and (5) inadequate disclosure of the basis of carrying inventories. The FASB now requires that companies carry securities portfolios at the lower of aggregate or market.

Investments. This category covers securities that are not liquid enough to be considered current. It may also include commitments in and advances to unconsolidated subsidiaries and more permanent investment holdings.

Fixed assets. These are land, buildings, machinery and equipment, and leaseholds. Fixed assets are now carried at cost. Those that are depreciable are shown at cost less depreciation allowance. Regulatory authorities have been reluctant to permit upward revaluation of fixed assets, which leads to an increase in surplus; state laws may prohibit payment of cash dividends from the surplus created in this fashion. In a striking departure from its traditional conservative stance, however, the Securities and Exchange Commission urged companies to disclose in their annual reports the effect of inflation on earnings because valuations at historical costs may be misleading in a period of rising prices. Subsequently, the commission went a step further by proposing that companies report replacement values in footnotes to their financial statements. The Financial Accounting Standards Board's current investigation of price-level accounting may lead to a requirement for supplemental disclosure of the effects of inflation on financial statements.

Intangible assets. These include assets that are identifiable, such as patents, trademarks, and franchises, and those that are not. Goodwill is the most common unidentifiable intangible asset and ordinarily represents the difference between the purchase price and determined net tangible asset value of a going business that has been acquired. The value of an intangible asset may stem from the favorable opinion of customers, the specialized knowledge of management, advantageous business locations, or monopolistic government grants embodied in patents and franchises. These considerations are qualitative, contributing a worth that is hard to gauge. Some indication of the value of intangible assets may be obtained by the difference between the capitalized value of a company's earnings and the stated value of its assets.

Prepaid expenses and deferred charges. These represent expenses for items that have been paid for but not consumed by the close of the accounting period. Prepaid expenses customarily arise from the normal operations of a business and include insurance premiums, interest, and rent. They are often grouped with current assets when they represent prepayments for services to be received within one year. Deferred charges usually arise outside the everyday activities of a corporation. They may comprise the unamortized portion of such things as bond discount, goodwill, and the expenses incurred in starting a new business. These items are typically small.

Liability Side

Current liabilities. These are obligations falling due within one year. They include notes and accounts payable, accrued liabilities (typically payrolls and taxes due), and miscellaneous debts, such as dividends declared. In the past, companies sometimes showed as noncurrent certain obligations due within one year that were expected to be refinanced, such as the maturing portion of long-term debt, construction loans, and commercial paper. To standardize this accounting practice, the FASB now requires such obligations to be included as a current liability, unless specified refinancing conditions are met.

Deferred income. This category includes income received for services that must be performed in the future. It appears as a liability that is gradually credited to income over a period of time.

Deferred credits. These amounts could be big and occur for different reasons. Deferred federal taxes on income arise from the timing differences between taxable income and book income. For example, a company may use accelerated methods of determining depreciation for tax purposes and a straight-line basis for public reporting, or it may defer income on installment sales for tax purposes while reporting it in the current year's income statement. In these circumstances, the creation of a deferred tax account is important in order to recognize the tax liability which will later arise when depreciation for public reporting exceeds depreciation for tax purposes, or when income on installment sales for public reporting is less than income for tax purposes. The devaluations of the dollar and subsequent changes in the exchange rates resulted in a number of companies recording net foreign currency translation gains. Given the generally unsettled currency relationships resulting from the introduction of floating rates, various companies, until recent FASB requirements were enacted, deferred counting exchange gains.

Long-term debt. This refers to the corporation's outstanding bonds. A detailed bond schedule often appears in a footnote.

Other liabilities. This category includes contingent liabilities, special accounts (such as accrued pension obligations), and rentals under long-term leases. Some of this information is omitted from published statements, but it is available in reports filed with the SEC. Following the issuance by the SEC in October 1973 of its requirement for expanded reporting of lease information, some companies began to show similar information in their annual reports.

After the SEC indicated that lease disclosures are necessary in annual reports to stockholders to comply with proxy rules, more companies disclosed this information in their 1974 reports. Peat, Marwick, Mitchell & Co. has indicated that for client companies with fiscal years ending on or after June 30, 1974, the information will constitute "generally accepted accounting principles" and will require a qualified opinion if not provided.[1] The FASB has also moved toward fuller lease disclosures.

Minority interest. Where this line appears, it generally is a relatively small item representing the equity of minority shareholders in consolidated subsidiaries.

Reserves. Historically, these comprised three broad categories. The first, valuation reserves, reduced to a realistic level the original cost of certain assets and are recorded as deductions from these assets. The second, proprietary reserves, earmark a portion of retained earnings to identify specified financial requirements. These reserves, appearing on the liability side of the balance sheet, are not now common, but they could be substantial. Phillips Petroleum, for example, reported in its 1974 balance sheet $60.3 million as a "reserve for contingencies." American Smelting and Refining (Asarco) showed a $21.9 million item called "reserves" in its 1973 balance sheet; a footnote explained that the bulk of these reserves had been provided that year to cover the anticipated losses from closure of the company's Baltimore and Amarillo plants. The FASB has provided some standards to govern the establishment of reserves against future expected losses. The third category, liability reserves, which were created to help meet pending obligations, also appeared on the liability side.

Current accounting practices accept only the second category covering proprietary reserves. The reserve captions in the modern annual report usually describe their purposes reasonably well, although some companies still show a vague account, such as the "Reserves and Deferred Liabilities" item in ITT's 1974 annual report.

Capital stock. This shows, for each class of equity security, the number of shares authorized, the number outstanding, and the stated or carrying value of the stock.

Other capital. This ordinarily arises from the issuance of stock at a premium. The account is also commonly called "additional paid-in capital" or "capital in excess of par value of common stocks." Sometimes companies, such as Robertson, still use the old term, "capital surplus." If it occurs in a special way, how it arose may be explained in a footnote. Asarco, for example, in its 1973 annual report, explains that "the 'additional capital' increase represents the gain on treasury stock used for corporate purposes." (Accounting doctrine ordinarily would not recognize this as a gain.)

Retained earnings. This represents profits kept in the business. Reflecting the tendency to drop technical terms, it may be described as "earnings employed in the business." The investor should ascertain whether there are any material provisions that limit the use of retained earnings for dividend payments and other corporate purposes. This information must be filed with the SEC and is characteristically inserted in published financial statements. For example, the long-term agreements of Engelhard restrict the payment of cash dividends and acquisition of the company's capital stock to the extent that stockholders' equity would be reduced below a required minimum balance; the debt agreements and the provisions of the preferred stocks of Foremost-McKesson contain restrictions as to maintenance of consolidated working capital, purchase of shares of the company's capital stock, and payment of dividends; the financing agreements of Mohawk Data Sciences with banks include provisions that restrict creation of additional borrowings, prohibit payment of dividends, and require maintenance of a minimum amount of consolidated tangible net worth as defined. The loan agreements of Wheelabrator-Frye with various banks contain restrictive covenants relating to working capital, tangible net worth, additional borrowings, and disposition of property. They also provide that beginning in 1973 the aggregate of cash dividends, and distributions on capital stock, plus purchases, redemptions, and other acquisition of shares of capital stock in any fiscal year, may not exceed 50 percent of consolidated income before extraordinary items. In most instances, some idea as to the effect of these restrictions is given.

Treasury stock. This represents shares of common or preferred stock that the company repurchased and has not retired. During the generally depressed market conditions of 1973 and 1974, many companies, apparently believing their stock to be undervalued, bought substantial amounts of their shares. As a result, it was quite common to see treasury stock, carried at cost, shown as a reduction of stockholders' equity.

USES IN ANALYZING SECURITIES

Investors are directly concerned with the return they receive from their purchases. Return depends on the earnings of a corporation. Earnings is a commodity of the income statement. This firmly joined chain of reasoning led to the dominance of the income statement in financial analysis. As a result, the balance sheet was in danger of becoming the forgotten instrument of securities analysis.

The collapse of the Penn-Central in mid-1970 abruptly resuscitated the balance sheet. Thereafter, as receding stock prices stymied equity financing and high interest rates placed barriers on the continued ability of corporations to roll over debt, liquidity as a phase of analysis assumed increasing importance. Moreover, it must be recognized that earnings flow from assets. The balance sheet lists these assets, together with their offsetting liabilities, and summarizes the net outcome of all income transactions. The statement thus provides a still-life picture of a company's status at the time its books are closed. It also furnishes the means of analyzing the dynamic qualities that created this picture of momentary equilibrium.

In the period of the mid-1970s, therefore, the balance sheet took a new lease on life. Lending institutions paid more attention to its implications in evaluating the credit worthiness of borrowers. As corporations extended their international activities, they found it necessary to examine the balance sheets of their overseas subsidiaries to detect their exposure to currency changes; management sought to place subsidiaries operating in weak currency areas in a net current borrowing position and subsidiaries in strong currency areas in a net current asset position.

Investors, in turn, may use the balance sheet to assay four important factors in determining the merits of an issue: (1) its tangible measures of value; (2) the corporation's financial strength; (3) the outlets into which earnings have gone; and (4) the influence of capital structure on profits.

Gauging the Tangible Asset Value of a Stock

The significance of tangible values usually is either greatly overrated or underrated. Tangible values are the actual worth of all or part of the assets that underlie each share of a corporation's stock. It follows, at least in theory, that the higher these values in relation to the market price of an issue, the greater the bargain the purchaser obtains. This conclusion would be valid only if the values indicated could be realized on liquidation and the corporation were contemplating such a step, or if the purchaser could acquire control of the corporation.

Because these eventualities rarely occur in combination, many investors veer toward the opposite extreme. They play down tangible values, sometimes even omitting these figures in their analyses of securities. As is usually the case, neither of these extreme courses seems wise. When used properly, tangible values are helpful analytic tools. The principal measures employed for this purpose are the book value, current asset value, and cash asset value.

Book value. Book values have two quite different sources of significance. First, a high figure relative to market value per share carries with it a potential for gain through the redeployment of assets. Second, since the value of most stocks comes from the flow of income expected from them,[2] the underlying assets, which are the basis of that income, are naturally important. For a number of industrial companies, such as those providing services, book values may not be indicative of earning power; in such instances, the figures have little meaning. The case is different for utilities or financial companies. Utility commissions gear income to asset values, and although they may use so-called fair value rather than book value, the two valuations are usually not so far apart as to deprive book value of its significance. The assets of financial companies consist of some mix of securities, mortgages, and loans, depending on the particular field of involvement; in general, carrying values have an important bearing on the market prices of these companies' shares.

Even though the book value of industrial stocks usually is a less useful bit of information than the book value of the stocks of utility or financial companies, the data should not be dismissed casually. It must be remembered that this value substantially represents the historical cumulation of retained earnings. It is illogical to maintain that retained earnings are important but the measure of their form is not.

Book value is calculated by subtracting from total assets all liabilities ranking prior to the common stock and dividing by the number of common shares outstanding. Some preliminary adjustments may be necessary. First, if the corporation groups treasury stock with assets, both the value of the assets and the number of shares of stock outstanding should be reduced by the amount of this item. When corporations show treasury stock as a deduction from the amount of shares issued, as is commonly done, this adjustment is unnecessary. Second, evaluation reserves should be deducted from their appropriate assets, whereas proprietary reserves that appear vague should be in retained earnings. (FASB requirements will reduce the use of such reserves.) This provides both for showing assets on a net basis and for standardizing their carrying values, regardless of the surplus adjustments a company may make for uncertain contingencies. Third, it is a common practice to lower assets by the value of intangible items. This procedure is simple, conservative, and uniform, permitting ready comparisons among companies regardless of how intangibles are valued, although sometimes it involves throwing out the baby with the bath water. Fourth, in recognition of their prior rank, senior securities should be deducted from assets on the basis of call or voluntary liquidating price, whichever is higher, plus any accumulated dividends. Noncallable issues should be valued at market.

The condensed balance sheet for General Motors, shown in Table 14-1, is used to illustrate the calculation of book value. The difficulty is that companies may carry certain assets at meaningless levels. IBM, which at one time reported patents and goodwill at $1, now does not even show the item, and yet it probably represents the company's most important asset. The investor has no real way of gauging this value; therefore, when it is clearly important, as in the case of IBM, its elimination from the book value calculation deprives the figure of much of its significance.

TABLE 14-1

Condensed Balance Sheet of General Motors, 1973

ASSETS	AMOUNT ($ MILLIONS)	LIABILITIES	AMOUNT ($ MILLIONS)
Total current assets*	12,166.6	Total current liabilities	5,969.6
		Other liabilities	462.5
Total investments and miscellaneous assets	1,465.6	Long-term debt	756.5
Common stock in treasury†	137.4	General reserve applicable to foreign operations	141.7
Net real estate and equipment (total property)	6,251.2	Deferred credit	399.7
		Preferred stock	283.6
Deferred income taxes and other deferred charges	238.1	Common stock $1 2/3 par value (287,617,041 shares)	479.4
Goodwill, patents, etc.	38.1	Capital surplus and retained earnings	11,804.0
Total assets	20,297.0	Total liabilities, reserves, and capital	20,297.0

*Includes prepaid expenses.

†Held for the incentive program.

SOURCE: Data taken from General Motors Corporation, *Annual Report 1973.*

Since the net worth of a corporation is the difference between its assets and liabilities, the investor may determine book value by using the net worth figure. He or she first adds the value of common stock and surplus (including retained earnings). The necessary adjustments are then made for treasury stock, proprietary reserves, intangibles, and the difference between the call and stated values of senior securities. Finally, this adjusted aggregate is divided by the number of common shares outstanding (less treasury stock). Table 14-2 illustrates the determination of book value by this procedure.

The investor may also base the calculation of book value on the direct subtraction of liabilities from assets. This procedure is equivalent to using net worth as indicated in the text. Since the book value represents a figure at a specific point in time, it does not seem necessary to use a weighted average. It is desirable, however, to include common stock equivalents and to calculate the figure on a fully diluted basis.

The fact that book value is the most commonly used of the tangible value figures underlines the importance of understanding its relation to

TABLE 14-2

Calculation of Book Value of General Motors Common Stock by Net Worth Method, 1973

ACCOUNT	VALUE ($ MILLIONS)
Common Stock	$ 479.4
Capital surplus and retained earnings	11,804.0
Net worth	12,283.4
Less treasury stock	137.4
Plus proprietary reserves*	141.7
Adjusted net worth	12,287.7
Less intangible assets	276.2
Tangible net worth	12,011.5
Less difference between call and stated value of preferred stock	36.7
Net book value of assets	$11,974.8
Number of shares of common stock outstanding, less treasury stock (millions)†	285.73
Book value per share	$41.91

*This is the general reserve applicable to foreign operations which was established in 1954. It is available to absorb extraordinary losses such as losses from discontinuing foreign operations in any locality, either voluntarily or because of conditions beyond the corporation's control. It is considered a proprietary reserve because there has been no change since its establishment.

†The company has no convertible securities. The effect of the assumed exercise of outstanding options and delivery of bonus awards and contingent credits under the Incentive program is not material.

market price. Under ordinary circumstances, one might reason that stocks of companies should sell above their book values because the benefits derived from an effective management team and personnel strengths do not appear in the balance sheet. In many cases, this intangible factor may be more important than the bricks and mortar that actually are reported. From the end of World War II through 1973, stocks generally did sell above their book values, even when prices were falling. For example, in 1957, a year which saw the Dow-Jones Industrial Average decline by 23 percent, 26 out of the 30 stocks in the average sold at or above book value at some time during the year, and 24 had market prices that were always above their book values. For 1962, a year in which the average dropped 15 percent, the corresponding totals were 26 and 22.

Figure 14-1 portrays the striking change that occurred as a result of the precipitous 1973-1974 market drop. At the beginning of 1973, with the Dow-Jones Industrial Average at about 1,000, there were 23 stocks in the average selling above their book values; by the close of September 1974, with the average at about 600, this number had shrunk to only 11. Moreover, the differential by which book value exceeded market value at the later date tended to be much narrower than at the earlier date. The stocks that showed a reversal in value are indicated by arrows in the figure.

Market value is volatile, shifting constantly as investors change their interpretations of future conditions. Book value is static, reflecting at any one time the summation of past events. For this reason, the book value figure is most useful as a statistical indicator of possible major discrepancies. It is particularly significant when the market price of a stock is well below its indicated book value and the company's assets are marketable. The sharp discrepancies between market and book values that emerged as a result of the 1973-1974 price rout suggested that either undervaluations were available or a business depression was in the offing. The ability of the analyst to reach a correct decision depended on individual judgment, the quality of which, after all the analytic work is done, distinguishes success from failure in the securities field.

It was not unusual for such undervaluations to be the precursors of takeover bids. For example, in early September 1975, Great Western United announced it was considering a tender offer for Bates Manufacturing common stock at $26.25 per share (Great Western subsequently announced it would not pursue the offer for the present; Bates's directors said they would not recommend the offer if made). The stock promptly rose six points to 28⅞ and, at the close of the month, sold at about 26 despite the abandonment of the proposal. On December 31, 1974, Bates had a tangible book value of about $30 a share and its coal properties were believed to be substantially understated. At about the same time, Emhart offered to purchase up to one million shares of USM at $23 a share–when the stock was selling at about 18–an offer that the latter corporation's president urged shareholders to reject. The stock responded by rising to approximately 20 and was selling at about 21 at the end of the month. USM's tangible book value on February 28, 1975 was about $40 a share.

Current asset value. A drawback of book value is the remote similarity that may exist between fixed assets and the amount actually realizable in the event of liquidation. To overcome this deficiency, the current asset value is sometimes used. This is calculated by determining total current assets, subtracting all liabilities preceding the common stock, and dividing by the number of common shares outstanding. Because the basis of the calculation is current assets, there is no need to adjust for the value of intangibles or treasury stock carried as an asset. It is still necessary to exclude proprietary reserves from liabilities, deduct senior securities at their call or voluntary liquidation prices, reduce the number of shares outstanding by the amount of any treasury stock counted by the corporation as an asset, and express the

FIGURE 14-1

Comparison of Market Value and Book Value of Common Stock

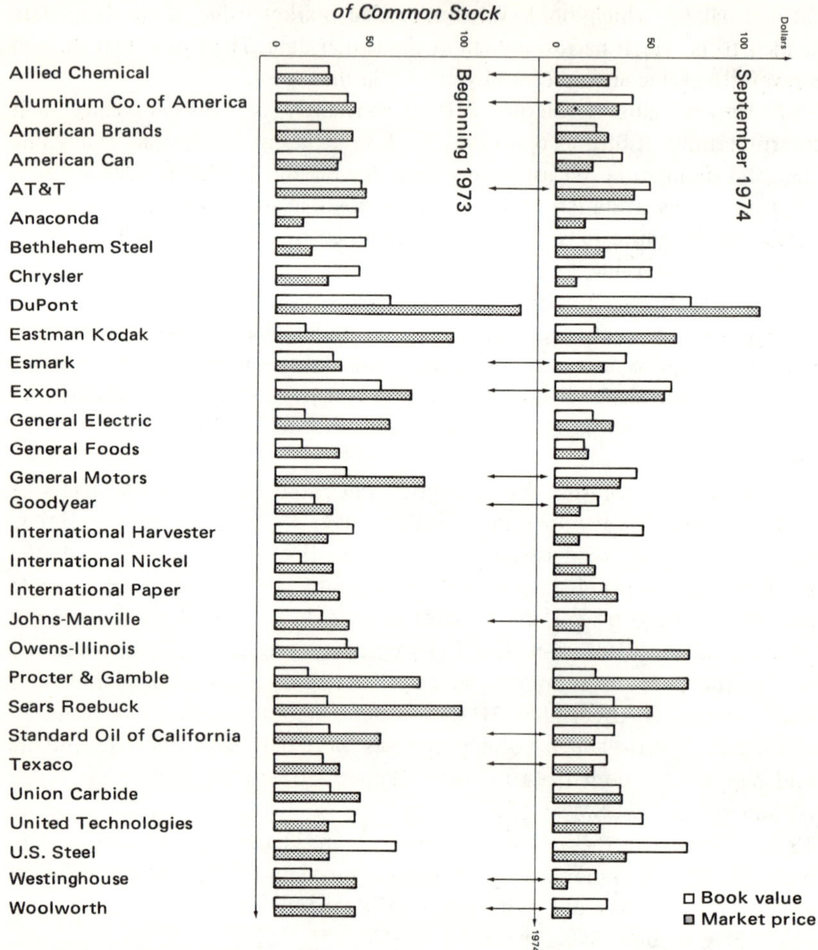

SOURCE: Book values from the ***Value Line Investment Survey***, January-April 1974; the 1974 figures are estimates. Book values for Exxon, Texaco, and Standard Oil of California were calculated based on data in Moody's.

shares on a fully diluted basis. Table 14-3 shows this calculation for General Motors common stock.

At the close of August 1974, the market price of General Motors common stock was about 40, or almost three times its current asset value. This discrepancy did not necessarily mean that the issue was overpriced, since many stocks sell at premiums over their current asset values, even when prices are depressed. Of special interest are those issues whose prices are at substantial discounts from their current asset values. These securities may

TABLE 14-3

Calculation of Current Asset Value of General Motors Corp., 1973

	VALUE (IN MILLIONS)
Total current assets	$12,166.6
Less liabilities*	7,588.3
	4,578.3
Less preferred stocks (at call price)	320.3
Total current assets applicable to common stock	4,258.0
Current asset value per share	$14.9

*Deferred credits are included in liabilities to be conservative and because they could be required to absorb future charges; the general reserve is excluded.

represent bargains if their low market prices are due to temporarily unfavorable developments that can be rectified. Since stocks may sell below their current asset values when a company's business is on the decline, the investor must be careful to investigate the cause of this condition.

Cash asset value. The cash asset value of a common stock is determined in a fashion similar to that used for current asset value; the only difference is that the basis of the calculation is cash and cash equivalents, rather than total current assets. Included in cash equivalents are liquid securities at market value, the cash surrender value of insurance policies, and other such readily disposable assets. Accounts receivable and inventories are pared down to levels that correspond more closely to their estimated realizable value in the event of liquidation. Excluded from the calculation are any assets that cannot readily be converted to cash. The cash asset value serves the same purpose as the net asset figure, but it represents a sterner measure.

Measuring a Corporation's Financial Strength

To carry on its everyday operations, a corporation must have sufficient current assets. The sum of these assets is generally called working capital. The financial strength of a corporation, its ability to obtain new financing, its capacity to meet the exigencies of economic fluctuations—all may depend on the relationship between current assets and current liabilities.

The simplest indication of financial capacity is the absolute difference between current assets and current liabilities, which is sometimes called *net working capital.* This figure has become a fairly popular measuring device in corporate finance. As we have seen, trust indentures and charters may limit dividends when net working capital falls below a designated level or a specified percentage of funded debt. Absolute measures, however, do not take into account the relation of current assets to current liabilities; hence, they do not accurately show how well a company can take care of its immediate obligations. For this purpose the "current asset" and "acid test" ratios are commonly employed.[3]

Current asset ratio. This ratio is calculated by dividing current assets by current liabilities. Acceptable minimum standards vary with different industries and types of companies although a ratio of 2.5/1 is by and large considered satisfactory for industrial companies. It is logical to expect high standards for manufacturing enterprises that finance their customers' purchases and hold substantial inventories for conversion into finished goods. Companies which discourage customer credits and do not require considerable inventories have a less urgent need for large amounts of working capital.

Some idea of these variations may be obtained from Table 14-4, which compares the current assets and liabilities of manufacturing companies,

TABLE 14-4

Comparison of Current Assets
(dollar amounts in millions)

	1974 MANU-FACTURING	1972 RAILROADS	1973 PUBLIC UTILITIES
Cash and deposits	28,124	113.4	
U.S. government securities and other investments	19,133	895.6	
Accounts and notes receivable	129,043	—	
Inventories	179,702	524.2	
Other current assets	19,366	486.9	
Total current assets	375,368	2,020.1	7,560
Notes and accounts payable	109,671	696.7	
Interest and taxes accrued	16,270	378.4	
Other current liabilities	66,737	2,486.0	
Total current liabilities	192,678	3,561.1	11,654
Current asset ratio	1.95	.57	.65

SOURCE: Data for manufacturing companies taken from Federal Trade Commission, ***Quarterly Financial Report for Manufacturing, Mining and Trade Corporations***, 1st quarter 1975; data for railroad companies taken from Moody's, ***Transportation 1974***; data for public utilities companies taken from Edison Electric Institute, ***Statistical Yearbook of the Electric Utility Industry***, 1973.

railroads, and public utilities. The relatively high current asset ratios of manufacturing companies, as compared with those of railroads and public utilities, reflect the differences in the activities of these enterprises. The activities of the manufacturing companies run through the standard working-capital cycle of inventories-receivables-cash-inventories. In contrast, both the railroads and public utilities are essentially service enterprises that have huge capital investments but comparatively little need for substantial amounts of working capital.

An investor may also want to check the ratios of a particular company against those of similar enterprises. For this purpose, the figures issued by many credit agencies and trade associations may be helpful. Finally, the investor may examine the trend of current asset ratios to find evidence of improvement or deterioration.

Acid test ratio. The acid test ratio, sometimes called the "quick" ratio, provides a more critical measure of the current financial strength of a company. It is calculated by dividing current assets, less inventories and miscellaneous items, by current liabilities. This ratio assumes that the remaining current assets—cash, marketable securities, and accounts receivable—are liquid, in which case they realistically offset current liabilities. For an industrial company, a ratio of 1:1 is considered satisfactory. It indicates that each dollar of current liabilities is at least covered by a similar sum of readily disposable assets.

Working-capital ratios are used primarily to show whether funds are adequate for operating purposes. They are not intended to show the value of the assets underlying each share of stock in case of liquidation or to reveal "bargain issues."

These ratios should be interpreted with caution. First, they are subject to fairly rapid deterioration. Second, high ratios may reflect inattentiveness on the part of management to the fact that the assets could be more profitably deployed in another fashion. High ratios may also indicate firms that can readily become take-over targets, which may impart to them a certain degree of speculative attraction.

Evaluating the Flow of Corporate Earnings

Because all the operations of a corporation are eventually reflected in its balance sheet, this statement enables an investor to observe the movement of corporate funds as they originate in different activities, and to follow their independent courses into the reservoir of total assets. An analysis of the sources and applications of funds furnishes a view of this ceaseless flow. The balance sheet is also a means of estimating earnings.

Sources and applications of funds. A skeleton statement of sources and applications of funds may be made by simply extending into two columns the differences between the balance sheet items of successive periods. In one column appear those factors that increase funds, in the other the elements that absorb them. For most corporations, typical sources of funds are net income, loans, depreciation, clearing of customers' carrying accounts, and sale of assets. Characteristic methods of disposing of these funds are dividend payments, plant expansion and improvements, payment of loans, and increases in net working capital.

A thorough analysis of the sources and applications of funds may require more detailed data from both balance sheets and income statements than the corporation publishes. Annual reports issued to stockholders usually show only net changes, and the investor may not be able to detect the influence of internal accounting transactions. For example, a company may spend much money on plant additions and improvements but may also retire a substantial amount of equipment during the same period. The net result of these transactions would be a small change in the plant and equipment account that was not at all representative of the funds actually expended.

Published reports do ordinarily provide the investor with enough information to develop a reasonable breakdown of the activities of a corporation over a designated period. This is particularly true because the modern report often contains a considerable amount of supplementary information in the president's financial review. SEC Forms 10 and 10-K call for statements of the sources and applications of funds, and the New York Stock Exchange now requires companies to include such statements in their annual reports to shareholders.

By providing an insight into a corporation's flow of funds, the statement of sources and applications of funds throws light on its liquidity ratios and helps in the forecast of future financial policies, particularly the payment of common dividends. Table 14-5, comparing the statements of IBM and General Instrument, suggests certain significant conclusions along these lines.

The liquidity ratios of both corporations were good. In 1973, IBM's current asset ratio was 2.3, and its acid test ratio was 2.1; the ratios of General Instrument for the fiscal year ending February 1974 were 3.7 and 1.8. The chief executive officers of General Instrument commented specifically on the current asset ratio, stating that "the financial condition of the Company remains excellent."

While the liquidity ratios of the two corporations do not show much difference between their financial positions, the sources and applications of funds statements reveal quite a different story. IBM obtained 87.2 percent of its funds from operations, while General Instrument derived only 33.5 percent from this source. IBM's sale of stock to employees provides a modest but continuing source of equity funds, whereas General Instrument does not raise any funds through the sale of stock to employees. Because of the relatively small amount that General Instrument obtains from operations and because of the absence of new equity capital, the corporation had to rely on long-term borrowing to a considerable degree. Thus, much of its liquidity

TABLE 14-5

Sources and Applications of Funds for General Instrument and IBM, 1973

	PERCENTAGE OF TOTAL	
SOURCE OF FUNDS	IBM	GENERAL INSTRUMENT
Net income	41.9	15.8
Depreciation and similar items	45.3	17.7
Total income from operations	87.2	33.5
Capital stock under employee plans	8.6	—
Long-term borrowings	4.2	63.6
Other	—	2.9
Total, nonoperating income	12.8	66.5
	100.0	100.0
APPLICATION OF FUNDS		
Fixed assets	54.7	21.7
Common dividends	17.4	—
Payment, long-term debt	7.4	10.9
Refinancing, long-term debt	—	7.1
Other	1.5	5.1
Increase in working capital	19.0	55.2
	100.0	100.0

SOURCE: Data taken from the 1973 annual reports of General Instrument Corp. and IBM.

strength stems from a weakening of its capital structure. Both corporations are in expanding fields and therefore probably require large expenditures on new plant and equipment. This policy is confirmed by the 54.7 percent of funds spent on fixed assets by IBM, compared with only 21.7 percent by General Instrument, which, in turn, had substantial refinancing and long-term debt maturities to handle. Because of the borrowing pressure on General Instrument, it paid no dividends and none seemed in sight, despite reported earnings of $1.82 a share. On the other hand, the comparatively low percentage of funds absorbed by IBM's common dividend payments suggested that the company might continue its policy of raising disbursements if economic conditions did not change materially.

Balance sheet appraisal of corporate earnings. The earnings of a corporation can be reconstructed by comparing its net worth at the beginning and the end of a designated period, adding back dividend payments, and subtracting stock transactions. Prior to the formation of the SEC, this technique was sometimes useful for estimating the profit or loss of corporations that did not report their income. All major companies with active markets for their securities now publish income statements, largely eliminating the need for determining earnings through balance sheet comparisons.

At one time, too, the analyst had to hunt for the extraordinary items affecting earnings, and changes in balance sheet reserves could help in this search. In accordance with various opinions of the Accounting Principles Board, however, it is now accepted accounting procedure to provide separate reporting of income before extraordinary items and net income, as well as earnings per share for extraordinary items (less applicable income taxes), although the definition of "extraordinary" remains unclear. Moreover, since 1973, the SEC has required registrants to show more detailed and timely information concerning extraordinary charges or credits to income. Balance sheet checks may help evaluate the implications of such transactions. Additionally, balance sheet analysis provides information on such items as potential dilution of outstanding shares, taxation, and the treatment of translation losses or gains, all of which affect reported earnings per share.

Assessing the Influence of the Capital Structure

The subject of capitalization frequently appears in discussions of securities analysis. The bond-stock capitalization ratio, discussed subsequently, is one of the standards used to gauge the quality of fixed-income securities. The adjustments required for certain changes in capitalization have already been described in connection with developing a consistent series of earnings. Our present concern is with the advantages and disadvantages to a common stockholder of a capitalization comprising different mixes of debt and equity.

Leverage arising from trading on equity. A decisive factor in the financial well-being of a corporation is the distribution of its capitalization among different types of securities. A large equity capitalization may limit the rate of the stockholder's return on investment, but it will not drive the enterprise into bankruptcy. A debt-heavy capitalization may increase the return under favorable conditions, but bankruptcy will constantly threaten the company if its earnings are not sufficient to meet fixed charges during periods of economic adversity.

Management's decision on future methods of financing hinges on the field in which the company operates. Public utilities, which have huge fixed-capital commitments, must raise a considerable portion of their financial requirements through long-term debt. Manufacturing companies have more flexibility and use equity securities more extensively. The effects of these different financing methods may be observed in the debt/equity ratios of different types of companies (Table 14-6).

TABLE 14-6

Comparison of Debt/Equity Ratios

	1974 MANUFACTURING		1973 PUBLIC UTILITIES		1972 RAILROADS	
	AMOUNT (IN MILLIONS)	PER-CENT	AMOUNT (IN MILLIONS)	PER-CENT	AMOUNT (IN MILLIONS)	PER-CENT
Long-term debt	130,119	24.2	56,910	52.9	10,594	40.5
Stockholders' equity	408,365	75.8	50,645	47.1	15,535	59.5
Total	538,484	100.0	107,555	100.0	26,129	100.0

SOURCE: Data for manufacturing companies taken from Federal Trade Commission, ***Quarterly Financial Report for Manufacturing, Mining and Trade Corporations***; data for railroad companies taken from Moody's, ***Transportation 1974***; data for public utilities companies taken from Edison Electric Institute, ***Statistical Yearbook of the Electric Utility Industry***, 1973.

The combination of a capitalization having a large percentage of debt (a thin-equity capitalization) and a fluctuating income both aggravates a corporation's financial problems and enhances its earnings potential. Such an enterprise has relatively large fixed charges, which it must defray regardless of economic conditions. During periods of business expansion, earnings will probably be above this rigid requirement; the resulting gap represents additional income for the stockholders. Conversely, during years of economic decline, earnings may fall below this requirement; the gap now constitutes a severe financial burden that may cause bankruptcy. A heavy base of fixed charges thus represents a leverage factor that accentuates the sharpness of net income fluctuations.[4]

A thin-equity capitalization enhances the speculative characteristics of a stock, particularly if the issuing corporation is engaged in a volatile industry. A classic illustration of dramatic change was provided by the heavily funded marginal railroads during the transition from depression to economic prosperity. The New York, Chicago & St. Louis, for example, which skirted bankruptcy in the 1930s, revealed a phenomenal improvement during the subsequent war and defense-inspired booms. In 1938 the railroad reported a deficit of $9.55 per share of common stock, and the issue sold as low as 7. Earnings skyrocketed to $55.88 per share by 1950. In the following year, after reaching a high of 236½, the common stock was split five-for-one.

Conversely, the earnings of a heavily leveraged company can decline precipitously. Pan American World Airways, for example, characteristically has a very large amount of long-term debt in its capitalization. In 1966 the company's stock reached, on an adjusted basis, a high of $40 per share, and the company reported earnings of $2.23 per share. By 1969 those earnings were converted to a deficit of 74 cents per share, and the stock hit a low of 11⅜. Thereafter, the company continued to experience financial problems, in part, at least, because of its heavy burden of fixed charges.

A thick equity is a conservative characteristic. Briggs & Stratton, for example, has a simple common stock capitalization and relatively stable earnings; its stock shows comparatively modest market fluctuations. Public utilities issue large amounts of fixed-income securities, but this speculative aspect of their capitalization is largely offset by the stability of their income, at least until the recent period of severe inflation, when rate adjustments tended to lag behind cost increases.

While the impact of leverage on the level and volatility of earnings is universally acknowledged, its influence on stock prices is a more controversial subject. Under certain assumptions, stock prices are unaffected by leverage, since the increase in earnings per share is offset by a corresponding rise in the capitalization rate or fall in the p/e ratio.[5] Such an offset is likely to occur when the injection of leverage raises a company's debt to a level that the market regards as risky. Until this point is reached, additional leverage even may have a positive effect on the p/e ratio. Modigliani and Miller, however, have denied that capitalization changes can affect stock prices. Their underlying proposition is the standard economic principle that identical commodities cannot sell for more than one price in a perfect market. As long as investors and corporations are equally capable of leveraging themselves, there can be no advantage for one to do it over the other. The stock of leveraged and unleveraged companies would then have to offer the same rate of return, or investors would create their own leverage and shift to the one with the highest yield, until equality was obtained. Even Modigliani and Miller have conceded that when interest is deductible for tax purposes, valuation will be affected by leverage.[6] The important thing to remember, however, is that their argument assumes perfect markets and no limit on the investor's ability to borrow. In the real world of financial markets, neither of these assumptions is likely to be true. Indeed, in preparing a company to go public, financial advisers will often recommend leverage to improve the earnings per share figure on the assumption that the p/e ratio will more likely rise because of the growth illusion than fall because of the risk effect.

Number of shares of stock outstanding. A corporation with a large amount of common stock must have substantial earning power to permit a high level of profits per share. Few industrial corporations could support the 287.6 million shares of common stock that General Motors had outstanding at the close of 1973. Yet General Motors, with its gigantic organization and sales in the billions of dollars, has been able to report satisfactory earnings for its stockholders and pay fairly liberal dividends since 1915.

Because corporate activity is a dynamic quality, it is not feasible to establish fixed limits on the number of shares of stock that may be issued. The importance of the common stock capitalization must be judged on the basis of a company's previous operations. In general, a persistent inability to raise earnings per share indicates overcapitalization.

A considerable amount of common stock creates an ample floating supply, necessitating a great demand to generate any important price movements. When the buyers of stock were primarily individuals, this factor could have more readily contributed to sluggish market movements. Now that demand is increasingly being concentrated among institutional investors, who require large floating supplies to insure liquidity, this factor has probably diminished in significance.

On the other hand, when a company has a small amount of shares outstanding, a relatively modest change in demand could generate sharp price fluctuations. It is not at all uncommon now for institutional investors to try to establish a position in a company considered attractive but to find that the resulting upward movement in the price of the stock makes it impossible to accumulate sufficient shares at the levels desired.

Bond maturities. It is important that the investor check the due dates of bond issues. When industrial conditions are favorable, most corporations can meet their maturities through refunding or readjustment plans. In years of economic adversity, the same corporations may exhaust their funds, issuance of new securities is often difficult, and bondholders are adverse to exchange offers.

Impending maturities may be a serious problem to marginal companies—and even to strong enterprises—during periods of poor business. Under these conditions, a conservative investor may prefer to avoid securities of such corporations until the maturity problem is clarified. However, this very problem will probably drive the issues to unusually low levels. At these depressed prices they may represent "bargain" opportunities to individuals who are willing to speculate on the corporation's eventual ability to meet maturing obligations.

Debt and inflation. Capitalization can assume special significance for those buying common stock as a hedge against inflation. To the extent that debt can be repaid in deflated dollars, the gain to the stockholder from inflated earnings is accentuated. However, capital structure is only part of the inflation-hedge picture. Gains accrue to stockholders only if corporations are *net* debtors. The investor must consider the inflation-resistant assets as well as the liabilities. If the cash held and credit extended by a corporation exceed its total indebtedness, the corporation is in fact a creditor, and its stock will hardly serve as an inflation hedge.

Complex capital structures. As the acquisition fever rose in the 1960s, a number of corporations issued a variety of convertible securities and warrants in exchange for the shares or assets of desired companies. In this way, conglomerates forged both formidable corporate empires and complex capital structures. The use of such instruments helped produce immediate, sharp per share gains, but they left considerable future supplies of stock overhanging the market if these privileges were ever exercised. Opinion no. 15 of the Accounting Principles Board now calls for the reporting of per share earnings on a fully diluted basis. This requirement has put a damper on the creation of complex capitalizations that include various privileged issues, since fully diluted reporting will eliminate much of the opportunity for showing the favorable earnings per share comparisons that were formerly possible.

MANAGEMENT'S RESPONSIBILITY IN DETERMINING AN OPTIMUM CAPITAL STRUCTURE

A decisive factor in the financial well-being of a corporation is the distribution of its capital structure between stocks and bonds. As we have seen, a substantial equity capitalization may limit the rate of a stockholder's return from investment, but it will not drive the enterprise into bankruptcy. A debt-heavy capitalization may increase the rate of return under favorable conditions, but bankruptcy will constantly threaten the company. Confronted with these alternatives, management sometimes tends to restrict its capitalization to common stock, thus reducing the threat of future financial difficulties.

This decision entails the resolution of an important financial dispute. If management has no responsibility for the market valuation of its stock, it may justly shun fixed-income securities. But if it has the responsibility of trying to maximize both the earnings of the stockholders relative to their risk exposure and the market's valuation of the common stock, the selection, for convenience, of a straight common stock capitalization may be an error.

It is our belief that management does have this responsibility. To recognize this obligation, management must develop an appropriate capitalization. Absence of senior securities from the capitalization of a corporation that is capable of issuing bonds is a deficiency. This omission suggests that management is either overly conservative or is unwilling to employ every means available for accelerating the flow of earnings to stockholders. (Even in the theoretically perfect market, there are tax advantages that must be considered.) Either policy is undesirable. This argument leads to a more general principle: investors must not be swayed to a corporation simply because it has capitalization entirely based on common stock. As a corollary, the presence of bonds is an investment virtue when the corporation appears able to meet its fixed charges during periods of economic adversity.

SUMMARY

The balance sheet summarizes the types and amounts of assets, liabilities, and capital of a company on a particular date. Its form and the composition of its major accounts are reasonably uniform. In recent years, the regulatory authorities have displayed an interest in reflecting the effects of inflation. They have also taken steps to standardize the reporting of current liabilities, expand the reporting of lease liabilities, and clarify the use of contingency reserves.

In securities analysis, the principal uses of the balance sheet are to measure the tangible value of a stock, gauge a corporation's financial strength, help determine the outlets into which earnings have gone, and assess the influence of capital structure on profits.

Tangible values indicate the actual worth of all or part of a company's assets that underlie its stock. In theory, the higher the ratio of the assets to the stock's market price, the greater the bargain the purchaser obtains. This conclusion is only valid, however, if the values could be realized on liquidation and the corporation were contemplating such a step, or if the purchaser could acquire control of the corporation. Because these eventualities rarely occur, tangible values are primarily useful either as supporting evidence to confirm evaluations or to suggest further investigation. The major measures of tangible value are book value, current asset value, and cash asset value.

To carry on its everyday operations, a corporation must have sufficient current assets. The sum of these assets is generally called working capital. The financial strength of a corporation, its ability to obtain new financing, its capacity to meet the exigencies of economic fluctuations—all may depend on the relationship between current assets and current liabilities. The basic measure of this relationship is the current asset ratio, which is calculated by dividing current assets by current liabilities. The acid test ratio, sometimes called the quick ratio, provides a more critical gauge of the current financial strength of a company. It is calculated by dividing current assets (less inventories and miscellaneous items) by current liabilities.

All the operations of a corporation eventually are reflected in the balance sheet. It is the basis of the sources and applications of funds statement. The latter enables an investor to observe the movement of corporate funds as they originate in different activities and to follow their independent courses into the reservoir of total assets. Although a comprehensive statement requires data from both the income statement and the balance sheet, a skeleton statement may be developed by simply extending into two columns the differences between the balance sheet items of two successive periods. Balance sheet comparisons are also useful in throwing light on reported earnings.

The major approach in assessing the capital structure of a company is to ascertain the relationship between its equity and debt segments. A large equity capitalization reduces the danger of bankruptcy. A debt-heavy capitalization may increase the return under favorable conditions, but bankruptcy will constantly threaten the company if its earnings are not sufficient to meet fixed charges during periods of economic adversity. It is a major responsibility of management to obtain a balanced relationship between debt and equity.

Other capitalization factors to consider in evaluating a stock are the number of shares outstanding, impending bond maturities, and the company's use of complex instruments, such as options, warrants, and convertible senior securities.

CHAPTER 15

Stock Appraisal: The Basic Considerations

It is easy to say that the intelligent investor should gather all the relevant facts, consider all the accounting pitfalls, and complete thorough statistical analysis before purchase of a security. Suppose, thinking these steps have been taken, the investor buys the stock. He or she still knows, as Borch has observed, that "there is necessarily a seller who thinks that at the present time and the present price it is right to sell the stock which we consider the best buy. If this seller is just as intelligent and smart as wer are, it may be useful to think twice."[1] There are so many imponderables surrounding the securities markets and so many alert people on the other side of the investing fence that it is difficult to reach decisions with any degree of certainty.

Moreover, the typical investor does not gather all the relevant facts, consider all the accounting pitfalls, or undertake a thorough analysis. For most people, investing is a part-time occupation. The effort spent on analyzing securities, therefore, will depend on the amount of money to be committed, the pressure of other concerns, and the pleasure derived from analysis. Even the institutional portfolio manager does not have enough time to study every stock that piques his interest, and so he depends on a steady flow of analysis and recommendations from outside sources.

Investors may purchase the services of advisory organizations or may obtain research from brokers who are reimbursed through the commissions charged. The Securities and Exchange Commission has asserted that broad-based securities research and its prompt and fair dissemination to both large and small investors is vital to efficient capital markets. The SEC has therefore endorsed the principle of paying for research through commissions.[2] The Securities Acts Amendments of 1975 have provided protection for money managers against being sued for paying more than the lowest obtainable commission for execution and research services.[3]

In the present chapter, we discuss how the investor may undertake independent analysis. Even if he employs a professional adviser, an understanding of research procedures will help him appraise the services he receives. Recognizing the differences in the needs of various investors, we offer methods of varying degrees of complexity. Moreover, an investor who is willing to undertake extensive research will find that not every security considered warrants careful examination.

WHAT STOCKS SHOULD BE INVESTIGATED?

There are more than 1,500 companies that have stocks listed on the New York Stock Exchange, and many thousands more whose stocks are traded over the counter.[4] Obviously, an investor can only investigate a small fraction of them.

In general, the approach suggested is to screen a large body of securities to define a list that merits further attention. The simpler methods of analysis that are discussed may then be employed to narrow the list still further. By this process, the securities that warrant careful examination may be reduced to a manageable number.

One type of filter to discriminate between the host of available securities is based on the needs of the investor. The terms of an agreement with a bank or the prospectus of a mutual fund will describe investment objectives that narrow the portfolio manager's scope of selection. Thus, the only stocks that the manager of a large income fund is likely to buy will be those of dividend-paying companies that have a sufficient number of shares outstanding to permit adequate liquidity. A conservative individual may also want to limit his purchases to issues of this sort. Aggressive investors, on the other hand, may want to concentrate on emerging situations more likely to be found in the OTC market than on the New York Stock Exchange.

Or the filter may be certain characteristics of a stock that appeal to the investor, such as a low price/earnings ratio or a high rate of earnings growth. Professor Henry Latané and two of his associates have devised a relatively simple device that combines these two features. For each stock they calculate the ratio of the latest earnings per share to the figure reported in the corresponding quarter of the preceding year. They also compute the ratio of the preceding period's earnings to the current quarter's price, defined as the "closing price at the end of the second month following the quarter under consideration."[5] These two ratios are then combined, and the stocks with the highest algebraic values become candidates for further investigation.

Still another approach stresses stocks of companies that have achieved more than expected earnings gains. For this purpose, a trend line may be fitted to quarterly earnings and the following quarter's earnings projected; stocks whose latest reported earnings exceed the projected quarterly figure by at least 1.5 standard errors of estimate are selected for continued investigation.[6]

Application of these broad scanning techniques is greatly facilitated by the use of a computer. But a filter cannot substitute for individual alertness in discovering companies with special attributes that can be translated into higher market values for the company's stock. The triggering factor may be a new product, like the dramatic innovations in electronics, photocopying machines, and photographic equipment. Or it may be a special cost advantage, like that gained by mail-order insurance; or a unique marketing technique, like Levitz Furniture's use of warehouse-showrooms.

The investor may come across ideas in different ways: among the companies in the industry where he works, in newspaper items, in trade or technical journals, or in the products that he finds attractive as a consumer. The method does not matter, so long as the investor is perceptive in recognizing potential opportunities and is quick to act. For example, as wine gained popularity in the United States, the investor might have been impressed by the number of times he came across cold duck and might therefore have been attracted to Franzia Brothers Winery, which produces various modest-priced sparkling wines, as well as generic and dessert wines. He might have waited in a long line before a Steak and Ale restaurant and so become interested in the company sponsoring this chain. Or he might have noticed the growing popularity of "African" wildlife preserves, leading him to Lion Country Safari, which has two such parks in the United States. As another illustration, in mid-1971 the money manager of a small aggressive fund discovered that he could not obtain reservations in a train carrying families and their automobiles between Washington, D.C. and Sanford, Florida, which is close to Disney World. On the basis of this information, he checked the sponsoring company, Auto-Train Corp., and found it an interesting vehicle for short-term speculation.

When the company that is responsible for the new product or novel technique is relatively small or has a short-term history, the problem of analysis is particularly difficult. As a result, the potential market risks and gains are both likely to be great. In these cases, if the stock is purchased, special care must be attached to the holding period, because as the company attracts increasing attention, its stock may be driven to unjustifiably high levels, or the company's early promise may fade.[7]

Careful analysis, good judgment, and a lot of luck is required to be able to steer a correct line between overholding and selling prematurely. In this connection, a helpful principle is that an investor cannot lose money by accepting market gains even if the stock continues to advance after he sells. Some may object to this implicit rejection of the concept of opportunity costs embodied in the profits foregone by selling securities that continue to move upward. The difficulty of correctly timing a high point is so great, however, that better results are likely to be achieved in the long run by the avoidance of overholding rather than by premature selling.

During booms, when stocks tend to sell at high price/earnings ratios, the investor has an incentive to seek relatively obscure companies whose stocks may flourish when the light of public attention is beamed upon them. On the other hand, when the market is at ebb tide, there is less need to assume the risk of buying the stocks of such companies, since issues of substantial enterprises are available at low price/earnings ratios, possibly below book value, and sometimes even below net current asset values. In both types of markets, of course, the irksome problem of timing remains, because all types of stocks tend to be carried along when prices are broadly advancing or declining.

THE FOCUS

Earlier, we noted that the worth of a share may be represented by discounting to the present time all the dividends to be received in a finite holding period and discounting the price for which the investment is expected to be liquidated. This latter value is often the more important.

For one thing, dividends are paid from earnings. Moreover, in the long pull, even if the investor gets no more from capital gains than from dividends, the aftertax net will be greater from the price appreciation. Then again, a company's dividends are likely to respond lethargically to expanding sales and earnings for two principal reasons. Either the company may want to retain a large portion of its enlarged profits for further expansion, or it may be reluctant to raise dividends to a level from which it may have to retreat if the change in its fortunes is transitory.

IBM, the locus classicus of growth companies, illustrates the greater potential importance of capital gains over dividends in evaluating a stock. During the 1961-1971 decade, the company's per share earnings, adjusted for stock splits and dividends, rose from $2.39 to $9.38. Reflecting its persistent rate of growth, the company raised its dividend payout ratio during this period gradually from 15.1 percent to 55.4 percent. On this basis, an investor who owned stock during the entire ten years received somewhat over $100 on each share held.[8] On the other hand, after taking into account stock splits and stock dividends, the market price of each share rose from a low point of $100 in 1961 to a high of about $1,890 in 1971.

In mid-1973, with short-term interest rates in the 8 percent range, analysts began to reconsider the importance of dividend payments.[9] They attributed, in part, the low price/earnings ratios that prevailed at that time to investors' desire for higher yields in common stocks to offset the high rates available from fixed-income securities. Some support was given to this theory when stocks spurted nearly 20 points, as measured by the Dow-Jones Industrial Average, following an announcement that the U.S. government was easing its restriction that had previously limited increases in payouts to no more than 4 percent. The rise was short-lived, however, and stocks soon resumed their sluggish course.

In considering a security, an investor cannot avoid looking into the distant future, since this will help throw light on the company's basic position in its field and its ability to survive the pressures of competition and expand its share of the market. But there are likely to be so many uncertainties in the picture that such a view is primarily useful to set the stage for a near-term forecast. In effect, securities should be scrutinized constantly to determine whether retention is warranted. The primary consideration is the return expected in the coming year (with allowance for risk). Thus, the investor must gauge (to the best of his ability) the price at which he can liquidate the stock one year hence and the dividends he will receive in the interim. Both these estimates, in turn, are heavily dependent on the company's expected earnings during this period, which therefore becomes the focus of the estimate. It should be realized, however, that stressing next year's earnings to determine terminal values of stocks demands that serious attention be given to what may happen in subsequent years, because the investor's long-term outlook is implicit in the expected price/earnings ratio for the following year.

THE BUSINESS ENVIRONMENT

Corporate earnings cannot be forecast in a vacuum. The fortunes of business firms depend on the environment in which those firms operate. From an investment viewpoint, perhaps the most important influences in this respect are general business conditions, inflation, and taxes. Clearly, all these factors are interrelated, but for purposes of analysis they may be considered separately.

General Business Conditions

Forecasting the general level of economic activity is a complex undertaking. In part, the future depends on the judgments of managers and consumers. Thus, if corporate managers are optimistic, they will raise their capital expenditures for plant and equipment, thereby setting in motion a chain reaction of increased activity by their suppliers, more employment, expanded consumer income, and a greater volume of money in circulation. If consumers, in turn, have confidence in the continuity of their jobs and income, they contribute to the upward spiral by spending more for housing, automobiles, and entertainment. To help the investor gauge such prospects, various expectations series are published. Thus, both the Department of Commerce and McGraw-Hill issue estimates of anticipated business expenditures for new plant and equipment, while the University of Michigan Survey Research Center provides a gauge of consumer sentiment.

Since 1938, the National Bureau of Economic Research has maintained a list of cyclical indicators that characteristically lead, lag behind, or coincide with the movements of aggregate economic activity. These series, as well as many others portraying all aspects of business conditions, appear in such publications as the *Survey of Current Business* and *Business Conditions Digest,* published by Bureau of Economic Analysis of the U.S. Department of Commerce; *Economic Indicators,* prepared for the Joint Economic Committee by the Council of Economic Advisers; *Monthly Labor Review,* issued by the Bureau of Labor Statistics; and the *Federal Reserve Bulletin.*

Nevertheless, even with the aid of these statistical props, tracking the course of the business cycle is no easy matter. Plans may be altered by subsequent events, and the policies of the government may have an important effect. General economic conditions are influenced by government decisions in both the fiscal and monetary areas. Fiscal policy affects economic activity through manipulation of taxes and government expenditures. Monetary policy operates through the volume of money made available. A debate has raged over the merits of these two channels of policy, but the consensus is that each has its role and its limitations.

There are a great number of ways of tampering with taxes, a major aspect of fiscal policy. Some techniques bear upon the ability of consumers to spend, while others are tied to business expenditures. These direct relationships are only the beginning, however, because a modification in one area is bound to have repercussions on the others. The government's decision to raise or lower expenditures on defense, welfare, education, Social Security, and various other areas will further affect the business picture.

Monetary policy, operating through the supply and availability of money, may influence (1) the cost of funds, and thus the demand for structures, equipment, and consumer durables; (2) the value of securities, which, in turn, has an influence on household net worth and, eventually, consumer expenditures; and (3) the allocation of credit, thereby affecting the market for housing and other durable goods.

This brief sketch of monetary and fiscal policy is intended merely to call attention to the scope of decision making involved and the uncertainty of actual outcomes. Integrating the decisions of corporate managers and individuals with the policies of government planners (which, in turn, have political and international overtones) is a vastly complicated and hazardous job, even for the professional economist. It is hardly an undertaking that the investor may assume with impunity. Recognizing the difficulty of this highly specialized area, the institutional money manager is likely to engage the services of professional economists. The investor, who is not in a position to have this personal assistance, may want to use the professional forecasts that appear in generally available publications. Such forecasts are issued by banks, brokerage firms, and investment advisers.

Over the past several decades, various government agencies, universities, and private business firms have fashioned elaborate, computer-solved econometric models to forecast business conditions. Models have been built by the Department of Commerce, the Federal Reserve System, the University of Pennsylvania (Wharton School), the University of Michigan, Chase Econometric Associates, and Data Resources, Inc.; the Federal Reserve Bank of St. Louis and RCA have developed models with a monetarist slant.[10] The Federal Reserve Bank of Richmond issues figures showing a "consensus" of forecasts made by others, as well as a compilation of representative forecasts, with names and details of estimates. Predicasts Inc. compiles historical data and composite forecasts on a great number of statistical series that are derived from a variety of sources and adjusted to a mutually consistent pattern; reports are issued quarterly, with an annual cumulative index. Figure 15-1 reproduces a Predicasts page covering financial instruments to illustrate the type of information provided. The National Planning Association Economic Projection Series is a continuing research activity of the Center for Economic Studies. The reports issued cover five- and ten-year forecasts of key indicators of economic and demographic growth for the nation, regions, states, and metropolitan areas.

Inflation

In the beginning of 1975, a major problem confronting investors was how to deal with the persistent advances of inflation. From about 1950 to

FIGURE 15-1

Page Showing Typical Forecasts of Predicasts, Inc.

				PREDICASTS									FORECAST ABSTRACTS	
SIC				YEARS			QUANTITIES			UNIT OF	SOURCE			Annual
NO	PRODUCT A	EVENT	PRODUCT B	B	S	L	B	S	L	MEASURE	JOURNAL	DATE	PAGE	Growth
	Nonconsumer Instruments													
60022 125	Commercial paper	funds from	capital & loan markets	73	74	75	5.3	1.5	2.5	bil $	Mfr Hanovr	2/ /74	15	−31.3%
60022 128	3 month commercial paper	rate		73	74	–	8.11	7.30	–	% yield	Fed Richmd	3/ /74	15	−9.9%
60022 128	3 month commercial paper	rate		–	74	–	–	7.5	–	% yield	Am Bank	2/15/74	72"b	– %
60022 158	3 month treasury bills	rate		73d	74a	74b	8.25	7.25	5.85	% yield	Am Bank	12/13/73	3"	−29.3%
60022 158	3 month treasury bills	rate		–	74d	–	–	5.25	–	% yield	Am Bank	11/20/73	3"b	– %
60022 158	3 month treasury bills	rate		72	73	74	4.86	7.60	5.15	% yield	Wells Frgo	11/ /73	2	−32.9%*
60022 158	3 month treasury bills	rate		73	74	–	7.07	6.35	–	% rate	Fed Richmd	3/ /74	15	−10.0%
60022 158	3 month treasury bills	rate		73	74	–	7.24	6.60	–	% yield	Bus Econ	1/ /74	77"	−8.3%
60022 158	3 month treasury bills	rate		72	73	74	3.25	8.75	7.00	% yield	Book Prod	5/ /74	22	−19.5%*
60022 158	3 month treasury bills	rate		73	74	75	7.04	6.8	6.15	% yield	UCLA 1974	3/21/74	T–1	−6.6%
	Stocks													
60023 005	Stocks	price		–	74	74d	–	109.	113.	S&P index	Am Bank	12/31/73	10	– %
60023 005	Stocks	price		–	74	–	–	875. ±	–	DJ index	United Bus	12/10/73	501	– %
60023 005	Stocks	price		–	74	–	–	1000. ±	–	DJ index	Wall St T	1/14/74	35596"	– %
60023 005	Stocks	price		–	74	74	–	792.	1200. ?	DJ index	Wall St T	12/17/73	35343"	– %
60023 005	Stocks	price		73d	74	74	900.	865.	1200. ?	DJ index	US News	11/19/73	98"	33.3%
60023 005	Stocks	price	(low)	73	74	75	788.	804.	950.	DJ index	UCLA 1974	3/21/74	T–1	9.8%
60023 005	Stocks	price	(high)	73	74	75	1052.	1050.	1100.	DJ index	UCLA 1974	3/21/74	T–1	2.3%
60023 005	Stocks	price		74a	75d	77d	975.	1190.	1500.	DJ index	Am Bank	12/ 3/73	15"	24.6%
60023 005	Stocks	funds from	capital & loan markets	72	73	74	10.2	9.	12.	bil $	UCB 1974	11/ /73	34	33.3%*
60023 005	Stocks	funds from	capital & loan markets	72	73	74	12.6	9.1	13.2	bil $	Bus Econ	1/ /74	60"	45.1%*
60023 005	Stocks	funds from	capital & loan markets	72	73	74	13.2	9.	19.	bil $	UCB 1974	11/ /73	34	★ %*
60023 005	Stocks	funds from	capital & loan markets	73	74	75	8.2	13.2	15.	bil $	Mfr Hanovr	2/ /74	15	35.3%
60023 005	Stocks	funds to	nonfinancial corporations	72	73	74	10.4	9.	13.	bil $	Wall St T	12/ 3/73	35198"	44.4%*
6010 BANKING INSTITUTIONS														
60100 004	Banking institutions	purchase of	transaction–oriented sys	–	–	76	–	–	200. +	mil $	Mod Data	11/ /73	29	– %
60100 004	Banking institutions	funds to	capital & loan markets	73	74	75	82.5	85.	89.	bil $	Mfr Hanovr	2/ /74	16	3.9%
60100 004	Banking institutions	funds to	capital & loan markets	73	74	–	100.	110.	–	index	Value Line	1/ 4/74	1903	10.0%
	Federal Reserve Banks													
60110 004	Federal Reserve Banks	funds to	capital & loan markets	72	73	74	.2	7.3	7.8	bil $	Bus Econ	1/ /74	60"	6.8%*
60110 004	Federal Reserve Banks	funds to	capital & loan markets	73	74	75	8.5	10.	9.	bil $	Mfr Hanovr	2/ /74	16	2.9%
	Commercial Banks													
60200 004	Commercial banks	expend for	computers & auxiliary eqp	73	74	–	100.	115.	–	index	EDP	3/27/74	5	15.0%
60200 004	Commercial banks	expend for	computer input devices	73	74	–	100.	119.	–	index	EDP	3/27/74	5	19.0%
60200 004	Commercial banks	expend for	data communications eqp	73	74	–	100.	160.	–	index	EDP	3/27/74	5	60.0%
60200 004	Commercial banks	employment		73	74	80	1138.	1172.	1380.	000 worker	US Outlook	10/ /73	357	2.8%
60200 004	Commercial banks	interest	(prime rate)	74a	74d	–	10.	7. –	–	% rate	Fin World	1/23/74	17	– %
60200 004	Commercial banks	interest	(prime rate)	73	74b	74d	9.75	8.	7.5	% rate	Am Bank	12/ 4/73	2"	−22.7%
60200 004	Commercial banks	interest	(prime rate)	–	74c	74d	–	11.5	7.5 ±	% rate	Outlook	6/24/74	706	– %
60200 004	Commercial banks	interest	(prime rate)	–	74d	–	–	8.5	–	% rate	Daily News	5/23/74	72"	– %
60200 004	Commercial banks	interest	(prime rate)	–	74d	–	–	8.75	–	% rate	Jrl Comm	3/13/74	11"	– %
60200 004	Commercial banks	interest	(prime rate)	74b	74d	–	7.5 ±	9.5 ±	–	% rate	Calif Bus	2/ 7/74	3	– %
60200 004	Commercial banks	interest	(prime rate)	73	74	–	8.01	7.34	–	% rate	Fed Richmd	3/ /74	15	−8.8%
60200 004	Commercial banks	deposits		73	74	75	100.	106.6	112.5 ±	index	Am Bank	2/15/74	59"	6.1%
60200 004	Commercial banks	liable for	demand deposits	73	74	80	288.	297.	379.	bil $	US Outlook	10/ /73	357	4.0%

SOURCE: From *Predicasts®: 1974 Annual Cumulative Edition* 56 (July 31, 1974): B-427. Copyright 1974 by Predicasts, Inc.

1964, the general price level rose at a modest annual rate of 1.6 percent per annum. After 1964, a sharp acceleration occurred; the annual growth rate reached a peak of 5.9 percent in 1969-1970, receded to about 3.3 percent in 1971-1972, then spurted ahead once more to attain "double-digit" levels, as the inflation rates of the mid-1970s have been popularly called.

Historically, investors have sought protection from inflation by acquiring real property, such as land, buildings, commodities, precious metals, and jewels. But these real assets are relatively illiquid, and in many cases do not provide any current return. Accordingly, in modern times, greater interest has centered on financial assets, particularly common stock. For this purpose, the degree to which common stock in general provides an offset to inflation may be distinguished from the effect of inflation on individual companies.

General effect of inflation on common stock. At one time, it was generally believed that common stocks afforded a good hedge against inflation, but evidence now emerging suggests that the relationship may be complex.[11] For example, during the 1939-1949 decade, which was dominated by World War II, consumer prices tended to rise more rapidly than stock values in most countries; stocks probably lagged, because of the adverse effect of wartime controls and taxes on corporate profits. During the following decades, from about 1950 to 1969, the relationship was reversed, as gains in stock values tended to outdistance the advances of consumer prices. In some countries, particularly the United States, the margins were substantial.

The total experience of 24 countries is portrayed in Figure 15-2 (only 13 of the countries are labeled), which shows the relationship between changes in consumer and stock prices for a long period ending in 1969. The 45-degree line separates those countries where stocks appreciated in real terms (above the line) from those where stocks depreciated in real terms (below the line). Wherever the annual inflation rate was below 5 percent, except for Denmark and Norway, the gains in stocks values were greater than the rises in consumer prices, but no distinct pattern seems evident. Wherever the inflation rate exceeded 5 percent, except for Austria and France, the gains in stock values were less than the rises in consumer prices, but there is a tendency for the two series to move upward together.

Several conclusions are suggested. Common stocks have not provided full hedges against rising consumer prices during periods of war and hyperinflation. Extensive consumer price rises, such as have occurred in various South American countries, are generally unhealthy because they create economic distortions and prevent both business firms and consumers from conducting normal activities. Stock prices can also be severely and adversely affected by inflation over the short run. This is particularly true when unemployment rises while inflation persists (a condition prevalent between 1971 and 1974 and sometimes called "stagflation"); much corporate gain in such a period represents unreliable inventory profits. When inflation is

FIGURE 15-2

Average Rates of Change of Stock Values and Consumer Prices, Pre-World War II to 1969

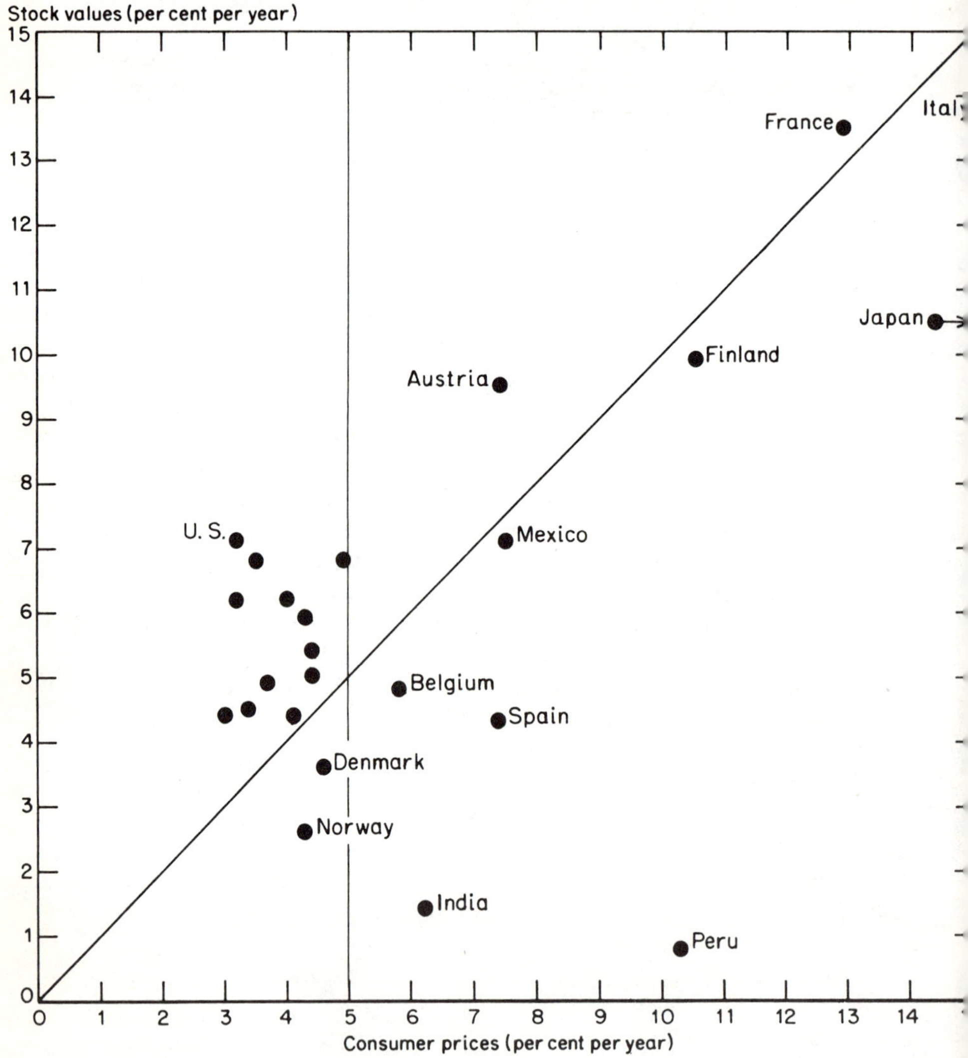

SOURCE: Phillip Cagan, "Common Stock Values and Inflation—The Historical Record of Many Companies," National Bureau of Economic Research Supplement to Report No. 13 (March 1974), p. 6. Copyright 1974 National Bureau of Economic Research. Reprinted by permission.

relatively moderate, stock prices appreciate in real terms; moreover, when lags do occur, apart from hyperinflation, common stock values eventually are likely to catch up with advances in commodity prices.

Effect of inflation on individual companies. Inflation rarely affects the prices of all goods evenly. The inflation may be worldwide or it may be confined to a single country. Whether prices respond to inflation depends, in part, on whether the good is traded on the world market or domestically only. How a particular company will be affected will depend on the proportions of its inputs and outputs that are subject to world market conditions.

The rampant inflation that characterized 1974 was marked by commodity shortages. Under such circumstances companies that had substantial raw material resources, such as mining operations or paper companies with their own timber lands, tended to benefit by price advances. In these circumstances, if no special governmental controls are imposed, such companies are likely to be able to raise the prices of the goods they produce faster than their operating costs increase. Conversely, companies that must constantly replenish their inventories may be harmed, because they may not be able to raise the prices of the goods they sell sufficiently to offset the rise in prices of the goods they buy. Gold producers are in a category of their own because of the special factors that affect the price of that metal. The traditional monetary role of gold creates a demand for gold, apart from its limited industrial and consumer uses, that is very difficult to assess.

Companies with substantial inventories may obtain a "one-shot" benefit from a sharp rise in the value of those inventories. If they do not have their own basic resources, however, this advantage disappears as the companies restock their inventories at higher prices. For example, in the first nine months of 1974, profits of the five biggest U.S. international oil companies leaped between 38 percent and 70 percent. Much of this gain, however, was caused by the price rises imposed by the Organization of Petroleum Exporting Countries (OPEC); these rises, in turn, triggered corresponding advances for the companies' big oil holdings in tanker firms and on tankers.[12] Subsequently, however, these companies' profits were adversely affected by rising costs.

In a number of enterprises, inflation may affect the prices of output and input uniformly. In these cases, the companies' reported earnings may be immediately benefited because depreciation charges, which are based on original rather than replacement values, tend to lag behind the growth of output and other costs. As inflation progresses, however, the relative benefit of the tax shelter provided by the depreciation is reduced. In the long run, therefore, the companies' cash flows will shrink, leading to possible reductions in dividends and the need to borrow at rising interest rates. If this condition is recognized by the market, the price/earnings ratios applied to the companies' stocks will fall and their market prices decline. These relationships may be simply demonstrated.

Without inflation a company's profits are

$$P = (1 - t)(S - CO - D),$$

where t = tax rate,
S = sales,
CO = cash outlays, and
D = depreciation.

The total cash flow (F) available for distribution to the stockholders is

$$F = (1 - t)(S - CO) + tD.$$

The first term on the right of the above expression, $(1 - t)(S - CO)$, exaggerates the tax bill because it does not take into account the effect of depreciation. Accordingly, the amount of the tax shelter, tD, provided by depreciation, must be added back. If the inflation rate is R, the inflated cash flow F' would be

$$F' = (1 - t)(1 + R)(S - CO) + tD.$$

This means that the cash flow increases by less than R.

$$\frac{F'}{F} = \frac{(1 - t)(1 + R)(S - CO) + tD}{(1 - t)(S - CO) + tD}.$$

F'/F would equal $(1 + R)$ only if depreciation increased at that rate. Furthermore, to the extent that depreciation is based on the original cost of the plant and equipment rather than on the current replacement cost, it is inadequate and profits are exaggerated. The net effect is that the tax rate paid by the company is implicitly increased.

Obviously, F'/F is greater than 1, so that if the investing public does not allow for inflation in its discount rate, the value of the stock will rise. However, if the discount rate is increased by the full amount R, the value of the stock will fall. There are two mitigating factors to this negative effect of inflation on cash flows. First, to the extent that a company uses accelerated depreciation, more of the tax dollars are saved at an early stage. Second, if the company's liabilities are greater than its financial assets, as is the case in about one-half the firms in the United States, it may be able to incur a gain by paying its debt in cheaper dollars.

In general, equities provide more protection against inflation than either cash or fixed-income securities, but the extent varies considerably with the type of company. To gauge the degree of protection afforded, therefore, the investor must analyze the differing effects that the price advance will have on the company's output of goods relative to its input of costs. In this analysis, it is important, as explained above, not to overlook the influence of depreciation.

Taxes

Taxation plays an important role in the investment field in various ways. It may affect the value of a security directly: the tax exemption of municipal bonds is an important influence on the price an investor is willing to pay for these securities. On the other hand, a low capital gains rate, a short required holding period, and allowed dividend credits enhance the attraction of equities. Taxation may also affect the value of a security indirectly, through its influence on earnings available for expansion and dividends; for example, the depletion allowance permitted mining and oil companies had an important influence on the companies' expenditure policies. The curtailment of those allowances in 1975 will force at least the large companies to find other sources of funds. Finally, taxation may have an effect on the overall economy; thus, generous investment credits may stimulate capital outlays by corporations and therefore provide a boost to the economy. In view of these circumstances, the investor must keep himself generally aware of the important tax areas and be alert for any possible changes that could have an influence on securities, companies, or the economy generally.

Then, too, the changes may apply to a particular type of company. As a case in point, the 1969 revisions to the Internal Revenue Code had considerable implications for the conglomerates. Among other things, these changes set a maximum of $5 million on the amount of interest that could be deducted for tax purposes on "acquisition indebtedness," defined as debentures meeting various criteria issued to effect an acquisition. In addition, marketable debt can no longer be used to effect an acquisition designed to capture the advantages of an installment sale. If marketable debt is used, the transaction is taxable in the year of the acquisition.

There are also complicated changes in the tax status of stock dividends. As a consequence the value of issuing the special types of securities that had been used for acquisitions in the past was reduced. All these changes meant that it would be more difficult for conglomerates like Litton and LTV to take advantage of such techniques to sustain their rate of growth. These companies would thus have run into trouble even if the economy and stock market had not behaved adversely.

Tax planning is an important phase of financial management. A good program can reduce a corporation's tax bill materially and improve its reported earnings per share. This influence is indicated in Table 15-1, which shows the impact of taxes on earnings of eight major drug companies. The difference between the growth rates of earnings per share in the first two columns reflects modifications effected, despite the fact that the basic federal statutory rate remained unchanged during the period covered. If it were not for a sharply reduced effective tax rate, for example, the growth in earnings per share of Abbott Laboratories would have been 1.2 percent rather than 7.4 percent.

As we have mentioned, the SEC now requires that companies show a reconciliation between reported taxes and those calculated at the statutory rate. The last three columns of the table measure the extent of these differences on the drug companies. In the case of Syntex, the tax differential amounts to $1.06 per share, equal to almost 70 percent of the company's 1973 earnings. Syntex has a contract with the Panamanian government which provides a very low tax rate on earnings brought into Panama from most other foreign countries. The principal sources of tax differentials for other companies are Puerto Rican tax exemptions and tax incentives in Ireland.

INDUSTRY CONSIDERATIONS

In determining the role of industry in the analytic process, various considerations are involved, including the nature of the industry and its life cycle.

Identifying the Industry

Traditional economics visualizes firms as profit-maximizing entities. Indiscriminate profit maximization, however, can result in the collection of unrelated activities, and some companies seem to have done just that. For example, Halliburton is best known as a leader in land-based oil services, but the company in 1973 had 21 divisions covering such other diverse areas as offshore drilling and power plant construction, insurance, pollution abatement, and diving services. Sometimes the unifying element is so broad as to be virtually meaningless. Thus, the activity of Rollins is confined to the service field. Its original business was radio and television broadcasting. In

TABLE 15-1

Earnings Growth Rates—Impact of Taxes on Earnings of Eight Major Drug Companies

	Earnings Per Share Growth Rate		1973 Tax Differentials**		
	1968–73 Earnings*	1968–73 Earnings Adj. to 1968 Tax Rate	Per Share	% of Rptd. Earnings Per Share	Millions
Ethical Companies					
Abbott Laboratories	7.4%	1.2%	$ .76	22.7%	$10.3
Eli Lilly	15.7	14.0	.34	15.0	23.4
Merck	12.9	9.9	.25	10.4	18.8
Schering-Plough	24.5(a)	18.6(a)	.27	13.7	14.4
G. D. Searle	14.1(b)	3.6(b)	.40	32.2	19.5
SmithKline	4.0	(3.5)	.83	23.4	12.3
Syntex (Jul.)	8.5	10.0	1.06	69.7	10.8
Upjohn	14.8	12.2	.14	6.0	4.3

*Includes pooled companies prior to year of pooling.

**The difference between taxes as reported and taxes at the U.S. Federal statutory rate of 48%.

(a) Growth rates for the 1969-73 period (results including Plough Inc. are not available for years prior to 1969).

(b) Growth rates for the 1969-73 period (results including Will Ross are not available for years prior to 1969).

SOURCE: Becker Securities Corporation, Investment Research Department, ***Basic Report: The Ethical Drug Industry***, August 19, 1974, p. 27. Reproduced with the permission of Becker Securities Corporation.

1964, however, it entered the pest control field with the acquisition of the largest business of this sort in the world; in 1965 it acquired a company engaged in janitorial services and maintenance; and in 1968 it moved into wall covering and decorating. In addition, Rollins is the fourth-largest outdoor advertising concern in the United States. Although, true enough, all these are service-related fields, it is somewhat difficult to detect a neat, unifying line that connects broadcasting, decorating, pest control, and outdoor advertising.

Another source of uncertainty regarding the long-term future of a company is the chance that it may completely abandon the industry it originally emphasized. As an illustration DWG, once called DWG Cigar, was long identified with the cigar business, but it sold this entire operation in 1968; today it is a holding company controlling enterprises that supply propane and butane gas, operate cold-storage facilities, and manufacture high-quality men's shirts and other furnishings. Such transformations often are hard to predict, and there may be little indication of change until news of negotiations emerge in the press. It probably is prudent, therefore, to avoid commitments in industries that are on the wane unless the analyst has considerable confidence in the adroitness of management to move into other areas and the stock's price adequately discounts the company's looming problems. On the other side of the coin, it may be feasible to detect companies that are ripe for take-overs, such as the cash-rich fire and casualty insurance companies during the 1960s.

We do not want to leave the impression that the abandonment by a company of a major industry line and the acquisition of a new one is as simple or quick as discarding old clothes and buying a new outfit. The metamorphosis of a company is likely to take place over a long time and involve the resolution of hard-fought policy decisions. In many instances, moreover, firms have more distinct profiles than can be achieved by random expansion, and it may still be possible to identify a diversified company with the primary industry or complex of industries in which it is engaged. For example, to broaden its original razor-blade concentration, Gillette has expanded into a general line of men's and women's toiletries and grooming aids. These product lines, which represent a common area, contributed 87 percent to profits in 1973. But, even here the signs point to a greater dilution of identity, since the company's products at home and abroad now include pens, personal leather goods, coffee makers, photoflash equipment, stereo hi-fi units, lighters, surgical equipment, and the Welcome Wagon community service business.

To the extent that an association can be made between an industry or group of industries and the firm under consideration, the analyst must take it into account, for over the long run the fate of the firm and the industry hangs together. Toward this end, the regulatory provisions that multi-industry firms supply breakdowns of revenues and earnings by major product lines is helpful. A major current difficulty with this requirement is that companies sometimes define product lines so loosely as to significantly reduce the usefulness of the data provided. Moreover, comparable cost breakdowns may be difficult to furnish. Reporting this information, however, is a step in the right direction, and more comprehensive data along these lines will be developed over the years. It is logical, therefore, in an evaluation of a company, to take as a starting point a determination of the industry or industries in which that company is primarily engaged; if the range is very broad, the analyst may then concentrate on those industries providing the bulk of revenues. If a company has not already provided the information in its annual report, the best publicly available alternative source of this information is the company's 10-K report.

Industrial Life Cycle

It is traditional to view an industry as passing through a life cycle. In its early pioneering stage, the industry grows rapidly for some period of time; the length of the span may vary considerably, depending upon the products handled. Eventually, a stage of maturity is reached and the rate of growth begins to diminish, as competing industries erode its market. A final stage of stabilization and then decline ensues, as the industry's problems increase and its rate of customer losses accelerates. The railroads are a classic illustration of an industry that has moved through these stages: swift growth in the second half of the nineteenth century, as the country's expansion virtually rode on the rails; a period of stabilization during the first part of the twentieth century; and the current decline, as competition from trucks, pipelines, and airplanes continues to eat into the once flourishing railroad market.

Life cycles, however, are not carved in granite. The stages often are not clearly marked; rates of change may rise or fall within a stage, or a receding industry may become rejuvenated and resume its period of growth. Despite its long history, the automotive industry has been able to fuel its constant expansion (although individual companies have died) by encouraging customers to turn over models and by moving into markets abroad. The chemical industry has taken new leases on life by its ability to develop new products that cater to the needs of consumers. There are so many instances of modifications in this "typical" life cycle that the concept can only be used as a background consideration. People must die, but there is no necessary terminal point to the life of an industry or of a company within it. The analyst simply starts with his judgment as to the industry's present stage of development based on its prior history; he then must evaluate all the relevant factors to determine the likelihood of the industry's continuing in its present phase, passing into a new one, or departing from the traditional pattern.

Factors Affecting Industry Development

Basic to a forecast of the future of an industry is an evaluation of its market. Here an important distinction may be made between direct demand and derivative demand. The automotive industry, for example, depends largely on direct purchases by the public, whereas the demand for steel from the steel industry derives from the market demand for automobiles and other products made of steel.

The direct market of an industry is related to the consuming population; sales potential varies with that population's size, character, and purchasing power. For example, there is a close correlation between consumption of liquor in the United States and the following factors: (1) the U.S. adult population, representing the size of the market; (2) the constituent age groups, representing the character of the market; and (3) discretionary income, representing its purchasing power. Any forecast of demand in the liquor industry, therefore, depends on a study of these elements. Based on changes in the U.S. population and the drinking proclivities of the different age categories, it is estimated that the number of persons drinking distilled spirits rose at an annual rate of 1.3 percent between 1960 and 1965 and 1.6 percent between 1966 and 1970.[13] While these percentages are small, they have a big influence on the actual amount of liquor consumed. Translating these changes in the drinking population into actual consumption, we find that consumption of distilled spirits in the United States during the decade of the 1960s grew by 5 to 6 percent annually. A retardation to a 2 to 3 percent rate of increase occurred in 1970 and 1971, reflecting a recessionary tendency, unemployment, higher taxes, and inflation; during the next three years it is estimated that consumption growth continued at less than 3 percent per year.

Within the framework of these changes, there has been a decided shift in the tastes of the U.S. drinking public. While "straights" and "blends" still constitute the largest segment of the market, their overall percentage has declined sharply during the past decade. On the other hand, substantial increases have been registered in the percentage of the market captured by Scotch, Canadians, vodka, and cordials, while gin's percentage has gained moderately. This trend toward "white" liquors and cordials is attributable to the growing importance of younger drinkers and of women. The younger drinkers, who have more diversified tastes than their parents, are inclined (as are women generally) toward sweeter drinks and light, mixable liquors like vodka. These factors typically are taken into account by analysts specializing in the industry. It is generally expected that gains in liquor consumption will occur as the economy expands, changes in the population mix result in a higher proportion of drinkers, people have more leisure time, and there is an increasingly permissive attitude toward drinking. The changing population mix and growing importance of women as drinkers, it is also believed, will continue the movement toward "whites" and cordials. Scotch and Canadians, particularly in bulk shipments, are also expected to show good growth, in part because of certain relative tax benefits given to bulk shipments. These factors also must be considered by the analyst.

To a significant degree, a major factor overshadowing forecasts at present is the uncertainty of foreign markets. As the technical efficiency and living standards of foreign populations improve, they may become an increasingly important market for the products of U.S. firms. Indeed, by the 1970s, foreign operations were contributing more than domestic operations to the income of a number of U.S. multinational companies. Forecasting a domestic market is hard enough, but forecasting the foreign market is even more difficult, because it means assessing areas of the world with which the U.S. analyst is unlikely to be familiar, as well as taking into account the influence of foreign taxes, currency restrictions, and international money markets. Even an industry specialist in most instances will have to concentrate on the relatively few major geographic areas to which his firm sells. He may gain his awareness of trends in economic conditions and financial restrictions from specialists in the international area of the firm, from financial institutions, or from published sources dealing with the foreign scene, such as bank letters.

Any industry is likely to have special problems, peculiar to its own development, which may burst forth at any time with serious repercussions for the operations of companies within its scope. In the period following World War II, for example, aluminum emerged as the wunderkind among metals. Demand rose swiftly, and companies embarked upon a program of robust expansion. Eventually, however, the demand slackened, as competition from other metals became stronger. Accordingly, during periods of general economic decline, companies in the industry found it necessary to cut back production. The unused capacity exerted a consequent downward pressure on prices and an upward pressure on costs, which had to be allocated over a lower output. At the extreme point of the 1970 economic recession (coinciding with a worldwide oversupply in aluminum) Reynolds Metals cut back primary aluminum production to 70 percent of capacity. The situation began to ease in 1972, but the supply-demand gap did not narrow enough to have a significant effect on price. Reflecting the interplay of these factors, the sales of Reynolds Metals continued to grow moderately during this period, but the company's ratio of net income to sales and its return on shareholders' equity experienced precipitous drops in both 1971 and 1972.[14]

The typical investor is not likely to be familiar with the technical factors influencing an industry. Nevertheless, if he does his own analysis, he should have some awareness of prevailing conditions and trends, so that he can relate them to the companies he is studying. In general, he can probably gain adequate insight into an industry by examining the industry reports of major research firms, such as Standard & Poor's, the studies issued by reputable brokerage firms, and trade journals.

Industry Approach to Analysis

One effect of the capital asset pricing model has been to shift attention in some quarters from the analysis of individual stocks to that of industries. Since selection of stocks to outperform the market has become increasingly difficult, some analysts have reasoned that better results could be obtained by seeking to identify whole industries that would respond favorably to changing economic and political conditions.

The point of departure in this approach is to break down a standard market index into its major industrial components. Investors' portfolios are divided into similar industrial categories. If the portfolio manager is uncertain of the market outlook, he "retreats into the market portfolio" by maintaining the same industrial breakdown as the index. He then shifts the percentages within the portfolio by judging which industries are likely to be benefited or hurt by changing economic and political conditions.

Table 15-2 summarizes the industry breakdown of the Standard & Poor's 500 stock index on December 31, 1974. The figure shows only the major groups, but actually over 80 different industrial categories are available.

TABLE 15-2

Industrial Breakdown of Standard & Poor's 500 Stock Index, December 31, 1974

	PERCENT OF MARKET VALUE
Credit sensitive	6.0
Consumer cyclicals	9.6
Consumer staples	7.0
Growth	24.7
Intermediate goods and services	26.6
Capital goods	7.9
Special situations	–
Foreign securities	–
Unclassified	18.2
Total	100.0

Depending on the size of the portfolio handled and the degree of diversification desired, the manager could choose how detailed the breakdown should be. For example, his comparison base might be the major categories of "credit sensitive," "consumer cyclicals," "consumer staples," and so forth. Or, within the "credit sensitive" area, he might distinguish between "housing" and "finance." Finally, he could provide a breakdown of the "housing" category into such components as "forest products," "building materials," "air conditioning," etc. (breakdowns provided by Oppenheimer Management Corp.).

This approach is not likely to produce dramatic results, since it leads to outcomes resembling those of the general market. Presumably, however, in the long run the portfolios should do better, because of the manager's judgment in arranging the industrial components and his ability to have "cash" as a component (absent in the market index). Extra benefits may accrue from the portfolio manager's specific stock selections.

FORECASTING COMPANY PERFORMANCE

After his investigation of the industry and its prospects, the investor is ready to proceed with an analysis of the company. His first step might be to obtain the company's annual reports for the past half dozen years. To a large extent, these documents now follow a common pattern, but within this uniform framework there are considerable variations in detail, accuracy, and language; these reflect the character of the company. (We have already noted that the grandiose reports of Litton prior to its debacle might have made an alert investor wonder about the image the company was trying to create.) The investor will check the statements, signed by the president or chairman of the board, from year to year to determine the accuracy of the forecasts, the degree to which problems are honestly set forth, and whether the officer tends to be forthright, boastful, or pessimistic. He will also examine management's discussion of its past operations in order to assess the adequacy of the explanations of prior problems. (See pp. 149-155 for a discussion of annual reports.) The description of products is helpful in understanding the company's operations. References to community affairs and employee services throw light on management's interest in social issues, which, in turn, at least suggests management's reaction to current developments. The financial analysis that is usually provided may indicate whether management is willing to portray the company's condition fairly.

Having gained some familiarity with the company and its products, the investor is ready to study its accounting policies in order to assess the quality of the company's earnings. As described previously, he will pay particular attention to the footnotes, auditor's statement, and the handling of sensitive areas such as depreciation and capitalization. It is desirable that he check the

10-Ks to determine whether there is additional significant information not included in the annual reports. As a result of this analysis, he may want to make some adjustments in the reported figures, or he may use the findings to help reach an appropriate price/earnings ratio for the company's stock.

This investigation is an important preliminary to an analysis of the major items in the company's financial statements, leading to an earnings forecast. When a professional analyst makes a careful study of a company she very likely will supplement her review of published data by a visit to the company's plant and a discussion with its principal officers. In view of SEC Rule 10b-5, which seeks to prevent the use of inside information by a privileged group to obtain market gains, companies now are cautious about revealing statistics that are not also disclosed to the public. Still, much can be learned through direct visits, which can provide the analyst with a better understanding of the company's plant, operation, products, and general management than she can obtain by just reading about them. The typical investor, however, will not be in a position to obtain direct access to the company, and his analysis will be largely confined to the published material. The major items of the income statement that enter into a forecast of earnings are sales, operating income, and net income.

Sales

A company's sales may be forecast either as a share of the market or directly. Most investors will find it difficult to use the market-share approach because ordinarily they do not have access to the requisite information. The typical point of departure is a tabulation over a period of time of industry sales and the portion of them absorbed by the company. If the company's portion has been stable, the average of the past five years might prove a reasonable forecast of the following year's results. If there is a trend, an appropriate upward or downward adjustment will have to be made. If there are any unusually large deviations from the average in the prior years, something peculiar may have occurred. Accordingly, the observation probably should be dropped from the calculation, and the market share recalculated.

The market-share method requires highly reliable data on both the industry and the company because a mistake in either set of figures could materially affect the results. Thus, if the forecast of company sales seems out of line, the error may lie in the forecast of either the industry or the company share of the market. To review the industry forecast, the analyst may check the trade journals once more and seek explanations from specialists in the area. In reviewing changes in the company's market share, data concerning competitors in the field will be particularly useful, since they will help the analyst gauge the appropriateness of the company forecast.

The market share of a company may depend on special factors. A small firm, for example, may pick up a lot of business when the economy is booming because large enterprises are working near capacity at that time. In these circumstances, the statistically inclined analyst might then make a forecast by regressing the sales of the company against the sales of the industry and the gross national product. An additional variable might be the ratio of industry sales to industry fixed capital. If such procedures are used, however, the analyst must remember that these calculations are primarily props. The determination of market share cannot be done on a mechanical basis; an understanding of what is happening in the industry and company is crucial. A change in management, for example, can substantially alter past relationships.

In the direct method of estimating sales, less reliance is placed upon industry benchmarks. This information, as well as market shares, still may be considered, but primarily as qualitative factors to place some limits on the direct sales forecasts. The direct approach may be used when accurate market-share information is not available, when the company is so diversified as to render the determination of separate market shares impracticable, or when internal conditions within the industry appear sufficiently stable to render unnecessary the added data. In the direct method, particular attention is given to the record of prior sales and the likelihood of any special developments occurring that could modify prior trends. An approach to forecasting operating income and net income is indicated in the Scott paper illustration below.

A FORECASTING ILLUSTRATION: SCOTT PAPER

Let us illustrate this forecasting technique by looking closely at Scott Paper, one of the world's leading companies engaged in the production of such paper items for consumers as toilet tissue, paper towels, wax paper, facial tissues, and sanitary napkins. Competition is keen and comes in part from companies outside the traditional paper field, such as Procter & Gamble. Scott has been aggressive abroad, and overseas sales have offset flagging domestic output at times. Because of the difficulty of defining the industry, the variety of products involved, and the uncertainty of the foreign markets, in 1971 Scott's sales were forecast by the direct method.

In the decade prior to 1971, the company's sales experienced mixed results. Between 1961 and 1964 the average annual rate of growth was about 5 percent. The rate jumped to almost 20 percent in 1965, fell back to about

6.5 percent in 1966, and then spurted to almost 27 percent in 1967. Growth was maintained in the 8 percent range in 1968 and 1969, but slumped to only 3.3 percent in 1970. In the absence of a market trend, 1971 rates were estimated in two ways: (1) by assuming that growth would be the same as that of the prior year, and (2) by assuming that growth would equal the average of the past five years. The forecast of a reputable service, Value Line, was also obtained. To show the difficulty of reaching accurate final net income results, the actual sales for 1971, which of course are now known, are also employed as a starting base (method I). These four methods are summarized as follows:

I. $\text{Est. sales}_{1971} = \text{Actual sales}_{1971}.$

II. $\text{Est. sales}_{1971} = \text{Sales}_{1970} \times \dfrac{\text{Sales 1970}}{\text{Sales 1969}}.$

III. Est. sales_{1971}

$$= \text{Sales}_{1970} \times 1/5 \left(\frac{\text{Sales 1970}}{\text{Sales 1969}} + \frac{\text{Sales 1969}}{\text{Sales 1968}} + \frac{\text{Sales 1968}}{\text{Sales 1967}} + \frac{\text{Sales 1967}}{\text{Sales 1966}} + \frac{\text{Sales 1966}}{\text{Sales 1965}}\right).$$

IV. Est. sales_{1971} = Value Line prediction, February 19, 1971.

All these estimates indicate the hazards of forecasting because, in fact, sales declined in 1971. From her perch in 1971, the analyst might well have surmised that the competitive difficulties of the company would continue and that the retardation in its rate of growth would be extended. It is unlikely, however, that she would have been able to foresee the shrinkage that actually was realized, because this represented a reversal of a long-term series of persistent gains. Estimate II, therefore, which simply repeated the modest growth of 1970, was the closest of those used to the actual outcome (except, of course, for method I, the actual 1971 sales).

FINPLAN, a corporate planning model, was used to transform these sales projections into the pro forma income statements in Table 15-3. The more important assumptions used in effecting this transformation are discussed below. The resulting figures in the table reflect the financing requirements of the company as well as its operating ratios.

Operating Income

Operating income is derived by deducting operating costs from sales. Typically, industrial companies report cost of goods sold, depreciation, and

TABLE 15-3

Comparison of Pro Forma Income Statements for Scott Paper for 1971 with Operating Results (000,000 omitted)

		I	II	III	IV
	ACTUAL OPERATING RESULTS	SALES ACCURATELY FORECAST	SALES RISE BY 1970 GROWTH RATE	SALES RISE BY AVERAGE 5-YEAR GROWTH RATE	SALES REPRESENT VALUE LINE PREDICTION
Sales	$746.66	$746.66	$780.74	$836.36	$800.01
Operating income	45.71	86.09[a]	90.02[a]	118.09[b]	112.96[b]
Interest expense	16.86	15.48	16.39	17.87	16.90
Income before taxes	28.85	70.61	73.63	100.22	96.06
Taxes	9.84	28.59	29.81	40.58	38.89
Net income from operations	19.01	42.02	43.82	59.64	57.17
Income from affiliates	7.36	7.90	7.90	7.90	7.90
Net income	26.38	49.92	51.71	67.54	65.06
Preferred dividends	.25	.25	.25	.25	.25
Available for common	26.12	49.66	51.46	67.28	64.81
Common dividends	30.22	32.78	33.96	44.41	42.77
Shares outstanding	34.55	34.14	35.01	35.95	35.24
Earnings per share	.76	1.45	1.47	1.87	1.84
Price per share with p/e ratio = 18.81[c]	14.30[d]	27.27	27.65	35.17	34.61

[a]Using same ratio as prevailed in 1970.

[b]Using average ratio of preceding 5 years.

[c]See p. 374.

[d]Average annual p/e ratio for 1971 was 27.9, giving a price of $21.20.

NOTE: FINPLAN, a corporate planning model, was used to transform the sales projections into the pro forma income statements.

selling and administrative expenses; other important items, such as the amounts spent on wages and on research, may also be shown. The extent to which the analyst forecasts each of these items separately will depend on how she assesses the figures and how much effort she wants to expend. The typical investor will find it difficult to analyze the interplay of the different costs involved. Ordinarily, therefore, he is likely to determine a ratio of operating income to sales by studying past relationships and to apply this ratio to his forecast of sales.

In the case of Scott Paper, the company's historic operating margin was quite steady, and therefore it was not considered necessary to employ a refined breakdown. The declining sales of the company had caused a curtailment of production during the second half of 1970, leading to excess capacity and an increase in unit costs. By 1971, however, it was expected that this condition would be ameliorated. Accordingly, it seemed reasonable to assume that the 1970 ratio of operating income to sales would prevail in 1971 or, if the company was particularly successful in controlling costs, that the ratio might actually improve to a level approaching the average of the prior five years. In Table 15-3 the 1970 ratio is applied to statement I (sales accurately forecast) and statement II (1970 growth repeated); the average ratio is applied to statement III (five-year average sales growth) and statement IV (Value Line sales prediction).

Net Income

Net income before taxes ordinarily varies from operating income because of the influence of financial items. On the revenue side, the most characteristic item is the interest that is earned on invested funds. Ordinarily this amount is not very large; a company prefers to have its money at work in its own operations, and if it has excess funds, they are likely to be placed in the short-term money market where returns historically have been low (the recent period is a conspicuous exception). Interest expense depends on the company's short- and long-term borrowings both in the United States and abroad; in certain cases this is an important amount. Scott Paper has relied upon external financing, and its interest expense is therefore relatively high. Because no significant plant expansion was in sight, however, the company debt was expected to remain substantially unchanged over the near term. Interest costs in 1971 were expected to run at about the same order of magnitude as in 1970, varying somewhat with sales because of short-term borrowing.

Taxes depend on both the tax rates in force and the company's ability to take advantage of allowable deductibles. Over the past five years, Scott was able to keep effective tax rate between 41 and 44 percent. In 1970 the rate was about 41 percent, and it was not expected that the rate for 1971 would be much different.

A company may elect to exclude the earnings of affiliated companies from its consolidated statements for various reasons, such as the existence of restrictions on the distribution of these earnings or a desire to keep operations as independent as possible. The equity method of accounting now requires the consolidated statement to reflect the parent's share in the income of its affiliates. Scott's interest in these earnings of its affiliated companies is relatively large, but no change in the 1970 level was expected in 1971. There was no reason to expect a halt in the distribution of preferred dividends, and the company's capitalization was likely to remain substantially the same.

The net result of these various forecasts for Scott Paper are shown in Table 15-3. Although the sales forecasts in Statements II and III differ by only 7 percent, the final forecasts of net earnings per share differ by 27 percent. This divergence indicates the considerable difficulty of tying together both revenue and cost changes. For comparative purposes, the actual results for 1971 are also shown. Not only did sales decline, but the company's ratio of operating income to sales also fell from 11.5 percent in 1970 to only 6.4 percent in 1971, because Scott was not able to maintain the expected control over costs. As a result, actual earnings per share amounted to 76 cents, compared with the $1.45 estimated in statement I, even though the starting sales figure was the same as that actually reported.

In the case of Scott Paper, the 1971 actual earnings per share were only about half the best estimate made a year previously. This is a bigger discrepancy than ordinarily might be expected from a forecast. The reason is attributable to the two major depressing changes: sales declined and relative costs rose. As 1970 progressed, these were inklings of problems that emerged in 1971; for example, in the fourth quarter of 1970, net income was 38 percent below that for the same period in 1969. It is clearly important for the forecaster not to rest content with her figures. Rather, she must follow the affairs of the company closely so long as she is interested in it, revising her figures as new information is obtained.

FORECASTING EARNINGS DIRECTLY

Most companies with actively traded securities show in their annual reports a record of earnings per share over the past five to ten years, adjusted for stock splits and dividends; the major statistical organizations show this same information in their different services. The analyst may use this historic record to make a forecast directly. Her purpose may be to supplement a more elaborate forecast made along the lines previously described; if there is a sharp divergence, she may then want to review her basic analysis to learn the reason. By direct forecasting she can highlight special factors of revenue or costs that caused the earnings per share to depart from normal patterns.

In this sense, the direct calculation is a simple and easily applied final check of the results of a more thorough study previously undertaken. Or the direct calculation may be employed beforehand, as a screening device to ferret out those companies whose earnings appear to be moving upward and therefore warrant more careful investigation.

It must be emphasized that no single forecasting method has been found very accurate.[15] Our own inclination, therefore, is to rely primarily on the basic analysis and to employ the direct forecast of earnings per share as a check or filter, as suggested above.

As would be expected, the direct methods are largely mechanistic. They involve making the prediction primarily on the basis of some combination of prior earnings, or by fitting a trend line to a time series of prior earnings. Within each of these approaches, many different techniques may be employed. We illustrate some of them below.

Predicting on the Basis of a Combination of Prior Earnings

In this approach, the analyst examines the past record and selects that projection of prior earnings which appears most reasonable to her. If the record is very stable, she may simply assume that earnings per share will not change over the coming year. If there is growth, she may assume that, depending upon the detected pattern, the rate of gain in the following year will be equal to that of the prior year or period of years. Several typical assumptions of this sort are listed below:

(1) Earnings will not change: $E_t = E_{t-1}$.

(2) The increment in year t will equal the increment in $t - 1$:

$$E_t = E_{t-1} + (E_{t-1} - E_{t-2}).$$

(3) The rate of growth in year t will equal the rate of growth in $t - 1$:

$$E_t = E_{t-1}\,(E_{t-1}/E_{t-2}).$$

(4) The rate of growth in year t will equal the geometric average of the rates of growth in the preceding five years:

$$E_t = E_{t-1}\,(E_{t-1}/E_{t-6})^{1/5}.$$

The results of using these assumptions to forecast the 1971 earnings of Scott Paper and four other companies arbitrarily selected are shown in the upper half of Table 15-4; in the upper half of Table 15-4a the forecast is shown as a percentage of the actual earnings per share.

In the case of Scott Paper, all the direct methods that utilize some combinations of prior earnings provide outcomes closer to 1971 actual earnings than those derived by the more elaborate forecast. The differences are not large, however, and the better performance achieved by the direct methods is caused by the implicit assumption underlying the basic analyses that the company would be able to correct its deteriorating position. In fact, this did not happen, and the company's earnings reeled under the combined pressures of shrinking sales and rising costs. Neither the direct nor the basic methods revealed this condition. The lower results of the direct methods, however, might have encouraged the analyst to use conservative assumptions in her basic procedures.

The erratic results of the different methods for Interstate Stores indicate that the company was in ferment, which made an accurate forecast difficult. On the other hand, the relatively consistent and reasonably close projections of Acme, du Pont, and Philadelphia Electric suggest that those companies were not experiencing major operating changes during that period.

Predicting on the Basis of Time-Series Analysis

Time-series models are based on the assumption that earnings will extend into the future along the same trend revealed in the past. Accordingly, the analyst fits various trend lines to the prior record of earnings, selects the one that provides the best fit, and obtains a forecast by projecting the trend to the future year. Typical models of this sort are summarized below:

(5) Earnings are a linear function of time: $E_t = a + bt$
(6) Earnings are an exponential function of time: $E_t = ae^{bt}$
(7) Earnings are a function of some power of time: $E_t = at^b$
(8) Earnings are a function of the reciprocal of time: $E_t = a + (b/t)$
(9) Earnings are a function of the reciprocal of a linear function of time:

$$E_t = 1/(a + bt) \text{ or } E_t = t/(a + bt).$$

The results obtained by fitting these curves to the past earnings of the selected companies are shown in the lower half of Table 15-4; the ratios of the projected earnings to those subsequently reported are shown in the lower half of Table 15-4a. As would be expected, these direct methods err by substantial margins in the cases of Interstate Stores and Scott Paper; they are

TABLE 15-4

Earnings Per Share Forecast for Selected Companies, 1971

FORECASTING METHOD	ACME*	DU PONT	INTERSTATE STORES	PHILADELPHIA ELECTRIC	SCOTT PAPER
Actual	4.39	7.14†	.11	2.10	.76
Based on prior rates of change					
$E_t = E_{t-1}$	3.69	6.76	.25	1.84	1.42
$E_t = E_{t-1} + (E_{t-1} - E_{t-2})$	4.12	6.17	−1.20	1.71	1.12
$E_t = E_{t-1} (E_{t-1}/E_{t-2})$	4.18	6.22	.04	1.72	1.17
$E_t = E_{t-1} (E_{t-1}/E_{t-6})^{1/5}$	3.66	6.44	.17	1.81	1.37
Based on trend					
$E_t = a + bt$	2.93	7.73	1.82	2.15	1.66
$E_t = ae^{bt}$	2.92	7.75	1.32	2.17	1.72
$E_t = at^b$	3.10	7.79	1.50	2.09	1.62
$E_t = a + (b/t)$	3.31	8.00	1.69	2.09	1.56
$E_t = 1/(a + bt)$	2.91	7.79	.66	2.20	1.68
$E_t = t/(a + bt)$	3.23	7.62	.99	1.99	1.56

*Adjusted for stock dividend issues up to and including 1971 fiscal year. Acme was renamed American Stores in December 1973.

†Adjusted. In 1971 the equity method for accounting for investment in affiliated companies not consolidated was adopted. As a result, earnings were increased in all years. The 1971 reported earnings were reduced by the ratio of the aggregate earnings per share for 1965-1970 before the accounting change to the aggregate for the same period after the accounting change.

TABLE 15-4a

Earnings Forecast as a Percentage of Actual for Selected Companies, 1971

FORECASTING METHOD	ACME	DU PONT	INTERSTATE STORES	PHILADELPHIA ELECTRIC	SCOTT PAPER	AVERAGE OF RATIOS
Based on prior rates of change						
$E_t = E_{t-1}$	.84	.95	2.27	.88	1.87	1.36
$E_t = E_{t-1} + (E_{t-1} - E_{t-2})$	.94	.86	−10.91*	.81	1.47	1.02
$E_t = E_{t-1}(E_{t-1}/E_{t-2})$	.95	.87	.36	.82	1.54	.91
$E_t = E_{t-1}(E_{t-1}/E_{t-6})^{1/5}$	.83	.90	1.55	.86	1.80	1.19
Based on trend						
$E_t = a + bt$	.67	1.08	16.55	1.02	2.18	4.30
$E_t = ae^{bt}$	.67	1.09	12.00	1.03	2.26	3.41
$E_t = at^b$	.71	1.09	13.64	1.00	2.13	3.71
$E_t = a + (b/t)$	.75	1.12	15.37	1.00	2.05	4.06
$E_t = 1/(a + bt)$	.66	1.09	6.00	1.05	2.21	2.20
$E_t = t/(a + bt)$	.74	1.07	9.00	.95	2.05	2.76
Column average of ratios	.78	1.01	8.52	.94	1.96	

*Not included in the computation of averages.

moderately off the actual earnings of Acme; and they provide rather good projections for du Pont and Philadelphia Electric.

In showing these different direct methods, we do not mean to imply that the analyst should use all of them either to screen companies or to supplement a basic analysis. The accuracy of the direct methods depends upon the pattern of earnings to which they are applied. An appropriate approach would be for the analyst to examine this pattern and then select the method or several methods that seem most logical. If one has access to a computer, their application is easy, since simple programs are available.

PUBLISHED FORECASTS OF EARNINGS

The various statistical services characteristically issue forecasts of earnings for major companies, while brokerage houses with research staffs make forecasts for the firms in which they are interested. A professional analyst undertaking his own investigation probably will want to examine some of these forecasts to see how they compare with his own, while an investor may have to rely on published forecasts to a much greater extent.

To control their financial activities, most business firms with actively traded securities use budgetary procedures that terminate in an earnings forecast. Not uncommonly, professional analysts employed by large institutions have been able to gain access to these forecasts through interviews with company officials or in talks given by them at closed meetings. This practice has declined because of SEC Rule 10b-5, which has made corporate officials hesitant about furnishing forecasts to analysts without at the same time making them available to the public.

Moving further in the direction of equalized disclosure, the SEC has veered sharply from its traditional ban on the inclusion of earnings forecasts in corporate statements filed with the commission. It has proposed that companies meeting certain standards be permitted to include forecasts of at least relevant net income in SEC filings; moreover, if they give or confirm forecasts to outsiders, the information would have to be made available to the public immediately and included in the company's filings. The commission proposed a so-called safe harbor rule whereby, under specified circumstances, a projection would not be considered untrue or misleading.

A major problem in this area is distinguishing between companies which make a genuine effort to forecast accurately but miss the mark by a wide margin and those which deliberately issue misleading forecasts. It is likely that considerable experience will have to be gained in this area before suitable guidelines can be worked out. As we have indicated, forecasting is an uncertain art under any circumstances.[16]

Corporations that make earnings projections for their internal use have found that the actual results often are substantially different. Accordingly, if corporations in the future follow a widespread policy of announcing projections publicly and reporting them in SEC statements, this information will be just one more tool available to the analyst. There is no assurance that the forecasts will prove accurate. The analyst will still have the responsibility of developing independent calculations to provide a check on corporate estimates. The forecasts probably will be of more use to the individual investor, who does not have access to this type of information now, but he, too, will hardly be able to relax his prior standards of investigation. As long as everyone has access to similar information, the more insightful analyst or investor is likely to win out in the long run. To provide a guideline for companies deciding to make financial forecasts, the FASB Accounting Standards Decision has issued a uniform set of procedures.

SUMMARY

Of the thousands of stocks that are actively traded, an analyst is only in a position to investigate a relatively small number with any care. To identify these issues, the analyst may screen the large body of securities through so-called filters, which may be based on the needs of the investor or the characteristics of the stock. But a broad-gauged filter cannot substitute for individual alertness in discovering companies with special attributes (such as a new product) or special cost advantages.

Having selected the stocks that appear potentially attractive, the analyst will initiate an analysis of particular companies by seeking to forecast the future amount of their earnings, which is likely to be a determining factor in the evaluation of their stock. In considering these earnings, the analyst considers long-term developments but primarily focuses on an estimate for the following year. To reach this estimate, the general economy, the industry, and the company must all be judged.

The fortunes of business firms depend on the economic environment in which they operate. To help anticipate the business trend, various statistical devices have been developed; these include expectations series, leading cyclical indicators, and elaborate econometric models.

Inflation has been a persistent economic consideration. In general, common stocks have not provided full hedges against rising consumer prices during periods of war and hyperinflation. When inflation has been relatively moderate, however, stock prices have appreciated in real terms; moreover, when lags have occurred (apart from hyperinflation), common stock values have usually caught up with advances in commodity prices. With respect to individual companies, those with substantial raw material resources tend to benefit by price advances. Conversely, companies that must constantly replenish their inventories may be harmed because they may not be able to raise the prices of the goods they sell fast enough to offset the rise in prices of the goods they buy.

Taxation is another important economic consideration which influences the earnings a company has available for expansion and dividends. The ability of a company to reduce its tax bite is one reflection of the acumen of its management.

Increasingly, firms have been diversifying into different fields of activity. Accordingly, in studying a particular company, the analyst first has to ascertain the contribution of its various lines of business; then, the analyst must investigate the outlook of the major industries in which it operates. For this purpose, he will check into such factors as the industry's life cycle, the market for its products, and any special problems that may exist. One effect of the capital asset pricing model has been to augment the attention given to the identification of industries that will respond favorably to changing economic and political conditions.

After completing an investigation of the industry and its prospects, the investor is ready to proceed with an analysis of the company. For this purpose, he must become familiar with its products and accounting policies and must analyze its financial statements. He will then use this information to project the major items of the income statement that enter the forecast of earnings. As a supplement to this approach, he may extrapolate earnings directly through various statistical methods. If the results are sharply different from his basic forecast, he may want to review his original analysis to ascertain the reason.

CHAPTER 16

Stock Appraisal: Forecasting Price and Dividends

In the world of theory, rational investors, all with equal access to information, competing in an efficient market, exit from stocks that are overpriced. As a result, prices are kept in line with earnings, and the current price of a stock is the best reflection of available information. In these circumstances, a primary role of securities analysis is to identify risk-return characteristics of securities; money managers then put together portfolios whose returns are simply dependent on the risk-return characteristics of the stocks held. In such a market, the effort to discover undervalued or overvalued issues is fruitless.

In the real world, things do not happen that way. For one thing, the theory does not prevent the appearance of exceptions; investors still misgauge future earnings, dividends, and discount rates. Then again, a stock may be in or out of market favor for psychological rather than economic reasons. Invariably, there are analysts who detect out-of-line cases and make wise decisions by buying or selling the stock before changing circumstances cause large bodies of investors to drive the price up or down. It is the mark of a good analyst that he is right more often than wrong in detecting these out-of-line issues. No analyst can expect to be always right. It is clear that without differences of opinion there would be no market, since all analysts would be recommending purchase or sale of the same stocks at the same time.

There is evidence of analytic foresight in the selection of specific stocks. Investors who recognized the future of the computer, photocopying machines, or "instant" photography at an early stage achieved large profits by purchasing stocks of IBM, Xerox, or Polaroid at very low prices when these corporations were developing. It is easy to dismiss these illustrations as hindsight, but the fact is that some of the investors who bought the securities before their substantial advances did anticipate these developments. On the other hand, serious losses have been avoided by investors who sold stocks that others still favored. Thus, some analysts were recommending Equity Funding up to the moment that trading was halted on March 27, 1973, while others, even without the benefit of inside information, had become skeptical about the company's intricate accounting policies, swift growth rate, and selling methods long before that fateful date.

It required alertness and good judgment not only to recognize the potential that Levitz Furniture's new concept of retailing brought to the stock when it was selling at 5, but also to become cautious about the company's ability to maintain a string of 50 percent quarterly earnings gains and to believe that the stock was overpriced at 60. There were analysts who foresaw the clouding outlook for New Process Co., a direct-mail retailer of clothing, before the stock collapsed from a high price of 70¾ in 1972 to below 10 in early 1973. Similarly, there were analysts who detected the financial weakness in Topper Corp. despite its tie-in with the popular *Sesame Street* educational television series; who were concerned about the questionable earnings base of Homes, a modular-home manufacturer; and who recognized the distended capitalization and costly superstructure of the gargantuan Pennsylvania Railroad-New York Central merger. Although at one time, the stocks of these last three companies were "high-flyers," all three eventually entered into bankruptcy, with substantial losses to the who did not anticipate the difficulties.

What is judged good performance depends upon the field of enterprise. Thus, a record of 40 percent successful operations would be poor for a surgeon, but a comparable record in baseball is an outstanding batting average. Competitive pressures in securities analysis have grown keener, but there is little reason to believe that opportunities have disappeared for the analyst who can anticipate changes in the factors affecting a company's stock before competitors can.

THE PRICE/EARNINGS RATIO

Our basic approach to gauge the future value of a stock is simple: forecast next year's earnings and apply the p/e ratio that will prevail at that time.

The simplicity, however, lies only in the arithmetic. We have already seen the problems in extrapolating earnings. Selecting the appropriate p/e ratio is equally troublesome.

Some Observations Regarding the P/E Ratio

There is nothing mysterious about the p/e ratio. It is the price investors pay for each dollar of a company's earnings. The price may relate to the reported or to the projected earnings. The higher the p/e ratio, the lower its reciprocal, the earnings/price ratio (e/p). Since companies rarely pay out more than they earn, the e/p ratio, in turn, is the upper limit of the dividend yield (when the earnings and the dividend pertain to the same period).

One of the most important factors affecting the p/e ratio is the growth prospects of the firm. While a firm with optimistic prospects may have a relatively low p/e ratio because of offsetting factors, such as involvement in a high-risk industry, a firm with little likelihood of growth probably will have a low p/e ratio. While the relationships between p/e and growth may be distorted by extraneous factors which cause the price of the stock to overreact either negatively or positively to the company's earnings potential, it is clear that, over the long run, a strong tie exists between the p/e ratio and the rate of growth.

A return on investment that is substantially in excess of a company's cost of capital is likely to attract competition and put pressure on that return. Even if the high return fails to draw in additional competitors, the development of new products or operating techniques—or the drying up of the company's market—may erode it. Then again, if the return continues high and competition is stifled, the federal government may bring antitrust charges. It is not easy, therefore, to anticipate how long a current rate of growth will be maintained. Nevertheless, all other things being equal, the longer a growth rate can be maintained, the more future earnings a current dollar of earnings represents and the higher the price it will command in the market; the shorter the growth period, the lower the price. The duration of growth is thus critical.

Earnings Growth and the P/E Ratio

Assume that the stocks of two companies, *G* and *A*, are in the same risk category, but that *G*'s stock sells at a higher p/e ratio than *A*'s. If the differential is justified, *G*'s earnings will have to grow more rapidly than *A*'s, which, let us further assume, grow at about the average rate for listed companies. It is unlikely that *G* will be able to maintain its high rate of growth indefinitely; presumably, after a period of time, the two rates will be about the same, and the two p/e ratios, all other things being equal, will also tend to be the same. It is useful to have some idea about the length this period must be to justify the differential in p/e's and the reality of expecting *G*'s growth rate to exceed *A*'s for that length of time.

As an illustration, assume that companies *G* and *A* have the same per share earnings but that the p/e ratio of *G* is three times that of *A*, while the rate of growth of *G*'s earnings is 1.20 times that of *A*'s. After a certain number of years, depending on the relative rates of growth, the ratio of per share earnings for the two companies will equal the initial ratio of p/e's. In our case, after about six years, the ratio of *G*'s per share earnings to *A*'s will be three. It can be shown that the number of years required to effect this equality of ratios is the minimum number of years the high rate of growth must be sustained to warrant the initial differential in p/e's. In any particular case, the number of years so required turns out to be the power to which the right-hand side of the following equation must be raised:[1]

$$\frac{P_g(0)/E_g(0)}{P_a(0)/E_a(0)} = \left(\frac{1 + \Delta E_g + D_g}{1 + \Delta E_a + D_a}\right)^{\tau},$$

where $P_g(0)$ = price of stock *G* in time 0,
$P_a(0)$ = price of stock *A* in time 0,
$E_g(0)$ = earnings per share of stock *G* in period 0,
$E_a(0)$ = earnings per share of stock *A* in period 0,
ΔE_g = growth rate of *G*'s earnings per share,
ΔE_a = growth rate of *A*'s earnings per share,
D_g = *G*'s dividend yield,
D_a = *A*'s dividend yield, and
τ = duration of growth.

Now consider RCA, which had a p/e ratio of 22.3 previously, and Youngstown Steel, a company of comparable risk, whose p/e ratio was merely 8.9. Let *g* represent RCA and *a* Youngstown Steel. Then, based upon the growth factors and dividend rates prevailing at that time:

$$1 + \Delta E_g + D_g = 1.00 + 0.30 + 0.02$$
$$1 + \Delta E_a + D_a = 1.00 + 0.13 + 0.05$$

Combining the earnings and dividend components, we find that the overall relative growth rate was 1.32/1.18 = 1.12, while the relative p/e ratio was 22.3/8.9 = 2.5. Putting these two factors into the equation:

$$2.5 = (1.12)^{\tau}$$
$$\tau \cong 8$$

Thus, the relative growth rate of RCA would have had to be sustained for eight years in order to warrant paying a p/e ratio for RCA 2.5 times that paid for Youngstown Steel. Inasmuch as Youngstown had been growing at a rate well above that of the GNP, it seemed unlikely to expect RCA to continue to grow 2.5 times as fast for almost a decade, despite the differences in the product mixes of the two companies. This relationship suggests that either RCA was overpriced or Youngstown Steel was underpriced. It was difficult to tell which condition existed, and a bit of both elements may have been involved.[2]

TABLE 16-1

Years of Earnings Growth Discounted, by Drug Stocks Relative to the Standard & Poor's 425 Stock Average

	RETURN ON EQUITY*	P/E RATIO AS OF 5/25/73	5-YEAR HISTORICAL GROWTH RATE IN EARNINGS PER SHARE	GAMMA FACTOR, OR YEARS TO DISCOUNT PREMIUM ON P/E MULTIPLE
Abbott	8.7%	25.2	3%	NA
American Home	25.3	38.5	11	15.0
Bristol-Myers	17.8	22.1	8	9.6
Eli Lilly	18.7	43.8	16	9.6
Merck	24.6	44.1	10	20.9
Chas. Pfizer	15.1	27.5	10	10.6
Richardson-Merrell	14.4	20.7	10	4.3
Schering-Plough	21.5	47.7	19	8.3
Searle	25.8	34.3	10	15.4
Sterling	14.1	27.8	9	13.5
Warner-Lambert	14.5	29.4	9	15.0

Assumptions: S&P 425 P/E = 17x;
S&P 425 Earnings Growth Rate = 5.1%

*Return on equity is net income/stockholders' equity, based on reported numbers in Moody's ***Handbook of Common Stocks***, 1973, 1st ed.

SOURCE: Robert M. Baylis and Suresh L. Bhirud, "Growth Stock Analysis: A New Approach," ***Financial Analysts Journal***, 29 (July/August 1973): 69. Reprinted by permission.

Table 16-1 provides some data for the drug industry with which to evaluate differences in p/e ratios. There is a slight modification in the method of calculation: the period of time represented by the gamma factor in column 4 represents the number of years the historical earnings growth rate of the company shown must continue, compared with that of the Standard & Poor's 425 stocks, in order to warrant the premium on the particular stock's p/e multiple, compared with the S&P 425 stock p/e multiple. It will be observed, for example, that in 1973 Ely Lilly's multiple appeared more appropriate than Merck's, based on historical growth rates, because only about ten year's more growth at the current rate was required to justify the premium on its multiple, compared with about twice that period for Merck.[3]

The implications that may be drawn from the relationship between the p/e ratios and the earnings growth ratios of two stocks is a useful check on the logic of the difference in the p/e ratios. An indication that a company must sustain a very high rate of growth for a long period of time to justify a high p/e ratio at least suggests the need for investigating the situation carefully. The outlook for the company might support the conclusion that the company could maintain the required rate of growth for the indicated period, or more careful checking might raise questions about the earnings forecasts. While useful as a checking device, the relationship does not provide a basis for selecting the appropriate p/e ratio to use.

Difficulties in Using P/E Ratios

Ordinarily, earnings are the outcome of economic and operating factors that tend to change gradually. Not only is the p/e ratio likely to react to such changes, but it is also sensitive to psychological factors. The ratio may advance swiftly, as investors' attitudes toward a particular company or the market generally become optimistic. Conversely, it may decline with equal swiftness, as pessimism develops.

FIGURE 16-1

Fluctuation of Price/Earnings Ratio Based on Dow-Jones Industrial Average at Year-End, 1949-1974

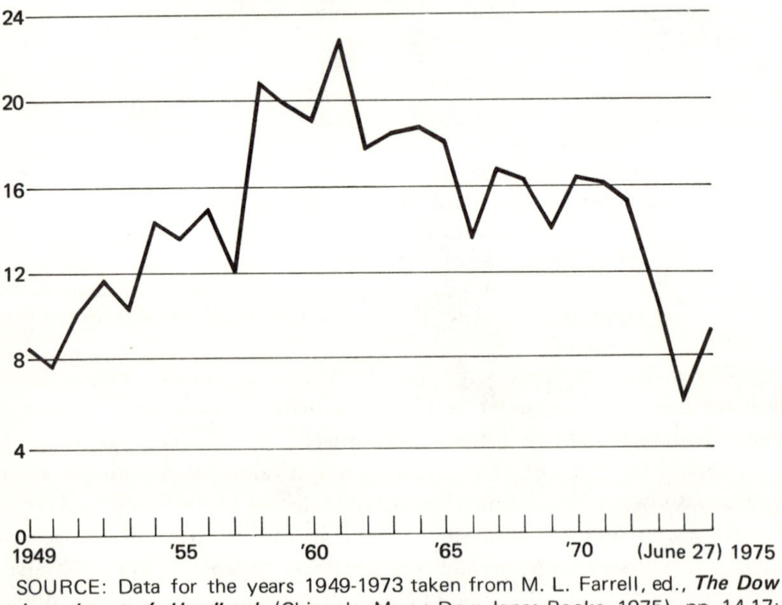

SOURCE: Data for the years 1949-1973 taken from M. L. Farrell, ed., ***The Dow Jones Investor's Handbook*** (Chicople, Mass.: Dow Jones Books, 1975), pp. 14-17; data for 1974 taken from ***Barron's Weekly***, December 30, 1974, p. 74; data for 1975 taken from ***Barron's Weekly***, June 30, 1975, p. 66.

On an overall basis, these movements may be observed in the wide swings of the p/e ratio of the Dow-Jones Industrials, as seen in Figure 16-1. Moving along a jagged line, the ratio expanded from about 8.5 in 1949 to 22.9 in 1961 and then experienced a long-term contraction, interrupted by minor upswings, until at the close of December 1974 the ratio fell to 6, a level that had not been approached for a quarter of a century. It has since recovered slightly. By and large, the stocks included in the Dow-Jones Industrials are of high quality and represent average outcomes for 30 companies. The relatively short-term fluctuations of particular issues over the past decade have reflected and even exceeded these considerable swings. As an illustration, between 1961 and 1962, the p/e ratio of IBM, a premier stock, shrank from a high of 66 to a low of 27; within the year 1966, Esquire's ratio declined from a high of 16 to a low of 5; from its 1968 high to its 1969 low, McDonnell Douglas's ratio dropped from 18 to 6; from its 1969 high to its 1970 low, Chock Full O'Nuts's ratio fell from 35 to 7; from its 1971 high to the 1972 low, the ratio for Alcoa, a Dow-Jones stock, went from 29 to 8; and, within the first nine months of 1974, Fairchild Camera moved between a high of 64 and a low of 19⅛. Conversely, Burroughs's ratio rose from a low of 13 in 1966 to a high of 45 in 1967; and Kaiser Aluminum & Chemical's ratio jumped from its 1970 low of 13 to a 1971 high of 66.

Underlying these swift changes in p/e ratios was the mood of investors. In the summer of 1973, for example, the stock market was in the doldrums following a period of persistent declines, despite a high level of economic activity and good corporate earnings. As a result, p/e ratios were driven to their lowest levels for the past two decades. Half the stocks on the New York Stock Exchange were selling at ten times their per share earnings or less; and several dozen issues at only three or four times earnings.[4] On the other hand, there was a small group of so-called high-quality growth stocks that still were priced at relatively high multiples. This condition, popularly called a two-tier market, created odd discrepancies in indicated values. For example, International Flavors & Fragrances, a first-tier growth stock, was selling at $98 per share on earnings expectations of $1.50, or 65 times earnings. The company had 18 million shares outstanding, providing a capitalized value of $1.8 billion; its 1972 sales were $128 million, and its earnings had been growing over the past ten years at an annual rate of about 15 percent. In comparison with this generous evaluation, Ford Motor Co. was selling at about $56 per share, or five times its expected earnings of $11.00 per share. The company had a total market value of $5.5 billion on 101 million shares outstanding, backed by sales of $20.2 billion in 1972. Although cyclical, Ford's earnings had grown at an annual rate of 7.7 percent over the past ten years. Even under relatively adverse conditions, the dividend return from Ford was likely to be substantially higher than that from International Flavors.[5]

This disparity between the price of the two stocks reflected investor attitudes at that time; they were willing to pay high multiples for a handful of favored issues, but only low multiples for cyclical stocks.[6] Regardless of a company's financial strength and prospects, then, an important decision in the evaluative process is the selection of an appropriate ratio. Should it be based on the return deemed suitable by the analyst or on the likely evaluation of the general body of investors? It seems unrealistic not to recognize that prices are created by the actions of buyers and sellers, and therefore the current circumstances that may be conditioning their attitudes cannot be overlooked. At the same time, it seems equally naïve not to take into account the other factors that may have varying degrees of influence, such as the financial characteristics of the company, the trend of the economy, and the prior record of p/e relationships in the company and industry.

By the fall of 1974, the two-tier market that had earlier attracted such attention had largely vanished. Continued declines in stock prices spread investor gloom, leading to the withdrawal of buyers and furthering the shrinkage in prices. All types of stocks suffered, and the sharp distinction between first- and second-tier stocks tended to disappear. As a result, the common stock of International Flavors & Fragrances slipped over 70 percent from its summer position, compared with a decline of about 30 percent in the Ford stock. At their new levels, the International Flavors issue sold at a p/e ratio of about 35; this was still about seven times the ratio of the Ford common, but the gap had narrowed perceptibly. Moreover, the attraction of International Flavors had weakened relative to other stocks of strong growth companies. At that time, for example, IBM was selling at 13 times its earnings, a historically low p/e ratio.

The considerable swings in price/earnings ratios in part reflect their susceptibility to the changing expectations of investors. This is carried to an extreme when an investor buys a stock that he knows has little intrinsic value solely because he believes it will appeal to the public, as has occurred in periods of hot issues. While we do not favor such a one-sided approach, we do believe that in selecting the p/e ratio to apply to a company's forecast earnings, the analyst should include, along with fundamental financial considerations, the stock's appeal in the prevailing investment climate. It is the subjective aspect of this phase that makes the selection of an appropriate p/e ratio such a personal and difficult undertaking.

SELECTING AN APPROPRIATE PRICE/EARNINGS RATIO

While various techniques are employed to forecast the p/e ratio, they may be broadly classified into the judgmental and statistical methods.

Judgmental Approach

There are three basic areas the analyst may explore to arrive at a judgment regarding a reasonable p/e ratio to employ in evaluating a stock. These are the prospects of the company, the record of prior p/e ratios, and the prevailing ratios for other companies in the same industry.

Company prospects. The p/e ratios of companies with favorable prospects will tend to be higher than those with dim outlooks. Thus, the point of departure for this approach is the analyst's determination of the financial condition and earnings potential of the company. On this basis, he reaches a conclusion about a reasonable return and converts this figure into a p/e ratio.

In the evaluation process, the p/e ratio will be applied to the forecast earnings of the company to arrive at a valuation base. Here caution must be exercised as to the earnings figure used. If it is for a future year, when much of the company's growth will be past, a high p/e ratio may involve double counting, incorporating both the company's growth prospects and the high level of earnings actually achieved.

This difficulty is eased when the ratio is applied to the expected earnings of the following year. Under these circumstances, the earnings growth is likely to continue, and there is justification for employing a relatively high p/e ratio to take into account the gains still expected to be achieved. The level of the ratio relative to other stocks then depends on the prospective growth rates of the related companies, and the formula described previously may serve as a gauge.

Record of prior p/e ratios. A useful check on the analyst's judgment is some average of p/e ratios that reflect prior relationships between the price of the stock and the earnings of the corporation. The choices of which period to use in the calculation and whether any expected future developments require a modification of the average derived then depend upon the judgment of the analyst; hence the label attached to this approach.

Assume, for example, that in early 1973, an analyst was examining the p/e ratios of the following companies: Exxon, Revco, and Alcoa. In the case of Exxon, a clear shrinkage of the ratio occurred in the period starting with 1967. For the five years prior to that time, the high p/e ratio moved between 15 and 19, while in the following six years the high moved between 12 and 15; in the earlier period, the range of the low p/e ratios was 12-15, compared with 8-11 in the later years. Since the p/e ratios were relatively stable and revealed no clear-cut trend during 1967-1972, the average of the annual high and low ratios in that period might have been an appropriate starting point to forecast a reasonable base ratio for the following year.

Revco is an aggressive discount drug chain. A decided breakpoint in the general level of its p/e ratio occurred 1968: in the four prior years for which price information is available, the ratio fluctuated between a low of 7 and a high of 18; between 1968 and 1972, however, the company gained stature and the low-high range was 14 to 41. In determining the starting level for a 1973 forecast, consideration would have to be given to the apparent improvement in the later period.

Alcoa presents still a different picture. There is a clear drop in its p/e ratios starting about 1968, but in 1971 the ratio took a sharp jump upward, bringing it within the range of the earlier period; in 1972 the ratio fell once more. Thus, a decision would have to be made whether 1971 should be excluded from the 1968-1972 average, or if the higher ratio for 1971 portended a higher level for the future, despite the 1972 fallback.

Once a reasonably uniform period has been selected for the calculation, the analyst must decide whether the resulting average represents a logical expectable figure for the following year or should be modified to reflect future possible changes. This decision is not an easy one. In the case of Scott Paper, for example, there was no sharp cleavage in the level of the ratios, as occurred in the illustrations described above. Rather, there was a gradual deterioration between 1962 and 1969 at an average annual rate of about 5 percent. The changes in the trend of Scott's earnings during this period did not seem to affect significantly the persistent decline in the p/e ratio. In 1970, moreover, the ratio rose despite a shrinkage in reported earnings per share, a rise that was perhaps generated by the booming general market prices during the latter part of the year.

Thus, between 1962 and 1970, the fluctuations in Scott's p/e ratio apparently reflected both the foibles of the marketplace and concern about the company's ability to sustain its earnings growth. Then, confronted with the need to forecast the 1971 p/e ratio, an analyst might have opted for the historic average of 21.9; a continuation of the long-term decline, which would have brought the ratio to about 15.5 in 1971; or a modification of the trend by some amount to reflect the 1970 improvement. The decision would be based primarily on the analyst's personal assessment of the condition and prospects of the company; in fact, the 1971 year-end ratio was about 21, approximating the long-term average.

Other companies in the same industry. Another check that might be made is to compare the ratio selected with those of other companies in the same industry to see if it is in line or if an indicated discrepancy is justified. For example, at the close of September 1974, the following p/e ratios existed in the petroleum industry: Exxon, 4; Phillips Petroleum, 7; Standard Oil of California, 3; Standard Oil of Indiana, 7; and Standard Oil of Ohio, 19. The range was broad, and an investor contemplating a purchase in the industry would want to check the reasons for the differences. In this case, the relatively high ratio of Standard Oil of Ohio probably reflected its disproportionately large Alaskan interests and its freedom from uncertainties in the Middle East.

Market prospects. After all these factors are considered, the p/e ratio will reflect the analyst's judgment regarding the company's prospects, the implications of prior ratios as well as those of other companies in the same industry, and the attitude of investors toward the stock analyzed. A question that arises is whether the general market outlook for the following year should be taken into account in determining the ratio. This is a troublesome issue. If the analyst expects a sharply rising market, he might raise the ratio modestly—say, not more than 10 percent, as an arbitrary figure. If the analyst expects a declining market, he had better avoid buying common stock and shift as much of his portfolio as possible into risk-free securities. If he is undecided or expects little change, the analytic procedures presumably would not be affected by market conditions.

Statistical Approach

The increasing availability of time-sharing computer facilities has broadened considerably the application of statistical techniques to financial analysis. In making forecasts, a common approach is to develop regression equations which relate the desired item to associated variables that presumably are easier to forecast directly. For example, we might hypothesize that the p/e ratio is dependent primarily upon its historic experience, the trend of the market, and the company's indicated growth rate. The resulting equation, based upon these assumptions, might take the following form:

$$\text{PE} = a + b_1(\text{AVG PE}) + b_2(\text{SAP} - \text{AVG}) + b_3(\text{GRO} - \text{AVG}) + e,$$

where PE = estimated p/e ratio,

AVG PE = average p/e ratio for the preceding five years,

SAP-AVG = return on Standard & Poor's 425 stocks minus the arithmetic average of the returns over the preceding five years (the return is simply the market relative, P_t/P_{t-1}, plus the dividend yield),

GRO-AVG = growth rate of earnings per share minus the geometric average of the growth rates for the preceding five years, and

e = random error.

To illustrate the application of this equation, the requisite data were collected for the years 1965 through 1970 for the stocks of 20 firms that embody roughly similar risks—that is, firms with comparable βs.[7] The β

coefficient of Scott was .796, and therefore we selected, at random, 20 companies with βs of .796 ± .05. This provided 120 observations.

The initial running of the equation resulted in an *a* value of 5.55643, which seemed unusually large since it would be reasonable for the intercept to be 0. As a consequence, we ran the equation without an intercept. This forced AVG PE to carry a larger portion of the burden. The resulting coefficients were:

COEFFICIENTS	*T* VALUES[8]
b_1 = 0.93261	32.59079
b_2 = 5.37753	1.36072
b_3 = −2.34249	−1.36840

At first glance, the results appear reasonable. One might surmise that the sign of b_1 would be positive and its coefficient close to 1 because of the direct relationship between a prior average and the current figure. The positive sign of b_2 (the rate of market growth) indicates the importance of buoyant markets. The negative sign of b_3 (the rate of company earnings growth) suggests that the market regards a growth rate for the current year that deviates from the historical average as transitory and therefore continues to price the stock on the basis of its historical average. Accordingly, if earnings grow more rapidly than expected, the ratio of price to current earnings is lowered, while if earnings decline more rapidly than expected, the ratio rises. Thus, on the basis of this equation, at least, investors apparently gave a more positive interpretation to a one-year advance in the market relative to its average than to a one-year growth in a company's earnings relative to its average.

To apply this forecasting equation to Scott, we used the following information, largely drawn from the data shown in Chapter 15:

	1971	AVERAGE, 1966-1970	COEFFICIENT OF *b*
PE	–	18.5510	18.5510 (AVG PE)
SAP	1.1013	1.0040	0.0973 (SAP-AVG)
GRO	0.5468	0.9687	– 0.4219 (GRO-AVG)

The only new information required was an estimate of SAP; the growth rate used for Scott's earning (GRO) was based on the assumption that in 1971 the actual results of 76 cents per share were correctly forecast (see p. 353). In these circumstances, the estimated p/e ratio worked out to 18.81. If GRO had been based on an inaccurate forecast of earnings, or if a much different prediction of market change (SAP) had been inserted, the resulting expected p/e ratio could have varied significantly. The dependence of the outcomes on the correctness of the inputs to the regression highlights the sensitivity of such equations to the variables and estimates employed.

DETERMINING THE PRICE OF THE STOCK

Having forecast next year's earnings and the p/e ratio likely to obtain at that time, the analyst derives the expected price of the stock by simply taking a product of these two factors (see the last row of Table 15-3). In determining the factors, we believe it desirable for the analyst to steer a careful course between the Scylla of undue subjectivity and the Charybdis of excessive statistical detail. In general, we veer toward simple but logical techniques that provide the analyst with a statistical base for his forecasts but allow the opportunity for personal judgment because of the enormous influence of intangibles on securities prices.

In the present state of the art, we are skeptical about relying too heavily on elaborate and presumably sophisticated methods. We believe it desirable for the analyst to be aware of these techniques. The analyst may be able to incorporate some of these devices into his own methodologies. As corporate reporting practices become more reliable and the market structure is improved, elaborate statistical tools may become increasingly useful.

There has been increasing experimentation with operational mathematical models in the area of finance. One model that is applicable to securities analysis, as well as to financial planning, was developed by Warren and Shelton and christened FINPLAN by them.[9] The model provides a simultaneous solution of a system of equations which portrays the functioning of a firm. Based upon assumptions regarding such variables as sales, operating ratios, p/e ratios, retention ratios, debt to equity ratios, and so forth, the model furnishes pro forma summary balance sheets and income statements, as well as certain other information, such as per share earnings and share prices. This model was useful to help project the earnings per share figures in Table 15-3.

The model recognizes the interdependence of financial relationships. For example, to produce a larger volume of sales, a firm needs more assets, and its method of financing these additional assets influences eventual income. If the assets are financed internally, all of earnings produced accrue to the existing shares, but if there is external financing, the effect on earnings will vary with the type of external funds issued. For purposes of securities analysis, a reiterative process may be necessary. Thus, the outcome of a particular run may suggest that the projected p/e ratio, which is one of the inputs, is not compatible with the indicated change in earnings per share. Under such circumstances, further experimentations would be required to obtain a p/e ratio that was consistent with earnings growth.

ROLE OF DIVIDENDS

In our basic evaluative process, involving primarily the application of a forecast p/e ratio to forecast earnings, no reference has been made to dividends. Yet, corporations have different dividend policies and the implications of this factor, of course, cannot be ignored. (See p. 107 for a discussion of corporate dividend policies.)

Effect of Dividends on the Multiplier

Unfortunately, the evidence on the impact of dividend policy on the multiplier is inconclusive. While one dollar of appreciation in the value of a stock yields a higher aftertax return than one dollar of dividends, capital gains is a less reliable source of income than dividend payments. Analysts have discerned that simple comparisons of the p/e ratios of high-payout stocks with those of low-payout stocks will not disclose the effect of payout policy. Reflecting this uncertainty, one careful study of the subject got mixed results, finding that in some industries liberal payout policies had a positive effect on the p/e ratio, in others the effect was negative, and in still others it appeared neutral.[10]

Benjamin Graham and David Dodd, the recognized fathers of securities analysis, have also exhibited ambivalence with respect to the weight given by investors to dividends. Originally they concluded that a dollar of earnings paid out as dividends was worth four times as much as a dollar retained in the business. After World War II, as the economy expanded, corporations tended to reduce their payouts to provide funds for the purchase of new equipment, and investors began to seek so-called growth stocks. Observing this new development, Graham and Dodd concluded that for stocks of this sort, dividends can be ignored and sole reliance placed on expected earnings.[11]

In mid-1973 analysts began to toy with the idea that another investment era was dawning and that emphasis would once more be given to dividends in determining the return that could reasonably be expected from a stock.[12] At that time, however, the validity of this notion was still in doubt. As mentioned previously, on June 21 a relaxation of federal restrictions on corporate dividend payments was announced; these provisions had originally been imposed as part of the government's inflation control policy. The new rules allowed payouts to be raised by more than the 4 percent to which they had been previously restricted. In the first session following this announcement, the Dow-Jones Industrial Average leaped ahead by 19 points within a half hour, but the boom soon subsided, and the net gain for the day was only 6 points. Thus, there is no evidence that the government's decision had a sustained impact.

In view of this changing and uncertain role of dividends, their treatment in the evaluative process seems properly a subjective consideration. As such, the company's dividend policy belongs in the package of factors used to determine the p/e ratio of a stock. If, in the judgment of the analyst, public fancy is veering toward the desire for a constant stream of income, she will tend to elevate the p/e ratio of the stock of a company with a generous policy. If growth issues are in the forefront, she will give little attention to the payout rate in determining the p/e ratio. If investor attitudes appear mixed, the significance of dividends in assigning a p/e ratio will depend on the financial characteristics of the company, particularly its internal rate of return, stability of earnings, current return, and need for funds.

Dividends as a Factor in the Rate of Return

Whatever the weight given dividend policy in selecting a p/e ratio, the amount of dividends that will be received in the following year is part of the investor's return. Therefore, it is important to gauge the likely level of disbursement.

Depending on state laws, corporations may pay larger amounts of dividends than their reported income or may continue disbursements during several years of deficit operations. This policy cannot be maintained for long without impairing capital; thus, the estimate of a corporation's basic earning power must exceed the level of probable dividend payments. The ratio between earnings and dividend payouts varies and is influenced by changing economic conditions: from 1960 to 1972, corporate dividends fluctuated between 42 percent and 62 percent of earnings, with payouts peaking in earnings troughs and reaching minima in earnings peaks. Since these are averages for all nonfinancial corporations, the range of actual payouts available to the investor is even greater. The 500 companies in Standard & Poor's Composite Index disbursed 41.4 percent of earnings in 1973, compared with 49.1 percent in 1972; the 60 utilities in the index paid out 64.6 percent in 1973, up slightly from 64.3 percent in 1972; and the 15 railroads reduced their payout to 45.2 percent from 49.6 percent.

Disbursement rates are also subject to specific factors, such as a corporation's financial condition, expansion program, or charter restrictions. For example, between 1963 and 1972, as IBM was increasingly able to meet its capital requirements through the large amount of funds it was generating internally, the company gradually raised its cash payout from 32.1 percent to 48.9. On the other hand, even though American Motors in 1972 reported earnings of $1.18 before an extraordinary income tax credit, the company paid no dividends. Retained earnings were not available for such payments because of restrictions in its debenture and bond agreements.[13]

The basic assumption in forecasting cash dividends for the ensuing year is that they will be at least the same as for the prior year. Only if the company has indicated that reduction is contemplated or a significant slackening of earnings is expected should the idea of a curtailment in the payout ratio be entertained. If a loss is projected and unusual cash drains are in sight, however, a distribution may even be abandoned. For example, American Seating, a manufacturer of institutional seating and classroom products, faced in mid-1973 with two successive quarterly losses and a newly instituted strike, omitted its third-quarter dividend, the first time it had ever made such an omission.[14]

In general, however, management is loath to move backwards on dividend payments because such a policy suggests financial weakness and may invite adverse stockholder reaction. From the opposite point of view, an improvement in operating conditions may well lead to a lifting of the dividend, particularly if the current rate is behind the industrial average. Thus, it is important for the investor to become familiar with payout policies. If the distribution rate of a particular corporation differs radically from the average for its field of activity, the reasons must be investigated to determine the possibility of a future departure from this conservative policy. The investor may also discover that the factor holding down payments soon will be eliminated, leading to a rise in the distribution rate. For example, according to Standard & Poor's, following the termination of dividend controls on April 30, 1974, the number of companies increasing dividend declarations in May rose to 242, up from 139 a year earlier; extra dividends were declared by 74 companies (compared with 53 previously), and over twice as many companies resumed payments. Examination of a company's statement of sources and applications of funds, ordinarily published in annual reports, may be of some help in ascertaining the direction of major outlays and the possibility of a reduction, thereby facilitating a future rise in the dividend payout rate.[15]

USING A RISK-ADJUSTED RATE OF RETURN

If the total of a stock's projected price plus dividends is below its current value, it obviously should not be purchased; the investor would do better to place his funds in a source that affords a positive return. If the projected results are greater than the stock's current value, its attraction then depends upon the return the investor will receive relative to the risks involved and the alternative opportunities available in the market.

As mentioned previously, the expected return of a stock is determined by means of the standard formula

$$R_t = \frac{P_t - P_{t-1} + D_t}{P_{t-1}},$$

where R_t = expected return, P_t = expected price, P_{t-1} = current price, and D_t = expected dividend. For example, if next year's expected price of a stock, purchased at \$20 (P_{t-1}), is \$22.50 (P_t), and no change is seen in the current dividend of 50 cents per share (D_t), the expected return (R_t) is 15 percent $\left(\frac{2.50 + .50}{20.00}\right)$. This return may then be compared with that available from alternative investment opportunities. For this purpose, the professional analyst will know the yields afforded by fixed-income securities and the range of returns on common stocks classified into different risk categories. The typical investor should have similar information, although it may not be as comprehensive as that used by the professional. If the investor does not have any idea of potential returns related to risk, he might prudently confine his equity commitments to the issues of investment companies.

The "risk-reward ratio" is an old and familiar Wall Street expression, but it is probably more widely applied as a rough criterion than as an actual figure. It is also true, however, that βs for individual stocks are becoming more generally available, and introduction of the beta concept certainly has focused interest on the role of risk in the selection of securities.

Using the Capital Asset Pricing Model

If the analyst is theoretically oriented, he may want to resort to the capital asset pricing model discussed in Chapter 10 despite its shortcomings. It will be remembered that, in equilibrium, the risk premium of a stock per unit of risk is equal to the risk premium of the general market. This equality is expressed by the following equation:

$$\frac{E(R_i) - S}{\beta_i} = E(R_m) - S,$$

where $E(R_i)$ = return of stock i, S = risk-free return, β_i = risk of stock i, and $E(R_m)$ = return of the market.

If a stock is expected to have a higher return than that suggested by its β, however, the left-hand side of the equation will exceed the right-hand side. As an illustration, let us assume that the previously mentioned stock with an expected return of 15.0 percent $[E(R_i)]$ had a beta value of 1.3 (β_i), meaning that over the past several years the rises and falls in its risk premium tended to be 30 percent greater than those of the general market. The yield on one-year Treasury notes, regarded as risk-free, was 8.8 percent (S), and the expected market return $[E(R_m)]$ was 11.0 percent.

On the basis of these figures, the relation between the risk premium per unit of risk on the stock concerned and the risk premium of the market is as follows:

$$\frac{15.0 - 8.8}{1.3} - (11.0 - 8.8) = 2.6$$

Thus, after adjusting for risk, the stock affords an expected return that is 2.6 percentage points greater than that of the general market. This relationship suggests that the issue is moderately attractive.

Allowing for a Margin of Error

In view of the uncertainties that underlie forecasting in the securities area, it seems prudent for the analyst to allow room for error. For this purpose, a distinction might be drawn between stocks that afford a high and a modest rate of return. If the expected return is substantially greater than that available from comparable securities, the current and forecast prices might be used as the indicated buy and sell levels, on the grounds that even if the forecast was optimistic, a curtailed return would still be satisfactory. In the event that the expected return was acceptable but not high, a 10 percent margin below the current price and above the forecast price might be established as the buy and sell levels. In the illustration cited above, for example, the forecast price for the stock concerned was \$22.50, the current price \$20, and the estimated dividend 50 cents, thereby affording an expected return of 15 percent. The analyst would then compare this return with that available from securities in comparable risk classes to determine whether it was sufficiently large to use the current and forecast prices to derive buy and sell levels.

If the capital asset pricing model was employed as described above, the analyst might use a decision rule that the excess of risk premium per unit of risk over the risk premium of the market would have to be at least five times the risk premium of the market to justify using the current and forecast prices as the buy and sell range. In the illustration, the market risk premium was 2.2 percent (11.0 – 8.8) and the adjusted risk premium on the stock was 4.8 percent $\left(\frac{15.0-8.8}{1.3}\right)$; the difference of 2.6 percent was considerably less than five times the market risk premium. Based upon the criterion suggested, the stock would not be worth buying unless the price dropped to approximately 18½ or about 10 percent below 20⅝, the price where the adjusted risk premium just about equals the market risk premium. At 18½, the total current yield would be 24.3 percent $\left(\frac{22.50-18.50+0.50}{18.50}\right)$; the adjusted risk premium would be 11.9 percent $\left(\frac{24.3-8.8}{1.3}\right)$; and this adjusted premium would be more than five times the market premium of 2.2 percent.

As noted, at a price of about 20⅝ adjusted risk premium about equals the market risk premium, and much of the stock's attraction to a holder would have evaporated. However, to allow for a margin of error, and to keep down transaction costs, the stock might be held until it reaches the forecast level of $22.50. In effect, this establishes a buy-sell range of $18.50-22.50, which is approximately 10 percent below and above the price of 20⅝. The range must be sufficiently broad to avoid the danger inherent in any feedback mechanism that might cause excessive transaction reversals and thereby chew up profits or compound losses with excess commission charges and taxes.

Buy and sell triggering points will change with both the fortunes of the company and market conditions. Moreover, unless the range is adjusted to accommodate the passage of time, the selling level may be reached by the realization of expectations. Accordingly, sooner or later the rule of thumb will not be a sufficient guideline, and a reevaluation of the stock will be necessary. Thus, the trigger buy and sell prices must be kept under constant surveillance.

Determining a Stock's Value

We strongly believe that investors should assign a tangible value to a security before buying it. This decision is a logical culmination of the process of securities analysis. The investor pays a specific price for a stock; he should be able to balance this figure against his own estimate of the issue's concrete value. If he cannot do this, he probably does not know enough about the stock to buy it.

Great mischief is wrought in the field of securities by well-meaning but uninformed persons who go through the motions of analysis without reaching valid conclusions. It may be comforting to obscure decisions with smoke screens of equivocation—and it may even preserve the reputations of some analysts—but such vagueness merely permits individuals to rationalize impulsive decisions and to be persuaded by superficial arguments.

We consider it only common sense that an evaluation of a security should indicate what it is worth. (Moreover, this disciplinary process of reaching a definite decision will dispel much of the fuzziness that sometimes characterizes analyses.) If the imponderables bulk so large that they prevent the investor from having a positive opinion, he will know that the security can be bought only on a chance or guesswork basis.

Admittedly, this procedure may create a semblance of certitude that does not really obtain in securities analysis. Some investors might place too much faith in these estimated values (although we consider this unlikely). However, since under any circumstances individuals will continue to buy and sell stock, their decisions should at least be clear-cut. To this end, the investor should be able to set price against value. The procedure, of course, will not prevent individual errors in analysis, but it should reduce the possibility of serious mistakes in the selection of securities.

SUMMARY

Having estimated a company's earnings per share for the following year, the analyst may gauge the market price of its stock by applying the expected price/earnings ratio to the forecast earnings. Simply, the p/e ratio is the typical relationship that the investor believes will prevail between the earnings of a company and the price of its stock.

An important factor affecting the p/e ratio is the growth prospects of a firm. All other things being equal, when a company's earnings are growing at a rapid rate, the p/e ratio of its stock will tend to be higher than that of a company whose earnings are growing more sluggishly. The analyst can calculate how long the company will have to maintain its relatively swift growth to justify the higher p/e ratio of its stock. Selecting the appropriate p/e ratio is troublesome because it is subject to wide changes as investor attitudes toward different stocks vary.

While various techniques are employed to forecast the p/e ratio, they may be broadly classified into the judgmental and statistical methods. The analyst may explore three basic areas to arrive at a judgment regarding a reasonable p/e ratio: the company's prospects, the record of prior p/e ratios, and the prevailing ratios for other companies in the same industry. A recommended statistical approach is to develop a regression which relates the p/e ratio to associated variables that presumably are easier to forecast directly.

Historically, dividends have had an inconsistent influence on the p/e ratio, depending on how investors value the relative importance of dividend income or capital gains in purchasing stock. Accordingly, a company's dividend policy is another subjective factor to be used in the determination of the appropriate p/e ratio. Whatever weight is assigned to dividend policy in selecting a p/e ratio, the dividends that will be received in the following year are part of the investor's return. Gaining an insight into a company's dividend policy, therefore, is an important part of the analytic process.

If the projected price and dividends of a stock are greater than its current value, the attraction of the stock depends on the amount of this expected return relative to alternative opportunities in the market. In making these comparisons, it is important to take into consideration the degree of risk associated with the different opportunities. In addition, some allowance should be made for error. For example, if the expected return is acceptable but not high, a 10 percent margin below the current price and above the forecast price might be established as the buy and sell levels.

CHAPTER 1

Stock Appraisal: Some Further Considerations in the Valuation Process

In the prior two chapters, the basic valuation stages–forecasting earnings and determining a price/earnings ratio–were discussed. The concepts are simple, but their applications are profoundly difficult and embrace the entire process of securities analysis. The emphasis was on a one-year horizon because of the decreasing reliability of extrapolations as they are extended for longer and longer periods. Nevertheless, we indicated that the distant future should be kept in mind by the analyst attempting to pluck aside the veil that obscures the coming year.

In the current chapter we give more specific consideration to certain underlying issues. This chapter suggests that before the analyst reaches a final valuation decision, he should give attention to the factors that might prevent the company from performing as expected. Toward this end, the analyst might ask whether the company has the management to sustain profitability and whether there are ingredients in the company's financial development that suggest its growth may not be sustainable. Even if we cannot quantify precisely the factors that influence sustainability, we can at least gain some understanding of their relative significance.

ASSESSING MANAGEMENT

The ingredient that transforms the bricks, mortar, and machinery of a business firm into a viable, profit-making organization is its management. For this reason, the ability to attract competent management may be the key element that enables a firm to achieve its profit goal, while the ability to keep management alert, aggressive, and competitive may be equally important in enabling the firm to sustain profits. Large shareholders are therefore reluctant to interfere with the policies of a management that has produced satisfactory earnings and dividends.[1]

Despite the importance of management, its qualitative nature makes it a particularly elusive factor for the analyst to evaluate. For this purpose, therefore, a direct visit is desirable, so that a personal judgment can be made as to the depth of management, its ability to respond to questions, its planning objectives, and general morale among employees. Whether or not a visit can be arranged, the analyst can obtain some insights by investigating the company's organizational structure, executives, and board of directors.

Organizational Structure

Various checks of organizational structure are possible. One is to assess the general framework the corporation has developed to handle its activities. For example, in the current era of diversification, there is the danger of a company's becoming mired in the details of supervising numerous lines of business. This problem contributed to the lagging sales and rising costs of Monsanto, a leading chemical producer, in the late 1960s and the beginning of 1970. During this period, the firm had a product-line organizational structure that created awkward administrative procedures and serious frictions. To resolve these problems, Monsanto instituted a major change in September 1970, by merging the numerous product lines into four largely autonomous companies, each with about $500 million in annual sales volume.[2]

Over the past several decades, U.S. enterprises have vigorously expanded their activities in distant lands; today a number of firms, such as IBM, derive a larger portion of their income from foreign than from domestic business. These firms have made corresponding changes in their organizational structures to handle their expanding interests abroad. By noting the organizational changes instituted by a company to control its multinational activities, the analyst can gain an idea of management's alertness in adapting to changing economic conditions.

In the initial period of overseas growth, the typical organizational ploy was to have a medium-level official serve as export manager within a structure that was essentially undisturbed. This approach was satisfactory so long as foreign sales were relatively modest, but as they expanded, the U.S. firms found that their foreign markets were threatened by competitors that had local manufacturing facilities. Accordingly, the U.S. firms began to establish their own producing facilities in overseas locations, commonly matching this development with the creation at headquarters of an international division to administer the foreign domain. Underlying this move was the assumption of a basic homogeneity to all offshore activities, which meant that the international division could be treated on a par with the other divisions of the firm. International divisions were established by some of the more experienced U.S. parent companies, such as General Motors and National Cash Register, prior to World War II, and their example was broadly followed by others in the postwar decade. As the foreign sector grew in size, however, supervision grew more difficult, and it became apparent that problems throughout the world were not necessarily the same. Out of this awareness emerged new organizational forms that, in the main, were based on geographic distinctions, product groupings, or some combination of these elements.[3]

The managerial group of a large organization is very small compared with the number of its employees. To exercise control over the company's activities and provide planning guidance, management typically relies on its budgetary system. Budgeting helps achieve these aims because it provides the basis for portraying expected sales, costs, profits, and asset changes through a unified body of reports. Because of their importance, budgeting procedures ordinarily are documented in formal manuals and eventually appear in a wide range of carefully designed reports in the preparation of which most of a company's executive and supervisory personnel play a part.

The professional analyst who pays a personal visit to a company and has direct discussions with its management ordinarily will include an assessment of these aspects of its organization in his review. He will check the structure devised to administer the production and marketing of its product lines; he will note management's agility in fashioning new organizational setups to control its spreading foreign empire; and he will examine its budgeting manuals. The investor who is not in a position to undertake personal visitations will experience greater difficulty in exploring these areas. Nevertheless, they constitute such an integral part of a company's planning and control efforts that much useful information about them is likely to appear in generally available sources, such as the company's annual reports, SEC records, newspaper articles, trade jounals, and the analyses of reputable brokerage firms.

Corporate Executives

To a large extent, the prospects of a company are tied up with the character and talents of the individuals at its helm. Accordingly, it behooves the analyst to know something about them and to reach some conclusion about their ability to cope with the problems of the firm. Industry specialists have attempted to develop concrete tests for identifying successful management. A particularly elaborate scheme of comparative management audits is used by the American Institute of Management, a nonprofit organization. Among its other activities, the institute studies the management of a large number of American corporations by means of some 300 checkpoints, grouped under the basic categories listed below, with specific weights assigned to each.[4] After analysis, the institute selects the enterprises whose management policies rate as excellent. Corporations with 7,500 or more points come under this classification.

	OPTIMUM RATING
Economic function	1,000 points
Corporate structure	500
Health of earnings	600
Service to stockholders	700
Research and development	800
Directorate effectiveness	800
Fiscal policies	1,000
Production efficiency	1,100
Sales vigor	1,300
Executive effectiveness	2,200
	10,000 points

Under the heading of "executive effectiveness"—the classification to which the institute assigns greatest weight—probing questions are raised concerning the talents of management. Some of these queries demand definite answers, such as the number of changes in executive personnel and the reasons for these changes. Other questions require qualitative responses. While all of this information is valuable, the average investor cannot obtain it. Nor, perhaps, is it even feasible to use direct quantitative standards to judge such abstractions as the abilities of the officers responsible for managing a company. The investors can, however, make an investigation to determine if certain typical trouble spots exist.

One problem area is the degree to which the firm may depend on the genius of a single person (whose talents may lie in product innovations, organization, finance, or marketing) without whom the firm's surviving power may be threatened. For example, much hope was pinned on the future of Sperry Rand in 1955 when a merger took place between Sperry Corp., a defense contractor, and Remington Rand, Inc., an office equipment manufacturer. Two years after the merger James H. Rand retired, leaving the important Univac Division virtually leaderless in its head-on struggle with IBM. In the following four years the new corporation had four chief executives, and it continued to be dogged by managerial problems that permitted competitors to eat into its markets. By 1965 the merged company reported less net income than Sperry Corp. had earned by itself a decade previously. In that year Frank Forster, its newly appointed chief executive, installed far-reaching managerial changes that enabled the company to operate for the first time with a carefully conceived organizational scheme.

From a different point of view, there is the danger that an executive may outlive his usefulness. For many years, Detroit Edison was headed by Walker L. Cisler, once regarded by the outside community as a visionary leader. In truth, however, he apparently paid little attention to financial issues and permitted the company's profit rate gradually to recede; by 1971 its return on equity was among the lowest in the industry. This factor, plus a survey by a major consulting firm that revealed to the company's directors the unfavorable light in which its management was held, led to the replacement of the 75-year-old Cisler by a younger executive who faced the problem of rebuilding the company's financial strength.[5] The concern with management overstaying its executive tenure is also seen in IBM's decision to have its chief executives retire at age 60 and in the replacement of CBS's 65-year-old vice-chairman, Frank Stanton, by a young president with a financial orientation.

The willingness of a company to revitalize its management team is at least indicative of its awareness of the need either to replace stodgy executives or to continue the energetic performance of those who have been replaced. The appearance of a new, relatively youthful face at the corporate helm, however, is no necessary indicator of future success. For example, in the spring of 1969, the Chase Manhattan Corp. replaced George Champion as a member of the institution's management team with 44-year-old Herbert P. Patterson, presumably to help close the performance gap that First National City had begun to open. But 3½ years later Patterson was replaced by Willard C. Butcher, as Citicorp continued to forge ahead, a condition reflected in the fact that investors were willing to pay 20 times earnings for Citicorp's stock, compared with only 13 times earnings for Chase's.[6]

An autocratic firm with a top management that issues decisions unilaterally is likely to run into more problems than one that takes into account the reactions of subordinates.[7] Members of a corporation's staff are not likely to identify wholly with the corporation, since there may be a conflict between their interests and the company's. A well-designed corporate organization therefore will seek to minimize these areas of conflict and to produce optimum action for the corporation. Top management is more likely to achieve such an organization and to sustain success if its objectives are set jointly with those who have the responsibility for meeting the prescribed goals. Moreover, an autocratic management may tend to exaggerate its own role and therefore take measures that are not in the best interests of the corporation. For example, G. W. Murphy, formerly chairman of the board and principal beneficial stockholder of G. W. Murphy Industries, Inc. (merged into Baker Oil Tools), a leading oil toolmaker, entered into a series of financial arrangements with the company that were of questionable benefit to it. As a result, he was ousted from the company and replaced by a new management team which described its efforts to develop an improved organization in this manner:

> At the same time we are strengthening our corporate staff, we are introducing a determined policy of decentralized operating management. Working with the corporate office early in the planning year, each divisional manager will establish specific and agreed upon objectives for his operation, and performance will be reviewed on a regular basis. From this point on, with the exception of certain legal and financial controls, he will assume full responsibility for the future growth and profit performance of his operation in line with these objectives.[8]

A managerial problem of a different sort arises when the firm is family controlled, since able executives may be blocked from action by the entrenched family hierarchy.

The existence of a problem area—a firm dependent on the genius of a single individual, an outmoded chief executive, an overly autocratic management, the lack of sufficient depth, domination by a family group—may be sufficiently serious to require potential investors to avoid buying the stock of a company until remedial steps are taken. If a new chief officer is introduced into the picture, his background should be examined to determine his prior posts and the reputation he achieved in handling these assignments. The number and kind of firms with which he was previously affiliated, the length of these affiliations, the record he achieved, and any comments written about his accomplishments all will help provide some insights into his possible success at his new office.

Board of Directors

State laws and recent federal court decisions make the board of directors responsible for guiding the corporation, and the board represents the final court of decision for policy directives. Moreover, as fiduciaries, it is expected that directors will conduct their responsibilities fairly and honestly. Accordingly, as part of the effort to evaluate management, a direct assessment of the quality of the board of directors may be attempted. In the American Institute of Management audits, the direct evaluation of the board is made under the heading of "Directorate effectiveness" and is one phase of the survey. For judging the board of directors, concrete tests include the composition of the board, the responsibilities of the directors, the stock ownership of its members, the age of the directors, the size of the board, its committees, the frequency of meetings, director compensation, the existence of an audit committee, and similar factors.

In general, analysts favor the "outside" board of directors, in which most of the members are chosen from other fields. It is claimed that the outside director can contribute a great deal to effective management by his counsel, independent views, expertise in his own field, and social interest.[9] Reflecting this attitude, the New York Stock Exchange encourages listed companies to have at least three outside directors, while many public companies have outsiders in as many as 50 percent of board positions.[10] This is an easy check for the investor to make, since the names and affiliations of the directors are usually included in the company's annual report.

Indicative of the importance some companies attach to their outside directors is this statement by Reed Tool Co. after the elimination of G. W. Murphy and a revamping of its managerial organization:

> During the year the Company made a transition from control by a single individual to that of a partnership of well-known and highly respected investors. Today all stockholders are represented by seven new members of the Board of Directors. . . .
>
> Each of the new Directors brings a particular strength to the direction of your company. Backgrounds of Finance, Corporate and Operating Management, Planning, Engineering, and specialized industry knowledge are all represented. Each member of today's Board owns stock or represents substantial ownership in the Company, and has a personal interest in maximizing the value of all shareholders' investment.[11]

An audit committee should consist solely of outside directors. This committee meets with the company's auditors and engages in a frank review of the company's audit. This gives the auditors an opportunity to speak openly about differences in opinion between the auditors and management regarding the treatment of certain items and about any misgivings the auditors may have concerning any aspect of the company's operations. The auditors thus have an opportunity to report fully on management's stewardship.

Beyond that, it is difficult to provide other standards for measuring the worth of a board. Youthful directors are vigorous, but older executives have the benefits of experience and ripened judgment. Large boards are unwieldy, but small ones do not provide the necessary diversity of backgrounds. Remuneration is desirable to attract qualified executives, but there comes a point beyond which the salary factor is not the primary inducement. Some observers, as suggested above by the management of Reed Tool, contend that the number of shares of stock of a corporation owned by members of the board is a reflection of their confidence in the company. It is further held that large stock interests create more attentive management. To set up share ownership as a criterion of management quality, however, would needlessly circumscribe the area of possible stock selection. Able people can render excellent service on a board of directors even if they do not believe that the company's stock suits their personal portfolios. In addition, it must be remembered that the interests of large and small stockholders are not necessarily identical. Tax decisions inapplicable to modest shareowners might justify conservative dividend policies for holders of substantial amounts of stock.

Overall Assessment

There is no easy solution to the problem of selecting standards for gauging the quality of management. Such an evaluation inevitably depends on intangible or controversial elements. It is prudent to review the organizational structure, determine the existence of any problem areas in the management team, check the names of the board of directors and top officers, note their current and previous business affiliations, and generally give attention to the interaction of these various aspects. In its disclosure forms, the Securities and Exchange Commission has evidenced its concern with providing information on the backgrounds of corporate managers as an aid to investors. The SEC requires such information as a ten-year litigation history pertaining to directors and executive officers; a statement regarding the nature of the responsibilities in prior positions of individuals occupying executive positions; and, for registrants which are not subject to the reporting provision, information concerning the prior experience of key personnel. The commission has also taken steps to standardize this reporting in its various forms.[12]

From another point of view, the quality of management is shown by the record of the corporation, since the most satisfactory measure of success is accomplishment. Based on this criterion, the capacity of management is reflected in a corporation's financial condition, the efficiency of its operations, its reported earnings and dividends, its relative share of the total sales market, its rate of growth, its acquisition of new products, and its development of enlarged outlets for its output.

ANALYSIS OF EARNINGS GROWTH

Essentially, there are three sources of earnings growth: increasing leverage, profitability, and new equity. Leverage may come from the use of any instrument senior to common equity, including preferred stock, debt, or lease. Profitability stems from the markup that a company places on the products it sells, from the degree to which it is able to utilize capacity (asset turnover), or from some combination of these two elements. New equity may take the form of stock that is sold or earnings that are retained.

If the earnings of a company grow, the effect on the price of its stock will depend on the source of the expansion. An earnings growth from increasing leverage probably will be beneficial to the price of the stock if the increase in leverage is modest, but the benefit will be limited because additional earnings variability will be created and the growth cannot be sustained. Growth from profitability in all likelihood will be viewed more favorably, but there are limits to the extent that it can be continued. The effects of the issuance of new stock depend on the price at which it is sold relative to its net asset value. Of these various sources, only growth through retained earnings can be sustained, and it therefore tends to have the most positive effect on a company's stock.

Use of Financial Leverage

The investor's principal concern is with return on equity, which, in turn, depends on the return on assets. It will be remembered that the introduction of leverage may either inflate or deflate that rate of return. (See p. 322 for a further discussion of leverage.) Consider a firm that earns 20 percent on \$100,000 of assets which are financed by \$40,000 of 5 percent debt (an illustrative rate, not intended to reflect any actual year) and \$60,000 of common equity. In column 3 of Table 17-1, it can be readily seen that the 20 percent earnings rate on assets is lifted to a 30 percent rate on equity

TABLE 17-1

Effect of Leverage on \$100,000 Investment

	1	2	3	4	5
Rate of return on assets (%)	18	19	20	21	22
Net operating income (\$)	18,000	19,000	20,000	21,000	22,000
Interest (\$)	2,000	2,000	2,000	2,000	2,000
Net income (\$)	16,000	17,000	18,000	19,000	20,000
Rate of return on equity (%)	26.7	28.3	30.0	31.7	33.3

because all $20,000 of earnings from the $100,000 investment (less the $2,000 of interest charges) now flows to the $60,000 of equity. Leverage thus adds to the stockholder's income so long as the earnings rate on assets is greater than the interest paid to the lenders.

Similarly, as the earnings rate on assets grows, the rate applicable to equity rises more rapidly because the total gain moves to the equity segment that is smaller than the asset base. Thus, a 1 percentage point increase in the rate of return on assets (shown in columns 4 and 5) is lifted to a 1.7 and 1.6 percentage point increase in the return on equity. On the other hand, the reverse situation prevails on the downside, as a 1 percentage point decline in the earnings rate on assets (columns 1 and 2) is reflected in a 1.7 and 1.6 point shrinkage in the return on equity. The introduction of taxes changes the numbers but not the principle.

By shifting our perspective, we can see how changing leverage can generate earnings for equity holders. First, assume that a company has a starting capitalization of only 1,000 shares, increases its assets each year through the sale of 100 additional shares at $100 per share, earns 20 percent on its assets, and pays taxes at a 50 percent rate. As seen in Table 17-2, the asset expansion financed by the sale of stock makes no contribution to the earnings growth.

TABLE 17-2

Asset Expansion Financed by Stock

	YEAR 1	YEAR 2	YEAR 3	YEAR 4	YEAR 5
Assets ($)	100,000	110,000	120,000	130,000	140,000
Earnings before interest and taxes (EBIT) ($)	20,000	22,000	24,000	26,000	28,000
Earnings after taxes (EAT) ($)	10,000	11,000	12,000	13,000	14,000
Number of shares outstanding	1,000	1,100	1,200	1,300	1,400
EAT per share ($)	10.00	10.00	10.00	10.00	10.00

Suppose, however, that the asset expansion, as shown in Table 17-3, is financed by debt except in the last year. EBIT rises by $2,000 and interest increases by $500 annually in years 2 through 4. All the EAT growth of $750 flows to the benefit of the existing equity holders in these years, resulting in an annual rise of 75 cents per share. This constant earnings gain applied to a widening earnings base, however, produces a declining rate of growth in earnings per share. In year 5 the policy changes, and the asset expansion is financed by new equity. The overall effect in that year is that net income after taxes rises by about 8 percent, compared with a 10 percent increase in outstanding stock, thereby producing a decline in per share earnings.

TABLE 17-3

Asset Expansion Financed by Debt at Constant Interest Rate

	YEAR 1	YEAR 2	YEAR 3	YEAR 4	YEAR 5
EBIT ($)	20,000	22,000	24,000	26,000	28,000
Debt ($)	0	10,000	20,000	30,000	30,000
Interest ($)	0	500	1,000	1,500	1,500
EAI ($)	20,000	21,500	23,000	24,500	26,500
EAT ($)	10,000	10,750	11,500	12,250	13,250
Number of shares outstanding	1,000	1,000	1,000	1,000	1,100
EAT per share ($)	10.00	10.75	11.50	12.25	12.05
Rate of growth (%)	0	7.5	7.0	6.5	−1.6

While increasing leverage in the prior illustration benefited earnings, there was some offset in the shrinking rate of growth and in the actual decline that occurred when a stock financing policy eventually was adopted. More seriously, leverage cannot be increased indefinitely, because eventually lenders will view with alarm the growing debt burden and will refuse to grant additional loans while investors will shy away from the stock. Before this stage is reached, moreover, the mounting debt probably would call forth higher interest rates. These increased rates would eat into the earnings benefits, as shown in Table 17-4, which restates years 2 through 4 on the assumption that the interest cost rises from 5 percent to 6.5 percent. As a result, the drop in the rate of growth is more precipitous than previously. Instead of falling by 0.5 percentage point each year, it now drops by 1 and then 1.5.

TABLE 17-4

Asset Expansion Financed by Debt as Interest Rate Increases

	YEAR 2	YEAR 3	YEAR 4
EBIT ($)	22,000	24,000	26,000
Debt ($)	10,000	20,000	30,000
Interest rate (%)	5.0	5.5	6.5
Interest ($)	500	1,100	1,950
EAI ($)	21,500	22,900	24,050
EAT ($)	10,750	11,450	12,025
Number of shares outstanding	1,000	1,000	1,000
EAT per share ($)	10.75	11.45	12.02
Rate of growth (%)	7.5	6.5	5.0

If increased leverage had its origin in preferred stock, the results would be roughly the same, with the difference arising primarily because preferred dividends are not deductible for tax purposes. Financing by leases also creates leverage, although the impact on balance sheets is concealed if the capitalized charges are not taken into account. The important thing, however, is that regardless of how leverage is created, the effect of the resulting earnings benefits on the price of a company's stock is partially offset by the fact that gains from this source cannot be sustained, and the riskiness of the equity is increased.

Profitability

Profitability stems from productivity. A common measure of productivity is the rate of return that a company is able to obtain from the assets at its disposal. This rate, in turn, is a consequence of two forces, markup and asset turnover.

$$\text{Productivity} = \frac{\text{EBIT}}{\text{Sales}} \times \frac{\text{Sales}}{\text{Assets}} = \frac{\text{EBIT}}{\text{Assets}}$$

The formula uses earnings before interest and taxes (EBIT) because the measure is intended to gauge operating efficiency rather than the ability to borrow at low costs or to minimize the tax burden. It is reasonable to employ total assets as the base, rather than only those assets most directly involved in producing the current period's earnings, because of the difficulty of making such a refinement and the broad character of the measure. There is some controversy as to whether the assets should be gross or net of depreciation, but the tendency is toward the gross figure because depreciation is heavily influenced by tax issues and the periodic charge is rarely a genuine reflection of a corresponding decline in productive capacity.

A troublesome question was the handling of leases. At one time, "accepted accounting principles" permitted the lease obligation incurred by a company that finances the acquisition of assets in this manner to be omitted from the balance sheet; therefore, the company's reported assets and liabilities were both understated. To calculate the asset-turnover ratio, or the return on assets, an adjustment was necessary to take into account the assets represented by the lease financing. A logical procedure followed by some analysts was to distinguish between two components of lease rentals; one, amounting to perhaps one-third of the rental, was taken to represent bond interest and sinking fund, while the other, covering taxes, insurance, and so forth, was included in operating expenses. The bond portion was then capitalized for the life of the lease at prevailing interest rates to obtain an imputed value for the debt and corresponding asset.

As a result of SEC requirements, companies must now disclose the present value of financing leases and the impact on net income of capitalizing such leases. Presumably this requirement is considered "accepted accounting principles." As discussed previously, the FASB has been developing extensive requirements of its own.[13]

The two components of productivity are helpful in throwing light on the characteristics of a company. It is to be expected that a company with a large investment in fixed assets, such as a public utility, would have a low asset-turnover ratio but a correspondingly high markup, as indicated by its ratio of earnings to sales. Conversely, a volume-oriented firm, such as a variety chain store, is likely to have a low profit margin but depend on a very rapid turnover of its assets to achieve an adequate rate of return. In the case of IBM, a breakdown of the components reveals that the company has a low turnover rate for an industrial enterprise, partly because of the considerable amount of funds invested in leased equipment and partly because of the enormous amount of short-term marketable investments it has characteristically carried. Accordingly, its outstanding performance has been achieved by an unusually high ratio of earnings to sales, rivaling that of a public utility.

Excess capacity, suggested by an asset-turnover ratio that is low compared with prior standards, could come about for various reasons: an economic slump may have reduced demand for the company's products; the company's market as a whole may not have developed as anticipated; or unusually aggressive competition may have been encountered. A common thread, of course, runs through all these influences, since a falling economy shrinks the market for a company's goods and leads to unexpectedly severe competition.

Profit margins may also narrow because of fading demand or rising competition when the economy is at high tide. Even if a company can maintain prices in the face of these conditions, the excess capacity likely to result means that overhead must be spread over fewer units of output, with detrimental effects on profits. On the other hand, excess utilization of assets may also curtail profit margins, as production bottlenecks develop and labor becomes less efficient. In the case of excess utilization of assets, however, only profit margins suffer, whereas in the case of excess capacity both ratios are likely to depress profitability. Accordingly, in order to evaluate the implications of changes in profitability, the analyst must investigate the factors leading to the changes in the underlying components.

Either an increase in the utilization of assets (until the point of excess utilization is reached), even if the profit margin remains unchanged, or a rise in the profit margin, even if asset utilization is the same, will bring about an increase in profitability. Over certain periods of time, gains from either or both of these two components may be achieved. This is particularly true for companies that are underutilizing assets or have experienced cost control problems. However, there are limits to the extent that a company can either utilize assets more efficiently or raise profit margins, although its influence over the latter ratio is usually greater. In Table 17-5, as an illustration, the bands within which these ratios move can be perceived for the companies covered. Over a nine-year period, the asset-turnover ratio of Acme (now traded under the name American Stores) was 3.6 at its lowest point and 4.0 at its highest, while Acme's profit margin moved from a low of 1.3 percent to a high of 2.7 percent; for Scott, the asset-turnover range was 0.7 to 0.8, while the profit margin ranged from 11.5 percent to 18.2 percent; for Philadelphia Electric, the asset-turnover range was unchanged, while the profit margin moved between 33.2 percent and 37.7.

For all three companies shown, the long-term earnings-sales ratio was downward. However, profit margins may be temporarily affected by special events in particular years which could lead to later benefits. In 1972, for example, Libby, McNeill & Libby incurred heavy expenses in the promotion of new corporate trademarks and labels; presumably these expenses would be reduced in future years, while the company's marketing efforts would be helped.[14] Profit margins can also be aided by more effective cost control. Thus, in 1970, the Harnischfeger Corp., a major producer of construction and mining equipment, inaugurated a cost-cutting program that benefited operating margins in that year as well as in 1971.[15]

This analysis indicates that there is considerable room for variation in the profitability of a company over time. As has been mentioned, under ordinary conditions a company is likely to have greater ability to influence profit margins than to improve asset utilization. It is questionable, however, whether profits generated from either of these two components can be sustained; turnover is limited by capacity and profit margins by competition. As benchmarks for potential gains, both the company's historical average and industry standards can be examined.

Sale of Stock

We have noted that when stock is sold, the effect on earnings depends on its price relative to its net asset value.

Sale at a price equal to net asset value. If there is no change in productivity and all earnings are distributed as dividends (so that there is no retention), the sale of shares at a price equal to its net asset value has no influence on earnings growth. This condition is illustrated in Table 17-6.

In year 0, the company has $100,000 of assets and 10,000 shares outstanding. It obtains a return of 10 percent on its assets, producing per share earnings of $1.00. Its stock sells at 10 times this figure, resulting in a price of $10.00, which is the same as the net assets per share. Each year thereafter the company expands its assets by 10 percent, entirely financed

TABLE 17-5

Productivity Changes of Three Companies, 1962-1970

	1962	1963	1964	1965	1966	1967	1968	1969	1970
ACME									
EBIT ($ mil.)	28.3	26.8	27.6	24.4	18.9	17.0	16.3	23.1	27.6
Assets (A) ($ mil.)	259.6	271.6	290.9	305.0	328.6	326.1	346.2	372.1	423.3
Sales (S) ($ mil.)	1,034.9	1,081.1	1,118.7	1,161.2	1,200.7	1,253.7	1,293.8	1,471.1	1,650.2
EBIT/S (%)	2.7	2.5	2.5	2.1	1.6	1.4	1.3	1.6	1.7
S/A	4.0	4.0	3.9	3.8	3.6	3.8	3.7	4.0	3.9
EBIT/A (%)	10.9	9.9	9.5	8.0	5.8	5.2	4.7	6.2	6.5
SCOTT									
EBIT ($ mil.)	64.6	67.3	68.2	72.0	95.1	99.3	98.3	108.5	87.2
Assets ($ mil.)	446.8	470.8	534.8	602.4	816.1	885.5	936.7	1,018.7	1,092.1
Sales ($ mil.)	354.4	370.0	428.6	461.0	591.9	623.4	684.6	731.5	755.7
EBIT/S (%)	18.2	18.2	15.9	15.6	16.1	15.9	14.4	14.8	11.5
S/A	0.8	0.8	0.8	0.8	0.7	0.7	0.7	0.7	0.7
EBIT/A (%)	14.5	14.3	12.8	12.0	11.7	11.2	10.5	10.7	8.0
PHILADELPHIA ELECTRIC									
EBIT ($ mil.)	114.4	116.7	120.6	125.3	131.5	139.0	141.9	155.1	167.6
Assets ($ mil.)	1,449.7	1,510.2	1,561.9	1,624.2	1,729.1	1,880.5	2,035.8	2,280.4	2,632.1
Sales ($ mil.)	303.2	314.4	323.9	340.9	357.9	376.5	405.2	440.5	504.4
EBIT/S (%)	37.7	37.1	37.2	36.8	36.7	36.9	35.0	35.2	33.2
S/A	0.2	0.2	0.2	0.2	0.2	0.2	0.2	0.2	0.2
EBIT/A (%)	7.9	7.7	7.7	7.7	7.6	7.4	7.0	6.8	6.4

SOURCE: Data taken from the Acme, Scott Paper, and Philadelphia Electric annual reports, 1962-1970.

by the sale of stock. The company continues to earn 10 percent on its assets, and therefore both assets and net operating income grow at this same rate. Since the stock is sold at a constant price of $10.00 which is the same as the net asset value, the outstanding shares also rise by 10 percent each year. As a result, both assets and earnings per share remain unchanged; there is no growth.

TABLE 17-6

Asset Expansion Financed by Sale of Stock at Price Equal to Assets per Share

	YEAR 0	YEAR 1	YEAR 2	YEAR 3	YEAR 4
(1) Assets (A) ($)*	100,000	110,000	121,000	133,100	146,410
(2) Net operating income (NOI) ($) (10% of line 1)	10,000	11,000	12,100	13,310	14,641
(3) Required equtiy ($) (Δ line 1)	—	10,000	11,000	12,100	13,310
(4) Shares outstanding (S)* (line 4 of preceding year + line 9)	10,000	11,000	12,100	13,310	14,641
(5) Earned per share (EPS) ($) (line 2 ÷ line 4)	1.00	1.00	1.00	1.00	1.00
(6) Price/earnings (p/e) ratio*	10	10	10	10	10
(7) Assets/share ($) (line 1 ÷ line 4)	10.00	10.00	10.00	10.00	10.00
(8) Price/share ($) (line 5 X line 6)	10.00	10.00	10.00	10.00	10.00
(9) Shares sold (beginning of year) (line 3 ÷ line 8 of preceding year)	—	1,000	1,100	1,210	1,331
(10) Dividend yield (%)† (line 5 ÷ line 8)	10	10	10	10	10
(11) EPS growth (%)	—	—	—	—	—

*At the outset, lines 1 and 4 of year 0 are given; line 6 is given and remains constant.
†All earnings paid out as dividends.

Sale at a price above net asset value. In Table 17-7, the same circumstances are assumed as in Table 17-6, with the conspicuous exception that this time the company is able to issue its stock at 11 times earnings, producing a sales price in year 1 of $11, compared with a net asset value of $10. As previously, assets and net operating income grow at a 10 percent rate. So long as this growth is financed by issuance of common stock, the percentage gain on a per share basis must be less than this rate. The magni-

TABLE 17-7

Asset Expansion Financed by Sale of Stock at Price Greater than Assets per Share

	YEAR 0	YEAR 1	YEAR 2	YEAR 3	YEAR 4
(1) Assets ($)*	100,000	110,000	121,000	133,100	146,410
(2) NOI ($) (10% of line 1)	10,000	11,000	12,100	13,310	14,641
(3) Required equity ($) (Δ line 1)	—	10,000	11,000	12,100	13,310
(4) Shares outstanding* (line 4 of preceding year + line 9)	10,000	10,909	11,901	12,983	14,163
(5) EPS ($) (line 2 ÷ line 4)	1.0000	1.0083	1.0167	1.0252	1.0338
(6) P/E ratio*	11	11	11	11	11
(7) Assets/share ($) (line 1 ÷ line 4)	10.000	10.083	10.167	10.252	10.338
(8) Price/share ($) (line 5 X line 6)	11.00	11.09	11.18	11.28	11.37
(9) Shares sold (beginning of year) (line 3 ÷ line 8 of preceding year)	—	909	992	1,082	1,180
(10) Dividend yield (%)† (line 5 ÷ line 8)	9.1	9.1	9.1	9.1	9.1
(11) EPS growth (%)	—	.83	.83	.84	.84

*At the outset, lines 1 and 4 of year 0 are given; line 6 is given and remains constant.
†All earnings paid out as dividends.

tude of the gain depends on the relationship between the percentage increase in assets and earnings (1.10) relative to the percentage increase in the number of shares outstanding (1.0909). This relationship (1.0083), in turn, depends on the difference between the sales price of the stock and its net asset value. When the sales price is only slightly above net asset value, the growth in shares outstanding will be close to that of the growth in assets and earnings, and the gains per share will be modest. The wider the gap between sales price and net asset value, the fewer shares needed to be issued and the swifter the rise in earnings per share. However, it is unlikely that this kind of growth can be sustained since eventually a persistent increase in outstanding shares will have an adverse effect on the price/earnings ratio and lead to a decline in the price of the stock relative to its earnings.

Issuance of stock for acquisitions. A rather different situation arises when new stock is issued to acquire other firms. In this case, the earnings effect depends on a variety of factors, including the relative size of the companies, their growth rates, and the exchange terms. Consider Table 17-8.

TABLE 17-8

The Transitory and Growth Effects of a Merger

			MERGED COMPANY			
	FIRM *A*	FIRM *B*	YEAR 0	YEAR 1	YEAR 2	YEAR 3
NOI ($)	40,000,000	20,000,000	60,000,000	67,000,000	74,850,000	83,657,500
Shares outstanding	30,000,000	30,000,000	37,500,000	37,500,000	37,500,000	37,500,000
EPS ($)	1.33	.67	1.60	1.79	2.00	2.23
P/E ratio	40	20	40			
Price per share ($)	53.20	13.40	64.00			
EPS growth (%)	—	—	—	34.0*	11.7	11.5

*Gain over *A*'s earnings of $1.33 per share.

Here it is assumed that firm *A* acquires firm *B* by paying one share of its stock for each four shares of *B*. *A* is the dominant enterprise in its field, its earnings outlook is for a consistent growth rate of 10 percent, and the stock sells at 40 times earnings. *B* is a relatively new entry in a very competitive field, and therefore its stock sells at only 20 times earnings, despite the fact that earnings are growing at a 15 percent rate. The terms may seem unattractive to *B*, since its shareholders surrender \$53.60 worth of shares for \$53.20 *A* stock. If investors give primary weight to *A*'s strong position and value the stock of the merged company at 40 times earnings, however, its stock will sell at \$64.00, and *B*'s shareholders will realize a gain of \$2.60 per share.

From *A*'s point of view, it obtains both a company growing more rapidly than itself and some diversification of activity. In year 0 of the merger, the new company has a net income of \$60 million and 37.5 million shares outstanding. Accordingly, its earnings per share in year 0 are \$1.60 compared with *A*'s \$1.33, an increase of 27 cents due entirely to the bargain struck and wholly independent of the growth rates of the two firms. In year 1, earnings rise an additional 19 cents to \$1.79, reflecting the growth rates of the firms and the exchange ratio which determines the number of *A* shares outstanding after the merger. Thus, the overall rise between *A*'s earnings of \$1.33 in year 0 and the combined company's earnings of \$1.79 in year 1 is 46 cents, or 34 percent, which, in turn is divided into two components: 27 cents, or 20 percent, because of the merger; and 19 cents, or 14 percent, which would have occurred without the merger and is due to the growth rate of the two firms.[16]

Of these two components, the one for 20 percent is transitory and has no effect in subsequent years; the one for 14 percent, in turn, may be broken into 10 percent, representing *A*'s basic growth rate, and 4 percent, which is the real incremental growth rate. In years 2 and 3 the overall rate of growth shrinks to 11.7 and 11.5 percent; the incremental effects, therefore, are only 1.7 and 1.5 percent, which are small compared with the transitory effect of 20 percent. Suppose then that a firm repeatedly acquires new firms; its maximum per share transitory growth is the ratio between the net income of the acquired firm and original firm, in this case 50 percent, and such an increase can only occur if the acquired firm is given to the conglomerate, a very remote possibility. More realistically, this ratio is reduced by the effect of the new shares that are issued for the acquired firm. Moreover, the size of the transitory effect is likely to diminish because as the conglomerate grows, it will have difficulty in finding target acquisitions that are sufficiently big to have meaningful earnings compared with those of the basic company. That is, no matter how large the conglomerate gets, the new acquisitions must maintain the same size, relative to the conglomerate, a condition that requires the discovery of successively larger firms. Such a conglomerate eventually would encompass the entire economy, and therefore this source of growth cannot be maintained.

Retention of Earnings

Another source of earnings growth is through the plow-back of earnings. To illustrate its implications, we employ in Table 17-9 a firm operating under the same assumptions as in Table 17-7, but this time its required new assets are financed through earnings retention rather than the sale of stock. Since net operating income grows and the number of shares outstanding is unchanged, earnings per share grow at the same rate as that of net operating income. In this case the rate is 10 percent, and it is maintained year after year.

TABLE 17-9

Asset Expansion Financed by Retained Earnings

	YEAR 0	YEAR 1	YEAR 2	YEAR 3	YEAR 4
(1) Assets ($)*	100,000	110,000	121,000	133,100	146,410
(2) NOI ($) (10% of line 1)	10,000	11,000	12,100	13,310	14,641
(3) Required equity ($) (Δ line 1)	—	10,000	11,000	12,100	13,310
(4) Shares outstanding (unchanged)*	10,000	10,000	10,000	10,000	10,000
(5) EPS ($) (line 2 ÷ line 4)	1.00	1.10	1.21	1.33	1.46
(6) P/E ratio*	11	11	11	11	11
(7) Assets/share ($) (line 1 ÷ line 4)	10.00	11.00	12.10	13.31	14.64
(8) Price/share ($) (line 5 X line 6)	11.00	12.10	13.31	14.63	16.06
(9) Shares sold	—	—	—	—	—
(10) Dividend yield (%)	—	—	—	—	—
(11) EPS growth (%)	—	10	10	10	10

*At the outset, line 1 is given; lines 4 and 6 are given and remain constant.

For purpose of the illustration, no dividend payment was assumed. So long, however, as a company disburses only a portion of its earnings, invests the amount retained in the business, and maintains its productivity, the company can continue to grow. This condition is easy to generalize:

$$E_1 = E_0 + rbE_0,$$

where E_1 = earnings in year 1, b = retention ratio, and r = return on new equity. In this equation, bE_0 is the additional equity used in the firm in year 1; therefore, rbE_0 represents the additional earnings of the firm in year 1. As a result,

$$E_1 = (1 + rb)E_0, \text{ and}$$

$$E_1/E_0 = (1 + g).$$

Clearly therefore $g = rb$, the rate of growth of earnings (and assets per share). While the growth, g, can be sustained, it may be affected by changes in the earnings rate and the dividend payout ratio. In the early years this latter ratio is apt to be low, gradually rising to perhaps 70 percent of earnings as the company approaches maturity.

Unraveling Growth

Growth cannot be unraveled in any easy way because of the interaction of its various sources. This difficulty may be indicated by several illustrations. At the outset, consider Table 17-10. This is the simple case of a company that has a debt-free capitalization of $100,000, does no new financing, and distributes all its earnings as dividends. The company earns 10 percent on its assets in year 1 and through improved productivity raises this return to 11 percent in year 2. As a result, net income per share increases from $1.00 in year 1 to $1.10 in year 2, or a gain of 10 percent.

TABLE 17-10

Effect of Increased Productivity with Assets Unchanged and No Leverage

	YEAR 1	YEAR 2
Assets ($)	100,000	100,000
Return on assets (%)	10	11
NOI ($)	10,000	11,000
Net income ($)	10,000	11,000
Total equity ($)	100,000	100,000
Retention ($)	0	0
Shares outstanding	10,000	10,000
Net assets/share ($)	10.00	10.00
EPS ($)	1.00	1.10
EPS growth (%)	—	10

In Table 17-11, the assumption is now made that the company's capitalization is equally composed of bonds and stock. The company pays interest of 5 percent on its debt, thereby reducing its net operating income each year by $2,500. Because half the capitalization is in debt, there are only 5,000 shares outstanding, compared with 10,000 in the previous case. As a result, earnings per share equal $1.50 in year 1 and $1.70 in year 2. The gain now is 13 percent, which is 2 percentage points greater than the original pure productivity effect.

TABLE 17-11

Effect of Increased Productivity with Assets Unchanged and Leverage

	YEAR 1	YEAR 2
Assets ($)	100,000	100,000
Return on assets (%)	10	11
NOI ($)	10,000	11,000
Debt at beginning ($)	50,000	50,000
Interest ($)	2,500	2,500
Net income ($)	7,500	8,500
Total equity ($)	50,000	50,000
Retention ($)	0	0
Shares outstanding	5,000	5,000
Net assets/share ($)	20.00	20.00
EPS ($)	1.50	1.70
EPS growth (%)	—	13

In Table 17-12 a new set of conditions is assumed. This time the company acquires additional assets which are financed in three different ways: by retained earnings, debt, and additional stock. When the acquisition of assets is financed through retained earnings, the per share gain in earnings is 5 percent; when the financing is through debt, the per share gain in earnings is 2.5 percent; and when the financing is through stock, the per share earnings are unchanged. Thus, an increase of productivity by itself produces a 10 percent improvement of per share earnings, while the acquisition of assets by itself contributes a 5 percent improvement if financed by retained earnings and a 2.5 percent improvement if financed by debt.

In Table 17-13 a further modification is introduced. It is now assumed that productivity gains by 10 percent and that additional assets of 5 percent are acquired, financed in the same three ways as previously. This time, per share earnings on an overall basis rise to $1.16, or by 16 percent, when the acquisition is financed by retained earnings; to $1.13, or by 13 percent, when the financing is by debt; and to $1.10, or by 10 percent, when the financing is by stock. Thus, the greatest gain occurs when the financing is through retained earnings. Moreover, the simultaneous increase in productivity and acquisition of assets financed by retained earnings results in a 1 percentage point greater gain in growth of per share earnings (16% – 15%) than the sum of the separate contributions, 10 percent from productivity improvement and 5 percent from new assets. Finally, a simultaneous increase in productivity and acquisition of assets financed by debt results in a 0.5 percentage point greater gain in growth of per share earnings (13.0% – 12.5%) than the sum of the separate contributions, 10 percent from productivity improvement, and 2.5 percent from increased leverage.

TABLE 17-12

Effect of Enlarged Assets Financed in Different Ways with No Change in Productivity

	YEAR			
	1	2a	2b	2c
		FINANCING METHOD		
		RETAINED EARNINGS	DEBT	STOCK
(1) Assets ($)	100,000	105,000	105,000	105,000
(2) Return on assets (%)	10	10	10	10
(3) NOI ($)	10,000	10,500	10,500	10,500
(4) Debt at beginning ($)	—	—	5,000	—
(5) Interest (5%)	—	—	250	—
(6) Net income ($)	10,000	10,500	10,250	10,500
(7) Net assets acquired ($)	—	5,000	5,000	5,000
(8) New debt incurred for current financing ($)	—	—	5,000	—
(9) Retention ($)	—	5,000	—	—
(10) New equity issued at beginning ($)	—	—	—	5,000
(11) Total equity ($)	100,000	105,000	100,000	105,000
(12) Shares outstanding at beginning	10,000	10,000	10,000	10,500
(13) Net assets/share ($)	10.00	10.50	10.00	10.00
(14) Number of shares sold at beginning*	—	—	—	500
(15) EPS ($)	1.00	1.05	1.025	1.00
(16) EPS growth (%)	—	5.0	2.5	0

*At a price equal to net assets/share; see line (13).

This analysis highlights two conclusions. One is that all other things being equal, an increase in assets will result in a greater rise in earnings per share if financed by retained earnings than if financed by debt. This difference is caused by the fact that all the additional income from the enlarged assets accrues to the existing shares when the assets are financed by retained earnings; the incremental interest must be deducted when the assets are financed by debt, while the additional income is offset by the rise in the number of shares when the financing is by stock sold at the same price as the net asset per share. The second conclusion is that the change in per share earnings from the interaction of these various factors—leverage and productivity or greater assets and productivity—is not equal to the sum of the separate contributions. Despite the difficulty of quantifying the contributions to per share earnings, an examination of the manner in which the contributory factors change is useful in throwing light on a company's intrinsic position and prospects. Such an analysis is illustrated in Table 17-14 for Acme and Philadelphia Electric; Scott is omitted because the substantial changes experienced by the company during the period covered made it difficult to obtain comparable asset/share and debt/share data.

TABLE 17-13

Effect of Increased Productivity and Enlarged Assets Financed in Different Ways

	YEAR			
	1	2a	2b	2c
		FINANCING METHOD		
		RETAINED EARNINGS	DEBT	STOCK
(1) Assets ($)	100,000	105,000	105,000	105,000
(2) Return on assets (%)	10	11	11	11
(3) NOI ($)	10,000	11,550	11,550	11,550
(4) Debt at beginning ($)	—	—	5,000	—
(5) Interest (5%)	—	—	250	—
(6) Net income ($)	10,000	11,550	11,300	11,550
(7) Net assets acquired ($)	—	5,000	5,000	5,000
(8) Net debt incurred for current financing ($)	—	—	5,000	—
(9) Retention ($)	—	5,000	—	—
(10) New equity issued at beginning ($)	—	—	—	5,000
(11) Total equity ($)	100,000	105,000	100,000	105,000
(12) Shares outstanding at beginning	10,000	10,000	10,000	10,500
(13) Net assets/share ($)	10.00	10.50	10.00	10.00
(14) Number of shares sold at beginning*	—	—	—	500
(15) EPS ($)	1.00	1.16	1.13	1.10
(16) EPS growth (%)	—	16.0	13.0	10.0

*At a price equal to net assets/share; see line (13).

From 1962 through 1968 the earnings per share of Acme declined steadily in the face of a consistent increase in assets per share. The source of the company's difficulty lay in a substantial decrease in productivity, from 10.9 percent in 1962 to 4.7 percent in 1968. The changes in leverage were mixed; on balance, debt tended to increase, thereby accentuating the effects of shrinking productivity. In 1969 and 1970 both productivity and leverage were

TABLE 17-14

Factors Contributing to Earnings per Share Growth for Two Companies, 1962-1970

	1962	1963	1964	1965	1966	1967	1968	1969	1970
ACME									
(1) Earnings per share ($)	3.94	3.85	3.99	3.84	3.08	2.82	2.55	3.25	3.69
(2) Change EPS (%)		−2.3	3.6	−3.8	−19.8	−8.4	−9.6	27.5	13.5
(3) Productivity (EBIT/A) (%)	10.9	9.9	9.5	8.0	5.8	5.2	4.7	6.2	6.5
(4) Change in productivity (%)		−9.2	−4.0	−15.8	−27.5	−10.3	−9.6	31.9	4.8
(5) Assets/share ($)	64.86	67.18	71.86	75.19	79.45	80.71	86.15	92.63	103.88
(6) Change A/S (%)		3.6	7.0	4.6	5.7	1.6	6.7	7.5	12.1
(7) Net assets/share ($)	40.79	43.31	45.94	48.23	48.89	50.21	51.08	52.63	54.56
(8) Change NA/S (%)		6.2	6.1	5.0	1.4	2.7	1.7	3.0	3.7
(9) Debt/share ($)*	22.80	21.79	23.19	23.65	27.04	26.73	31.20	36.16	45.57
(10) Change D/S (%)		−4.4	6.4	2.0	14.3	−1.1	16.7	15.9	26.0
(11) Debt/asset (%)	35.2	32.4	32.3	31.5	34.0	33.1	36.2	39.0	43.9
(12) Change D/A (%)		−8.0	−0.3	−2.5	7.9	−2.6	9.4	7.7	12.6
PHILADELPHIA ELECTRIC									
(1) Earnings per share ($)	1.61	1.71	1.79	1.92	2.08	2.13	1.94	1.97	1.84
(2) Change EPS (%)		6.2	4.7	7.3	8.3	2.4	−8.9	1.5	−6.6
(3) Productivity (EBIT/A) (%)	7.9	7.7	7.7	7.7	7.6	7.4	7.0	6.8	6.4
(4) Change in productivity (%)		−2.5	0	0	−1.3	−2.6	−5.4	−2.9	−5.9
(5) Assets/share ($)	41.22	42.59	43.71	44.94	47.73	51.33	53.52	59.92	64.26
(6) Change A/S (%)		3.3	2.6	2.8	6.2	7.5	4.3	12.0	7.2
(7) Net assets/share ($)	14.49	15.17	15.52	16.00	16.73	18.39	18.15	20.30	20.45
(8) Change NA/S (%)		4.7	2.3	3.1	4.6	9.9	−1.3	11.8	0.7
(9) Debt/share ($)*	22.31	22.96	23.71	24.42	26.46	28.30	31.08	34.11	36.85
(10) Change D/S (%)		2.9	3.3	3.0	8.4	7.0	9.8	9.7	8.0
(11) Debt/asset (%)	54.1	53.9	54.2	54.3	55.4	55.1	58.1	56.9	57.3
(12) Change D/A (%)		−0.4	0.6	0.2	2.0	−0.5	5.4	−2.1	0.7

*Based on total debt.

lifted, and per share earnings therefore experienced substantial gains. The combination of more resources at its disposal and more leverage brought Acme's 1970 earnings per share to a level close to that of 1962. Productivity of 6.5 percent in 1970, however, was still well below the 10.9 percent of 1962. This difference, in turn, was largely due to reduced profit margins rather than failure to utilize assets fully. Thus, the outlook for the company depended to a large extent on its ability to meet competitive pressures and gain more effective control over costs, a condition that was accentuated by its much larger debt-equity ratio.

The Philadelphia Electric story is somewhat different. Between 1962 and 1967 the company was able to raise its per share earnings at a persistent although mixed rate. Since productivity changes were negative during most of these years, the gain was caused primarily by the growth of assets/share. In 1968 and 1970, however, productivity declined with relative sharpness; per share earnings also suffered, although they remained somewhat higher than in 1962 because of the offsetting effects of the enlarged assets/share. Thus, the components of profitability tended to offset each other to a greater extent in Philadelphia Electric's case than in Acme's. The ability of the company to change its productivity was inhibited by the presence of a utility commission that largely controlled its rate of return. Since it was likely that assets/share would do no more than continue a steady rate of growth, no basic change in reported earnings/share appeared on the horizon.

To the securities analyst, unraveling growth has important implications. Ordinarily, he will not be able to ascribe exact percentages to the different factors contributing to the growth. Through analysis, however, he will be able to get some insights into their relative importance. He will be most impressed by a company that is able to maintain a high level of productivity and to finance a major portion of its growth through retained earnings. At the same time, he will prefer that the company make adroit use of capitalization changes through modest employment of leverage and the sale of limited amounts of stock at prices well above net assets/share.

SUMMARY

The analyst must consider not only the short-term performance of a company but also certain underlying issues: whether the company has the management to sustain profitability, and whether there are ingredients in the company's financial development that suggest its growth may not be sustainable.

Despite the importance of management, its qualitative nature makes it a particularly elusive factor to evaluate. Where possible, therefore, a direct visit is desirable so that a personal judgment can be made regarding the depth of management and its general ability to respond to questions. Even if such a visit cannot be arranged, helpful information may be gathered from generally available sources, such as the company's annual reports, SEC records, newspaper articles, trade journals, and the analyses of reputable brokerage firms. By examining these sources, the analyst may gain insights into such areas as the company's organizational structure, its chief executives, and its board of directors.

From another point of view, the quality of management is shown by the record of the corporation, since the most satisfactory measure of success is accomplishment. Based on this criterion, the capacity of management is reflected in such factors as a corporation's financial condition, its reported earnings and dividends, and its rate of growth. Probably the most prudent approach in evaluating management is both direct, through a review of its organization and personnel, and indirect, through an appraisal of its statistical record.

There are essentially three sources of earnings growth. Leverage may come from the use of any instrument senior to common equity, including preferred stock, debt, or lease. Profitability stems from the markup that a company places on the products it sells, as well as from its ability to utilize its capacity. New equity may take the form of stock that is sold or earnings that are retained.

Earnings growth from leverage probably will be beneficial to the price of the stock if the increase in leverage is modest, but the benefit will be limited because additional earnings variability will be created. Growth from profitability in all likelihood will be viewed more favorably, but there are limits to the extent such growth can be continued. The effects of the issuance of new stock depend on the price at which it is sold relative to its net asset value. So long as the price of the stock exceeds its asset value, earnings per share will rise by the ratio of the earnings rate on assets to the earnings yield of the stock. It is unlikely that this rate can be kept high indefinitely, however, because eventually a persistent increase in outstanding shares will have an adverse effect on the price/earnings ratio. As a result, the price of the stock will decline relative to its earnings. Of the various sources of earnings growth, only growth through retained earnings can be sustained. Therefore, this method tends to have the most positive effect on a company's stock.

Part Four

ANALYZING FIXED-INCOME SECURITIES

With interest rates at generally high levels, increasing attention in recent years has been focused on fixed-income securities, including those of corporations, the U.S. government, and state and local governments, broadly classified under the rubric "municipals." The first two chapters of this section establish the principles for evaluating corporate obligations. In the course of conducting its massive financing operations, the U.S. government has issued a myriad of marketable and nonmarketable issues; to take advantage of the investment opportunities afforded by this array of securities requires an understanding of their major features, which are reviewed in the following chapter. The tax-exempt privileges of municipal bonds endow them with special appeal to investors in the high-income tax bracket; the special considerations involved in appraising these obligations are described in Chapter 21. This section closes with a discussion of preferred stock, a form of fixed-income security that requires special analytic treatment because of its mixed bond-stock characteristics.

CHAPTER 18

Introduction to Bond Analysis

The complete contract between a borrowing corporation and the holder of its obligations is evidenced by two instruments: (1) the bond, which contains the corporation's promise to pay a stipulated amount to either bearer or registered holder; and (2) the trust indenture, which is made out to a trustee with the bondholders as beneficiaries. Holders usually see only the bond. They might even find it difficult to obtain a copy of the indenture. The size which such documents sometimes attain makes it prohibitively expensive to print many copies. Moreover, the average investor is not likely to understand the indenture's complex legal phraseology.

The owner of a corporate obligation has two sets of rights, one arising out of the bond, the other from the indenture. The modern bond refers to the indenture in several instances, thus clearly notifying the holder of its existence. The courts have generally construed the two documents as representing a single instrument embodying the full rights of the owner.

CORPORATE BOND

A *corporate bond* represents a debt of the issuing corporation. It is an instrument usually but not necessarily under seal, in which the corporation promises to pay a fixed amount of money at a designated time with interest until a specified maturity date. In addition to these essential legal requirements, a typical bond may contain a good deal of supporting information, including a summary of its important characteristics, such as redemption, registration, and conversion features; a statement of the rights of holders; the procedure in the event of default; authorization to modify some of the terms of the contract on approval of a specified percentage of holders; and a statement that recourse may not be had to any stockholder, director, or officer for payment of principal or interest.

Bond Denominations

The denomination of a bond is the value indicated on its face, which the corporation will pay at maturity. The most common denomination is $1,000, although some corporations have issued obligations with lesser denominations. This practice has not been widely adopted, because it entails increased expense to the issuer. In recent years, more interest has been shown in small denominations, to attract individual investors who have increased their participation in the bond market. Corporations commonly offer bonds of higher denominations to meet the needs of institutions whose transactions may be large. The companies usually permit denominations to be interchanged within certain broad limits, and the New York Stock Exchange has established special rules governing the deliverability of bonds of different denominations. The unit of trading for bonds listed on the NYSE is $1,000 original principal amount, except in special cases, when higher trading units may be designated by the exchange. Since bonds are ordinarily traded in large amounts, the NYSE permits orders for the purchase or sale of ten bonds or more to be executed off the floor without the necessity of obtaining prior consent. The principal market for bonds, therefore, is over the counter.

Coupon Bonds and Registered Bonds

Most bonds are issued with *coupons*. These are small rectangular slips of uniform size attached to a bond. Each coupon represents the corporation's promise to pay a specified amount of interest to the bearer. The owner of a bond must detach these coupons on interest dates and forward them to the designated paying agent or obtain collection through the facilities of a commercial bank, much as he would cash a check. Coupon bonds are transferable by delivery.

Registered bonds are payable to specified persons. The name of the payee appears on the face of the bond and is entered in the bond register kept by the company or its paying agent. Bonds may be registered as to both principal and interest or only as to principal.

Registered bonds may be transferred by endorsement of the owner. If the bond is registered as to principal only, the coupons may be detached and presented for payment. In the case of bonds registered as to interest as well, payments are made directly to the registered owner. Interchangeability of registered and coupon bonds is governed by the terms of the trust indenture.

Interest Payment Dates

Interest on bonds is generally paid semiannually on the first of the month. Typical payment dates are January and July, February and August, March and September, April and October, May and November, and June and December.

Occasionally, interest is payable annually, especially in the case of income or real estate bonds. A domestic issue with an annual payment is the Chicago Great Western General Income 4½s due 2038. Annual payments are also common on Eurobonds, which are issues floated abroad, possibly in several countries by international underwriting syndicates. The market in Eurobonds emerged in 1963, when various foreign public and private enterprises which were limited by the interest equalization tax from borrowing in the United States began to issue securities in Europe.[1] The market was further stimulated by the introduction of the voluntary Department of Commerce foreign direct investment control program, which led U.S. corporations to raise capital abroad. Thereafter, the market flourished, and since the elimination of U.S. restraints it has remained an alternative source of funds for American firms.

The investor must be careful to note that an annual bond does not provide the same yield as a bond with the same interest paid semiannually. As an illustration, a bond selling at par with a 6 percent coupon payable annually and maturing in 20 years provides a yield equivalent to a bond with a 5.913 percent coupon payable semiannually and identical in all other respects. The reason lies in the effect of compound interest.

TRUST INDENTURE

The trust indenture is the supplementary document. It is an agreement between the corporation and the trustees representing the bondholders in which the terms of the issue, together with the rights and responsibilities of the parties involved, are described in detail. The indenture permits a single trustee to serve in place of numerous bondholders located over wide geographic areas. Many of these holders own but a few bonds and are neither sufficiently informed nor able to act for themselves.

Through the trust indenture and the vesting of certain powers in the trustee, much expense and duplication of effort are avoided. Because there is no need to make a separate contract with each holder, the rights of the parties can be fully explained and various modification clauses inserted. Where bonds are nationally distributed, use of the trust indenture is a practical necessity. In the case of obligations of national or local governments, trust indentures are rarely used. The rights of holders of these bonds are governed by the legislation authorizing their issuance.

Corporate Trustee

It was formerly common practice to name individuals as trustees under corporate trust indentures. At present, a banking institution or trust company is generally appointed, although some states still require individual co-trustees.

Corporate trustees perform three types of functions: (1) they certify that the bond is one of the issue described in the trust indenture (bonds require this authentication to make them valid); (2) they assume certain operational responsibilities, such as payment of taxes and insurance and, often, the handling of interest, sinking funds, and redeemed bonds; and (3) they serve the bondholder in special matters, including notifying him in the event of default and taking the necessary steps to protect his interests. Prior to 1939, corporate trustees were sometimes lax in fulfilling their responsibilities. This led to passage of the Trust Indenture Act of 1939, which sets up legislative requirements governing the selection and conduct of corporate trustees.

Importance of Trust Indenture Provisions in the Analysis of a Bond

The principal criterion used in selecting high-grade corporate bonds is the ability of a company to meet its contractual requirements, as indicated by the standards outlined in the following chapter. In addition, the investor should be familiar with the major provisions of the trust indenture. In most instances these provisions will not affect him directly, but in specific cases problems may arise whose solution depends on the terms of the agreement between the bondholder and the corporation.

The provisions of the trust indenture may be classified into five major categories: (1) the mortgage, (2) protective features, (3) the rights of the bondholder, (4) the general characteristics of the issue, and (5) special privileges.

Mortgage. The terms of the mortgage provide a description of the property pledged as security for the loan and a summary of the following important factors: the right of the corporation to effect releases or substitutions; limitations that may be present on the maximum amount of bonds permissible under the mortgage; and an after-acquired clause, if one exists, which places all property acquired in the future under the lien of the mortgage.

Investors and analysts often exaggerate the importance of a mortgage. As an example, a corporation's unsecured bonds may receive less favorable investment ratings and sell at prices that afford higher yields then its secured obligations. This relationship suggests the advantage of buying the higher-yielding junior or unsecured bonds, *provided that they pass the tests of a high-grade issue*. The same reasoning does not apply to securities that are not of top quality, because if bankruptcy occurs these bonds will probably receive poorer treatment than prior-ranking obligations in the eventual reorganization. Interest may even be maintained on senior obligations during the period of bankruptcy proceedings.

Unsecured bonds, called *debentures*, are backed by the general credit of the issuer but have no specific pledge of real or personal property. Industrial corporations often use them because the value of their properties tends to be relatively low in relation to the size of their business. Public utilities offer debentures in moderate amounts; railroads occasionally use them. At times, subordinated debentures convertible into common stocks have been a relatively popular financing medium. Secondary corporations are compelled to provide extensive mortgage protection for their obligations in order to facilitate sale to investors, who are under the illusion that a comprehensive mortgage may offset a poor earnings record. Because strong enterprises are not under similar pressures, their debentures frequently have unchallenged credit ratings.

Protective features. Protective features are provisions intended to prevent the corporation from taking steps that will impair the status of the bonds in relation to that of other outstanding securities. Typical restrictions limit the payment of dividends when disbursements would reduce the working capital of the corporation to less than a specified amount, require that the net current assets of the corporation bear a specified relation to the outstanding bonds, and stipulate that common stock plus surplus must represent a minimum percentage of the total capitalization. Because debentures have no specific asset security, their trust indentures often limit the amount of funded debt that may be outstanding and grant holders a prior or equal mortgage on the corporation's properties if any mortgage bonds are subsequently issued.

Rights of the bondholder. These rights cover his remedies in case of default and the power of specified percentages of holders to amend certain terms of the indenture.

General characteristics. Among the most important items in this category are the redemption provisions. These may establish optional or sinking fund call prices, both of which may be on a sliding scale. The optional call price tends to be above the sinking fund price. Noncallable bonds are unusual because corporations desire the flexibility of being able to modify their debt structure as they desire.

Usually, optional calls may be exercised in whole or in part. A clause may be provided restricting the right of the corporation to call the bonds to some specified term, ordinarily five to ten years after issue. Corporations are likely to call bonds during periods of low interest rates, when satisfactory investment outlets are not easy to find. Accordingly, during periods of high interest rates, investors are apprehensive that subsequent declines may invite calls, and they prefer obligations with relatively long restrictive call provisions. Recognizing this attitude, Illinois Power provided a ten-year protection against redemption in its 10.50 percent bonds offered in September 1974. The *Wall Street Journal* referred to this provision as "a sign of the times for electric utilities," noting that "in recent months [they] generally have been forced to double their more traditional five-year guarantee to holders."[2]

On the other hand, a redemption price puts a ceiling on the market level of an issue, although the pressure of low interest rates sometimes causes its price to penetrate this ceiling. It is generally prudent to avoid bonds that sell much above their call prices, in order to prevent the risk of a capital loss if the bonds are redeemed prior to maturity. Sometimes the redemption provision has a no-refunding clause. In such cases, the corporation can redeem the bonds if it no longer needs the money or if it wishes to eliminate an objectionable clause in the indenture, but it may not redeem in order to refund at a lower rate of interest.

A substantial sinking fund provides a buoying market influence when bonds are selling below call price and affords some assurance that a corporation will be able to meet the maturity of its obligations. On the negative side, the periodic retirement of a bond issue through a large sinking fund may eliminate an investment of considerable merit, thereby requiring the owner to discover new investment outlets. The advantages of a strong sinking fund overshadow this possible inconvenience. Ordinarily the indenture will specify the amounts to be called, the years of call, and the available method. This may be by lot, purchase in the open market, or by tender, a widely advertised offer to buy the amount wanted at a specific price.

Special privileges. Typical bondholder privileges are the authority to convert to common stock and *warrants* permitting the purchase of new common stock. It is imperative that the bondholder be thoroughly familiar with these provisions, which may change over a period of time.

Variable-Interest Bonds

Frequent periods of inflation occurring throughout the world have attracted attention to the subject of *indexing*. Its basic concept is simple, although many of its applications are not. Indexing means abandonment of the fiction that a currency, the dollar in the case of the United States, has a constant value. Instead, items such as taxes, wages, rents, and interest rates are adjusted periodically, based on the movements of a generally accepted price-level index.

The form of indexing most common in the United States is the cost-of-living escalator clause in collective bargaining aggreements; indexed bonds have been used extensively in Finland, Israel, and Brazil. Back in 1925, the Rand-Kardex Co. of Buffalo, New York, attracted considerable attention by proposing a debenture linked to the Bureau of Labor Statistics wholesale price index. The issue was withdrawn, however, because of public unfamiliarity with this type of financing. Some legislative attention has been given to the possibility of adjusting the principal and interest on government securities in line with a price index. The Treasury Department, however, has manifested little interest in such proposals.[3]

A kinsman of the indexed security that achieved some popularity in the United States for a while is the floating-rate note with a put feature (the right to sell the note back to the user after a specified period of time.) In such notes, however, the put is characteristically at par, and the return on the instrument is tied to the money market rather than to price changes (see pp. 125-126).

Prior to 1933, the year when private ownership of gold was banned in the United States, it was not uncommon for a debt instrument to have a gold clause. This provided for payment of the contract terms in gold, or for the payment to be varied in accordance with the price of gold. In 1933, Congress enacted the Gold Clause Joint Resolution (31 U.S.C. 463), which invalidated such clauses. Lifting of the prohibition against holding gold after December 31, 1974, paved the way for a revival of securities with the gold clause, as well as for the introduction of securities which provide for payment in the currencies of a number of different countries (such securities have been employed in the international financial markets). The Treasury's interpretation of the Gold Clause Resolution is that domestic use of both these types of instruments still is invalid. Despite this stand, the question of the application of the gold clause is not completely free from doubt.[4]

INVESTMENT STATUS OF BONDS

The bond is the traditional instrument of investment for institutions and safety-minded individuals. As we have seen, the shackles of this tradition are being broken by the need to adjust portfolios to changing economic conditions. Increasing recognition is being given to the fact that even without the binding obligation of a contract, certain corporations appear both able and willing to disburse dividends on stocks, regardless of the movements of the business cycle.

Variations in Quality of Bonds

Bondholders are creditors. Within the same corporation, therefore, the bond occupies a stronger position than stock. In two comparable corporations, a bond well protected by earnings is undoubtedly more conservative than a similarly protected stock. However, the bond contract by itself offers no assurance that the corporation will be able to meet its interest and principal requirements. Consequently, bonds vary from the highest-grade security, such as U.S. government obligations, to those of dubious value, such as the Kreuger & Toll 5s of 1959, which were offered at 98 in 1929 and were selling at about 4 in mid-1974.

Between these two extremes is a wide range of different obligations. There are medium-grade issues affording a high yield but on which some question exists about the issuer's ability to continue payments; bonds on which disbursements are being maintained on a partial basis; income bonds comparable in some respects to preferred stock; and defaulted obligations selling at very low levels and interesting only as outright speculations on the grounds of possible market appreciation. Therefore, although an issue may be a bond and have an impressive descriptive title, its investment merit can be ascertained only by analysis.

Bond Ratings

Moody's and Standard & Poor's, as well as a third rating agency, the Fitch Investors Service, issue ratings indicative of the quality of bonds.[5] Only fairly large issues are rated. At one time, the subscription fees to the agencies' various publications subsidized the rating services, but as costs of meeting the demand for rating services increased, the agencies instituted fee schedules for ratings. Bonds sold privately are rated on request, and confidential ratings may be provided; the purchaser is free to sustain the confidentiality of the rating or to publish it. In rating bonds the services presumably take into account all the financial, economic, and legal factors pertaining to the issue.

The ratings are represented by letter designations that by and large follow a similar format and have similar implications. The Standard & Poor's corporate bond ratings and their meanings are shown in Figure 18-1. Fitch also employs capital letters, as shown in the Standard & Poor's tabulation. In the case of Moody's, the first letter is a capital, followed by a lowercase designation; Aaa, Aa, A, and Baa represent the top four categories.

Accurate ratings serve a useful purpose. In their absence, each investor would have to undertake his own presumably careful investigation of the quality of an issue. Many individual investors, however, are not in a position to make such a study, while institutions would duplicate each other's efforts.

Thus, the publication of ratings permits a substantial reduction in the costs of information. It is true that complete reliance cannot be placed on the ratings, because there are fine qualitative differences between bonds that the agencies, which must review a great number of issues, may not recognize. Generally, however, verifying the quality of an issue is less costly than the initial determination of that quality. Furthermore, investors who confine their commitments to issues of specified quality will find that the ratings are a convenient screening device, because they eliminate the necessity of even a cursory examination of a large number of issues.

Finally, in the absence of ratings, investors who have neither the time nor the skill to determine the quality of an issue might choose to ignore it as an investment instrument. Accordingly, to the extent that their funds were invested outside the bond market, the cost of money to issuers would increase. More positively, nationally accepted ratings keep drawing new investors into the market and therefore tend to reduce borrowing rates.

Issuers are very much concerned about a bond's rating, since it will influence both the price at which it will sell and its marketability. As an illustration, Standard & Poor's assigned a triple-A rating to Kraftco Corp. (formerly National Dairy), while Moody's carried a double-A rating. In early 1971 the company announced plans for a $50 million public offering of 25-year sinking fund debentures. Considerable interest was displayed in the possibility that Moody's would revise its rating upward because, as was pointed out, "the prestigious triple-A enables a concern to sell its debt issues at the lowest prevailing interest cost." Analysts estimated that the upgrading would result in a total savings of about $1,250,000 in interest payments over the issue's life.[6]

Similarly, in early 1973, Standard & Poor's downgraded Consolidated Edison's credit rating by one notch, from A to BBB. The head of Standard & Poor's corporate rating section stated that the action was necessary "in view of the inadequate level of earnings protection afforded to bondholders since early 1970." An official of Consolidated Edison indicated that he was not surprised at the move "because of the effect of higher operating costs, and

FIGURE 18-1

STANDARD & POOR'S BOND RATINGS

To provide more detailed indications of credit quality, our traditional bond letter ratings may be modified by the addition of a plus or a minus sign, when appropriate to show relative standing within the major rating categories, the only exceptions being in the "AAA" – Prime Grade category and the lesser categories below "BB"

CORPORATE BONDS

BANK QUALITY BONDS– Under present commercial bank regulations bonds rated in the top four categories (AAA, AA, A, BBB or their equivalent) generally are regarded as eligible for bank investment.

AAA Bonds rated AAA are highest grade obligations. They possess the ultimate degree of protection as to principal and interest. Marketwise they move with interest rates, and hence provide the maximum safety on all counts.

AA Bonds rated AA also qualify as high grade obligations, and in the majority of instances differ from AAA issues only in small degree. Here, too, prices move with the long term money market.

A Bonds rated A are regarded as upper medium grade. They have considerable investment strength but are not entirely free from adverse effects of changes in economic and trade conditions. Interest and principal are regarded as safe. They predominantly reflect money rates in their market behavior, but to some extent, also economic conditions.

BBB The BBB, or medium grade category is borderline between definitely sound obligations and those where the speculative element begins to predominate. These bonds have adequate asset coverage and normally are protected by satisfactory earnings. Their susceptibility to changing conditions, particularly to depressions, necessitates constant watching. Marketwise, the bonds are more responsive to business and trade conditions than to interest rates. This group is the lowest which qualifies for commercial bank investment.

BB Bonds given a BB rating are regarded as lower medium grade. They have only minor investment characteristics. In the case of utilities, interest is earned consistently but by narrow margins. In the case of other types of obligors, charges are earned on average by a fair margin, but in poor periods deficit operations are possible.

B Bonds rated as low as B are speculative. Payment of interest cannot be assured under difficult economic conditions.

CCC-CC Bonds rated CCC and CC are outright speculations, with the lower rating denoting the more speculative. Interest is paid, but continuation is questionable in periods of poor trade conditions. In the case of CC ratings the bonds may be on an income basis and the payment may be small.

C The rating of C is reserved for income bonds on which no interest is being paid.

DDD-D All bonds rated DDD, DD and D are in default, with the rating indicating the relative salvage value.

NR– Not Rated.

Canadian corporate bonds are rated on the same basis as American corporate issues. The ratings measure the intrinsic value of the bonds, but they do not take into account exchange and other uncertainties.

SOURCE: Standard & Poor's Corporation, *Bond Guide* 39 (September 1975): 6. Reprinted by permission.

the pressure of having to obtain large sums of new capital for our construction program." Of interest is the fact that only a month earlier, the New York State Public Service Commission had granted the company a $110 million interim rate increase, in part to preserve the utility's interest coverage and protect its bond rating. Analysts estimated that the rating drop could raise financing costs by 10 to 15 basis points (100 basis points = 1 percentage point); a rise of 10 basis points on the forthcoming $150 million bond issue could add $4,500,000 without compounding in interest over the life of the loan.[7]

When economic conditions are favorable, investors tend to bid up the prices of lower-rated bonds, and their yields decline relative to those of the higher-rated issues. On the other hand, as the economy recedes, investors seek the shelter of prime bonds and bid up their prices; therefore, their yields fall relative to those of the lower-rated issues. Reflecting a gloomy business outlook, for example, the A-rated bonds of Monongahela Power were forced in November 1974 to yield a shocking 1.1 percentage points more than the AA-rated bonds of Cincinnati Gas & Electric; this differential was nearly six times the prevailing spread over the previous twelve months.[8]

Ratings are not intended as recommendations. It is recognized that investors may decide against buying a bond despite a high-quality designation. The return may be too low or may be less than that available on comparable issues; the obligation may be selling above its call price, with redemption a reasonable possibility; or the investor's own analysis may suggest that the published rating is inaccurate. On the other hand, an issue with a low rating may have interesting appreciation potentialities. Ratings should be considered as guides in ascertaining the preliminary characteristics of an obligation prior to actual purchase. It is desirable to analyze the status of all bonds, regardless of the rating.

FACTORS CAUSING CHANGES IN PRICES OF HIGH-GRADE BONDS

Bonds may be roughly divided into high-grade (or prime) and secondary obligations. Because bonds lend themselves to conservative investments, attention is focused on *high-grade securities*—that is, issues of considerable soundness on which continued interest disbursements are highly probable and payment of principal on maturity is quite certain. In this category may be grouped U.S. government obligations and municipal and corporate securities with at least an A rating. Relatively few preferred issues may be classified with high-grade bonds. Individual common stocks are excluded because their dividend distributions vary too closely with earnings. The New York City case raised the question of whether A-rated municipals belonged in this select group.

The yields of high-grade bonds sometimes have more than modest swings. In view of the unassailable quality of these obligations, the breadth of their market fluctuations may appear surprising. For example, between 1967 and 1970, Moody's Corporate Aaa Bond yields advanced swiftly from about 5.51 to 8.04 percent; then yields dropped to about 7.08 percent at the end of 1972, rose almost without interruption thereafter until they reached 9.27 in October 1974 and fluctuated at a level about 50 basis points lower in the first half of 1975.

Influence of Interest Rates on Prices of High-Grade Bonds

Fluctuations in the prices of high-grade bonds are tied to the movements of interest rates. This relationship originates in the fact that governments and corporations pay a fixed and presumably certain amount of dollar income on these issues during their lifetimes. Holders may be expected to retain their commitments as long as they provide a rate of return that is similar to that available on other investments of comparable quality. If new obligations affording a better return appear in the market, investors will logically switch out of their current holdings in order to buy the higher-yielding securities. This process will continue until the prices of the older obligations decline to a level that permits the same rate of return as that afforded by the more recently offered issues. Thus, as interest rates rise, the prices of high-grade, fixed-income securities decline; conversely, as interest rates drop, the prices of prime securities rise. To ascertain the outlook for such obligations, therefore, it is necessary to evaluate the trend of interest rates; this, in turn, requires some knowledge of the nature of these rates and of the theory underlying their movements.

The Interest Rate Structure

Although interest rates are often referred to as a single concept, actually a conglomerate of rates exists. There are independent rates for bankers' certificates of deposit (CD's), bankers' acceptances, commercial paper (short-term unsecured notes of established corporations), and federal funds (reserves at the Federal Reserve banks that member banks buy and sell); for short-term government obligations, long-term government issues, and high-grade corporate bonds; and for various other classes of debtors on different types of loans. These rates are all interwoven into a pattern referred to as the interest rate structure. A comparison of the levels that have prevailed in some important rates is shown in Table 18-1.

TABLE 18-1

Interest Rate Structure, June 28, 1975

TYPE	PERCENTAGE
Federal funds	5.72
U.S. Treasury bills, 3-month	5.80
Prime bankers' acceptances, 90-day	6.03
Finance company paper, 3-6 month	5.63
Prime commercial paper, 4-6-month	6.18
U.S. Treasury bills, 1-year	6.32
U.S. Treasury 5-7-year issues	7.49
Corporate bonds, Aaa	8.75

SOURCE: *Federal Reserve Bulletin* 61 (July 1975): A27-A28.

Transactions in short-term loans form the basis of the nation's money market, which is largely concentrated in New York City. The money market is closely related to the long-term capital market, where new securities are floated, and to the securities markets, where stocks and bonds already issued are traded. As an indication of this relationship, commission brokers and investment bankers may obtain short-term bank loans to finance their own operations in long-term securities. Thus, changes in the interest rate level of one market are reflected in corresponding adjustments in rates prevailing in the other markets.

At different periods of time, however, special factors may cause rates in various sectors of the market to diverge. For example, federal government policy may stress short-term rates at the expense of long-term rates, or a housing boom may create an unusual demand for mortgages and cause their rates to move out of line, or the need for equipment may cause heavy long-term corporate borrowing, with rising rates in that sector of the market. Even though different categories of interest rates tend to move in the same direction, the differentials between them may change substantially, at least partly because of such factors. Thus, in February 1964 the spread between yields on new issues of Aa utility bonds and long-term U.S. government bonds was 3 basis points, but the spread rose to 110 basis points in September 1966, fell to 58 basis points in February 1967, increased to 212 basis points in November 1970, and fell to 140 basis points in January 1973. Between February 1973 and the last week in July 1975 the spread increased by 62 basis points.[9]

Government Control of Interest Rates

In the modern era, exercise of some degree of economic control has become an accepted national responsibility. Governments throughout the world are reluctant to permit a completely automatic adjustment of interest rates, since these rates are regarded as important instruments for regulating the movements of the business cycle. Reflecting this viewpoint, national treasuries and central banks have jointly formulated methods of influencing the interest rate level in accordance with predetermined aims.

In the first decade after World War II, an economic philosophy based on the belief that low interest rates are a powerful means of generating a high level of business activity was fostered in this country. Exponents of this philosophy occupied important government posts and exerted their influence during this period to keep rates low. Changing economic conditions brought a gradual shift in attitude, and the pegging of interest rates was abandoned in 1951. While rates nevertheless continued to be largely subject to government control, they have maintained a generally upward course which has, to be sure, been periodically interrupted.

Typically these interruptions have occurred during periods of lagging business, when the low-interest philosophy tended to gain strength. The Nixon years marked the rise of a new economic philosophy, at least partially continued in the following administration. This philosophy stresses control of the supply of money (monetary aggregates) as a major vehicle through which monetary policy seeks to affect prices and economic activity. The continued burden of military appropriations, an upward wage-price spiral, commodity scarcities, and errors in timing of tax-rate changes all have led to sharp fluctuations in the handling of the money supply and have contributed to economic instability. These factors, in turn, have contributed to the persistence of interest rate fluctuations around a relatively high base. Reflecting these conditions, the Senate and House adopted a "sense of Congress" resolution in the spring of 1975 telling the Federal Reserve Board to pursue policies that would encourage lower long-term rates and, over the long run, keep money and credit growing fast enough to finance stable economic growth.

Interest Rate Theory

Interest rates represent the price paid for the use of money. They are determined by complex economic forces. Rates will move to a level at which the amount of funds actually demanded and the amount actually supplied (which are always equal to each other) are also equal not only to the demand and supply that the community wants (this demand and supply are not necessarily equal) but also to the real savings and real investment the community wants (which, unlike realized savings and investment, may not always equal each other). Government authorities exert an important influence on interest rates through their control over bank reserves, which can be changed directly within specified limits or through open-market operations. The purchase of securities by the Federal Reserve not only expands bank reserves but also lowers yields and may add to the buying pressure and raise prices. The injection of funds may take place anywhere in the spectrum of maturities and, with varying degrees of effectiveness, depending in part on the degree of segmentation of the market, will be felt throughout the whole range. The consequent fall of interest rates is likely to be only the first in a long sequence of events. Repercussions will be felt on the gross national product, the savings of individuals, investment by corporations, and the flow of funds through the various financial institutions. However, the yield investors seek tends to reflect the rate of inflation anticipated. As a consequence, the expansion of the money supply by the Fed may generate expectations of inflation which produce higher rather than lower interest rates. A decline in the money supply following open-market sales by the Federal Reserve will generally increase pressure on prices, push bond prices down and interest rates up.

The Fed's effectiveness is limited. It can exercise reasonable control over interest rates in the short run, but its control over long periods is quite limited. Similarly, while the Fed is reasonably quite effective controlling money aggregates over long periods, it may not be equally effective in the short run. In determining its open-market operations, the board projects such things as bank reserves, but these factors are volatile and hard to predict. They are influenced by float (uncollected balances in the process of collection), the movements of funds into and out of Treasury loan accounts, the flow of funds between country and city banks, and international currency movements. All these elements are subject to sudden changes that can affect bank reserves seriously and offset the effects of short-term board decisions.

The volume of funds available for investment for the most part stems from individual savings. The impact on interest rates of changes in this volume, in turn, depends upon the disposition of savings; differing effects may be felt if individuals invest directly than if they use various institutional channels. Not only do individuals and institutions have dissimilar portfolio structures, but those of institutions also differ among themselves. As a result, the channels through which savings flow have important implications for the yields on various financial instruments and the allocation of funds to various investment outlets.

On the demand side, the primary force prompting the search for capital is anticipation of the efficiency with which funds may be employed. The demand for capital will increase with expectations of a larger return without a commensurate increase in risk. Opportunities for economic profits become more abundant when the economy is buoyant. At such times, the competition for additional funds intensifies, and this contributes to rising interest rates.

Some idea of the general direction in which interest rates are likely to move may be obtained from projections of the sources and uses of funds in the economy. For a number of years the Federal Reserve Board has been publishing detailed tables in this area, technically called the flow of funds. The financial community also makes projections of fund flows. One widely used analysis is *Credit and Capital Markets*, published annually by the Bankers Trust Co. A typical summary form is reproduced in Figure 18-2.

This presentation is buttressed by more than two dozen supplementary breakdowns which examine the sources and uses of funds in the various markets and the sources and uses of funds by the major sectors of the economy. A general rule of thumb that can be used for forecasting the direction of interest rates is that if the projection calls for the absorption of a considerable volume of debt funds by residual investors–individuals and others–there will be upward pressure on interest rates; thus, the substantial residual funds shown in the table under "individuals and others" in 1969 and the amount estimated for 1973 foreshadowed the subsequent high rate levels. Like most rules of thumb, however, the relationship is not conclusive, and discrepancies may occur. A recent analysis indicates that "market professionals" have made large errors for all interest rates–larger in absolute terms for short-term rates, but larger relative to the size of the rate fluctuation for long-term rates. Moreover, in a substantial percentage of cases, the direction of rate movements was inaccurate. Even when the experts correctly foresaw the direction of movements, they tended to underestimate the magnitude of the rate changes.[10]

YIELD CURVES

Studying the outlook for interest rates will help the investor determine what type of bond he wants. If he expects a decline in rates, he will choose longer maturities, so that he may continue to obtain the benefits of a high return as other rates drop or profit from the rise in bond prices. If he expects a rise in rates, he will select shorter-term securities, in order to use the funds released from his maturing obligations to acquire higher-yielding issues as rates advance and minimize losses from the fall in bond prices. This strategy of lengthening or shortening maturities depending on the outlook for interest rate is basic to bond management. Other strategies primarily involve swapping bonds. Compared with common stock, bonds may be more readily grouped into similar quality or risk classes, and those issues that appear to be selling out of line may be more easily identified. Various types of shifts may then be

FIGURE 18-2

Analysis of Fund Flows

SUMMARY OF FINANCING REQUIREMENTS - TOTAL FUNDS

(in billions of dollars)

	1967	1968	1969	1970	1971	1972	1973 (est.)	1974 (proj.)
ES (FUNDS RAISED)								
vestment funds	51.7	54.6	61.1	66.5	101.8	112.7	111.6	126.8
ort-term funds	16.7	26.3	37.8	19.9	20.7	42.3	72.8	39.4
S. Government and budget agency securities, privately held	7.7	8.7	-8.8	6.9	16.7	20.2	-.5	6.9
Total uses	76.1	89.6	90.1	93.3	139.2	175.1	183.9	173.1
JRCES (FUNDS SUPPLIED)								
surance companies and pension funds								
fe insurance companies	8.5	8.7	8.7	9.0	11.9	13.4	15.1	16.3
ivate noninsured pension funds	6.0	7.0	6.4	7.8	8.6	9.3	9.2	10.0
ate and local retirement funds	4.0	4.8	5.1	6.1	6.9	7.3	9.0	10.3
re and casualty insurance companies	2.2	2.5	2.3	4.0	6.2	6.2	6.7	7.1
Total	20.7	23.1	22.5	26.9	33.6	36.2	40.0	43.7
rift institutions								
vings and loan associations	9.3	10.2	9.5	11.5	28.3	35.9	26.4	30.0
tual savings banks	5.2	4.4	2.8	4.2	9.8	10.2	4.7	8.2
edit unions	.8	1.5	1.8	1.6	2.5	3.1	3.1	2.9
Total	15.2	16.0	14.2	17.3	40.7	49.1	34.2	41.1
vestment companies	1.0	2.4	3.5	1.7	.4	-.2	.2	1.3
her financial intermediaries								
nance companies	.6	5.1	8.1	.7	3.4	7.9	8.8	4.8
al estate investment trusts	--	.2	.8	2.1	2.5	4.9	4.5	2.0
Total	.6	5.3	8.9	2.8	5.9	12.8	13.3	6.8
mercial banks	36.8	40.1	17.3	36.6	51.4	74.6	75.0	69.1
siness								
siness corporations	3.5	7.0	5.9	2.6	7.0	7.4	22.8	13.4
ncorporate business	.4	.5	.6	.6	.7	1.1	1.2	1.0
Total	3.9	7.5	6.5	3.2	7.7	8.5	24.0	14.4
vernment								
. Government	1.1	1.4	1.4	.4	.5	.1	-.5	.2
budget agencies	2.5	2.3	4.7	8.4	3.0	4.4	10.9	5.6
ate and local general funds	.7	1.9	2.9	.7	.3	5.2	3.3	2.2
Total	4.3	5.6	9.0	9.5	3.8	9.7	13.7	8.0
eign investors	2.0	1.5	.1	11.0	27.1	10.5	5.0	-2.9
sidual: Individuals and others	-6.0	-1.0	31.4	-4.0	-20.1	.2	9.3	7.6
Total gross sources	78.6	100.6	113.3	105.0	150.4	201.4	214.7	189.1
s: Funds raised by financial intermediaries								
estment funds	1.3	1.4	2.5	4.1	6.1	8.5	3.7	5.8
rt-term funds	1.6	6.4	10.4	-.7	4.5	14.9	11.4	5.6
budget agency securities, privately held	-.5	3.1	10.4	8.3	.6	2.9	15.7	4.6
Total	2.4	10.9	23.3	11.7	11.2	26.3	30.8	16.0
Total net sources	76.1	89.6	90.1	93.3	139.2	175.1	183.9	173.1

SOURCE: Bankers Trust Company, Economics Division, ***Bankers Trust Credit and Capital Markets 1974***, February 28, 1974, p. T1.

worked out from the overpriced to the underpriced issue. In arranging these moves, consideration is given to the shape of the yield curve and the effect of interest on interest.

For bonds of similar quality and indenture provisions, yields differ primarily because of maturity. These differences give rise to what is known as the *term structure* of interest rates, often referred to as *yield curves*, which are carefully watched by the investment community. As illustrated in Figure 18-3, these curves may take different shapes. The most common, at least since the 1930s, has been the ascending curve. The descending curve generally obtains when the full spectrum of interest rates is relatively high; such curves were common in this country from about 1906 to 1929. As curves change from the ascending to descending form or vice versa, they may temporarily become flat, but this shape is relatively uncommon. In recent years, a humped curve has made a frequent appearance. This pattern, like the descending curve, is likely to appear when interest rates are very high. Shifts in formation result from movements in the whole spectrum of rates and the greater volatility of short-term over long-term rates.

There are a number of explanations for these changing shapes. One widely accepted theory maintains that the rate for any particular maturity is the average of the short-period rates that are expected to prevail between the current period and maturity. Thus, if short rates are expected to fall steadily over the next ten years, the ten-year rate will be less than that for any shorter maturity. The five-year rate will be the average of the rates that are expected to prevail in the first five years. Since these are all higher than the rates that are expected to prevail in the last five years of the decade under consideration, the five-year rate will be higher than the ten-year rate, and the yield curve will be descending over the ten-year range.

According to this theory, if the yield curve does not reflect investors' expectations regarding the short-term rates as described above, forces will be set in motion that produce the descending yield. Suppose that long rates are high relative to the short rates expected. Buyers of the long-term securities will thus enjoy a relatively favorable return as long as they hold their investment, whereas buyers of short-term obligations will be rolling them over into new short-term issues with declining rates as time passes. On the other hand, an investor who sells a long-term security prior to maturity stands to realize a capital appreciation at that time; the longer the maturity relative to the holding period, the more he is likely to gain. If the investor originally purchased a ten-year bond at par with a 6 percent coupon and disposed of it after five years, when the yield on five-year maturities had fallen to 4 percent, he would receive \$108.90 for his bond. In these circumstances, investors would find long-term bonds attractive, bid up their prices, and in the process reduce their yields. This process will continue until the long-term yield affords no advantage over holding a succession of short-term investments.

FIGURE 18-3

Typical Yield Patterns of U.S. Government Securities

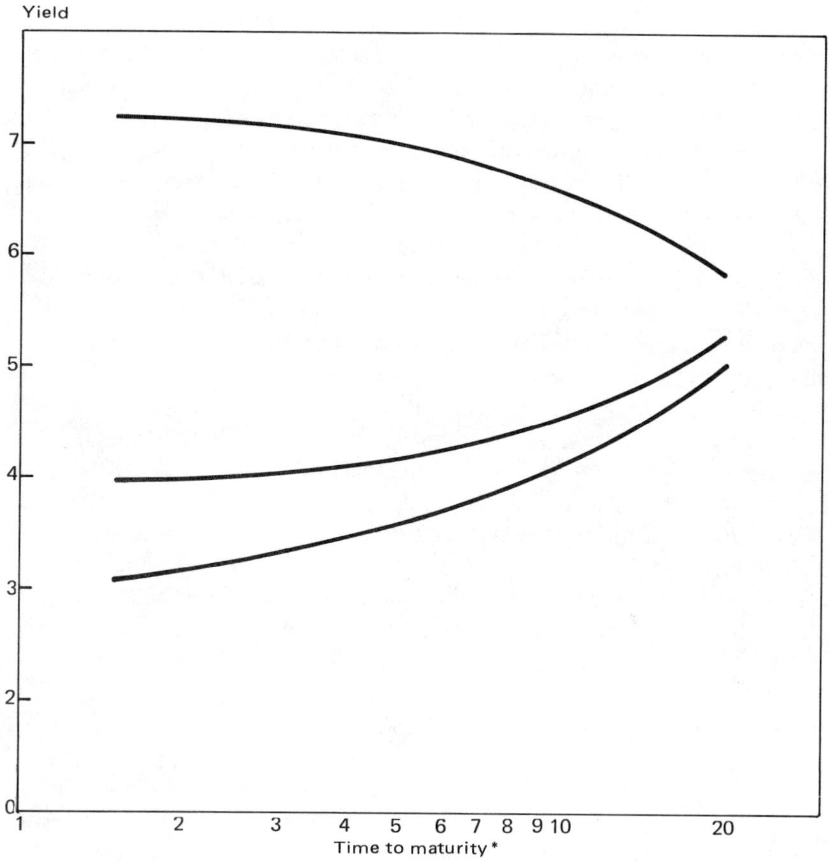

*Time to maturity is plotted on a logarithmic scale on which equal distances represent equal percentage changes in time to maturity.

Thus, the yield curve will have become a descending one. Corresponding forces would cause the curve to be ascending when short-term rates are expected to rise.

Another theory views the capital market as substantially segmented, with institutions choosing maturity structures suited to their liabilities. Certain institutions which have long-term liabilities, such as life insurance companies and pension funds, are primarily interested in the long-term sector of the market. Commercial banks, on the other hand, prefer short-term obligations because a large portion of their liabilities is of a demand nature. The shape of the yield curve then depends on the strength of supply and demand in the various sectors of the market. Adherents of this theory do not believe that arbitrageurs will have sufficient funds available to flatten the curve significantly.

A third school feels that the ascending curve is the natural one. At the short end of the maturity spectrum, investors are ready to accept a lower yield because of the liquidity provided. Moreover, the sensitivity of a security to interest rate changes is a function of its maturity. Consequently, according to this theory, for any given shift in interest rates, the price change at its long end will be greater than that at the short end. To compensate for this additional risk and to take into account the benefits of early liquidation, investors require a higher rate of return for long-term obligations.

The truth is probably a mixture of these theories. Since most investors probably are risk averters, there is very likely a normal tendency to desire a premium on long-term obligations as some compensation for the uncertainties of the future. However, money-market factors, such as an easing of Federal Reserve policies, may lead to expectations of a decline in rates. If the weight of such opinion is very strong, it may generate enough demand for long maturities to offset the risk premium associated with uncertainties of the future. Moreover, while it is undoubtedly true that the structure of liabilities of a financial institution creates a preference for a corresponding distribution of maturities in its assets, there is evidence that this preference is not overriding. Firms seem perfectly willing to shift funds whenever the interest rates in the various maturities appear to be out of line.

"Riding the Yield Curve"

When the interest rate curve has a sharp upward sweep, investors may obtain capital gains by purchasing medium- or long-term issues, holding them for several years, and selling them at the relatively higher price that prevails for shorter-term securities. This strategy was common after World War II, when the yield curve had a sharp upward sweep. To demonstrate the principle, let us assume that an investment officer who had been studying the interest rate curve for December 31, 1948, decided to buy the 2¾s of 1958 - 1963 at a price of 109.02 because they afforded a return of 1.71 percent (relatively attractive at that time) for an issue with a maturity of about ten years. Let us further assume that on June 15, 1954, four years prior to the issue's first call date, the interest rate curve showed the same general configuration as on the day of purchase. During this entire period the institution had regularly amortized the premium at which the bonds were originally acquired. As far as its books were concerned, the yield to the call date was the same, regardless of the prevailing rates of interest for short-term money.

On the basis of the interest rate curve, a bond with a four-year maturity afforded a yield of about 1.24 percent. However, the 2¾s which were then callable in four years still provided the institution with their original return of 1.71 percent. Capitalizing these yields, the market price of a four-year Treasury security bearing a 2¾ percent coupon and yielding 1.71 percent was about 104, whereas the value of an issue yielding 1.24 percent was approximately 106. If the investment officer wished, he could sell the bond at a gross profit of about 2 points. This practice is called "riding the yield curve" and entails a swap based on yield realignments as a result of changing maturities. So long as the curve has a sharp upward slant, investors may buy long-term securities and sell them several years prior to maturity at a profit. The steeper the slope, the greater the potential gains. As the spread between long- and short-term rates narrows, the curve straightens out, and the opportunity of "riding" its slope disappears.

Further Application of Yield Curves

The yield curve is a helpful tool for identifying issues which are selling out of line and which therefore afford opportunities for shifts based on these pure yield discrepancies. Let us now assume that we are sitting next to an institutional investment officer as he studies the curve in Figure 18-4. (Because

FIGURE 18-4

Hypothetical Interest Rate Curves

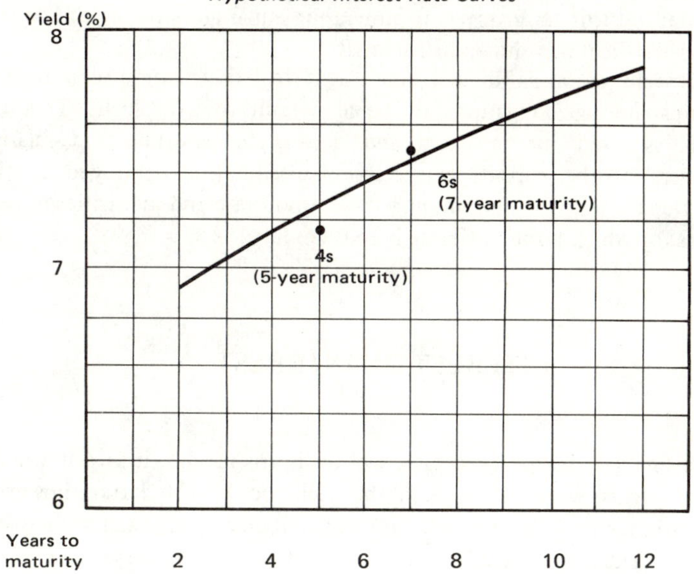

interest rates are subject to change, we have used hypothetical relationships and levels.) If the yields on all the bonds were selling in line, the interest rate curve would pass through each point designating a yield. However, examination of the curve reveals clearly that several of the yields are either below or above their theoretical norm. Under these circumstances, a switch from the lower to the higher-yield issues may be advantageous, provided that it conforms with the maturity pattern of the institution's portfolio. However, a switch should never be made without an investigation to determine whether there is some peculiarity about the bond or its market that warrants the deviation from the yield curve.

According to the curve, the Treasury 4s with a 5-year maturity afford a relatively low return, as compared with the 6s due in 7 years. Both these obligations fall within the medium-term maturity bracket. This relationship suggests a more detailed investigation. The 4s are priced at 86.63, providing a yield of 7.18 percent to maturity, the 6s are priced at 92.00, for a yield of 7.49 percent to maturity. Lengthening the indicated due date by less than two years increases the gross yield by 31 basis points. Because of the higher yield of the 6s, an investor could buy 10 of these bonds and obtain a return comparable to that available from 11 of the 4s. He could then obtain an extra return on the money saved by buying the 10 bonds instead of the 11; for convenience, it is simply assumed that this return is 5 percent on bank deposits. This package combination of maturities would increase his dollar income and provide more flexibility if the investment officer's expectation of declining rates is not realized and interest rates actually rise. A comparison of the indicated returns to an investor purchasing equal amounts of the 4s and the 6s plus certificates is shown in Table 18-2.

The yield curve is thus a convenient technique for evaluating the relationships among obligations of equal default risk (typically Treasury issues). It is used by investors and dealers to ascertain the relative attractiveness of the various marketable issues and is employed by the Treasury Department for determining the coupon rate and maturities of new obligations for which public offering is contemplated.

INTEREST ON INTEREST

While the analysis in the preceding section is traditional, it is not wholly valid. The yields were taken from the yield book. The latter, however, crucially assumes that the proceeds from all coupons are invested at the yield to maturity. Thus, presumably, the coupons from the 4s were invested at 7.18 percent and the coupons from the 6s were invested at 7.49 percent.

TABLE 18-2

Comparison of Results of Switching from Hypothetical 5-Year 4s to 7-Year 6s

5-YEAR 4s		7-YEAR 6s	
Purchase 11 bonds at 86.63*	$9,529.30	Purchase 10 bonds at 92.00*	$9,200.00
Average return per year from yield to maturity of 7.18% (7.18% X $9,529.30)	684.20	Average return per year from yield to maturity of 7.49% (7.49% X $9,200)	689.08
		Additional income provided from bank deposits (5% X $300)	15.00
		Average return per year from total yield to maturity of 7.41% from bonds and deposits	704.08

*Price decimals are usually 32nds, but these are cents on the dollar.

However, if the proceeds from the coupons of the 6s could be invested at 7.49 percent, why should an investor holding 4s be satisfied with 7.18 percent? A valid assumption therefore might be that the interest payments received will be invested at the best yield possible, regardless of the so-called yield to maturity of the bond from which the interest came.

Accordingly, in evaluating swapping opportunities, consideration might be given to the effect of the interest that can actually be earned on the interest received. This critical factor is the *reinvestment rate*, and its importance may be gauged from Table 18-3. This shows the effective yield* as well as the cash that would be produced by reinvesting, at varying rates, the coupons received from purchase of an 8 percent, 20-year bond. Thus, if the reinvestment rate rises by one-third, from 6 percent to 8 percent, the amount of interest on interest rises by about one-half, from $1,416 to $2,201, and the effective yield is increased by almost a full percentage point, from 7.07 percent to 8.00 percent.

*The effective yield is that rate at which interest on a bond at par, if reinvested at the yield to maturity, will produce the same amount as the actual interest on the bond under consideration will produce if reinvested at the explicitly assumed reinvestment rate; e.g., 20-year 7.53s, noncallable bonds purchased at par in which the interest was reinvested at 7.53 percent would produce the same amount of cash at the end of 20 years as 20-year 8s in which the interest was reinvested at 7 percent. This concept contrasts with the yield to maturity, which assumes reinvestment at the yield at maturity. Of course, if the reinvestment rate is assumed to be the yield to maturity, the latter and the effective yield are the same.

TABLE 18-3

*Cash Available at Maturity from 20-Year 8s, Noncallable, Bonds Purchased at Par to Yield 8 Percent**

REINVEST-MENT RATE	TOTAL	CASH FLOW		INTEREST ON INTEREST AS PERCENTAGE OF TOTAL CASH FLOW	EFFECTIVE YIELD
		COUPONS	INTEREST ON INTEREST		
0%	$1,600	$1,600	$ 0	0%	4.84%
5	2,696	1,600	1,096	41	6.64
6	3,016	1,600	1,416	47	7.07
7	3,382	1,600	1,782	53	7.53
8	3,801	1,600	2,201	58	8.00
9	4,281	1,600	2,681	63	8.50
10	4,832	1,600	3,232	67	9.01

*Disregarding income taxes and transaction costs.

SOURCE: Based on Table 1 from the book ***Inside the Yield Book***, by Sidney Homer and Martin L. Leibowitz, Ph.D., p. 22. © 1972 by Prentice-Hall, Inc. Published by Prentice-Hall, Inc., Englewood Cliffs, New Jersey.

Various kinds of swaps take into account the reinvestment rate. Perhaps the simplest is the substitution swap, which involves comparisons of securities within the same quality class.

Substitution Swaps

A substitution swap depends on imperfections in the market which result in two equivalent securities temporarily selling at different yields. For example, compare a 7-year, 4 percent bond priced at 86.63 and a 7-year, 6 percent bond price at 92.00, assuming that the reinvestment rate is 6 percent. To make an appropriate comparison, we assume in Table 18-4 that the 14 coupons are each invested at 6 percent per year as they come due. The value to which this will accumulate by the maturity date is found on line (3): $341.72 and $512.58 for the 4s and 6s respectively. We now know that by maturity, which is the same in both cases, we will end up with either $1,341.72 for the 4s or $1.512.58 for the 6s. The lower figure would have cost us $866.30, while the larger amount would have cost $920.00. Thus, the eventual investment values per dollar of original investment are 1.5488 and 1.6441, respectively; $1 invested at 6.43 percent for 7 years results in the first figure, $1 invested at 7.36 percent in the second. Thus, the 6s have a 93-basis point advantage over the 4s.

It is interesting to note that if both securities were priced to yield 7.49 percent to maturity, there would be no apparent advantage to swapping. At

TABLE 18-4

*Effects of Swapping Hypothetical 7-Year 4s for 7-Year 6s, with a Reinvestment Rate of 6%**

	7-YEAR 4s	7-YEAR 6s
(1) Semiannual coupon payment	$ 20.00	$ 30.00
(2) 7-year future value of $1 per period for 14 periods at 3 percent for period	$ 17.086	$ 17.086
(3) 7-year future value of coupons and interest on interest (line 1 X line 2)	$ 341.72	$ 512.58
(4) Principal at maturity	$1,000.00	$1,000.00
(5) Total value 7 years hence (line 3 + line 4)	$1,341.72	$1,512.58
(6) Original cost	$ 866.30	$ 920.00
(7) 7-year future value per dollar (line 5 ÷ line 6)	$ 1.5488	$ 1.6441
(8) Effective yield	6.43%	7.36%

*Disregarding income taxes and transaction costs.

a reinvestment rate of 6 percent per period the 4s would actually have a 7-basis point advantage in terms of effective yield. Furthermore, the lower the reinvestment rate, the greater would be the advantage. This is because only the coupon income is subject to the vagaries of the reinvestment rate. The income from capital accrual is fixed, and the lower the coupon (for a given maturity and yield), the larger the part of the total income that comes from the accrual of capital gain.

This swap is sometimes complicated by a discrepancy in the maturities of the two securities involved. Suppose, for example, that the 4s had a 5-year rather than a 7-year maturity. To take proper cognizance of the reinvestment rate, one can assume either that the 7s are sold at the end of the fifth year, which involves guessing the market price that will prevail, or that the proceeds from the 4s at maturity are reinvested in a 2-year note, which necessitates making an assumption about the yield on the note and the reinvestment rate. In Table 18-5, the 4s are rolled over into a 2-year note at par; a 6 percent reinvestment rate is still assumed. It is also assumed that fractional shares of a note can be purchased. Under these assumptions, the advantage of the 6s is decreased by 20 basis points.

Finally, when two bonds of equivalent quality are not selling in line with each other, the possibility exists that the differential will be corrected before maturity. If this occurs, the original differential will be magnified. Thus, assume the availability of a 7 percent, 30-year bond selling at par and a comparable issue priced to afford a yield to maturity of 7.10 percent. If the price differential is corrected in one year, the effective yield of the underpriced security would be 8.29 percent (assuming that the coupons were

TABLE 18-5

*Results of Purchasing Hypothetical 5-Year 4s with Reinvestment Rate of 6% and Conversion of 4s at Maturity into 2-Year 5s**

	5-YEAR 4s
(1) Semiannual coupon payment	$ 20.00
(2) 5-year future value of $1 per period for 10 periods at 3% per period	$ 11.464
(3) 5-year future value of coupons and interest on interest (line 1 X line 2)	$ 229.28
(4) Principal at maturity	$1,000.00
(5) Total value 5 years hence (line 3 + line 4)	$1,229.28
RESULTS OF INVESTMENT IN 2-YEAR 5s	2-YEAR 5s
(6) Semiannual coupon (on principal of $1,229.28)	$ 30.73
(7) 2-year future value of $1 per period for 4 periods at 3% per period	$ 4.184
(8) 2-year future value of coupons and interest on interest (line 6 X line 7)	$ 128.58
	COMBINED INVESTMENT
(9) Total value 7 years hence (line 5 + line 8)	$1,357.86
(10) Original cost	$ 866.30
(11) 7-year future value per dollar (line 9 ÷ line 10)	$ 1.5674
(12) Effective yield (interest rate for $1 to reach line 11)	6.63%

*Disregarding income taxes and transaction costs.

reinvested at 7 percent). Accordingly, the actual differential would be 129 basis points, instead of the 10 points originally indicated.

Other Swaps

Other types of swaps involve added considerations. For example, the intermarket spread involves shifts between bonds in different quality groups that appear out of line. Suppose that the investor has in her portfolio 25-year 5s priced at $815.90 to yield 6.50 percent, and comes across a lower-quality bond with the same maturity selling at par to yield 7 percent. She believes this spread of 50 basis points is excessive. Expecting that the spread will shrink by 15 basis points within a year, she considers a switch. To evaluate the implications of such a move, she prepares Table 18-6 and discovers that the swap will improve her yield to 232 basis points. (Of this differential, 50

TABLE 18-6

*Value of a Sample Intermarket Yield Pickup Swap, 25-Year 7s vs. 25-Year 5s**

	25-YEAR 7s AT 7%	25-YEAR 5s AT 6.50%
(1) Initial yield to maturity	7.00%	6.50%
(2) Expected yield 1 year later	6.90%	6.55%
(3) Original investment	$1,000.00	$ 815.90
(4) Interest received during year	$ 70.00	$ 50.00
(5) Interest on interest at 7% (1 coupon @ 7%)	$ 1.23	$ .88
(6) Price at year-end (based on expected yield)	$1,012.50	$ 813.70
(7) Total value at year-end (lines 4 + 5 + 6)	$1,083.73	$ 864.58
(8) 1-year future value per dollar (line 7 ÷ line 3)	1.0837	1.0597
(9) Effective yield (interest rate for $1 to reach line 9)	8.20%	5.88%
(10) Basis point gain	232 basis points	

*Disregarding income taxes and transaction costs.

basis points will be realized even if there is no change in spread; the swap is in a "yield pickup" direction.) In considering this move, she must weigh the potential gain against the risk of moving into a lower-quality bond.

The swap could also be in the other direction. This time assume that the investor holds the 7s and believes that the spread is too narrow. She expects it to widen by 15 basis points and therefore is considering a switch into the 6.50 issue. Her calculations are found in Table 18-7. Despite a sacrifice of yield to maturity, the swap would produce a gain of 138 basis points if the expected workout time of one year is realized. The investor, however, is now exposed to the risk of loss arising from her sacrifice of yield to maturity. Time, therefore, is working against her, and she may lose basis points if the workout period to achieve the expected narrowing of spreads becomes extended. The intermarket spread swap is often made between U.S. Treasury and corporate bonds.

Still another swap is the rate-anticipation type, mentioned earlier in the chapter. This involves shifts between bonds of different maturities to take advantage of expected changes in the yield relationships of long- and short-term issues. Obviously, if the investor's forecasts are wrong, the strategy can be costly. Although this kind of swap could be profitable, it is also quite risky.

Interest in the type of bond-trading opportunities described above began to rise in the 1970s as uncertainties clouded the outlook for stock.

TABLE 18-7

*Value of a Sample Intermarket Yield Give-up Swap, 25-Year 7s vs. 25-Year 5s**

	25-YEAR 7s AT 7%	25-YEAR 5s AT 6.50%
(1) Initial yield to maturity	7.00%	6.50%
(2) Expected yield 1 year later	7.00%	6.35%
(3) Original investment	$1,000.00	$ 815.90
(4) Interest received during year	$ 70.00	$ 50.00
(5) Interest on interest at 7% (1 coupon X 7%)	$ 1.23	$ .88
(6) Price at year-end (based on expected yield)	$1,000.00	$ 834.80
(7) Total value 1 year hence (lines 4 + 5 + 6)	$1,071.23	$ 885.68
(8) 1-year future value per dollar (line 7 ÷ line 3)	$ 1.0712	$ 1.0855
(9) Effective yield (interest rate for $1 to reach line 9)	$ 7.000	$ 8.380
(10) Basis point gain		138 basis points

*Disregarding income taxes and transaction costs.

Swapping bonds, however, is the province of the professional. The practice involves careful calculation of break-even points, interest-rate movements, and the costs involved. Moreover, because of the substantial amounts required to justify the swaps, participation is largely confined to large financial institutions with a background in bond trading. (Anything less than a million dollars is generally considered an odd lot in bond trading.)

Swaps might be called to the attention of institutions by the major bond dealers who follow the market closely. Aware of the institutions' portfolios, moreover, the dealers might also uncover other trading routes, or such routes could be found by the institutions themselves as they gained sophistication in this area. For example, bonds could be accumulated at discounts in anticipation of submitting them to corporations that had to enter the market for sinking fund purposes. Or, research could point to bonds that appeared likely candidates for lowered ratings with consequent adverse market reaction.

SUMMARY

The complete contract between a borrowing corporation and the holder of its obligations is evidenced by two instruments: the bond, which contains the corporation's promise to pay principal and interest; and the trust indenture, which is made out to a trustee with the bondholders as beneficiaries and which provides a description of the terms of the issue and the rights and responsibilities of the parties involved.

Among the terms of the issue, it is now common to include protective features intended to prevent the corporation from taking steps that will impair the status of the bonds relative to other outstanding securities. A typical restriction limits the payment of dividends when disbursements would reduce the working capital of the corporation to less than a specified amount. Other important items are the redemption provisions, sinking fund requirements, and special privileges, such as the right to convert to common stock.

In recent years, increasing attention has been given to the effect of inflation on bonds because of their characteristic fixed payments. One possible modification is to adjust bond principal and interest requirements to a price index. Another form, which has made some headway in the United States, is a floating-rate note, with the holder given the right to sell the note back to the issuer after a specified period.

Various private agencies issue ratings that indicate the quality of bonds. Because investors make extensive use of them, the ratings have an important influence on the market status of the bonds. Municipal and corporate securities with at least an A rating and U.S. government issues may be regarded as high-grade. The fluctuations in the prices of these bonds are tied primarily to the movements of interest rates.

The interest rates for different types and maturities of securities are interwoven into a pattern commonly called the term structure of rates. This structure is largely determined by the demand for and supply of funds. As economic conditions change, the supply of securities coming to the market will vary, as will the demand of investors for obligations of different qualities and maturities. In this area, the federal government exerts an important influence through its control over both banks and the volume and types of securities it brings to the market. To anticipate the direction of interest rates, analysts assess the attitude of the government and project the sources and uses of funds in the economy.

Compared with common stock, bonds may be more readily grouped into similar quality or risk classes, and issues that appear to be selling out of line may be identified. To make such analyses, curves are commonly plotted showing the relationship between the yields and maturities of comparable obligations. In these curves, the yields used ordinarily are based on the assumption that the proceeds from all coupons are invested at the yield to maturity. Analyses may also assume that the coupons are reinvested at the best yield possible, rather than the yield to maturity.

CHAPTER 1

Corporate Obligations

We live in a world of uncertainty. It is impossible to be sure of a corporation's ability to pay interest and principal. As a consequence, it does not seem reasonable to assert, as is sometimes done, that the investor should avoid buying an issue as a conservative commitment, regardless of the bond's other attractions, if there is any doubt of the corporation's ability to pay interest and principal. The most any investor can expect is that the probability of default will be less than some predetermined low level. The maximum tolerable probability of default depends on the investor's risk aversion. It really makes little difference whether one is dealing with a high-grade or low-grade bond. If the investor is looking for a low-risk bond to put into his portfolio, any issue with a probability of default less than the critical amount is an eligible candidate. Actually, however, the number of instances in which industrial bonds have defaulted is surprisingly low, regardless of grade.

IMPORTANCE OF SPECIFIC STANDARDS IN SELECTING HIGH-GRADE CORPORATE BONDS

At one time, it was popular to say that high-grade bond investment was a negative art, in contrast to the positive art of common stock investment. This meant that the approach to the purchase of a high-grade bond was to measure it against required tests; if it passed, the issue could be considered high-grade and might be acquired, provided that its yield was relatively favorable within its quality bracket. On the other hand, to find an undervalued common stock required an aggressive, searching effort to explore the potential of the issuing corporation.

While the distinction still has some validity, its sharpness has been considerably blunted. The uncertain economic climate of the early 1970s caused abrupt changes in the quality ratings of even top-quality obligations. For example, during this period, some newly issued securities of utilities, such as those of Cleveland Electric, were downgraded by Standard & Poor's in only six months; even worse, others were downgraded more than once. Revisions of this sort led bond managers to rely less on the published ratings and more on their own research, "regardless of what the little red Moody's book says," as one manager observed.[1]

To ascertain the issuing corporation's future financial capacity, the investor may employ various quantitative measures. For this purpose, the basic test is fixed charge coverage. Other major tests include: the capitalization ratio, the size of the company, and the company's financial condition. A number of analysts also use the margin of safety test.

FIXED-CHARGE COVERAGE: A BASIC TEST

The principal statistical gauge of a corporation's ability to meet its contractual obligations is the *fixed-charge coverage test*, or the number of times that earnings available for charges exceed these charges. A high ratio indicates that fixed charges are not consuming a large portion of income and that the corporation appears able to meet its basic financial needs. A low ratio suggests that fixed charges are a burden on the company and indicates difficulty in meeting interest and related requirements, with bankruptcy looming as a possibility.

The fixed-charge coverage is determined by dividing total fixed charges for the year into the net income available for fixed charges. Analysts rely on this simple test in their evaluation of bonds. Thus, in September 1974, Standard & Poor's determined that the quality of the New York State Gas and Electric bonds had been lowered and therefore revised their rating downward from double-A to single-A. The reason, the service indicated, was a marked decline in fixed-charge coverage over the past several years.[2]

The main problem in making the calculation is to isolate the elements entering into the ratio. Accountants and analysts have varying practices that sometimes result in their reporting different figures for the same company's fixed charges or for the net income available for these charges. For a valid comparison of fixed-charge coverage ratios, major differences of this kind must be eliminated, so that the two factors may be calculated as uniformly as possible.

Determination of Fixed Charges

Fixed-charge requirements refer to the recurring payments that a corporation must make to meet its debt and other long-term contractual arrangements. The principal amount of the debt, as such, is not a part of these charges, but periodic allocations of a sinking fund toward eventual retirement of principal should be included when they are required by the terms of the indenture. (For simplicity, these payments often are excluded.)

Interest is generally the major charge. In addition to interest and sinking fund disbursements, the corporation may be required to make other payments arising out of leases, guaranties, and rentals. Leases represent a contractual charge and therefore are important in evaluating a company's debt. The handling of leases in financial statements is an accounting bugaboo and has been a topic of debate for a long time. Even after the Financial Accounting Standards Board issues a final statement on the subject, the security analyst may have to adjust items in reported statements to reflect his judgment of financial realities.

The essential problem is to put on a comparable basis the interest costs of a company (lessee) that finances itself by means of leases with the interest costs of a company that finances by means of debt. Toward this end, for some time the prevailing practice (which had been accepted by the SEC) was to count one-third of rental payments as interest costs, with the remainder representing such charges as depreciation and maintenance applicable to operations.

In October 1973, the commission issued Accounting Release no. 147 which, for all noncapitalized financing leases (similar to the FASB capital leases), requires the disclosure of the present values of the minimum lease commitments in the aggregate and by major categories of properties, such as real estate, aircraft, truck fleets and other equipment. Financing leases are defined as those which, during the noncancellable period, either cover 75 percent or more of the economic life of the property or have terms which assure the lessor a full recovery of the property plus a reasonable return on the use of the assets invested. The present values are computed by discounting net lease payments (after subtracting the estimated or actual amounts of operating expenses, such as taxes, insurance, and maintenance) at the interest rate implicit in the terms of the lease at the time of entering into the agreement. This disclosure, however, is not required if the present value of the minimum lease commitments is less than 5 percent of the sum of long-term debt, stockholders' equity, and the present value of the minimum lease commitments, and if the impact on net income is less than 3 percent of the average net income for the most recent three years.

These disclosures provide the basis for making reasonable estimates of the portion of rentals which represent interest. Accordingly, in Accounting Release no. 155, issued in April of the following year, the SEC stated that in the specifications for fixed charges in the calculation of the ratio of earnings to fixed charges, the criterion for the interest factor of one-third of all rentals was deleted. In lieu of this provision, the amended Regulation S-X, governing the accounting instructions for SEC forms, requires that fixed charges include "such portion of rentals as can be demonstrated to be representative of the interest factor in the particular case."

The analyst could estimate this interest factor by multiplying the present value of minimum rental commitments on long-term financing by the weighted average interest rate used in discounting the leases; both items are ordinarily shown in footnotes to reported financial statements. For example, in its 1974 annual report, TRW, Inc. estimated that the present values of the net fixed minimum rental commitments for all noncapitalized financing leases were $71.1 million for real estate and $2.0 million for machinery and equipment. Applying the average interest rate of 6.6 percent, used to estimate the real estate and the 11.5 percent used for machinery and equipment, to the capitalized figures produces an imputed interest cost of $4.9 million. This figure is over 10 percent of the reported interest expense of $48.3 million for the year.

The FASB Exposure Draft takes a different tack. It requires that the lessee, at the inception of the lease, record in the balance sheet a capital lease as an asset and a corresponding obligation, classified as long- or short-term as the case may be. The amount recorded is equal to the present value of the minimum lease payments (excluding such operating expenses as insurance, maintenance, and taxes to be paid by the lessor) plus the present value of any payment called for by a bargain purchase option. The discount rate is the lessee's incremental borrowing rate which is the rate that would be paid for a current borrowing of a similar amount for a similar term. Except for land, the asset is amortized in accordance with the lessee's normal depreciation policy. The difference between the total net minimum lease payments and the present value of these payments, as reflected in the balance sheet, represents the total interest involved. The amortization of this amount in proportion to the remaining balance of the obligation in the balance sheet is counted as interest expense for the current period.

Other expenses, such as amortization of debt discount and the miscellaneous costs involved in borrowing, are sometimes grouped with bond interest. These expenses may not be recurring obligations, but their close relationship to debt is often taken as justification for including them in the fixed-charge category. This practice is questionable. The issue is whether the company is exposed to default—that is, whether the company will be able to make the cash outlays required by the terms of its outstanding debt. Amortization is a noncash charge. While it may affect the interest of the investor in the company's equity, it has no influence on the company's ability to service its debt. Nevertheless, it is often difficult to segregate these noncash charges; they generally are not large, and therefore it is a conservative policy to include them. In its definition of fixed charges (Accounting Release no. 155), the SEC includes amortization of debt discount expense and premiums on all indebtedness.

The principle of consolidating parent and subsidiary company financial reports into a single statement involves the aggregating of comparable accounts in the different statements. This practice provides a realistic income statement but may be deceptive in regard to bonds of corporations which have subsidiaries. It is important to remember that earnings cannot go upstream until all the claims against the subsidiary which rank ahead of those of its stockholders are honored. Thus, the holders of the preferred shares of a subsidiary have a prior claim to its earnings over the holders of a first mortgage bond of the parent. If a subsidiary's income is to be counted upon for paying the interest obligation of a parent, all the charges against the operating income of the subsidiary which have priority over the stockholders' claims should be included in the fixed charges of the parent. For example, the Western Union Telegraph Co., which is the principal subsidiary of Western Union Corp., has a relatively large issue of preferred stock outstanding. In the parent company's income statement, dividend payments on this issue are shown as a deduction from income after taxes. In calculating coverage, these dividends should be counted with interest expense. In 1973, they amounted to $3 million, compared with consolidated interest charges of $10.4 million.

To illustrate the charges that may be encountered, Table 19-1 shows typical items listed in a random sampling of corporate income statements.

Determination of Earnings Available for Fixed Charges

A basic figure in every corporate income statement is the annual net income. To provide a consistent procedure, the earnings available for fixed charges may be calculated by adding to the net income for the year the aggregate of the fixed charges, federal and state income taxes, and any other charges that the company deducted but might be appropriately counted as income for the year; sometimes, too, the net income figure may have to be credited or debited as discussed below. The quality of a corporation's earnings was discussed in Chapters 11 and 12 as part of the process of evaluating its stocks. Here, consideration is given to some items especially pertinent to the determination of earnings available for fixed charges.

TABLE 19-1

Items Included in Fixed Charges by Selected Companies, 1972

NAME	INDUSTRY	ITEM	AMOUNT (IN MILLIONS)
Dayco	Industrial	Interest and loan expense	$ 7.6
General Instrument	Industrial	Interest and amortization of debt expense	7.7
Allied Chemical	Industrial	Interest and other financial charges	30.3
Dearborn-Storm	Industrial	Interest and amortization of debt discount and expense	4.2
Northeast Utilities	Public utility	Interest on long-term debt; amortization of debt discount and expense; other interest	81.9
Seabord Coast Line Railroad	Transportation	Rents for leased roads and equipment; interest on debt; amortization of discount on funded debt	24.5

Proprietary reserves. Corporations have varying reserve policies that can seriously distort reported earnings. Proprietary reserves may be properly segregated from retained earnings to guard against contingencies, but corporations sometimes adopt the questionable procedure of charging these reserves against earnings. In this event, the investor is justified in making a reverse entry to increase the earnings available for fixed charges by the value of these proprietary reserves.

Nonrecurring profits and losses. Net income should be increased by the nonrecurring losses and reduced by the nonrecurring profits that the company has included in its income statement. It is sometimes necessary, however, to distinguish between ordinary and extraordinary items.

Income taxes. Analysts often deduct income taxes from earnings prior to the calculation of the fixed-charge coverage. They hold that this procedure is conservative and makes it easier to determine the fixed-charge coverage of preferred stock. When income taxes were low these arguments had sufficient weight to justify the policy, but the height of present levies materially affects the resulting ratio. To exemplify the extent of these differences, Table 19-2 shows the fixed-charge coverages of a number of companies, calculated on the basis of income before and after taxes.

TABLE 19-2

Fixed-Charge Coverage Ratios for Selected Companies, Calculated Before and After Federal Income Taxes, 1973

COMPANY	PRETAX RATIO	AFTERTAX RATIO
Amstar	7.34	4.46
Celanese	5.29	3.14
Continental Oil	9.19	4.71
Quaker Oats	7.66	4.28
Missouri Pacific Railroad	2.64	2.40
Western Air Lines	3.38	2.38
Leaseway Transportation	3.25	2.44
Rochester Gas & Electric	3.12	2.61
New Jersey Power & Light	2.54	2.44
General Telephone Co. of Calif.	3.14	2.16

SOURCE: Moody's, ***Industrial, Public Utility, and Transportation Manuals,*** 1974.

Bond interest is a deductible charge in the calculation of net income, subject to income taxes. Determination of the fixed-charge coverage prior to taxes portrays more realistically the actual earnings protection afforded holders of bonds. Consider a simple example of a firm whose operating income before interest and taxes was just sufficient to cover the interest bill. Under these circumstances, its tax bill would be zero, and the company would have sufficient funds to pay its interest. In other words, *the creditor has a prior claim over the government on operating income.* One difficulty with this approach, however, should be noted. Allocations for sinking funds must come out of aftertax earnings. Thus, if the fixed charges include sinking fund requirements, the use of pretax earnings will overstate the coverage and the use of aftertax earnings will understate the coverage. One way of solving this problem is to include in the fixed charges, instead of the straight sinking fund allocation, the pretax earnings the firm will have to realize in order to have enough left over after paying taxes to make the sinking fund payments. (This adjustment is discussed in greater detail in Chapter 22, dealing with preferred stock.)

As a matter of historical interest, New York State in April 1953 revised its statutes governing investments of savings banks to provide for railroads calculating their earnings available for fixed charges without deducting federal income taxes. Before this change was adopted, the statutes established tests based on railroads covering their fixed charges *after* deducting federal income taxes and on public utilities covering their fixed charges *before* federal and state income taxes. The probable reason for this disparity was that the section dealing with rail investments was enacted earlier than the public utility statutes. The revision was very desirable because it placed the calculation of the fixed-charge coverage test on a more uniform basis throughout the law.

Minority interest. If a corporation does not own the entire equity of a consolidated subsidiary, allowance must be made for the interest of the minority stockholder. There is no uniformity in the treatment of minority interest in corporate income statements. It may be shown as a separate deduction after all other charges, as in the annual reports of General Mills, Hoover, and Owens-Illinois; often it is grouped under a common heading with various other costs of the corporation (Carnation, Exxon, W. R. Grace); and no allowance may be provided in the income statement, even though the account appears in the balance sheet (Cabot Corp., Pillsbury, Rohm & Haas, Sunbeam). Minority interest may be handled in various ways in the calculation of fixed-charge coverage: (1) it may be deducted after earnings available for fixed charges (Method 1 in Table 19-3); (2) it may be treated as an income deduction prior to determining earnings available for fixed charges (Method 2); or (3) both the subsidiary companies' income included in earnings available for fixed charges and their fixed charges may be reduced proportionately by the minority interest (Method 3). Although each method produces the same consolidated net income for parent company stockholders, each results in a different fixed-charge coverage, as indicated in Table 19-3.

Method 3 is the most logical, because it correctly allocates the minority stockholders' interest in both earnings and fixed charges. In most cases, however, enough data for this procedure are not easily available, and either Method 1 or 2 is employed. Standard & Poor's follows the practice of reporting fixed-charge coverage prior to any deduction for minority interest, whereas Moody's deducts minority interest in arriving at earnings available for fixed charges.

In most cases, the method used will not materially affect the results, since minority interest is likely to be small. At times, however—particularly during periods of low earnings—the method chosen may significantly alter reported results. Since it is prudent to use conservative procedures in establishing standards for gauging high-grade bonds, the suggested practice is to deduct minority interest from earnings available for fixed charges.

Depreciation. The method of taking depreciation will importantly affect the earnings figures. If one company uses straight-line depreciation while another employs a liberalized procedure, it may be advisable to define earnings before rather than after depreciation. This approach, however, is recommended only for comparisons. It is true that the cash flow associated with the depreciation is available for the payment of interest and, therefore, that the utilization of such funds can ward off a default. Unfortunately, such course of action can be taken only at the price of abandoning or delaying

TABLE 19-3

Effect of Minority Interest on Fixed-Charge Coverage

			CONSOLIDATED COMPANY		
	PARENT COMPANY A (IN MILLIONS)	SUBSIDIARY COMPANY B (IN MILLIONS)	METHOD 1*	METHOD 2† (IN MILLIONS)	METHOD 3‡
Net income	$300	$200	$500	$500	$420
Minority interest				72	
Earnings available for fixed charges	300	200	500	428	420
Fixed charges	90	20	110	110	102
Net income after fixed charges	210	180	390	318	318
Minority interest			72		
Net income for stock	$210	$180	$318	$318	$318
Fixed-charge coverage			4.5 times	3.9 times	4.1 times

*Minority interest deducted after earnings available for fixed charges.

†Minority interest deducted prior to earnings available for fixed charges.

‡Minority interest deducted proportionately from both earnings and fixed charges.

NOTE: Minority stockholders own 40 percent of the outstanding common stock of the subsidiary.

capital expenditures, with consequent deleterious effects on the future returns to the firm. A failure to replace equipment now may impair the ability of the firm to meet its interest obligation at some future date. Moreover, excluding depreciation is the conservative policy.

Equity interest in unconsolidated subsidiaries. In the equity method of accounting for unconsolidated subsidiaries, the corporation recognizes its share of the earnings or losses of the subsidiary in the period for which they are reported in the financial statement rather than when the subsidiary declares a dividend (see pp. 252-254). As in the case of minority interest, the amount of earnings available for equity does not vary with the line in the income statement where the corporation's equity in net earnings of affiliated companies appears. Reporting practices do affect the earnings available for fixed charges, and corporations follow different policies in their annual reports. Some include the equity in earnings in gross income (General Refractories, Libby, McNeill & Libby, Westinghouse Electric); others add it to net income from operations and taxes (Archer Daniels Midland Co., Chemetron, Scott Paper); while still others report the figure as a credit to operating income after deducting interest to arrive at income before taxes (Hercules, Inc.).

How the equity figure is treated can make a substantial difference in determining the earnings available for consolidated fixed charges. For example, for the year ended 1972, Sprague Electric Co. reported operating income before interest and taxes of $4.4 million. The company's equity in the net earnings of affiliates, carried in the income statement after this figure, amounted to $1.1 million, or one-fourth of its operating income.

In a number of instances, corporations indicate that they have no intention of having their overseas subsidiaries remit dividends. So long as the corporation exercises a significant influence over the policies of the subsidiary, however, the corporation could provide for dividends if such payments were financially desirable. Accordingly, it seems appropriate as a consistent policy for analytic purposes to include in earnings available for fixed charges a company's equity in the earnings of unconsolidated subsidiaries, unless there is a provision in a subsidiary's bond indenture or a restriction imposed by a host government that prevents the parent from tapping these earnings. A caveat is to exercise caution when the bulk of earnings comes from a company's equity in its nonconsolidated subsidiaries. In 1973, for example, Kaiser Industries covered its fixed charges by almost 10 times, an excellent showing. Some $52.7 million of earnings available for fixed charges, however, came from its equity in nonconsolidated subsidiaries, compared with a bare $100,000 from the consolidated system's operation. While the company expected to withdraw the funds represented by this equity, the dividends would be received after the subsidiaries had paid interest on their own debt. As a result, the parent's bondholders were in a secondary position relative to the bondholders of the nonconsolidated subsidiaries; the high interest coverage was, in effect, calculated on the deceptive prior-deductions method.

The lease adjustment. As discussed previously for leases outstanding unaffected by the FASB draft, fixed charges must be adjusted to include the interest factor implicit in financing-lease payments. Since this factor is added to fixed charges, it must be deducted from operating costs. No adjustment need be made for ordinary leases which are presumed to be an operating cost.

The process of capitalizing leases and allowing for amortization of related properties as well as the implied interest costs may affect income. As a result, among the provisions called for by SEC Accounting Release no. 147 was a requirement to show the impact upon net income if all noncapitalized financing leases were capitalized, related assets were amortized on a straight-line basis, and interest costs were accrued on the basis of the outstanding lease liabilities. If the impact on net income is less than 3 percent of the average net income for the most recent three years, the SEC permits this fact to be stated in lieu of the disclosure.

To illustrate how this calculation is made, assume that a company has minimum rental commitments arising from noncancelable financing leases for the next 30 years. These future leases are discounted at interest rates ranging from 8.1 percent to 9.1 percent, depending upon the type of the property involved. The present value of these future requirements discounted at the indicated interest rates is $59.8 million (after allowing for the present value of sublease rentals to be received). The impact on net income for the current year of this capitalizing procedure is determined by amortizing the above value, including the amount of implicit interest, allowing for the indicated tax expense, and deducting the actual rental paid for the year. In the example shown below, the amount of amortization and interest based on the capitalized values for the entire period exceeds the current year's rentals by somewhat over $1 million.[3]

CHARGES AGAINST INCOME	AMOUNT (IN THOUSANDS) CURRENT YEAR
Amortization of lease rights	$4,051
Interest costs	5,943
	9,994
Rental expense	8,056
	1,938
Income tax expense	930
Reduction of net income	$1,008

In its August 1975 Exposure Draft on "Accounting for Leases," the FASB noted that a number of respondents to its request for lease information opposed requiring disclosure of the estimated effect on net income of capitalizing certain leases. The board then indicated that it agreed with this view. The SEC has stated that after the FASB develops standards of accounting for leases, it expects to reconsider its own disclosure requirements.

The FASB Exposure Draft indicates that its provisions do not apply to leases outstanding prior to the effective date of the new statement. Accordingly, for a number of years to come, the accounting for leases in financial statements may follow prior policies for old leases and new policies for current leases. In these circumstances, the analyst will have to make the adjustment for the implicit interest factor as described above for old leases. This adjustment will not be necessary for new leases because interest will be included in the income statement to reflect the indicated lease obligation in the balance sheet. The lack of comparability has been the subject of criticism.

Interest charged to construction. Public utilities are permitted to capitalize an allowance for funds used during construction equivalent to the cost of funds devoted to plant under construction. The allowance is added to the company's fixed investment and the offsetting credit entry is to the account "interest charged to construction." The SEC has indicated (Accounting Release no. 155) that these credits should be added to gross income and not deducted from interest in the calculation of the fixed-charge coverage ratio.

Calculating Fixed-Charge Coverage

An example of the calculation of the fixed-charge coverage is shown in Table 19-4 for Phillips Petroleum. To the reported net earnings after taxes of $429.8 million are added interest of $52.8 million and $13.8 million for unusual losses. (This is a nonrecurring item.) In its annual report, the company shows that the present value of the basic rental commitments under noncancelable leases (after allowing for subleasing income) was $273.1 million and that the weighted average interest rate used in arriving at this figure was 6.3 percent. The product of these two items is $1.7 million, which represents the imputed interest charge. This figure is added to fixed charges and to the net earnings available for fixed charges. Income taxes are also included in net earnings because these taxes are calculated after interest is deducted. No capitalized lease obligation is shown in the balance sheet. The company indicates that capitalizing its financing leases had a negligible effect on income. After making the required adjustments, the earnings available for fixed charges are $854.1 million and the fixed charges are $54.5 million. The fixed-charge coverage ratio is therefore a very respectable 15.7.

Calculating Fixed-Charge Coverage When Several Bond Issues Are Outstanding

When a corporation has several bond issues outstanding, the fixed-charge coverage may be calculated in three ways, called the prior-deduction, cumulative, and overall methods. Before the Securities Act of 1933 was passed, investment bankers often used the prior-deduction method, which involved breaking down the interest charges of a corporation to show the amount of earnings available for interest on each issue of bonds in order of priority. Because of the misleading implications of this calculation, its use could be interpreted as an effort to deceive the buyer. The practice is no longer employed. In the cumulative method, sometimes used by analysts, charges are segregated so that the coverage of interest may be calculated for the senior bond alone and the coverage of interest on each subsequent issue

TABLE 19-4

Income Statement and Fixed-Charge Coverage Calculation: Phillips Petroleum, Year Ended December 31, 1974

	AMOUNT (IN MILLIONS)
Gross operating revenues	$4,980.7
Equity in earnings of nonconsolidated subsidiaries	59.7
Other revenues	65.3
Total revenues	5,105.7
Costs and operating expenses	3,583.4
Selling, general, and administrative expenses	311.6
Depreciation, depletion, amortization, and retirements	273.5
Taxes other than income	84.8
Interest and expense on indebtedness	52.8
Unusual items*	13.8
Provision for income taxes	356.0
Total costs and expenses	4,675.9
Net earnings after taxes	$ 429.8

CALCULATION OF FIXED-CHARGE COVERAGE	
Net earnings after taxes	$ 429.8
Unusual items	13.8
Reported interest	52.8
Interest implicit in financing leases	1.7
Income taxes	356.0
Earnings available for fixed charges	854.1
Reported interest plus interest implicit in financing leases	$ 54.5
Fixed-charge coverage	15.7 times

*Net loss from the closing or disposal of plants and interests.

NOTE: For simplicity, sinking fund payments are not considered; also, a company is not likely to be forced into bankruptcy because of a sinking fund default.

SOURCE: Phillips Petroleum Company, ***Annual Report***, 1974, pp. 27, 31, 32.

may be determined cumulatively with that of the preceding obligation. The third, or overall method, is the most conservative and most widely used. It calls for ascertaining the coverage by aggregating all the fixed charges of a company.

To illustrate the implications of these methods, let us assume that a corporation has the following two issues of bonds outstanding:

$10,000,000 8% first-mortgage bonds, due in 1985;
$1,000,000 10% debentures, due in 1990.

If $2,000,000 is available for fixed charges in a given year, the coverage of bond interest under each method is determined as in Table 19-5.

TABLE 19-5

Calculation of Fixed Charges by Prior-Deduction, Cumulative, and Overall Methods

	AMOUNT	COVERAGE
Prior deduction		
Earnings available for fixed charges	$2,000,000	
Interest on senior bonds	800,000	
Fixed-charge coverage of senior bonds		2.5 times
Earnings available for fixed charges on debentures	1,200,000	
Interest on debentures	100,000	
Fixed-charge coverage of debentures		12.0 times
Cumulative		
Earnings available for fixed charges	$2,000,000	
Interest on senior bonds	800,000	
Fixed-charge coverage of senior bonds		2.5 times
Interest on debentures	100,000	
Total interest	900,000	
Fixed-charge coverage of debentures		2.2 times
Overall		
Earnings available for fixed charges	$2,000,000	
Total interest	900,000	
Fixed-charge coverage of senior bonds and debentures		2.2 times

Using the prior-deduction method, we find that the fixed-charge coverage of the debentures is 12.0 times, as compared with only 2.5 times for the senior issue. This is clearly absurd; it suggests that the junior bonds are stronger than the senior obligations. Typically, the difference in the coverages of the two issues is great if the junior obligations are small compared with the prior-ranking bonds.

The cumulative method produces the same coverage of 2.5 times for the senior bonds but reduces that of the junior obligations to 2.2 times. Although this procedure always yields more conservative results for junior bonds, it overstates the strength of the senior issue. Failure to pay the fixed requirements of a lowly junior debenture could drive a corporation into bankruptcy as readily as default on a senior issue.

Reorganization proceedings are likely to affect adversely the market values of both senior and junior obligations. Hence the true gauge of the safety of a bond is the ability of the issuing corporation to meet all the interest charges. This ability is best measured by the overall method, which establishes the same coverage for both senior and junior bonds. In our illustration, this procedure gives a coverage of 2.2 times for either the senior bonds or the debentures.

Selecting the Period for Measuring the Fixed-Charge Coverage

Top-quality bonds are storm cellars for investment funds. When business conditions are depressed, commodity prices tumbling, and dividend omissions widespread, investors still expect interest and principal payments on high-grade obligations. Indeed, under these conditions, prime issues have their greatest appeal because of their relative market immunity to the economic decline and the increased purchasing power of the interest income they provide. Earnings of very few enterprises are completely invulnerable to the disturbances created by business fluctuations. However, the income shrinkages of corporations whose bonds are actually of high-grade caliber will be relatively modest, of brief duration, and largely offset by the power and duration of subsequent rises in earnings.

For a realistic appraisal of the caliber of a bond, the investor must consider the ability of the issuing corporation to meet its fixed charges under varying conditions. No fixed period can be recommended for this purpose. Generally, one should go far back enough to include a period of real adversity. Examination of the fixed-charge coverage of the company at such times provides an insight into its ability to handle its debt requirements under unfavorable circumstances. Calculating the average results for the entire period reveals the company's sustained earnings power after balancing both good and bad years. It is suggested that the fixed-charge coverage test of a bond take into account the issuing corporation's ability to earn its requirements both by a stipulated minimum margin during the worst year and by an average margin during the entire period.

Obtaining such a view of a corporation's earnings variability may entail reaching back many years to a time when the corporation under study differed significantly from its present condition. However, the alternative of not providing any gauge of corporate earnings during periods of severe economic restraint is far more unsatisfactory. If the investor is convinced that a company has changed so drastically, through expansion or diversification of its activities, that information for earlier years is useless, he must estimate how great a decline might occur under adverse conditions. For this purpose, he might note the shrinkage in income experienced by comparable enterprises and apply this same percentage to the corporation's current level of income.

Using this test may arbitrarily exclude certain bonds from the prime category. Such an error is not serious in the field of fixed-income securities, in which most high-grade issues afford comparable returns. The saddest error in this field of analysis is to purchase a bond in the belief that it is a prime obligation only to find that the issuing corporation subsequently defaults.

Treatment of Fixed Charges in Calculating Averages

A practical problem encountered in calculating the average fixed-charge coverage of a bond is whether the average of the fixed-charge coverage of individual years should be determined or the requirements of the current year should be related to the average earnings over the designated period. The difference between the two methods may be indicated by a simple illustration. Let us assume the following earnings and fixed-charge coverage record of a company for three successive years:

YEAR	EARNINGS AVAILABLE FOR FIXED CHARGES	FIXED CHARGES	FIXED-CHARGE COVERAGE
1974	$12 million	$6 million	2 times
1973	9	3	3
1972	6	1	6
Average	9	3.3	2.7

The average fixed-charge coverage ratio during the period is 2.7 times, whereas that obtained by relating the 1974 charges to the average earnings for the period is 1.5 times. The theory underlying the first method is that earnings and fixed charges are interdependent and should be treated as a unit in determining the average coverage for a number of years. In the second method, stress is placed on the current charges of the corporation. If these have been reduced, the company's position is thought to have been strengthened, and this should be reflected in a higher average coverage. If the charges have been increased, as in the preceding illustration, its financial status is less favorable, and the average coverage should be lower.

A corporation whose fixed charges have risen because of new financing may have greater earning power if the additional funds are used for expansion. By the same token, the corporation may now find itself with a debt-heavy capital structure and large added costs that enhance its vulnerability in the event of a business decline. The conservative practice would be to determine the average fixed-charge coverage by relating current debt requirements to average earnings over the full period used in the calculation. The rate of corporate change has become so rapid, however, that in many cases this relationship would be misleading. Accordingly, the analyst has little choice but to calculate an average fixed-charge coverage and to rely on the capitalization ratio to provide a gauge of the capital structure.

Influence of Coupon Rates

The fixed-charge coverages of two corporations with the same amounts of earnings and outstanding debt will vary if the coupon rates of the two issues are different. It is even conceivable that a secondary bond, through refunding into lower-coupon debt, may be transformed into a prime obligation. This result may seem illogical, but it represents no more than ordinary changes in securities' quality that spring from the operating and financial activities of corporations. The ability of an enterprise to finance at low interest rates is a favorable indication of its financial strength or of the astuteness of its management. This condition may be considered as much a part of the company's characteristics as low labor costs. For this reason, it seems entirely proper to determine fixed-charge coverage on the basis of requirements created by applying actual coupon rates to the amount of bonds outstanding.

Establishment of this rule does not eliminate the necessity of the investor's taking into account the chances of change. In analyzing securities, the future is always important. Thus, the likelihood that additional rounds of wage increases will occur is an essential factor in the analysis of plants with high labor costs. Similarly, during periods of rising interest rates, the investor cannot ignore the probable effects on a corporation's fixed-charge coverage of the impending need to refund a low-interest-bearing bond with a higher-coupon issue. The inevitable increase in fixed charges may lower the issue's coverage sufficiently to alter its present rating.

Using Forecast Earnings

The difficulty with the traditional fixed-charge coverage (as well as the margin-of-safety test described below) is that it fails to recognize the stochastic or uncertain character of a firm's earnings. Whether tests cover a single year or a period of years, the variability of the underlying earnings figures is ignored. To take this factor into account, two principal methods have been developed.

In one method, pro forma cash-flow statements are projected in order to determine the funds that will be available for the payment of principal and interest over the years ahead. The major components of one such statement are shown in Figure 19-1.

The critical figure is the net operating cash flow, which is the amount produced by the business that is available for servicing debt. The changes in

FIGURE 19-1

Format for Cash-Flow Statement

ITEM	AMOUNT
Nonfinancial cash inflows	
Sales	
+ Other revenues	
+ Reduction of accounts receivable	
− Increase in other current assets	
Total	
Operating cash outlays	
Cost of sales	
− Depreciation	
+ Selling and general expense	
+ Income taxes	
+ Increase in inventories	
+ Miscellaneous	
+ Decrease in current liabilities	
Total	
Net operating cash flow	
Financial outlays	
Interest	
+ Repayment of long-term debt	
+ Repayment of other debt	
Total	
Discretionary outlays	
Cash dividends	
+ Capital expenditures	
+ Other investments	
Total	
Financial receipts	
New long-term debt	
+ Increase in other debt	
Total	
Cash position	
Net cash flow	
+ Discrepancy	
+ Beginning cash items	
= Ending cash balance	

SOURCE: Adapted from J. E. Walter, ***The Investment Process*** (Boston: Harvard Business School, 1962), p. 368.

the ending cash balance, however, are also of interest. In order to sustain operations over the long term, a company invariably experiences other flows, as suggested in Figure 19-1. Persistent cash drains or heavy borrowings have unfavorable implications for the quality of a bond.

Projecting pro forma statements of this sort is a complicated undertaking. Many items are interrelated. If a growing volume of sales requires the construction of plant and equipment that must be financed externally, a decision has to be reached on how these funds will be raised. Depending on the measures taken, the future flow of earnings will, of course, be affected. Then again, a probability distribution may be assigned to the net operating cash flow, and that probability distribution, in turn, depends on the probability distributions of each of the several interdependent items that enter into the computation of the net operating flow. Because this type of forecasting relies on computers, investors ordinarily do not have the facilities for the necessary calculations. At best, therefore, use of this technique is limited to corporate managers seeking to determine financing methods or to institutional investors concerned with the position of marginal bonds selling at depressed levels that have substantial appreciation potential. To appraise a high-grade obligation, simpler methods are preferable.

For this purpose, consider the ratio $(\bar{E} - K\sigma)/F$, where $\bar{E}$ represents expected earnings, K an arbitrary multiple, σ the standard deviation of earnings, and F the fixed charges of the firm. With $K = O$, the formula represents the expected fixed-charge coverage. If the probability distribution of earnings is normal, expected earnings plus or minus one standard deviation should cover realized earnings 68 percent of the time. Plus or minus two standard deviations should cover realized earnings 95 percent of the time. If $K = 2$, the numerator represents the level below which earnings are likely to fall only 2.5 percent of the time. (We use 2.5 percent instead of 5 percent because we are only concerned with earnings minus 2 standard deviations, not with earnings plus or minus 2 standard deviations.)

The intuitive appeal of this ratio comes from the fact that (1) as $\bar{E}$ (expected earnings) increases, all other things being equal, safety is improved and the value of the ratio increases; (2) as σ increases, all other things being equal, safety deteriorates and the value of the ratio decreases; and (3) as F increases, all other things being equal, safety deteriorates and the value of the ratio decreases.

The investor can set K at any level he desires; the value he sets will be directly related to his willingness to take risks. Because the higher the value of the ratio, the safer the security, this ratio can be considered a safety factor rather than a risk factor. He can project the safety factor as many years into the future as he is willing to forecast earnings and their potential range.

Much of what was said above in relation to the simpler measures of fixed-charge coverage applies here. The estimated $\bar{E}$ may be either cash flows or earnings. Earnings may be projected by any of the methods discussed in the chapters on analyzing common stock. Whichever method is used, it should be remembered that the standard deviation of earnings is likely to grow along with earnings. Provisions for such growth should be made even if it only involves assuming that the standard deviation remains proportional to expected earnings instead of being fixed for all time.

CAPITALIZATION RATIO TEST

The *capitalization ratio*, the relationship between the stock and bond portions of a corporation's capital structure, is a supporting test. The test throws light on two factors. First, it reflects the degree of asset protection for the bonds; the larger the equity portion of the capital structure, the smaller the amount of bonds outstanding and the greater the value of assets underlying these bonds. Second, it measures the volume of capital contributed by the stockholders in relation to that advanced by the bondholders.

This test is used by federal and state regulatory agencies and, as we have mentioned, is sometimes included in bond indentures to protect bondholders.[4] The Securities and Exchange Commission has established the criterion that the percentage of equity in total capital should be at least 25 percent for public utilities falling within its jurisdiction.[5] The New York State law that governs investments eligible for purchase by savings banks requires that the outstanding capital stock and surplus of a public utility equal at least two-thirds of the total secured debt. A typical instance of a protective feature in a bond is contained in the indenture of New England Gas & Electric Association, which prevents the issuance of additional obligations when the ratio of consolidated debt to total capitalization, including surplus, exceeds 60 percent.

In these tests, the value of the outstanding securities is generally taken as the amount stated in the corporation's books. However, this value may not accurately reflect the current worth of listed assets. The going value of a corporation may be more realistically gauged by using the market prices of its stock in determining the capitalization ratio. Funded debt may be calculated at stated rather than market value, because it is both convenient and conservative to assume that high-grade bonds are carried at par. A troublesome question is the treatment in the lessee's balance sheet of leases that do not appear as debt. For such leases, disclosure requirements now permit the analyst to show an obligation reflecting the present values of noncapitalized financing (capital) leases at the interest rates implicit in the lease arrangement. For leases falling under new FASB requirements, as indicated in its Exposure Profit, lessees must report the indicated asset and related obligation in the balance sheet.

Calculation of the capitalization ratio for Phillips Petroleum is shown in Table 19-6. In order to simplify the calculation, minority interest is included

TABLE 19-6

Calculation of Bond Capitalization Ratio of Phillips Petroleum 1974

	AMOUNT (IN MILLIONS)
Total long-term debt reported in balance sheet	$ 658.2
Minority interest in consolidated subsidiaries	8.0
Net capitalized value of financing leases	273.1*
Total long-term debt	939.3
Common stock (76,102,207 shares outstanding)	3,144.6†
Total capitalization	$4,083.9
Bonds as percentage of total capitalization	23.0%

*As reported in footnotes to financial statements representing the present value of basic rental commitments less subleasing income; the weighted average interest rate used to capitalize rentals was 6.3%.

†Based on the average of the high and low of the market price of the common stock in the fourth quarter of 1974.

SOURCE: Data taken from Phillips Petroleum Corporation, *Annual Report 1974*.

with total funded debt. Employing the market value of common shares automatically gives recognition to retained earnings, which need not be added to the value of the capital stock thus calculated. If the issue sells below book value, this procedure penalizes a company because of the negative reaction of the market to the carrying value of its assets. A high bond capitalization ratio raises some doubt about a corporation's long-term ability to meet fixed charges in the event of a severe business contraction. This stems from the fact that the net operating income of any company is essentially a variable quantity. Given the probability distribution of this net operating income, the probability of its failing to cover the interest charges on a strong corporation's limited volume of outstanding debt is small. All other things being equal, the larger the debt element in the capital structure, the greater is the probability that fixed charges will not be covered.

SIZE OF THE COMPANY

On the surface, the size of a corporation provides little indication of the quality of its obligations. Huge corporations may have difficulty in covering fixed-charge requirements, whereas small enterprises may easily be able to meet them.

However, the size of a company may affect the stability of its operations. Small companies often suffer more heavily during periods of economic stress. Moreover, adequate information on the financial background of very small organizations may not be readily available, their securities may not have a satisfactory market (making the raising of additional equity difficult at times), and the position of the company in the industry is not likely to be so well established as the positions of larger units in the field.

In view of these circumstances, it is suggested that a minimum size be established for corporations whose securities are regarded as high-grade investments. This test is not intended to distinguish between the obligations of the very large and medium-sized companies, but merely to exclude issues of very small enterprises from the prime category. This requirement may result in specific issues of excellent caliber falling by the wayside. In the quest for high-grade obligations, however, the investor need not incur the extra burden of studying securities of very small enterprises.

FINANCIAL POSITION

If a corporation is able to pass the fixed-charge coverage and capitalization ratio tests, its financial position is probably strong enough to meet debt requirements without undue strain. Nevertheless, the liquid resources of a company may be drained even when earnings are good. Such a condition can be particularly serious for industrial enterprises which must constantly finance current operations or are expanding rapidly.

The financial requirements of public utilities and railroads extend over longer periods. Even in these cases, a shortage of liquid funds may prove embarrassing; hence it is prudent to restrict purchase of high-grade corporate bonds to issues of enterprises in a satisfactory financial position, although the typical public utility probably requires less working capital for its operations than comparable railroads or industrial concerns. Use of balance sheet ratios to assess financial condition is discussed in Chapter 14.

MARGIN OF SAFETY

In lieu of the fixed-charge coverage, some analysts employ the *margin-of-safety test.* This measure is calculated by dividing the balance after fixed charges by gross revenues. The ratio indicates the extent to which revenues may decline (without an offsetting reduction in expenses) before a corporation fails to cover its fixed charges. The higher the ratio, the greater the margin of safety.

It is conceivable that two corporations with the same fixed-charge coverage might have sharply differing margins of safety because of variations in the percentage of total revenues absorbed by operating costs. This condition is illustrated in Table 19-7.

TABLE 19-7

Comparison of Fixed-Charge Coverage and Margin-of-Safety Tests

ACCOUNT	CORPORATION A	CORPORATION B
Gross revenues	$100,000,000	$50,000,000
Operating expenses	70,000,000	20,000,000
Operating income*	30,000,000	30,000,000
Bond interest	10,000,000	10,000,000
Balance after fixed charges	$ 20,000,000	$20,000,000
Margin of safety	20%	40%
Fixed-charge coverage	3 times	3 times

*Income, prior to taxes, available for fixed charges.

Corporation *A* has twice the gross revenues of Corporation *B*, but its operating expenses are substantially heavier. As a consequence, both corporations report the same operating income and have the same fixed-charge coverage, but the margin of safety of *A* is 20 percent, whereas that of *B* is 40 percent. This differential indicates that *B* could experience a considerably greater decline in revenues before its operating income failed to cover fixed charges.

The margin-of-safety test reveals both the ability of a corporation to meet its fixed charges and the control it exercises over costs. The test is commonly applied to railroads, which may have both high operating costs and large income available for fixed charges; this combination of factors creates a deceptively liberal fixed-charge coverage that could be obliterated by a modest decline in gross revenues. A major drawback of the margin-of-safety measure is that it ignores the ability of a corporation to shrink its operating expenses in response to a decline in operating revenue. For a given expense, one company may have a lower margin of safety than a second. However, when full cognizance is taken of its ability to retrench expenses, the resulting fixed-charge coverage may be larger than that of the second corporation at lower levels of gross revenue.

RELATIONSHIP BETWEEN QUANTITATIVE STANDARDS AND INDUSTRY

The industry in which a corporation operates affects its earnings. Consumption of residential electric power, gas, and water, for example, is generally more stable than the demand for freight transportation or the manufacture of industrial products. Reflecting this difference, earnings of corporations in the public utility field ordinarily fluctuate less than those of most railroads or industrial enterprises.[6]

Listing quantitative standards on an industry-wide basis could be misleading. The profits of certain industrial corporations engaged in staple consumer-goods fields may be more consistent than those of some public utility enterprises whose output is sold primarily to industrial users. Moreover, many companies have such diverse activities that it is difficult to assign these firms to any particular industry. Despite such divergences, it is common practice to apply standards based on field of operations, since they simplify the problem of distinguishing between bonds of different caliber. This approach is also tilted in the direction of conservatism.

After World War II, the National Bureau of Economic Research undertook a major study of the history and characteristics of corporate bond financing.[7] Although an old study (the last year covered was 1943), it is still pertinent because the generally high level of earnings since World War II has resulted in relatively few defaults. These findings revealed shifts in the earnings cycles of different corporations. From 1900 to 1929 the average annual rate at which railroad bonds went into default was only 0.9 percent of outstanding issues, as compared with 1.5 percent for public utilities and 2.1 percent for industrials. This favorable performance of railroads accounts for their common inclusion, at that time, in legal lists of bonds eligible for savings banks and trust fund investments. Between 1930 and 1943 conditions changed strikingly, and the record of public utilities was considerably better than that of the railroads or industrials, neither of which did well during the period. The default rate for industrials was 3.5 percent, compared with 3.2 percent for railroads, whereas the default rate for public utilities increased only by one-tenth of 1 percent.

State legislative yardsticks governing eligibility of bonds for purchase by savings banks recognize industry variations. Legislative requirements, however, are sometimes based on traditional rather than current conditions. The New York State Banking Law, for example, requires virtually the same fixed-charge coverage requirements for both railroads and public utilities. Nor does the basic law admit obligations of industrial corporations.

The similar requirements for railroads and public utilities and the admission of industrial bonds only under special provision do not appear to reflect the current entrenchment of utilities in the nation's economy, the emergence of a number of industrial enterprises of outstanding financial strength, or the increased problems of railroads. As we have observed, New York State has attempted to modernize its requirements through amendments which make the legal list much more flexible. It is still questionable whether the legislation has gone far enough in the right direction. Although establishment of industry-wide standards seems desirable, it is equally important that these requirements do not lag behind the growth of American industry.

MINIMUM SUGGESTED STANDARDS

The nature of the probability approach makes the determination of minimum standards difficult. What is acceptable depends partly on the investor's risk aversion and partly what is available in the market. Nevertheless, since the probability approach is not universally accepted and investors find guidelines helpful, we suggest the following standards, broadly differentiated between industrial, railroad, and public utility issues.

Industrial Bonds

To qualify as a prime industrial bond, an individual company must have maintained an average coverage, prior to income taxes, of at least 6.0 times over the previous five years; must have earned its charges by at least 4.0 times in four out of the previous five years, including the year immediately preceding the investment; and (as the supplementary test) must have covered current fixed charges on the average of at least 2.0 times in "depression-level" earnings.

The one-year exemption recognizes the erratic nature of industrial income and the possibility that unusual conditions in a single year might disrupt an otherwise excellent record. We insist that the minimum required coverage must have been maintained in the previous year because the investor has no certain way of knowing whether a current earnings dip is temporary or represents the beginning of a downward trend. If earnings in the latest year fall below the minimum margin, the investment status of the bonds must be suspended until the company once more shows that it can cover its charges by the requisite amount.

With respect to the capitalization ratio, the bonds should constitute not more than 35 percent of the total capital structure. While strong industrial corporations could meet this test, the ratio appears sufficiently low to weed out companies with overfunded capitalizations.

As a gesture in the direction of conservatism, it is suggested that a company's minimum gross sales be at least $50 million for its securities to be ranked in the top category.

Railroad Bonds

The minimum pretax earnings requirements suggested for railroads are as follows: an average five-year coverage of 4.0 times; an annual coverage requirement of 3.0 times for four out of the previous five years, including the year immediately preceding the investment; and an average coverage of 2.0 times for the depression-equated period. Owing to the cyclical nature of the railroad field, the supplementary test is of particular importance. At the present time, very few railroads satisfy these criteria; but then, there are probably very few railroad bonds that may justifiably be considered high-grade.

To qualify as high-grade, the bonds should represent not more than 50 percent of a railroad's capitalization. In prior years, carriers as a group have been outstandingly remiss in permitting their debt to become overheavy.

A road that obtains at least $20 million in railway operating revenues meets the standard of size. This test is more rigorous than the New York State law, which requires a road to report at least $10 million of revenues for five out of the six previous fiscal years or to operate not less than 500 miles of standard-gauge line within the United States.

Public Utility Bonds

In the case of prime public utility bonds, the pretax earnings of a corporation must cover fixed charges by at least 3.0 times during each of the five previous years. This test is severe because it makes no allowance for any temporary lapse in a company's income. Its inflexibility is counterbalanced by the steadiness of public utility earnings and the modest numerical coverage demanded. The minimum requirement for the supplementary test is an average coverage of 2.0 times during the depression-equated period.

The funded debt of a public utility should not exceed 55 percent of its capitalization. The height of this ratio also reflects the industry's stability and its capacity to assume a relatively large debt burden.

The minimum size for public utilities issuing high-grade bonds is measured in terms of gross operating revenues, which must be at least $10 million. In order to qualify for inclusion in the legal list, the New York State Banking Law requires that the gross operating revenues of electric and gas companies should have averaged at least $2 million, and those of telephone companies $5 million, during the five years preceding the investment.

These standards are summarized in Table 19-8.

TABLE 19-8

Standards for Selection of High-Grade Corporate Bonds

FIXED-CHARGE COVERAGE (excluding sinking fund)				
		PRECEDING 5 YEARS		DEPRESSION-EQUATED YEAR
CATEGORY	PRECEDING YEAR	AVERAGE	EACH YEAR	AVERAGE
Industrials	4.0 times	6.0 times	4.0 times*	2.0 times
Railroads	3.0	4.0	3.0*	2.0
Utilities	3.0	3.0	3.0	2.0

CAPITALIZATION RATIO	
	BONDS AS A PERCENTAGE OF TOTAL CAPITALIZATION DURING PRECEDING YEAR
Industrials	35%
Railroads	50
Utilities	55

SIZE OF COMPANY	
	PRECEDING YEAR
Industrials	$50 million gross sales
Railroads	$20 million railway operating revenues
Utilities	$10 million gross operating revenues

*Requirements must be met in 4 out of the 5 preceding years.

LOW-QUALITY BONDS

For assurance of income, there is no substitute for quality in high-grade bonds. If an issue fails to meet the quantitative standards prescribed, it should not be considered a prime obligation. Nevertheless, if its yield is commensurate with its risk, an investor may be willing to include it in his portfolio. However, the investor must realize that he is taking more risks with respect to market action, continuity of interest disbursement, and payment on maturity than with a high-grade bond.

There is not much point in developing quantitative standards for medium-grade and speculative obligations. Such standards would be meaningless. Bonds that do not fall in the high-grade classification may automatically be considered in the secondary category. The methods of analyzing these issues are essentially no different from those of analyzing high-grade issues. It should be recognized, however, that the legal classification of an instrument as a bond does not necessarily make it a superior investment to a stock. If a bond of a given risk does not promise a yield so great as that of a stock of comparable quality, there is simply no point in buying the bond. Moreover, bonds in default or in a very marginal financial condition should be analyzed as if they were common stocks rather than bonds.

The investor should not overlook the fact that if the expected yield on a bond is more than commensurate with the risk, a well-diversified portfolio of such bonds should, on the average, return to the investor a realized yield more than commensurate with the risk taken, even if some bonds in the portfolio default.

SPECIAL TYPES OF BONDS

Thus far, in our discussion of fixed-income securities, we have developed methods of analysis centered on the issuer. This course exemplifies the modern belief that the nature of the issuer, rather than the form of the security, governs the quality of a senior obligation. We now shift our perspective. In certain instances the form of the bond may become important because it modifies in some way the role of the issuer. Three types of securities fall in this category.

First are issues whose collateral significantly affects the quality of the bond; examples are equipment obligations, collateral trust bonds, and some real estate issues. Of this group, only railroad equipment obligations are consistently high-grade. The second type consists of guaranteed issues in which the primary obligation for payment is shifted to another party and in which the form of the guaranty is of significance. The third type includes income bonds in which the nature of the contract permits the corporation to omit interest payments without incurring legal penalties.

Equipment Obligations

Railroads issue most of their equipment obligations to finance the purchase of rolling stock. The popularity of this method of financing in the railroad field has led to its employment by other industries; for example, airlines use it to acquire flying equipment, and oil companies use it to obtain tank cars.

Equipment obligations are usually sold through the so-called Philadelphia plan.[8] The railroad orders the equipment from a manufacturer. After the order is filled, the manufacturer transfers title to a trust company, which obtains most of the funds to pay the manufacturer by means of *equipment trust certificates*; these mature serially and are guaranteed as to principal and interest by the railroad. The trust company leases the equipment to the carrier in exchange for an initial down payment and a contract for periodic rent payments sufficient to meet interest on the certificates and provide for their complete amortization. After the terms of the lease are fulfilled, title passes to the railroad.[9]

Equipment trust certificates have an excellent financial record. During the depression of the 1930s—the most rigorous economic test in modern American history—railroads occasionally had to extend the maturities of these instruments or provide for their exchange into other securities, but on only one issue were holders compelled to accept a loss of principal. Even the hapless Penn Central (now the Penn Central Transportation Co.), which entered into bankruptcy proceedings in June 1970, was under court order to continue payments on some $1.2 billion of equipment trust agreements, conditional sales contracts, and leases covering most of its railroad freight cars and locomotives. While the road took advantage of "grace periods" provided in some of the contracts in order to conserve its dwindling cash resources, it did not actually default on these obligations.[10]

Three major factors contribute to the strength of equipment trust certificates: (1) the original deposit made by the railroad permits initial issuance of a smaller amount of certificates than the value of the equipment serving as collateral; (2) thereafter, this margin of safety increases because the certificates are retired at a rate more rapid than that of the collateral's depreciation in value; and (3) the equipment is standard, necessary for continued operations, and easily disposed of to other roads.

The strength of the certificates is reflected in their relatively high investment rating compared with other obligations within the same system. This fact is revealed in Table 19-9, which shows the Standard & Poor's rating of certificates for selected carriers, along with the best rating assigned to the road's other direct obligations. In each case, the rating of the certificate is at least one classification higher than that accorded the senior bonds in the system's capital structure.

TABLE 19-9

Comparison of Standard & Poor's Rating of Equipment Trust Certificates with That of Highest-Rated Direct Bond in the Same System, August 1975

	EQUIPMENT TRUST CERTIFICATE	BOND
Atchison, Topeka & Santa Fe	AAA	AA
Atlantic Coast Line	AA	BBB
Burlington Northern	AA	A
Chicago, Burlington & Quincy	AA	A
Denver & Rio Grande Western	AAA	A
Gulf, Mobile & Ohio	AA	A
Missouri Pacific	A+	BBB
Southern Railway	AA+	A+
Texas & Pacific Railway	A	BBB

SOURCE: Data taken from Standard & Poor's Corporation, ***Bond Guide*** 39 (September 1975).

In recent years, because of the generally high calibre of equipment trust certificates, railroad companies have been able to sell large amounts of these securities, even though the bond market has been unsettled. In the first half of 1975, according to the Association of American Railroads, the carriers put $727 million of new equipment into service. ($685 million had been financed in 1974.) Despite a broadened new-issue market for the certificates, their subsequent trading market has continued to be less liquid than, say, the sector for corporate industrial bonds. This limitation has not posed a marketing problem, however, since the bulk of the certificates have been purchased by institutional investors who plan their purchases so that repayment coincides with the institution's need for funds.

Despite the outstanding record of equipment trust certificates and the potential for recovery in case of default, investing in a company that might default is to be avoided as much when choosing among equipment trust certificates as when choosing among bonds. The instruments of weak companies are more subject to default than those issued by stronger ones. Indeed, suitable maturities, at only a comparatively slight sacrifice in yield, can often be found among the instruments of stronger corporations. In evaluating certificates, attention must be given to the type of equipment serving as collateral and the possibility of technological obsolescence, the relation between the amortization period and the life of the equipment, the size of the down payment, and the overall demand for that type of equipment. Thus, Pan American World Airways has certificates outstanding secured by Boeing 747 aircraft. Despite the importance of this collateral, the certificates carry a Standard & Poor's B rating, compared with a BB rating for the bankrupt Pennsylvania Railroad's equipment trust certificates (the road's bonds, on the other hand, are rated DDD). In part, this low rating reflects Pan American's precarious financial position; for example, when the certificates were issued in 1970 their prospectus stated that " . . . Pan Am did not in 1969, and expects that it will not in 1970, generate sufficient earnings to cover its fixed charges in those years." In part, also, unlike the rolling stock of railroads, the long-term future of the 747s is uncertain in view of the rapid technological changes characteristic of the air transportation field.

Collateral Trust Bonds

Collateral trust obligations are secured by personal, intangible property that usually takes the form of stocks and bonds. These securities are deposited with a corporate trustee, who is usually authorized to liquidate them in the event of default. Most indentures now contain protective features to prevent any deterioration of the collateral. Indentures may also provide that the market value of collateral must not fall below a minimum level in relation to the principal value of outstanding obligations.

The unique feature of a collateral trust bond arises when the collateral, rather than the issuer, determines the quality of the bond. This condition may occur when the collateral represents a major asset of the issuer. For example, the Pennsylvania Co. collateral trust 5¼s of 1985 are secured by Norfolk & Western common stock, which must equal at least 150 percent of the principal value of outstanding bonds. This stock is a major asset of the Pennsylvania Co.; therefore, analysis of the collateral trust bonds requires an evaluation of Norfolk & Western common stock.

The value of the collateral may stem from the fact that it represents a stronger company than the issuer. Thus, in July 1970 the Baltimore & Ohio offered $27 million collateral trust 11s due 1977, backed by an equal amount of Chesapeake & Ohio refunding and improvement bonds, also due 1977. Reflecting the strength of the C&O, the collateral trust obligations have a Standard & Poor's rating of A, compared with one of BB for the Baltimore & Ohio's other bonds.

Debenture obligations of investment companies are, in effect, collateral trust bonds. The merits of these debentures depend on the securities in the company's portfolio. When the market value of stocks and bonds held is high relative to the amount of obligations outstanding, and when the quality of these portfolio securities is good, an investment company's debentures may be considered of first-grade caliber. Under the Investment Company Act of 1940, closed-end funds may issue bonds provided they have a net asset coverage of 300 percent. The financial services are reluctant to assign a quality rating to an investment company's bonds because of the uncertainty of the success of the institution's investment policy.

Real Estate

Loans to acquire, construct, or improve real estate–comprising land and buildings–are commonly secured by pledge of the property involved. (This discussion does not include farm mortgages, which constitute an independent and highly specialized subject.) Disastrous consequences have followed the granting of these loans without adequate analysis of the financial integrity of the issuer and the prevailing economic environment. In making an evaluation, the investor should take account of certain historical tendencies. Loans granted at the peak of real estate cycles have resulted in notably large losses. Foreclosure rates have been higher for loans on properties located near the centers of large cities; this reflects the current trend toward municipal decentralization of both population and industry. More favorable results have come from mortgages granted on owner-occupied houses, newer properties, less expensive dwellings, and properties in which land is a relatively small percentage of the total appraised valuation.

If a borrower defaults on a real estate loan, the lender may acquire the property by foreclosure and sell it to recover the value of his loan. His indemnification then depends on both the worth and the marketability of the mortgaged real estate. Hence, the mortgage is of some significance as regards the quality of these bonds. Legislation regulating investments of financial institutions generally limits real estate loans to a specified percentage of the appraised value of the property. These loans may be direct mortgage bonds or leasehold mortgages. In addition, to get around the uncertainties arising from dependence on single mortgages, real estate trusts became popular during the 1960s. Another type of enterprise that has come to the forefront is the land development company. Such commitments generally entail high risks.

The most common type of real estate financing is a direct loan secured by a pledge of residential property. Institutional investors, such as savings and loan associations, life insurance companies, and mutual savings banks, grant these loans. Their terms have been liberalized by provisions for government insurance or guarantees, which may be granted in several ways.

Direct mortgage loans. These are made by individuals on an accommodation basis, as loans are made by one member of a family to another. These loans also may be granted as outright investments when the interest rate is attractive and the real estate collateral is sound. When these are considered as investments, careful study must be made of the value of the property serving as backing. This analysis should include checking the construction of the property, the quality of its maintenance, the outlook for the neighborhood, the existence of zoning restrictions, and the character of other properties in the vicinity. Appraisals are notably subjective, and the amateur may easily be misled. It is questionable whether direct mortgages represent suitable investment outlets for persons not specially trained in the real estate field.

Mortgage bond. A mortgage bond is like a direct mortgage, except that it is issued to cover a large property or group of properties, and the mortgagor's promise to pay is represented by bonds rather than a note. Mortgage bonds may be offered to finance the erection or purchase of large commercial properties, such as hotels or buildings.[11] High levels of business prosperity stimulate this type of construction. As a result, mortgage bonds are often issued during boom periods, when the value of the underlying property is exaggerated by liberal appraisals, high rentals, and inflated construction costs.

Mortgage bonds have been particularly vulnerable to the impact of economic declines, and their record is studded with defaults. Commercial property is specialized, and disposal may be difficult if default becomes necessary; hence, the indicated value of the collateral underlying a mortgage bond does not influence the quality of the issue as much as does a mortgage on residential properties. The quality of these bonds depends more directly on whether the underlying properties produce sufficient earnings to permit payment of service charges without difficulty.[12] Making this analysis involves applying tests similar to those developed for corporate obligations. In view of the poor prior record of mortgage bonds, the investor should regard them with great caution.

Leasehold bonds. These are often issued to finance the construction of large commercial buildings. Such bonds are usually secured by a first lien on the building and by a long-term lease on the ground. In the event of default the bondholders could take title to the buildings, but they would still be liable for continuation of rental payments under the lease. Default of rental payments would permit the owners of the ground to take title to the buildings. This relationship makes the position of the landowners senior to that of the holders of the leasehold bonds.

Land trust. In certain metropolitan areas where land is very valuable, land trust certificates may be used as a means of financing. In this case, the owner of the land leases it to another person, transfers title to a trustee, and sells to the public a number of certificates, each of which represents an interest in the land. The lessee must continue his regular payments or forfeit the building erected on the leased land. The value of this construction is usually good; the lessee is reluctant to default on rentals, and the certificates characteristically occupy a strong position. These arrangements sometimes grant the issuer a subsequent right to redeem the certificates or give the lessee an eventual right to buy the land at a stipulated price.

Real estate investment trust (REIT). REITs are trusts in the true sense of the word, since shareholders receive certificates of beneficial interest. Such trusts are exempt from paying income taxes if they distribute at least 90 percent of ordinary income to shareholders, who then pay taxes on the payments they receive.

An REIT may either own real estate, lend money on it, or both. The loans may be long-term mortgages or short-term for construction or development purposes. Equity trusts engage primarily in the ownership of real estate; they earn income from the normal excess of rents over operating costs and obtain tax benefits from depreciation. Mortgage trusts, which have attracted attention because of high interest rates in recent years, profit from the spread between the cost of raising funds and the interest they receive on loans. However, as borrowing costs soared in the 1970s but income from mortgages and rentals remained fixed, many REITs experienced financial difficulties.

GUARANTEED SECURITIES

There has been some proliferation of commitments that are not immediately apparent on the examination of a balance sheet. While they may have little or no impact on the traditional tests, they may have a significant impact on the fortunes of the committed firm and the investor. The commitment made in so-called project financing is one such phenomenon. Sometimes, when projects have to be undertaken, such as the Canadian Arctic Pipeline, several firms in a given industry will cooperate and a new corporation will be formed. The participating corporations then make firm commitments to use the product of the project, signing "take or pay" contracts or something similar. This means that the product or service will be paid for whether or not it is used to the extent originally planned. This is a subtle way of guaranteeing a cash flow to a project with which the project can service the debt that was incurred in the construction of the project.

The guarantee of a subsidiary's issues is another phenomenon of this sort. The guarantee has an impact on the quality of both the issuer's bonds and the guarantor's bonds. The impact on the guarantor depends, of course, on the nature of the guarantee. The SEC requires that, under certain conditions, a ratio of earnings to fixed charges should be calculated on a "total enterprise" basis. This means that a company guaranteeing the debt of an affiliated credit company or of a major supplier would include the fixed charges of such a "related" company in computing the fixed-charge ratio. This calculation is called for if it materially affects the coverage.

Guaranteeing securities is a practice common to all fields of enterprise. Mortgage companies may provide guarantees on real estate loans. Throughout the history of the railroads, guarantees have been used for loans on particularly important properties. Parent companies in public utility holding-company systems have guaranteed the obligations of less-known subsidiaries to facilitate the sale of their securities. In the public field, the credit of the U.S. government backs certain federal agency bonds. Practically all Eurobonds issued by private corporations are guaranteed. Usually the bonds are floated by specially incorporated financing subsidiaries whose credit standing alone would not warrant the terms obtained on these bonds.

A guarantee by another company enhances the quality of an issue when the guarantor has a stronger credit rating than the issuing corporation. In these circumstances, the investment merits of the bonds depend on the guarantor's strength rather than the issuer's. A number of corporations may guarantee a single issue. For example, Kansas City Terminal Railway Co. bonds were guaranteed by 12 railroads. While the presence of different guaranties raises the caliber of an issue, the dominant consideration is the financial standing of the strongest guarantors. A mere accretion of weak guarantees may not materially alter the quality of the bond.

On the other hand, unless the fortunes of the two companies are perfectly correlated, a guarantee by a company financially weaker than the issuer may strengthen the bond. The weaker company is more likely to default than the stronger, but the probability that the stronger company will go bankrupt while the weaker company survives is hardly zero; thus, the latter's guarantee may have some meaning. However, where the guarantors are all in the same industry (like the railroads) and their fortunes are highly correlated, focusing attention on the stronger guarantor has merit.

Analysis of a guaranteed obligation begins with a review of the terms of the guaranty, including the names of the guarantors, the extent of the guaranty, the firmness and duration of the agreement, and the existence of any contingent requirements. Unsatisfactory provisions may weaken the investment status of a bond. Once the guaranty has been evaluated, the analytic procedures are the same as those for other bonds representing issuers in the same field of activity.

INCOME BONDS

Income bonds reflect the acumen of corporate management, which has created an instrument that is considered a bond by the investor but does not burden the corporation with the inflexible requirements of the typical bond contract. Like any other type of bond, income obligations have a fixed maturity for payment of principal, but this date may be so far removed from the time of issuance that it is no source of concern to incumbent managers.

These issues differ from most bonds in that interest on them is payable only if earned.

The indenture agreements underlying income bonds may include a number of protective features. In many instances, management must pay interest to the extent earned and may have the authority to make payments even if not earned. Interest is usually cumulative to a designated level, thus providing pressure for holders to be paid in full, even though temporary lapses may occur. The procedure for determining income is commonly set forth in the trust indenture; this obviates the danger that management might manipulate the accounts to minimize the earnings available for these bonds. A capital fund may also be required, to prevent the dissipation of earnings on contingent interest payments while the corporation's properties deteriorate.

Table 19-10 contains a list of representative railroad income bonds and a summary of some of their leading characteristics. Interest on railroad income bonds is generally payable annually in April or May. Purchasers may not have to pay the accrued interest, because most bonds are traded "flat." It will be remembered that the prices of issues selling on this basis drop by the amount of the interest payment on the ex-date, but over a year this decline tends to be erased.

Income bonds have a special tax aspect that may be advantageous to some investors: the portion of interest received applicable to the period prior to the date of purchase is considered a capital adjustment. For example, assume that on December 31, 1972, an individual purchased a 4.5 percent income bond at a price of 61, with interest payable annually on May 1. Two-thirds of the annual interest payment on May 1 would be treated as a capital return; this would result in a reduction in the purchase price of approximately 3 points for tax purposes. Only one-third of the payment, or $15, representing the amount for the period after the purchase date, would be considered income. Thereafter, if the investor sold the bonds for 62½ immediately prior to the next interest date, the difference between his adjusted purchase price of 58 and the sales price of 62½ would be treated as a capital gain.

Analysis of income bonds proceeds along the same lines as that of preferred stocks, which is discussed in Chapter 22. The investor must, however, give particular attention to the indenture provisions of the income obligations. It is highly desirable that these bonds be cumulative, grant the right to receive interest whether earned or not, and entitle the holder to sinking fund payments. The first two characteristics afford the holder some basis for expecting that the corporation will continue disbursements even if earnings diminish temporarily. Fulfilling the terms of a sinking fund over a period of years will gradually enhance the status of the dwindling supply of bonds still outstanding.

TABLE 19-10

Characteristic Features of Railroad Income Bonds

NAME	STANDARD & POOR'S RATING	CUMULATIVE FEATURES	ANNUAL SINKING FUND	INTEREST STATUS
Central of Georgia 4½s, 2020	BB	Cumulative up to 13.5%; interest paid after first-mortgage interest and sinking fund.	0.5% of maximum amount outstanding out of available net income.	Paying.
Chicago Great Western 4½s, 2038	CCC	Cumulative up to 13.5%; interest paid after first-mortgage interest, sinking fund, and capital fund.	0.25% of maximum amount outstanding, dependent on income.	Paid 1969-1970 interest April 1971.
Chicago, Indianapolis & Louisville 4s, 1983	B	Fully cumulative; interest paid out of available income.	$50,000 out of available net income.	Paying.
Chicago, Milwaukee, St Paul & Pacific 4½s, 2019	CCC	Cumulative up to 13.5%; interest paid after first-mortgage interest, betterment, sinking fund.	0.5% of A and B income bonds originally issued, but only to extent earned; 50% of common dividends divided between A and B as contingent sinking fund.	Paying.
Chicago, Rock Island & Pacific 4½s, 1995	DD	Cumulative up to 18% and payable to extent earned in ensuing year.	Varying cash amounts, contingent upon earnings and cumulative up to a maximum of $4,000,000.	No interest paid since September 1967.
St. Louis-San Francisco 5s, 2006	B	Cumulative up to 15%.	0.5 of 1% of maximum Series A debentures issued.	Paying.
Western Pacific Railroad 5s, 1984	B	Cumulative up to 20% interest paid after capital fund requirement.	$800,000 payable to extent earned after fixed charges plus optional payments of 50% of required payments.	Paying.

SOURCE: Rating and interest status taken from Standard & Poor's, ***Bond Guide*** 39 (September 1975).

SUMMARY

In gauging the quality of a corporation's bonds, the basic tests suggested are: fixed-charge coverage, the capitalization ratio, the size, and the company's financial condition.

The fixed-charge coverage is calculated by dividing total fixed charges into the net income available for these charges. The concept is simple, and the main problem is to ascertain the items entering into the numerator and denominator of the ratio.

Fixed charges are the recurring payments that a corporation must make to meet its debt and other long-term contractual requirements. In addition to interest and sinking fund allocations, the corporation may be required to make other payments arising out of leases, guaranties, and rentals. Recent accounting regulations mandate that a public company provide considerable information, not available previously, concerning its leases. It is now possible to estimate lease payments by multiplying the present value of minimum rental commitments on long-term financing leases, as reported by the company, by the weighted average interest rate used in discounting the leases.

To provide a basis for comparison, the earnings available for fixed charges may be calculated by adding to the net income for the year the aggregate of the fixed charges, federal and state income taxes, and any other charges that the company deducted but might appropriately be counted as income for the year, such as charges against earnings for proprietary reserves.

When a corporation has several issues of bonds outstanding, the fixed-charge coverage should be calculated by the overall method. This calls for using the same earnings figure for all the issues and including in fixed charges the requirements applicable to all the issues. In effect, therefore, a single coverage is established for both senior and junior bonds, on the theory that failure to meet the requirements of either category could drive a corporation into bankruptcy. In determining minimum standards for the fixed-charge coverage test, consideration is given to the company's ability to cover its charges in depressed economic periods.

The fixed-charge coverage (and margin-of-safety test) has been criticized because it fails to recognize the stochastic or uncertain character of a firm's earnings. To take this factor into account, pro forma cash-flow statements may be projected and an allowance made for expected future variations in earnings.

The capitalization ratio is calculated by determining the relationship between the stock and bond portions of a corporation's capitalization. This test reflects the degree of asset protection of the bonds. It also measures the volume of capital contributed by the stockholders in relation to that advanced by the bondholders. The size of a company and its financial position are checked to exclude bonds of very small or weak enterprises from the top category.

Other measures may be used along with the fixed-charge coverage. The margin-of-safety test is calculated by dividing the balance after fixed charges by gross revenues; the ratio indicates the extent to which a corporation's revenues may decline before it fails to cover its fixed charges.

Specific standards are suggested for the selection of high-grade corporate bonds. This approach reflects the modern belief that the nature of the issuer, rather than the form of the security, governs the quality of a senior obligation. Consideration, however, is also given to certain cases where the form of the bond is important. These include equipment obligations, collateral trust bonds, and some real estate issues.

Some bonds are guaranteed by the parent of the issuer or another party that has reason for doing so. Such guarantees improve the quality of bonds, but the exact nature of the guarantees should always be examined carefully.

Bonds in which the issuer has to pay only if it has earned sufficient income are known as income bonds. The principal difference between such bonds and preferred stock is that the issuer has no discretion about paying interest when sufficient income has been earned. That is not so in the case of preferred stock.

CHAPTER 20

United States Government and Related Obligations

The history of the United States public debt mirrors the great physical and economic struggles that have shaped the rise of the nation itself. During these years of development the public debt has been the cause of sporadic factional conflicts. Apologists for economy have favored limited expenditures, balanced budgets, and, in some instances, increased taxation. Proponents of a more expansive monetary philosophy have veered toward borrowing and, in the early years, toward high tariffs as means of financing enlarged government spending.

Although the debt has occasionally declined, it has generally grown at a rate that depended on the prevailing economic circumstances and fiscal philosophies. Moreover, despite efforts at maturity stretching, the average length of the privately held marketable debt has shrunk over the past decade along a jaggedly declining line, from five years nine months in June 1965 to three years in July 1975.[1] The general maturity picture is portrayed in Figure 20-1, showing particularly the sharp rise in obligations due in less than one year. In 1975 pressure was exerted on the entire long-term bond market, including government and corporate issues, by the huge Treasury financing program to meet antirecessionary budget deficits.

FIGURE 20-1

Maturity Groupings of U.S. Government Marketable and Convertible Debt

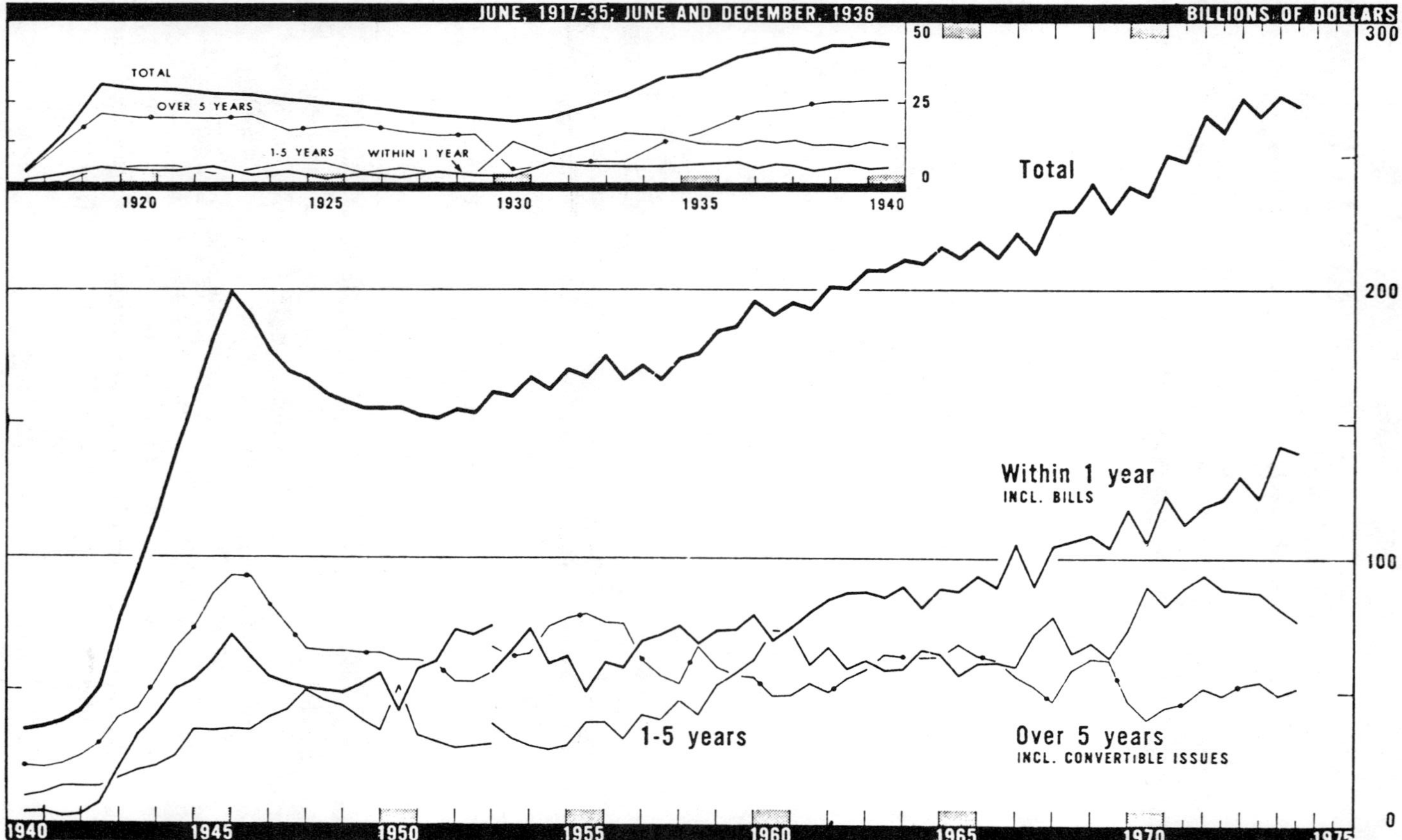

NOTE: Par value based on Treasury Department, "Daily Statement of the United States Treasury." Maturity classification based on period to first call before 1953; thereafter on period to maturity.

SOURCE: Board of Governors of the Federal Reserve System, ***1974 Historical Chart Book*** (Washington, D.C.: Government Printing

TYPES OF U.S. GOVERNMENT OBLIGATIONS

The secretary of the Treasury, with the permission of the president in certain instances, has considerable authority to issue securities of various forms and characteristics; Congress has adopted further broadening amendments. This latitude in treating different types of securities that may be offered enables the Treasury to "tailor" obligations to the nation's needs. Within the framework of existing market conditions, therefore, the Treasury has consistently attempted to adapt its financing program to meet the requirements of individual and institutional investors. It has issued a number of different obligations, broadly divided into the marketable and nonmarketable categories.

Marketable securities provide the investor with flexible instruments that he may buy or sell at prices immediately responsive to changing economic conditions. By permitting free interchange among investors, these bonds contribute to the fluidity of the capital markets. Both the Federal Reserve and the Treasury use them to implement credit control policies. The primary disadvantages of marketable obligations originate in their price variations, which discourage some investors from holding them. Moreover, they may be available only in minimum amounts that may be too large for the small investor. For example, in 1970, the government raised the minimum purchase of Treasury bills from $1,000 to $10,000 in order to check the flow of potential mortgage money from savings deposits. Of the various Treasury and agency issues, only the Federal Housing Administration debentures are available in denominations of less than $1,000, while only a few other issues are available in denominations of $1,000.

Nonmarketable bonds enable investors to obtain a secure form of income that is free from market risks; they also enable foreign governments to buy large amounts of Treasury obligations without upsetting their price structure. On the other hand, the nonmarketable bonds do not have the flexibility of marketable issues. Many are payable on demand, thus confronting the Treasury with the threat of huge redemptions. Nor are they suitable instruments for effectuating credit control policies.

The changing mix of Treasury securities outstanding is shown in Figure 20-2. Since 1965, savings bonds have been substantially steady, except for a modest rise in recent years. Marketable bonds have declined perceptibly. Substantial increases have occurred in special issues and in notes, certificates, and bills. To use Treasury and agency securities effectively as investment media, the investor must be familiar with their characteristics and understand the principles underlying the debt-management decisions of the government. Table 20-1 lists the issues currently included in the public debt. As the debt has grown, the statutory debt limit has been repeatedly raised.

FIGURE 20-2

Interest-Bearing Debt of the U.S. Government, June 30 and December 31

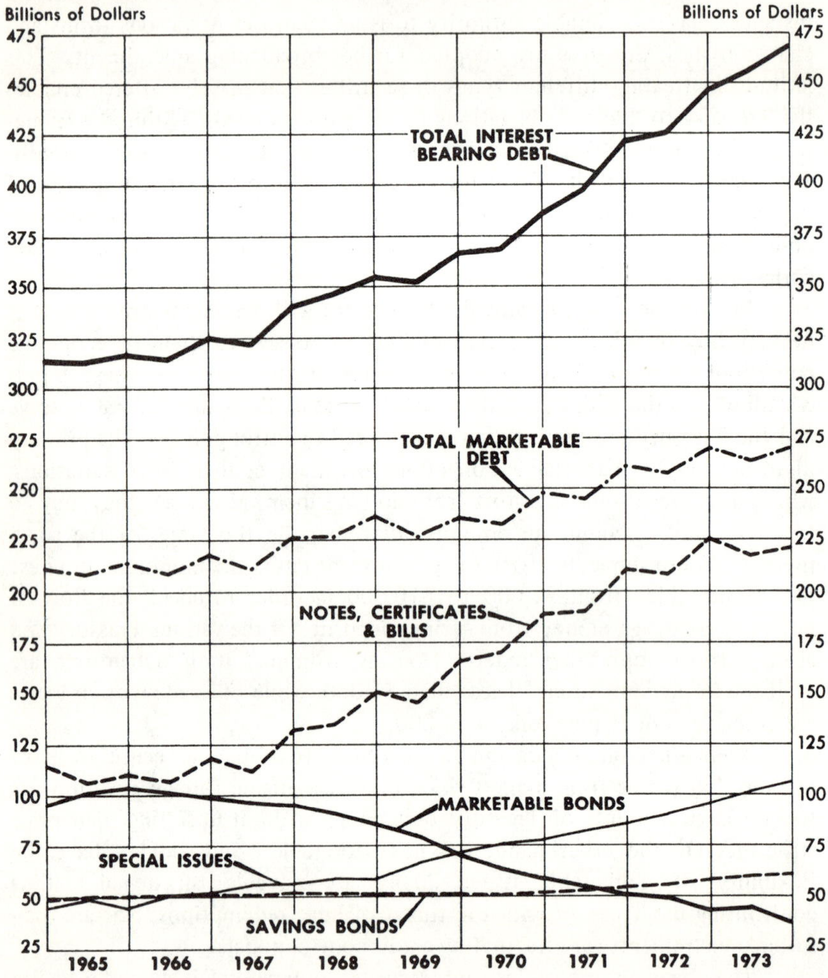

SOURCE: The First Boston Corporation, ***Handbook of Securities of the United States Government and Federal Agencies and Related Money Market Instruments***, 26th ed. (1974), p. 40. Reprinted by permission.

TABLE 20-1

Public Debt of the United States as of March 31, 1975
(Detail, rounded in millions, may not add to totals)

ISSUE	AMOUNT OUTSTANDING (IN MILLIONS)
Interest bearing debt	
Treasury bills	$123,972
Treasury notes	141,915
Treasury bonds[1]	34,103
Total marketable issues	299,989
Depository series	17
Foreign government series	
Dollar denominated	22,370
Foreign currency denominated	1,599[2]
Government account series[3]	116,812
Investment series	2,268
R.E.A. series	12
State and local government series	605
U.S. individual retirement bonds	*
U.S. retirement plan bonds	96
U.S. savings bonds	64,371
U.S. savings notes	442
Total nonmarketable	208,592
Total interest-bearing debt	508,581
Noninterest-bearing debt	
Matured debt	361
Other	727
Total noninterest-bearing debt	1,079
Total public debt outstanding	509,660
Public debt subject to limit	
Public debt outstanding	509,660
Less amounts not subject to limit	
Treasury	616
Federal Financing Bank	65
Total public debt subject to limit	508,979
Other debt subject to limit	
Guaranteed debt of Government agencies	488
Specified participation certificates[4]	1,135
Total other debt subject to limit[5]	1,623
Total debt subject to limit	510,602
Statutory debt limit[6]	531,000
Balance of statutory debt limit	20,396

[1]Pursuant to 31 U.S.C. 752, the face amount of Treasury bonds held by the public with interest rates exceeding 4¼ percent per annum may not exceed $10,000 million. As of March 31, 1975, $6,625 million was held by the public.

[2]Dollar equivalent of Treasury notes issued and payable in the amount of 5,403 million Swiss francs.

[3]Includes special issues to government agencies and trust funds.

[4]Pursuant to 12 U.S.C. 1717(c) and 31 U.S.C. 757b-1.

[5]Notes issued to International Monetary Fund were redeemed and a letter of credit in an equal amount was issued.

[6]Pursuant to 31 U.S.C. 757b. By Act of February 19, 1975, the statutory debt limit established at $400,000 million was temporarily increased to $531,000 million through June 30, 1975.

*$500 thousand or less.

SOURCE: U.S. Treasury Department, ***"U.S. Treasury Department Monthly Statement of the Public Debt of the United States,"*** March 31, 1975.

Treasury Bills

Treasury bills are non-interest-bearing securities sold principally by competitive bidding on a discount basis. They may have maturities of up to one year. Various series have been used; typical of recent years are 13-week and 26-week bills auctioned weekly and 52-week bills auctioned every four weeks. Yields are usually quoted on an annualized basis, with a year considered to have 360 days. In order to determine the yield of a Treasury bill, the following formula may be utilized:

$$\frac{100 - \text{price}}{100} \times \frac{360}{\text{days to maturity}}.$$

Thus, if the price of a 270-day Treasury bill was \$94.500 (competitive tenders must be expressed on the basis of 100, with no more than three decimals) the yield would be:

$$\frac{100 - 94.500}{100} \times \frac{360}{270} = 7.33\%.$$

Although this figure is generally called the "yield" of a bill, it is actually more like a bank discount rate. Since yields on most coupon issues are calculated on a 365-day year and use the purchase price as a base, their yields and those for Treasury bills are not strictly comparable. Approximate equivalence can be obtained by converting the bill calculation to a 365-day basis by means of the following formula:

$$\frac{365 \times \text{bill rate}}{360 - (\text{bill rate} \times \text{days to maturity})}.$$

Using the prior illustration, we find that the comparable yield on a coupon bond* works out to be

$$\frac{365 \times 7.33\%}{360 - (7.33\% \times 270)} = 7.86\%.$$

Investors may desire to determine their return if they sell bills before maturity at a different rate from that at which they were purchased. The following formula can be used for this purpose:

$$\frac{\text{Days to maturity} - \text{days held}}{\text{days held}} \times \text{Difference between rates at which bills are purchased and sold.}$$

*This formula does not take into account the fact that on coupon issues interest is paid every six months, while on bills the interest is not earned until maturity. For bills with more than six months to maturity, therefore, the actual bond equivalent yield is somewhat lower than that obtained from the formula shown.

The result is a differential factor that is subtracted from the original return if the bills are sold at a higher rate and added if they are sold at a lower rate. Thus, let us assume in the original illustration that the 270-day bills, bought at 7.33 percent, are held 60 days and sold on a 7.00 percent basis. Using the prior formula we have:

$$\frac{270 - 60}{60} \times .33\% = 1.155\%.$$

Since the bills were sold at a lower rate than they were bought, the differential is added to the original return of 7.33 percent to obtain 8.485 percent.

In 1951 the Treasury offered a tax anticipation series of bills (TAB) which could be accepted at face value in payment of taxes on the specified tax date or submitted for cash several days later. These bills have been sold under competitive bidding, as regular bills are. The TABs generally mature on the 22nd of the month; since the tax payment date is the 15th of the month, the taxpayer receives seven days free interest. The Treasury has also issued a "strip" of bills, which is a package containing a number of different maturities. In buying strips the investor is required to bid for the package as a whole.

When the Treasury sells bills, it accepts the highest bids offered up to the amount desired. Noncompetitive tenders, recently up to $500,000 without stated prices, are allocated in full at the average price of those sold on a competitive basis. Since April 1974 the Federal Reserve has been permitted to bid noncompetitively to "roll over" maturity bills which it owns or are owned by its governmental customers, primarily foreign monetary authorities.

Bills afford the Treasury a flexible means of financing and provide the investor with a highly liquid, risk-free investment. Bank depositors in various states hold them periodically when their deposits are subject to certain taxes. The extra demand created at those times may temporarily force yields to unusually low levels.

Coupon Issues

Coupon issues include certificates, notes, and bonds which may be issued for cash subscription or in exchange for outstanding or maturing obligations. Ordinarily, the Treasury announces an offering one to three weeks before actual issuance. It specifies a date until which the books are kept open for subscription at the Treasury's announced price or for entry of bids if the price is to be determined by auction. In recent years, the latter method has not been used for new-money offerings and only occasionally for refundings. In general, individuals and corporate buyers must post deposits running up to 10 percent; commercial banks normally may submit subscriptions for customers. Oversubscriptions often occur on fixed-price offerings, leading to percentage allotments with an initial portion, usually $200,000, allotted in full. Preferential allotments may be made to certain categories of investors, such as the Federal Reserve and governmental subscribers.

Certificates of indebtedness. These instruments have maturities of up to one year and have been issued without coupons. None was outstanding on June 30, 1975.

Treasury notes. Traditionally restricted to maturities between one and five years, Treasury notes may now be issued with maturities of up to seven years. Their relatively short terms are attractive to the commercial banks, which consistently have held large amounts of these issues. They are usually sold at auctions under rules similar to those for bills. The Treasury introduced an innovation, however, in its September 1974 refunding, which represented the first rollover of the quarterly cycle of two-year maturities begun in 1972. For that auction, the Treasury did not fix a coupon interest rate in advance but instead invited bidders to state the percentage yield they would accept; the coupon was established after the auction. The aim of this procedure was to accommodate any wide fluctuations in interest rates between the date on which the financing was announced and the auction date.[2]

The government uses notes to provide a convenient maturity spread between its very short-term and its longer-term obligations. In the face of rising interest rates, the Treasury has found it necessary to raise the coupon rates of notes over recent years. The first 5 percent issue received such an enthusiastic reception among individual investors that they became known as the "Magic Fives." This rate, however, is modest compared with the 9 percent notes due August 1980, which had the largest coupon of all notes outstanding June 30, 1975.

Treasury bonds. Although these obligations may bear any maturity, they generally have been issued with original due dates of more than seven years. Some issues are callable by the Treasury at par several years prior to maturity. For example, the 4s of 1988-1993 mature for payment on February 15, 1993, but may be redeemed at the option of the United States on or after February 15, 1988, in whole or in part, at par and accrued interest, on any interest day, on four months' notice.

For many years Treasury bonds were always issued at par. As interest rates began their long-term rise in the latter part of the 1950s, this practice, plus the use of coupons (whose terms varied by an even 1/8 of 1 percent), made it impossible to market the bonds economically. Private industry adjusts the difference in coupon and market yield by selling bonds at a premium or discount; shading the yield by 1/16 of 1 percent on an issue of $1 billion represents a saving of $625,000 per year. As a consequence, the Treasury began to permit discounts and premiums in 1958.

In an effort to "redevelop the longer-term market," the Treasury at the beginning of 1973 offered a 6.75 percent, 20-year issue under a new auction technique, the "uniform price" method. The Treasury, as in the case of bills, accepts the highest tenders and then moves down to lower-priced bids, until the total accepted bids equal the amount of the sale. However, instead of awarding each accepted tender at the bid price, as is customary, the Treasury awards all tenders at the price of the lowest accepted bid. In this method, therefore, all accepted tenders are awarded at the low price, even if the bids were higher. This method is designed to appeal to pension funds, personal trusts, savings banks, and other investors in long-term securities that are not as experienced as commercial banks in submitting competitive bids.[3]

Nonmarketable issues. In addition to savings bonds, the only nonmarketable issues of any magnitude outstanding are special issues, the foreign and foreign currency series, and an investment series.

U.S. savings bonds. These obligations are issued only in registered form but may be held in the name of a single owner, with or without a beneficiary, or in the name of co-owners. They may not be owned by commercial banks, which may, however, purchase them in a fiduciary capacity. The bonds are noncallable and nontransferable. Since 1935, when they were first offered, the Treasury has sold various series of savings bonds, with different terms. Changes have been primarily to increase the effective rate of return, ordinarily by shortening maturities, although in 1968 and 1970 bonus payments were given to those who held to maturity.

The Series E bonds may be bought only by investors other than commercial banks; there is an annual limit on new purchases of $10,000 issue price for each investor. The bonds are sold at a 75 percent discount from their maturity value, which is par; they have a current duration (effective December 1, 1973) of five years and may be cashed by the holder at stated redemption prices without notice at any time not less than two months from issue date. The yields of these bonds depend on the length of time they are retained. If held to maturity, they afford a yield of 6 percent compounded semiannually. Any bonds not submitted for cash at their original maturity are automatically extended at the new rate.

Once a bond has been bought, its yield must be calculated from the date of its current redemption value to the period left to maturity. On this basis, the yield to maturity at any particular time after purchase is higher than the initial yield to maturity; this is because redemption values have been set to yield less than the full 6 percent if the bonds are sold prior to maturity. Investors who wish to liquidate a portion of their investment in savings bonds should always check the tables showing yields from that time to maturity and dispose of those that have the lowest yield.

Series H bonds were first made available on June 1, 1952. They may be bought by investors other than commercial banks up to a current annual limit of $10,000. The bonds are issued at par; they have a duration of ten years; and they may be cashed by the holder at par on written notice after six months from the issue date. The requirement of notice is intended to discourage premature redemptions. Interest is paid semiannually on a rising scale, to provide a yield of 6 percent per annum if retained to maturity. The Series H bond is intended to obviate the drawback, inherent in the Series E issue, of no current interest payments. Holders of Series E bonds may exchange them at current redemption values for the Series H issue.

A holder who is considering redeeming a Series H issue must figure his yield on face value from each interest payment date to maturity. After an individual has held a Series H bond for a number of years, his effective yield for the remaining life exceeds 6 percent.

Holders of Series H bonds have been granted extended maturity terms.

Special issues to government agencies and trust funds (government account series). Various agencies and trust funds of the government buy public-debt securities. The most important purchasers include the Federal Old-Age and Survivors Insurance Trust Fund, the Highway Trust Fund, the Federal Employees' Retirement Funds, the National Service Life Insurance Fund, and the Federal Hospital Insurance Trust Fund. On any given day these agencies may be in possession of very substantial sums which, if applied to the purchase of marketable government obligations, could seriously disturb the price structure of these securities. To avoid this danger, the Treasury issues special nonmarketable securities for the investment of these funds as they become available.

Foreign Series. These securities were issued beginning January 1962 to meet the needs of foreign governments and monetary authorities. There are two kinds, which may be offered in the form of certificates of indebtedness, notes, or bonds. One is payable in U.S. dollars ("Foreign Series"), the other in the currency of the buyer ("Foreign Currency Series"). Large amounts of foreign series bonds have been issued since 1971, as various central banks have reinvested dollars acquired in supporting the foreign exchange rate of the dollar and, more recently, as oil-rich governments have sought investment outlets.

Treasury bonds: Investment Series. The Treasury has thus far offered two series of nonmarketable investment bonds, but only the second is still outstanding. The Investment Series B 1975-1980 issue was initially offered in 1951 in exchange for two long-term marketable 2½ bonds that were overhanging the market. The Investment Series bonds, which have been callable on any interest date since April 1975, bear an interest rate of 2.75 percent, and are nontransferable and nonredeemable by the holder, although they may be exchanged at any time for marketable 1.5 percent five-year Treasury notes. The Series B bonds were offered again in 1952 on designated terms. This offering was not very successful, reflecting the continued rise in interest rates during this period.

U.S. retirement plan bonds. In 1962, Congress passed the Self-Employed Individuals Tax Retirement Act. This law, as amended, permits self-employed persons to contribute an amount up to 15 percent of earned income or \$7,500 per year (whichever is less) to retirement funds. The full amount of these contributions is deductible from taxable income, thereby postponing the tax until the income is used. In 1963 the Treasury issued a new type of savings bond specially tailored for this market, the *U.S. retirement plan bond.*

Bonds are issued in denominations ranging from \$50 to \$1,000. The earliest issues earned 3.75 percent; bonds sold from June 1966 to December 1969 yield 4.15 percent; those sold on or after January 1, 1970, provide a yield of 5 percent compounded semiannually. They are more like Series E than Series H bonds, since the interest takes the form of an excess of redemption value over purchase price (which is par), rather than detachable coupons. When an investor draws his retirement fund, he pays taxes on the interest of these bonds and on the amount of the deduction taken when the bonds were purchased. The typical self-employed individual can expect to earn much less in retirement than during his working years and will thus be in a lower tax bracket. Thus, not only does he get the advantage of the postponement of the income that went into his retirement fund, but it is also taxed at a reduced rate. A retirement plan bond cannot be cashed until the investor is over 59½ years old, unless he becomes significantly disabled or the secretary of the Treasury authorizes a redemption to prevent unnecessary hardship. Should the investor die before reaching 59½, the heirs are free to cash the bonds.

Depositary bonds. These bear interest at the rate of 2 percent and mature in 12 years; they are redeemable by the Treasury or the owner at any time on 30 to 60 days' notice, at par and accrued interest. These bonds may be purchased by banks designated as depositaries and financial agents of the government as a means of offsetting the costs incurred by them in handling government business. The bonds may serve as collateral to obtain deposits of federal funds.

Treasury bonds: R.E.A. Series. These bonds were issued at various times, beginning July 1, 1960, in connection with the financing of the Rural Electrification Administration.

State and Local Government Series. These nonmarketable certificates, notes, and bonds have been issued since August 1972. They afford state and local governments the opportunity of temporarily investing in higher-yielding taxable securities, the funds derived from the advance refunding of their own tax-exempt obligations.

Other Treasury Issues

The Treasury obligations previously described constitute the total interest-bearing public debt. The remaining issues either are of a technical nature or are outstanding in very small amounts.

Some guaranteed securities are outstanding. The relatively small number of these bonds reflects the Treasury's policy, inaugurated in October 1941, of providing funds directly to government corporations instead of selling guaranteed issues in the open market.

The debt not subject to statutory limitations primarily includes U.S. notes, which represent part of the nation's money supply; government deposits for retirement of national bank notes, Federal Reserve bank notes, and silver certificates; and Federal Financing Bank bonds.

U.S. GOVERNMENT AGENCIES

The U.S. government has established a number of agencies that serve as intermediaries to channel funds from the public to certain critical economic sectors. Originally, these agencies were designed to provide financial assistance to those sectors of the economy where credit flows from private sources were considered inadequate. More recently, however, this objective has been broadened to cover efforts at influencing the allocation of resources for social rather than economic purposes.[4]

Federal agencies have been in existence for a long time, but their composition and functions have experienced considerable changes. In general, their role has been expanding, and the volume of securities issued by those institutions has grown considerably in recent years. Table 20-2 shows the amounts outstanding of various government agencies and sponsored corporations. While the bulk of such obligations are not guaranteed by the U.S. government, some form of backing often is provided; for example, the Treasury may be authorized to buy the securities or the agency may be allowed to borrow directly from the Treasury. The agricultural and housing agencies have by far the largest volume of securities outstanding.

Major Agricultural Agencies

The Farm Credit Administration supervises three kinds of banks: federal land banks, federal intermediate credit banks, and banks for cooperatives.

TABLE 20-2

Outstanding Securities of Government Agencies and Sponsored Corporations, December 31, 1973 (in millions)

Banks for cooperatives consolidated bonds	$ 2,670
Federal intermediate credit banks consolidated bonds	6,860
Federal land banks consolidated bonds	9,837
Farmers Home Administration	5,557
Federal home loan banks consolidated bonds	15,362
Federal National Mortgage Association debentures	20,849
Federal National Mortgage Association discount notes	2,153
Government National Mortgage Association	4,390
Federal Housing Administration debentures	415
Local authority project notes	3,870
Local authority bonds	8,300
Local public agency notes	3,470
New communities debentures	222
Merchant marine bonds and notes	1,134
Small Business Administration guaranteed debentures	185
Tennessee Valley Authority bonds and notes	2,535
Washington Metropolitan Area Transit Authority guaranteed bonds	595
U.S. Postal Service nonguaranteed bonds	250
Student Loan Marketing Association notes	182
Export-Import Bank obligations	2,645
District of Columbia Armory Board bonds	20

SOURCE: Data taken from the First Boston Corporation, ***Handbook of Securities of the United States Government and Federal Agencies and Related Money Market Instruments***, 26th ed. (1974), pp. 62-89.

Federal land banks (FLB). The 12 federal land banks were organized pursuant to the Federal Farm Loan Act of 1916 and are owned by federal land bank associations, through which borrowers apply for loans. Consolidated federal farm loan bonds are not guaranteed by the U.S. government They are, however, the joint and several obligations of the 12 banks, and are issued only against suitable collateral. Interest on the bonds is exempt from state, municipal, and local income taxes but is subject to federal taxation.

Federal intermediate credit banks (FICB). The 12 federal intermediate credit banks were authorized by the Agricultural Credit Act of 1923. They make loans to and discount paper for production credit associations (which own their stock), national and state banks, and various agricultural financing institutions. The consolidated debentures are not guaranteed by the U.S. government. They are, however, the joint and several obligations of the 12 banks and are secured by suitable collateral. Interest is exempt from state, municipal, and local income taxes but is subject to federal taxation.

Banks for cooperatives (COOP). The 13 banks for cooperatives were organized under the Farm Credit Act of 1933; they are now owned by cooperative associations. The banks make and service loans to eligible cooperative associations owned by farmers. The consolidated collateral trust debentures are not guaranteed by the U.S. government but are joint and several obligations of the 13 banks and are secured by suitable collateral. Interest is exempt from state, municipal, and local income taxes but is subject to federal taxation.

Farmers Home Administration (FHDA). This agency of the Department of Agriculture extends loans in rural areas for farms, homes, and community facilities. It issues loan notes that are fully insured by the U.S. government. In 1973, Congress authorized the sale of certificates of beneficial ownershp in trusts of FHDA notes, and this has become the established method of financing. Interest is subject to federal income tax as well as to state and local taxes.

Major Housing Agencies

Federal home loan banks (FHLB). The 12 federal home loan banks were organized under the Federal Home Loan Bank Act of 1932. They serve as a credit reserve system for their members, which include savings and loan associations and certain other institutions. The consolidated notes (bonds with an original maturity of one year or less are also called notes) and bonds are joint and several obligations of all the banks. The amount issued may not exceed 12 times the total paid-in capital stock and reserves of the banks and is secured by an equal amount of suitable collateral. Beginning May 1974 the banks introduced consolidated discount notes. The banks' obligations are not guaranteed by the U.S. government, which, however, may buy up to $4 billion of them. Interest is exempt from state, municipal, and local income taxes but is subject to federal taxation.

Federal National Mortgage Association (FNMA, or Fannie Mae). This agency was originally chartered in 1938, rechartered in 1954, and partitioned into two companies in 1968: the Federal National Mortgage Association and the Government National Mortgage Association (GNMA). The FNMA is empowered to purchase or make purchase commitments and sell (as the need arises) government guaranteed or insured and, since 1970, conventional mortgages. Sellers of mortgages to and borrowers from the association must subscribe to its common stock. The association finances its activities by the sale of debentures and short-term discount notes in an amount that cannot exceed 25 times the sum of its capital and surplus and cannot be greater than its holdings of specified assets. Its obligations are not guaranteed by the U.S. government, but under certain conditions the FNMA may sell them to the secretary of the Treasury. Interest is subject to federal taxation, and there is no exemption under federal law with respect to local taxes.

Government National Mortgage Association (GNMA, or Ginnie

Mae). The GNMA is wholly owned by the U.S. government and was established in 1968 to take over the special assistance functions and management and liquidating functions of the Federal National Mortgage Association. The special assistance programs, intended to help in the financing of certain types of home mortgages, has largely involved acquiring mortgages from private lenders at prices above the market and selling them at prevailing market prices. GNMA obtains funds for financing these functions by borrowing from the Treasury. The management and liquidating functions involve mortgages acquired under contract prior to November 1, 1954; they also include acquiring mortgages and loans from any federal instrumentality and managing and selling these assets. GNMA also conducts two types of guaranty operations. First, it guarantees mortgage-backed bonds issued by FNMA and the Federal Home Loan Mortgage Corporation (FHLMC). Second, it provides guarantees for pass-through certificates issued by private lenders; on these, interest and principal payments collected on mortgages underlying the certificates are passed through to the holders.

A futures market in Ginny Mae pass-through certificates developed on the Chicago Board of Trade in the fall of 1975. The contracts call for the delivery of certificates representing $100,000 of government-backed mortgages at a given price which, if sold at par, would yield 8 percent to maturity.

An investor, expecting to receive funds for investment at a future date, can lock in a rate close to the prevailing one by buying futures. The alternative is to wait until the future date arrives and to take whatever yield prevails at that time.

Similarly, an investor can sell such a contract. If she already owns a certificate and sells a futures contract, she can lock in a yield close to the prevailing one. If she waits to sell the certificate, she might realize a higher or lower yield, thereby creating a degree of uncertainty. It would all depend on what happens to interest rates between the time she considers selling the futures contract and the date the certificate is sold.

While the spread between yields on various instruments varies, the correlation is quite high. As a consequence, Ginny Mae futures can be used to hedge the yield on a wide range of financial instruments.

The Chicago Mercantile Exchange has developed futures in 90-day Treasury bills, which can be used to protect against interest changes or for speculation.

Federal Home Loan Mortgage Corporation (FHLMC, or Freddie Mac). The FHLMC was created in 1970 to strengthen the existing secondary market in government guaranteed or insured residential mortgages and to assist in the development of secondary markets for conventional mortgages. Its capital stock is owned by the 12 federal home loan banks. The corporation raises funds through the sale of two types of securities: (1) mortgage-backed bonds not exempted from federal, state, or local taxes, guaranteed as to principal and interest by GNMA, and constituting general obligations of the United States supported by its full faith and credit; (2) participation sale certificates, representing interests in pools of conventional and government guaranteed or insured mortgages. FHLMC guarantees the payment of principal and interest, but the certificates do not carry a guaranty of the U.S. government.

Public housing agencies (local authorities). These issue short-term project notes as well as long-term bonds. Bids are invited monthly on a large number of project notes to be issued by various local agencies. The bonds usually are 40-year serial issues that provide permanent financing for low-rent housing projects that are near completion. Both notes and bonds are secured by the pledge of the federal government to pay to the local authorities annual contributions that are enough to meet principal and interest payments. Urban renewal agencies (local public agencies) issue only short-term project notes to provide temporary financing for slum clearance and urban redevelopment. Eventually, funds to repay the temporary loans are obtained from the sale of land in the urban renewal area and from the provision of a federal capital grant that places behind the notes the full faith and credit of the U.S. government. Interest on project notes is exempt from federal income tax and usually from state taxes in the state of issuance. Additionally, the notes issued by local agencies in the District of Columbia, Puerto Rico, the Virgin Islands, and the various American Indian nations are exempt from taxation by any state or territory.

Federal Housing Administration (FHA). The FHA, established in 1934, encourages improvements in housing standards and provides a system of mutual mortgage insurance to stimulate the flow of private capital into residential financing. The FHA may pay insurance claims in debentures that are fully guaranteed as to principal and interest by the U.S. government.

New communities debentures. These debentures, backed by the full faith and credit of the federal government, are issued to finance new communities that meet certain standards. Interest from the debentures is subject to federal income taxes, and they carry no specific exemption from any taxes imposed by a state or local taxing authority.

Other Agencies

In addition to the major agricultural and housing agencies, which dominate the market for such obligations, other agencies engaged in different fields have issued securities.

U.S. Postal Service. In 1971 the U.S. Postal Service took over operations of the country's postal system. To conduct its activities, the Postal Service may issue obligations and may request the U.S. government to provide a full guaranty. Although the agency has offered bonds publicly, they are not guaranteed by the government.

Export-Import Bank (Eximbank). The Export-Import Bank was founded in 1934 to assist exports through loans, guaranties, and credit insurance. The bank has borrowed from the U.S. Treasury and has sold certificates of beneficial interest (CBIs) and participation certificates (PCs) in its own portfolio, both with and without its own guaranty. The bank has also issued its own debentures.

Small Business Administration (SBA). The SBA was created in 1953 primarily to provide financial and managerial assistance to small business concerns. As part of its program, the administration makes loans to small business investment companies (SBICs), which are privately owned, and to SBA-licensed and regulated companies that provide capital to small firms. Under authority granted in 1971, the Small Business Administration may guarantee payment of principal and interest on debentures of SBICs; these debentures may be pooled and sold publicly through issuance of debentures guaranteed as to principal and interest by the SBA and secured by the full faith and credit of the United States. Interest on SBA debentures is subject to federal income taxes but is exempt from state and local income taxes.

Tennessee Valley Authority (TVA). The TVA was established by an act of Congress in 1933 to assist in the development of the Tennessee River and adjacent areas. The TVA periodically sells issues of long-term bonds at competitive bidding and each month issues short-term discount notes in an auction similar to that employed for Treasury bills. Advances up to $150 million may be obtained from the Treasury; service payments due on these advances are subordinated to the principal and interest on the agency's publicly outstanding bonds and notes.

Student Loan Marketing Association (SLMA, or Sallie Mae). The SLMA was created in 1972 to foster a secondary market for student loans. The agency both purchases loans outright and makes advances to lenders collateralized by these lenders' portfolios of student loans. The agency may issue common stock of limited transferability to eligible financial and educational institutions; it made an initial offering in the first quarter of 1974. Nonvoting preferred stock that has no ownership restrictions and is fully transferable also may be issued. There are no restrictions on the maturities or interest rates of the SLMA's obligations, which are backed by the full faith and credit of the United States.

District of Columbia Armory Board. This board, created by Congress in June 1948, was authorized under the District of Columbia Stadium Act of 1957 to construct a stadium and to operate it for a period of 30 years from July 1, 1960. To finance the project, $19.8 million in 4.20 percent stadium bonds of 1970-1979 were offered in July 1960. These bonds are guaranteed as to both principal and interest by the United States. Interest is subject to federal income taxes.

General Services Administration (GSA). The GSA was established in 1949 to provide the federal government with an efficient system for the management of its property, including the construction and operation of buildings. In 1972 the GSA was authorized to undertake a program for the construction of a number of public buildings and their long-term purchase by the government. To finance this program, the agency has issued participation certificates in the buildings; the purchase prices of these certificates are backed by the full faith and credit of the United States and they are considered government securities.

Merchant Marine bonds. These bonds were formerly secured by ship mortgages insured by the United States, but in 1972 the approach was changed to a direct federal guaranty of the obligations. Each series of bonds is secured by a first preferred mortgage on a ship; in the event of default, bondholders would be entitled to receive cash payments from the secretary of the Treasury. Various series of bonds, notes, and obligations have been offered since 1958.

Washington Metropolitan Area Transit Authority. This authority was established in 1967 to plan, finance, and provide for the operation of mass transit facilities in the greater Washington, D.C., metropolitan area. In part, the facilities have been financed by issuance of federally guaranteed transit bonds.

Federal Financing Bank. The Federal Financing Bank was established in late 1973 to consolidate the financing of various federal agencies and other borrowers whose obligations are guaranteed by the U.S. government. The original concept was for the bank, itself, to go to the market directly for funds to lend the agencies. But after one offering that was sold at a somewhat higher rate than on comparable Treasury issues, a new procedure was developed. Employing funds borrowed from the Treasury, the bank now regularly advances them to the agencies through loans, purchase of securities, and commitments. By this means, the bulk of government agency borrowing is done through the bank. As a result, the proliferation of government agency entries into the market has been reduced and the agencies have been able to obtain funds at somewhat lower rates.

OTHER ASPECTS OF GOVERNMENT SECURITIES

There are certain other aspects of Treasury issues that might be briefly mentioned to complete the picture of these obligations.

Method of Trading

Although Treasury issues are listed on the New York Stock Exchange, virtually all trading occurs in the over-the-counter market. The focus of this market is a group of dealer firms that includes several large banks. These firms maintain primary markets in government obligations, dealing directly with large institutional investors and indirectly with small investors through their local banks or securities firms. Dealers customarily buy and sell at net prices; transactions do not involve any commissions, but service charges or price adjustments are applied to small odd-lot transactions or those in registered securities.

Payment for and delivery of government obligations occur on the next full business day following the day of the transaction, except in cases of "cash" or "delayed delivery" transactions. Odd-lot transactions usually have a settlement period of five business days. Payment ordinarily is made in Federal funds representing bank funds on deposit in a Federal Reserve bank. This permits prompt clearance. The alternative is to make payments in clearing-house funds. The dealer receiving such funds cannot draw on them until the following day. Federal funds may be used immediately. Accrued interest to the delivery date is added to the price of coupon obligations. To assist dealers who cannot deliver a security because of delays in transit ("fails"), the Federal Reserve lends securities from its own portfolio to recognized dealers at a small fee. The Federal Reserve, commercial banks, and securities dealers have been cooperating to create a "book-entry" system for government securities that would reduce the costs and risks of transactions. All the large New York City banks, including those handling most of the transactions of the major government securities dealers, are now participating in a system of this sort. They clear most of their transactions in government securities with each other and with the Federal Reserve through the telegraphic Government Securities Clearing Arrangement and a book-entry method maintained by the Federal Reserve Bank of New York.

Most agency issues, particularly those that bear coupons, are first issued through financial specialists known as fiscal agents. The agent, in turn, brings together a group of securities firms to distribute the securities to the investor. After they have been initially distributed, the agency issues are traded in the secondary market in a similar manner as direct U.S. government obligations. Most dealers in Treasury issues also make markets in agency issues.

Quotations

The prices quoted for Treasury obligations are exclusive of interest accrued. Generally, the price is stated in percentage form, but care must be exercised in the interpretation of the decimal. A price of 99.3 is not the same as 99.30. The first means 99$^{3}/_{32}$ percent; the second, 99$^{30}/_{32}$ percent. ($^{1}/_{32}$ of 1 percentage point represents 31.25 cents on a $1,000 bond). On occasion, the quotation will be in sixty-fourths. Thus, a quotation of 98.26+ means that the bond will sell for 98$^{52}/_{64}$ plus $^{1}/_{64}$th of $1,000, or a total of $988.28. These quotations do not apply to Treasury bills, which, as mentioned previously, are traded on a discount basis. A typical quotation sheet of the First Boston Corp., a dealer firm, is shown in Figures 20-3 and 20-3a.*

Dealers usually publish both the bid and ask prices. The yield is conventionally computed at the ask price to the maturity date. When a redeemable bond sells at a premium, however, the yield is computed to the optional call date. The difference between the bid and ask prices, called the spread, reflects the activity and characteristics of the different issues; the spread on short-term issues may be $^{1}/_{32}$ to $^{4}/_{32}$ a point ($312.50 to $1,250 per $1 million), and that on long-term or inactive issues somewhat greater—sometimes as much as ½ a point.

Accrued interest is calculated by formula. If the period of accrual is exactly three, six, or 12 months, each month is treated equally, regardless of the number of days in the calendar period; in other cases, the accrued interest is based on the exact fraction of the period for which interest is accrued. Periods are counted from the day after the date of issue and the date after payments are due.

Tax Status of U.S. Treasury Obligations

The taxation of a U.S. government security may be affected by the act authorizing its issuance and by local laws. For tax purposes, therefore, the investor must check the status of each individual issue. The following principles, however, may be used as a general guideline:

(1) Income is subject to federal income tax but exempt from state and local taxes.
(2) Securities are subject to both federal and state capital gains,[5] inheritance, gift, and excise taxes.
(3) Securities are exempt from state and local property taxes.
(4) Securities may be subject to state and local franchise taxes imposed on the privilege of doing business in the area.

*In this figure, yield after corporate taxes reflects deductions of (1) the 48 percent corporate profits tax from coupon income, and (2) the 30 percent capital gains tax payable by nonbank corporations on the recovery of discounts from issue price or par. The "corporate tax equivalent" column shows the coupon that a new issue priced at par, with the full return subject to corporate income tax, would have to carry to match the aftertax yield shown in the preceding column.

The income on Treasury bills, which is the excess of the liquidation over the purchase price, is treated as an ordinary gain or loss, regardless of the length of time the security is held. The investor can choose between paying income taxes on the accrual value of savings bonds or deferring the tax until maturity or redemption.

A number of Treasury obligations are of special interest to estate planners. Picturesquely described as "flower bonds," these issues, when owned by a decedent and part of his estate, are redeemable at par and accrued interest when the proceeds are applied to payment of federal estate taxes. This feature has attracted a special demand for such discount bonds, driving the near-term issues of this sort to levels that are close to par. Accordingly, desirable maturities are often hard to obtain. The supply of these bonds is being reduced because the Treasury no longer issues them, and they are constantly being submitted for estate tax purposes. Nevertheless, suitable issues sometimes become available when institutional holders find sufficiently attractive yields elsewhere to warrant reducing their commitments, even at a loss.

THE APPEARANCE OF THE SMALL INVESTOR

Faced with rising inflation, consumers in the early 1970s tended to reduce or curtail their spending on nonnecessities and to save a larger percentage of their discretionary income. In lieu of depositing these funds in savings institutions, however, consumers became increasingly interested in the money market, once the domain of institutions and large investors.

To combat this tendency, federal regulators not only raised the rates that banks and other thrift institutions could pay but also permitted these institutions to remove, within specified limits, the interest ceiling on savings certificates with minimum required maturities. Some banks even tied their rates to those in the money market. Nevertheless, the funds of small investors continued to flow to the money market so long as high rates were available. In the fall of 1973, for example, an official of Merrill Lynch, Pierce, Fenner & Smith, the nation's largest securities firm, reported that trading activity by individual investors in the government securities area had tripled in recent weeks, and other firms echoed this judgment.[6]

This new interest of small investors in the money market had a number of repercussions. It influenced the Treasury to consider how the terms of new issues might affect the small investor. For example, to help stem an outflow of funds from hard-pressed savings institutions, the Treasury raised the

FIGURE 20-3

Quotation Sheet of Treasury Securities

First Boston
MEMBER NEW YORK STOCK EXCHANGE INC

United States Treasury Securities

Coupon	Maturity	Bid	Asked	Chg.	Yield To Mat.	Yield After Tax ■	Corp. Tax Equiv.	Yield Value Per 1/32	1973-74 Range High	1973-74 Range Low	Amt. of Issue Total	Amt. of Issue Pub. Held ⊕
N 5 5/8	8-15-74	99- 5	99- 7	-2	8.68	4.51	8.68	.1263	99-22	96-16	10284	4331
N 6	9-30-74	98-30	99- 0	-2	8.71	4.53	8.71	.0869	100- 7	96-18	2060	1931
♦ B 3 7/8	11-15-74	97-19	97-23	...	8.66	4.50	8.66	.0671	98-11	94- 6	1213	1066
N 5 3/4	11-15-74	98-14	98-16	-3	8.90	4.63	8.90	.0666	99-26	96- 1	5442	3231
N 5 7/8	12-31-74	98- 5	98- 7	...	8.85	5.14	9.88	.0534	99-28	96- 1	2102	2043
N 5 3/4	2-15-75	97-25	97-27	-2	8.76	5.10	9.80	.0447	99-24	95-23	4015	2472
N 5 7/8	2-15-75	97-28	97-30	-1	8.75	5.07	9.75	.0446	100- 0	96- 1	1222	1107
N 5 7/8	5-15-75	97- 7	97-11	-5	8.71	5.04	9.69	.0341	99-26	95-17	1776	1643
N 6	5-15-75	97-11	97-15	-2	8.70	5.01	9.64	.0341	100- 2	95-22	6760	2242
N 5 7/8	8-15-75	96-20	96-24	-5	8.67	5.01	9.63	.0276	99-22	95- 1	7679	4928
N 8 3/8	9-30-75	99-24	99-28	-1	8.46	4.41	8.49	.0246	103- 0	99- 1	2042	2008
N 7	11-15-75	97-25	97-30	-3	8.49	4.69	9.01	.0230	102-22	96- 0	3115	2372
N 7	12-31-75	97-24	97-28	-4	8.42	4.63	8.91	.0213	100-31	97- 2	1731	1493
N 5 7/8	2-15-76	95-19	95-23	-6	8.55	4.93	9.48	.0202	99-16	94- 4	4945	3771
N 6 1/4	2-15-76	96-12	96-20	-4	8.35	4.72	9.08	.0200	100-24	95- 4	3739	382
N 8	3-31-76	99-12	99-16	-6	8.28	4.36	8.38	.0184	100- 8	98-26	1500	1500
N 5 3/4	5-15-76	95- 4	95-12	-4	8.31	4.78	9.20	.0178	99-22	93-12	2802	2228
N 6 1/2	5-15-76	96-14	96-22	-6	8.33	4.66	8.97	.0177	101-10	95-10	2697	1889
N 8 3/4	6-30-76	100-13	100-17	-6	8.46	4.40	8.46	.0163	100-23	99-26	N/A	N/A
N 6 1/2	8-15-76	95-30	96- 6	-6	8.39	4.70	9.04	.0159	99-30	95- 4	3883	2063
N 7 1/2	8-15-76	97-30	98- 6	-4	8.39	4.52	8.70	.0157	104-16	95-18	4194	2544
N 6 1/4	11-15-76	95- 4	95-12	-8	8.34	4.71	9.06	.0145	100-11	94- 4	4325	4058
N 8	2-15-77	99-16	99-24	-4	8.09	4.23	8.13	.0129	106-30	96-18	5163	2106
N 6 7/8	5-15-77	96- 6	96-14	-10	8.24	4.53	8.71	.0123	100-19	95- 6	2565	2190
N 7 3/4	8-15-77	98-16	98-14	-16	8.30	4.42	8.49	.0113	106-24	97-12	4913	3308
N 6 1/4	2-15-78	93-30	94- 6	-10	8.07	4.52	8.70	.0102	100- 2	92- 8	8389	5017
N 8 3/4	8-15-78	101-16	101-24	-16	8.25	4.29	8.25	.0088	102- 8	99-30	N/A	N/A
N 6	11-15-78	92- 0	92- 8	-8	8.09	4.58	8.81	.0088	99- 0	90- 8	8207	4609
N 6 1/4	8-15-79	92- 2	92-10	-10	8.07	4.52	8.70	.0078	100- 4	90-16	4559	2781
N 6 5/8	11-15-79	93- 0	93- 8	-12	8.17	4.53	8.71	.0075	100-14	91-20	1604	516
N 7	11-15-79	94-22	94-30	-20	8.16	4.45	8.56	.0074	101-16	91-10	2241	1977
♦ B 4	2-15-80	81-16	82- 0	...	7.96	4.85	9.33	.0077	93- 0	80-12	2573	1713
N 6 7/8	5-15-80	94- 8	94-16	-16	8.05	4.40	8.45	.0069	100-23	93- 0	7265	1811
♦ B 3 1/2	11-15-80	77-16	78-16	-8	7.78	4.81	9.26	.0072	84- 0	76-23	1896	1147
N 7	2-15-81	94- 8	94-16	-20	8.07	4.39	8.44	.0063	100-29	93- 2	1842	1475
B 7	8-15-81	94-16	95-16	-16	7.82	4.21	8.11	.0059	105- 4	93- 0	807	400
B 6 3/8	2-15-82	91-24	92-24	-8	7.63	4.19	8.06	.0057	100- 8	91- 0	2702	1661
♦ B 3 1/4	6-15-83/78	72- 8	73- 8	-8	7.33	4.55	8.75	.0057	79-12	63-24	1479	1205
B 6 3/8	8-15-84	91- 0	92- 0	-16	7.50	4.11	7.90	.0047	99- 8	90- 8	2353	978
♦ B 3 1/4	5-15-85	71-24	72-24	-16	6.81	4.18	8.04	.0050	79- 4	68-24	950	721
♦ B 4 1/4	5-15-85/75	75- 0	76- 0	-8	7.49	4.48	8.61	.0050	83- 4	74- 0	1201	708
B 6 1/8	11-15-86	88-24	89-24	-16	7.39	4.07	7.83	.0042	99-12	76- 8	1216	340
♦ B 3 1/2	2-15-90	71-16	72-16	-16	6.27	3.76	7.23	.0039	79- 0	63- 0	3954	2824
♦ B 4 1/4	8-15-92/87	71-24	72-24	-16	6.90	4.06	7.81	.0038	80-16	70- 0	3685	2256
♦ B 4	2-15-93/88	71-16	72-16	-8	6.57	3.88	7.46	.0036	80-12	69-16	227	159
B 6 3/4	2-15-93	86-28	87-28	-12	8.01	4.39	8.44	.0036	99-20	85-24	627	464
B 7 1/2	8-15-93/88	94-16	95- 0	-16	8.01	4.26	8.19	.0033	105- 8	93- 8	1914	801
♦ B 4 1/8	5-15-94/89	71-20	72-20	-12	6.61	3.89	7.47	.0035	80- 0	68- 8	1459	909
♦ B 3	2-15-95	71-16	72-16	-16	5.18	3.08	5.93	.0030	79- 0	68- 0	832	695
B 7	5-15-98/93	88-24	89-24	-16	7.96	4.31	8.30	.0032	100- 8	88- 0	692	446
♦ B 3 1/2	11-15-98	71-16	72-16	-16	5.57	3.27	6.29	.0029	79- 0	68- 0	3031	2209
B 8 1/2	5-15-99/94	103- 0	103-16	-20	8.14	4.23	8.14	.0031	104- 4	102-24	N/A	N/A
N 1 1/2	10- 1-74	96- 0	97- 0	...	9.73	5.06	9.73	.0884	97-14	92-16	42	42
N 1 1/2	4- 1-75	93-24	94-24	...	7.81	5.20	9.99	.0392	95- 0	90- 8	8	8
N 1 1/2	10- 1-75	91-24	92-24	...	7.12	4.71	9.07	.0255	92-24	84- 4	30	30
N 1 1/2	4- 1-76	89-20	90-20	...	6.91	4.57	8.78	.0192	90-20	85-24	27	27
N 1 1/2	10- 1-76	87-12	88-12	...	6.88	4.55	8.75	.0156	88-16	83-16	11	11
N 1 1/2	4- 1-77	85- 0	86- 0	...	6.95	4.60	8.84	.0133	86-16	81- 0	5	5
N 1 1/2	10- 1-77	83- 0	84- 0	...	6.89	4.55	8.76	.0117	84-16	79- 0	17	17
N 1 1/2	4- 1-78	81- 0	82- 0	...	6.87	4.54	8.72	.0105	82-24	77- 0	15	15
N 1 1/2	10- 1-78	79- 8	80- 8	...	6.79	4.48	8.62	.0095	81- 0	78- 0	3	3
N 1 1/2	4- 1-79	77- 8	78- 8	...	6.82	4.50	8.66	.0088	78-16	77- 8	N/A	N/A

Minimum denomination on new issues $1,000. Exempt from state and local income tax.
\# Premium above zero yield to maturity or call.
B Bonds. C Certificates. N Notes. WI When issued.

♦ When owned by a decedent and part of his estate, redeemable at par in payment of Federal estate tax.
⊕ Data for publicly held lags several months behind the figure for total outstanding. Amounts in millions.

■ Yield after corporate profits tax of 48%. For obligations selling at a discount from par, and which are more than six months from maturity, effect is given to the corporate capital gains tax of 30%.

U.S. TREASURY BILLS

Amt. of Issue	Days	Maturity	Bid	Asked	Eq. Bd. Yld.
4300	7	5-23-74	8.80	7.80	7.92
4300	14	5-30-74	8.80	7.80	7.93
1300	19	6- 4-74	8.50	7.50	7.63
4300	21	6- 6-74	8.50	7.50	7.64
4300	28	6-13-74	8.50	7.50	7.65
4300	35	6-20-74	8.50	7.50	7.66
4500	36 TAB	6-21-74 (a)	8.10	7.70	7.87
4300	42	6-27-74	8.20	7.80	7.98
1800	47	7- 2-74	8.20	7.80	7.99
4300	50	7- 5-74	8.20	7.80	7.99
4300	56	7-11-74	8.20	7.80	8.01
4300	63	7-18-74	8.20	7.80	8.02
4300	70	7-25-74	8.20	7.80	8.03
1800	75	7-30-74	8.20	7.80	8.04
4300	77	8- 1-74	8.30	8.00	8.25
4300	84	8- 8-74	8.30	8.00	8.27
4400	91 3 mos.	8-15-74	8.20	8.10	8.38
1800	98	8-22-74	8.40	8.00	8.29
1800	103	8-27-74	8.40	8.00	8.30
1800	105	8-29-74	8.40	8.00	8.30

(a) YIELD TO 6-17-74 8.85

Amt. of Issue	Days	Maturity	Bid	Asked	Eq. Bd. Yld.
1800	112	9- 5-74	8.40	8.00	8.32
1800	119	9-12-74	8.40	8.00	8.33
1800	126	9-19-74	8.40	8.00	8.34
1800	131	9-24-74	8.40	8.00	8.35
1800	133	9-26-74	8.40	8.00	8.36
1800	140	10- 3-74	8.40	8.00	8.37
1800	147	10-10-74	8.40	8.00	8.39
1800	154	10-17-74	8.40	8.00	8.40
1800	159	10-22-74	8.40	8.00	8.41
1800	161	10-24-74	8.40	8.00	8.41
1800	168	10-31-74	8.40	8.00	8.43
1800	175	11- 7-74	8.30	8.10	8.55
W.I	182 6 mos.	11-14-74	8.25	8.15	8.62
1800	187	11-19-74	8.40	8.10	8.57
1800	215	12-17-74	8.40	8.10	8.60
1800	243	1-14-75	8.40	8.10	8.63
1800	271	2-11-75	8.40	8.10	8.66
1800	299	3-11-75	8.40	8.10	8.69
1800	327	4- 8-75	8.40	8.10	8.71
1800	355	5- 6-75	8.25	8.15	8.80

Amounts in millions. Minimum denomination $10,000. All earnings on Treasury bills are subject to Federal income tax, but exempt from state and local income tax.

CLOSING QUOTATIONS - TUESDAY MAY 14, 1974 YIELDS FOR DELIVERY - THURSDAY MAY 16, 1974

DECIMAL EQUIVALENTS of 32nds and 64ths per $100

+	$.015625	4+	$.140625	8+	$.265625	12+	$.390625	16+	$.515625	20+	$.640625	24+	$.765625	28+	$.890625
1	.031250	5	.156250	9	.281250	13	.406250	17	.531250	21	.656250	25	.781250	29	.906250
1+	.046875	5+	.171875	9+	.296875	13+	.421875	17+	.546875	21+	.671875	25+	.796875	29+	.921875
2	.062500	6	.187500	10	.312500	14	.437500	18	.562500	22	.687500	26	.812500	30	.937500
2+	.078125	6+	.203125	10+	.328125	14+	.453125	18+	.578125	22+	.703125	26+	.828125	30+	.953125
3	.093750	7	.218750	11	.343750	15	.468750	19	.593750	23	.718750	27	.843750	31	.968750
3+	.109375	7+	.234375	11+	.359375	15+	.484375	19+	.609375	23+	.734375	27+	.859375	31+	.984375
4	.125000	8	.250000	12	.375000	16	.500000	20	.625000	24	.750000	28	.875000	32	1.00000

Coupon Rate %	Interest Per Million Per Day*	Nbr. Days* to Equal 1/32nd	Coupon Rate %	Interest Per Million Per Day*	Nbr. Days* to Equal 1/32nd	Coupon Rate %	Interest Per Million Per Day*	Nbr. Days* to Equal 1/32nd
1½	$ 41.09589	7.6	6¼	$171.23288	1.8	9¼	$253.42466	1.2
2	54.79452	5.7	6½	178.08219	1.8	9½	260.27397	1.2
2½	68.49315	4.6	6¾	184.93151	1.7	9¾	267.12329	1.2
3	82.19178	3.8	7	191.78082	1.6	10	273.97260	1.1
3½	95.89041	3.2	7¼	198.63014	1.6	10¼	280.82192	1.1
4	109.58904	2.9	7½	205.47945	1.5	10½	287.67123	1.1
4½	123.28767	2.6	7¾	212.32877	1.5	10¾	294.52055	1.1
5	136.98630	2.3	8	219.17808	1.4	11	301.36986	1.0
5¼	143.83562	2.2	8¼	226.02740	1.4	11¼	308.21918	1.0
5½	150.68493	2.1	8½	232.87671	1.3	11½	315.06849	1.0
5¾	157.53425	2.0	8¾	239.72603	1.3	11¾	321.91781	1.0
6	164.38356	1.9	9	246.57534	1.3	12	328.76712	1.0

* 365 day basis

SOURCE: The First Boston Corporation, *Handbook of Securities of the United States Government and Federal Agencies and Related Money Market Instruments*, 26th ed. (1974), p. 138. Reprinted by permission.

FIGURE 20-3a

Quotation Sheet of Agency Securities

Federal Agency And Related Issues

♦FEDERAL HOME LOAN BANKS

Coupon	Maturity	Bid	Asked	Chg.	Yield To Mat.	Yield After Tax ■	Yield Per 1/32	Amt. Of Issue
6.35	5-27-74	99-25	99-29		9.15	4.76	.9971	300C
6.45	5-28-74	99-26	99-30		8.09	4.21	.9133	700B
7.65	8-25-74	99- 8	99-20		8.89	4.62	.1149	181B
5 3/8	8-26-74	98-20	99- 4		8.50	4.42	.1148	400C
9 5/8	8-26-74	99-30	100- 6	+ 2	8.75	4.55	.1126	800C
7.05	11-25-74	98-16	99-	+ 4	9.04	5.06	.0628	1000C
8	11-25-74	99-	99-16	+ 4	8.99	4.85	.0625	227B
5 7/8	2-25-75	97-12	97-28		8.75	5.07	.0432	400C
6.10	2-25-75	97-16	98-		8.80	5.06	.0432	250C
8.20	2-25-75	99- 4	99-20	+ 4	8.68	4.60	.0425	500C
8.05	5-26-75	98-20	99-12	+ 4	8.69	4.64	.0325	265C
6.80	5-27-75	97-20	98- 4	+ 8	8.74	4.89	.0328	300C
7.15	5-27-75	97-28	98-28	+16	8.31	4.53	.0325	700C
7.15	8-25-75	97- 8	98-		8.83	4.89	.0267	400C
7 7/8	8-25-75	98- 4	98-28	- 4	8.81	4.75	.0266	500C
7.95	8-25-75	98- 4	98-28	- 4	8.88	4.79	.0266	300C
6 1/2	11-25-75	96- 4	96-28	+ 4	8.73	4.94	.0223	350C
7.05	11-25-75	96-28	97-20	+ 4	8.74	4.85	.0226	600B
WI9.10	11-25-75	100- 8	100-12	- 4	8.83	4.59	.0222	C
7 3/8	2-25-76	97-	97-24	- 4	8.76	4.80	.0196	300C
8 3/4	2-25-76	99-16	100-16	- 4	8.43	4.38	.0192	300C
7.20	5-25-76	96-28	97-16	+ 4	8.57	4.70	.0174	600C
7.45	5-25-76	97- 8	97-28	+ 4	8.61	4.69	.0173	300C
7.80	8-25-76	97-24	98-12	+ 4	8.59	4.61	.0155	500C
7.20	2-25-77	95-28	96-20	- 4	8.58	4.71	.0131	500C
6.95	5-25-77	95-	95-24	- 4	8.57	4.75	.0122	200C
7.15	8-25-77	95- 8	96-	- 4	8.57	4.71	.0114	300C
WI8.80	8-25-77	100- 6	100-14	- 6	8.64	4.49	.0111	C
6 3/4	11-25-77	93-28	94-16	- 4	8.59	4.80	.0108	300B
7.45	11-25-77	95-20	96-20	- 8	8.58	4.66	.0106	300C
7.60	5-25-78	96- 8	97-	- 8	8.49	4.58	.0095	500C
WI8 3/4	5-25-79	100-20	101-	- 4	8.50	4.42	.0077	C
7.05	2-25-80	92-20	93-20	-16	8.46	4.66	.0072	300C
7 3/4	2-25-80	95-28	96-28	-16	8.44	4.51	.0070	350B
7.80	10-15-80	95-24	96-24	-16	8.46	4.52	.0065	200C
6.60	11-27-81	88-24	89-24	-24	8.47	4.74	.0060	200C
7.30	5-25-83	91-20	92-20	-24	8.49	4.63	.0052	200C
WI8 3/4	5-25-84	100- 8	100-20	-12	8.65	4.50	.0047	C
7 3/8	11-26-93/83	88-24	89-24	-16	8.46	4.59	.0035	400C

FEDERAL NATIONAL MORTGAGE ASSOCIATION

Coupon	Maturity	Bid	Asked	Chg.	Yield To Mat.	Yield After Tax ■	Yield Per 1/32	Amt. Of Issue
5.70	6-10-74	99-21	99-25		8.78	4.57	.4612	350C
7.90	6-10-74	99-26	99-30		8.55	4.45	.4562	400C
5.65	9-10-74	98-20	98-28		9.21	4.79	.1016	300C
7.85	9-10-74	99-10	99-18		9.14	4.75	.1005	250B
6.10	12-10-74	97-28	98-12		9.09	5.27	.0586	250C
6.45	12-10-74	98- 4	98-20		8.98	5.12	.0584	450C
6.35	3-10-75	97-16	98- 8	+ 4	8.59	4.87	.0409	600C
7.55	3-10-75	98-16	99- 8		8.50	4.59	.0405	300C
CD6	4- 1-75	98-12	99-12		8.74	4.68	.0379	200C
5 1/4	6-10-75	95-24	96-16	+ 4	8.75	5.18	.0321	500C
6.80	9-10-75	96-28	97-16	+ 4	8.84	4.96	.0260	650C
7 1/2	9-10-75	97-24	98-12		8.82	4.82	.0259	350C
5.70	12-10-75	94-28	95-20	+ 4	8.74	5.09	.0224	500C
8 1/4	12-10-75	98-20	99-12	+ 4	8.68	4.59	.0218	300C
5.65	3-10-76	94- 8	95-	+ 4	8.68	5.06	.0195	500C
7 1/8	3-10-76	96-24	97-12		8.71	4.81	.0192	400C
5.85	6-10-76	94- 4	94-28	+ 4	8.61	4.97	.0174	450C
6.70	6-10-76	95-24	96-16	+ 4	8.58	4.80	.0172	250C
5.85	9-10-76	93-20	94-12	+ 4	8.57	4.95	.0157	500C
6 1/8	9-10-76	94- 4	94-28	+ 4	8.60	4.92	.0156	300C
6 1/4	12-10-76	93-28	94-20	+ 4	8.63	4.91	.0143	500C
7.45	12-10-76	96-16	97-16	- 4	8.55	4.64	.0140	300C
4 1/2	2-10-77	89-12	90-12	- 4	8.52	5.15	.0138	198A
6.30	3-10-77	93-20	94-12	- 8	8.58	4.88	.0131	500C
7.05	3-10-77	95-28	96- 8	-16	8.57	4.73	.0130	400C
6 3/8	6-10-77	93-12	94- 4	- 8	8.59	4.87	.0122	250C
6 1/2	6-10-77	93-24	94-16	- 4	8.57	4.83	.0122	150C
7.20	6-10-77	95-16	96- 8	- 4	8.61	4.73	.0120	500C
6 7/8	9-12-77	94-12	95- 4	- 4	8.59	4.77	.0113	300C
7.85	9-12-77	97- 4	97-28	- 8	8.59	4.60	.0111	400C
7 1/4	12-12-77	95- 8	96-	- 4	8.57	4.69	.0106	500C
7.55	12-12-77	96- 4	96-28	- 4	8.58	4.65	.0105	500C
7.15	6-12-78	94-16	95-16	- 8	8.48	4.65	.0094	600C
7.15	9-11-78	94-24	95- 4	- 8	8.52	4.68	.0090	550C
6 3/4	12-11-78	92-16	93-16	-12	8.49	4.73	.0087	300C
7 1/4	3-12-79	94- 8	95- 8	- 8	8.47	4.62	.0082	500C
7.85	6-11-79	96- 8	97- 8	-20	8.53	4.56	.0078	300C
6.40	9-10-79	90- 4	91- 4	-16	8.51	4.80	.0078	300C
6.55	12-10-79	90-16	91-16	-12	8.50	4.77	.0075	350C
6 7/8	3-10-80	91-28	92-28	-16	8.45	4.68	.0072	250C
7 1/2	9-10-80	94-12	95-12	-16	8.46	4.57	.0066	400C
6.60	12-10-80	89-24	90-24	-16	8.46	4.74	.0066	300C
7.05	3-10-81	91-24	92-24	-24	8.47	4.66	.0064	350C
7 1/4	6-10-81	92-16	93-16	-24	8.49	4.64	.0062	250C
7 1/4	9-10-81	92-12	93-12	-24	8.48	4.63	.0060	250C
7.30	12-10-81	93- 4	93-16	-20	8.48	4.62	.0059	250C
6.65	6-10-82	88-12	89-12	-24	8.49	4.75	.0058	250C
6.80	9-10-82	89-	90-	-24	8.50	4.72	.0056	200C
7.35	12-10-82	92- 4	93- 4	-24	8.49	4.62	.0054	300C
6 3/4	6-10-83	88- 4	89- 4	-24	8.49	4.73	.0053	200C
7.30	6-10-83	91-20	92-20	-24	8.48	4.62	.0052	300C
6 3/4	9-12-83	87-28	88-28	-24	8.50	4.73	.0053	250C
6 1/4	6-11-84	84-	85-	-24	8.49	4.82	.0051	200C
6.90	12-10-84	88-	89-	-28	8.50	4.71	.0048	250C
7	3-10-92	86-	87-	-16	8.42	4.63	.0037	200C
7.05	6-10-92	86-12	87-12	-16	8.42	4.63	.0037	200C
CD7.40	10- 1-97/82	87-24	88-24	-16	8.52	4.63	.0034	250C
7.10	12-10-97/82	85-16	86-16	-16	8.43	4.62	.0034	200C

GOVERNMENT NATIONAL MORTGAGE ASSOCIATION†

Coupon	Maturity	Bid	Asked	Chg.	Yield To Mat.	Yield After Tax ■	Yield Per 1/32	Amt. Of Issue
FH5.30	8-26-74	98-22	98-30		9.11	4.74	.1152	200D
FH8 3/8	6- 2-75	98-24	99-16		8.88	4.71	.0320	250D
FH7.05	8-25-76	95-28	96-20		8.71	4.83	.0157	400D
FH6.15	2-25-77	93-	94-	- 8	8.62	4.93	.0133	350D
FH8 5/8	10- 1-90/80	98-12	100-12	-12	8.54	4.44	.0064	200D
FH8.60	11-27-95/83	98- 8	100- 8	-16	8.56	4.45	.0048	140D
FH7 3/4	8-26-96/84	90-12	92-12	-16	8.52	4.57	.0033	150D
FH7.15	5-26-97/82	84- 4	86- 4	-16	8.54	4.69	.0035	150D

♦FEDERAL LAND BANKS

Coupon	Maturity	Bid	Asked	Chg.	Yield To Mat.	Yield After Tax ■	Yield Per 1/32	Amt. Of Issue
5.85	7-22-74	99- 6	99-14		8.80	4.58	.1710	326A
5.30	*10-21-74	98- 4	98-16		8.88	4.62	.0762	300A
7.15	1-20-75	98-16	99-		8.67	4.78	.0487	300A
8 3/8	1-20-75	99- 8	99-24		8.73	4.60	.0484	220A
4 3/8	4-21-75	95-16	96- 8		8.65	5.27	.0367	200A
7.65	4-21-75	98-16	99- 8		8.49	4.57	.0358	300A
5.70	7-21-75	95-24	96-16	- 4	8.87	5.19	.0291	425A
8.30	7-21-75	99-24	100-	+ 2	8.28	4.31	.0282	300A
7.20	10-20-75	97- 8	98-	+ 4	8.71	4.80	.0240	300A
7.40	10-20-75	97-20	98-12	+ 4	8.63	4.71	.0239	362A
6 1/4	1-20-76	95-16	96- 8		8.69	4.96	.0209	300A
5	2-24-76	92-24	93-24		8.88	5.32	.0202	123A
6 1/4	4-20-76	95-	95-24	- 4	8.69	4.96	.0184	373A
8 1/4	4-20-76	99-10	99-18	- 4	8.49	4.46	.0179	400A
5 3/8	7-20-76	92-20	93-20	+ 4	8.64	5.08	.0167	150A
7.05	7-20-76	95- 8	96- 8	-16	8.97	5.01	.0165	360A
7.15	10-20-76	95-28	96-28		8.60	4.73	.0148	450A
8 1/4	4-20-77	99- 4	99-16	- 8	8.44	4.42	.0123	565A
7 1/2	7-20-77	96- 8	97-	- 8	8.59	4.66	.0116	550A
6.35	10-20-77	92-20	93-12	- 8	8.62	4.89	.0111	300A
4 1/8	2-20-78/73	85- 4	86- 4	- 8	8.51	5.21	.0108	148A
5 1/8	4-20-78	87-24	88-24	-12	8.56	5.07	.0102	150A
6.40	7-20-78	91-24	92-24	-12	8.49	4.79	.0094	269A
7.35	10-19-78	94-12	95-12	-12	8.63	4.72	.0088	550A
5	1-22-79	85-20	86-20	-12	8.52	5.06	.0089	205A
7.10	1-22-79	93-28	94-28	-12	8.44	4.63	.0084	300A
6.85	4-23-79	92-12	93-12	-16	8.52	4.73	.0082	235A
7.15	7-23-79	93-20	94-12	-12	8.51	4.67	.0078	389A
6.80	10-23-79	91-24	92-24	-12	8.49	4.72	.0076	400A
6.70	1-21-80	91- 8	92- 8	-16	8.44	4.70	.0073	300A
7 1/2	7-21-80	94-16	95-16	-16	8.45	4.56	.0067	250A
6.70	4-20-81	89-28	90-28	-24	8.47	4.72	.0064	224A
6.90	4-20-82	89-28	90-28	-24	8.50	4.71	.0058	200A
7.30	10-20-82	89-28	90-28	-88	8.06	4.09	.0056	239A
7.30	10-20-83	91-12	92-12	-24	8.49	4.63	.0051	300A

♦BANKS FOR COOPERATIVES

Coupon	Maturity	Bid	Asked	Chg.	Yield To Mat.	Yield After Tax ■	Yield Per 1/32	Amt. Of Issue
.8780	6- 3-74	99-28	100-		8.46	4.40	.6391	617B
7.95	7- 1-74	99-23	99-27		8.95	4.65	.2459	469B
8.15	8- 1-74	99-20	99-24	- 1	9.16	4.76	.1498	559B
7.15	9- 3-74	99- 8	99-12		9.18	4.77	.1071	349B
8.20	10- 1-74	99-16	99-20		9.14	4.75	.0856	251B
8.65	11- 4-74	99-25	99-27	+ 2	8.97	4.66	.0696	211B
7.70	4- 4-77	97- 4	97-24	- 4	8.59	4.63	.0126	200B

FEDERAL INTERMEDIATE CREDIT BANKS

Coupon	Maturity	Bid	Asked	Chg.	Yield To Mat.	Yield After Tax ■	Yield Per 1/32	Amt. Of Issue
9 3/4	6- 3-74	99-29	100-		9.13	4.75	.6223	626D
5.95	7- 1-74	99-12	99-20		8.79	4.57	.2482	224D
9 3/4	7- 1-74	99-30	100- 2		8.71	4.53	.2381	699D
7.95	8- 1-74	99-18	99-22		9.09	4.73	.1470	503D
8.60	9- 3-74	99-19	99-23		9.21	4.79	.1042	520D
7.95	10- 1-74	99-11	99-15		9.14	4.76	.0841	616D
8	11- 4-74	99-10	99-14	+ 1	9.05	4.71	.0686	754D
7.15	12- 2-74	98-27	98-31	+ 2	9.01	5.02	.0599	785D
6.05	1- 2-75	97-28	98-12		8.75	5.03	.0529	240D
8.15	1- 2-75	99-10	99-14		9.00	4.84	.0523	608D
8.80	2- 3-75	99-26	99-28	+ 1	8.95	4.68	.0464	674D
5.70	7- 1-75	95-28	96-16	- 8	9.03	5.30	.0305	302D
6.65	1- 5-76	96- 4	96-24	- 4	8.82	4.97	.0213	261D
7.10	1- 3-77	95-28	96-16	- 4	8.61	4.75	.0132	236D
7.10	1- 3-78	95-	95-24	- 8	8.48	4.66	.0104	406D

EXPORT-IMPORT BANK†

Coupon	Maturity	Bid	Asked	Chg.	Yield To Mat.	Yield After Tax ■	Yield Per 1/32	Amt. Of Issue
5.30	2- 3-75	97- 4	97-16	+ 4	8.97	5.33	.0470	300D
5.70	12- 1-76	92- 4	93- 4	- 4	8.77	5.12	.0146	300D
6 1/4	8- 2-77	92-12	93-12	- 4	8.65	4.93	.0118	400D
6.45	2- 1-78	92- 8	93- 8	-12	8.61	4.87	.0104	300D
8.35	8-28-78	98- 4	99- 4	-12	8.59	4.51	.0089	300D
7.30	11-27-78	94-20	95-20	-12	8.48	4.62	.0086	300D
7	3- 7-79	94-	95-		8.28	4.53	.0082	400D
6.60	5- 3-79	91-	92-	-16	8.61	4.84	.0082	200D
PC5.10	2-20-82	79-12	80-12	-24	8.62	5.11	.0064	250D

FARMERS HOME ADMINISTRATION (FHDA)†‡

Coupon	Maturity	Bid	Asked	Chg.	Yield To Mat.	Yield After Tax ■	Yield Per 1/32	Amt. Of Issue
8 7/8	1-31-75	99- 4	99-28		8.76	4.53	.0452	200G
6 5/8	8-31-76	94- 8	95- 8	+ 4	8.79	4.96	.0155	150F
6.35	3-31-77	92-24	93-24	- 4	8.71	4.95	.0128	400F
6.45	6-30-77	92-16	93-16	- 4	8.72	4.95	.0119	300F
6 7/8	8-31-77	93-12	94-12	- 4	8.71	4.86	.0113	400F
6.55	12-29-77	91-28	92-28	- 4	8.73	4.93	.0105	400E
7.20	3-21-78	93-20	94-20	-12	8.71	4.80	.0098	300E
7 1/4	5-12-78	93-20	94-20	-12	8.72	4.80	.0095	300E
7.35	7- 5-78	93-24	94-24	-12	8.72	4.78	.0092	300E
7.30	12-28-78	93- 8	94- 8	-12	8.66	4.75	.0084	300D
8.90	1-31-80	98-28	100-28	-16	8.50	4.42	.0068	150G
7	11-30-80	89-24	91-24	-16	8.51	4.70	.0065	300F
6.40	3-31-81	86- 8	88- 8	-24	8.56	4.84	.0064	200F
7 7/8	6-30-81	93-20	95-20	-24	8.54	4.56	.0059	250F
7.10	1- 4-82	89-	91-	-24	8.57	4.72	.0053	350F
8 5/8	7-31-85	96-24	98-24	-24	8.61	4.48	.0043	300G
7 1/2	8-31-86	88-16	90-16	-24	8.60	4.67	.0043	150F
7 1/8	12-29-87	85-	87-	-16	8.60	4.74	.0042	200F
7 1/2	3-21-88	87-24	89-24	-16	8.62	4.68	.0041	200E
7 1/2	5-12-88	87-24	89-24	-16	8.62	4.68	.0041	200F
7 3/4	12-28-88	89-24	91-24	-16	8.58	4.61	.0039	200D
9	4-23-89	101- 8	102- 8	- 8	8.54	4.44	.0036	200D

WASHINGTON METRO AREA TRANSIT AUTHORITY†

Coupon	Maturity	Bid	Asked	Chg.	Yield To Mat.	Yield After Tax ■	Yield Per 1/32	Amt. Of Issue
7.30	7- 1-12	87-	87-16	- 8	8.40	4.56	.0030	225
7.35	7- 1-12	87-16	88-	- 8	8.40	4.56	.0030	220
7 3/4	7- 1-13	91-	92-	- 8	8.45	4.52	.0029	150
8.15	7- 1-14	95-28	96-12	-16	8.47	4.46	.0023	225

■ Yield after corporate profits tax of 48%. For obligations selling at a discount from par, and which are more than six months from maturity effect is given to the corporate capital gains tax of 30%.

♦ Interest exempt from state and local income tax.
* Yield to first call for callable issues quoted at a premium.
Minimum denominations: A—$1,000; B—$5,000; C—$10,000; D—$25,000; E—$100,000; F—$500,000; G—$1 million

CD—Capital debenture. PC—Participation certificate. WI—When issued.
† Backed by the full faith and credit of the U.S. Government.
‡ Coupon paid annually—yield calculated on semiannual payment basis.

First Boston
MEMBER NEW YORK STOCK EXCHANGE INC

THE FIRST BOSTON CORPORATION 20 Exchange Place New York N.Y. 10005 (212) 344-1515 Cable Firstcorp N.Y.

BOSTON (617) 542-7200 · CHICAGO (312) 372-6640 · CLEVELAND (216) 696-8822 · LONDON 588 0101 · LOS ANGELES (213) 485-9696 · MELBOURNE 62 4848 · MONTREAL* (514) 871-1561 · PHILADELPHIA (215) 563-9700 · PITTSBURGH (412) 471-8800 · SAN FRANCISCO (415) 981-0700 · TOKYO 216-4708/4709 · ZURICH 36 48 90

*Subsidiary First Boston (Canada) Limited

SOURCE: The First Boston Corporation, *Handbook of Securities of the United States Government and Federal Agencies and Related Money Market Instruments*, 26th ed. (1974), p. 139. Reprinted by permission.

minimum purchase of notes in its September 1974 auction, returning to the $1,000 minimum denomination the following month. The interest of small investors in the money market contributed to substantial withdrawals of funds from savings institutions; this restricted their ability to grant mortgage loans and led to special measures to aid the ailing mortgage market. A special crop of investment companies arose that offered to place the funds of their stockholders in money-market instruments not ordinarily available to small investors. Banks subject to Federal Reserve control over interest rates paid on deposits exerted pressure to have the limits relaxed so that they could compete for investors' funds. The participation of small investors in the money market meant that they remained aloof from the stock market, thereby contributing to the steep slide of prices in 1973-1974.

To a large extent, also, the move of the small investors to the money market reflected their greater sophistication in the securities area. As business education has spread and business publications have gained broad readership, investors have become more knowledgeable about financial matters. Accordingly, it is to be expected that they will be increasingly sensitive to differentials in investment returns, suggesting the need to eliminate competitive barriers between institutions. The increased sophistication of the small investors also points to the importance of building their confidence in the stock market through the creation of a strong central market and through firm regulatory measures that permit the investors to obtain full and equal disclosure of corporate affairs.

INTERNATIONAL AGENCY BONDS

The U.S. government has an interest in certain institutions which borrow worldwide to finance their activities. Preeminent among them is the International Bank for Reconstruction and Development (World Bank); also of interest are the Asian Development Bank and the Inter-American Development Bank.

International Bank for Reconstruction and Development

In July 1944 the United Nations Monetary and Financial Conference at Bretton Woods, New Hampshire, drafted the Articles of Agreement of the International Bank for Reconstruction and Development. In June 1946 the bank began formal operations, holding its first annual meeting in September of the same year with representatives present from its entire membership of 38 countries. Thereafter, membership has grown steadily, embracing 68 countries by June 30, 1961, and 125 countries by June 30, 1975. The Soviet Union and the Chinese People's Republic are the conspicuous powers outside the fold.

The bank maintains headquarters in Washington, D.C. It is an international cooperative institution formed to help in rehabilitating war-torn countries, aid in the development of economically backward nations, promote private foreign investment, and stimulate long-range balanced growth of international trade. With the passage of time, emphasis has shifted from reconstruction of war-damaged countries to building industry in underdeveloped areas. Within the developmental area, the focus—which in the 1950s was predominantly on infrastructure, particularly transportation and electric power—has broadened to include agriculture, education, and technological improvement.

Subject to prescribed conditions, the World Bank may guarantee, participate in, or make loans to member countries or their political subdivisions, or to private enterprises located in member countries. Loans to private organizations must be guaranteed by the member government or by some acceptable agency within the country, such as its central bank. Except for special circumstances, a World Bank loan must be for a specific project that is technically and economically sound as well as of high priority for the member country's economic development. To date, the bank has incurred no losses on its loans, and only a very few have been rescheduled.

The bank's original authorized capital of $10 billion has been increased several times and amounted to $27 billion on June 30, 1975 (gold weight and fineness in effect on July 1, 1944), of which $25.5 billion (in 1944 dollars) was subscribed. Of the amount subscribed, 10 percent has been paid in; the 90 percent unpaid portion is callable only to meet the bank's own obligations. With respect to the 10 percent portion that has been paid, about 1 percent is in gold or U.S. dollars immediately available for lending, while 9 percent is in the national currencies of members, which can be used only with the consent of the nations whose currency is involved.

The bank obtains its funds from usable capital subscriptions, net borrowings in world capital markets, net income, sales of loans to other investors, and repayment of outstanding loans. Of these sources, the largest portion comes from borrowings, which may be in the form of public offerings through investment bankers or private sales to central banks, governments, or governmental agencies, and, in recent years, petroleum-exporting countries. The bulk of World Bank bonds are medium-term issues, payable in a specified currency (principally U.S. dollars, German marks, or Japanese yen), and with interest rates that reflect prevailing money-market conditions.

Investors are primarily interested in the obligations that the bank distributes directly in the open market. These bonds are not secured by any particular collateral but are general obligations backed by the institution's full resources. These assets comprise (1) the bank's portfolio of loans; (2) the bank's liquid assets of cash and marketable issues; and (3) the unremitted portion of its capital stock, which may be called if the assets previously listed are not adequate to meet the bank's obligations.

On June 30, 1975, the current liabilities of the bank, comprising for the most part the undistributed balances of loans, were $7.7 billion; the total volume of bonds outstanding amounted to $12.3 billion. Against this total of $20 billion, the bank had total assets of $26 billion, of which $19.9 billion represented outstanding loans. Moreover, the $23 billion (in 1944 dollars) of subscriptions subject to call represents a powerful protection for the integrity of the bank's bonds. For the fiscal year ended June 30, 1975, the bank earned $275 million, of which $115.8 million was allocated to the Supplemental Reserve Against Losses on Loans and from Currency Devaluations and $100 million was transferred to the International Development Association (IDA).

The bank's obligations are amply covered by assets that appear sound and have the added bulwark of the uncalled subscriptions. This substantial protection gives the bonds a high-grade quality for U.S. investors. They are, however, exempt from the registration and other provisions of the Securities Act. Several factors contribute to their marketability: national and state member banks of the Federal Reserve System may invest in and underwrite these securities up to 10 percent of their capital and surplus; and subject to various qualifications, the securities are permitted investments for commercial banks, savings banks, insurance companies, and trust funds in most states. Interest paid on World Bank bonds to residents of the United States is fully taxable.

In 1956 the bank established its first affiliate, the International Finance Corporation (IFC), to work with private enterprise in developing countries. In September 1969 the bank's second affiliate, the International Development Association (IDA), was created to lend on concessionary terms. In the fiscal year beginning July 1, 1975, the bank established, on a tentative basis, a "third window" to provide development assistance on terms intermediate between those of the bank and the IDA.

The International Monetary Fund (IMF) is a separate institution concerned with stabilizing international exchange. Its functions are complementary to those of the bank, and only members of the IMF may become members of the bank. The IMF has no outstanding obligations and assumes no responsibility for those of the bank.

Asian Development Bank

The Asian Development Bank was established in 1966 to encourage regional economic cooperation in Asia and the Far East. It seeks to help the economic growth of its developing members by making loans, promoting investment, and providing technical assistance. The United States participated actively in the organization of the bank and is, with Japan, one of the two largest subscribers to its capital stock. As in the case of the World Bank, the subscribed segment of the Asian Development Bank's capital is divided into paid-in and callable portions. The callable portion may be used only to meet obligations on borrowings and guaranties. The bank has raised funds in various countries, including the United States.

Inter-American Development Bank

Composed of American governments, the Inter-American Development Bank is intended to further the economic and social development of its member countries, primarily through the grant of loans. The bank, which operates under an agreement effective December 30, 1959, has raised funds in a number of different countries, including the United States. The bank's borrowing is limited to not more than the amount of the uncalled subscription of the United States. This amount, in turn, is callable only to meet the bank's obligations arising from its borrowing operations.

SUMMARY

The ability of the U.S. government to meet the service requirements on its outstanding debt is unquestioned. Accordingly, U.S. government securities represent premier obligations. Their attraction to investors seeking a safe investment haven, therefore, depends upon their returns relative to those of other prime bonds. The government has issued a great many different kinds of securities. Accordingly, within this group, the investor has a multiplicity of choices to suit his own needs.

Nonmarketable bonds provide secure income that is free from market risks; they also enable foreign governments to buy large amounts of Treasury obligations without upsetting their price structure. On the other hand, these bonds do not possess the flexibility of issues that are traded in the open market. Among the marketable bonds, an important consideration to the investor is the maturity desired.

Treasury bills are non-interest-bearing securities that have maturities of up to one year. Their yield depends on the depth of the discount at which they are sold. Treasury notes have traditionally had maturities of between one and five years, but they may now be issued with maturities of up to seven years. Their relatively short terms are particularly attractive to commercial banks. Treasury bonds may bear any maturity but generally have been issued with original due dates of more than seven years.

The government has established a number of agencies that serve as intermediaries, channeling funds from the public to certain critical economic sectors. In general, their role has been expanding, and the volume of securities issued by them has grown considerably in recent years. While the bulk of such obligations are not guaranteed by the U.S. government, some form of backing often is provided. For example, the Treasury may be authorized to buy the securities, or the agency may be allowed to borrow directly from the Treasury.

The U.S. government has an interest in various international financial institutions. The dominant one is the International Bank for Reconstruction and Development (World Bank), which has been a large issuer of bonds. Because of the World Bank's substantial assets and its right, if necessary, to call upon subscribers, including the United States, for additional payments, the bank's bonds are considered high-grade.

CHAPTER 21

Municipal Obligations

Obligations of states, municipalities, and other local governments are marketed through municipal bond dealers, who purchase the bonds from issuing governments for subsequent resale to the public. Most dealers in municipal securities indicate their bond offering (asked) prices in the *Blue List of Current Municipal Offerings*, issued after the close of each business day. This list provides the basis for ascertaining the current interests of dealers and facilitates the conduct of transactions. At the close of 1975, the *Blue List* carried 12,644 listings for an aggregate face value of $959 million. The securities which the municipal bond dealer distributes are referred to in financial circles as *municipal bonds*.

Commercial banks may also serve as dealers, but they are limited by the Glass-Steagall Act of 1933 to handling, for their own accounts, the general obligations of a state or its political subdivisions. Legislation which would amend the Glass-Steagall Act to permit commercial banks to underwrite state and local revenue bonds has been introduced almost continuously in Congress since the passage of the Glass-Steagall Act. The present prohibition against the underwriting of revenue bonds does not arise from specific language in the 1933 act but rather from the fact that the term "revenue obligation" was omitted from the legislation.

SCOPE OF THE MUNICIPAL FIELD

The term "municipal bond" applies to many different kinds of obligations. Included are the bonds of states, political subdivisions of states, local housing authorities, and U.S. territories and insular possessions. Political subdivisions of states embrace cities, counties, towns, villages, and boroughs. In addition, civil governments may create districts of various types, such as school districts, road districts, and water districts, all of which may issue bonds that are considered "municipals."

Municipal bonds may be *general obligations* backed by the limited or unlimited taxing power of a political entity, or they may be payable from the revenues of specified assets. Sometimes the pledge of revenues from particular assets furnishes the chief basis for principal and interest distributions, but the issuer agrees to supplement these payments from other income sources if the primary source of earnings proves insufficient. Tax-raising powers also may vary considerably. These differences are fundamental, and they provide securities of radically differing quality.

Besides the dealer banks, there are securities firms that deal in municipal securities, buying and selling for their own accounts, and bond brokers, which serve only as agents for investors. The total community in the municipal field consists of about 1,200 firms of varying sizes and characteristics, with about three times as many nonbanks as banks.[1] Some 125 firms dominate both the underwriting of new municipal issues and the maintenance of secondary markets in these issues.

The methods of syndicating and distributing municipal securities are usually determined by state law. Ordinarily, general obligation bonds must be sold by competitive bidding, while arrangements for the distribution of revenue bonds are made by negotiation. In many ways, the underwriting of municipal and corporate issues is similar, but there are significant differences in their secondary trading markets. The varied characteristics of each municipal bond issue—rating, yield, term, and other factors relating to the securities themselves—and the differences of the various series within each particular issue make municipal bonds less fungible than corporate securities. Moreover, although municipal obligations ordinarily are traded in rather large denominations (a trade of less than $10,000 is considered an odd lot), the volume of secondary trades is small compared with the trading volume in corporate securities.

Pricing Municipal Bonds

Municipal bonds are usually issued in serial form, with specified amounts falling due each year. These bonds, particularly the earlier maturities, are generally traded on a yield basis. This means that they are bought and sold in terms of the yield they afford rather than their actual dollar price. An investor wishing to buy municipal securities must convert the yield to an actual dollar price in order to determine how much he has to pay. For quotation purposes, the dollar prices derived from yields usually are approximate; the exact price related to the exact period remaining in the life of the bond is determined on the day of the transaction.

In the fall of 1975, Connecticut State issued $100 million of various purpose bonds, dated September 15 and maturing serially from 1975 through 2023. The bonds falling due in October 1985 bore a 6.10 percent coupon and were offered on the yield basis of 5.80 percent. Their capital value was 102.25, representing the price equivalent of a 6.10 percent issue due in ten years and yielding 5.80 percent. An individual able to buy these securities five years later, on September 15, 1980, at the same yield basis of 5.80 percent would pay 101.29. At this price, a 6.10 percent bond due in five years would afford a yield of 5.80 percent. In order to obtain the actual purchase price, as for most bonds, the accrued interest to date of purchase is added. In the case of a 6.10 percent bond, this is $0.1671 per day per $1,000 bond.

On the same day, the city of Lawrence, Kansas, offered its serial hospital revenue bonds, Series A, 1975. Not considered to be of equal quality with the State of Connecticut issue, the Lawrence bonds due in 1985 bore an 8.50 coupon and were priced at par to yield 7.90 percent to maturity. An investor who bought these bonds would also have to pay the accrued interest to the date of purchase. For the issue under consideration, with a coupon of 7.90 percent, interest accumulates at the rate of $0.2164 per day on each $1,000 bond.

Figure 21-1 illustrates the form of announcement of the sale of a new issue of municipal securities. It shows the amount of bonds maturing serially each year, their coupon rates, and their yields or prices. As in this case, it is also common to provide a statement regarding the tax status of the bonds (here the tax exemption does not apply to a "substantial user of facilities" or to a "related person"), the denominations available, registration features, and some "boiler-plate" legal disclaimers. The statement also displays the hierarchy of the underwriters.

Portfolio managers are often interested in municipal obligations because their serial form permits convenient maturity distributions. The great number of different issues outstanding also makes it easy to introduce geographic diversification into a portfolio.

Legal Opinions

Numerous legal restrictions govern the issuance of municipal obligations. Violation of even one technical provision could invalidate an entire

FIGURE 21-1

Announcement of Sale of New Municipal Securities Issue

Interest exempt, in the opinion of Bond Counsel, from federal income tax as presently enacted and construed, except as provided in Section 103(c)(7) of the Internal Revenue Code as to any Series A, 1975 Bond held by a substantial user of Industrial Development Projects or by a related person. A ruling to this effect with respect to the Series A, 1975 Bonds has been secured from the Internal Revenue Service. The Series A, 1975 Bonds, their transfer and the income therefrom (including any profit made on the sale thereof) are, in the opinion of Bond Counsel, free from taxation within the Commonwealth of Pennsylvania under the laws of the Commonwealth as presently enacted and construed, except with respect to inheritance or estate tax.

NEW ISSUE

$40,000,000

The Pennsylvania Industrial Development Authority

Revenue Bonds, Series A, 1975

(Lots A1-A40)

The Series A, 1975 Bonds will be special obligations of the Authority and not a debt of the Commonwealth of Pennsylvania or any political subdivision thereof other than the Authority. The Bonds will be payable solely from revenues of the Authority and will be secured under the provisions of the Resolution as described in the Official Statement.

Dated: July 1, 1975 — Due: January 1 and July 1, as shown below

Coupon bonds in the denomination of $5,000 registrable as to principal only, or as to principal and interest. Principal and semi-annual interest (July 1 and January 1, first coupon January 1, 1976, interest accrues from July 1, 1975) payable at First Pennsylvania Bank, N.A., Trustee and Paying Agent and at the option of the holder, unless registered, at the principal office of Chemical Bank, Co-Paying Agent.

Amount	Due	Interest Rate	Yield or Price	Amount	Due	Interest Rate	Price	Amount	Due	Interest Rate	Price
$2,000,000	Jan. 1, 1977	6%	5.70%	$1,000,000	July 1, 1980	6.40%	100%	$1,000,000	July 1, 1983	7%	100%
2,000,000	July 1, 1977	6	5.80	1,000,000	Jan. 1, 1981	6.60	100	1,000,000	Jan. 1, 1984	7.20	100
1,750,000	Jan. 1, 1978	6	5.90	1,000,000	July 1, 1981	6.60	100	1,000,000	July 1, 1984	7.20	100
1,750,000	July 1, 1978	6	100	1,000,000	Jan. 1, 1982	6.80	100	1,500,000	Jan. 1, 1985	7.40	100
1,250,000	Jan. 1, 1979	6.20	100	1,000,000	July 1, 1982	6.80	100	1,500,000	July 1, 1985	7.40	100
1,250,000	July 1, 1979	6.20	100	1,000,000	Jan. 1, 1983	7	100	1,500,000	Jan. 1, 1986	7½	100
1,250,000	Jan. 1, 1980	6.40	100					1,500,000	July 1, 1986	7½	100

$13,750,000 7¾% Term Bonds Due July 1, 1990 at 100%

(Accrued interest to be added)

The Bonds maturing after July 1, 1985, are subject to redemption prior to maturity beginning on July 1, 1985, as more fully described in the Official Statement.

These Bonds are offered when, as and if issued and received by the Underwriters, subject to prior sale, to withdrawal or modification of the offer without notice, and to the approval of legality of the Bonds by Messrs. Ballard, Spahr, Andrews & Ingersoll, Philadelphia, Pennsylvania, Bond Counsel. Certain legal matters will be passed upon for Authority by its Counsel, Messrs. Ruffin, Hazlett, Perry & Lonergan, Pittsburgh, Pennsylvania. Certain legal matters will be passed upon for the Underwriters by their counsel, Messrs. Hawkins, Delafield & Wood, New York, New York.

The offering of these Bonds is made only by the Official Statement, copies of which may be obtained in any State from such of the undersigned as may lawfully offer these securities in such State.

Goldman, Sachs & Co. — **Butcher & Singer**

Arthurs, Lestrange & Short — Bear, Stearns & Co. — A. G. Becker & Co. Municipal Securities Inc. — Blyth Eastman Dillon & Co. Incorporated — Alex. Brown & Sons

Donaldson, Lufkin & Jenrette Securities Corporation — Drexel Burnham & Co. Incorporated — Elkins, Stroud, Suplee & Co. — The First Boston Corporation

Halsey, Stuart & Co. Inc. Affiliate of Bache & Co. Incorporated — Hornblower & Weeks-Hemphill, Noyes Incorporated — E. F. Hutton & Company Inc. — Kidder, Peabody & Co. Incorporated

Kuhn, Loeb & Co. — Lazard Frères & Co. — Loeb, Rhoades & Co. — McDonald & Company — Merrill Lynch, Pierce, Fenner & Smith Incorporated

Moore, Leonard & Lynch, Incorporated — W. H. Morton & Co. (Div. of American Express Co.) — John Nuveen & Co. Incorporated — Paine, Webber, Jackson & Curtis Incorporated — R. W. Pressprich & Co. Incorporated

Reynolds Securities Inc. — L. F. Rothschild & Co. — Salomon Brothers — Shearson Hayden Stone Inc.

Thomson & McKinnon Auchincloss Kohlmeyer Inc. — Weeden & Co. Incorporated — Wertheim & Co., Inc. — White, Weld & Co. Incorporated — Dean Witter & Co. Incorporated

July 14, 1975

SOURCE: *Wall Street Journal*, July 14, 1975, p. 17.

issue. To avoid this danger, it is the practice of issuers to obtain the opinion of a firm of attorneys concerning the legality of the issue. Because of the complicated nature of the field and the importance of having the opinions readily accepted, they are usually prepared by recognized firms specializing in this type of work. Buyers may require a notarized copy of the opinion to accompany the bond; alternatively, the opinion may be printed on the bond, a practice which has become common in recent years. In the case of state issues, the opinion is sometimes provided by the state attorney general.

In 1973 the U.S. Supreme Court ruled that the states have the responsibility of providing equal educational opportunities for their residents. Starting from this premise, some state courts have asserted that the local property tax stands in the way of this objective because of the disparity of funds that can be raised in wealthy and poor areas. Accordingly, lawmakers in such states have been instructed to discover alternative ways of paying for public education. In these circumstances, legal opinions have tended to assert that elimination of the property tax as a source of school revenue would not invalidate already outstanding bonds collateralized by the tax.

TAX STATUS OF MUNICIPAL BONDS

Municipal obligations have special exemptions from both federal and state income taxes. Under the original income tax legislation, this preferred status did not attract wide attention. Tax rates were low, and wealthy investors could obtain better net yields from certain types of taxable securities. Sharp rises in tax rates, however, have endowed the exemption privilege with an advantage that has focused increased attention on the municipals.

Exemption from Federal Income Taxes

Interest on the obligations of states, cities, and their political subdivisions is completely free from federal income taxes. The case for constitutional exemption is founded on Chief Justice John Marshall's enunciation of the doctrine of reciprocal exemption in *McCulloch* v. *Maryland* (4 Wheaton 316 at 431), in which he stated that "power to tax involves the power to destroy. . . ." The doctrine thus created holds that the federal government may not tax the issues of state or local governments and that these governments may not tax obligations of the national government. Subsequently, after enactment of the income tax amendment, Congress, in the Internal Revenue Code, specifically exempted from federal income taxes the interest paid by state or local governments on their outstanding bonds. Interest on obligations of housing authorities and those of territories and insular possessions is also exempt; in these cases, the exemption is written into the acts authorizing the bonds. The U.S. Treasury now contends that the statutory provision is the sole source of the exemption and that it can be eliminated by a legislative change. Congress has periodically evidenced some interest in the adoption of such a change.

The tax exemption endows the issues with particular appeal for corporations and individuals in the upper-income brackets. The extent of the tax advantage is indicated in Figure 21-2, which shows for different income-tax brackets the yield that a taxable bond must afford to provide the same return as that available from municipal obligations. This equality is determined by dividing the tax-free yield by 100 percent minus the investor's marginal tax rate.

In the last week of August 1975, the Bond Buyer's Index, representing an average of the yields of 20 representative municipal bonds, was 7.18 percent. On the basis of tax rates prevailing at that time, an investor in the $44,000 to $52,000 income-tax bracket filing a joint return would have to realize a yield of 14.36 percent from a taxable security to receive a comparable return (7.18)/(100% – 50%). The tax exemption on municipal bonds allows a wealthy investor to purchase a security that affords the safety of a prime fixed-income obligation but provides the aftertax return of a medium to low-grade corporate bond.

The significance of the tax-exemption privilege for municipal obligations was clearly demonstrated by their sharp price rise after the Korean war began, when values of U.S. government and high-grade corporate bonds were declining. The outbreak of hostilities had aroused the expectation of increased federal income taxes to cover the enlarged military expenditures that would inevitably ensue. A more subtle reflection was the speculative interest in housing bonds in mid-1974 on the possibility that the tax-free variety would gain scarcity value if the new Federal Financing Bank began funding the housing program by selling taxable obligations.[2]

If the purchaser of a municipal bond selling at a discount holds the bond to maturity (providing the taxation on municipal securities does not change), the increase in capital value will be taxed as a capital gain by the federal government. It is only the income accruing from the coupon that is exempt from taxation. Thus, to offset the tax cost, the yield on low-coupon bonds is likely to be higher than that on high-coupon bonds of the same quality and maturity. On the other hand, the amount above par on a premium bond is not considered a capital loss but is incorporated in the yield.

If a bond is originally issued below par, the federal government recognizes the discount as a part of the interest payment, and the recovery of this discount is tax-exempt. However, if an original issue at 100 is found to be overpriced and a new syndicate is formed to reoffer the bonds, the recovery of the discount from the reoffering is not tax-exempt. A similar situation prevails in the case of serial issues when the price paid by the underwriting syndicate for the whole issue is equal to the par value of the issue and no specific prices are attached to the individual maturity. Under these circumstances, if some of the maturities are reoffered at a discount, the recovery of that discount is not tax-exempt.

Efforts to Eliminate the Federal Income Tax Exemption

The exemption privilege has come under increasing attack, and the case against the privilege has changed over time. Originally it was asserted that the attraction of municipal bonds for wealthy individuals cut off the stream of venture capital that these investors might otherwise provide. It was also held that the resulting loss of revenue to the federal government indirectly augmented this tendency by contributing toward higher tax rates, which are an important impediment to the flow of venture capital. Finally, the feature was condemned because it weakened the financial structure of many municipalities by tempting them to rely excessively on low-interest bonds for additional funds.

Another argument against the privilege has been in terms of equity and costs. Critics have asserted that a number of very wealthy individuals are substantially minimizing their tax burden, a condition that is objectionable on equity grounds. Some writers have also contended that the very considerable volume of funds which state and local governments must raise on the capital markets has led to the sale of bonds to investors in relatively lower tax brackets. To these investors, the tax-exemption privilege is not as attractive as to the rich individual who has long been viewed as the primary market for municipal obligations. As a consequence, the claim is made that the federal government is losing more revenue than the state and local governments have been gaining through decreased interest costs. Therefore, the federal government can subsidize the municipal bond issuers more cheaply directly than by continuing to allow the tax exemption.

For several years, starting in 1938, the Roosevelt administration attempted to persuade Congress to adopt legislation authorizing the federal government to tax all future issues of state or local governments. In return, the administration was willing to grant these local governments similar taxing power over future issues of the federal government. This effort was unsuccessful. Pressure was subsequently renewed in early 1942 to obtain passage of much broader legislation permitting taxation of all issues of municipal obligations. This proposal also failed. In addition, in 1941 the Treasury sought to impose income taxes on certain obligations of the Port of

FIGURE 21-2

Tax-Free Bonds vs. Taxable Securities

Tax-Exempt vs. Taxable Income

Under federal income taxes effective December 1973
the comparable yields are:

(Taxable income in thousands)

Joint Return	$8 to $12	$12 to $16	$16 to $20	$20 to $24	$24 to $28	$28 to $32	$32 to $36	$36 to $40	$40 to $44	$44 to $52	$52 to $64	$64 to $76	$76 to $88	$88 to $100	$100 to $120	$120 to $140	$140 to $160	$160 to $180	$180 to $200	Over $200
Separate Return*	$4 to $6	$6 to $8	$8 to $10	$10 to $12	$12 to $14	$14 to $16	$16 to $18	$18 to $20	$20 to $22	$22 to $26	$26 to $32	$32 to $38	$38 to $44	$44 to $50	$50 to $60	$60 to $70	$70 to $80	$80 to $90	$90 to $100	Over $100
% Tax Bracket	22	25	28	32	36	39	42	45	48	50	53	55	58	60	62	64	66	68	69	70
TAX-EXEMPT YIELDS																				
4.00%	5.13	5.33	5.56	5.88	6.25	6.56	6.90	7.27	7.69	8.00	8.51	8.89	9.52	10.00	10.53	11.11	11.76	12.50	12.90	13.33
4.10	5.26	5.47	5.69	6.03	6.41	6.72	7.07	7.45	7.88	8.20	8.72	9.11	9.76	10.25	10.79	11.39	12.06	12.81	13.23	13.67
4.20	5.38	5.60	5.83	6.18	6.56	6.89	7.24	7.64	8.08	8.40	8.94	9.33	10.00	10.50	11.05	11.67	12.35	13.13	13.55	14.00
4.30	5.51	5.73	5.97	6.32	6.72	7.05	7.41	7.82	8.27	8.60	9.15	9.56	10.24	10.75	11.32	11.94	12.65	13.44	13.87	14.33
4.40	5.64	5.87	6.11	6.47	6.88	7.21	7.59	8.00	8.46	8.80	9.36	9.78	10.48	11.00	11.58	12.22	12.94	13.75	14.19	14.67
4.50	5.77	6.00	6.25	6.62	7.03	7.38	7.76	8.18	8.65	9.00	9.57	10.00	10.71	11.25	11.84	12.50	13.24	14.06	14.52	15.00
4.60	5.90	6.13	6.39	6.76	7.19	7.54	7.93	8.36	8.85	9.20	9.79	10.22	10.95	11.50	12.11	12.78	13.53	14.38	14.84	15.33
4.70	6.03	6.27	6.53	6.91	7.34	7.70	8.10	8.55	9.04	9.40	10.00	10.44	11.19	11.75	12.37	13.06	13.82	14.69	15.16	15.67
4.80	6.15	6.40	6.67	7.06	7.50	7.87	8.28	8.73	9.23	9.60	10.21	10.67	11.43	12.00	12.63	13.33	14.12	15.00	15.48	16.00
4.90	6.28	6.53	6.81	7.21	7.66	8.03	8.45	8.91	9.42	9.80	10.43	10.89	11.67	12.25	12.89	13.61	14.41	15.31	15.81	16.33
5.00	6.41	6.67	6.94	7.35	7.81	8.20	8.62	9.09	9.62	10.00	10.64	11.11	11.90	12.50	13.16	13.89	14.71	15.63	16.13	16.67
5.10	6.54	6.80	7.08	7.50	7.97	8.36	8.79	9.27	9.81	10.20	10.85	11.33	12.14	12.75	13.42	14.17	15.00	15.94	16.45	17.00
5.20	6.67	6.93	7.22	7.65	8.13	8.52	8.97	9.45	10.00	10.40	11.06	11.56	12.38	13.00	13.68	14.44	15.29	16.25	16.77	17.33
5.30	6.79	7.07	7.36	7.79	8.28	8.69	9.14	9.64	10.19	10.60	11.28	11.78	12.62	13.25	13.95	14.72	15.59	16.56	17.10	17.67
5.40	6.92	7.20	7.50	7.94	8.44	8.85	9.31	9.82	10.38	10.80	11.49	12.00	12.86	13.50	14.21	15.00	15.88	16.88	17.42	18.00
5.50	7.05	7.33	7.64	8.09	8.59	9.02	9.48	10.00	10.58	11.00	11.70	12.22	13.10	13.75	14.47	15.28	16.18	17.19	17.74	18.33
5.60	7.18	7.47	7.78	8.24	8.75	9.18	9.66	10.18	10.77	11.20	11.91	12.44	13.33	14.00	14.74	15.56	16.47	17.50	18.06	18.67
5.70	7.31	7.60	7.92	8.38	8.91	9.34	9.83	10.36	10.96	11.40	12.13	12.67	13.57	14.25	15.00	15.83	16.76	17.81	18.39	19.00
5.80	7.44	7.73	8.06	8.53	9.06	9.51	10.00	10.55	11.15	11.60	12.34	12.89	13.81	14.50	15.26	16.11	17.06	18.13	18.71	19.33
5.90	7.56	7.87	8.19	8.68	9.22	9.67	10.17	10.73	11.35	11.80	12.55	13.11	14.05	14.75	15.53	16.39	17.35	18.44	19.03	19.67
6.00	7.69	8.00	8.33	8.82	9.38	9.84	10.34	10.91	11.54	12.00	12.77	13.33	14.29	15.00	15.79	16.67	17.65	18.75	19.35	20.00
6.10	7.82	8.13	8.47	8.97	9.53	10.00	10.52	11.09	11.73	12.20	12.98	13.56	14.52	15.25	16.05	16.94	17.94	19.06	19.68	20.33
6.20	7.95	8.27	8.61	9.12	9.69	10.16	10.69	11.27	11.92	12.40	13.19	13.78	14.76	15.50	16.32	17.22	18.24	19.38	20.00	20.67
6.30	8.08	8.40	8.75	9.26	9.84	10.33	10.86	11.45	12.12	12.60	13.40	14.00	15.00	15.75	16.58	17.50	18.53	19.69	20.32	21.00
6.40	8.21	8.53	8.89	9.41	10.00	10.49	11.03	11.64	12.31	12.80	13.62	14.22	15.24	16.00	16.84	17.78	18.82	20.00	20.65	21.33
6.50	8.33	8.67	9.03	9.56	10.16	10.66	11.21	11.82	12.50	13.00	13.83	14.44	15.48	16.25	17.11	18.06	19.12	20.31	20.97	21.67
6.60	8.46	8.80	9.17	9.71	10.31	10.82	11.38	12.00	12.69	13.20	14.04	14.67	15.71	16.50	17.37	18.33	19.41	20.63	21.29	22.00
6.70	8.59	8.93	9.31	9.85	10.47	10.98	11.55	12.18	12.88	13.40	14.26	14.89	15.95	16.75	17.63	18.61	19.71	20.94	21.61	22.33
6.80	8.72	9.07	9.44	10.00	10.63	11.15	11.72	12.36	13.08	13.60	14.47	15.11	16.19	17.00	17.89	18.89	20.00	21.25	21.94	22.67
6.90	8.85	9.20	9.58	10.15	10.78	11.31	11.90	12.55	13.27	13.80	14.68	15.33	16.43	17.25	18.16	19.17	20.29	21.56	22.26	23.00
7.00	8.97	9.33	9.72	10.29	10.94	11.48	12.07	12.73	13.46	14.00	14.89	15.56	16.67	17.50	18.42	19.44	20.59	21.88	22.58	23.33
7.10	9.10	9.47	9.86	10.44	11.09	11.64	12.24	12.91	13.65	14.20	15.11	15.78	16.90	17.75	18.68	19.72	20.88	22.19	22.90	23.67
7.20	9.23	9.60	10.00	10.59	11.25	11.80	12.41	13.09	13.85	14.40	15.32	16.00	17.14	18.00	18.95	20.00	21.18	22.50	23.23	24.00
7.30	9.36	9.73	10.14	10.74	11.41	11.97	12.59	13.27	14.04	14.60	15.53	16.22	17.38	18.25	19.21	20.28	21.47	22.81	23.55	24.33
7.40	9.49	9.87	10.28	10.88	11.56	12.13	12.76	13.45	14.23	14.80	15.74	16.44	17.62	18.50	19.47	20.56	21.76	23.13	23.87	24.67
7.50	9.62	10.00	10.42	11.03	11.72	12.30	12.93	13.64	14.42	15.00	15.96	16.67	17.86	18.75	19.74	20.83	22.06	23.44	24.19	25.00
7.60	9.74	10.13	10.56	11.18	11.88	12.46	13.10	13.82	14.62	15.20	16.17	16.89	18.10	19.00	20.00	21.11	22.35	23.75	24.52	25.33
7.70	9.87	10.27	10.69	11.32	12.03	12.62	13.28	14.00	14.81	15.40	16.38	17.11	18.33	19.25	20.26	21.39	22.65	24.06	24.84	25.67
7.80	10.00	10.40	10.83	11.47	12.19	12.79	13.45	14.18	15.00	15.60	16.60	17.33	18.57	19.50	20.53	21.67	22.94	24.38	25.16	26.00
7.90	10.13	10.53	10.97	11.62	12.34	12.95	13.62	14.36	15.19	15.80	16.81	17.56	18.81	19.75	20.79	21.94	23.24	24.69	25.48	26.33
8.00	10.26	10.67	11.11	11.76	12.50	13.11	13.79	14.55	15.38	16.00	17.02	17.78	19.05	20.00	21.05	22.22	23.53	25.00	25.81	26.67
8.10	10.38	10.80	11.25	11.91	12.66	13.28	13.97	14.73	15.58	16.20	17.23	18.00	19.29	20.25	21.32	22.50	23.82	25.31	26.13	27.00
8.20	10.51	10.93	11.39	12.06	12.81	13.44	14.14	14.91	15.77	16.40	17.45	18.22	19.52	20.50	21.58	22.78	24.12	25.63	26.45	27.33
8.30	10.64	11.07	11.53	12.21	12.97	13.61	14.31	15.09	15.96	16.60	17.66	18.44	19.76	20.75	21.84	23.06	24.41	25.94	26.77	27.67
8.40	10.77	11.20	11.67	12.35	13.13	13.77	14.48	15.27	16.15	16.80	17.87	18.67	20.00	21.00	22.11	23.33	24.71	26.25	27.10	28.00
8.50	10.90	11.33	11.81	12.50	13.28	13.93	14.66	15.45	16.35	17.00	18.09	18.89	20.24	21.25	22.37	23.61	25.00	26.56	27.42	28.33
8.60	11.03	11.47	11.94	12.65	13.44	14.10	14.83	15.64	16.54	17.20	18.30	19.11	20.48	21.50	22.63	23.89	25.29	26.88	27.74	28.67
8.70	11.15	11.60	12.08	12.79	13.59	14.26	15.00	15.82	16.73	17.40	18.51	19.33	20.71	21.75	22.89	24.17	25.59	27.19	28.06	29.00
8.80	11.28	11.73	12.22	12.94	13.75	14.43	15.17	16.00	16.92	17.60	18.72	19.56	20.95	22.00	23.16	24.44	25.88	27.50	28.39	29.33
8.90	11.41	11.87	12.36	13.09	13.91	14.59	15.34	16.18	17.12	17.80	18.94	19.78	21.19	22.25	23.42	24.72	26.18	27.81	28.71	29.67
9.00	11.54	12.00	12.50	13.24	14.06	14.75	15.52	16.36	17.31	18.00	19.15	20.00	21.43	22.50	23.68	25.00	26.47	28.13	29.03	30.00
9.10	11.67	12.13	12.64	13.38	14.22	14.92	15.69	16.55	17.50	18.20	19.36	20.22	21.67	22.75	23.95	25.28	26.76	28.44	29.35	30.33
9.20	11.79	12.27	12.78	13.53	14.38	15.08	15.86	16.73	17.69	18.40	19.57	20.44	21.90	23.00	24.21	25.56	27.06	28.75	29.68	30.67
9.30	11.92	12.40	12.92	13.68	14.53	15.25	16.03	16.91	17.88	18.60	19.79	20.67	22.14	23.25	24.47	25.83	27.35	29.06	30.00	31.00
9.40	12.05	12.53	13.06	13.82	14.69	15.41	16.21	17.09	18.08	18.80	20.00	20.89	22.38	23.50	24.74	26.11	27.65	29.38	30.32	31.33

*Applies only to married persons filing separate returns.

Note: Interest on state and local government securities is exempt from federal income taxes. This table gives the approximate yields which taxable securities must earn in various income brackets to produce, after tax, yields equal to those on tax-free bonds yielding from 4 percent to 10 percent.

The table is computed on the theory that the taxpayer's highest-bracket tax rate is applicable to the entire amount of any increase or decrease in his taxable income resulting from a switching from taxable to tax-free securities, or vice versa.

SOURCE: Securities Industry Association, Inc., *Tax Exempt Securities and the Investor*, 1974, pp. 22-23. Copyright 1974 Securities Industry Association, Inc. Reprinted by permission.

New York Authority and the Triborough Bridge Authority. It was the Treasury's contention that securities of public authorities and state agencies did not qualify for tax exemption under existing law and that the exemption of states and municipalities had no constitutional immunity. These claims were denied by the lower courts, and the U.S. Supreme Court refused to review the case.

Thereafter, efforts have periodically been made to eliminate or at least modify the exemption. In 1974 a bill sponsored by Senator William Proxmire was introduced in Congress which offered municipalities the option of selling taxable or tax-exempt obligations. If they elected to go the taxable route, the federal government would provide a subsidy by paying one-third of the cost of borrowing. The bill, however, would have had no effect on the tax status of existing bonds or of those issued by municipalities that preferred to offer taxable bonds. The bill never became law, but a similar idea was later revived.

If the attack on the tax status of municipal bonds proves successful, the effect on previously issued bonds would, of course, depend on their treatment. If bonds issued prior to the repeal were permitted to retain their tax-exempt privilege, they would gain a scarcity value that would improve their market position. On the other hand, if the exemption were not attached to the bonds themselves but given to holders who bought before the repeal, the effect would be far different. In this case, a large number of potential buyers would withdraw from the market, adversely affecting the market prices of the bonds and reducing their marketability. The possibility also exists—although it appears less likely—that all holders, regardless of date of purchase, and all bonds, regardless of when they were issued, would be subject to the tax.

The courts have been careful to prevent abuse of the tax-exempt privilege. Thus, an investor cannot deduct interest on funds borrowed to buy a municipal bond, since this would provide a double benefit. Similarly, a town cannot sell tax-free bonds and use the proceeds to invest in higher-yielding securities.

Exemption from State Taxes

Provisions of state laws vary with respect to taxation of their own bonds and those of other states. Most states do not tax interest on their own obligations or on those of subdivisions within the state, but they do impose taxes on the interest paid by other states and their subdivisions. Sometimes differences exist in the treatment of individuals and corporations. For example, individuals do not pay a tax on the income from bonds issued by New York State, but such income is taxable for corporate franchise purposes. Figure 21-3, a chart prepared by Coopers & Lybrand, summarizes the taxation policies affecting municipal issues of the 50 states.

BORROWING RECORD OF STATE AND LOCAL GOVERNMENTS

A brief history of municipal bonds will provide a background for a discussion of the methods of analyzing these issues. From the ratification of the Constitution in 1789 to about 1830, the conservatism that dominated government fiscal policies resulted in a very small amount of public financing. State governments were the first to loosen this restraint; they borrowed heavily during the ensuing years, particularly to help in developing the railways, turnpikes, and canals that formed the basis of the country's rapidly growing transportation system. In the general economic declines set off by the panics of 1837 and 1873, the strain resulted in successive waves of repudiation and default.

Lessons derived from bitter financial experience exerted a sobering influence on the state governments, which subsequently restricted their borrowing programs. A step-up in the financing activity of local political units filled the void. Because of these diverse trends, by the turn of the century local debts constituted the largest segment of outstanding government loans. Local entities, particularly cities, continued to dominate public borrowing until the federal government came to the forefront, spurred by World War I military needs.

After the war, both state and local governments once again borrowed large amounts to extend their community services, until the depression of 1932 led to a new series of defaults on the part of several large and well-established political units, such as the state of Arkansas and the city of Detroit.[3] The maximum amount of interest and principal deferred at any one time was $320 million, which represented 16 percent of the obligations due but only 1.7 percent of the debt outstanding. In most cases, however, bondholders eventually received payment and permanent losses amounted to less than 1 percent.[4]

The depression period gave way to World War II. Municipal financing was held back until 1947, when voters, in the early optimism of the postwar years, authorized a record volume of new bonds to obtain funds for veterans' bonuses, schools, roads, water supply systems, and various capital improvement projects. This resurgence of municipal activity was overshadowed by the enormously broadened scope of federal government participation in the economic life of the country, augmented over a period of 35 years by a shattering depression, two world wars, and the need to maintain the nation in constant military preparedness. As a result, by 1950, as shown in Table 21-1, the federal debt constituted over 90 percent of the total U.S. public debt. Thereafter, however, the trend was reversed, and by 1972 the federal portion had shrunk to 70.9 percent. Indicative of the extraordinary growth of municipal financing is the fact that approximately $23 billion of total

FIGURE 21-3

State and Local Taxation of Municipal Bonds

(T — TAXABLE NT — NOT TAXABLE)

State	Corporations						Individuals					
	State Tax on Income		Property Tax		Local Tax on Income		State Income Tax		Property Tax		Local Income Tax	
	Own State	Other States	Own State	Other States	Own State	Other States	Own State	Other States	Own State	Other States	Own State	Other States
labama	NT	T	NT	T	None	None	NT	T	NT	T	None	None
laska	NT	NT	None	None	None	None	NT	NT	None	None	None	None
rizona	NT	T	None	None	None	None	NT	T	None	None	None	None
rkansas	NT	T	T	T	None	None	NT	T	T	T	None	None
alifornia:												
Franchise Tax	T	T	NT	NT	None	None	NT	T	NT	NT	None	None
Income Tax	NT	T										
olorado	T(1)	T	None	None	None	None	T(1)	T	None	None	None	None
onnecticut	T	T	None	None	None	None	None	None	None	None	None	None
elaware	NT	T	None	None	NT	NT	NT	T	None	None	NT	NT
istrict of Columbia	NT	NT	None	None			NT	NT	None	None		
lorida	T	T	NT	T	None	None	None	None	NT	T	None	None
eorgia	NT	T	NT	T	None	None	NT	T	NT	T	None	None
awaii	NT	T	None	None	None	None	NT	T	None	None	None	None
daho	T	T	T	T	None	None	T	T	T	T	None	None
linois	T	T	T	T	None	None	T	T	None	None	None	None
ndiana	NT	NT	NT	T	None	None	NT	NT	NT	T	None	None
wa	T	T	None	None	None	None	T	T	None	None	None	None
ansas	T(1)	T	NT	T	None	None	T(1)	T	NT	T	None	None
entucky	NT	T	NT	T	NT	NT	NT	T	NT	T	NT	NT
ouisiana	NT	T	NT	T	None	None	NT	T	NT	T	None	None
laine	NT	NT	None	None	None	None	NT	T	None	None	None	None
laryland	NT	NT	None	None	None	None	NT	T	None	None	NT	T
assachusetts	T	T	NT	NT	None	None	NT	T	NT	NT	None	None
ichigan	NT	T	NT	T	NT	NT	NT	T	NT	T	NT	NT
innesota	T	T	None	None	None	None	NT	T	None	None	None	None
ississippi	NT	T	NT	NT	None	None	NT	T	NT	NT	None	None
issouri	NT	T	T(2)	T(2)	NT	T	NT	T	T(2)	T(2)	NT	NT
ontana	NT	T	T	T	None	None	NT	T	T	T	None	None
ebraska	NT	NT	None	None	None	None	NT	NT	None	None	None	None
evada	None	None	NT	NT	None	None	None	None	NT	NT	None	None
ew Hampshire	NT	NT	None	None	None	None	NT	T	None	None	None	None
ew Jersey	T	T	None	None	None	None	None	None	None	None	None	None
ew Mexico	NT	NT	NT	NT	None	None	NT	NT	NT	NT	None	None
ew York	T	T	None	None			NT	T	None	None		
New York City					T	T					NT	T
rth Carolina	NT	T	NT	T	None	None	NT	T	NT	T	None	None
rth Dakota	NT	T	NT	NT	None	None	NT	T	NT	NT	None	None
hio	NT	NT	T	T	NT	NT	NT	NT	T	T	NT	NT
klahoma	T	T	None	None	None	None	T	T	None	None	None	None
regon	T	T	None	None			NT	T	None	None		
Portland					T	T					None	None
ennsylvania	NT	NT	None	None	None	None	NT	T	NT	T	NT	NT
Philadelphia (School District)											NT	T
hode Island	T	T	None	None	None	None	NT	T	None	None	None	None
uth Carolina	NT	T	None	None	None	None	NT	T	None	None	None	None
uth Dakota	None	None	NT	T	None	None	None	None	NT	T	None	None
nnessee	NT	T	NT	NT	None	None	NT	T	NT	NT	None	None
xas	None	None	T	T	None	None	None	None	T	T	None	None
ah	T	T	None	None	None	None	NT	NT	None	None	None	None
rmont	NT	NT	None	None	None	None	NT	NT	None	None	None	None
rginia	NT	T	NT	T	None	None	NT	T	NT	NT	None	None
ashington	None	None	None	None	None	None	None	None	None	None	None	None
est Virginia	NT	T	NT	T	None	None	NT	T	NT	T	None	None
sconsin	T	T	None	None	None	None	T	T	None	None	None	None
oming	None	None	NT	T	None	None	None	None	NT	T	None	None

(1) General obligation bonds

(2) Tax repealed effective January 1, 1975

SOURCE: Securities Industry Association, Inc., *Tax-Exempt Securities & the Investor*, 1974, pp. 20-21. Copyright 1974 Securities Industry Association, Inc. Reprinted by permission.

long-term municipal securities were issued in 1973, compared with $25 billion of new corporate securities, including bonds and stocks, offered publicly in that year.

In 1975 an unfortunate combination of circumstances, including business recession, inflation, the pressure for more services, and sometimes poor budgeting practices placed a number of big municipalities, especially New York City, in financial difficulties. As a result, some state and local government borrowers had to pay unusually high rates of interest to attract buyers. In some cases these rates were competitive with those available on high-grade, taxable corporate issues.

TABLE 21-1

*Distribution of U.S. Public Debt, 1942-1972**
(in percentages)

	1942	1950	1955	1960	1965	1966	1967	1968	1969	1970	1971	1972
Federal	78.9	91.4	86.1	80.4	76.1	74.9	74.2	74.2	72.6	72.1	71.5	70.9
State	3.6	1.8	3.5	5.2	6.5	7.0	7.3	7.6	8.2	8.1	8.6	9.0
Local	17.5	6.8	10.4	14.4	17.4	18.1	18.7	18.2	19.2	19.8	19.9	19.9
Total	100.0	100.0	100.0	100.0	100.0	100.0	100.0	100.0	100.0	100.0	100.0	100.0

*At end of fiscal year.

NOTE: Details may not add to totals because of rounding.

SOURCE: U.S. Bureau of the Census.

Expanded Scope of State and Local Borrowing

States, cities, and their political subdivisions are confronted by an urgent need for large-scale expenditures to meet the requirements of expanded populations living in communities often unequipped to cope with this growth; these governments must also face the almost overwhelming problems of urban rehabilitation and environmental protection. Various pressures may impose temporary checks on the volume of new state and local government financing, but in the long run it is likely to continue high. This tendency entails the danger that some communities may overborrow, exposing themselves to debt-service difficulties in the event of severe economic reversals, or may find themselves unable to cope with the problems they face. Recognition of the desirability of some restraint in public financing has contributed to the pressure by local governments for revenue-sharing with the federal government.

One factor leading to the growing volume of municipal debt is the expansion of purposes for which the bonds have been issued. Today bonds may be created for parking lots, golf courses, beach improvements, water pollution control, and various services relating to transportation. A relatively unhealthy development is the authorization by a number of states for municipalities to issue bonds (either general obligations or revenue bonds) for financing private corporations. These funds are not loaned directly to the corporation but are used to acquire or to construct plants which, in turn, are leased to the corporation. Not only does this create a potential interest burden if the corporation should flounder, but it also removes the property from the tax rolls. To restrain this practice, Congress in 1968 amended the Internal Revenue Code to eliminate the tax exemption on such new issues in excess of $5 million. Since then, however, Congress has considered liberalizing the ceiling. Moreover, the ceiling does not apply to specified areas, including facilities for air and water pollution control, sewage disposal, and water treatment, as well as certain transportation facilities, certain sports and trade show installations, and certain industrial parks.

At first, only modest use was made of the pollution bonds, but as the interest-rate differential between tax-exempt and taxable issues widened, corporations found them quite attractive. Bethlehem Steel, for example, which sold about $100 million of such issues in 1972 and 1973, estimated that it saved $40-50 million in interest payments. As major corporations used them, sales mounted rapidly, reaching an estimated $2.5-3.0 billion in 1974, compared with only $88 million in 1971. Moreover, corporations began to probe the possibility of broadening the interpretation of what constituted pollution control. The increasing percentage of the tax-exempt market represented by these bonds has attracted the regulatory attention of both federal and state authorities.[5]

Remedies in the Event of Default

The legal remedies for holders of bonds issued by state and city governments differ considerably. Under the U.S. Constitution, individuals may not sue a state. Hence, if a state defaults, a bondholder may seek legal redress only with the state's own permission. Other states owning the defaulted bonds may bring suit, or individual holders may take action against officials of the defaulting state.

Individuals may sue a city or other political subdivision of a state that fails to discharge its contractual requirements. The usual procedure for the bondholders or their representatives is to establish their claims in the appropriate court and to obtain a writ of mandamus requiring the local government to impose sufficient taxes to meet service payments. The effectiveness of this right is limited by the fact that suits may be lengthy and costly.

Local governments, including cities, political subdivisions, and taxing districts, may also file plans of composition under the Municipal Bankruptcy Act. These plans may provide for the modification or alteration of the rights of creditors, generally or as a class, through either issuance of new securities or other methods. If approved by a specified percentage of affected creditors and found fair and equitable by the courts, the plan becomes binding on all creditors. Municipalities have preferred not to effect debt settlements through this measure because its use might create a credit stigma. In 1974 no municipality was operating under this act. In 1975 New York City tottered on the brink of default. In early September it was clear that if neither the state nor the federal government came to its rescue, default was inevitable. Only after the mayor's budgetary power was stripped from him and transferred to the Emergency Financial Control Board, the state was committed to raising money to help the city, the possible fiduciary liability of the state comptroller for buying bonds of the Municipal Assistance Corp. (MAC—which had been set up by the state to help the city) for the state pension funds was lifted, and a number of other arrangements made was New York City given a breather. Existing law makes it difficult for a city to cope with the aftermath of default. For this reason, and to facilitate voluntary default by New York City, Congress considered amending the law. The cliff-hanging rescue of New York deferred action, leaving still on the books the cumbersome provisions of the legislation.

REGULATION OF MUNICIPAL SECURITIES

Until the passage of the Securities Acts Amendments of 1975, local government financing to the public was virtually unregulated except for the antifraud provisions of the securities laws. For a number of years, this freedom from regulation did not seem to be a serious problem because the field was largely the preserve of large institutions, which presumably could fend for themselves. Conditions began to change in the 1970s, as individuals found the high interest rates of municipal bonds, coupled with their tax-exempt status, increasingly attractive. In 1973, for example, individuals held \$50.7 billion in tax-exempt notes and bonds, up from \$31.4 billion ten years earlier.[6] The entrance of individuals into the market encouraged unprincipled promoters to employ high-pressure and questionable sales tactics, primarily in the Memphis area. As a result, the Tennessee legislature enacted regulatory legislation, effective September 1972, but this led to the dispersal of unethical dealers into other geographic areas.

The SEC became concerned about the extent of "boiler room" practices in the municipal field and brought action against various firms, alleging fraud in their municipal securities dealings.[7] These difficulties led to various reform proposals, some of which were incorporated in the 1975 securities legislation. For various reasons, this phase of the law is a patchwork affair: banks, which are important dealers in municipal securities, have their own supervisory authorities; the National Association of Securities Dealers already functions in the over-the-counter area, where municipals are traded; and the issuers of these obligations, as government officials in their own right, although at a local level, vigorously opposed any direct or even indirect control.

The 1975 amendments did establish a new, self-regulatory body, the Municipal Securities Rulemaking Board. Initially, board members are appointed by the SEC for two-year terms; subsequently, the size, term, and method of election will be determined by the board itself. At all times, however, board membership must be equally divided among public, broker-dealer, and bank representatives. Moreover, the public members are subject to SEC approval and must include at least one representative of investors in municipal securities and one representative of issuers. Municipal securities dealers must register with the SEC unless they are already registered as a result of their general securities business.

The board has broad powers, covering such areas as prevention of fraudulent and manipulative acts, establishment of standards for entry into the municipal securities business, regulation of selling and underwriting practices, provision for the form and content of municipal quotations, and prescription of the records that municipal securities dealers must keep. The SEC's powers over the board generally are similar to its relationships with the other self-regulatory agencies.

The board has the authority to adopt rules affecting the activities of municipal securities dealers (defined to include a separately identifiable department or division of a bank), but it does not have inspection enforcement responsibilities. Responsibility for conducting inspections and enforcing board rules is given to the NASD for its member firms and to the bank regulatory agencies for bank municipal securities dealers. The SEC, in turn, may review the enforcement procedures of the NASD, but not of the bank regulatory agencies. However, the commission can take action against any municipal securities dealer with the proviso that if the dealer is a bank, the SEC must first give notice to and consult with the appropriate banking agency.

To a large extent, the new measure extends the basic coverage of the Securities Exchange Act of 1934 to the securities firms and banks that underwrite and trade municipal securities. Departing from the precedent set by the disclosure provisions of the Securities Act of 1933, which apply to corporate securities, the new law provides that neither the commission nor the Municipal Securities Rulemaking Board can require an issuer of municipal obligations, directly or indirectly through a purchaser, to file information in connection with the distribution of such issues. The closest thing to such disclosure is a provision of the act that enables the board to require securities firms and departments of banks which underwrite and trade municipal securities to furnish to the board or prospective purchasers generally available information.

As a consequence of the New York City tragicomedy, the question of the need for disclosure legislation has arisen. The question whether the hidden deficit, caused by overstating aid from the federal and state governments and by other bookkeeping gimmicks, was $600 million, $1.8 billion, or $2.1 billion casts grave doubts on the integrity of municipal financial statements.

ANALYSIS OF MUNICIPAL BONDS

Like the yields of any other fixed-income securities, the yields of municipal bonds are subject to changes in interest rates, which, in turn, are influenced by federal monetary policy. There are special factors, however, which also play upon the municipal bond market.

Some Special Factors Affecting Bond Yields

The most important purchasers of municipal bonds are the commercial banks, fire and casualty companies, municipal bond investment funds, personal trust funds, and individuals. Traditionally, the commercial banks became large-scale buyers of tax-exempt bonds when the demand for their own funds was low; they held the bonds until maturity and abstained from the market when the demand for loans was high. In recent years, however, they have become more willing to liquidate their holdings of tax-exempts as loan demand increases. Moreover, the 1969 Revenue Act contains a provision limiting the extent to which the commercial banks can offset losses from the sale of tax-exempts against their securities profits. This factor, plus the general uncertainty regarding the future of the tax-exempt benefit, has dampened their interest in these bonds. These developments pose additional risks for all investors in the tax-exempt market and have exerted upward pressure on the yields of municipals.

A bond which banks find useful for portfolio adjustments to offset fluctuations in the demand for loans will be riskier than a comparable security which is not used in this way. On the other hand, if banks are not interested in a particular bond, its marketability may be impaired. As a result, a relatively modest amount of trading may bring about costly deviations from quoted prices.

The activity of the commercial banks is not the only institutional factor contributing to shifting municipal bond yields. To some extent, instability in bond yields is absorbed by large swings in the inventories of municipal bond dealers. Much of the dealer activity, in turn, is in response to fluctuating costs of their own funds and to changing condidions. At any particular time, therefore, and with respect to particular issues, yield fluctuations may be attributable to the policies and positions of the dealers.

For municipal bonds to be sold, they must be competitive with other securities. The yield on tax-exempts is therefore partly dependent on the supply and demand for corporate and U.S. government securities. In addition, the relative merits of the options available to the investor depend on the structure of income taxes. When tax rates are high, the ratio of municipal yields to corporate yields will tend to fall; when the rates are low, the opposite will happen.

Evaluating Particular Bonds

In analyzing specific municipal bonds, investors have traditionally focused on the characteristics of the issuer, not on the underlying factors that enable a community to service its debt. Yet Adam Smith recognized long ago that the wealth of a nation lay in its ability to generate product or (on the other side of the same coin) income. A community's taxes must ultimately be paid by its human and institutional residents out of the income that they earn. The value of taxable land and buildings, as well as the revenue potential of sales taxes, derive from the income-generating power of the community. The ability of a government to service its debt depends on its ability to raise taxes, which, in turn, depends on the ability of the community to earn income. The amount of taxes required is also related to the community's propensities to consume public goods; this, in turn, may be a function of the socioeconomic characteristics of its residents. Thus, a projection of the revenue-producing potential of a community involves economic, political, and behavioral factors that are hard to evaluate.

Adding to the difficulty of evaluation is the inadequacy of available data in this area. Periodic reports on per capita and overall state income are available, but similar statistics for local subdivisions, such as school districts, are often hard to come by. Such measures as the assessed value of a community's property are essentially proxy variables. Not only are they inadequate substitutes for income, but they also give little guidance as to the quality of that income.

Finally, the caliber of a municipal bond is strongly influenced by the fiscal policies of the issuing government. Interpreting these policies is a technical undertaking that involves a knowledge of budgeting procedures, legal restrictions, and financial principles not encountered in the corporate field. For all these reasons, many investors and securities analysts have preferred to avoid the evaluation of municipal obligations and have concentrated on equities where interest was considerably broader. Hence, a comparatively small group of municipal specialists influences the credit ratings of state and local governments. Nonspecializing firms often obtain and transmit to their own clients the opinions of these specialists.

Because of the esoteric nature of the field, the ratings assigned by the major services have a particularly important influence on the price of a bond. For a long time, therefore, New York City officials sought to have the city's bonds graded A. Moody's was the first to believe that the city's improving credit status justified this rating; it took another year before Standard & Poor's, in December 1973, finally assigned the bonds the coveted A rating, upgrading them from BBB. To obtain the rating change, the retiring and prospective budget directors made a detailed analysis to Standard & Poor's, pointing to improvements in a long list of economic factors. For example, the tax to income ratio of purely local taxes on residents of the city had risen only one-fourth as fast in the past decade as the burden of state taxes; despite concern over the exodus of the middle class from New York, the ratio of families with real income over $10,000 a year, on the basis of constant 1970 dollars, had risen.[8]

Nevertheless, little more than a year after receiving its improved rating, New York City was confronted with the possibility of bankruptcy. In May 1975, when its borrowing capacity seemed exhausted, the city had the awesome job of meeting $1.5 billion of debt falling due by the end of its fiscal year (June 30) and another $1.5 billion by Labor Day. On the one hand, it seemed impossible for the city to dig itself out of a fiscal hole this deep. On the other hand, it seemed equally incredible that federal, state, and banking authorities, whatever their public comments, would permit the country's "Empire City" to default, because of the uncertain impact such an event would have on the country's capital market and, possibly, its economy. The two major rating agencies split in their evaluation of the situation: Standard & Poor's withdrew its rating, while Moody's stuck to its A classification for the time being. Shortly before maturity, city notes were available at a price of $975, with few if any retail buyers, despite the extraordinary high annualized yield afforded at this price. The financial cliffhanger was at least temporarily resolved by the creation of a new state agency, the

Municipal Assistance Corporation (generally referred to as "Big MAC"), designed to assume responsibility for converting the city's $3 billion of short-term debts into long-term obligations.

In retrospect, commentators pointed to various factors that had signaled the city's impending distress. Typical was the following summary, compiled on June 1 by Eileen Shanahan, a leading financial writer for the *New York Times*:[9]

- New York's deficits are very large compared with its total receipts, 8 to 10 per cent in recent years. A deficit of 5 per cent is considered a warning signal.
- New York's deficits have persisted over many years. Two years in a row is considered a danger sign.
- New York has repeatedly closed out its fiscal year with short-term loans still outstanding. Doing this even once is considered a symptom of deadly serious financial illness.
- The amount that New York City has to pay to service its debt (interest plus principal coming due on long-term obligations) exceeds 17 per cent of its current budget expenditures. Anything over 15 per cent is enough to make those who rate the quality of municipal bonds take a scared new look.
- The delinquency rate on property-tax collections is rising in New York. This is considered a certain sign of municipal financial distress.
- New York City's outstanding short-term debt . . . has risen more than twelvefold in the last decade. There is no record like that in any other city.

But, as indicated above, the city's rating had been raised less than 18 months earlier, and financial bankers had bought huge amounts of its bonds. Presumably, they did not anticipate the sequel described above (see p. 522). In these circumstances, it would appear that legislation requiring full and clear disclosure of the status of local governments that issue securities should replace the statutory exemption from disclosure that presently exists.

The subsequent difficulties were not solely due to the discovery of bookkeeping gimmickry. A profound skepticism about the willingness and capacity of the mayor to undertake the economies necessary to put the city on a sound financial basis led to difficulties in rolling over the debt and hence the realistic possibility of default and bankruptcy. These forces combined to necessitate the transfer of fiscal authority from the mayor to the Emergency Control Board. Surprisingly, in spite of a growing fear that default by the city would undermine the entire municipal market and force other cities and even states into default, the federal government persisted in taking the stance that the problem was not Washington's. The market's attitude was, however, reflected in the fact that the State of New York one-year notes to raise funds to help the city were sold at a yield of 8 percent, even though the interest was tax free. Salomon Brothers reported that on September 12, 1975, the business day prior to the New York State offering, one-year prime municipal securities were yielding 4.20 percent.

By the close of the year, the city and state fashioned a complex financial package involving a legally contested state law suspending payment of principal on city notes; a plan offering the noteholders a choice between extending their notes for at least 3 years at a reduced 6-percent interest rate or exchanging them for 8-percent MAC bonds due in 10 years; as well as various other agreements by the city to economize and by institutions to accept debt-modifying terms. Based upon these draconian steps, the federal government adopted legislation authorizing direct loans for the next 3 fiscal years to tide the city over its default months. These loans have to be fully repaid by the end of each fiscal year out of subsequent tax collections. Although these measures may avert a cash crisis for three years, the city still faces the harsh reality of putting its financial house in sufficiently good order to permit reentry into the credit market. In the interim, the state, burdened by its own financial troubles, sought a program of tax increases and spending cuts to balance its budget.

In the process of establishing ratings for thousands of obligations, municipal bond specialists may make serious errors. Since these issues are often bought in large amounts, such errors can have grave consequences. Hence, even though analysis of such securities is especially complicated, it is desirable that the investor have some knowledge of the issues in which he is interested.

As a guide to the analysis of municipal bonds, some traditional methods of assessing them are described below. We emphasize the general obligations of states and local governments because these issues comprise the bulk of municipal obligations. Thereafter we consider the other major types of securities in this field, including revenue bonds, special assessment bonds, tax district obligations, and local housing authority issues.

GENERAL OBLIGATIONS

An issuing government pledges its full faith and credit to support the service payments of its direct or general obligations. Continuance of disbursements depends on both the desire and the ability of the issuer to pay. Civil governments within the United States rarely default through unwillingness to discharge their contractual responsibilities. In addition to being understandably reluctant to be charged with bad faith, they have a practical reason for scrupulously observing bond service requirements. Once the credit rating of a political unit is blemished, it usually remains so for a long time, since a government cannot, like a corporation, reorganize under a new name and establish a new financial life. Defaulting governments, even though they eventually clear their debts, would probably have to pay relatively high interest rates on any funds borrowed for a considerable period of time; these rates, in turn, would necessitate more and higher taxes on their populations.

Under these circumstances, the primary reason for default on the part of local governments is economic pressure. This is shown by the fact that defaults usually occur in periods of business adversity. Thus, the first consideration in evaluating a municipal obligation is whether the government can continue interest and principal payments even when business conditions are poor. We suggest three criteria for this judgment: (1) the basic economic strength of the community; (2) its revenue-raising potential; and (3) the relative magnitude of its fixed-charge requirements.

A Community's Basic Economic Strength

The economic character of a community provides an indication of its long-term ability to handle its funded debt. A prosperous, growing state is more likely to be able to withstand a business decline than one that is economically backward. In addition, the progressive community will be better able to whittle down a debt that was perhaps unduly heavy when originally issued.

There are various means of measuring the internal economic strength of a community. The community's location is important; for example, is it well situated with respect to transportation facilities and natural resources, and is it in an area of the country that is expanding or declining? The analyst must study the industries from which the bulk of the population's income is derived. Are these industries diversified? Do they include consumer-goods companies, which create a base of economic stability, as well as heavy-goods enterprises, whose output may be expected to vary with the economic cycle? There is an element of weakness in the economy of a single-industry city like Detroit, regardless of any current prosperity. Financial aspects should also be considered. To what extent does a community's budget history reveal an ability to meet operating costs by taxes? For what purposes has money been borrowed? Do expenditures appear to have been carefully supervised? How strong and aggressive are the unions? Are the fringe benefits going to create problems for future administrations? The existence of strong local banks reflects creditably on the financial status of a community.

The investor should supplement these general observations by studying specific economic indicators of local business conditions. Typical data of this sort are per capita income, retail sales, unemployment, bank deposits and debits, population, automobile registrations, telephones in service, electric power production, and newspaper advertising. The significance of these statistics for a particular community may be more clearly ascertained by examining their trends and making comparisons with figures for similar communities and for the country as a whole. Information on local conditions may be obtained from the local chamber of commerce, the business research bureaus of nearby universities, and Moody's *Government Manual.*

Changes in the economic environment may occur gradually and escape the investor's attention. The potential drains on the vitality of a community are as important as its historical achievements. The economic base is subject to erosion. One of the great problems facing many communities is a tendency for the tax base to deteriorate as the need for taxes increases. This condition can result from shortsightedness at various levels of government and from inability or refusal to recognize the interdependence of the urban center and its surrounding communities. In many areas the moderately wealthy citizens have deserted the urban core for the surrounding suburbs, with a consequent deterioration of values and tax base. As a result, the city is not able to sustain a satisfactory living environment, thereby accelerating the efflux of that part of the population which can best afford to pay taxes. Attempts to raise rates still further have led many business firms to depart. Accordingly, many cities today face formidable problems. School buildings often are obsolete and overcrowded; redevelopment needs and welfare requirements are staggering. On the other hand, since the political weight of the cities may not match that of the suburban and rural vote, adequate state and federal aid may not be forthcoming. Possible solutions include broadened revenue-sharing with the federal government or statewide real estate assessment and tax collection. Such developments would ease the financial problems of local political subdivisions and therefore help raise the quality of their obligations.

Even when the bond under consideration is a general obligation, it must not be assumed that the entire tax-raising ability of the community is available to service the issue. In some instances, constitutional or statutory provisions limit the amount of taxes the government may impose for debt purposes. Nor are all claims of equal priority. While both a city and a county may collect funds for itself as well as its subdivisions, the important consideration is not who is the collecting agency but who has the prior claim against the collection; it is the junior party that bears the burden of delinquencies. This order of priority is not uniform throughout the country.

It is, of course, very important to consider both the tax rates and the tax basis. An examination of the rate by itself is not enough. The relationship between assessed and market values of taxable property varies substantially from one government unit to another. Some units have high assessments and low tax rates; others have high tax rates and low assessments. Finally, any evidence of the community's willingness to impose taxes should be carefully gauged. For a local government to stress borrowing in its fund-raising program suggests a reluctance on the part of the administration to face financial realities.

A Community's Revenue-Raising Ability

For a number of years now, the costs of operating local government have risen rapidly because of inflationary price movements, expansions in services, and increases in population. Both state and city governments have had to augment their income accordingly. This problem has been solved, in part, by raising the existing tax rates. In many instances, these increases have been insufficient to meet the community's needs, and different types of taxes have been required.

New taxes create special problems. Established interests often oppose adoption of these levies and, even when they are enacted, attempt to eliminate them through legal devices or by marshaling public support for repeal campaigns. This customarily hostile reaction puts new taxes in jeopardy during the initial years after adoption. Hence, the investor must be wary of buying obligations of a community which derives a substantial portion of its revenues from taxes that are still under attack. Once a tax has survived a reasonable testing period, the investor has more assurance that it is a permanent part of the community's financial structure.

To cure some of the regressive characteristics of the property tax, a number of states have adopted so-called "circuit breaker" legislation, providing property tax relief related to the income and age characteristics of property owners. A tax relief program in Michigan, for example, provides that taxpayers 65 years and over with less than $3,000 annual income are entirely exempt from property taxes. To accomplish this objective, the states are restructuring their revenue systems with new taxes and using federal revenue-sharing funds.[10]

Departures from traditional revenue sources reduce the importance of some of the established yardsticks used in appraising the credit position of state or local governments. Because of differences in the income composition of individual communities, studies of their revenue-raising potential will vary in emphasis. Despite these differences, the following factors should be examined: sources of revenue, per capita revenue, the tax rate, the record of tax collections, and any pertinent tax limitations.

Sources of revenue. In the 1972-1973 fiscal year, state and local governments obtained their general revenues from three major categories: income, sales, and property taxes contributed 58.2 percent; governmental aid, chiefly from federal sources, produced 20.6 percent; and miscellaneous charges yielded 21.1 percent.[11]

Outstripping all other tax sources for the states was the general sales or gross receipts levy, which is applicable, with prescribed exceptions, to all types of goods, services, or gross income rather than to selected commodities and services. Property taxes comprise the single most important levy for municipalities, accounting for the bulk of all tax money raised by local governments to defray the costs of schools, police, fire protection, and other services. The sharp rise of these taxes has contributed to the exodus of industry from urban areas and has discouraged landlords from maintaining their properties, thereby accelerating the physical deterioration of cities. Moreover, the property tax is considered a regressive levy because it leans heavily upon residents of poor areas; as a result, they cannot support good school systems, which means that the children of low-income families receive a less satisfactory education. These factors have led cities to request massive financial support from their states, which, in turn, desire to share revenues with the federal government. The property tax has thus been described as an "outmoded levy,"[12] and state and local governments, in their quest for revenue sources, have increasingly resorted to other taxes, including those on income, amusements, and consumption.

The tax distributions of many areas do not conform to a standard pattern. Moreover, different forms of taxation have tended to come to the forefront over the years. These differences emphasize the importance of first ascertaining a community's source of income in order to determine what features to stress in the subsequent analysis.

Per capita revenue. Per capita revenue is the ratio of revenues to population. When confined to taxes, it indicates the relative contribution of each member of a community to operating and fixed expenses. Its size is limited by the population's income-paying ability. A high ratio, however, may be caused by factors, such as burdensome taxes, that are not truly descriptive of the community's wealth. Used by itself, the ratio may be misleading and must be interpreted in conjunction with the general economic picture of the community obtained from the overall analysis. As shown in Table 21-2, the figures for different states cover a wide range. for example, in fiscal 1972 the per capita revenue of New York was $608, while Ohio's was $329.

Tax rate. Assessed valuations include both real and personal property. Of these, real property is considerably the more important. The tax on real property is expressed in terms of a charge per $100 of assessed valuation. The basis of the valuation is commonly set at some stated percentage of the actual assessed value of the property. For this reason, the tax rate must be adjusted to a 100 percent valuation basis to permit valid comparisons. A tax rate of $3.00 per $100 assessed on a valuation base of 80 percent is equivalent to a tax rate of $3.75 per $100 on a valuation base of 100 percent.

Local conditions often change a community's ability to pay designated rates; thus, it is impractical to specify at what point a particular rate becomes onerous. An indication of the flexibility of these rates may be obtained from their trend over a period of time. A downward trend suggests that the local government will be able to raise taxes if circumstances require. Advancing rates mean that the community is moving toward the point beyond which further increases may induce neutralizing rises in unpaid taxes.

TABLE 21-2

Revenue of State Governments for Fiscal Years 1972

STATE	TOTAL AMOUNT (IN MILLIONS)	PER CAPITA*	STATE	TOTAL AMOUNT (IN MILLIONS)	PER CAPITA†
1 United States	$112,309	$ 475			
2 Alabama	1,707	433	27 Montana	465	539
3 Alaska	458	1,282	28 Nebraska	602	380
4 Arizona	1,076	485	29 Nevada	367	555
5 Arkansas	870	411	30 New Hampshire	388	352
6 California	13,730	567	31 New Jersey	3,502	393
7 Colorado	1,295	486	32 New Mexico	747	648
8 Connecticut	1,639	481	33 New York	12,795	608
9 Delaware	410	702	34 North Carolina	2,497	435
10 Florida	3,149	394	35 North Dakota	367	536
11 Georgia	2,178	428	36 Ohio	4,798	329
12 Hawaii	754	824	37 Oklahoma	1,331	482
13 Idaho	419	471	38 Oregon	1,291	456
14 Illinois	5,859	480	39 Pennsylvania	6,645	471
15 Indiana	2,069	365	40 Rhode Island	559	508
16 Iowa	1,393	423	41 South Carolina	1,210	415
17 Kansas	962	396	42 South Dakota	311	445
18 Kentucky	1,607	453	43 Tennessee	1,636	375
19 Louisiana	2,137	532	44 Texas	4,684	376
20 Maine	581	488	45 Utah	695	540
21 Maryland	2,093	479	46 Vermont	348	663
22 Massachusetts	3,175	504	47 Virginia	2,245	414
23 Michigan	5,473	516	48 Washington	2,370	560
24 Minnesota	2,336	553	49 West Virginia	1,108	527
25 Mississippi	1,192	473	50 Wisconsin	2,635	531
26 Missouri	1,885	362	51 Wyoming	266	676

*Includes liquor stores and insurance trust activities.

†Based on resident population as of July 1.

SOURCE: Bureau of the Census, ***Statistical Abstract of the United States:*** 1974, Washington, D.C.: U.S. Government Printing Office, 1974, p. 258.

Tax collection. The ability of a community to maintain a high rate of tax collections reflects favorably on both the level of its tax rates and the income-paying capacity of its population. As might be expected, when business is good this problem is not severe and tax delinquencies are low. As economic conditions deteriorate, however, the rate of delinquencies rises. A tax collection rate that is unusually sensitive to changing economic conditions lowers the caliber of a community's general obligations. A relatively stable rate is a constructive factor.

Tax limitations. In some instances, constitutional or statutory tax limitations hamper the revenue-raising ability of a civil government. If debt requirements are not specifically exempt from these restrictions and existing taxes prove insufficient to meet debt service payments, a government has several choices. It may amend these limitations, reduce its operating expenses, raise assessed valuations, or discover alternative tax sources. If it cannot take any of these steps or if they prove inadequate, default may be the outcome.

Recognition of the weakening influence of tax limitations on the caliber of a civil bond is shown in the New York Banking Law. This statute provides that savings banks in New York may not purchase obligations of any city, county, school district, or other municipality of any state other than New York unless the issuer has power to levy taxes on real property for payment of its bonds without limitation of rate or amount.

Special limitations may apply to different types of bonds. For example, a municipality may issue tax-anticipation notes, which, as the name implies, are securities designed to raise funds before future taxes, from which they will be paid, are received. New York City has used these obligations extensively to tide it over when revenue from taxes has been slow. The city's statutes require that the volume of outstanding tax-anticipation notes cannot exceed estimated real estate revenues over a certain period. In early 1975, New York was forced by a bank syndicate to cancel a proposed issue of $260 million of such securities. The reason offered by the syndicate was the city's inability at that time to meet the revenue test.[13]

Relative Size of a Community's Fixed-Charge Requirements

To evaluate the caliber of a civil bond, the community's revenue-raising ability must be compared with the size of its debt. The bonds of a prosperous community may not meet accepted investment standards if its debt drains off a substantial portion of the inhabitants' income for service requirements. Three measures of the debt burden of a community are suggested: (1) the ratio of debt service to operating expenses; (2) the ratio of net debt to assessed valuation; and (3) the per capita debt.

Ratio of debt service to operating expenses. The debt service requirements of a civil government comprise interest, principal payments on maturing issues, and sinking fund appropriations. Usually these payments rank with operating expenses as legal claims on the community. In some states, service payments are given legal precedence over operating expenses.

The ratio of debt service to operating and capital expenditures is a gauge of the pressure of the debt on the community's financial capacity. If the burden is heavy, a reduction in tax collection may necessitate an extreme sacrifice in operating expenses or capital improvements in order to maintain fixed-charge requirements. Continuation of this situation could lead to debt default. On the other hand, a low ratio makes it easier for a community to absorb increased tax delinquencies by adjusting expenses and capital improvements.

One of the difficulties with this measure is that the fraction of total expenditures undertaken by a state or local government but financed by the federal government varies from one state or locality to another. Two governments with the same ratio may have quite different fractions of their total revenue coming from federal subsidies or grants-in-aid. The more federal financing a civil government relies upon, the greater is its dependence on a revenue source over which it has little control.

Additionally, the difficulty with this measure may be compounded if the government has resorted to lease financing. The lease payments should be treated as debt service charges, but the payments may not be clearly identified.

Ratio of net debt to assessed valuation. We have mentioned that the property tax, despite its declining importance, is still the principal source of income for most city governments. Since this tax is based on the assessed value of real property, a commonly used gauge of a community's borrowing load is the ratio of net debt to assessed valuation.

The net debt refers to the total funded debt of the community, less amounts in the sinking fund and self-supporting debt (where service may be met by revenues from the properties financed). Conservative practice is further to adjust the net debt to take into account both underlying and overlapping debt. Underlying debt includes the obligations of smaller political units within the community; the charges on this debt are paid from taxes on the same property that serves as the basis of the community's taxes. Overlapping debt comprises the community's share of the debt of a larger political unit in which the community is located. This share is estimated by multiplying the net debt of the larger political unit by the ratio of the assessed valuation of the community's property to the assessed valuation of the property of the larger political unit. Typical additions to the net debt of a city are the underlying debt of school districts within the city and the overlapping debt of the county in which the city is located.

It is difficult to establish precise standards for the ratio of net debt to assessed valuation. Higher ratios are more justified in larger communities with relatively diversified and stable property values. The accuracy of the ratio also depends on assessment methods, which may vary substantially among political entities. In general, the overall net debt should not exceed 10 percent of estimated actual valuations.[14]

Such generalizations should, however, be treated with caution. A proper analysis of a community's debt burden includes the debt and operations of the self-sustaining undertakings of the community. The utilization of revenues from such operations to service revenue bonds may impair the general revenue-raising capacity of the community. If revenue bonds are included in the numerator, the assessed valuation loses some of its relevance for the denominator. Moreover, with the proliferation of authorities, the identification of the debt burden of a specific geographic area becomes increasingly complex.

Per capita debt. The per capita debt is calculated by dividing net debt by total population. The lower the resultant figure, the less the burden on each member of the community. For the 1972 fiscal year the average per capita debt of U.S. state and local governments was $888. Individual variations were great. Delaware had a per capita debt of $1,488 while the comparable figure for South Dakota was $219. Even among large cities the range was wide.[15]

In view of the breadth of the differences, the ratios must be considered in conjunction with other factors, such as the wealth of the community, trends in population, and the rate of industrial growth. Per capita debt may be compared specifically with per capita revenues to throw light on the relation between revenue-producing capacity and debt burden. A sharply rising per capita debt indicates that the investor should ascertain whether the community's volume of borrowing is outdistancing its rate of growth.

Other Factors

Other measurements of the quality of civil government obligations include the size of the community, the debt record, and the maturity of the bond as compared with the life of the improvement financed.

The size of a community does not necessarily indicate the quality of its indebtedness. But larger communities—for instance, those with populations of at least 50,000—are likely to have a greater diversification of industries and higher concentration of wealth than smaller political units. Moreover, available data will probably be more comprehensive for larger communities, thereby facilitating the analysis.

The default record of a government throws light on its previous willingness and ability to meet service payments. Long histories of successful debt liquidation reflect creditably on the caliber of an obligation. In this connection, the New York State Banking Law establishes default-free periods to govern the eligibility requirements of obligations of states and cities outside New York. The law provides that states must not have defaulted in payment of principal or interest for more than 90 days during the 10 years prior to the investment,[16] and that cities must not have defaulted for more than 120 days during the 25 years preceding the investment.[17]

It is also sound practice to buy a bond whose maturity is less than the life of the improvement. In the case of a general obligation, issuance of a bond with a longer maturity than the underlying capital equipment does not mean that the community will necessarily have difficulty in meeting its fixed requirements after the capital depreciation period expires. Nevertheless, making continued payments on an obligation for which there is no capital-goods offset is a drain on a community's finances. Furthermore, if the improvement has to be extended, the replacement may be financed with a new issue, so that the community may be servicing two debts.

Many investment analysts maintain that the most important information relative to the quality of a corporate security is information on the quality of management. In certain respects this is also true in the evaluation of tax-exempt obligations. Since governments in the United States are elected at periodic intervals, the quality of "management" cannot be determined in quite the same way as in the case of corporations. Nevertheless, although men and women come and go, the style in which a municipality is governed has some durability. The critically important thing which may prevent the finances of a municipality from getting out of hand is the care with which the expenditures are planned. It is therefore important to determine whether the local officials have adopted systems of program budgeting–or, as it is widely known, the planning, programming, and budgeting system (PPBS). Program budgeting does not produce magic. It creates no revenue where there was no revenue before. It does not make mistakes impossible. It does force upon the local administration a systematic consideration of the costs and benefits to be derived from each item in the capital program, and it does contribute to a more systematic comparison of the relative merits of the options available to the community. Thus, it helps avoid the kind of problem that confronted New York City in 1975, which was caused, at least in part, by careless budgeting and accounting, apparently under a series of mayors.

REVENUE BONDS

Revenue bonds are obligations issued by a governmental body for the purpose of acquiring, improving, or constructing a particular project to be operated in the public service, with the understanding that the revenues derived from its operations will be used to meet bond interest and principal requirements. Since a governmental body is the issuer, the bond may bear the government's name, but the bond need not have the government's backing. For example, the New York State Dormitory Authority issues revenue bonds for dormitory and educational facilities throughout the state; the New York State Housing Finance Agency issues revenue bonds for hospitals, mental institutions, and public buildings; the New York State Urban Development Corporation has issued revenue bonds for residential and civic projects. None of these bonds is a general obligation of the state, and their service requirements depend on the income received from the project financed.

A common thread underlying these issues was the desire to avoid a public vote on controversial new financing. In the first part of the 1960s, to make palatable the large volume of public housing issues then coming to the market, John Mitchell, a Wall Street bond attorney before he joined the Nixon administration, devised the so-called "moral obligation" bond. It included a commitment that if a deficit occurred in a reserve fund to meet debt service on the bonds, the governor would ask the legislature to make up the difference. There was no legal requirement that the legislature do so, but a moral obligation was presumed to exist.

In early 1975, New York's Urban Development Corporation (UDC), the country's largest public housing developer, defaulted on $105 million of notes and $30 million of bank borrowings. The agency had sold $1.1 billion of such bonds, and at least 12 other New York State agencies had a total of $6 billion in "moral obligation" bonds outstanding. Moreover, public authorities in about 30 states, following New York's lead, had used this type of bond to raise funds to build housing, schools, hospitals, and other special projects. The UDC default not only had repercussions throughout this area but also cast a pall over the entire municipal bond market.[18] Eventually, the default was cured by a combination of commercial bank and state loans, and an agency was created to issue bonds to repay the bank loans. Despite the ability of UDC to free itself of impending financial difficulties, unease in the municipal market continued, as investors viewed the UDC episode and New York City's continued financial plight as signs of vulnerability in municipal securities.

Uses of Revenue Bonds

These bonds are employed by states, political subdivisions of states, and specially created governmental instrumentalities, such as boards, commissions, and authorities. The types of project financed include water, electric power, turnpike, bridge, terminal, educational, airport, recreational, and sewer facilities. State highway bonds, payable from gasoline taxes or motor vehicle fees, are often included among revenue bonds, despite the fact that the source of payment is a tax rather than a charge based on service. The reason for this classification is that these bonds are sold for the purpose of road construction or improvement and are financed by persons using the road.

The increasing popularity of revenue bonds is reflected in their expanded use. Between 1953 and 1973 the amount of these obligations increased 6.3 times, and in 1973 they accounted for 43.67 percent of the total state and local long-term issues.[19] This growth may be ascribed to four principal reasons: (1) a more general acceptance of the principle that governmental burdens should be apportioned on the basis of benefits received; (2) the high level of property taxes, which forces communities to discover alternative means of financing public improvements without tax increases; (3) imposition of municipal debt restrictions, which necessitates raising local funds without incurring debt chargeable to public revenues; (4) the growing vigor with which local governments are entering the public service field.

Evaluation

Revenue bonds are intended to be self-liquidating. Presumably the projects financed are initiated after careful study. If the financing has been properly planned, there is little difficulty in meeting interest and retiring the issue prior to the termination of the life of the project. These bonds often have excellent records of continued payments and may be accorded high credit ratings. On the other hand, inadequate planning may lead to servicing difficulties and poorly rated issues.

The properties serving as the basis of a revenue bond must be economically self-supporting if service requirements are to be met; rates charged users are established in relation to the service requirements of the obligation. Even though a project is endowed with public interest, the local government is not likely to provide aid toward meeting its contractual liabilities. For this reason, the analysis of a revenue bond resembles more closely the analysis of a private corporate obligation than that of a local government issue.

Several distinct characteristics of revenue bonds may be noted. First, the number of times that fixed charges are covered is less significant than the consistency of earnings, because the rates of a public project are intended to permit payment of fixed charges but not to produce a wide margin of coverage. Net earnings 1.75 times greater than annual interest requirements therefore are considered "respectable" coverage for revenue bonds.[20] Second, many public revenue bonds are secured by revenues only, and generally no mortgage is placed on the physical properties. An asset pledge would be of little practical consequence, since the courts are reluctant to permit attachment of public property. Finally, unlike the bonds of a typical private corporation, revenue bonds may have a principal value initially approximating that of the underlying assets, because public property is not usually financed by equity funds. Over a period of time the net asset coverage rises as the bonds are retired.

The investor must pay attention to certain provisions of the bond indenture, authorizing resolution, or act that establishes the responsibilities of the issuer. Of particular significance are the rate stipulations and the order of application of revenues. Rates must be sufficient to cover operating expenses, depreciation, and debt service, as well as to permit the creation of a reserve for a margin of safety. Engineers' estimates of projected revenues and costs provide some indications of future operations. The investor must be aware of any prior-ranking obligations and of the issuer's authority actually to issue any securities of this sort. It is also important that safeguards exist against construction of competing projects. Investors might justifiably hesitate to purchase bonds issued to build a bridge if a competing span is likely to be erected in the vicinity. Revenue bonds may also have governmental backing, through a subsidy by a state or city, for example, or a provision for the legislature to vote to make up any deficiencies. The support features of a particular issue must be judged on their own investment merits.

Until the summer of 1974, the aforementioned UDC bonds were popular and were bought by major banks. The combination of inflationary trends in the housing industry, a fading economy, and managerial problems apparently led to the agency's difficulties. The sharp reversal in its fortunes and the questionable value of the "moral obligation" suggest the difficulty of assessing the varied factors that affect the quality of revenue bonds.

SPECIAL ASSESSMENT BONDS

Special assessment issues are designed to finance specific property improvements and may be outside the statutory debt limit. Income to service these bonds comes from levies on the property subject to improvement. These assessments are made without consideration of the benefits to users. If property owners do not pay their assessments, collection may be enforced through sale of the property in accordance with state laws. Special assessment bonds are issued to finance sewers, sidewalks, streets, and similar improvements.

The caliber of these bonds depends on the character of the neighborhood and the likelihood that property values will be maintained at a sufficiently high level to support bond charges. Because the revenue used to service special assessment bonds is derived from a specific section of property, the bonds are not considered equal in quality to general obligations. Sometimes, however, the local government agrees to make up any deficit in the taxes from which the special assessment bonds are primarily paid. In these cases, the bonds may assume the status of general obligations, depending on the nature of the agreement.

TAX DISTRICT OBLIGATIONS

A specialized form of state political subdivision is the *tax district.* These districts do not have the generalized powers of cities or towns that are incorporated to serve the needs of a local population. Tax districts are usually established to perform a specific function, such as operating schools, constructing roads, or irrigating agricultural areas. The districts may be carved out of a portion of a city, may be coterminous with the city, or may embrace several cities. Revenue to service the bonds issued by tax districts is obtained from levies against property within the district. As we have seen, the same property may be subject to several layers of taxation.

The investment position of tax district bonds depends on the purpose for which the bonds are issued, the value of the properties in the district, and the outlook for the section. The special character of these bonds lowers their investment caliber. Obligations of school districts have favorable records; the history of irrigation, drainage, and road district bonds has been less satisfactory.

LOCAL HOUSING AUTHORITY ISSUES

Under the United States Housing Act of 1937, as amended, the federal government is empowered to provide financial assistance to help states and their political subdivisions to carry out an extensive program of constructing low-cost multiple-unit housing for low-income families.[21] The responsibility for the administration of this program is placed with the Department of Housing and Urban Development (HUD). This agency discharges its responsibilities under the act by means of financial assistance contracts with local housing authorities created by cities, counties, and other specified political subdivisions in accordance with state law.

Local housing authorities are authorized to borrow money to implement their slum clearance programs. For this purpose, the various authorities have issued three types of bonds: (1) those dependent on assistance contracts with a state; (2) those directly guaranteed or assumed by a state or local government; and (3) those issued under annual contributional contracts with HUD.

The quality of the first two types of obligations is directly related to the credit rating of the sponsoring state or local government. Most local housing authority financing is now confined to obligations issued under contracts prescribed in the 1937 Housing Act. These obligations may take the form of short-term project notes and long-term bonds.

The agreement underlying the project notes provides that the U.S. government will make a loan to the local authority in an amount sufficient to pay principal and interest on the notes to maturity. Proceeds of the project notes are used to pay the development costs of a project or to refund outstanding notes.

The local authority ordinarily obtains permanent financing for low-rent housing projects by offering long-term bonds at or near the time when construction or modernization of the project is near completion. These bonds are secured by an annual pledge of net rental revenues of the local housing authority and by an annual contribution contract which provides annual federal contributions that are sufficient to meet principal and interest on the outstanding bonds. The act also strengthens the pledge of the U.S. government to continue payments despite any contractual breach by a local authority. In view of this firm provision, the bonds are considered of a high caliber.

HUD also administers the program of federal financial assistance to local public agencies, which issue notes to finance slum clearance and urban redevelopment and renewal projects as authorized by the Housing Act of 1949, as amended. Although the notes are obligations of the local public agencies, they are secured by a pledge of the proceeds of loans which the U.S. government makes pursuant to loan and grant contracts with a local public agency. A payment agreement obligates the federal government to pay principal and interest of such obligations at maturity.

All local authority project notes and bonds and urban renewal project notes are exempt from federal income taxes.

SUMMARY

The term "municipal bond" includes the obligations of states, political subdivisions of states, local housing authorities, and U.S. insular possessions. These securities are usually issued in serial form, with specified amounts falling due each year. While the issuers of these bonds are exempt from registration under the federal securities laws, the Securities Acts Amendments of 1975 extended the basic coverage of the Exchange Act to securities firms that underwrite and trade these bonds.

The prime attraction of municipal obligations lies in their privileged tax status. Interest is exempt from federal income taxes, and most states do not tax interest on their own obligations. The exemption privilege has increasingly come under attack, and any rescinding of this privilege would have a severe influence on the prices of the bonds affected. Thus far, however, efforts to bring about repeal have been unsuccessful.

An issuing government pledges its full faith and credit to support the service payments of its direct or general obligations. Accordingly, the prime consideration in evaluating such obligations is the ability of the government to maintain interest and principal payments in the face of economic adversity. Ordinarily, the major criteria for assessing this ability are the community's basic economic strength, its revenue-raising potential, and the relative magnitude of its fixed-charge requirements.

In contrast to general obligations, the interest and principal of revenue bonds are payable from the income produced by a specific project. Even though a project is endowed with public interest, a local government may not provide aid toward meeting that project's contractual liabilities. The 1975 default of New York's Urban Development Corporation, the country's largest public housing developer, is a grim illustration of this fact. Accordingly, the type of analysis applied to a revenue bond resembles more closely that used for a corporate obligation than for a local government issue.

Various specialized issues are also classified as municipal bonds. Special assessment issues are designed to finance specific property improvements; their caliber depends on the character of the neighborhood and the likelihood that property values will be maintained. Tax districts sell bonds to obtain funds to perform specific functions, such as operating schools, constructing roads, or irrigating agricultural areas. The investment position of these bonds depends on the purpose for which they were issued, the value of the properties in the district, and the outlook for the section. Local housing authorities, permitted to borrow money to implement slum clearance programs, have issued various types of bonds. The most prominent, in effect, have the backing of the federal government and therefore are considered of high caliber.

Because of the complexity of analyzing municipal bonds, the ratings assigned by the major services have a particularly important influence on the prices of these issues.

CHAPTER 22

Preferred Stock Analysis

In the previous chapters, we examined those instances in which the bond form is an important analytic consideration. This discussion provides the background for an evaluation of preferred stock, whose hybrid form creates its own special problems.

CHARACTERISTICS OF PREFERRED STOCK

Unless specifically prevented by law or charter, the shareholders of a corporation may endow one class of stock with preference over others. In order to provide the corporation with financing flexibility, a common procedure is for the shareholders to approve an issue of preferred stock that management is contemplating for possible future use. For example, the stockholders of the Carnation Co., at a special meeting in 1972, authorized 2 million shares of a new class of preferred stock without par value, but as of December 1974 no such shares were outstanding. The expression *preferred stock* is reserved for the class of stock on which dividends must be paid at a designated rate, within the framework of appropriate state law, before any distributions are made to common stockholders, and which has priority as to assets over the common stock in the event of dissolution of the corporation. In addition to these two basic features, the board of directors may establish various other attributes, such as voting rights, redemption prices, sinking funds, conversion privileges, and liquidation rights.

Use of preferred stock declined significantly with the rise in the corporate tax rate. Since preferred stock dividends are not deductible and interest payments are, many companies shifted their financing in favor of debt issues. To some extent, this tendency has been modified by the fact that corporate investors can deduct, for tax purposes, 85 percent of the dividends they receive. Indicative of the renewed interest in preferred stock is the growth in the number of companies that report one class of preferred in their capital structures and the shrinkage in the number of companies that have no preferred stock. This change is shown in Table 22-1.

TABLE 22-1

Changing Capital Structures of Corporations, 1969-1972

COMPANIES OFFERING COMMON STOCK WITH:	1972	1971	1970	1969
No preferred stock	164	164	165	197
One class of preferred stock	327	309	314	268
Two classes of preferred stock	81	92	88	98
Three or more classes of preferred stock	28	35	33	37
Total	600	600	600	600

SOURCE: American Institute of Certified Public Accountants, ***Accounting Trends and Techniques*** (New York, 1973), p. 180. Copyright 1973 by the American Institute of Certified Public Accountants, Inc. Reprinted by permission.

A variant that has gained some popularity is the convertible preferred. A large number of these issues came into being through tax laws that permit the consummation of an acquisition or merger by an exchange of voting stock without subjecting the selling stockholders to either ordinary or capital gains taxes. Acquiring corporations found it convenient, as a consequence, to use a voting convertible as a medium of exchange.[1] This approach is limited, however, by the adoption of accounting rules which, among other things, prescribe pooling as a method of accounting for mergers or combinations that involve only the exchange of common stock. (See p. 273 for a discussion of pooling.)

Despite this limitation, convertible preferred stock is a useful financing vehicle, since it permits a corporation to finance an operation at a fixed rate during its developmental period and then to set the stage for a shift into common stock as expanding earnings justify such a change. The shift may come about through market forces, as rising common stock prices and dividend payments reflect the company's improving position. Or the company may force conversion by calling the preferred if the issue sells above its redemption price as a result of a rise in the price of the common stock into which it is convertible. When Hygrade Food Products wanted to encourage conversion in order to build up the common stock segment of its capital structure, the company adopted the unusual procedure of offering an additional payment of $8 cash for each share of preferred stock converted between December 9, 1971, and January 11, 1972.

Preferred Stock Nomenclature

Although there are two distinct types of stocks, common and preferred, different classes of common may exist with no preference as to dividends. Home Oil, for example, has a class A that is identical to class B except for voting rights. In other instances, a class A stock may resemble a preferred more closely than a common issue; the Curtiss-Wright class A, for example, is entitled to $2 noncumulative annual dividends prior to any payments to the common stock.

A company may also have outstanding preferred stock of different series that could have varying characteristics. Long Island Lighting, for example, has 11 series of preferred stock, bearing dividend rates that range from 4.25 percent to 8.40 percent; additionally, the 5.75 percent Series I issue is convertible. On the other hand, W. R. Grace has three series of $100 par preferred outstanding: the 6 percent issue is cumulative and has 80 votes per share; the 8 percent, class A issue is cumulative and has 8 votes per share; and the 8 percent, class B issue is noncumulative and has 8 votes per share. The company's certificate of incorporation also authorizes a class C issue, without par value. While the required payments on preferred stock may be in odd amounts, the prescribed rates usually do not vary by less than ¼ of 1 percent. Moreover, as indicated in Table 22-1, the tendency has been for a decline in complex capital structures with several classes of preferred stock.

The title of a stock may describe it inadequately. A complete description of its terms is found in the corporate charter and resolutions of the board of directors. For most investors, however, reference to these sources is both impractical and unnecessary. They may obtain suitable summaries of the major features of a security from more convenient sources, such as the manuals of the financial services and the company's prospectuses and listing statements.

Three distinctive aspects of preferred stock merit comment because of the influence they may exert on its market price: cumulative features, protective provisions, and the fixed retirement terms. Preferred stocks occasionally have special dividend features, such as participating in further distributions after the stipulated dividend has been paid. Borden, for example, has a small Series A preferred that has an interesting feature of this sort; not only is the issue convertible but it is also entitled to receive annually, until January 14, 1976, cumulative dividends per share of one-half the per share common stock dividend or 60 cents, whichever is greater. Thereafter, the dividend is determined by the board of directors, but in no event is it less than 60 cents per share. The methods of analyzing these provisions are discussed in the chapter on privileged securities.

Cumulative Provision

As in the case of common stock, authority for disbursement of preferred dividends rests with the board of directors, whose decision must conform to state statutes. In most instances, courts have recognized the rights of directors to withhold preferred dividends despite the availability of earnings as long as the decision appears to reflect the directors' sincere belief that suspension of payments is in the corporation's best interests.

This reliance on the decision of directors is indicated in the results of two old but important decisions that are worth restating. In 1949, Illinois Central preferred stockholders brought suit, claiming dividends for the years 1937 through 1947. The stockholders contended that the railroad had earned dividends in each of these 11 years by a satisfactory margin and that payment was mandatory even though the stock was noncumulative. The federal court dismissed this claim, declaring that the directors "acted in their best judgment, indeed seeking financial advice from other experts in the field of finance in order to make their conclusions doubly certain."[2]

The courts displayed equal reluctance to halt payment of dividends declared by directors in good faith. In 1948 a holder of the $4.00 preferred stock of Standard Gas & Electric sought an injunction to restrain the company from paying dividends to the prior preferred stockholders on the ground that payment would be out of capital, thereby violating Delaware law. In denying the injunction, it was held that "this court cannot substitute either plaintiff's or its own opinion of value for that reached by the directors [who] must be given reasonable latitude in ascertaining value."[3]

To counterbalance this freedom, corporate charters ordinarily provide that preferred stock must be cumulative. This feature means that if the designated rate is not paid in any one year, the deficiency accumulates and must be fully cleared prior to any common dividend distributions. In the case of noncumulative preferred stocks, dividends do not accumulate even though earnings were available in the years in which payments were skipped. The Great Western United Corp. $1.88 cumulative preferred is an unusual issue in that payment of dividends is mandatory if there is a surplus available; this requirement is in contrast to the company's $3.00 serial convertible preferred, on which, like most issues, payments are within the discretion of the board of directors.

During periods of business prosperity the cumulative feature is not important. Corporations are then able to pay dividends regularly, and preferred stocks with accumulations are rare. When the economy slips into a recession, corporations are more likely to have to defer payments on their preferred stocks. In this event, without protection of the cumulative feature the investor could probably never recover the value of the lapsed payments, even during subsequent years of revival.

Dividend arrearages may mount to high levels. Cash distributions required to eliminate these accumulations may become prohibitively large. Hence, corporations often do not clear substantial arrearages by cash disbursements; instead, they find it expedient to provide for these accruals through capital adjustments. These plans usually involve either a combination offer of cash and securities in settlement of the arrears, or a complete exchange of the old preferred plus accumulations for new common stock or a combination of cash and securities. For example, on January 12, 1973, the shareholders of ASG Industries approved a plan of recapitalization which amended the certificate of incorporation to eliminate the 5 percent cumulative preferred stock, including dividend arrearages of $2.1 million, by reclassifying each share of preferred into three shares of common stock.

The bundle of new issues received in the exchange often has substantial value. Therefore, inclusion of the cumulative feature in a preferred stock may add tangibly to the value of the issue. This benefit could be especially important for marginal companies and those engaged in highly cyclical industries, in which earnings are sensitive to changing economic conditions.

Protective Features

The preferred stock is essentially a weak instrument. It possesses neither the legal force of a bond, to help in securing regular dividend payments, nor the profit potentialities of common stock. To offset such inherent inadequacies, corporations often insert special provisions in their charters.

Protective features may include the voting privilege on default of a specified number of dividend payments, the right to approve issuance of any bond or prior-ranking preferred stock, and restrictions on payment of common stock dividends. These restrictions often become operative when the capital structure is overburdened by a large funded debt or when payment would reduce current assets below a designated level. The preferred stock restrictions may be similar to those applicable to the agreements underlying the company's bonds and bank notes. The terms of the Reynolds Metals preferred provide that dividends on common stock may not be paid during any period when the sinking fund for the preferred may be in default. These protective features cannot of themselves raise an issue from the medium to the top-quality bracket. They do—particularly in the case of marginal companies—exert pressure on management to maintain preferred dividend payments whenever economically possible, help to produce sound capitalizations, and provide some assurance that the capital structure will not be materially altered to the detriment of the preferred stockholder.

Fixed Retirement Terms

The fixed retirement terms of bonds may be oppressive to a company if they mature during unfavorable business conditions. Complete elimination of this responsibility, however, even though it creates additional pressures, is not necessarily desirable. Static capital structures in an economic era marked by abrupt changes could lead to impairment of a corporation's financial condition. The set maturities of bonds, with the associated compulsion of undertaking periodic payments to facilitate eventual principal retirements, create an automatic means of adjusting capital structures to the economic environment.

Management's need to retain control over a corporation's capitalization is recognized in present-day charters. These ordinarily permit the preferred stock, which usually has no specified due date, to be eliminated through call or sinking funds. Charters also establish the prices at which preferred stock may be retired in the event of the corporation's voluntary or involuntary dissolution.

Redemption

The redemption privilege permits a corporation to take advantage of declining interest rates to substitute issues that pay lower dividends for those bearing high rates.[4] In calling a stock, the corporation usually must provide the holder with some advance notice. Redemption prices are commonly above issue price, to afford the owner some compensation for retirement of an issue that he may desire to retain. A premium as high as 10 percent, which is gradually reduced over a period of time, is not unusual.

During periods of declining interest rates, the call feature places a ceiling on the market value of a stock. Should the price rise materially above its redemption level, the corporation would be in a position to refund the stock at a lower dividend rate. Barring existence of some special privilege, such as a conversion feature, the market value will rarely exceed the redemption price by more than a narrow margin.

A small number of noncallable preferred stocks are still outstanding. For the most part, they represent strong issues that were distributed during periods of high interest rates and have been outstanding for long periods of time. Despite their good quality, their prices have experienced wide swings, reflecting changing interest rate relationships. Thus, the Liggett & Myers 7 percent preferred, which once sold as high as 210½ and still commanded a premium price of 164½ in 1965, hit a low of about 74 in 1975. To avoid having to pay generous dividends during periods of low interest rates, most corporations now make their preferred callable for retirement. The SEC recognizes that noncallable preferred stocks or bonds may prevent corporations from taking advantage of low interest rates in raising capital. For this reason, it has criticized issuance of noncallable senior securities and has indicated that it will insist that corporations try to eliminate this undesirable feature from future financing.

In recent years, new offerings have customarily carried a five-year and sometimes even a ten-year protection against refunding at a lower interest or dividend rate. This feature is intended to make the shares more palatable to investors, who were apprehensive that corporations would otherwise take such steps in the event interest rates declined.

Sinking Fund

Modern preferred issues often offset the lack of a fixed maturity date by including provisions for a sinking fund. Terms of these funds may differ. They may include specified annual dollar amounts or numbers of shares, application of a designated percentage to the number of outstanding shares or to the company's net earnings, or a combination of these methods. A typical provision calls for an amount equal to 3 percent of the greatest number of shares previously issued; a retirement program that annually eliminates less than 3 percent of an issue is inadequate. Another innovation appearing in 1974 was the creation of a preferred stock with an accelerated sinking fund pattern designed to retire the security within ten years of issuance. This innovation reflected investors' reluctance at that time to buy long-term preferred stocks because of the uncertainties of the future.

To provide financing flexibility, authority is likely to be provided for the sinking fund to operate through call, which may be at a level that is below optional redemption, or through open-market purchases.

Voluntary vs. Involuntary Retirement

Corporate charters ordinarily provide that preferred stockholders will receive a higher price in the event of voluntary dissolution than in the event of involuntary dissolution. The differential may be very sharp. For example, the $2.40 preferred stock issue of Sybron Corp. is redeemable at the option of the corporation after November 1, 1973, at $70 per share plus accrued dividends. The voluntary liquidation price is also set at $70, but in the case of involuntary liquidation the price is $22 per share. Similarly, the Ingersoll-Rand $2.35 preference stock is redeemable after January 2, 1974, at $47.50 per share plus accrued dividends, and it is entitled to the same price on voluntary liquidation. In the event of involuntary liquidation, however, the price drops to $20 per share. The differential is intended to deter a corporation from voluntarily dissolving to eliminate an issue and then reorganizing. Management might conceivably be tempted to take this step if the voluntary call price was very low. However, corporations do not customarily liquidate, and a premium for voluntary dissolution is not usually important.

The Various Stated Values

When a corporation issues a preferred stock, it must be carried in the financial statement at a specified value; this is likely to be a technical figure with little legal significance. Various redemption prices will also be provided, but there may be little relationship among these various levels. For example, the Engelhard Minerals & Chemicals Corp. $4.25 cumulative convertible preferred stock has an assigned value of $6.18 per share, equivalent to the par value of the 6.18 shares of common stock into which each share of preferred is convertible. The preferred stock is also redeemable at the company's option on or after September 27, 1974, at $104.25 per share the first year, reduced by 85 cents per share in each of the following five years. In the event of liquidation, dissolution, or winding up of business, holders of the preferred stock are entitled to receive $60 per share, plus accrued dividends, out of available distributable assets before any distribution is made to common shareholders.

EVALUATION OF PREFERRED STOCKS

Since the preferred is a fixed-income security, it is subject to the same analytic principles as a bond, except for differences necessitated by the absence of any legal authority to compel regular dividend payments and the omission of a definite maturity. Accordingly, the newer analytic methods for bonds are also applicable to preferred stocks. However, as indicated previously, these approaches are complex, and simpler tools are therefore employed by the individual investor. He or she would ordinarily use the fixed-charge coverage and capitalization ratio tests, as well as measures of size and financial strength.

Application of the Fixed-Charge Coverage Test to Preferred Stock

The most important measure of the quality of a security is the ability of the issuing corporation to continue interest or dividend payments. To test ability to meet bond interest, the fixed-charge coverage test should be used. To gauge the protection of common stock dividend disbursements, earnings per share of common stock are calculated.

The shortcomings inherent in the use of per share earnings data make it advisable, as in the case of a bond, to use the fixed-charge coverage test to gauge the earnings protection of a preferred stock. In applying this test, it is necessary to use the cumulative rather than the overall method. In effect, to make the calculation, the investor first compares a corporation's fixed charges arising from its funded debt with the earnings available for fixed charges. Pretax earnings needed for preferred dividends are added to fixed-charge requirements, and this total is compared with available pretax earnings. If the corporation has several classes of preferred stock with different priorities, the pretax earnings requirements are cumulated for each class and compared with pretax earnings available for fixed charges.

It is desirable to use the cumulative method in analyzing a preferred stock because dividends are not fixed charges. Corporations can and often do maintain interest payments while preferred dividends are in arrears. Similarly, a corporation may, without exposing itself to legal proceedings, pay dividends on a senior preferred and suspend disbursements on its junior issue.

Use of the fixed-charge coverage method to calculate the earnings protection on preferred dividends reduces the exaggerated percentage fluctuations that occur when the per share data are employed. When bond and preferred dividend charges are cumulated, there is no possibility that the earnings protection of a junior security can exceed that of a senior issue. These results are logical. Within a corporation, bond interest payments are necessarily more secure than first preferred dividends, which must be paid prior to any disbursement on the second preferred stock.

The question sometimes is raised as to whether indicated common stock dividends should be included in the cumulative figure for payment requirements. The reason advanced for doing so is that sometimes corporations may pay dividends on the preferred because of a desire to maintain common stock distributions. Thus, if the payment of a preferred dividend will leave the corporation unable to pay the common dividend, the organization may choose to pay neither. We do not believe this procedure advisable. Where the preferred is cumulative, the corporation does not have the alleged motivation for withholding the preferred dividend. Furthermore, dividends on common stock are not prescribed in any contractual arrangement and may vary considerably. Accordingly, it is difficult to determine the level of future distributions, and they do not belong in any fixed-charge coverage test. At best, the pressure to maintain common payments may be considered a qualitative factor in judging the underlying strength of the preferred issue.

Treatment of income taxes. When a corporation has no debt, aftertax earnings may be used to calculate the dividend coverage of preferred stocks. When the senior segment of a corporation has both bonds and preferred shares outstanding, the appropriate procedure is not so clear-cut. It is important that the investor recognize the implications of these different approaches.

Let us consider three industrial corporations, each of which must pay $100,000 of senior charges. Corporation *A* has only bond interest and Corporation *B* only preferred dividends, whereas the senior requirements of Corporation *C* comprise $80,000 of bond interest and $20,000 of preferred dividends. Assuming an income tax rate of 50 percent, the distributions of earnings and charges are shown in Table 22-2, as well as the fixed-charge coverage of the bonds and preferred stock on an aftertax basis.

TABLE 22-2

Calculation of Bond and Preferred Stock Fixed-Charge Coverage

ACCOUNT	CORPORATION A	CORPORATION B	CORPORATION C
Income available for fixed charges	$800,000	$1,600,000	$1,600,000
Bond interest	100,000	—	80,000
Income after bond interest	700,000	1,600,000	1,520,000
Income taxes (50%)	350,000	800,000	760,000
Net income for preferred stock	350,000	800,000	760,000
Preferred dividends	—	100,000	20,000
Net income for common stock	350,000	700,000	740,000
Bond fixed-charge coverage	8.0 times	—	20.0 times
Preferred fixed-charge coverage	—	8.0 times	—
Preferred fixed-charge coverage (adjusted)	—	—	13.3 times

Corporation *A* covers its bond interest 8 times prior to any deductions for taxes. The income available for fixed charges of Corporation *B* is twice that of Corporation *A*, but taxes absorb a large portion of the income of *B*, yielding a preferred dividend coverage of 8 times. The similarity of coverage in the face of the vast difference in gross earnings is a striking indication of the influence of a corporation's capitalization on the quality of its securities. The requirement that aftertax earnings must cover preferred dividends by the same margin by which earnings prior to taxes cover bond interest means that the earnings of the first company must exceed those of the second by an amount sufficient to take care of income taxes.

Corporation *C* has $760,000 net income for preferred dividends. This amount is 38 times greater than its preferred dividend requirements of $20,000, but the indicated coverage is clearly too high, since the interest coverage on the bonds is only 20 times. The calculation illustrates the deceptive aspects of the prior-deduction method of determining fixed-charge coverage. Another way to determine net income available for the preferred fixed charges might be to add bond interest to net income after taxes. In the case of Corporation *C*, this sum yields $840,000, which, compared with the aggregate of bond interest and preferred dividends, yields a coverage of 8.4 times. This figure is inaccurate because it employs net income after taxes but includes bond interest (properly deductible before taxes) in the preferred fixed-charge requirements. When taxes and interest are high, the distortion may be serious.

This shrinkage is also misleading. If we consider interest alone, coverage is twenty times. The inclusion of the small preferred dividend requirements should not lead to so abrupt a drop in coverage. Since bond interest comprises 80 percent of fixed charges, the preferred coverage clearly should be closer to that of the bond. One method of obtaining more realistic results is to use income available for fixed charges before income taxes. The lack of tax savings implicit in the existence of preferred stock, rather than bonds, may then be taken into account by increasing preferred dividends by the amount required to provide the total income which would cover both taxes and preferred dividends. This may be done by dividing preferred dividends by the expression (1 – tax rate).[5] In the case of Corporation *C*, preferred dividends are raised to $40,000, which brings total charges to $120,000. This figure is divided into income available for charges before taxes to give an overall coverage of 13.3 times, which is more in line with the bond interest coverage alone. The SEC has indicated that in computing the combined ratio of fixed charges and preferred dividend requirements, the preferred dividends should be "grossed up" for the tax effect as described above.

In calculating the fixed-charge coverage of bonds, there are some grounds for excluding sinking fund payments, even though they are a contractual requirement. So long as interest payments are maintained, bondholders are not likely to enforce these payments if such a step would drive the corporation into bankruptcy. The corporation, however, is likely to meet its sinking fund requirements (or at least a substantial portion of them) on the bonds, even though such payments limit the payment of preferred dividends. Accordingly, recognition should be given to sinking fund requirements in determining the fixed-charge coverage of preferred stock; since sinking fund payments are not deductible for tax purposes, they must be stepped up by the (1 – tax rate) factor.

El Paso Natural Gas: an example of the calculation of preferred fixed-charge coverage. The capital structure of the El Paso Natural Gas Co. (now called El Paso Co.), a leading public utility, is displayed in Table 22-3. As of December 31, 1973, the company not only had outstanding long-term debt but also had both senior and junior cumulative preferred stock. The calculation of the coverage is displayed in Table 22-4. The debt, first preferred, and second preferred coverages are .86, .80, and .80, respectively; the amount of second preferred outstanding is too small to change the coverage. In estimating these coverages, we adjusted the sinking fund and the dividend payments for taxes. As noted, these are not deductible items. For each dollar of such charges the company must earn enough before taxes to have $1 left over after taxes—that is, it must earn $1.92 = $1/(1 – 0.48).

Inadequacies of Per Share Earnings Data for Preferred Stock

The investor may still find reports of preferred stock earnings per share for the purpose of measuring a corporation's capacity to pay preferred dividends. If the company has both a senior and a junior preferred in its capital structure, the earnings per share of the senior stock are first reported; the dividend requirements of the senior issue are deducted from the company's net income; and the earnings per share of the junior stock are then calculated by dividing the net income available for the junior preferred by the number of junior shares outstanding.

This method has several serious shortcomings. The per share figures for a preferred stock in themselves do not have much meaning. The size of the per share earnings does not indicate the amount of dividends that will be paid, since preferred dividends are limited to a specific rate. Furthermore, such comparisons of per share earnings with per share dividend requirements are distorted when a corporation has both bonds and preferred stock outstanding. The calculations in Table 22-5 are quite misleading. The per share earnings of the second preferred are an unbelievably whopping but substantially meaningless –$831.59. Dividends were nevertheless paid. These figures reflect the deceptive influence of the prior-deduction method when the junior issue is small. In fact, as shown in Table 22-4, the company is almost able to cover its overall bond interest, sinking fund payments, and preferred dividend requirements out of income from continuing operations. However, when income from operations divested or to be divested and extraordinary items

TABLE 22-3

Capitalization of El Paso Natural Gas Co., December 31, 1973

CAPITALIZATION	AS REPORTED	CLOSING PRICE	AMOUNT (IN THOUSANDS)	PERCENTAGE OF TOTAL CAPITAL	CUMULATIVE PERCENTAGE
Long-term debt	$877,628,000	*	$877,628	62.31	99.9
$5\frac{1}{8}$ cumulative preferred stock ($100 par)	555,000 shs.	*	55,500	3.94	
$10\frac{3}{4}$ cumulative preferred stock ($100 par)	250,000 shs.	*	25,000	1.77	37.68
$8\frac{1}{4}$ cumulative preferred stock ($100 par)	230,000 shs.	*	23,000	1.63	
$5 second preferred stock (no par; stated value $100)	17,214 shs.†	*	1,721	.12	30.34
Common stock	27,909,669 shs.	$15.25‡	425,622†	30.22	30.22

* Book value.

† After deducting 3,336 treasury shares.

‡ Market value (average of high and low for the fourth quarter of 1973).

NOTE: The name of the company was changed to El Paso Co. after merger in June 1974 of wholly owned E G Inc. into the El Paso Natural Gas Co.

SOURCE: El Paso Natural Gas Company, ***Annual Report***, 1974.

TABLE 22-4

Illustration of Calculation of Preferred Fixed-Charge Coverage of El Paso Natural Gas Co., for Period Ending December 31, 1973

		AMOUNT (IN THOUSANDS)	COVERAGE
Net Income*†		$ 53,094	
Interest and debt expense		69,184	
Federal income tax (net of investment credit)		36,105	
Less minority interest in income of subsidiaries		(–958)	
Earnings before interest and taxes (EBIT)		157,425	
Fixed charges adjusted for taxes:			
Interest and debt expense	$ 69,184		
Interest coverage (157,425/69,184) =			2.28
Estimated sinking fund payments (59,003/0.52)‡	113,467		
Total debt charges		182,651	
Debt fixed-charge coverage (157,425/182,651) =			.86
Dividend on first preferred (7,448/0.52)§		14,323	
Total debt and first preferred charges		196,974	
Total debt and first preferred charge coverage (157,425/196,974) =			.80
Dividend on second preferred (94/0.52)§		181	
Total debt and preferred charges		197,055	
Total debt and preferred charge coverage (157,425/197,055) =			.80

*Includes $822,000 allowance for funds used during construction. As permitted by the Federal Power Commission Uniform Systems of Accounts, the company capitalizes the cost of funds used to finance construction expenditures and reports it as this item. Inclusion of the amount in net earnings available for fixed charges seems appropriate so long as this source of nonoperating income is minor.

†Does not include income from operations divested or to be divested or extraordinary items.

‡Current maturities of long-term debt. The statutory tax rate of 0.48 is used in determining the step-up factor (1–0.48).

§The company reported total cash dividends of $7,542,000 on preferred stock in 1973.

NOTE: The name of the company was changed to El Paso Co. after merger in June 1974 of wholly owned E.G. Inc. into the El Paso Natural Gas Co.

SOURCE: El Paso Natural Gas Company, *Annual Report, 1973.*

TABLE 22-5

Estimate of Preferred Stock Earnings per Share for El Paso Natural Gas Co., for Period Ending December 31, 1973

		AMOUNT (IN THOUSANDS)
EBIT		$157,425
Less:		
Interest and debt expenses	$69,184	
Federal income taxes	36,105	105,289
Aftertax income		52,136
Less:		
Estimated sinking fund payments		59,003
Earnings available for preferred		−6,867
Less:		
Dividends on first preferred		7,448
Earnings available for second preferred		−14,315
Earnings per share of first preferred (−6,867/1,035) = −6.64		
Earnings per share of second preferred (−14,315/17.214) = −831.59		

SOURCE: El Paso Natural Gas Company, *Annual Report, 1973.*

are included, net income per share of common stock before provision for sinking fund was $1.91.

The earnings per share of preferred will show greater percentage fluctuations than the fixed-charge coverage figures. Even though the absolute changes in the amounts available for coverage are the same, the base used in calculating the percentage changes for preferred stock is less by the amount of bond fixed charges. For example, assume that in three successive years a corporation reports $10 million, $14 million, and $20 million available for fixed charges. If fixed charges are $8 million, the amounts available for preferred stockholders, disregarding income taxes, are $2 million, $6 million, and $12 million. In the second and third years earnings expand by $4 million and $6 million, respectively. The percentage increases in the funds available for fixed charges during these years are 40 percent and 43 percent, whereas the corresponding gains in funds available for preferred dividends are 200 percent and 100 percent.

Comparison of Bond and Preferred Stock Fixed-Charge Coverage Standards

Because of the lack of legal compulsion for payment of regular dividends, their association with the income stream of a company is much more uncertain than is the association of interest on a bond issue of the same company. Whether a preferred share of one company is riskier than a bond of another, however, depends upon the basic riskiness of the two companies and the degree to which the debt issuer has extended itself. As we have stated previously, it is wrong to assume that securities can be arbitrarily graded on the basis of risk by their legal form alone. Some preferred shares are less risky than some outstanding bonds.

An issue cannot be considered high-grade if the investor may have to resort to legal proceedings to protect his rights. Nevertheless, the inflexible terms of bonds strengthen such issues. Their absence in preferred stock gives management the prerogative of deferring dividends in circumstances where deferring bond interest would be unthinkable. This extra uncertainty about payment of preferred dividends suggests that the investor should require high quantitative standards for the selection of preferred stocks.

Stern fixed-charge coverage requirements were recommended in the selection of corporate bonds (see p. 468). Similar yardsticks are suggested in selecting preferred stocks. The resulting preferred stock standards, however, are more rigid. The income available for bond interest and preferred dividends is less than that available for bond interest alone, by the amount of the bond charges plus income taxes. Conceptually, preferred fixed charges include those applicable to both bonds and preferred stock, whereas bond fixed charges comprise only those applicable to bonds. As a consequence, a corporation requires a considerably higher earning power to cover preferred fixed charges by the minimum margin than it needs to meet comparable bond fixed charges alone. Relatively few preferred stocks can meet such standards.

Capitalization Ratio: The Second Test of a Preferred Stock

The preferred stock capitalization ratio estimated in Table 22-3 measures the volume of capital contributed by common stockholders relative to that contributed by bondholders and preferred stockholders. This test is used primarily for evaluating prime securities. In determining this ratio, as has been indicated, it is desirable to include common stock at market value and bonds at their principal value of $1,000. In the case of preferred stock, market or redemption values seem appropriate. For high-grade issues, these values often will be similar, unless a sharp rise of interest rates causes market prices to fall.

In some instances, as in the case of El Paso, the market value of the preferred stocks may not be available. The El Paso senior preferred shares had a par value of $100; the junior preferred, which had no par value, was carried at a stated value of $100. The preference in involuntary liquidation for these issues was $100 per share plus accrued dividends. In these circumstances, it seemed reasonable to use $100 as the valuation base of the El Paso preferred stocks.

Within a corporation, the protective cushion of the bond is necessarily higher than that of the preferred. We nevertheless suggest that the investor use the same capitalization ratio standards for both bonds and preferred stock. This requirement means that when a corporation has both types of securities outstanding, the bonds must occupy a much smaller percentage of the total capitalization than that required for a high-grade issue if the preferred stock is to meet the capitalization ratio test.

The equity cushion underlying the long-term debt and preferred stocks of El Paso was 30 percent; the amount of second preferred was too small to affect the calculation. For a public utility, an equity backing for the senior securities of at least 45 percent is desirable. The 30 percent common stock capitalization ratio of El Paso, therefore, is on the low side. This factor, coupled with the inadequate fixed-charge coverage, indicates that the preferred stocks are not of high-grade quality.

When corporations have two classes of preferred stock outstanding, one senior to the other with respect to dividend payments and asset distribution in the event of liquidation, the investor should calculate the capitalization ratio of each class separately, thereby establishing the junior stock as a portion of the protective cushion behind the prior-ranking issues, as we have done in Table 22-3. The cumulative percentages show the proportion of the total capital acting as such a cushion.

Other Standards for Selecting High-Grade Preferred Stock

Two further tests are the financial condition and the size of the issuing corporation. There is no need to differentiate preferred stock and bonds in applying these measures. By using bond standards to judge the adequacy of the dividend coverage and capitalization ratios of preferred stock, we actually impose higher requirements on these issues. This step-up effect does not occur in calculating the financial condition and size of a company, because these measures do not involve the leverage embodied in capitalization. In view of the secondary importance of these tests, it does not seem necessary to develop special requirements for preferred stock.

SUMMARY

Preferred stockholders are entitled to dividends at a designated rate before any distribution is made to common stockholders, and they have priority as to assets in the event of the company's dissolution. Ordinarily, dividends are cumulative, which means that if the designated rate is not paid in any one year, the deficiency accumulates and must be fully cleared before any distributions to the common stock. The board of directors may also establish various other attributes, such as voting rights, redemption prices, sinking funds, conversion privileges, and liquidation rights.

Since the preferred is a fixed-income security, it is subject to the same analytic principles as a bond, except for differences necessitated by the absence of any legal authority to compel regular dividend payments and the omission of a definite maturity. In gauging the quality of a preferred stock, the primary test is the company's ability to pay income taxes and the stipulated dividend requirements. Another important test involves a breakdown of the company's capital structure to assess the financial implications of the amount of bonds preceding the preferred stock and the amount of common equity following it. Further considerations are the financial condition of the company and its size.

For these tests, the same standards for high-grade preferred stocks are suggested as were used in the appraisal of bonds. This means that sterner requirements are imposed for dividend coverage and capitalization ratios than the bonds had to meet. The reason is that interest, sinking fund, and taxes are included in the coverage tests, and the amount of bonds outstanding is grouped with the preferred in the capitalization test.

Part Five

ALTERNATIVE INVESTMENT METHODS AND TECHNIQUES

Typically, the field of securities analysis embraces the development of methods for appraising the fundamental merits of stocks and bonds, as described in the preceding chapters. The investor, however, has alternative paths available to him. Instead of developing his own portfolio of securities, he may prefer to buy the shares of an investment company, which itself owns portfolios of securities. Chapter 23 provides a description of these companies, a risk-adjusted method for evaluating their performance, and a technique for analyzing the securities of different types of investment companies. Alternatively, the investor may find attractive the unique features of privileged instruments like convertible securities and warrants, which are reviewed in Chapter 24. Still another way open to him, discussed in Chapter 25, is to investigate stock options, which have gained new legitimacy with the advent of their formal trading in registered exchanges. The value of a privilege rests primarily upon the value of its related security; as we have stressed, this involves a fundamental appraisal of the issuer's underlying financial strength and earnings. In addition to or in lieu of this fundamental approach, the investor may want to employ technical analysis, which involves appraising securities by their prior price configurations. Although generally dismissed by academicians, this method is treated in the final chapter because there is a cult of practitioners who favors its use.

CHAPTER 23

Understanding Investment Companies

An *investment company* is any arrangement in which a group of persons pool their funds in order to invest them in securities. The term "company" is used in a broad context because the company may assume various legal forms. Most are corporations, while a significant minority are trusts; some are unincorporated associations. Within this flexible organizational framework, investment companies may be grouped in different ways.

TYPES OF INVESTMENT COMPANIES

The Investment Company Act of 1940 divides registered investment companies into three categories: face-amount certificate companies, unit investment trusts, and management companies.

Face-amount certificate companies issue contracts binding the company to pay a fixed sum at maturity to buyers who have made a single payment or a series of payments over time. These certificates are debt instruments that provide a largely predetermined and relatively low rate of interest, with no opportunity for capital appreciation. This field—whose volume of business is comparatively small—is dominated by the giant Investors Diversified Services, Inc. (IDS), and its wholly owned subsidiary, Investors Syndicate of America, Inc.

There are two types of *unit investment trusts.* One sells a redeemable interest in the shares of a single company, usually a management investment company, which, in turn, manages a portfolio of securities. This type of trust issues periodic payment plan certificates (popularly known as contractual plans), which enable investors to buy the shares of a mutual fund on an installment basis; purchase could also be made through a lump sum, called a single-payment plan. The other type of unit investment trust holds a designated list of securities. In the early 1930s it was common for this list to consist of common stock, but now the list is likely to be a package of municipal bonds. For example, the first series of the Nuveen Tax Exempt Bond Fund was offered in mid-1961; subsequent series have been issued as each prior offering has been sold. The Nuveen funds, as well as the other municipal bond funds, typically hold a larger percentage of revenue bonds than general obligations; in most cases, these portfolios have a wide geographic diversification. Starting about 1971, these tax-exempt funds have gained considerable popularity as investors have sought relatively secure high returns. Under the tax laws, such a fund at present cannot offer its shares continuously and still pass through the tax-exempt status of its income. Amendments have been under consideration, however, to grant mutual fund shareholders a "pass-through treatment," thereby exempting them from federal income tax on the portion of the fund's income distribution represented by municipal bond income.

Investment companies that are neither face-amount certificate enterprises nor unit investment trusts are classified as *management companies.* These, in turn, are categorized in two ways, one by portfolio holdings, and the other by operating method. With respect to portfolio holdings, the 1940 law distinguishes between a diversified company, which meets a designated minimum test for the distribution of its assets, and a nondiversified company, which does not meet the test. A company is diversified for purposes of the Investment Company Act if, with respect to 75 percent of its total assets, it invests not more than 5 percent of its total assets in the securities of any one company and holds no more than 10 percent of the outstanding voting securities of any one company. The operating-method provision creates a distinction between an open-end company, which permits a holder to redeem a security for its proportionate share in the issuer's net current assets, and a closed-end company, which does not have this provision. These categories are overlapping, so that an open-end or closed-end company may be diversified or nondiversified.

Of the major categories, by far the most important is the management company. These companies have been ingenious in developing different types of funds (not defined by the act) to appeal to the tastes of different investors. There are general purpose funds, which invest primarily in common stocks but which may stress growth, income, or some combination of both; there are also balanced funds, which shift their investments between bonds and stocks, depending upon their judgment regarding the future of equities and interest rates; there are special purpose funds that may emphasize particular industries, such as insurance, or specific geographic areas, like Japan.

As economic conditions change, the securities mix is likely to change. Thus, specialized industry funds have come and gone. For a number of years, little interest was displayed in bond funds because of their conservative bias. In the early 1970s, however, these funds began to flourish because they enabled small investors to take advantage of high long-term interest rates by indirectly purchasing bonds which ordinarily are sold only in large denominations. A number of these funds have also extended their activities by aggressively managing fixed-income portfolios. Their strategy is to seek swapping opportunities between different components of the bond market where yield spreads are temporarily out of line (see pp. 434-440). As would be expected, the turnover of the holdings of these funds is high compared to that of the more staid income fund that has remained aloof from the new strategies. In September 1974 there were at least 76 bond funds with total assets of roughly \$5.1 billion, compared with only a handful ten years previously.[1]

In 1967 a number of *dual purpose funds* were established. These funds have two classes of stock: income shares, which receive all of the fund's net investment income, and capital shares, which reflect all of the capital appreciation or depreciation of the fund. The income shares have a minimum dividend, which is cumulative, and the shares are callable after a specific period of time. When the shares are called, their holders are entitled to receive the full original net asset value of the shares, plus the amount, if any, of the cumulative minimum dividend that is in arrears. The capital shares are entitled to divide the remaining net assets of the fund. Typically, the capital shares had a 2:1 leverage at inception, a ratio, of course, that changes as the asset value of the fund changes. To the extent that a fund increases its asset value, the income shares stand to receive the greater income generated on the greater assets; the capital shares benefit because all the capital appreciation is allocated to them. These funds are all closed-end.

During this same period, at one time or another, investors showed interest in real estate investment trusts, tax shelters, and combined fund shares and insurance programs. Reflecting academic skepticism about the ability of money managers to select undervalued securities, some so-called "index" funds, intended to match the performance of a popular market index, also made an appearance.

High short-term interest rates at that time spurred the creation of *money-market funds.* These funds normally restrict their investments to Treasury bills, commercial paper, and other high-quality, short-term debt instruments. During 1974 about 25 such funds were created, of which the 10 largest accumulated over $2 billion in assets. Most of these funds were offered without sales charge and provided for the declaration of daily dividends. As interest rates declined, the money-market funds sought other competitive devices, such as granting holders the privilege of writing checks of specified minimum amounts. In June 1975 the Securities and Exchange Commission proposed guidelines to standardize reporting of yields by these funds. These guidelines created the concept of yield to average life, which means the rate of return that would be received by shareholders in the investment company if all the securities currently in the company's portfolio, valued at market, were held to maturity and redeemed at par value, with the proceeds distributed to such shareholders.

THE MUTUAL FUND COMPLEX

While redemption of their own shares is the primary distinguishing feature of open-end companies, they characteristically keep large amounts of unissued stock that enable them to engage in a continuous selling operation. Perhaps because of these characteristics, they are usually described as mutual funds, although for tax purposes, where the mutual concept may have originated, they are treated the same way as closed-end companies. An investment company is normally externally managed—that is, the investment company enters into an agreement with a separate management company to provide investment advice as well as general corporate administration. Since the management company receives an important source of income from the fee charged for supervising the company's portfolio of securities, it is advantageous for the management company to market the mutual fund shares aggressively, in order to expand the asset base on which its fee is computed. For this reason and because of their ability to fashion packages that appeal to investors, the mutual funds have grown much more rapidly than the closed-end funds and today constitute the bulk of the industry. Indicative of the effort to provide such packages is the introduction of an insurance program that furnishes protection, within certain limits, against loss on a long-term investment in mutual fund shares.

Over the years, the mutual funds have developed a complex organizational structure. Typically, a management company that is a separate corporate entity, provides investment advice for a fee to a single fund (which may issue shares in separate series) or to a group of separate funds. Only a small number of funds are serviced internally by their own officers and employees. In addition to supervising the portfolio, the management company, directly or through a subsidiary, usually serves as the principal underwriter and arranges the mechanics of stockholder relationships. Acting as a wholesaler, the principal underwriter seeks to develop a dealer network which may embrace hundreds of firms, including large brokerage houses and small owner-operated units, all of which sell to the public. In some cases, the principal underwriter markets the funds' shares directly to the consumer through its own sales staff. *No-load funds* are distributed without a principal underwriter and have no sales charge.

At their inception, the management companies, responsible for forming the funds, were small, privately held enterprises. They obtained their income principally from portfolio-supervision fees and sales commissions, although many of these commission fees were, in turn, passed on to the selling dealer organizations. In the two years following a 1958 court decision (*SEC* vs. *Insurance Securities, Inc.*) which held the 1940 Investment Company Act did not prevent the sellers of a controlling block of stock of a management company from retaining all the consideration, a number of such companies made public offerings of their stock.

As the funds grew, the income of the management companies from portfolio supervision expanded correspondingly; not uncommonly, these companies then entered other lines of activity. As a result, some management companies have become giant enterprises engaged in diverse business fields. While IDS, for example, is best known as the investment adviser and exclusive distributor for various mutual funds that had net assets at the close of 1974 of over $6 billion, it also engages in life insurance, real estate, and mortgage banking. The company once owned but later sold Jefferies & Co., Inc. which now deals in the third market and provides execution services for institutional customers.[2]

THE INVESTOR AND THE INVESTMENT COMPANY

The ingenuity and zeal displayed by promoters of mutual funds have drawn much investor attention. Between 1940 and 1971 the number of publicly offered funds rose from approximately 70 to more than 600, while the assets under their management expanded from $500 million to over $55 billion. The size of these assets depends on both the inflow of new investment dollars and on the value of the securities in the portfolio. Until 1972 this inflow was consistent; mutual fund sales had exceeded redemptions in every year since record keeping began.[3] In 1972, however, the boom seemed to subside. Following a period in which offshore funds (those sold abroad) fell into some disrepute, a number of so-called "go-go" funds stressing swift capital gains experienced financial setbacks, and funds generally found it difficult to demonstrate good performance. For the first time in history, investors cashed in more shares than they bought, and the funds closed the year in a net redemption position; gross sales for the year totaled $4.89 billion compared with redemptions of $6.56 billion, producing a deficiency of $1.67 billion.[4] The trend continued through 1974 (without counting sale of money-market funds).

This negative reaction, however, does not necessarily indicate that shares of mutual funds are poor investment vehicles. What it does suggest is the need for an investor to ascertain how he can best use these securities. In order to reach this decision, he should be able to answer three basic questions: Should he buy the stock of an investment company? If so, should he choose a closed-end or open-end fund? Within each classification, which issues will be most attractive to him?

Advisability of Purchasing the Stock of an Investment Company

Sponsors of investment companies once made extravagant claims about both the safety of the principal and the size of the income afforded by their securities. This condition led the Securities and Exchange Commission, with the assistance of the National Association of Securities Dealers, to investigate the advertising methods and sales literature employed. In order to correct the abuses that were uncovered, the SEC in 1950 issued a statement of policy (since amended several times) to set standards of fairness and prohibit the use of misleading statements in mutual fund sales material.

The statutory basis for mutual fund advertising is contained in the Securities Act of 1933, which applies to all public securities offerings. That statute calls for public disclosure of all material information concerning the security offered through issuance of a prospectus. Rule 134 under the act, however, provides for an exception to the prospectus requirement by permitting an advertisement that simply announces an offering; such an advertisement is commonly called a "tombstone" because of the austerity required. Investment companies have chafed at the stern limitations on the descriptive material they may include.[5] While there was some relaxation of requirements over the years, the industry's advertising shackles were loosened more perceptibly in 1972 by amendments to Rule 134 and the adoption of the new Rule 135A. Specifically, these modifications increased the information which could be included in tombstone advertising and allowed underwriters to engage in generic advertising, which discusses the industry in general terms; mutual funds were also permitted to use a summary prospectus.[6] In subsequent years, the SEC further modified Rule 134 to permit an investment company to include in its tombstone advertisement a description of its own special attributes, method of operation, and services, as well as a general description of investment companies and material concerning economic conditions, retirement plans or other goals, and certain pictorial illustrations. A new Rule 425B was also issued, providing for a simplified prospectus.[7]

This wavering between sternness and looseness reflects the reality of the funds' investment role. On the one hand, shares of these institutions are no nostrums to cure financial ills. Except for certain specialized funds, companies cannot provide an assured income return or promise future definite market value. Accordingly, these securities tend to embody either the customary risks of equity commitments or the uncertainty of interest rate fluctuations. In addition, investment company shares have a handicap arising from the limited ability of an institution to cope with changing economic conditions. Even though the economic outlook may appear gloomy, the management of a stock fund rarely has sufficient confidence in the accuracy of a bearish forecast—or else lacks the audacity—to shift substantially into cash or high-grade bonds. If the move turned out to be unwarranted, it might reduce a company's returns from its own investments and might shake the confidence of its stockholders. Moreover, in the case of large funds, massive changes are not easy because of the size of their individual commitments. For these reasons, investment company shares afford no special advantage to an institution or a pension fund that has a competent staff of its own, or to a person with the training, temperament, and financial resources to develop, adequately diversify, and supervise his or her own portfolio.

On the other hand, the institution or the pension fund may not be equipped to handle its own investments or may desire to place a portion of its money with outside advisers in order to check the relative performance of its internal staff.[8] Similarly, it would be folly for an individual to manage his or her own financial program independently when not in a position to do so. For that matter, the investor would be equally foolhardy to enter any business or profession without the necessary qualifications. Thus, the institution or individual may find it expedient to obtain the services of some independent adviser or to place at least a portion of the available capital with an investment company. In the case of the small investor, access to an independent adviser is difficult and the only recourse may be to an investment company.

The decision to use an investment company, however, does not eliminate but only reduces the investor's responsibilities toward the securities portfolio. If he decides to buy the stock of an investment company, he must still determine which one suits his needs. After buying these shares, he must also follow the company's affairs to make certain that management is living up to his expectations. If not, a shift to another fund may be called for. It is a mistake to believe that one's financial requirements are well served by acquiring investment company shares without adequate analysis.

Relative Advantages of Closed-End and Open-End Funds

If the investor has decided to buy the shares of an investment company, he must choose between the closed-end and open-end funds. Each affords certain advantages.

One merit of buying closed-end companies is that costs of transactions in these shares are likely to be lower than costs of dealing in securities of open-end institutions. Total charges for buying and selling 100 shares of stock listed on the New York Stock Exchange and valued at $5,000 amount to about 1.6 percent of the principal, as compared with the typical sale load of about 9 percent of the principal for buying and selling the same amount of a mutual fund. In the latter case, the charge or load usually is imposed on purchase, and there is no cost attached to redemption. This comparison may be considered inaccurate because it overlooks the fact that the shares of traded securities are purchased at the asked price but sold at the bid, and that odd-lot differentials may be involved. Although these conditions make positive comparisons difficult, the difference between most load charges and commission rates is large enough to indicate that costs are lighter in buying and selling shares of closed-end funds than of open-end funds (except for no-load funds). Shares of many closed-end companies may also be acquired at a substantial discount from net asset value. This is never the case with open-end issues.

Open-end funds may have a special problem because of their policy of constantly issuing new shares for sale and redeeming outstanding stock at any time. During periods of advancing prices, a contagious optimism leads to large increases in the purchase of investment companies' stock, thereby increasing the funds these institutions have available for buying new securities. Declining prices spread pessimism, inducing investors to convert their stock to cash. These tendencies leave the open-end funds with ample supplies of money for investment when prices are high but may compel them to liquidate portions of their portfolios to obtain cash for meeting share redemptions when prices are low. Closed-end institutions are free of this unfavorable two-way pressure because they make no commitment to sell or redeem their shares. Thus, there is no possibility that a "run" on a closed-end company could force it to liquidate portfolio securities against its judgment, as could occur in the case of an open-end company.

Nevertheless, prices of closed-end stocks do fluctuate because of changes in their underlying asset values and because of shifts in the demand for and supply of these shares in the securities markets. These dual forces may exaggerate the effects of temporary market fluctuations on the prices of closed-end shares. In contrast to this condition, the constant repurchase policy of open-end companies makes their shares largely immune to the direct influence of price flurries, although their redemption prices will reflect movements indirectly through changes in the market values of the underlying portfolio.

At one time, a number of closed-end funds had complex structures that created highly leveraged common stock. The availability of such issues has been vanishing as senior securities have been eliminated. To the extent that continuing leverage is still available, however, it is in the closed-end area.

Specialized types of companies with closed-end characteristics may appeal to certain classes of investors. In this group is the real estate investment trust (REIT). Short-term mortgage trusts invest primarily in construction and development loans; long-term trusts stress permanent mortgages; and equity trusts concentrate on real estate equities. Since REITs raise funds through both short- and long-term borrowing, their outstanding stocks may possess considerable leverage. Qualifying trusts receive tax treatment substantially similar to that of investment companies. The REITs initially experienced rapid growth but then ran into serious financial difficulties, as high interest rates and inflationary conditions raised their costs and unfavorable economic conditions curtailed the sale of properties. Another close relative of the closed-end fund is the small business investment company, which offers investors the opportunity to participate in the fortunes of relatively small, privately held, venture-type enterprises. In a sense, any firm that has a large portion of its assets in securities, such as those of fire and casualty companies, may be considered as a kind of closed-end fund. (At least this aspect of their business requires close attention when evaluating securities of fire and casualty companies.)

Open-end funds may also be advantageous for certain investors. One reason is that purchases may be made in small amounts. While some funds establish fairly substantial initial minimum requirements, they usually permit subsequent acquisitions to be made in modest sums. Brokers, on the other hand, are often loath to execute stock transactions for, say $50. Lowered sales charges typically are available in open-end funds for large purchases. If the buyer provides a letter of intent, he may effect these purchases over time.

Open-end funds ordinarily do not issue stock certificates unless specifically requested; rather, they credit the shares for each purchaser to accounts maintained by banks or other independent transfer agents. Thereafter, information is provided regularly as to the investor's holdings. This arrangement avoids the nuisance of either keeping a stock certificate or having it in "street name" with a broker. The right of redemption provides immediate liquidity usually without costs and without the need of going through a broker.

Dividends of most open-end (and some closed-end funds) may be reinvested automatically in full and fractional shares at net asset value. A large investor probably could make arrangements with his broker to hold his shares of a closed-end fund, receive the dividends, and reinvest them automatically. But he would have to pay commissions, and such an arrangement probably would not be feasible for the small investor. Corporations also have introduced dividend reinvestment plans, but they ordinarily involve a transaction cost.

Plans are available to permit the systematic accumulation of the shares of open-end funds through voluntary regular or periodic investments on a monthly, quarterly, or other basis. While the installment purchase plans provided by some New York Stock Exchange firms tend to offset this advantage, the mutual fund programs are likely to prove more flexible. For investors who prefer the pressure of forced savings, contractual plans are available.

Automatic withdrawal plans are also likely to be available. In these, the shareholder who owns a minimum specified amount may receive a monthly or quarterly check in a stated amount on a selected date. Or the shareholder may elect a variable plan, whereby withdrawals are made on the basis of a selected percentage of net asset value instead of in fixed dollar amounts.

Open-end complexes often give the investor a choice of different types of investments. For instance, he can switch from a growth fund to an income fund when his investment objectives change. This variety also permits him to construct his whole portfolio by using stocks of multiple investment companies to represent the aggressive and defensive elements. Furthermore, an open-end fund may introduce leverage into its portfolio by borrowing from banks at a fixed rate of interest. Under the Investment Company Act, such borrowing can only be made to the extent that a fund's total assets (including the borrowings) are equal to at least 300 percent of all borrowings.

After examining the relative virtues and shortcomings of closed-end and open-end funds, the investor must determine which type he prefers. This decision depends on his own desires. In general, closed-end funds may represent better intrinsic values when their shares can be bought at unusual discounts from valuations; conversely, the shares of closed-end funds may be overpriced when selling at relatively modest discounts or at premiums. Because they are not exposed to uncertain money inflows or outflows, closed-end funds may avoid certain market pressures. On the other hand, open-end companies appear more suitable when the investor finds their purchase programs helpful or is interested in some special type of fund available in no other form.

SELECTING THE MOST ATTRACTIVE INVESTMENT COMPANY STOCK

Having determined the type of fund desired, the investor must next decide which particular companies in the chosen category appear most attractive for his or her purpose. This decision requires an evaluation of the relative characteristics of the different funds, including management performance, portfolio composition, extent of leverage, discount from net asset value, dividend return, and operating expenses.

Management Performance

The buyer of an investment company stock shifts the burden of making investment decisions from himself to the institution. He must have confidence in the judgment of the management to which he entrusts this responsibility. To this end, he should learn something about the background of the company's executive officers, its methods of obtaining research advice, and its ways of reaching investment decisions. This information is helpful, but it does not in itself guarantee the ability of management to handle a large portfolio of securities.

To gauge the talent of management in supervising portfolios, analysts have employed quantitative measures of actual past experience. One method of evaluation is simply to rank the different funds on the basis of these measures. Another approach is to compare the record of a particular fund with that of an overall index of market activity, such as the Standard & Poor's Industrial Index of 425 stocks; a fund is considered to have performed poorly if it advances less than the index in a rising market, but to have performed well if it falls less than the index in a declining market.

In its Institutional Investor Study, the SEC pointed out that past investors had tended to equate "performance" with "price action," without adjusting for the risk borne by the portfolio. The commission followed the academic practice of identifying risk with portfolio volatility and indicated that improved disclosure would require the separation of this element from investment returns.[9] The SEC described one method of handling volatility in the measurement of performance that indicates the commission's general approach.[10]

In essence, this method applies the beta concept to the measurement of portfolio results. It will be remembered that the volatility of a portfolio is related to the amount of nondiversifiable risk the investor bears; this volatility, in turn, can be measured by the beta coefficient. Thus, a volatility coefficient of 0.5 might be expected of an income fund, indicating that changes in its rate of return move more sluggishly than changes in that of the market. On the other hand, a coefficient of 2.0 might be expected of a capital gains-oriented fund, indicating that its rate of return is likely to change more rapidly than that of the market return. On the basis of these relationships, if one knows the return on the market index and the volatility coefficient of the institutional portfolio, it should be possible to predict the rate of return that would be obtained on an unmanaged portfolio that has the same volatility as an institutional portfolio. This unmanaged portfolio then could be used as a standard to evaluate the performance of a particular institutional portfolio with the same volatility.

The approach developed to obtain the standard portfolio is to combine a riskless and risky unmanaged portfolio in the appropriate proportions to obtain a mixed portfolio with the same degree of volatility as that of the fund being evaluated. For this purpose, Treasury bills are assumed to represent the risk-free segment, which has a volatility coefficient of 0.

The rate of return on the standard portfolio is the sum of the rates of return on the components of Treasury bills and the market index, weighted by the percent of the value of the total portfolio in each of these components. This rate of return can be shown to be equal to the risk-free rate plus the product of volatility coefficient of the standard portfolio times the risk premium of the market portfolio, represented by the difference between the return on the market index and Treasury bills.

In terms of the formulas used in Chapter 11, let

$$r_s = S + \beta_s(r_m - S), \text{ where}$$

r_s = the return on a standard portfolio,
r_m = the return on the market portfolio,
S = the return on a risk-free asset, and
β_s = the volatility coefficient of the standard portfolio.

It can easily be seen that the volatility of the standard portfolio is the same as the percentage of that portfolio invested in the market portfolio. Let x represent the percent invested in the market portfolio. Then,

$$\begin{aligned} r_s &= xr_m + (1 - x)S \\ &= xr_m + S - xS \\ &= S + x(r_m - S). \end{aligned}$$

If the right-hand side of this equation is compared with the right-hand side of the first equation above, it is clear that $\beta_s = x$.

Table 23-1 shows the rates of return and volatility coefficients of various standard unmanaged portfolios with varying sums of money invested in Treasury bills and the market index.

TABLE 23-1

Rates of Return and Volatility of Standard Unmanaged Portfolios

STANDARD PORTFOLIO NUMBER	PERCENTAGE IN TREASURY BILLS	RATE OF RETURN ON TREASURY BILLS	PERCENTAGE IN MARKET INDEX (β_S)	RATE OF RETURN ON MARKET INDEX	RATE OF RETURN ON STANDARD UNMANAGED PORTFOLIO	VOLATILITY OF STANDARD UNMANAGED PORTFOLIO
1	100%	4.2%	0%	10.5%	4.2%	0.00
2	75	4.2	25	10.5	5.8	0.25
3	50	4.2	50	10.5	7.4	0.50
4	25	4.2	75	10.5	8.9	0.75
5	0	4.2	100	10.5	10.5	1.00
6	−25	4.2	125	10.5	12.1	1.25
7	−50	4.2	150	10.5	13.7	1.50

When 0% of the standard unmanaged portfolio is in the market index, the return on the portfolio is 4.2% (the same as the return on Treasury bills), and the portfolio's volatility is 0. When 100% of the standard unmanaged portfolio is in the market index, the return on the portfolio is 10.5%, the same as the return on the market index, and the portfolio's volatility is 1.00. Volatilities greater than 1.00 can be achieved through leverage by borrowing at the risk-free rate and placing the funds in the market index.

The relationship between the rate of return on standard unmanaged portfolios and their volatility is shown in graphic form in Figure 23-1. Actual portfolios with superior performance would have rates of return lying above

FIGURE 23-1

Evaluation of Fund Performance

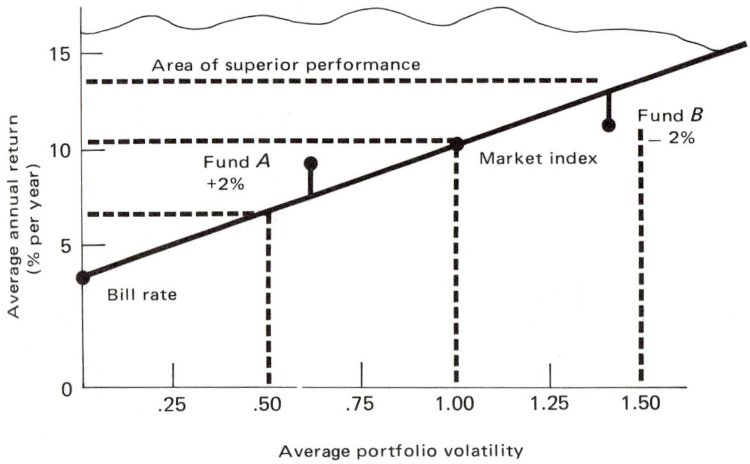

SOURCE: U.S. Congress, House, Committee on Interstate and Foreign Commerce, *Institutional Investor Study Report of the Securities and Exchange Commission,* 92d Cong., 1st sess. (Washington, D.C.: Government Printing Office, 1971), p. 406.

the line of neutral performance that connect the returns on the standard portfolios. Actual portfolios with inferior performance would have returns falling below this line of neutrality. The results of two actual portfolios are shown in the graph. The absolute return of fund *B* is greater than that of fund *A*, but when adjusted for volatility the results are reversed; on this basis, fund *A* reveals a superior performance, while fund *B* has an inferior record.

The SEC has not as yet taken any steps to require the use of volatility-adjusted comparison standards in determining performance fees. This approach coincides with the efficient-market theory of the academician, which holds that portfolio managers cannot consistently outperform the market and can vary the returns they receive only by varying the distribution of their portfolios between risk-free and risky securities.

There are major difficulties with this approach. First it fails to distinguish between the portfolio manager's skill in selecting stocks and his skill in anticipating market fluctuations. A manager with good judgment of the market can switch from aggressive to defensive stock or the reverse at the appropriate time with profit. Second, such a strategy would make it difficult to measure the β with which to adjust for the portfolio's risk. Third, as Friend, Blume, and others have shown, this approach would tend to underrate the performance of high-risk portfolios in the long run.

Portfolio Composition

When an investor buys the shares of an investment company, he acquires a partial interest in a portfolio of securities. Portfolio policies, of course, may change drastically over the years, depending on the decisions of management and on restrictions written into the articles of organization. When the investment climate appears particularly dour or uncertain, even aggressive investment companies may stress cash, government securities, or commercial paper. Nevertheless, over the long run, the portfolio of a company is likely to reflect its fundamental policies, which are clearly set forth in the prospectus issued in connection with the sale of shares.

As an illustration, the Oppenheimer Management Corp. is the investment adviser for a family of funds that have varying investment policies. Within this group, both the Oppenheimer Fund and the Oppenheimer Time Fund have similar objectives of capital appreciation, but the risk each is willing to assume to reach these objectives varies. Thus, the Oppenheimer Fund prospectus includes the following statement of investment policy:

> Oppenheimer Fund's goal is to seek capital growth consistent with what it considers prudence. It is designed for an investor who, aware of the risk, looks for this growth of investment value over the years rather than current income. While current income is not a primary objective, it is hoped that growth in income will accompany growth in capital.

On the other hand, the Oppenheimer Time Fund prospectus states the following:

> The investment objective of the Fund is to seek growth of capital. Current income is not a consideration in the selection of portfolio securities. . . . The securities acquired may include listed and unlisted

> securities, and securities of small and unseasoned companies as well as those of large and well-known companies. . . . The Fund is not intended as a complete investment program but is designed for investors who are willing to accept greater risks in the hope of greater gains. This investment policy is speculative and involves substantial risks.

Reflecting these differences in stated policies, the portfolio of the Time Fund ordinarily has contained a much larger percentage of securities that are listed on the American Stock Exchange or are traded over-the-counter. In contrast to both these funds' emphases on capital appreciation, the Oppenheimer Income Fund subordinates capital appreciation to obtain a relatively high and consistent flow of current income to its holders. Its prospectus indicates the following:

> The investment objective of the Fund is to provide as much current income as possible consistent with reasonable safety of capital. A secondary, although important objective is growth of income and capital.

Depending upon his objectives and interests, the investor has a broad range of portfolios within which to move. There are balanced funds, which characteristically hold both senior securities and common stock; capital appreciation-oriented funds, like the Oppenheimer Fund and the Oppenheimer Time Fund, which ordinarily emphasize common stock; income funds, which ordinarily hold relatively large amounts of senior securities and stress dividend-paying stocks in their equity group; and the new money-market funds, which invest in short-term debt instruments and reduce considerably the risk of capital loss.

Every investment company embraces to some degree the principle of diversification, in order to gain the protection of large numbers and minimize the effects of errors in choosing securities. The company pays for this reduction of risk through the additional costs involved in buying and supervising many issues rather than a few. Some institutions, however, give less recognition to diversification, preferring to rely more strongly on the principle of selection. These institutions seek protection through good judgment in choosing a relatively small number of securities or industries which seem outstandingly attractive. (Big funds may have to stress particular industries rather than stocks because of the problem of liquidity.) Such funds concede the inevitability of error but believe that, in the long run, discriminating selections will not only counterbalance losses but provide greater gains.

The investor must weigh carefully the virtues of diversification and selectivity. He may question the worth of a management that spreads its holdings thinly over a standard group of stocks and characteristically keeps a representation in most of the major industry groups; he may feel that this policy could overplay the mechanics of large numbers at the expense of personal initiative. A management that favors buying fewer issues or industries avoids expensive use of mechanistic devices for protection against losses; it has more confidence in its own decisions. Although its mistakes could lead to a serious erosion of capital, foresighted purchases, particularly of "special situations," could produce huge profits. Stocks of companies stressing this policy tend to appeal to the aggressive investor, whereas the balanced or more broadly diversified funds attract more conservative investors.

Leverage

Leverage could be important for an investment company. The principle operates in this way. An institution that has senior securities in its capitalization or borrows from a bank has a correspondingly smaller proportion of its net assets accruing to the benefit of its common stockholders. This relationship balloons fluctuations in the value of total assets into greater percentage changes in the assets available to the common stock. Differentials grow as the proportion of senior securities or bank debt increases. Regardless of the changes in total net assets, the same amount is required to cover the principal value of the institution's outstanding senior obligations, leaving a larger amount to the common stockholders. This condition is illustrated in Figure 23-2, which shows how a specified gain or loss in the total net assets of three investment companies is translated into corresponding changes in the net assets available for common stock.

All three companies have the same amount of total assets, but the amount in the senior segment varies, as does the number of shares of common stock outstanding. All three companies have a starting net asset value of $10 per common share. If there is a 20 percent increase in total assets, the net asset value of company *A*'s common stock, with no leverage, rises by the same percentage, to $12 per share; the net asset value of company *B*'s common stock, with some leverage, rises by 22.2 percent, to $12.22 per share; and the net asset value of company *C*'s common stock, with more leverage, rises by 25 percent, to $12.50 per share. Of course, if total assets shrink, net asset values per common share fall in the same proportions.

Leverage thus gives a speculative hue to the common shares of an investment company. Under the Investment Company Act, closed-end companies can issue debt securities that have an asset coverage of at least 300 percent. As mentioned previously, however, closed-end funds have been gradually eliminating senior issues; leverage has therefore disappeared as a permanent part of their capitalizations. Open-end funds can obtain leverage

FIGURE 23-2

Effects of Leverage on Three Investment Companies

Company *A*: $100 million total assets; no senior segment; 10 million shares of stock.

Company *B*: $100 million total assets; $10 million senior segment; 9 million shares of stock.

Company *C*: $100 million total assets; $20 million senior segment; 8 million shares of stock.

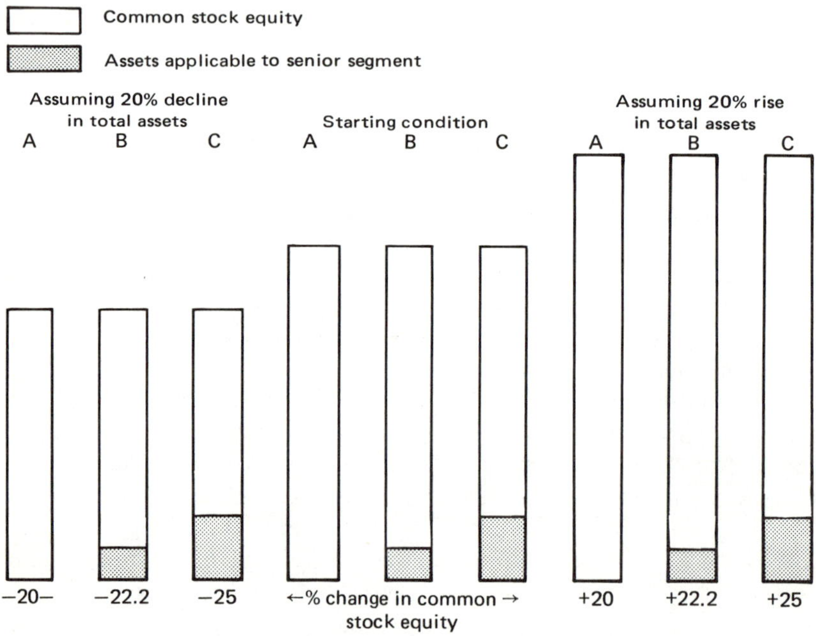

by borrowing from banks, provided the loan has a 300 percent asset coverage. As a policy, however, most funds of either type borrow rather sparingly.

Discount from Net Asset Value

We have stressed that the principal criteria for the desirability of different funds are their suitability to the investor's requirements and their performance. Once these features are known, cost becomes a consideration. Prices of open-end shares are fixed by their liquidating values. Discounts do not exist, and premiums are determined by sales commissions added to the purchase price. By contrast, net asset values and prices of closed-end funds may differ sharply, as shown in Table 23-2.

Important influences on the relationship between net asset value and price are the market outlook, the reputation of management, and the

TABLE 23-2

Market Prices and Net Asset Values of Selected Closed-End Investment Companies, September 5, 1975

COMPANY	MARKET PRICE	NET-ASSET VALUE PER SHARE	DISCOUNT OR PREMIUM (P) (PERCENTAGE)
Adams Express	$9\frac{5}{8}$	12.68	24.1
Advance Investors	$7\frac{3}{4}$	10.53	26.4
Carriers & General	$11\frac{1}{4}$	14.72	23.6
Central Securities	4	6.50	38.5
International Holdings	$11\frac{1}{2}$	13.16	12.6
Lehman	$10\frac{7}{8}$	13.43	19.0
Niagara Share	$12\frac{3}{4}$	12.59	1.3P
Tri-Continental	$18\frac{3}{8}$	22.08	16.8
United Corp.	$6\frac{5}{8}$	9.36	29.2
U.S. and Foreign Securities	$14\frac{3}{4}$	19.46	24.2

SOURCE: *Wall Street Journal*, September 8, 1975.

character of the portfolio. The stock will sell at a discount below or a premium above net asset value, depending on whether the net impact of these factors is negative or positive. Over a period of years, discounts or premiums will change in size, and the same stock may sell at a discount at one time and at a premium at another.

The variety of influences affecting the relationship between market prices and net asset values makes it clear that the investor must determine the cause of a discount or premium before deciding on its significance. In the absence of any discernible reason, such as a poor prior record, a sizable discount is a favorable pricing factor. It signifies that large assets are at work in relation to the market value of outstanding stock. This factor enhances the stockholder's potential return. In addition, if the discount from net asset value is greater than that normally prevailing, the price of his shares may benefit from the tendency for big discounts to narrow as conditions change.

Similarly, the fact that a stock sells at a premium above net asset value is of itself a negative factor. This condition indicates that the amount of money paid per share of stock is greater than the tangible assets received. Presumably, investors buying stocks that sell at premiums have great confidence in the quality of the issuing company's management.

Dividend Return

The Internal Revenue Code recognizes that investment companies may serve as a conduit for distributing the income they receive from their portfolio companies to their shareholders. Accordingly, if such a company disburses as taxable dividends not less than 90 percent of its net income, exclusive of capital gains, for any taxable year, and meets certain requirements to qualify as a "regulated investment company" (the diversification standards of the Internal Revenue Code are similar but not identical to those of the Investment Company Act), its tax liability on the income distributed is passed on to its shareholders, who are taxed on both the income and net realized capital gains received. The company pays tax only on amounts not distributed to shareholders.

Investment companies pay dividends out of their two principal earnings sources: interest and dividends received from their own investments and capital gains resulting from securities transactions. To ensure adequate disclosure to the shareholders, the Investment Company Act requires that a written statement accompany any disbursement that does not come from investment income. The investor must know the source of these distributions for several reasons.

First, the capital gains of an investment company are erratic. Depending primarily on the status of the market, they have both exceeded and fallen substantially below investment income at different periods. A number of the major companies have reported investment income consistently, but few, if any, have avoided for long at least a single year of net losses from purchase and sale of securities. Because capital gains are a capricious source of income, the 1970 amendments to the Investment Company Act authorize the SEC to prohibit the distribution of long-term capital gains more than once a year; investment income distributions may occur more frequently. Acting under this authority, the SEC in November 1972 adopted Rule 19(b)-1, under the Investment Company Act providing that in any single taxable year a fund may distribute one capital gains dividend plus one supplemental distribution that is not more than 10 percent of the prior distribution.

A second reason for identifying the source of dividends is that distributions from profits on securities transactions actually represent a reduction of capital investment. Assume, for example, that a fund pays to its shareholders the $300,000 of capital gains resulting from the sale, at $70 per share, of 10,000 shares of stock in a particular company originally purchased at $40. If the holders fail to reinvest the $300,000 in the same fund, the company will have only the original $400,000 available for buying new securities. Recognizing this fact, many open-end funds allow their shareholders to reinvest dividends from capital gains without paying a sales load, while closed-end funds often disburse optional stock or cash dividends; both policies effectively result in the automatic reinvestment of distributions.

A third reason for noting carefully the sources of dividends involves the different methods of taxing these distributions. As mentioned previously, the portion of a dividend emanating from investment income is subject to the ordinary income tax, whereas the portion representing the excess of net long-term capital gains over net short-term capital losses is subject to the lower tax rate on capital gains. A "regulated investment company" may retain its realized long-term capital gains without any tax penalty to its shareholders, who only experience some extra bookkeeping complications in recording their own tax status.

For most capital appreciation funds, dividend income is relatively unimportant. In appraising an income fund, however, dividends and interest are major considerations.

Operating Expenses

The principal expense of an investment company is the management fee paid to its investment adviser. In addition to portfolio supervision, the fee may include all normal operating expenses of the fund except those attributable to the principal underwriter and taxes; in other cases, the fee may pay only for investment management. Between these two extremes, the nonadvisory services covered by the fee may vary widely. Typically, the fee includes salaries and compensation of officers, occupancy and office rental, clerical and bookkeeping services, determination of offering and redemption prices, accounting services, and stationery, supplies, and printing. Services ordinarily not covered and paid directly by the fund include such things as registration and filing fees, salaries and compensation of disinterested directors, legal fees, reports to shareholders, auditing, stock transfer and dividend disbursing fees, and expenses relating to the custodianship of securities. The primary control of these expenses is through state securities regulations, which often establish maximum expense ratios.

At the close of 1974, the average advisory fee as calculated by CCMP, a management consulting firm, for 15 large growth funds was .42 percent, while the total expense ratio was .59 percent. The ratios for small funds (with assets between $15 million and $50 million) were substantially higher, particularly for nonadvisory expenses: .54 percent for the average advisory fee and 1.06 percent for total expenses.

Relatively few funds keep an internal management structure. Those that do, on the average, have lower management costs and expense ratios than the externally managed funds, possibly because the relatively large size of some internally managed companies gives them the opportunity to take advantage of the economies of scale.

To the extent that a fund can keep its operating costs down or shift them to its adviser, the investor receives the benefit. This area, however, is much less important than performance. Moreover, a high expense ratio is not necessarily an unfavorable sign, since the enlarged costs may provide better management; it is doubtful, however, that the size of these expenses and the performance of a fund are closely related.

SPECIAL ASPECTS OF THE INVESTMENT COMPANY INDUSTRY

We have now completed our discussion of the approach to analyzing the common stock of investment companies. In order to understand the investment company industry, the investor should also understand the various special factors affecting it. These are briefly discussed below.

Regulatory Status

An investment company which offers shares to the public is subject to the disclosure and antifraud provisions of the Securities Act of 1933; its underwriter is subject to the Securities Exchange Act of 1934; and its investment adviser is subject to the Investment Advisers Act of 1940. All three entities, however, are directly regulated by the Investment Company Act of 1940. This act was primarily intended to eliminate abuses that had previously existed in the industry. Toward this end, the act provides controls to eliminate dishonesty and to limit the transactions which investment companies may have with affiliated persons; it set up safeguards to prevent unsound capital structures, and it seeks to curb the power of management by providing for unaffiliated membership on an investment company's board of directors. Thirty years later, the Investment Company Amendments Act of 1970 strengthened regulation of three major areas: management fees charged by investment advisers to their affiliated funds; determination of the load charged in the sale of mutual funds; and certain provisions of contractual plans, to permit the sale of advisory contracts at a profit, provided specified statutory guidelines are met.

Management fees. In the original act, the standard for determining the legality of the fee charged a fund by the investment adviser was "gross misconduct or gross abuse of trust." The amendments introduce a new yardstick of "fiduciary duty." The requirement that nonaffiliated directors annually approve the advisory fee is made mandatory (formerly approval could be secured from shareholders). The directors now have the duty of requesting the information necessary to evaluate the terms of the advisory contract, and the investment adviser must furnish this information. Moreover, a new Section 2(a) (19) introduces the concept of an "interested person" and sets limits on the number of such persons who can be included on a board of directors. The new concept is broader than the concept of "affiliated persons" it replaces.

Some funds have incorporated into the compensation program of their adviser so-called performance fees. In this arrangement, the adviser receives a basic fee (fulcrum fee) and an additional payment (performance fee) if it outperforms a securities index by designated margins. Corresponding reimbursements are given by the adviser to the fund for poor performance. The 1970 law permits a contract for performance fees under prescribed conditions. The fee may be based on fund assets that are averaged over a designated period; provision must also be made for the fee to increase and decrease proportionately with the performance of the fund relative to that of the selected index.

At one time, the popular practice in determining performance fees was for growth funds simply to measure changes in their net asset values per share during the relevant periods. These changes were adjusted to compensate for distributions of capital gains by assuming that all such distributions were reinvested in shares of the fund at the net asset value per share then prevailing. Since no other adjustment was made, the net asset value at the end of each fiscal year reflected the undistributed net income (the net income of the fund less the dividends paid during the year). The performance of the index, in turn, was measured by the difference between its value at the beginning and end of the period, without taking into account any dividends paid on the stocks included, except insofar as the index automatically adjusted for the dividends.

In August 1972 the Securities and Exchange Commission adopted Investment Advisers Act Rule 205-1, which defined the statutory terms "investment performance" of an investment company and "investment record" of the index of securities prices.[11] In a major procedural modification, the SEC required that the reinvested value of cash distributions had to be added to both the change in the net asset values of the fund and the change in the level of the index during the period under consideration. In this arrangement, however, since a fund's dividends are from net income, the performance results of the fund are burdened with the costs of operations and of dividend distributions, while the performance of the index is not. Prior to the enunciation of the rule, the funds had an implicit advantage arising from the fact that dividend payments were not considered in measuring performance and that, on the average, the distributions of growth funds tended to be less than those on the stocks comprising an index. By requiring the inclusion of dividends in determining performance, the SEC eliminated this advantage, but the commission did not provide for counting costs in the calculation of index results. This discrimination in effecting comparisons has discouraged the use of performance fees.

Sales load. In general investment company practices, mutual fund sales loads are based on a percentage of the total purchase price, not on the actual cost to a buyer. Thus, if an investor purchases the stock of a mutual fund at $10 per share and is charged the usual load of 8.5 percent of the public offering price, he actually pays 9.3 percent on his net investment. Most funds reduce the basic charge for bigger purchases. This charge is considered necessary by many companies to provide an incentive to salesmen to market fund shares. However, there are a number of companies that do not charge a load, relying instead on advertisements as their principal marketing tool.

To regulate the sales load, the Investment Company Act originally gave the SEC and the NASD (or any other registered securities association) rule-making authority to prevent "unconscionable or grossly excessive" charges. In lieu of this standard, the 1970 amendments authorized the NASD, subject to SEC oversight, to regulate permissible commissions to prevent "excessive sales loads." Following an extensive study of the subject, the NASD proposed to the SEC a rule which would set the maximum sales charge at 6.25 percent unless the fund offered one or more of these services: reinvestment of dividends at net asset value, quantity discounts, and the right to accumulate later purchases to obtain the lowered sales charge. If all three services were offered, a maximum charge of 8.5 percent of the amount invested could be imposed. (A charge in between could be provided depending on the services offered.) In October 1975 the SEC indicated its approval of the proposed NASD rule.

Another statutory control in the original act, Section 22(d), provides for resale price maintenance by prohibiting dealers from selling mutual fund shares at less than the current offering price as defined by the fund in its proposal. In a study of this provision requested by the Senate Banking Committee, the SEC staff in November 1972 concluded that there was no compelling public interest in continued retail price maintenance and that repeal of Section 22(d) would on balance be desirable. Acting on this evidence, the commission then inaugurated a series of hearings on the entire question of mutual fund distribution and in November 1974 expanded the types of groups to which funds could offer their shares at quantity discounts. At the same time, the commission indicated that it would not recommend repeal of section 22(d) but would attempt to move funds gradually toward greater retail price competition.

In the following year, the SEC proposed to let funds set up "open season." Funds or their underwriters would be allowed to charge a set fee on sales to new investors, but they could charge a reduced fee, or eliminate the fee entirely, on additional sales to established shareholders. The idea was to enable repeat investors to share in the distribution economies that may accompany additional sales to fund shareholders. A different attack came from the Justice Department. In early 1973, it brought an antitrust suit against various larger funds and brokerage houses, alleging that they had conspired to prevent the development of a secondary market in fund shares where investors could buy and sell their shares at prices determined by competition, like the shares of any other stock. Eventually the case was brought to the Supreme Court, which decided in 1975 that the industry was immune from antitrust liability because its authority to conduct such restrictive practices was implicit in the Investment Company Act.[12]

Contractual plan. Investors not uncommonly acquire shares of investment company stock pursuant to a regular investment program, which may be voluntary or contractual. In the former case, arrangements are made for systematic purchases, but there is no formal plan objective and a regular-level sales load is incurred. A contractual plan (front-end load periodic payment play certificate), on the other hand, provides for a designated number of payments to be made over a period of time, and group coverage usually may be acquired to insure completion of the program. Ordinarily, however, there is no penalty for delinquent payments, and completion of a plan may be accelerated if the investor desires.

The primary characteristic of a contractual plan is the handling of the sales load. While this charge is about the same for those who complete the plan as for those who purchase their shares directly, a relatively large portion is applicable to the initial payments. Prior to the 1970 amendments it was customary for about one-half of the investor's first 13 monthly payments to be deducted. As a result, if he redeemed his shares at an early stage, the applicable sales cost was relatively high.

The 1970 act permits two types of contractual plans. In the first type, a 50 percent front-end load may be offered, but a holder is entitled to a refund of the net asset value of the shares in his account plus all the sales charges paid if he elects to redeem his shares within a specified short period of time; if he redeems within the first 18 months, he may obtain a refund of the net asset value of his shares plus an amount equal to the portion of the sales charge that exceeded 15 percent of his payments to date. The second type permits a so-called "spread load" plan, under which no more than 20 percent of each of the first 48 monthly payments may represent sales charges, subject to the further limitation that the entire sales deduction for the initial four years may not average more than 16 percent of total payments. Accordingly, if a charge of 20 percent is imposed during the first three years of payment, no more than 4 percent may be applied in the last year, with the remaining sales charge spread equally over the subsequent monthly payments.

The investment company industry offers contractual plans because of the incentives they provide to salesmen. In effect, such a plan establishes an arrangement similar to the front-end commission deduction employed in the insurance industry. An investor may achieve the same results through a voluntary plan that he systematically carries out.

Use of Brokerage

In the course of buying and selling securities, investment companies, like other institutional investors, generate substantial amounts of brokerage commissions. Determination of an appropriate method for handling this business has been a nagging industry problem.

At one time, particularly during the era of fixed minimum commissions on all transactions, commission allocation practices were subject to little regulation. Brokers were eager to get this business, since it represented a lucrative source of income for which investment companies found they could obtain reciprocal benefits in the form of various services, primarily research, or through the sale of their shares. The simplest arrangement was for the investment company to assign the commissions to those firms that returned the desired benefits. This direct relationship often was difficult, particularly in the area of research and/or sales, because many different brokers might be engaged in the distribution of the investment company's shares, and it was impractical to keep direct brokerage ties with all of them. Accordingly, various practices were devised whereby the investment company would direct a "lead broker" to give up a portion of its commissions to other brokers to whom the investment company owed a favor. With NYSE member firms, direct give-ups from other NYSE firms were permissible; for regional only or over-the-counter firms, the give-ups would have to be arranged through members of regional exchanges, since some of these exchanges allowed give-ups to be made to nonmembers.

As the intricacy of these arrangements came to light, the regulatory authorities became concerned, and in December 1968 the NYSE, under pressure by the SEC, prohibited the practice of give-ups. In February 1972, in an important statement on the structure of the securities industry, the SEC requested the NASD to direct its members to discontinue the use of reciprocal portfolio brokerage for the sale of investment company shares. Some months later, the NASD proposed and adopted a rule that carried out this injunction but did not necessarily prohibit the execution of portfolio transactions by members who also sell shares of the investment company. In 1974 the SEC held hearings on this rule to determine if a limited relaxation should be permitted.

As a fiduciary of its affiliated funds, an investment adviser is required to obtain the best execution of the funds' portfolio transactions. In its February 1972 statement, the commission indicated that even under competitive commission rates, it might be appropriate for an investment company to pay higher commissions for research. This apparent willingness to countenance higher commissions in exchange for investment advice raised the question as to whether such a policy sanctioned the disregard of an adviser's obligation to seek the "best price and execution" of portfolio transactions on accounts it manages. To clarify this uncertainty, the commission issued a statement indicating that while it did not sanction disregard of the obligation to seek best price, it did believe " . . . that an investment manager should have discretion, in assigning an execution or negotiating the commission to be paid therefor, to consider the full range and quality of a broker's services which benefit the account under management and need not solicit competitive bids on each transaction."[13]

As indicated previously, the Securities Acts Amendments of 1975 state that is not a breach of an investment adviser's fiduciary obligation for a managed account to pay a higher commission than that charged by other brokers. However, the adviser must have received valuable research or brokerage services in return; pursuant to SEC rules, the circumstances in which and the services for which the higher fees were paid must be disclosed.

When an investment company or any other institution pays higher commissions than it would otherwise incur, particularly under competitive rates, it is, in effect, paying for the research with "hard" rather than "soft" dollars. The dollars are "hard" because the institution could have executed the transaction at a lower rate; they were "soft" under noncompetitive rates, since costs were the same everywhere within the confines of the primary market. This change has made institutions more careful in allocating commissions for research.

A related issue that has arisen in this area is the degree to which an investment company is obligated to recapture brokerage. If the investment company has an affiliated broker, it can recapture brokerage, for example, by reducing the company's advisory fees or costs by all or a portion of the income earned by the affiliated broker from the fund's portfolio transactions. In a landmark case, the First Circuit Court of Appeals partially agreed with and partially reversed an original district court decision. Involved was a derivative action by shareholders of Fidelity Fund who alleged violations of the Investment Company Act arising out of Fidelity's use of reciprocals to stimulate sales or obtain research and its failure to recapture give-ups for the benefit of the fund (the practice had not yet been banned). Both the lower and higher courts agreed that Fidelity's grant of reciprocals was unobjectionable and that the fund, as determined by its directors, was not obligated to use an affiliated broker as its investment adviser for the purpose of the recapture. Reversing the lower court, however, the circuit court held that management of the investment adviser had committed a "gross abuse of trust" in failing to notify the directors that a portion of fund brokerage could have been recaptured for the benefit of the fund by directing give-ups in transactions on either the PBW or Pacific exchanges to its underwriter, which was a subsidiary of the investment adviser and a member of the NASD.[14]

At present, therefore, it is clear that, at a minimum, the disinterested directors should be informed of all recapture opportunities and that in negotiated transactions the charges imposed by the affiliated broker should be competitive.[15] As indicated previously, however, this problem eventually will be eliminated, since the Securities Acts Amendments of 1975 provide for the termination of all portfolio transactions between a broker and its affiliated fund within a three-year period.

Sale of a Management Company

The principal assets of a management company are the know-how of its management and its investment advisory contract, which must be approved at least annually by the investment company's board of directors, including a majority of the board's disinterested members. Ordinarily, contracts are renewed regularly. As the affiliated fund grows, the value of the management company correspondingly increases because its principal source of income is the management fee, which is usually based on the amount of the fund's assets.

In 1966, Lazard Freres decided to withdraw from serving as investment adviser to the Lazard Fund, the shares of which were not being continuously offered. The reason for this move was that the fund's assets had been shrinking. Lazard had determined that a continuous offering of shares was desirable but did not consider itself in a position to undertake this function. Accordingly, an arrangement was made with Dun & Bradstreet to merge the Lazard Fund into the Moody's Capital Fund, a new, continuously offered fund to be formed by the Moody's Investors Service, Inc., a wholly owned subsidiary of Dun & Bradstreet, for stock valued at about $3 million. The arrangement was approved by more than 80 percent of the outstanding shares of the Lazard Fund, with less than 1 percent voting against it. When suit was brought to upset the plan, the district court concluded that since there was proper shareholder approval of the new advisory arrangement, there was no violation of the act. On appeal, however, the U.S. Court of Appeals for the Second Circuit in 1971 reversed the decision (*Rosenfeld* v. *Black*, 445 F. 2d 1337 [2d Cir. 1971]), ruling that since an investment adviser has a fiduciary relationship with its affiliated mutual fund, the adviser cannot profit by the transfer of its office to, or the use of its influence in, obtaining the approval of a successor adviser. This conclusion was different from that reached in the Insurance Securities, Inc. case mentioned previously (see p. 569).

To get around this limitation and to clarify the attendant legal uncertainties,[16] the 1975 amendments make clear that an investment adviser may incur a profit on the sale of its business subject to two major safeguards to protect the investment company and its shareholders. The first requires that after the sale, 75 percent of the investment company's directors must be independent for a period of three years. The second is that neither the transaction nor any implied or expressed conditions impose any "unfair burden" on the investment company. Included in the meaning of "unfair burden" is any arrangement during the subsequent two-year period whereby the investment adviser or any related parties receive any compensation directly or indirectly.

SUMMARY

An investment company is any arrangement in which a group of persons pool their funds in order to invest them in securities. Of the different types of companies, the most important is the management company. It may be classified, in turn, as an open-end company (usually called a mutual fund), which permits a holder to redeem a security for its proportionate share in the issuer's net assets, or as a closed-end company, which does not have this provision. In addition, open-end funds characteristically keep large amounts of unissued stock that enable them to offer shares continuously; ordinarily distribute stock through dealers at net asset value plus a sales charge or load (although some, called no-load funds, distribute stock without any charge); and typically are part of a complex organizational structure that includes a separate management company which provides the fund with investment advice for a fee. The shares of a closed-end company are traded in the open market and may sell at a discount from their net asset value.

The stock of an investment company is primarily useful to an investor who is not in a position to manage a portfolio. In evaluating the relative merits of different companies, primary consideration should be given to their relative performance, which must be considered in the light of their objectives. Depending on these objectives, the investment policies of the companies embody different degrees of riskiness which affect the returns that may appropriately be expected. To establish a standard to gauge these returns, the investor may predict the rate of return that would be obtained on an unmanaged portfolio that had the same degree of risk (volatility) as the portfolio of the company under study.

At present, there are many cross-currents affecting various areas of the investment company industry, including the relationship between the investment adviser and the funds it manages, the use of brokerage, and the handling of the charges imposed. While these factors are important, they are not vital considerations to the investor, whose prime concerns are the reliability of the adviser and its ability to perform well over a long period of time.

CHAPTER 24

Special Aspects of Privileged Securities

Senior securities represent a mixture of benefits and drawbacks to both the corporation and the investor. For the corporation, bond financing is a cheap way of raising new money, since it provides an income tax deduction. For the stockholder, this financing method may increase the amount of earnings carried to his benefit. These advantages justify including bonds in capital structures up to an amount that can be supported by earnings. The grave danger of this policy is that corporations may exceed their borrowing limit. Preferred stock financing is a means of raising fixed-income funds without infringing on the possibility of selling bonds in the future.

Declining business activity often draws individuals to the investment shelter of fixed-income securities. Corporations seeking funds at such times may succumb to the insistence of the market and sell senior issues, despite their preference for common stock. To obtain the benefits of favorable rates, it may be necessary to grant these senior securities certain common stock attributes or to give holders an opportunity to exchange them for common stock. Bonds or preferred issues having these features are called privileged securities.

As the economic outlook brightens, enterprises often wish to take advantage of improving market conditions by whittling down cumbersome debts. Capital structures must be pliant in order to accommodate these changing individual and business needs. To create flexibility, corporations may reserve the authority to call senior securities, obtain authorization for more common stock than needed at the time, issue income bonds, or establish the means for amending some features of the trust indenture. In addition, many companies have found, as will be explained later, that privileged securities may facilitate adjusting capital structures to varying economic conditions.

Privileged securities are important instruments of corporate finance. Although we have referred to their role in the capital-raising programs of corporations, our primary concern is to examine them from the investor's point of view. For this purpose we discuss senior issues with participating privileges, stock purchase warrants, and conversion features. We then consider stock rights and warrants as independent trading media.

PARTICIPATING SECURITIES

Endowing a senior security with a *participating privilege* enables the holder to share in a corporation's expanding earnings without losing his previous status in the capital structure. A typical privilege calls for the preferred stock to receive its designated dividend rate and for the common shares to obtain a similar distribution; thereafter, the two classes of securities divide any further disbursements equally. Minor variations often occur. The preferred stock may not participate fully in subsequent distributions; after the preferred issue has been paid at a designated rate, both it and the common stock may share immediately on an equal or proportionate basis in subsequent disbursements; or the common shareholders may receive smaller initial dividend payments than those obtained by the preferred stockholders, prior to sharing in future distributions.

The participating issue has been used primarily to facilitate the exchange of securities arising out of corporate reorganizations and to "sweeten" new offerings. An important crop of these issues grew out of the numerous railroad reorganizations following the 1929-1933 depression. Continued business prosperity has lessened their usefulness, and they are not a popular financing medium at present.

Method of Appraisal

In analyzing a participating preferred stock, the investor must first estimate the worth of the senior security without considering the attendant privilege. He then evaluates the participating feature as a separate common stock entity and finally combines these two elements into a single overall value. The technique of this calculation depends on the terms of the participation. If the preferred and common share equally in earnings after the basic dividend of the preferred has been paid, the value of a privilege is roughly similar to that of a common, with the number of shares outstanding equal to the combined amount of both types of stock. Allowance may have to be made for differences in voting rights and other privileges that may accrue to the common and not to the preferred, such as the preemptive right to subscribe to new offerings of common stock. Consideration might also be given to the degree of protection against small stock dividends. Adjustments for these factors, however, are likely to be small and ordinarily may be ignored.

As a general illustration, assume that a corporation has outstanding 1 million shares of participating preferred stock entitled to fixed dividends of $8.00 per share; thereafter, it divides earnings equally with 1 million shares of common stock. The investor first calculates the fixed-charge coverage of the $8 million required payment and assigns a value to this senior segment along the lines described for a straight preferred stock. To ascertain the participating earnings per share, he subtracts $8 million from the net earnings after taxes available for equity and divides the remaining amount by the sum of the number of preferred and common shares outstanding. Next, he develops a value for the participating portion in the same manner as for an ordinary common stock. By combining these two parts, he obtains an overall evaluation of the participating preferred stock.

This procedure may have to be adjusted to take into account different participating terms. For example, assume that the common stock is entitled to a specific payment prior to any further distribution to the preferred; in this case, the earnings that are shared by the common and preferred holders are reduced by the amounts to which the common stock is first entitled. To these lowered figures the investor must apply the appropriate common stock capitalization rate in order to derive a value for the participating segment applicable to the preferred.

Record of Participating Issues

Participating preferred stocks seem to have interesting possibilities for the investor; they permit retention of a senior position in a company's capital structure while providing the opportunity of sharing in any increased earnings. In actuality, purported benefits have often proved fictitious.

To a large degree, participating issues are employed by companies of limited earnings capacity. Thus, of ten industrial participating preferreds appearing in both Moody's *Manual* for 1974 and the Standard & Poor's *Stock Record*, only three received a Standard & Poor's rating above BB. Favorable economic conditions over a long period of time have resulted in a considerable reduction in the number of companies using participatory preferreds and in some enhancement of their caliber. Despite this improvement, most of the enterprises using the instrument are of modest size and have erratic records. These preferreds are characteristically speculative, and their participating features emphasize their dominant common stock characteristics.

SENIOR SECURITIES WITH STOCK PURCHASE WARRANTS

The common stock aspect of a participating preferred stock is inherent in the issue. Owners of the preferred stock automatically share with common stockholders the benefits of increased dividend payments beyond designated levels. A senior security with warrants provides a different type of privilege. The basic instrument is an ordinary bond or preferred stock. The privilege is created through attached *warrants* which give a holder the option of buying common stock on some specified basis. Instead of cash, the holder sometimes is permitted to purchase the stock by submitting the related senior security. For example, Tenneco, Inc. has outstanding warrants which permit a holder to tender Tenneco 6s79 at face value instead of cash. If the holder of a warrant does not exercise his privilege, he receives no additional equity in the income of the company.

Sometimes a holder may only exercise warrants by turning them in with his senior security. In other cases he may separate the warrants from the senior issue and submit them separately to obtain the common stock. Detachable warrants, as they are called, customarily command separate market prices, since holders remove them from, and sell them independently of, the senior security.

Corporations employ warrants to make more attractive an issue that might be hard to sell. Corporations may also offer warrants directly, as part of an exchange plan to effect mergers or reorganizations; or they may use warrants to compensate underwriters, promoters, and management.

Senior securities with warrants have had a resurgence of popularity in recent years. A noteworthy case was the sale by American Telephone & Telegraph in May 1970 of a large amount of bonds; each $1,000 bond had warrants attached enabling a holder to buy 20 shares of stock at $52 per share plus the bond until May 15, 1975. At that time the stock was selling at about $47. Inclusion of the privilege enabled the giant utility to market the obligation by means of subscription to its stockholders. For the first time, moreover, the New York Stock Exchange was willing to list a warrant.

For some time prior to the expiration date, the AT&T stock continued to sell somewhat below $52. Morgan Stanley undertook to head a syndicate to attempt to persuade holders to exercise their warrants even if the price was a shade less than $52. The theory behind this move was that the exercise of the warrant at this level would result in a lower net cost than would have to be paid in an open-market purchase after the investor added the commission on such a purchase. AT&T could pay Morgan Stanley to conduct this operation because the cost to the company would be less than if the warrants expired and it had to issue stock for the same amount of equity funds. Although the price of the stock rose to $52 for a short period just before the warrants expired, the operation was not as successful as had been anticipated. Only about 10 percent of the warrants were exercised.

A warrant has certain implications for the financing of the issuer. For one thing, when a warrant is exercised, the senior security to which it was originally attached may remain outstanding; therefore, the company's fixed-income capital structure is unchanged. Then again, conversion of warrants cannot be forced, although pressure in that direction may be exerted by an increase in dividend payments or a change in the exercise price previously provided. However, in the first instance the holder may still prefer to retain the warrant, and in the second, exercise depends on the terms of the original agreement. Consequently, the company has relatively little control over when it will receive the cash, and its financial planning is made difficult. It might appear that this limitation need not concern the company, since the warrant is likely to be exercised when the stock price is high—that is, at a time when the company is prospering and rapidly expanding and probably can use the money. Sometimes, however, the exercise of the warrants is simply the result of arbitrage.

CONVERTIBLE SECURITIES

A *convertible security* is an instrument which the holder may exchange at his own discretion on some specified basis for another type of issue, usually common stock. Because the privilege involves a shift from one security to another, a holder who exercises the conversion option loses his prior status in the company's capital structure. This feature represents an important distinction between the convertible security and the senior issue with warrants. In many respects, however, the two instruments are similar; they both provide for purchase of designated amounts of common stock, over specified periods of time, and at prices that on original issuance are usually somewhat above the prevailing market. Moreover, to encourage their use, privileges often contain a series of purchase prices that are scaled upward in accordance with a prescribed schedule. For example, Litton Industries subordinated 3½s/1987 are convertible into common stock at $42.50 a share until April 1, 1982, and at $45 thereafter until maturity on April 1, 1987.[1]

Corporations Using Convertible Securities

When the convertible security first became popular, corporations used it as they did the other types of privileged securities–to make their offerings more attractive. In recent years, the convertible security has assumed increasing stature as a financing vehicle. Many leading corporations have been reluctant to use common stock to finance plant enlargements. This hesitancy reflects their fear that the resulting increase in the number of equity shares might prevent maintenance of dividend payments during the interim period of plan construction, when earnings have not yet begun to flow from the new properties. On the other hand, an overly enthusiastic reliance on interest-bearing senior obligations could build up a permanent deadweight of fixed charges that might endanger financial solvency during periods of business reaction.

A number of corporations have resolved this dilemma through convertible securities. They have been able to sell these issues at favorable rates, reducing dilution during the early nonproductive period of plant construction. The new properties contribute to income, and the corporations are able to increase dividend payments. Reflecting these improvements, the market prices of their common stocks tend to rise, and conversion becomes attractive. As a result, holders of senior securities find it profitable to turn in their issues for common stock, thus cutting debt and augmenting the equity base. Employed in this way, convertible securities have been helpful in developing capital structures that reflect the changing earnings pattern of corporations.

American Telephone & Telegraph has been a conspicuous user of convertible obligations. A broadening demand for efficient means of communication has necessitated a tremendous expansion of AT&T's facilities. To provide the capital for this purpose, the company has relied heavily on the sale of convertible debentures. If no offsetting reductions had taken place, the amount outstanding would have created a formidable debt even for such a corporate giant. A large number of debenture holders, however, have converted their securities into common stock, thereby easing considerably the company's fixed-charge burden.

The roster of corporations that have employed convertible securities reads like an elite register of American business. Included are companies in varied fields, such as Abbott Laboratories, Alcoa, Chemical New York Corp., Connecticut Light & Power, Consolidated Gas Electric Light & Power of Baltimore, Ford Motor Credit, International Paper, R. H. Macy & Co., Standard Oil Co. of Indiana, and Union Pacific. The list of corporations that have utilized participating issues or senior securities with warrants contains relatively few such prominent names.

Some Conversion Terms

Conversion parity generally means the market price of the common stock which, on the basis of the conversion terms, is equivalent to the current value of the senior security. This figure is obtained by dividing the market price of the senior issue by the number of common shares into which it is convertible. The term *common stock value* (or *conversion value*) refers to the market value of the common stock into which the senior security may be converted; it is also called the stock value of the senior security. To determine this figure, the number of shares into which the senior issue is convertible is multiplied by the market price of the common stock.

Sometimes the statement of conversion terms does not directly give the number of shares for which the senior issue may be exchanged but shows the equivalent price of the common stock at which the transfer may take place. This price has no significance in itself but is only a circuitous means of indicating the number of shares into which the senior security may be converted. Thus, the fact that a $1,000 bond has a conversion price of $40 merely shows that the bond is convertible into 25 shares of stock. The relationship between the face value of the security and the conversion price of the stock is also known as the *conversion ratio.*

These terms represent relationships that are important in the evaluation of a convertible security. In Table 24-1, they, as well as several other descriptive features, are shown for a number of convertible securities.

An examination of the table reveals several things about the convertible securities listed. In most instances, they were selling on a yield basis that was relatively low for issues of their caliber, reflecting the influence of the conversion feature. That the conversion feature had promise is indicated by the fact that conversion parity (except for Chemical) was either just about at or only modestly above the price of the common stock. Moreover, except for the Union Pacific issue, the yields on the convertibles were above those of the related common, and in the case of Union Pacific the differential was small. Thus, the convertible securities not only provided a senior position relative to

TABLE 24-1

Selective Features of Convertible Securities

CONVERTIBLE SECURITY	QUALITY RATING	CONVERTIBLE SECURITY PRICE	SHARES OF COMMON PER CONVERTIBLE SECURITY	CONVERSION PARITY	COMMON PRICE	COMMON STOCK VALUE OF CONVERTIBLE	PREMIUM	CURRENT YIELD CONVERTIBLE	YIELD COMMON
Allied Stores 4½s/92	BBB	63	22.47	28	24½	550½	14.4%	7.14%	6.19%
AT&T $4.00 pfd.	AA	46½	1.05	44¼	41⅜	43⅜	7.2	8.60	8.22
Chemical New York Corp. 5½s/96	NR	69¾	13.51	51⅝	37⅛	501½	39.1	7.89	7.76
Crane Co. 5s/93	B	105	40.00	26¼	26⅝	1065	–	4.76	3.76
Ethyl Corp. $2.40 pfd.	BB	28¼	1.30	21¾	20¼	26¼	7.6	8.50	5.93
International Minerals & Chemical Corp. 4s/91	BB	82	19.68	41⅝	36⅞	725¾	13.5	4.88	3.47
Union Pacific 4¾s/99	A	99	17.50	56½	56½	988¾	0.1	4.80	4.96

NR: Not rated.

SOURCE: Data taken from Standard & Poor's Corporation, ***Fixed Income Investor*** (Fall 1974, various issues).

the common but also generally afforded comparable appreciation potential, plus a higher and more secure return.

Investment Value

Since the price paid for a convertible security consists of the value of the senior segment plus the option, the issuer ordinarily is able to provide a lower payment than on a straight issue. As a result, if the convertible were stripped of its privilege, the price would fall so that the yield would be the same as that of a comparable straight security; the price that would result is known as its *investment value*.

A convertible security's sale price tends to exceed not only its investment value but also its common stock value. The excess of the market price over the common stock value, as a percentage of the common stock value, is known as the *conversion premium.* If it is negative, an arbitrage is indicated. Assume that the convertible bond mentioned previously had a market price of $1,010 when the stock sold at $41. The common stock value is $1,025 (41 X 25) and the conversion premium is –1.46 percent = [(1,010/1,025) X 100%]. Such a situation very rarely occurs because professional arbitrageurs constantly check these relationships; if the securities are out of line, the arbitrageurs will immediately buy the bonds and sell the stock short. Thus, for practical purposes, the floor of a convertible bond is almost always at least its investment or common stock value, whichever is higher.

Table 24-2 shows a comparison of the investment values of selected convertible bonds, as determined by Standard & Poor's, compared with their market prices. Standard & Poor's gauges the issues' investment values by averaging the yields of similar quality bonds without the conversion feature. By and large, in 1974 the investment values of the public utility convertible bonds were fairly close to their recent prices, whereas the investment values of the industrial convertibles, with several exceptions (such as the Air Reduction and Allied Stores issues), tended to be well below their market prices. This differentiation probably reflected the greater stability of the utility obligations.

The price of a convertible security can be decomposed into three parts: the investment value, the excess of the common stock value over the investment value, and the conversion premium in dollars. The sum of the last two items constitutes the value of the option. On this basis, the price of a convertible may also be expressed as the sum of the investment value and the value of the option, or the sum of the common stock value plus the conversion premium in dollars.

To illustrate these terms, let us now assume a market price of $1,050 for a 6 percent bond convertible at $40 per share into common stock (25

TABLE 24-2

Investment Worth of Selected Convertible Bonds, 1974

	INVEST-MENT WORTH	RECENT PRICE
Utility Issues		
AA rated		
Houston Lighting & Pwr. 5½s, 1985	69	76
A		
Northern Indiana Pub. Ser. 4¼s, 1992	48	51
Rochester Telephone 4¾s, 1994	49	52
Southern Calif. Edison 3⅛s, 1980	66	67½
BBB		
Carolina Tel. & Tel. 5¾s, 1988	59¼	66
Central Hudson G & E 5¾s, 1978	80	82½
Central Hudson G & E 4⅜s, 1981	60½	65
Florida Power 4⅜s, 1986	59¾	65
Hawaiian Electric 4⅛s, 1982	46	49
Virginia Elec. Power 3⅝s, 1986	53¼	55
Industrials		
AA		
Standard Oil (Ind.) 5s, 1996	59	102¼
A		
Combined Insurance (Amer.) 4¼s, 1998	44½	65
Pfizer 4s, 1997	47¼	69¾
Sinclair Oil (now Atlantic Richfield) 4⅜s, 1986	61⅝	119
Trane Co. 4s, 1992	44½	53
Union Pacific Corp. 4¾s, 1999	52	103
Xerox Corp. 6s, 1995	66⅞	104⅞
Will Ross (now Searle, G.D.) 5¼s, 1989	56½	60½
Will Ross (now Searle, G.D.) 4½s, 1992	48½	53½
Industrials (continued)		
BBB		
Air Reduction 3⅞s, 1987	49	52
Allied Stores 4½s, 1981	70	71
Allied Stores 4½s, 1992	49	52
Aluminum Co. Am. 5¼s, 1991	59	83½
Amerace Corp. 5s, 1992	50	58½
ARA Services 4⅝s, 1996	49	61¾
Ashland Oil Inc. 4¾s, 1993	50½	54
Baxter Laboratories 4s, 1987	54¼	172½
Baxter Laboratories 4¾s, 1990	60	83
Baxter Laboratories 4⅜s, 1991	58	83
Becton Dickinson 4⅛s, 1988	55	65
Becton Dickinson 5s, 1989	61	70
Burlington Industries 5s, 1991	59¼	63
Burlington Northern 5¼s, 1992	56¼	68
Carrier Corp. 5⅛s, 1989	48	52
Dart Industries 4¼s, 1997	46½	74½
Engelhard Mineral & Chem. 5¼s, 1997	57	64
FMC Corp. 4¼s, 1992	46½	50
Ford Motor Credit 4½s, 1996	48¼	54½
Ford Motor Credit 4⅞s, 1998	48	59½
General Amer. Transp. 5¾s, 1999	58	63⅝
Great Northern Nekoosa 4¼s, 1991	49¼	78½
International Paper 4¼s, 1996	63¼	67½
Jostens' Inc. 4¾s, 1988	46¾	55
Kirsch Co. 6s, 1995	53¾	55
Macmillan Inc. 4s, 1992	59¼	65
Macy (R.H.) & Co. 4¼s, 1990	43	47
Macy (R.H.) & Co. 5s, 1992	50	55
Marcor 5s, 1996	53¾	60

SOURCE: Standard & Poor's Corp., ***The Fixed-Income Investor***, September 21, 1974, p. 431. Reprinted by permission.

shares) selling at $41 per share. Based upon the quantitative tests described previously, it is determined that as a straight bond with a 10-year maturity, it would yield 7.44 percent to maturity. Therefore, the investment value is $900. The excess of the common stock value (25 shares × $41 per share) over the investment value is $125 ($1,025 – $900), and the conversion premium in dollars is $25 ($1,050 – $1,025). The price of the bond may be expressed as the investment value of $900 plus the value of the option $150 ($125 + $25), or as the common stock value of $1,025 plus the conversion premium of $25.

Some Theoretical Aspects of the Convertible Security

As has been indicated, the strategy underlying the issuer's sale of a convertible security is for the purchaser to retain possession until earnings expand, when conversion may become desirable to reduce the debt. To ensure that such a retention period occurs, the corporation probably will provide an initial contractual income that exceeds the dividends paid on the underlying stock. As a result, the issue probably will sell at a conversion premium which, in essence, represents the cost to the investor of buying the convertible rather than the stock.

Against this cost, the investor must measure her potential gains. If she buys the senior security, she obtains a contractual income stream plus the common stock to be delivered at some future time when conversion occurs; if she buys the common stock directly, she obtains dividends (if paid) and has the same stock that she would have received at the future time under the other option. In addition, if she buys the convertible and, having failed to convert for some period of time, finds that the investment value of the bond exceeds the conversion value for the remainder of the life, her liquidation value from the buying-the-bond strategy will be greater than from the buying-the-stock strategy. The degree of uncertainty associated with the value of the convertible instrument at any future date is less than that associated with the underlying stock at such a date. The downside movement of the instrument is muted, since it cannot fall below the straight bond value, though it must be remembered that that value is a variable rather than a fixed quantum because it will vary with fluctuations in the prevailing interest rates (though, of course, it goes to par at maturity.) There is also much less uncertainty associated with the contractual income than with the dividend stream. Thus, while the dividends should be discounted at a rate appropriate to stock, the contractual stream should be discounted at a rate appropriate to a senior security. Consequently, the present value of the income stream of the convertible will usually be larger than that of the dividend stream on two counts: the undiscounted income until time of conversion will usually be bigger, and the discount rate is smaller. The investor then may measure his cost of buying the convertible against the amount by which the present value of the convertible exceeds that of the stock over the conversion period.

If, as the company expects, the company grows and dividends increase, the present value of the expected dividend stream will eventually be worth more than that of the contractual stream. As this differential widens, presumably, most holders of the convertible will elect to exchange their senior security for the related stock, thereby bringing the issuer's original strategy to fruition. However, some strongly risk-averse holders still may prefer to retain the senior issue because its investment value provides a floor that otherwise would not exist. Thus, once an obligation sells on a conversion basis, its price advance will match that of the underlying stock. For this reason, at any future point in time, the theoretical market price of the senior security is no greater than that of the underlying stock. But the extent of any potential decline is limited by virtue of its investment value which is, in turn, responsive to changes in market yields of securities of comparable quality. The theoretical superiority of the senior security, when it sells on a conversion basis, may be shown by the following case, which requires an elementary knowledge of probability theory.

No investor can know with certainty the future price of a stock, but conceptually it may be expressed as $\sum_i P_i \pi_i$, where P_i is one possible price that may obtain and π_i is its probability of occurrence. The products of each price and its associated probability are summed over all possible prices. Now introduce a bond which permits the investor to surrender it for either its investment value which is assumed to be \$100 (assuming interest rates never change) or a specified number of shares (x), whichever is desired. The expected price of the bond on the cash-out date becomes:

$$\sum_{\substack{i \\ xP_i \geqslant 100}} xP_i \pi_i + \sum_{\substack{i \\ xP_i < 100}} \$100\pi_i,$$

where the notation under the first $\sum$ indicates the summation begins with the initial value of i for which xP_i is equal to or greater than \$100. It is assumed that all possible prices are numbered sequentially, with the value of i rising with the value of P. This new expression has a higher value than the previous one because for each value of i for which $xP_i < 100$, the product $xP_i\pi_i$ in the first expression is replaced by $\$100\pi_i$ in the second. Moreover, since the high price in the second case is unchanged but the low level is raised, the dispersion of the resulting probability range of fluctuations is reduced.

As an illustration, assume that an investor believes that the probability distribution of prices for this common stock at some specified future date is as follows:

PRICE (P_i)	PROBABILITY (π_i)	WEIGHTED PROBABILITY ($P_i\pi_i$)
\$120	40%	\$ 48
110	30	33
90	20	18
80	10	8
Total	100%	\$107 = $\Sigma P_i\pi_i$

The investor is given the alternative of buying a \$100 principal amount bond that may be converted into one share of stock and that has an investment value of \$100 established by analysis. Since the bond may always be sold for \$100, the investor will only convert when the stock sells above this level. Using the second expression as our valuation base, we find that:

$$\sum_{\substack{i \\ P_i > 100}} P_i\pi_i,$$

representing all prices above \$100, equals \$81 (\$48 + \$33). On the other hand, if the price falls below this level, the investor can sell the bond at \$100, represented by:

$$\sum_{\substack{i \\ P_i < 100}} \$100\pi_i,$$

which is equivalent to \$30 (\$100 X 30%.) Thus, the expected value of the bond is \$111, compared with \$107 for the stock. The range for the bond runs from \$120 to \$100; for the stock, from \$120 to \$80. Because of this reduced dispersion, it is appropriate to use a lower discount rate to determine the present value of the expected stock equivalent value of the bond (\$111) than that used for the present value of the expected price of the stock (\$107). On balance, the risk-averse investor would have to weigh the present value of the increased dividend stream he would receive by holding the common stock after the income parity stage has been reached against the present value of the reduced principal of his investment if he switches from the bond to the stock.

The cost of buying the convertible rather than the company's straight bond consists of the conversion premium plus the excess of the conversion value over the investment value. By assuming this cost, the investor obtains an offsetting potential gain determined by the expected price of the stock at some designated future, since he could always convert to obtain this amount.

With respect to the typical convertible security, the investment value may be less than $100 for each $100 principal amount of bonds, but the conceptual approach is the same. The value of a convertible preferred can be analyzed in the same way as long as the investor remembers that the income stream is not so assured as for a bond but more certain than for the same company's stock, and that the cash-out value of the preferred is more ambiguous than that of a bond. There is no maturity to a preferred, but a floor of sorts nevertheless exists. If the company runs into trouble, the preferred is likely to be worth more as a senior security than as a common stock.

An Interesting Convertible Security

The severe market decline in 1974 drove the market prices of a number of convertible bonds close to their investment worth, as may be seen in Table 24-2. A particularly interesting case was the Storm Drilling & Marine (formerly Dearborn Computer & Marine Corp.) 5¼ percent subordinated debentures convertible into common stock at $24.07 per share (the privilege was protected against dilution). In the fiscal years ending October 1973 and 1972, the company's interest and related charges were covered about 3 times, but its depreciation charges were heavy, and on a cash basis the coverage was about 5 times. The company also had substantial bank maturities that were constantly being rolled over. Storm Drilling originally was formed as a computer leasing enterprise but had abandoned this business; in 1973 it was, for the first time, entirely concentrated in offshore drilling and marine services. On a fully diluted basis, earnings per share were $1.54 for the fiscal year. Because of the speculative nature of Storm Drilling's business, the short period of time it had been involved in these activities, and the company's fairly heavy debt structure, its bonds were considered to be of low medium-grade quality; they were rated CCC by Standard & Poor's.

Reeling under general market declines, Storm Drilling's common stock hit a low of 8¾ in September 1974. At that level, the conversion value of the company's debentures was $363. Interest charges, however, were amply covered, the company's financial position was good, and its earnings prospects bright. In these circumstances, it seemed reasonable to assume that the investment worth of the debentures was not less than $500; at this level, the issue would afford a current return of 10.5 percent, which seemed generous in view of its good protection. Reflecting the decline of the common stock, the debentures also fell sharply, but at their low point they remained several points above the indicated investment value of $500. Within a month, however, despite a continued general market depression, the debentures almost doubled in value, as reports emerged that a favorable tender offer by another company was on the verge of completion. In view of the strong position of the company in an interesting industry and the company's relatively modest size, such a move had seemed a reasonable prospect for some time.[2]

FACTORS TO CONSIDER IN EVALUATING A PRIVILEGE

The method of evaluating senior issues with conversion privileges or warrants follows the pattern outlined for participating stocks. First, the investor must judge the senior security on its own investment merits, thereby establishing a minimum price at which it would probably sell if the conversion or subscription privilege were not included. Second, he must gauge the value of the privilege separately. The following checkpoints may be used for this latter purpose.

Leverage Potential

The outstanding attraction of warrants lies in their leverage potential. Since the warrant represents a call on the related stock, the prices of both instruments move in tandem, but since the warrant must sell at a lower level, its percentage change is higher. For example, consider a warrant that entitles the holder to buy a common stock at $25 a share and assume for purpose of the illustration that the warrant's price is always its exercise value. In fact, warrants ordinarily are valued at a premium, but this differential would not materially change the percentage effects. As the termination date approaches, the premium tends to disappear. Table 24-3 shows the price and percentage changes in the stock and warrant.

The absolute price changes of the stock and warrant are the same, but the percentage changes of the warrant are steeper. The sharpness of this differential is very great at first but narrows as the prices of the instruments rise. On the declining phase, the process is duplicated in a reverse direction, except that the percentage shrinkage can never exceed 100, whereas the gains can be greater.

Moving from theory to fact, we can find many cases of warrants that have experienced much sharper changes than their related stock. This relationship is indicated in Table 24-4, which shows the price changes in the warrants and common stocks of a number of companies between their high

TABLE 24-3

Percentage Change in Common Stock and Related Warrant

COMMON STOCK		WARRANT	
MARKET PRICE	PERCENTAGE CHANGE	MARKET PRICE	PERCENTAGE CHANGE
30	– %	5	– %
40	+33	15	+200
50	+25	25	+67
60	+20	35	+40
70	+17	45	+29
60	−14	35	−22
50	−17	25	−29
40	−20	15	−40
30	−25	5	−67

and low points in 1973. It is possible to augment the leverage inherent in a warrant if the instrument may be purchased on margin, thereby requiring the deposit of only a portion of the purchase price.

TABLE 24-4

Price Changes of Warrants and Common Stocks of Selected Companies, 1974

	WARRANTS			STOCKS		
	PRICE RANGE		PER-CENTAGE CHANGE	PRICE RANGE		PER-CENTAGE CHANGE
	HIGH	LOW		HIGH	LOW	
AT&T	4⅞	⅜	1200%	53	39⅝	34%
Avco Corp.	2	⅜	433	8⅞	2	344
Chrysler	6⅜	1	538	20⅛	7	188
City Invest	2	⅜	433	14	4	250
Greyhound	4⅜	1⅛	289	18⅝	9¾	91
No. Cen. Air	1⅞	¾	150	4	2⅛	88
Tenneco	4⅝	1	463	24¾	16¾	48
United Telec.	3⅜	⅜	800	17⅜	10⅝	64
Wms. Cos.	56⅞	27⅛	110	77	45⅜	70

The nature of the warrant makes it a more speculative instrument than the related common stock. In addition to its greater percentage movements in price, the warrant ordinarily has a limited life, and it is not entitled to dividends or various of the other benefits of common stock. On the other hand, a convertible security ordinarily is less speculative than its related common stock, but it does not afford the leverage potential of the warrant. The *option segment* of a convertible security is the difference between its market and investment values, and the percentage changes in this segment are likely to be greater than those of the related common stock. In order to acquire this segment, however, the investor must buy the senior security, and the need for this outlay deprives the convertible of the leverage potential inherent in a warrant.

Changes in Terms of the Privilege

When the market price of a senior security has risen because of benefits from a common stock privilege, any lessening in the value of this feature will cause a corresponding decline in the price of the senior issue. To avoid an impairment of capital for this reason, the holder of a senior security whose market price reflects a common stock privilege must be familiar with its provisions. This information will enable him to know when he must sell the senior security or exercise the privilege to prevent a loss from a scheduled unfavorable change in conversion terms.

The American Telephone & Telegraph $3\frac{1}{8}$ percent debenture is an old case, but it illustrates well the importance of keeping abreast of conversion terms. The issue was convertible into common stock at a price of $130 per share through June 19, 1951, and at $140 thereafter; this privilege called for payment by surrender of $100 principal amount of debentures and cash equal to the difference between the conversion price in effect and 100. On June 19 the bonds closed on the New York Stock Exchange at $123\frac{7}{8}$, providing a yield of 0.15 percent to maturity. On the basis of the bond price of $123\frac{7}{8}$, the conversion parity of the common was $153\frac{7}{8}$; the closing price of the common on that day was $154\frac{3}{8}$.

The favorable conversion feature clearly produced the high price and extremely low return on the bonds. It was logical to assume that the 10-point rise in the conversion price of the common stock scheduled for the next day would produce a corresponding decline in the value of the bonds. On the following day, when the change in the conversion price became effective, the common stock closed at $154\frac{1}{8}$, virtually the same level as on the previous day; the bonds, reflecting the lowered conversion price, dropped $9\frac{3}{4}$ points to a new price of $114\frac{1}{8}$. To avoid this decline, the bondholders had the choice of converting into common stock or disposing of their holdings before June 20.

Protection Against Dilution

A capitalization change, such as a stock dividend or split, that materially decreases the market price of a company's common stock will reduce correspondingly the value of a common stock privilege. It is standard practice for corporations to protect against dilutions of this sort by reducing the conversion or subscription price in proportion to the increase in the number of common shares outstanding. It is prudent for the investor to check the terms of the privilege to make certain that the antidilution clause exists.

Duration of the Privilege

The duration of a common stock privilege establishes the period within which the holder must exercise his option. When this interval runs for several years, there is greater opportunity for the market price of the common stock to rise above its conversion or subscription level. It is particularly important for the privilege on a new issue to be long enough for the earnings of a corporation to benefit from its additional financing. The investor must always consider the length of the privilege in conjunction with the relationship between the market price and the subscription price or conversion parity. A privilege permitting acquisition of common stock only moderately below the existing market level may be of little value if it is scheduled to expire shortly. However, when the exercise period is very long, the gap between market and conversion or subscription price may be wider and still be profitable ultimately.

A classic illustration of the value embodied in the length of time a privilege runs is the perpetual warrant. At one time a number of such instruments were outstanding, but their existence constantly overhung a company's capital structure, and many of them have therefore been retired through exchange offers. The fact that such warrants give the holder a call on the underlying stock *forever* enormously augments their leverage potential. For example, Tri-Continental, a large closed-end investment company, still has perpetual warrants outstanding. In 1942 each warrant entitled the holder to buy 1.22 shares of stock at $18.46. Since the price of the stock ranged between ¾ and 2⅛, the likelihood of the warrants ever having any intrinsic value appeared very remote, and at their low for the year they sold at about 3 cents. Over time, the growth of the American economy and circumstances peculiar to the company have been reflected in a striking rise in the price of the common stock. The warrants are protected against dilution. Since there were several changes in capitalization, each warrant in 1973 entitled a holder to buy 3.46 shares of common stock at $6.51 per share. In that year the price for the common stock was much higher. Reflecting its related value, the warrant reached a high in 1973 of 82¾. Thus, over the 31-year period, from a low price in 1942 to a high price in 1973, the warrants experienced a dramatic rise from a negligible to a substantial value.

Call Price of the Senior Security

Retaining a privileged senior security selling at a substantial premium over call price is dangerous if at the same time the market level of the related common stock is below its conversion parity or subscription price for nondetachable warrants. The holder of such an issue exposes himself to the possibility of a loss that is equal to the difference between the market and redemption or privilege price, whichever is greater.[3] This hazard does not exist when the related common stock is selling at about its parity price. In that event, if the corporation calls the senior issue, the holder may still exercise his option of obtaining the common stock at an equivalent price during the period of time normally intervening between announcement and redemption date. To avoid losses through carelessness, the investor should act promptly after the call notice.

In late 1974, Standard Oil of Indiana announced its intention to retire, on March 23 of the following year, the remainder of its outstanding convertible debentures 5s due 1996 at $1042.50 plus interest. The common stock privilege, scheduled to expire on November 29, provided for conversion of the bond into 14.184 shares of common stock. The bonds were selling at about $1,210; the conversion parity and market price of the common stock equaled 85. To avoid a loss of about $163 per bond, holders had to convert to common stock or liquidate the bonds before the expiration date.

Expected Price Movements of the Common Stock

The factors thus far discussed are primarily objective in nature. The value of an option is also influenced significantly by the subjective judgment of the market regarding the price movements of the related stock. In this respect, the two major judgments involve price appreciation and volatility. These two factors interact differently on warrants and convertible securities.

The value of both a warrant and the option privilege inherent in a convertible is directly dependent upon expectations regarding the appreciation potential of the related stock. To the extent that this aspect is believed to be favorable, the warrant is likely to command a premium, and the sum of its market and exercise prices will exceed the market price of the related common stock. Similarly, the convertible issue will have a positive conversion premium that adds to the value of the instrument's option privilege.

Generally, bonds with detachable warrants provide investors with better options than do convertible securities. In periods of high bond prices, holders of warrants can dispose of any or all of their bonds, if they have any, without surrendering the exercise privilege. The holder of the convertible cannot. Because the straight bond can be disposed of at will, the investor has greater opportunity for leverage with warrants than with convertibles. In both cases the investor can lose the entire privilege value if the stock price does not rise to the exercise price.

Volatility has similar effects on the two types of investments, but because of the warrant's greater leverage, the impact is likely to be greater on the value of the warrants. All other things being equal, the values of both the conversion privilege and the warrant increase with the volatility of the stock.

COMMON STOCK PRIVILEGES AS INDEPENDENT TRADING MEDIA

We now shift from studying senior securities with common stock purchase privileges to viewing these options as separate trading media. Privileges that may be bought or sold independently of other securities arise for several reasons: holders of detachable warrants may disengage them from their senior securities; companies may issue warrants directly; or corporations may give their stockholders rights that embody certain benefits.

Warrants

Stock purchase warrants embody the privilege of purchasing another security at a specified price or at a changing scale of prices; this privilege may be effective for a limited period or may have no time limit. Compared with rights, the stock purchase warrant generally has a longer life span, provides for the purchase of the other security at a higher price than that prevailing at the date of issuance, and is usually traded in units that entitle the holder to purchase one full share of the additional security.

A warrant has no compensating advantages over the related common stock and is not entitled to dividends that the latter may receive. Accordingly, the warrant should never sell above the stock. On the other hand, at a minimum, the warrant is worth the excess of the market price of the stock over the exercise price. If the warrant sells for less, an investor can easily make a profit through buying the warrant, selling the stock short, and exercising the warrant to cover the short position. The market price of a warrant, however, may be greater than the difference between the market price of the stock and the exercise price, because speculators are willing to pay a premium for the greater percentage gains that may be realized from the warrant. Thus, assume that a warrant provides for the purchase of one share of common stock at $20 and that the stock is selling at $25. The stock's price of $25 clearly sets an upper limit to the value of the warrant. At the other extreme, exclusive of the costs of buying and selling, the warrant is worth at least $5 ($25 – $20).

Between the maximum and minimum extremes, the warrant's price movements reflect those of the related stock. The level of the curve, however, gradually declines as the number of months before expiration is reduced until it approaches the minimum value line. Typical price curves for a hypothetical warrant are shown in Figure 24-1. Analysts have attempted to take advantage of this pattern by trading schemes that involve buying the stock and selling the warrant short when it incorporates a high premium.[4]

FIGURE 24-1

Typical Price Pattern of Hypothetical Warrant

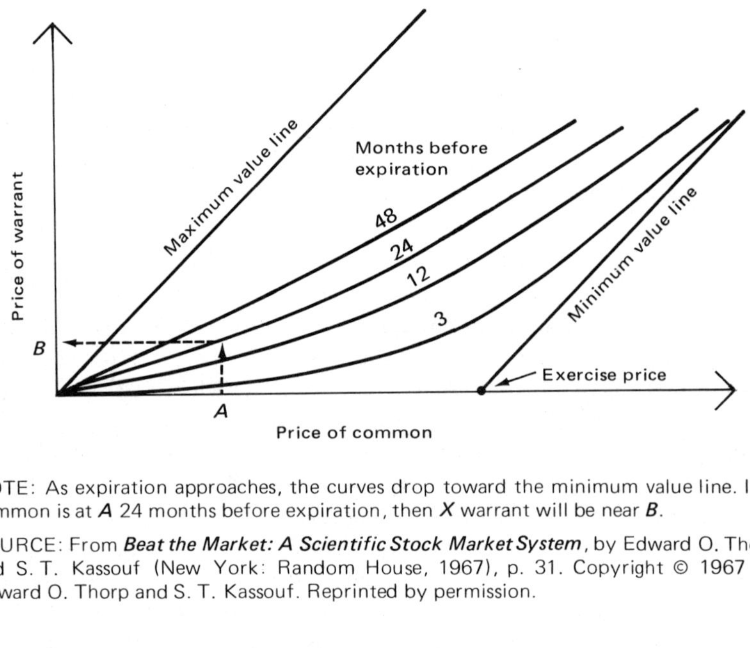

NOTE: As expiration approaches, the curves drop toward the minimum value line. If *X* common is at *A* 24 months before expiration, then *X* warrant will be near *B*.

SOURCE: From ***Beat the Market: A Scientific Stock Market System***, by Edward O. Thorp and S. T. Kassouf (New York: Random House, 1967), p. 31. Copyright © 1967 by Edward O. Thorp and S. T. Kassouf. Reprinted by permission.

As an illustration, let us assume that in period 1 the market price of a stock is less than the subscription price ($MP_1 < SP$); the resulting premium equals the subscription price plus the price of the warrant (W_1) less the market price of the stock ($P = SP + W_1 - MP_1$). If an individual buys the stock and goes short on the warrants, he would experience the following effects at a time 2 immediately prior to the expiration date, depending upon the price movements of the stock:

(1) *The stock advances in period 2 to a level above its exercise price ($MP_2 > SP$).*
The warrant sells at its intrinsic value ($W_2 = MP_2 - SP$). The holder incurs a profit on the stock ($MP_2 - MP_1$). When he sold the warrant

short he received $(P - SP + MP_1)$. When he covered, he had to pay $(MP_2 - SP)$ for the warrant. His gain on the short sale is $(P - SP + MP_1 - MP_2 + SP)$, which in this case is negative. It reduces to $(P + MP_1 - MP_2)$. His net gain is the sum of the gains on stock and on the warrant $(MP_2 - MP_1 + P + MP_1 - MP_2)$, which reduces to P, the original premium on the warrant.

(2) *The stock advances to not more than its exercise price* $(MP_2 > MP_1$ but $MP_2 \leqslant SP)$.
The warrant has no intrinsic value. The holder incurs a profit on the stock and a gain on the short sale equal to the original value of the warrant. His net gain is the sum of these two elements $(MP_2 - MP_1 + W_1)$.

(3) *The stock declines by not more than the original value of the warrant* $[MP_2 < MP_1$ but $MP_2 \geqslant MP_1 - W_1)]$.
The warrant has no intrinsic value. The holder incurs a loss on the stock $(MP_1 - MP_2)$ that at maximum is equal to the original value of the warrant. Therefore, either a net gain results equal to the profit on the short sale less the loss on the common $(W_1 - MP_1 + MP_2)$, or there is a standoff $(W_1 - W_1)$.

(4) *The stock declines by more than the original value of the warrant* $[(MP_2 < MP_1$ and $MP_2 < MP_1 - W_1)]$.
The warrant has no intrinsic value. The holder incurs a loss on the stock that is greater than the value of the warrant. Therefore, his net loss is the decline of the common less the value of the warrant $(MP_1 - MP_2 - W_1)$.

To illustrate these various conditions, let us assume that an individual sells a warrant short at \$5 that has an exercise price of \$12 and buys the related common stock at \$8. Under conditions described in case (1) above, the stock advances to \$25. The warrant sells at its intrinsic value of \$13. The holder incurs a profit of \$17 on each share of common stock (\$25 – \$8) and loses \$8 on the short sale of the warrant (\$5 – \$13), for a net gain of \$9, which is equal to the original premium of the warrant (\$12 + \$5 – \$8). In case (2) the stock rises to \$11, \$1 less than the exercise price. He makes a profit of \$3 on the common stock. Since the warrant has no intrinsic value, he gains the original value of the warrant on the short sale. His net gain is \$8 (\$5 + \$3). In case (3) the stock declines to \$3. He loses \$5 on the stock but makes \$5 on the short sale. He therefore breaks even. In (4) the stock declines to \$1. He loses \$7 on the stock but makes \$5 on the short sale. His net loss is \$2.

Analysts who favor this type of transaction point out that only in the case of extreme declines in the price of the stock (4) does a net loss occur. An individual who actually undertook this maneuver would have to take into account the costs of buying and selling and would have to be able to retain his short position during the entire time.

Stock Rights

Stock rights are transferable privileges authorizing stockholders to purchase another security or a portion of another security at a designated price for a specified period of time. Corporations often use them as the physical means of implementing the stockholders' preemptive right to subscribe to additional shares of stock in proportion to their present holdings. Companies also issue rights that give stockholders the opportunity of acquiring assets in the process of liquidation.

Unless it is expressly denied by state statute or corporate charter, owners of equity issues have the preemptive right. A number of corporations have limited this right in order to enhance the flexibility of their financing programs. By freeing themselves from the restriction of first offering additional stock to existing shareholders, corporations also eliminate the expense of preparing transferable subscriptions and increase the number and geographic diversification of their stockholders.

Calculating the Value of Rights

Since subscription rights do not entitle the holder to any direct participation in the earnings or assets of the issuing corporation, their value depends directly on the price of the security which may be bought and on the terms of the privilege. A holder may have to determine the value of rights under these principal conditions: (1) when the rights permit him to acquire common stock of the issuing corporation and the stock sells "cum-rights," or "rights-on"; (2) when the rights permit him to acquire the common stock of the issuing corporation and the stock sells "ex-rights"; and (3) when the rights permit him to buy an asset or security other than the common stock of the issuing corporation.

Rights to purchase common stock of the issuing corporation: stock selling "cum-rights." Corporations announce the distribution of rights just as they announce dividend payments. A notice is issued to the effect that shareholders whose names are recorded on the books of the corporation as of a specified future date will receive rights to purchase additional stock on a designated basis. After this announcement, a purchaser of the original shares knows that he will receive the privilege if he obtains the stock before it goes "ex-rights." The date on which a security sells "ex-rights" is established by the New York Stock Exchange, just as in the case of dividends. It represents the date on which the purchaser of stock is no longer entitled to receive the rights or dividends to be issued by a corporation.

In the case of a rights offering, however, the corporation must issue new stock, which has to be registered with the Securities and Exchange Commission. Ordinarily, corporations do not include in the registration statement first filed with the commission the complete subscription terms for securities to be offered by means of subscription rights. Until these terms are released, there is no way of determining the value of the rights. This information is often announced and made public at a later time through an amendment to the registration statement. The amendment is usually filed on or just prior to the date on which the registration statement becomes effective, which is frequently used as the record date to determine which stockholders are entitled to the rights.

When the effective registration and record dates coincide, the New York Stock Exchange ordinarily provides that the beneficiary security trades "ex-rights" at the first full business day after the effective date, which ordinarily is also the first day of trading on the exchange. A "due bill" must then accompany certificates delivered after the record date in settlement of contracts made prior to the ex-date.

In these circumstances, a common stock ordinarily will trade "cum-rights" for not more than one full business day. For example, let us assume that on January 1, 1975, a corporation announces an offering of 100,000 shares of new common stock which holders of record on January 15 may purchase in the ratio of one new share for each ten shares held. Let us further assume that registration of the security becomes effective on January 15 with an exercise price of $15 per share and the NYSE approves trading for that date. The stock will then sell "ex-rights" on January 16, the first full business day after the effective date.

During the short period that the stock sells "cum-rights," its value may be determined by $V = (M_0 - S)/(R + 1)$, where V is the value of one right, M_0 represents the market price of the common stock with rights on which the holder of each right is entitled to purchase, S is the subscription price at which the holder may exercise his right to acquire additional common stock, and R is the number of shares of stock required to obtain one new share.[5] This formula represents the ratio between the shares already oustanding and those to be issued.

To illustrate the application of this formula, assume that on January 15, when trading in the stock "cum-rights" occurs, the market price of the stock is $20 per share. On that date, the value of each right is determined as follows: $V = (20 - 15)/(10 + 1) = 0.45$.

Rights to purchase common stock of the issuer: stock selling "ex-rights." After a common stock goes "ex-rights," its market price no longer includes any privilege allowance. At that time, the difference between the market and subscription prices of the stock equals the value of the rights required to buy one full share of the stock by subscription. The value of a single right may be determined by dividing this difference by the number of rights necessary to obtain one share of stock. The formula may be stated as follows: $V = (M_e - S)/R$, where M_e represents the market price of the stock ex-rights.

The results of this formula can be compared with those obtained in the previous example. On January 16, when the stock sells "ex-rights," its market price drops by the value of one right, which was calculated to equal 45 cents, reducing the M in the equation to about \$19.50.[6] We now divide by R alone. Since M_e is a price that already reflects the exercise of the rights, it represents the value received when a right is exercised. The value of the rights used in acquiring the stock is the excess of M_e over the subscription price. The value of a single right is, therefore, the ratio of that excess to the number of rights needed to buy a share, namely R, not $(R + 1)$. On the rights-on case, the market price cum rights is *not* the consideration that is received when the rights are exercised. The excess of the cum-rights price over the ex-rights price is scheduled to evaporate on the day the stock goes ex-rights. The ratio of the excess of the cum-rights price over the exercise price to the number of rights needed to purchase a share is thus greater than the value of a single right. An adjustment factor is needed. As can be seen in note 5, the adjustment is effected by dividing by $R + 1$ instead of R. The value of the right is thus $(19.50 - 15)/10$, or 0.45, the figure reached when the stock sold "cum-rights." In practice, this relationship may not work out exactly, because the numerous forces influencing the price of a stock may offset a complete adjustment after the issue sells "ex-rights."

Rights to purchase securities other than the common stock of the issuer. Rights also may be distributed to stockholders that entitle them to acquire a security other than the common stock of the issuing corporation. During the years of active public utility holding company simplification, parent companies often gave their shareholders rights to buy subsidiary securities that had to be liquidated. More recently, corporations have distributed rights of this sort to enable common stockholders to obtain new issues of convertible obligations. In most cases, the value of rights should be calculated by the ex-rights formula, in which the denominator is simply R instead of $(R + 1)$. When the rights entitle the stockholder to buy the securities of a company other than the issuer of the rights, the issuer of the securities is rarely the recipient of the subscription price. For example, if company S is a subsidiary of company H and the latter issues rights which entitle the H stockholders to buy the stock of S held by company H, S will receive no cash and the number of its shares outstanding will not change. Under the circumstances, there is no reason why the value of its stock should change as a consequence of the rights offered. The excess of the value of its stock over the subscription price, therefore, measures the gain H stockholders obtain from having been issued the rights to buy that share. The gain per share must be divided by the number of rights needed to purchase one share of S in order to determine the gain per right. That gain per right is its value.

As a consequence of this type of transaction, the value of H stock should be expected to fall. For each share of S disposed of, H loses the value of that share and receives in exchange only the subscription price, which, presumably, is less.

In this type of financing, the corporation is likely to offer its stockholders the right to buy a security that has never before been publicly traded. The corporation either may have held the issue as an asset in its own portfolio or may be offering a new obligation of its own. For this reason the price of those securities used in the computation is often based on "when distributed" or "when issued" prices. This is the equivalent of the ex-rights price; therefore, one must use R rather than $(R + 1)$ in the denominator.

Transfer of Stock Rights

Each right that is traded in the stock exchange usually embodies the privilege of buying only a fractional share of new stock. The certificates evidencing these rights are called warrants;[7] they may be issued in registered form, assignable and transferable, or in bearer form. Individuals who do not receive rights in the proper multiples to purchase full shares of stock must either dispose of the excess number or buy enough additional rights to make up the deficiency.

The New York Stock Exchange allows use of a single warrant to represent full and fractional subscription rights, provided that arrangements are made so that at subscription the residual rights called for by the warrant may be sold for the benefit of the subscriber. The exchange also recommends that the means be provided for holders to purchase additional rights up to the next full unit. To carry out these stipulations, corporations often make arrangements with the financial institution serving as subscription agent to buy additional rights for subscribers or to sell, with no charge or only a small fee, the excess rights not required for subscriptions. In undertaking these transactions, the subscription agent tries to offset buying and selling orders. When an individual is ready to exercise his warrants, he surrenders them properly executed, accompanied by the full subscription price. Because rights have no value after their expiration date, holders must decide to sell or exercise them prior to this time.

Stock rights have the same type of leverage as stock purchase warrants. In addition, the low price of rights and their brief duration encourage concentrated speculative activity. Price fluctuations of rights tend to be considerably more violent than those of the senior securities with which they are associated. Nevertheless, the longer duration of stock warrants relative to rights affords warrants the opportunities for substantial market gains over longer periods of time.

SUMMARY

Of the various privileged securities, a senior issue with participating privileges theoretically embodies the most favorable technical terms. The holder is under no pressure to take positive action, since he always retains senior status while automatically sharing in any corporate earnings improvement.

The senior issue with detachable warrants is the next most attractive type of security. Instead of automatically receiving benefits, the owner of an issue with warrants must make a definite decision. To be certain that he benefits from his privilege, he must either detach the warrant and sell it or exercise his privilege of obtaining common stock and eventually dispose of the stock. If he keeps the common issue obtained by exercising his option, his current gains may later be eliminated by market declines. However, the warrant holder has the unique advantage of being able to "cash in" his common stock privilege without endangering his priority position in the capitalization of the company. The holder of a convertible security does not have this choice; he either retains his senior securities or exchanges them for common stock, thereby losing his higher status.

In practice, investors have not been able to exploit to any large degree the special qualities of a participating privilege. As has been observed, relatively few (and often the less prominent) corporations tend to use this feature. By contrast, many leading enterprises do use convertible securities in their financing programs. Moreover, conversion terms are often favorable, enabling investors to purchase sound senior securities with market enhancement possibilities. Warrants provide considerable opportunity for leverage and can therefore be attractive, depending on their duration.

Rights and warrants obtain their value indirectly, through their claims on other securities, and they cannot provide any current income; hence, they are not suitable holdings for the average investor. However, they have considerable leverage and may yield substantial market gains. As independent trading vehicles, therefore, they may be attractive to the venturesome investor.

CHAPTER 25

The New Popularity of Options

In general, an *option* represents a contract in which the buyer is granted the privilege of obtaining some benefit from the seller for a specified period of time in exchange for an agreed fee. The major forms of options are the *call*, entitling the holder to buy something at a definite price for a fixed period of time, and the *put*, which gives him a similar privilege on the sell side. Combinations of puts and calls have also been worked out. These terms, as well as others that are involved in securities option trading, are defined more explicitly in the appendix to this chapter.

BACKGROUND

An article on options in the *Institutional Investor* noted that the first reference to such a contract probably occurs in the Bible. Jacob promised to work for Rachel's father for seven years in return for a call on her hand in marriage at the end of that time. After the contract expired, however, the father refused to honor the terms of the agreement and insisted that Jacob first marry the elder daughter, Leah. "Thus," the author observed, "did options begin to acquire a reputation for being high-risk vehicles of uncertain return."[1]

The authors wish to acknowledge the aid of Richard Carrigan, a partner of the Tortoise Fund, in the preparation of this chapter.

While there is no record of how options may have been used in the years following Jacob's unfortunate experience, we do know that securities options have been actively traded for the past century in Europe, where, before World War II, the principal markets were in London, Paris, and Amsterdam. Recently, some European financial centers, especially London, have been investigating the possibility of adapting the method of trading options on exchanges used in the United States to their own markets. When options were introduced into the United States, they earned an unsavory reputation because of early abuses. Accordingly, in the original drafts of the Securities Exchange Act of 1934, Congress contemplated outlawing the purchase or sale of options through an exchange or in connection with exchange-traded securities.[2] Recognizing that options also had legitimate uses, Congress finally compromised by giving the Securities and Exchange Commission broad powers under Sections 9(b) and 9(c) to regulate their trading.

For 40 years following passage of the Exchange Act, option trading was concentrated in the over-the-counter market, but it was an esoteric field that attracted little public attention. Largely ignored by the SEC, the market was primarily self-regulated by some 20 specialty firms which served as middlemen between option buyers and sellers. In 1932 these firms established the Put and Call Brokers and Dealers Association to provide a formal regulatory structure. Gradually, investors began to show more interest in the field; reflecting this trend, about 75 member firms had established departments for options by the early 1970s.[3] Still, they were not widely used. Besides lack of knowledge, the major deterrents to investors were the relatively high costs of trading and the cumbersome nature of the market. Moreover, option sellers and buyers were largely locked into their contracts; sellers had to wait until the options they had written expired or were exercised, while buyers had difficulty disposing of unexpired options, even when they had value.

As described below, inauguration of the Chicago Board Options Exchange (CBOE) on April 26, 1973, changed the picture considerably. Several months before that, the SEC had granted the application of the CBOE to register as a national securities exchange "to permit it to test the market for such options within a controlled environment." As part of a surveillance program, the first rule emanating from the commission was Rule 9b-1, which, among other things, requires an exchange which wants to trade options to obtain approval of a plan for their regulation.[4]

The stock exchanges, then in a period of low volume, were attracted to the CBOE operation; the American Stock Exchange was the first to file a plan with the commission for option trading. Approval was granted pursuant to Rule 9b-1, and the AMEX commenced trading in January 1975. PBW was given approval to begin operations in June, and the Pacific Stock Exchange was expected to initiate its option program in 1976.

In its studies, the commission has raised several questions about options, such as the suitability of such trading for the nonprofessional investor,[5] the degree of disclosure that should be provided, the impact of option trading on the liquidity of the markets for the underlying stocks, the economic function served by the writing and purchasing of options, and the conditions which should govern trading in multiple exchanges. The commission did not release specific findings, but in April 1974 the staff (with the apparent approval of the commission) requested the AMEX and the CBOE (which was seeking to expand its program) to meet goals relating to the use of a common tape, standardization of option terms, a common clearing system, and availability of option quotations to nonmembers. Following this request, the AMEX and CBOE established a common clearing faculty, the Options Clearing Corp. (OCC), based on the preexisting CBOE Clearing Corp. Provision was made for other exchanges to become participants in the OCC.[6] Options traded on the PBW are issued by the OCC and are subject to its rules.

CHICAGO BOARD OPTIONS EXCHANGE

CBOE is the nation's first organized (and still dominant) exchange for the trading of options. Its method of operations is discussed in some detail because it represents the pattern that is being followed by the other exchanges that deal in options.

The Chicago Board Options Exchange is a nonstock corporation organized under the laws of Delaware. The OCC, the common clearing facility for exchange-traded options, not only provides for the settlement of CBOE transactions but also is the legal issuer of the options. As such, it provides a blanket prospectus, which covers all options traded on the exchanges. The prospectus is updated periodically and must be given by a member firm to any investor who attempts to open an account.

The CBOE was developed by the Chicago Board of Trade, and a member of that organization who qualifies is automatically entitled to membership on the CBOE. At the outset, 165 memberships were acquired through this affiliation, and these may only be transferred as a package; 217 memberships were sold by the exchange at a price of $10,000 in two stages; in June 1973, several months after trading began, 50 additional memberships were authorized at a price of $15,000. Thereafter, transactions in outstanding memberships began to occur, and the market price of membership rose very rapidly.

Each exchange determines from time to time the underlying stocks to be used for its options, which at present are only calls. All the underlying stocks must be listed on an exchange, approved by the SEC, and meet various requirements, including certain earnings tests. At the outset, the CBOE approved call options in 34 stocks; it then initiated transactions in 16 stocks and shortly thereafter added another 16. Each exchange adds stock from time to time and plans, as institutions and the public become more familiar with its operations, to initiate trading in puts as well. By the fall of 1975 call options in over 100 stocks were traded on the exchanges.

In the first week of trading, calls on the CBOE averaged roughly 100,000 shares of stock per day (every call is an option on 100 shares of stock). By the close of the year, volume was running about 1 million shares a day (10,000 contracts). Activity has continued to rise and on October 23, 1974, exceeded 6.2 million shares (62,000 contracts), causing the exchange at that time to prohibit for a while the entry of all stop orders, in order to maintain a "fair and orderly market."[7] The CBOE is now doing the largest volume per listing of any registered securities exchange in the United States. Option volume in the AMEX rose during the first three months of activity to almost one-fifth that of the CBOE; by the end of the summer of 1975, it rose to over one-third of the CBOE volume. The CBOE volume has, at times, approached 10 million and the Amex, 2.5 million shares.

Participants in the Option Transaction

The listed call option entitles the holder (buyer) to purchase from the Options Clearing Corp. a fixed number of shares of a specified security (the underlying stock) for a prescribed price (the exercise or striking price) prior to a determined time (the expiration date). For legal purposes, the arrangement is made with the OCC. Since the corporation does not actually own the stock, however, there must be another party to the transaction who has evidenced her willingness to provide the stock on the specified terms. This party is the seller (writer) of the option. If she owns the stock, the option is covered; if she does not, the option is referred to as uncovered (naked). In the latter case she is, in effect, "short" the stock and is subject to the exchange's margin requirements.

The buyer pays a price (premium) for the call option which is given to the writer. The intrinsic factors determining the size of the premium are the duration of the option, the difference between the exercise price and the market price of the underlying stock, and the characteristics of the underlying stock, particularly its volatility. Within this framework, at any particular time, the amount of the premium reflects the demand for and supply of the option in the exchange's auction market. Thus, writers and buyers gain an idea from the intrinsic factors as to what the option is worth; then the premium is worked out through the competitive bids and offers submitted in the exchange market.

The customer's broker is required to approve an account before the investor may write or buy an option on the exchange. For this purpose, the broker obtains information as to the investor's objectives and financial condition, to make certain of her "suitability" for option trading. The broker may also impose special requirements, such as a minimum amount in an account. The account executive with whom the customer is to deal must have passed an examination administered by the firm's option supervisor. The option supervisor appointed by a broker must pass an examination prepared and administered by the National Association of Securities Dealers.

Standardizing the Transaction

The major contribution of the CBOE was to make the option a fungible instrument that could be easily bought and sold in a secondary market at prices that are susceptible to routine reporting in the daily newspapers. This feat was accomplished by standardizing the striking prices and expiration dates. Unlike conventional options that can terminate on any business day, all exchange options expire at 4:00 P.M. Eastern Standard Time on the Saturday immediately following the third Friday of the expiration month. This represents the time by which notice must be received by the OCC. An investor can exercise an option only through the brokers handling his or her account.

Initially, the only permissible expiration months were January, April, July, and October. To relieve the burden of paperwork and administrative supervision that began to result from the large volume of trading that developed in the opening months of 1975, a second cycle of expiration months—February, May, August, and November—was introduced. This distributed the weight of the work more evenly over the year. A March, June, September, and December cycle remains in reserve and will be introduced if the volume warrants it. Options in any particular stock can have only one cycle on a given exchange. Currently, no option is traded on more than one exchange, though multiple exchange trading is certainly contemplated. Indeed, the CBOE has been planning to introduce trading in Boise Cascade options similar to those already traded on the PBW.

Since trading in options of a particular month starts approximately nine months earlier, at any one time options with up to three different expiration months are available for trading.

The exercise prices are established at 5-point intervals for stocks trading below 50, 10-point intervals for stocks trading between 50 and 100, and 20-

point intervals above 100; the CBOE has asked the SEC for permission to extend the 10-point interval to 200. The exercise price is fixed by the exchange at the dollar per share figure most closely approximating the market price of the underlying stock at the time the call is written. Thus, if the market price of ABC stock is 53 when trading is initiated in October options, the exercise price would be set at 50. If the price of the underlying stock is at or near the middle of an interval, an exchange may open trading in options with exercise prices at each end of the interval, especially if both exercise prices for another month are currently being traded.

As the expiration date of an option approaches, the amount of open interest in it diminishes. This tendency occurs regardless of the market price of the underlying stock. If the market price is above the exercise price, writers may use the secondary market to buy options, thereby eliminating their obligation, while holders may sell their options rather than exercise; if the market price is below the exercise price, holders may seek to recover a portion of the premium, since exercise is not likely to be a practical alternative. Thus, Figure 25-1 shows the fading open interest in July Telephone 50s during the month of July, compared with the mounting interest in the October and January options.

When significant price movements take place in an underlying stock during the quarterly periods between the introduction of new expiration months, additional options may be opened for trading at the price intervals stated above for one or more of the expiration months already the subject of trading. For example, with respect to the ABC October 50s (that is, a call for 100 shares of ABC stock at $50 per share which expires at the end of October), if the market price of ABC stock were subsequently to decline to 45, trading in ABC Octobers might be introduced at that exercise price, and if the market price were then to rise to 60, ABC Octobers might also be introduced at that exercise price. Indeed, trading in a single striking price for a given expiration month is the exception rather than the rule, except, perhaps, shortly after trading in a given expiration month has been introduced. The number of options for a given underlying stock traded any one time may be quite large. In the first week of September 1975, 14 different options for McDonald's stock were traded on the CBOE. Over 800 options are typically available for exchange trading. Once trading in a given month and price has been initiated, new options at those terms may subsequently be written, regardless of the stock price prevailing at the time.

The striking price of exchange-traded options is adjusted to reflect stock dividends and splits but not any cash dividends paid on the underlying security. Trading in options with the same terms may continue until 4 P.M. on the day prior to expiration of the contract.[8]

FIGURE 25-1

Open Interest, Telephone 50s

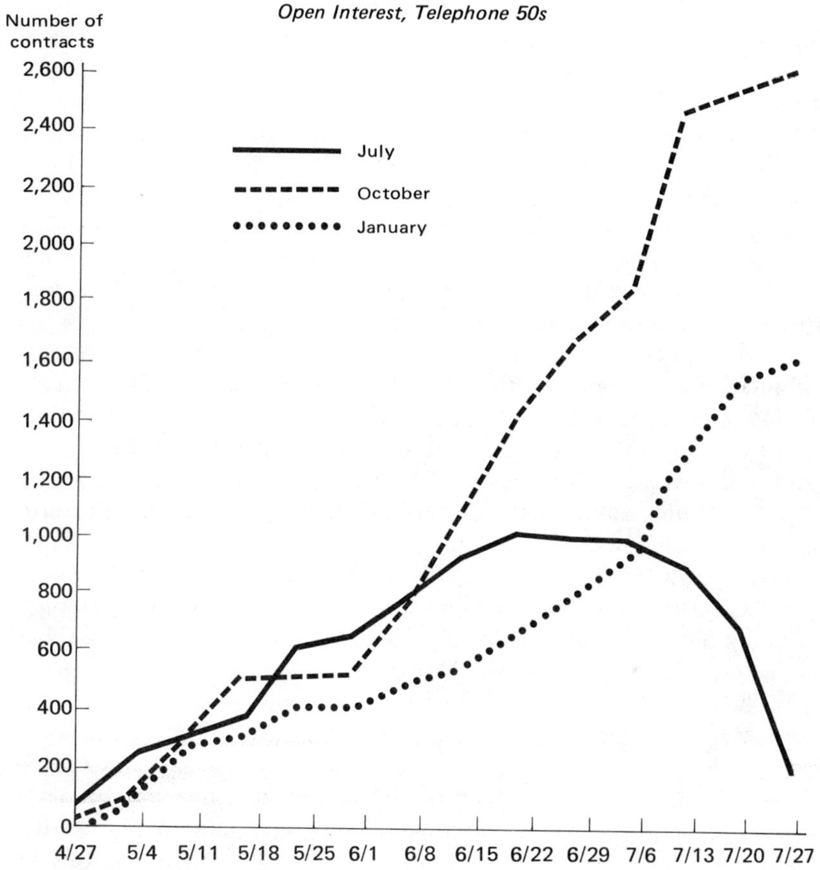

SOURCE: Chicago Board Options Exchange, ***Chicago Board Options Exchange: The First Three Months***, Appendix 5, 1973. Courtesy of the CBOE.

Determinants of Call Premiums

A premium less than the exercise value, the excess of the market value of the underlying stock over the exercise price of the option, cannot persist for long. Arbitrageurs will recognize the profit to be made by buying the option and selling the underlying stock short. The demand thus generated and the decrease in the supply resulting from the exercise of options will raise the premium until it is at least as great as the exercise value. It can easily be seen why the exercise value is sometimes known as the intrinsic value or tangible value.

If the premium consisted solely of the exercise value, no investor would buy such an option if this value were negative. Obviously, however, they do; indeed they buy options that are "out of the money"—that is, with an exercise price greater than the market price—by fairly substantial amounts.

Indeed, the typical premium exceeds its exercise value. The reason is that the exercise value is only one of the components of option value.

The second component of option value is called its time value. The premium paid for an option is pure time value when the market price of the stock and the exercise price of the option are the same. The time value derives from certain properties of the option. At any point in time during the life of the option, the downside risk is the current price of the option. For the duration of the option's life, the investor can reap any benefits that may develop from appreciation of the price of the stock and suffer limited consequences if the price of the stock falls. All other things being equal, the longer this is true, the more the option is worth.

In addition, options have the capacity for magnifying the rate of return on the underlying stock. To see this, consider the IBM April 180s, which on September 5, 1975 closed at 21⅜. The underlying stock closed that day at 180. Thus, investors had a choice of buying the April 180s or the stock itself. The April 180s obviously had no exchange or intrinsic value. Suppose that just before the option expired, the stock had risen to 210. If we ignore transaction costs, then the investor in stock would have realized a 16⅔ percent capital appreciation. The buyer of options would have realized a capital appreciation of about 40 percent, but he would have had to buy almost 3.5 contracts to realize the same dollar profit as could have been made on a single round lot of IBM stock. Another way of looking at it is that the investor gets the action on 180 stock for only 74⅜. In effect, he gets an intrinsic free loan of $105.19 on each share of stock. He could have bought on margin. Had he done so, however, he would not have been able to borrow as much, and the loan would not have been interest free. Second, the margined investor in stock has more to lose even if a stop loss order is used, but he has greater opportunity to recoup.

The ability to profit from this magnification potential depends upon the option remaining alive long enough for the price appreciation to take place. This can be seen if we consider the IBM April 180s again. If IBM were to be selling for 180 the day before the April 180s were due to expire, the options would be worthless. It is the fact that the option provides for a span of time in which gains are possible that gives the option a value over and above its exchange value. The longer the time allowed, the greater is the time value. One would therefore expect that the IBM October 180s, which were due to expire six months before the April 180s, would trade for much less. And indeed they did. On September 5, they closed at 9⅛, less than half the value of the April 180s. The January 180s, which had an intermediate maturity, sold at an intermediate price that day: 15⅞. Clearly, if an opportunity to profit from the options arose prior to the expiration of the October 180s, that opportunity would have been available to the January and April 180s as well. The longer options always permit investors to reap benefits available to the shorter options, but also permit the investors to reap benefits that might occur after the shorter options expire. Hence, they are worth more.

The investor will not typically exercise his option to reap the benefit of the appreciation of value of the underlying stock. Generally, it pays to exercise the option before it goes ex-dividend, if the ex-dividend date is close to the expiration date (since the exercise price is not adjusted for cash dividends). The larger the dividend, the greater the lead time between the ex-dividend date and expiration date that warrants the exercise of the option. Usually, however, as long as liquidation is desired in advance of the expiration date, it pays to sell the option instead. Only in this way can the holder of options realize the time value of the option as well as the exchange value. The latter is all that the investor can get by exercising the option.

Time value is at a maximum when the market price of the stock equals the exercise price. To see that this is so, assume that it is not so. On September 5 the investor could have purchased IBM October 160s or October 180s. As we noted, the October 180s closed at 9⅛. The exchange value of the 160s was 20. If the time value of the two options were the same, the 160s would have sold for 29⅛. If IBM then rose to 210 just before expiring, the holder of the 160s would have realized an appreciation of almost 72 percent, but the holder of the 180s would have realized an appreciation of almost 229 percent. The investor in the 180s risks less and makes more. If the prices were the same as assumed, no one would buy the 160s. Under such circumstances, it is to be expected that the time value of the 180s should exceed that of the 160s. Indeed, they did because the 160s traded at only 24⅛, with a time value of 4⅛ instead of 9⅛. Similarly, the time value will fall if the striking price exceeds the market price. If an option is out of the money, increases in the price of the underlying stock do not increase the exchange value of the option. For any given rate of increase in the price of the underlying stock, the more an option is out of the money, the more time will be required before any given exercise value is reached. That is the same as shortening the life of the option. Once again, this phenomenon can be seen easily by comparing the IBM April 200s with the 180s on September 5. As we noted above, the premium of 21⅜ on the 180s represents pure time value. The premium on the 200s was only 12. Since there is really no such thing as a negative exchange value, 12 must represent the time value of the 200s.

All other things being equal, the time value of a contract is a function of the price of the stock. Thus, if IBM had a three-for-one split and the exercise price was adjusted accordingly, as indeed it would be under the OCC rules, it would take three contracts on September 5 at one-third of the price of the October 180s to have achieved the same absolute and relative results discussed above. It is difficult to see why the market would have paid any more or less than 3 for the option subsequent to the three for one split. With decimal pricing, the price would have fallen to 3.04; rounded to the nearest eighth, this is 3. However, there is some evidence to suggest that option buyers are willing to pay proportionately higher premiums for options on low- rather than high-priced stocks.

Suppose that on September 5, IBM had traded at 160 instead of 180. The exercise value of the 160s would have been zero, and the entire premium would have consisted of time value. If we take the time value of the 180s on September 5 as our guide, we may assume that on that day the time value of the 160s would have been roughly 8⅛. The 20-point increase in the price of IBM, which brought the premium on the 160s to 24⅛, would then have resulted in only a 16-point rise in the value of the option. As we illustrated above, the time value diminishes as the exercise value increases. As long as an option has a time value, the increase in the premium will be less than the increase in the price of the underlying stock. The difference in the increases diminishes as the exercise value of the option increases. In addition, the time value of an option is dependent on prevailing interest rates and the volatility of the price of the underlying stock. It is not as easy to illustrate this dependence on interest rates and price volatility as it was to illustrate the dependence on the other factors. However, recall that a purchase of the IBM April 180s at 21⅜, when the stock was selling at 180, implied obtaining a substantial interest-free loan. The value of such loans to investors depends on the interest saved. (The interest saved is a function of the rate of interest investors would have to pay if the money was borrowed from the usual channels.) The higher the interest rate, the more saved.

Similarly, we can reason that the greater the volatility of the price of the underlying stock, the greater the earnings potential of the option on the upside and the greater the protection on the downside.

A variety of formulae have been derived to ascertain whether an option is overpriced or underpriced. The investor then has the option of buying the former or writing the latter. These formulae generally include the price of the stock, the volatility of that price, the expiration time, the striking price, and the interest rate. A formula widely used on the street was developed by Fischer Black and Myron Scholes.[9]

Mechanics of Trading

In order to buy a stock on option contract, the customer gives his broker an order that specifies the underlying stock, expiration date, exercise price, and number of contracts desired. The order should also state whether it will result in a new position for a holder (an "opening" transaction) or extinguish a writer's preexisting position (a "closing" transaction).

The broker transmits the order via telephone or wire to one of the posts on the floor of an exchange. On the Amex and PBW the order is handled in the same fashion as an order to trade in stock. On the CBOE two to four classes of options (each class representing a particular underlying stock) are traded at each post. On the CBOE floor there are three types of members: floor brokers, who execute orders on an agency basis; board brokers, each of whom maintains a book of limit orders for each class of options assigned to him and acts solely as an agent in executing such orders; and market makers, who trade for their own accounts to maintain a fair and orderly market in those classes of options to which they are assigned. In the CBOE, unlike the exchanges, more than one market maker is assigned to each stock; furthermore, he serves only as a dealer, while the agency function of the specialist is handled by the board broker.

The floor broker who receives the order seeks to reach agreement on the floor with a writer or his broker through the auction process. If a premium is established, a binding trade takes place. The brokers for both parties file a report with the Options Clearing Corporation, and the broker for the buyer pays the premium at the OCC prior to 9:00 A.M. of the following business day. If the reports coincide and the premium is paid, the option is issued by the OCC at 10:00 A.M. Central Time on the business day following the trade. If the reports do not match, they must be reconciled, and the option will be issued at 10:00 A.M. on the first business day following the day on which the OCC is notified that the differences have been eliminated.

Ordinarily, the Options Clearing Corporation does not provide certificates to evidence the CBOE options that have been issued. Instead, the OCC maintains daily records of options issued in each of the accounts of its clearing members, who, in turn, must keep a continuous record of their customers' positions in the options. Ordinarily, therefore, ownership is evidenced by the confirmations and periodic statements which brokers furnish to their customers.

The holder of an option may only exercise it through his broker, who tenders an exercise notice to the OCC, which is the obligor on every option. The exercise notice is then assigned randomly to a clearing member (the "assigned clearing member") which has an account with the OCC that reflects the writing of an option with the same terms as the one exercised. The assigned clearing member, in turn, allocates the exercise notice to a customer maintaining a position as a writer in the account; this allocation also may be random or by any other method (such as first in, first out) that is fair and equitable to the customer. The assigned clearing member must also deliver to the exercising clearing member, against payment of the aggregate exercise price, the underlying stock in good form on or before 12:00 noon on the "exercise settlement date"; this is the fifth business day following the date on which the exercise notice is properly tendered to the OCC, unless there is a permissible exception. The OCC has made arrangements for exercise settlement through correspondent clearing corporations. The Midwest Clearing Corporation and the Midwest Securities Trust Company, which together operate a clearing and depository system, have such arrangements.

The mechanics of trading on the exchanges and the settlement procedures of the Options Clearing Corporation have been so arranged as to ensure that in the aggregate there are always enough writers to meet the demand for stock should all holders of options exercise their call privileges. Once an exercise notice for an option is assigned to a particular writer, he is contractually obligated to his clearing member to perform the terms of the option. In turn, the clearing member is responsible, whether or not his customer performs, to carry out the OCC's obligation on an assigned option.

The exchanges have established limitations governing the maximum number of options on the same underlying stock that may be exercised by an investor or a group of investors in any five consecutive business days. For most stocks the limit is 1,000 contracts (which represents 100,000 shares), regardless of expiration date. In particular instances, different limits may be established.

Members of the exchanges charge commissions on the purchase or sale of options. The rates are based on the price of the option, not the underlying stock. Thus, before May 1, 1975 the commission to purchase 1,000 shares of a stock selling at \$13 would have been about the same as the charge to buy 10 calls at \$13. A holder who elects to exercise his option avoids the commission that would have been paid on the liquidating transaction but must pay the regular stock exchange commission on exercise of the option and on the subsequent sale of the stock acquired. The writer of a called stock similarly avoids the option commission that would be imposed on a closing transaction but pays the regular stock exchange commission on the stock delivered to the holder.

Since option trading was initiated on the AMEX and PBW, prices and volume of all exchange option transactions have appeared together on an "options tape." This is shown on the floor of each exchange and also appears on the information-retrieval devices furnished to subscribers by vendors. At present, the exchanges have listed options for different stocks, but it is contemplated that options for a number of the same underlying stocks will eventually be listed. At that time, if the options have the same expiration dates and exercise prices, a position created on one exchange could be liquidated on the other.[10]

CONVENTIONAL OPTIONS

Despite the advent of option trading on exchanges, transactions in conventional options still occur in the over-the-counter market. For one thing, different underlying stocks may be available; then again, puts as well as various combinations of puts and calls may be acquired. Activity in the CBOE, however, runs at a much higher level than in the conventional OTC market. For example in early 1974, a typical CBOE volume of 10,000 contracts per day represented about 90 percent of the monthly OTC figure.[11]

Conventional option contracts assume a standard form that is issued by the Put and Call Brokers and Dealers Association to its members and serialized by number. The contract shows the name of the stock, its striking price, and the expiration date. These terms, as well as the premium paid for the contract, are subject to negotiation. In a conventional contract, the premium the buyer pays and the amount the writer receives may differ by the amount of any transaction fee charged by the broker to the purchaser, by the amount kept by the broker who arranges the transaction, and by any endorsement fee paid to the endorser. Before such a contract may be sold, it must be endorsed by a member of the NYSE, who guarantees performance.

The writer and endorser of a conventional contract are obligated to the holder of the particular option written and endorsed by them. Accordingly, to the extent a secondary market is available, it is very limited.[12] Suppose that an individual buys a conventional call on ABC at $50 for 190 days and that after 90 days the price has risen to $60. If he tries to capture the $10 appreciation by exercising his option, he sacrifices a privilege which still has 100 days to run. It would have been preferable to purchase a 90-day option, which presumably would have been cheaper. The exchanges enable an individual to recapture the premium for the unused portion of the period by selling the option in the secondary market rather than exercising it.

In the fall of 1975, the National Association of Securities Dealers announced plans for establishing a standardized market for trading options in OTC securities. The program would be instituted on a pilot basis involving call options on a group of actively traded OTC stocks. Procedures would generally be patterned after those in the CBOE and the quotations would be carried in the NASDAQ system.

USES AND RISKS OF OPTIONS TO THE HOLDER

Options may be used aggressively to obtain greater percentage gains than would be derived from a direct investment of the same amount of money in the underlying stock. Or they can be used defensively to protect against adverse price changes—a decline in the price of a stock the investor owns or a rise in the price of a stock he has sold short. Some of these strategies and their related risks are discussed below.

Obtaining Added Leverage

We noted above that an investor who, on September 5, 1975, expected IBM to rise could purchase stock directly or buy an April 180 call on it. We noted the extent to which the option permitted the investor to receive a magnified return. On the other hand, suppose that by the expiration date the price of IBM had fallen to 162. The holder of the call would lose his entire investment in the call, $2,137 for each contract, and there would be no possibility of recovery. The stockholder, on the other hand, would have suffered a loss of $1,800; moreover, he or she could recoup the loss on a subsequent recovery.

An investor who expects the price of a stock to fall can sell short or buy a put. If a decline should occur, he would incur a greater percentage gain from the put compared with the short sale, for reasons similar to those described above for the purchase. On the other hand, if the price rises, there would be no ceiling to his potential loss from the short sale, while the most he could lose on the put would be the premium price.

Limiting the Loss on a "Short" Position

An individual who sells short is exposed to a large potential loss if the stock should rise in price. He can protect himself by purchase of a call. In these circumstances, he is not concerned about how high the stock may rise because the striking price of the call establishes the limit of his loss. On the other hand, if the price of the stock falls, the individual's profit is reduced by the premium paid for the call less the price he receives if it can be sold in the secondary market. Several short sales may be protected by a given call option so long as they are made within its duration period. In this way, the investor can take advantage of the wide swings of a volatile stock by selling short at high levels and buying back as the price falls, while keeping the same call protection. To be fully protected against an increase in price, the calls must be for the number of shares sold short, and the striking price of the calls must not be greater than the price at which the short sale was effected.[13]

Limiting the Loss on a Long Position

Unlike the short-seller who, at least in theory, has no ceiling on his potential loss, the buyer of a stock knows that he cannot lose more than the price paid, and a loss of that magnitude would only occur if the stock had no value, which is not likely. Nevertheless, he may desire to protect himself against a loss of a designated amount. For this purpose, he could place a stop-loss order at a certain number of points below his purchase price. Such an order, however, becomes a market order when the specified price is reached or passed, and so there would still be some element of uncertainty. When the investor buys a put, the size of his potential loss is limited to the premium paid plus the difference between the purchase price of the stock and the striking price of the put. On the other hand, if the price of the stock rises, the amount of the gain is reduced by the premium paid for the put, whereas there is no cost for placing a stop-loss order.

Taking a Profit and Staying Invested

Assume that an investor bought 100 shares of MMM stock at $43 and that in early September it is $54. He does not believe that the stock is "played out," but he nevertheless wants to assure himself of the profits he has earned so far, or at least a portion of them. He may, therefore, sell the stock at a profit of $1,100 and with, say, $250 of the profits buy an MMM October 55. If the price of the stock goes up more than $1.00, he obtains a further gain, but if the price falls, he is nevertheless left with $850 profit, exclusive of costs.

Taking a Profit and Staying Short

Just as a call can be used to maintain a long position in a stock at a limited risk when confidence in an upward trend has diminished, a put can serve a similar purpose during a declining trend. Suppose an investor is confident that MMM, currently selling for $54 will decline to $40 and probably to $30. He sells short, and the expected fall to $40 is realized. He is now less confident in the downward trend than he was when the stock was selling at $50. There are several alternatives open to him. He could cover his position, but then he loses the opportunity of further gains if the falling trend continues. He could maintain his position, but then his profit may be eliminated if the downward trend is reversed. Another possibility is to buy an OTC put, thereby maintaining his ability to benefit by a further shrinkage in the price of the stock. If the trend does turn around, he loses only the premium paid for the put.

USES AND RISKS OF WRITING OPTIONS

The writer of a call option undertakes to sell the stock on the designated terms to the holder, while the writer of a put undertakes to buy the stock on the designated terms from the holder.[14] The writers of options are primarily institutions which have portfolios of stocks, while the holders of options tend to be individuals. A call option is covered if the writer already owns the stock that he may be required to deliver, and a put option is covered by effecting a short sale in the stock the writer may be required to buy. The margin requirements of the Federal Reserve Board, the CBOE, and the other exchanges to which a broker may belong apply to a customer's position as an option writer. Additionally, many brokers impose their own requirements, which may be more stringent than those of the regulatory agencies. As a result, all writing transactions must be conducted in a margin account, unless the writer owns the underlying stock in full and has agreed to deposit it under specified arrangements. The objectives and risks of writers of covered and uncovered options differ.

Covered Calls

The objectives and method of operation of the writer of a covered call depend upon his attitude toward the underlying stock. In any case, the writer desires to realize, through the receipt of premium income, a greater return than would be earned on the stock alone. The writer may be interested in disposing of the stock; for example, he may have achieved a gain and may be contemplating a sale should the stock advance a few more points. In this case, he wants the stock to be called and hopes to hold it until that happens. On the other hand, the writer may be fundamentally optimistic about the stock's prospects and desire to retain it. To eliminate his obligation, therefore, he could execute a closing purchase transaction. In this case, he probably will do so near the termination date of the contract, when the option's time has diminished; the premium he pays is therefore likely to be lower than the premium he originally received. Facilitating this approach is the fact that call holders who exercise their options tend to do so close to the expiration dates.

While the writer of a covered call receives premium income, he may forgo the possibility of gain on the underlying stock above the exercise price. At the same time, he is exposed to the risk of a decrease in the price of the stock below the purchase price. Assume, for example, that an institution has in its portfolio Baxter stock that is currently trading at $50 and writes a call against it at an exercise price of $50 for a $600 premium (less commissions). If Baxter rises to $60 per share and the writer does not execute a closing purchase, the call probably will be exercised (costing the writer additional commissions), and it will have forgone any of the $1,000 increase in value of the underlying stock. On the other hand, should Baxter fall to $40 per share, the call will not be exercised, and the writer will have suffered an unrealized loss of $1,000 in its stock position.

Uncovered Calls

The objective of an uncovered writer is to realize income from the writing transaction without having to commit capital to the underlying stock, except for the margin requirements. Moreover, he avoids the risk of incurring a loss if the price of the underlying stock should decline. On the other hand, such a writer assumes the risk of an increase in the price of the stock above its exercise price, and, in theory at least, this risk is unlimited. Assume, for example, that an uncovered call is written on Baxter stock at an exercise price of $50 per share for a $600 premium (less commissions). The stock thereafter moves upward sharply, and if the writer does not execute a closing purchase, he is at the mercy of the holder, who could exercise his call at any time prior to the expiration date. The writer then would have to buy the stock at the advanced price and sell it to the holder at the lower exercise price. In this case, not only would the writer have incurred an actual capital loss but he would also have had to pay three sets of commissions—on the original sale of the option, on the purchase of the underlying stock, and on the sale of the underlying stock to the holder.

Covered Puts

The writer of a put who covers by effecting a short sale presumably believes that he may use the stock put to him to meet his short position. Except for his premium income, however, such a writer has no protection against swiftly rising prices, and, in theory at least, this risk is unlimited. Moreover, he forgoes the possibility of gain resulting from closing the short position at a price lower than the exercise price.

Assume that a writer sells short 100 shares of ABC at $50 per share (paying a commission) and writes a put covering the shares at an exercise price of $50 per share (less commissions). If ABC subsequently rises, the put will not be exercised, but eventually the writer will have to buy back the stock (paying a commission) to cover his short position, and there is no way of knowing what this price will be. On the other hand, should ABC decline to $40, the put will be exercised at $50 (costing the writer a commission), and he will have forgone any of the $1,000 unrealized profit on his short position. At present, there is no secondary market in puts that would have permitted him to close his position.

Uncovered Puts

The writer of an uncovered put earns a premium income, net of costs, in the event of a rise in the price of the underlying stock which would make it unprofitable for the holder to exercise his option. If the price of the stock declines sufficiently, however, the holder will exercise the option. In this case, the writer will have to buy the stock (paying a commission) at market price. If he does not wish to keep the stock in his portfolio, he will have to sell it at the then current market price (paying another commission). He will thus incur a loss on the transaction and will have had to pay three sets of commissions. These negative factors are likely to be only partially offset by the writer's premium income.

OPTION HEDGING

A hedge represents offsetting transactions in assets that are related in some way. They may, for example, be the same instrument traded in different markets or different instruments where one is exchangeable for the other. The purpose of the hedge is to reduce the risk of loss. Hedging in warrants and in the stocks they entitle a holder to buy has been practiced for a long time. The creation of a secondary market in calls on an exchange has also paved the way for a similar type of hedging in these options and their underlying stocks.

The point of departure in option hedging is to establish a fundamental value for the option by analyzing the price movements of various call options and their underlying stocks. Based upon this analysis, the options determined to be overvalued are sold, while those that appear undervalued are bought. Against the short options, some portion of the underlying stock is bought as a hedge; against the long options, some portion of the underlying stock is sold short as a hedge.

A common strategy is to write two or more calls against each long position of 100 shares of stock; the greater the apparent overvaluation of the options, the higher will be the ratio of options written to stock held. Table 25-1 provides an illustration of some outcomes from a 1:5 ratio hedge, representing the purchase of 100 shares of Ford common stock at 52⅜ and the sale of 500 January Ford 60s. In this strategy, three factors determine the potential profit or loss of the hedge: (1) the premium received on the calls that are written; (2) the difference between the proceeds realized from sale of the long stock to the option holder at the striking price and the price at which the stock was bought; and (3) the loss from covering the naked calls at a price in excess of the striking price.

TABLE 25-1

Some Outcomes from a 1:5 Option Hedge
(write call, buy stock)
Example: Ford Jan/60 vs. Ford common

SUMMARY	
Current date	October 31, 1975
Option maturity date	January 31, 1976
Time to maturity	3 months
Market price of common	52⅜
Market price of option/per share	2⅛
Strategy	1:5 hedge (i.e., sell five calls representing 500 shares; buy 100 shares of common)
Break-even parameters at maturity	
Upside break-even	64½
Downside break-even	41¾
Profitability range	22¾
Maximum profit	$1,825
Investment required	$5,576.88
Maximum return on investment	32.7%
Maximum annualized return on investment	130.8%

NOTE: Expenses and dividends (which writer retains) have been excluded for simplicity.

The contribution of the premium to the profits achieved simply depends on the number of options written and is independent of the price movements of the stock subsequent to the writing of the call. The striking price is fixed for the duration of the option. Given the expiration month, therefore, the outcome of this maneuver depends upon the price movements of the underlying stock during the life of the option. Accordingly, the profit or loss results can be computed at different levels, thereby permitting a determination of the upside break-even, the downside break-even, and the maximum profit obtainable.

The upside break-even occurs at the price of the stock when the first two factors listed above—the premium received plus the profits from the long position—equal the third, the loss from covering the naked calls. If the price of the stock falls below the striking price, the calls will not be exercised. Accordingly, the downside break-even is determined by the premium received for all the calls written. As the price of the underlying stock advances beyond its cost level, the profit on the long position grows. Once the striking price is passed, however, the loss from covering the naked calls creates an offset to this profit. On the other hand, as the price of the underlying stock falls away from its original cost, the loss on the long position erodes the profit contribution of the premium received on the calls. The maximum profit, therefore, results when the closing price of the underlying stock equals the striking price of the option.

Figure 25-2 gives the formula for determining the upside and downside break-evens, as well as the calculations for Table 25-1.[15] The upside break-even is \$64.50 per share. At this level, a loss of \$4.50 per share (\$64.50 – \$60.00) is incurred on each naked call that has to be covered. Since there are four such calls, representing 400 shares, the total loss from the covering operation is \$1,800. Against this, a profit of \$762.50 is obtained from the long position (\$6,000 – \$5,237.50), plus \$1,062.50 from the premiums on the five calls written (\$2.125 × 500). The total profit, therefore, is \$1,825, which just about equals the covering loss of \$1,800.

FIGURE 25-2

Formula and Calculations for Determining Upside and Downside Break-evens

Upside break-even:

$$= \begin{bmatrix}\text{market price}\\ \text{of common}\end{bmatrix} + \frac{\begin{bmatrix}\text{strike price} - \text{market price of common} + \text{call premium}\end{bmatrix}}{\begin{bmatrix}1 - \dfrac{\text{common bought}}{\text{calls sold}}\end{bmatrix}}$$

$$= 52\tfrac{3}{8} + \frac{60 - 52\tfrac{3}{8} + 2\tfrac{1}{8}}{1 - \dfrac{100}{500}}$$

$$= 64\tfrac{1}{2} \quad \text{(23.2\% above current price)}$$

Downside break-even:

$$= \begin{bmatrix}\text{market price}\\ \text{of common}\end{bmatrix} - \begin{bmatrix}\dfrac{\text{calls sold}}{\text{common bought}}\end{bmatrix} \times \begin{bmatrix}\text{call premium}\end{bmatrix}$$

$$= 52\tfrac{3}{8} - \begin{bmatrix}\dfrac{500}{100}\end{bmatrix} \times 2\tfrac{1}{8}$$

$$= 41\tfrac{3}{4} \quad \text{(20.3\% below current price)}$$

The downside break-even is \$41.75 per share. At this level, a loss of \$1,062.50 is incurred on the long position (\$5,237.50 – \$4,175.00). This amount equals exactly the premiums received from writing the five calls (\$2.125 × 500).

Figure 25-3 shows the calculation for determining the maximum profit obtainable. This profit is reached when the market price for the underlying stock is at the striking price for the options. At this level, a gain of \$762.50 is incurred on the long position (\$6,000 – \$5,237.50); beyond this point, the options would be exercisable, resulting in a loss on the covering transaction. The premium income on the options written is \$1,062.50. The total profit is the sum of these two elements, or \$1,825.

FIGURE 25-3

Formula and Calculation for Determining Maximum Profits

Maximum Profit:

(Ford closes at \$60, the strike price, on January 31, 1974)

= Profit/(loss) on common + Profit/(loss) on option

$$= \left[\text{number of common shares}\right] \times \left[\text{closing price of common, January 31, 1974} - \text{purchase price of common, October 31, 1973}\right]$$

$$+ \left[\text{number of options sold}\right] \times \left[\text{call premium, October 31, 1973} - \text{call premium, January 31, 1974}\right] \times \left[100\right]$$

$$= (100)\,(60 - 52\tfrac{3}{8})$$

$$+ (5)\,(2\tfrac{1}{8} - 0)\,(100)$$

$$= 762.50 + 1{,}062.50$$

$$= \$1{,}825$$

The rate of return on the transaction depends upon the profits achieved, as described above, and on the actual amount of money that is invested. The size of this investment, in turn, depends on the margin requirements for the long position and the margin requirements for the various calls. In Figure 25-4, the amount required is calculated to be \$5,576.88. This figure is based on the margin rules that were applicable at the time the calculation was originally made. The margin requirements of the Federal Reserve Board and the exchanges are neither simple nor uniform but are subject to change from time to time. Sometimes, special margin requirements may be imposed on particular options. The margin requirements imposed by the exchanges may be greater than those imposed by the Federal Reserve. They do not have the authority to relax the Federal Reserve requirements. Similarly, brokerage houses are free to impose greater requirements than those imposed by the exchanges. Such variations will affect the numerical outcome, but not the basic structure, of the calculations that have been laid out in Figure 25-4. However, the investment requirements will be affected by the practice of marking to the market to determine margin requirements. The sum of the amounts needed to carry the stock held and the uncovered options sold is reduced by the premium received for the options.

To help him reach a decision, an investor who contemplated in October 1973 the advisability of undertaking a 1/5 hedge in Ford January 60s, might

FIGURE 25-4

Formula and Calculation for Determining the Investment Required

Investment Required:

$$
\begin{aligned}
= & \begin{bmatrix}\text{market price}\\ \text{of common}\end{bmatrix} \begin{bmatrix}\text{margin}\\ \text{requirement}\end{bmatrix} \begin{bmatrix}\text{number of}\\ \text{common shares}\end{bmatrix} \\
+ & \begin{bmatrix}\text{number of}\\ \text{naked calls}\end{bmatrix} \begin{bmatrix}\text{margin maintenance}\\ \text{requirement}\end{bmatrix} \begin{bmatrix}\text{market price}\\ \text{of common}\end{bmatrix} \begin{bmatrix}100\end{bmatrix} \\
+ & \begin{bmatrix}\text{number of}\\ \text{naked calls}\end{bmatrix} \begin{bmatrix}\text{market price}\\ \text{of common}\end{bmatrix} - \begin{bmatrix}\text{strike}\\ \text{price}\end{bmatrix} \begin{bmatrix}100\end{bmatrix} \\
- & \begin{bmatrix}\text{number of}\\ \text{calls sold}\end{bmatrix} \begin{bmatrix}\text{market price}\\ \text{of option}\end{bmatrix} \begin{bmatrix}100\end{bmatrix} \\
= & (52\tfrac{3}{8})(65\%)(100) + (4)(30\%)(52\tfrac{3}{8})(100) \\
+ & (4)(52\tfrac{3}{8} - 60)(100) - (5)(2\tfrac{1}{8})(100) \\
= & 3404.38 + 6{,}285 - 3{,}050 - 1{,}062.50 \\
= & \$5{,}576.88
\end{aligned}
$$

have prepared a summary sheet like that shown in Table 25-5. At that time, the stock was selling at about 52. The range of prices over which he calculates the outcomes of this strategy is limited by the break-even levels of 42 and 64. (For simplicity, trading costs are not included.) This means that the stock could advance by 23 percent or decline by about 20 percent from the base price of 52 and he would still earn a profit on the operation. Only a single loss figure is indicated at either end, because the investor could readily terminate his risk exposure. If the price of the underlying stock threatens to exceed the upper break-even, he could limit his loss by purchasing additional stock so that the remaining options were covered, or he could purchase closing calls to match those written, thereby canceling his obligation. On the other hand, should the stock fall to the lower break-even, the investor could sell his long position and permit his calls to expire. The maximum profit that the investor could realize at a closing price of 60 is \$1,825, which would mean a rate of return of approximately 33 percent for the three-month period and a very substantial 131 percent annualized return.

The illustration provides a gauge of the opportunities available in hedged options involving a combination of long positions in stocks with short positions in options. In effect, the packaged operation modifies the risks that would otherwise be involved in a speculative instrument like an option. In order to exploit these arrangements, however, the investor needs considerable agility in entering into and closing out positions. With volatile securities, this dexterity may be hard to attain. Moreover, transaction costs would be incurred that reduce the indicated profit potentials.

TABLE 25-5

Profit Summary

(Ford Jan/60 vs. Ford common, 1:5 hedge)

CLOSING PRICE, JANUARY 31, 1974	PROFIT/ (LOSS)	RETURN ON INVESTMENT	
		3-MONTH	ANNUALIZED
$66	$ (575)	(10.3)%	(41.2)%
64	225	4.0	16.0
62	1,025	18.4	73.6
60	1,825	32.7	130.8
58	1,625	29.1	116.4
56	1,425	25.6	102.4
54	1,225	22.0	88.0
52	1,025	18.4	73.6
50	825	14.8	59.2
48	625	11.2	44.8
46	425	7.6	30.4
44	225	4.0	16.0
42	25	.4	1.6
40	(175)	(3.1)	(12.4)

Neutral Hedging

The fact that the time value of an option diminishes as the market price of the stock and the exercise price of the option diverge has considerable significance for hedging operations. Consider a neutral hedge as one that produces low risk for small movements in stock prices. To effect such a hedge, the investor must have a number of option contracts. That number depends on the rate at which the time value changes as the exercise price and market value of the stock diverge. Thus, suppose that a $1 increase in the price of the stock, and hence in the exercise of value of an in-the-money option, will diminish the time value by 50¢, and a $1 fall in the stock price will increase the time value by 50¢. In effect, this means that for a small change in the price of the stock in either direction, the option value will change by half of that amount in the same direction. The ratio of change in option price to the change in stock price is known as *the hedge ratio*; its reciprocal represents the number of option contracts required for a neutral hedge. To guard against a $1 fall in the price of the stock, the investor must write two option contracts.

In Table 25-1, no attempt was made to achieve a neutral hedge. The rate at which the price of an option contract responds to changes in the price of the underlying stock varies as the exercise and stock prices diverge. Consequently, what was a neutral hedge for a given price of the stock ceases to be a neutral hedge as the divergence changes. Assume, for example, that an investor had set up a neutral hedge when the hedge ratio was 1:2 and maintained this ratio as the hedge ratio moved up to 1:4. If the price of the stock then fell by $1, and the investor chose to liquidate, he would have lost $1 on the price retreat of the stock, but he could cover his short position in options more cheaply. If he had written four options, the savings of 25¢ on each would have completely offset the setback in the stock, but since he had written only two, the offset is only 50¢.

It should be clear from the above that there are two ways of looking at hedging. An investor may try to hedge his initial position. Or an investor may adjust a hedge continuously and, in effect, reconsider exposure or risk daily.

Writing a naked option is not risky per se. Indeed, whenever the hedge ratio is less than 1, writing one or more naked options may be necessary to achieve a neutral hedge. Finally, even a so-called neutral hedge is not actually a riskless investment, unless the neutrality of the hedge is maintained as the hedge ratio changes. Otherwise, if the stock price moves only slightly, the hedger's return will be affected only slightly, but if the stock price experiences a large move, the hedger's return will be affected significantly.

A neutral hedge does not necessarily involve taking a long position in stock and a short position in options. An investor may short the stock and buy contracts instead. If the options are overpriced, the hedge with the short in options is preferable. If the options are underpriced, it is better to be a buyer than a writer.

A hedge does not necessarily involve taking opposite positions in options and the underlying stock. One may offset one option with another. This is known as *spreading.* Options have three identifying characteristics: the underlying stock, the maturity, and the striking price. Spreading may involve positioning options with different maturities or different striking prices. If the investor takes a long position in one maturity and a short position in another maturity with the same stock and striking price, he has a *time spread* or *calendar spread.* If the two positions differ in striking price, instead of maturity, the investor has a *money spread.* A *butterfly spread* can be achieved in either striking price or maturity. This involves taking a position in an option with a given maturity or striking price and taking the opposite positions with both a longer and shorter maturity or a higher and lower striking price, respectively. In establishing spreads, investors seek combinations of options in which one is relatively more overpriced than the other(s) in the combination. The most overpriced is sold and the most underpriced is bought.

TAXATION OF OPTIONS

The tax consequences of buying or selling options are based on laws and interpretations that are subject to change. We therefore consider only the basic principles applicable to holders and writers.

Taxation of Holders of Options[16]

An option is a capital asset. If it is sold within six months, therefore, the realized capital gain or loss is short-term; after six months, long-term. An option that expires is treated as having been sold on the expiration date and, if held for more than six months, represents a long-term loss. Upon the exercise of an option, the holding period of the acquired stock begins on the date the call is exercised. The tax base is the price of the stock plus the premium paid for the option.

Consider a call on ABC October 50s purchased for $600 in January. Suppose that the price of the underlying stock is $60 just prior to the expiration date. If the investor exercises the option and sells the stock immediately, the proceeds would exceed the tax base by $400 ($6,000 – $5,600) and the gain would be short-term, since the stock would have been held for only one day. Alternatively, the investor could sell the call for roughly $1,000, which would also yield a profit of $400, but this time the profit would be considered long-term. Actually, the price would probably be somewhat under $1,000 in order to make it sufficiently attractive for buyers to purchase the option and exercise it.

If the price of ABC rises to only $54 and the investor desires a capital loss for tax purposes, he could sell the option for roughly $400 and realize a loss of $200. He must execute the transaction prior to six months, however, in order to preserve the short-term nature of the loss. If six months has expired and he desires to show a short-term loss, he can exercise the call at $50 and sell the stock at $54, securing a loss of $200. Since the holding period for the stock begins only after the call is exercised, it does not make any difference when exercise takes place. On the downside, if the price of ABC stock falls below the striking price of $50, the investor might want to sell the option before six months in order to obtain a short-term loss. Allowing the option to expire would produce a long-term loss.

Taxation of Writers

The premium received for writing an option is not included in income at the time of receipt (when the option is written) but is deferred until such time as the writer's obligation terminates. The writer's obligation may terminate (1) by the passage of time, (2) by delivery of the underlying stock pursuant to the terms of the call, or (3) through a closing purchase transaction (repurchasing a call with the same terms as the one sold at an earlier date).

If a writer's obligation terminates by reason of the passage of time, the premium constitutes ordinary income to the writer realized on the day of expiration. If the option is exercised, the premium received by the writer is treated as an increase in the proceeds realized upon the sale of the underlying stock in the exercise transaction. The gain or loss on such sale constitutes a capital gain or loss, long-term or short-term, depending upon how long the stock has been held. If a writer engages in a closing purchase transaction, thereby terminating his obligation, the difference between the premium received in the original writing transaction and the amount paid in the closing transaction is ordinary income or loss realized on the day of the closing transaction.

If a call is written when the underlying stock or a call on that stock has been held for six months or less, or if the underlying stock or call on that stock is acquired subsequent to the writing of the call but before it is exercised or expires, the writing of the call does not affect the holding period of the underlying stock or a call on it held by the writer.

Converting Short-Term Gains into Long-Term Gains

By combining options with other moves, the investor may convert short-term gains into long-term gains. For example, suppose an investor buys a 9-month call on ABC at $50 for a premium of $600. At the end of five months the price of the stock rises to $75, and the investor fears that the price will retreat before the option expires. If he immediately sells or exercises the option, however, his profit will be short-term; his problem is to preserve the gain but convert it to a long-term basis. A possible solution is to sell the stock short at $75, wait until the option is at least six months old, and then cover the short position in the open market and sell the call. The result would be:

	PRICE FALLS TO $70	PRICE REMAINS THE SAME	PRICE RISES TO $80
Proceeds from short sale	$7,500	$7,500	$7,500
Proceeds from sale of call*	2,000	2,500	3,000
Less cost of covering in the market	7,000	7,500	8,000
Less cost of call	600	600	600
Short-term gain (or loss)	500	—	(500)
Long-term gain	1,400	1,900	2,400

*With large tangible values, time value can be ignored.

As the price of the stock rises or falls (but is far above $50), the value of the option will tend to change in the same direction dollar-for-dollar. As long as the stock's price is so much over $50, the total gain is $1,900 because the results from the option purchase and short sale are offsetting, but most of the gains will be long-term. If the price falls below $50, all gains come from the short sale and are short-term; the greater the price decline, the larger the gains. Thus, we have an asymmetry: there is a downside limit to the loss that can be experienced in the call, but there is no corresponding upside limit to the profit from the short sale.

A short-term gain may also be converted into a long-term gain by selling a call. Suppose that the writer has a long position in ABC which he originally acquired at $50 and that three months after purchase the stock is trading at $75. If the writer liquidates, the gain is short-term. If he writes a call and the price is sustained or rises, he will be paid after the six-month period is up and will have the premium as additional profit. If the price falls, the premium at least provides a buffer against any loss. If the call is exercised before the writer has the stock for six months, he is still ahead by the amount of the premium.

SUMMARY

The two major forms of option contracts are calls and puts. A call enables a holder to buy a security at a specific price for a prescribed period of time. A put is a similar privilege that applies to sellers. Various combinations of puts and calls are also available.

For many years, option trading was an esoteric field that was concentrated in the over-the-counter market. The inauguration of the CBOE, followed by the introduction of option trading on the AMEX and PBW, has changed this picture. Under the surveillance of the SEC, the move now is toward standardized practices, common clearing facilities, and full disclosure of prices and quotations.

At present, option trading on exchanges occurs only in calls that apply to stocks listed on a national securities exchange. The buyer pays a price (premium) for the option, which is given to a seller (writer) who has evidenced his willingness to provide the stocks on the specified terms. The intrinsic factors that influence buyers and writers in determining the size of the premium are the option's duration, the difference between the exercise and the market price of the underlying stock, and the nature of the stock.

Despite the advent of option trading on exchanges, transactions in conventional options still take place in the over-the-counter market. These conventional options may cover different underlying stocks, as well as puts and combinations of puts and calls.

Options have various uses. They provide leverage because the percentage changes in the premium of an option that has value will be greater than those of the underlying security. They also can play a role in certain types of transactions, such as purchase of a call to protect a short position or purchase of a put to protect a long position. The creation of a secondary market in options has also paved the way for their use in hedging operations. In such operations, options believed after analysis to be overvalued are sold short, while some portion of the underlying stock is bought as a hedge; options believed undervalued are purchased, while a portion of the underlying stock is sold short as a hedge.

For tax purposes an option is considered a distinct capital asset for a holder, and profits or losses are treated as short- or long-term, depending on the length of time the option was held. If an option is not exercised, the writer's gains or losses resulting from the termination of the option are treated as ordinary income or loss realized on the day the option is terminated. If the option is exercised, the premium is added to the proceeds from the sale of the underlying stock. It augments a capital gain or diminishes a loss. Whether the gain or loss is short- or long-term depends entirely on the holding period of the underlying stock.

APPENDIX: Glossary of Terms Used on the Option Market

Call Option

A call option (or a call) is a contract which entitles the holder to purchase 100 shares of the optioned stock at a price specified in the contract (the striking price) within the named period. The buyer is entitled to that price regardless of the prevailing market price at the time he exercises his privilege. The price paid for the call option is known as the *premium.*

Conversion

Transformation of a put into a call. Brokers effect conversions by buying a put, going long the stock, and selling a call. The striking price of the put and call must be the same as the price paid for the long position. Converters take no risk. If the price rises, the call will be exercised, so the long position is sold out at the price paid for it. The put will expire. If the price falls, the long position will be sold to the writer of the put, and the call will expire. The converter makes his money from the fee he charges. This can be quite high, since he requires the seller of the put to pay him at least 0.5 percent more than the call money rate for the initial value of the stock position and all the brokerage fees the investor would have incurred in buying and selling the stock. He also makes some money on the fact that the premium on the put he buys is less than on the call he sells.

Downside-out Calls and Upside-out Puts

Conventional calls and puts except for two features: (1) the downside-out call is canceled if the specified stock trades at less than 90 percent of the striking price during the period of the call; (2) the upside-out put is canceled if the specified stock trades at more than 110 percent of the striking price during the period of the put. As long as the put or call has not been canceled, the dealer is obligated to repurchase the option at a premium whose ratio to the original premium is equal to the ratio of the unexpired period of the option to the original period. For example, suppose that an investor buys a 190-day downside-out call on ABC at $50. This would require a premium of $600 (12 percent of $5,000). Suppose that at the end of 95 days the price of ABC has risen to $75 and the investor wishes to cash in. He can resell the option to the dealer who sold it to him and receive back $300 of the premium. He would, of course, receive $2,800, less the standard two commissions he would have incurred in exercising his call. The $2,800 would reflect the $2,500 appreciation in the value of the stock and the $300 rebate of premium. If ABC trades below $45 (90 percent of the exercise price), the option is canceled and the premium is lost. Downside-out calls and upside-out puts have been developed to provide the same recoupment potential for conventional options.

Endorser

A broker or dealer who signs an over-the-counter option, thereby guaranteeing the performance of the writer if the option is exercised. Usually, the OTC options are endorsed by NYSE member firms.

Open Interest

The amount of outstanding option contracts in a particular stock. It is usually reported in terms of the number of shares involved.

Put Option

A put is a contract which entitles the holder to sell 100 shares of the optioned stock at a price specified in the contract (striking price) within the named period. The price paid for a put is also known as the premium.

Spread

A combination of put and call options in a single contract, with the striking price of the put usually less than the striking price of the call. The premium on a spread is usually smaller than the premium on a straddle.

Straddle

A straddle (like a spread) is a combination of put and call options in a single contract. The specified striking prices and periods of time are the same for the put and call features, and the seller receives a single premium.

Straps and Strips

Combinations of two calls and one put and combinations of two puts and one call, respectively.

Striking Price

The price at which an option may be exercised to obtain the underlying stock. This price is also called the exercise price, which should be distinguished from the exercise value (defined as the difference between the market and striking prices).

CHAPTER 26

Technical Analysis

Technical analysis is the study of past market price performance and securities trading in graphic form to establish bases for meaningful projections of prices. The analysis includes the use of a variety of indexes and indicators which may provide information on supply and demand conditions in the market.

Technical analysts maintain that graphs of the fluctuations of securities prices and volume, reflecting the decisions of millions of investors, afford the most tangible clues to future price movements. They believe that the motivations governing investors' activities—confidence, caution, or doubt—are revealed in the form and patterns of these movements and that all pertinent economic and financial information has already been taken into account by the market and is reflected in the price movements of stocks.

Some technicians reject any fundamental information about the companies they study on the grounds that it impairs their ability to interpret the message provided by prior price performance. A less extreme position is that technical analysis is an additional tool which can help identify interesting market situations, but that final investment decisions should not be made until fundamental data have also been examined.

Technical analysis has come under significant attack in recent years. The two principal analytic onslaughts on the technical approach are the random walk and capital asset pricing model studies. Theories by themselves would hardly suffice to undermine a long-established doctrine. However, the empirical work in relation to these theories also suggests the limitations of technical analysis. For example, Fama observed that "the weight of the empirical evidence [in the random walk literature] is such that economists would generally agree that whatever dependence exists in series of historical returns cannot be used to make profitable predictions of the future."[1]

The nature of the rationalizations and the type of data observed confine the usefulness of most technical analyses largely to listed securities. It is precisely these securities that are most likely to reflect the totality of available information at all times. Much technical analysis is based on the speed of market absorption of information and invariably presupposes extended periods of absorption. Yet statistical evidence suggests that the absorption period is too short to enable investors to profit by a strategy based on market reactions to new developments. Investigations using the capital asset pricing model also suggest that the stock market is relatively efficient and offer some support to the contention that prices reflect all available information very quickly.

In addition, the structure of the market has changed substantially in recent years. We have noted its growing institutionalization. This development undermines the rationalizations of technical analysis, since these rationalizations presume a market dominated by individuals.

For these reasons, despite the growing use of computers for technical analysis, we are reluctant to give much attention to the subject. Still, technical analysis has a strong following. We have, therefore, chosen to discuss some of the prominent approaches in order to offer the investor some idea of the kinds of methods employed.

TECHNICAL ANALYSIS OF THE GENERAL MARKET

Technical analysis began with the attempt to forecast the general market, as opposed to the future price performance of a single security. The Dow Theory is the best-known approach that seeks to characterize existing trends in the general market area.

The Dow Theory: A Method of Characterizing Existing Trends

Charles H. Dow, editor of the *Wall Street Journal* from 1889 to 1902, is generally recognized as the founder of technical analysis. He initiated the famous Dow-Jones averages and used the Dow-Jones Industrial Average in conjunction with the rail average in attempting to evaluate market trends. Dow's ideas were expanded and developed by W. P. Hamilton and Robert Rhea into an elaborate system that has influenced investors for almost half a century.

The Dow Theory is frequently portrayed by a comparison of the movement of prices in the stock market with those of the ocean: there are tides (major trends), waves (intermediate corrections), and ripples (minor fluctuations). The basic idea is to identify the direction of the major trends (tides) as bullish or bearish and to invest accordingly.

Trends. Three basic trends are postulated. The primary or major trend is a sweeping movement of the Dow-Jones averages in one general direction, usually lasting from slightly less than one year to several years. An upward tilt in this trend is alleged to represent a bull market; a downward slant is supposed to indicate a bear market. Once the averages give a bull or bear "signal" by penetrating a previous high or low point, the orthodox theorist holds that the trend remains unchanged until a new high or low point is established and subsequently pierced.

Secondary trends interrupt the vigorous pace of an upward or downward primary move. They tend to retrace one-third to two-thirds of the preceding primary swing and normally terminate within two months. These intermediate corrective moves serve to drain the energy from the speculative excesses that the force of the primary trends may have created.

Minor trends are the short-lived changes–usually of only several days' duration–that comprise the secondary movements. Ordinarily, these saw-tooth-like minor fluctuations are not considered to have much significance. Sometimes, however, they form an indeterminate sidewise trend that is the basis of line formations, which are discussed later.

A bull market is likely when the peak of each secondary rally is higher than the previous one and the low point of each decline is higher than that of its predecessor. Contrariwise, there is greater likelihood of a bear market when the intermediate reactions have successively lower bottoms and tops. Sometimes these secondary cycles obscure the basic trend, and the chartist has the problem of determining whether the trend itself will continue or end.

Phases. Each bull or bear market is divided into three principal phases. During the first phase of the upside, the confidence of farsighted investors revives, and they begin to buy securities; in the second phase, stock prices start to rise because of a noticeable improvement in industrial activity; in the third, favorable financial news begets investor optimism, thereby attracting wider public buying, greatly increasing speculation, and causing unjustified price advances. On the reverse side, during the first phase of a bear market, farsighted investors begin to sell at the first indication that business earnings have passed their peak; in the second phase, unfavorable business signs are clear-cut, inducing public unloading and precipitous price declines;

and in the third, the downward movement decelerates but the leveling pressure on better-grade stocks continues because investors must dispose of their securities to realize cash.

Strict observance of Dow Theory rules can result in long periods of inactivity despite relatively sharp changes in securities prices. Even orthodox chartists, therefore, may veer a little from its principles. A typical instance of this sort is the willingness of some technicians to act during a third-phase movement before a primary turning point is confirmed.

Lines. These formations represent limited movements that occur for several weeks. The maximum and minimum degrees of allowable fluctuations are not precisely known, but they generally fall within a 5 percent range. Penetration of the upper or lower limits of a line formation indicates a secondary reaction.

Confirmation. Originally this was an important part of the Dow Theory. Confirmation meant that a change in a primary trend was not validly signaled until both industrial and rail averages had passed the allowable 5 percent limits. As a rule, when one average moved through the limit, the other was expected to follow shortly. However, as railroads played a smaller role in the economy, some Dow Theory followers became willing to waive the requirement of confirmation by the rails. Presumably, the current transportation index, which includes railroads, airlines, and bus companies, could be used in lieu of the former railroad index.

Volume. According to this feature, trading in securities accelerates as prices change in conformance with the established primary trend. Accordingly, during a bull market, turnover expands as prices rise and shrinks as they fall. Conversely, during a bear market, activity grows as prices decline and diminishes as they advance. Volume data are important primarily as supporting evidence; only price movements can confirm trend changes.

Price and volume momentum. Technicians sometimes view price and volume in a somewhat different way. Price momentum is alleged to show the growth or deterioration of prices, and volume momentum is thought to show the growth or deterioration of volume. When the figures suggest that the average price or volume for the preceding month is greater than the average for the past six months, there is allegedly a quickening of momentum. When the two momentums are mutually confirming, a trend is supposedly established. This role of momentum is not part of the Dow Theory.

Other Methods of Characterizing Existing Movements

Other methods, less elaborate than the Dow Theory and developed subsequent to it, also have as their primary purpose the characterization of existing movements.

Barron's Confidence Index. This is measured by the spread between yields to maturity of high- and low-grade bonds and is supposed to indicate bondholders' evaluation of the economy. Since bondholders are primarily financial institutions, which presumably have access to economic information that may not be easily available to the individual investor, this group of investors may anticipate future economic conditions more realistically. Confidence leads institutional buyers to expect that issuers of secondary bonds will be able to cope with their indebtedness. The investors shift to those obligations that provide a high return, thereby driving prices up and yields down. As a result, the yield differential between high- and low-grade bonds becomes relatively narrow. Conversely, lack of confidence induces bondholders to adjust their portfolios toward high-grade securities. Consequently, their yields decline, those on secondary issues rise, and the differential widens.

Index vs. moving average. A comparison may be made between the movements of the Dow-Jones index (or indexes for the New York Stock Exchange or the American Stock Exchange) and their 200-day moving averages. Investor optimism is indicated by the ability of an index to penetrate and move away from its moving average on the upside. Pessimism is suggested by a reverse relationship.

NYSE firms' free credit balances. This is money that is temporarily left in the hands of brokers, usually after securities have been sold. Customers are believed to let more money lie idle during the early stages of a bull cycle and then to reduce these balances as the cycle advances.

NYSE firms' debit balances. This is money loaned by brokers to their customers for the purpose of buying securities on margin. Logically, these balances should move inversely with free credit balances and rise as the business cycle advances. Instead, debit balances are reputed to grow during the early stages of the business cycle, as expected, but to fall off in the later stages.

Odd-lot index and odd-lot short sales index. The theory of contrary opinion assumes that the public is generally wrong. Accordingly, the intelligent investor should be selling when the public is bullish and should be buying when the public is bearish. The use of odd-lot statistics carries the theory of contrary opinion one step further by assuming that the small investor will consistently buy and sell at precisely the wrong time. The key is consistency. A consistently wrong forecastor can be used as effectively as one who is consistently right. The response to the forecast is simply reversed.

The odd-lot index is the ratio of odd-lot sales to odd-lot purchases. A ratio of more than 1.00 is considered a positive indication that market prices will rise in the future. The strongest bull signal occurs when odd-lotters are not only net sellers but also become short-sellers. The odd-lot short sale index is usually calculated by comparing odd-lot short sales to total odd-lot sales. The higher the ratio of short sales to total sales, the more bearish odd-lotters are perceived to be and, in line with the application of the contrary opinion theory, the greater the probability of a market rise.

Short interest. Since investors sell short when they expect prices to fall, a rise in the short interest suggests that many investors are bearish. Low short interest points, however, have accompanied major market peaks. This does not speak well for the prognostication talents of the short-sellers. A short interest also indicates potential future market support, since the short-sellers will have to cover their short positions. Technicians, therefore, calculate the ratio of total short interest to the average daily volume of the period for which the short interest has been tallied. They consider a ratio below 1.00 bearish and a ratio above 1.00 bullish. A ratio of above 2.00 is considered especially bullish.

Methods of Anticipating Turning-Points of Established Trends

Dow theorists profess only to characterize preexisting movements. Other technicians have gone a step further. They have developed methods intended to identify imminent changes in established trends. These techniques are chiefly based on the theory that the relative strength of buyers and sellers governs the direction of stock market movements. According to this theory, if analysis of falling prices indicates that buyers are becoming more aggressive, an upturn is likely to develop. Conversely, it is reasoned, gathering selling power will eventually reverse an upward trend of market values. To reveal these conditions, various comparisons are made of statistical series designed to measure the buying and selling power underlying market fluctuations.

Advance-decline line (breadth). A characteristic of the market often noted is its so-called breadth, the net number of stocks that advance or decline. In its simplest form, the advance-decline indicator is simply the cumulative net difference between the number of common stocks which have experienced a price rise and the number of stocks which have experienced a price decline in a given time interval. The typical time period is either a day or a week.

If the number of issues traded in a day was 1,200, of which 700 advanced, 400 declined, and 100 remained unchanged, the net advance in the daily index would have been +300. If, on the following day, 1,350 issues were traded, with 440 advancing, 660 declining, and 250 unchanged, the net for the day would be –220 and the cumulative index for the two days would be +80. The cumulative advance-decline line is compared with some market index, such as the Dow Jones average or the Standard & Poor's indexes. A shrinking advance-decline line with an advancing index has been taken as a general warning of an impending downturn.

The calculation of this index gives no consideration to either the relative significance of the price change or the market value of the outstanding shares. Thus, the same weight is given to a half-point change in IBM's market price as to a ½-point change in the price of Allied Stores. An attempt to test empirically the effectiveness of the advance-decline line produced no support for its predictive value.[2]

Advance-decline ratio. This is the ratio of a ten-day moving average of total advances to a 10-day moving average of total declines for both the New York and American stock exchanges. Index values in excess of 1.00 are supposed to indicate an overbought condition, thereby suggesting an impending decline, while values below 1.00 are supposed to indicate an oversold condition, thereby suggesting an impending advance. For this reason, the index is sometimes called the "overbought-oversold index."

Comparison of different types of securities. When economic prospects are bright, individuals are willing to buy speculative stocks, but as the outlook becomes gloomy, they seek more conservative issues. To gauge the attitude of investors, some market technicians study the relationship between speculative and conservative securities. A typical procedure is to calculate the ratios over a period of time between the average prices of low- and high-priced stocks or between AMEX and NYSE stocks. If these ratios decline in the face of generally advancing prices, a sell signal is indicated on the grounds of apparently waning public confidence in market prospects. It is considered a favorable sign if the ratios expand while prices drop.

Stocks vs. bonds. The spread between the dividend yield on the Standard & Poor's index of stock prices and the yield to maturity of AAA corporate bonds used to be considered a significant indicator of turning points in either the stock market or the money markets. During the 1950s and the early 1960s there was a widespread belief that whenever dividend yields on common stocks were less than the yields to maturity on high-grade bonds, stocks were overpriced and would inevitably decline.

The investment logic at that time assumed that the risk differential between stocks and bonds not only was so great that investors in common stocks should receive a higher current return on their investment but that market price appreciation was also both a natural and necessary supplement to their potential realized rate of return. Capital gains were considered to be the unanticipated frosting on the cake for investors in common stocks.

As investors in common stocks began to accept anticipated appreciation as a part of their predictable returns, the logic of comparing the dividend yield on stocks with the yields of corporate bonds disappeared. As a result, over the past decade the dividend yield on common stock has not uncommonly been below the yield to maturity on high-grade corporate bonds.

Comparison of price and volume data. A simple method involving this relationship is to compare curves of stock prices and trading volume. When volume drops while prices rise, a reversal movement is supposed to be forming. Technicians also measure the volume of turnover required to raise and lower securities prices. For this purpose, the daily gains and losses of all active stocks are segregated. Total gains are divided by the volume of trading in this group to obtain the average rise per share of stocks showing an improvement for the day. A similar average is made for issues that exhibited net losses during the day. If the average gain per share traded exceeds the average loss per share, prices are expected to move upward.

TECHNICAL MARKET ANALYSIS—INDIVIDUAL SECURITIES

In addition to analyzing the general securities markets, technicians study a number of graphic formations covering specific securities. It is claimed that characteristic patterns invariably occur when an established trend is waning and a reversal is in prospect, or when a consolidation period is in effect and a renewed drive in the same direction is likely. These formations are called reversal area patterns when they point to a turn in the established trend; they are called consolidation patterns when they indicate the probable continuation of the trend. Area patterns commonly include head and shoulders, triangles, rectangles, and flags and pennants. Technicians also use other devices, such as gaps and resistance levels, to clarify area patterns and identify trading opportunities. To gauge the nature of a movement, still other measures, such as relative strength and point and figure charts, are used.

The skilled chartist has great confidence in his tools. At one extreme, he may even claim that if the statistical record is accurate and long enough, he does not have to know the name of a stock to interpret its fluctuations and trade profitably in it. In view of these assertions and the frequent references to technical market analysis, a description of some of the more prominent formations and devices might be of interest.

Head and Shoulders

This formation is an important reversal area pattern. It is called a head and shoulders top when signaling the transition from rising to falling prices, and a head and shoulders bottom when it augurs a change from a declining to an advancing trend.

A typical head and shoulders top appears in Pattern A of Figure 26-1. This formation comprises four basic elements. The first, the left shoulder, represents a rally marked by heavy trading that climaxes the established trend and precedes a drop in prices on receding volume. The second is the head, which includes a second vigorous rise that carries beyond the top of the left shoulder but promptly turns into a decline, marked by shrinking volume to a level below the left shoulder top. The third phase, the right shoulder, comprises another rally that fails to reach the height of the head and is characterized by relatively light volume. Finally, the decline is continued through the neckline, represented by a line drawn across the bottom of the recessionary moves. A decisive final penetration of the neckline signifies a "breakout" into a declining trend of prices.

Triangles

The symmetrical triangle is the most familiar of these formations. As shown in Pattern B of Figure 26-1, it is composed of a series of short-term rallies whose tops reach successively lower levels and whose bottoms halt at successively higher levels. Downward and upward sloping lines may be drawn through these tops and bottoms, converging at an apex to form a clearly defined symmetrical triangle. While the formation is developing, the volume of trading gradually dries up until the breakout occurs; the direction of the breakout may continue or reverse the previous trend. Downside breaks are not generally marked by much increase in volume, whereas the upside movements are usually accompanied by a sharp rise in turnover. Triangles are relatively easy to discern, but it is difficult to anticipate the direction of the eventual penetration.

When the arms of the triangle are asymmetrical, the formation is called a right-angle triangle, and the probable direction of the breakout is indicated more clearly. If the top line of the triangle is horizontal and the bottom line slants upward to meet it at the apex, the pattern is of the ascending type; this denotes a breakout to a rising price trend. Conversely, when the lower line is horizontal and the upper line slopes downward to the apex, the formation is descending; this relationship heralds falling prices.

Rectangles

Closely related to the preceding type of movement is the rectangle. As shown in Pattern C, it comprises a series of indecisive price fluctuations bounded by lines which are parallel or have only a very slight slant. Like

FIGURE 26-1

Typical Graphic Patterns Used in Technical Market Analysis

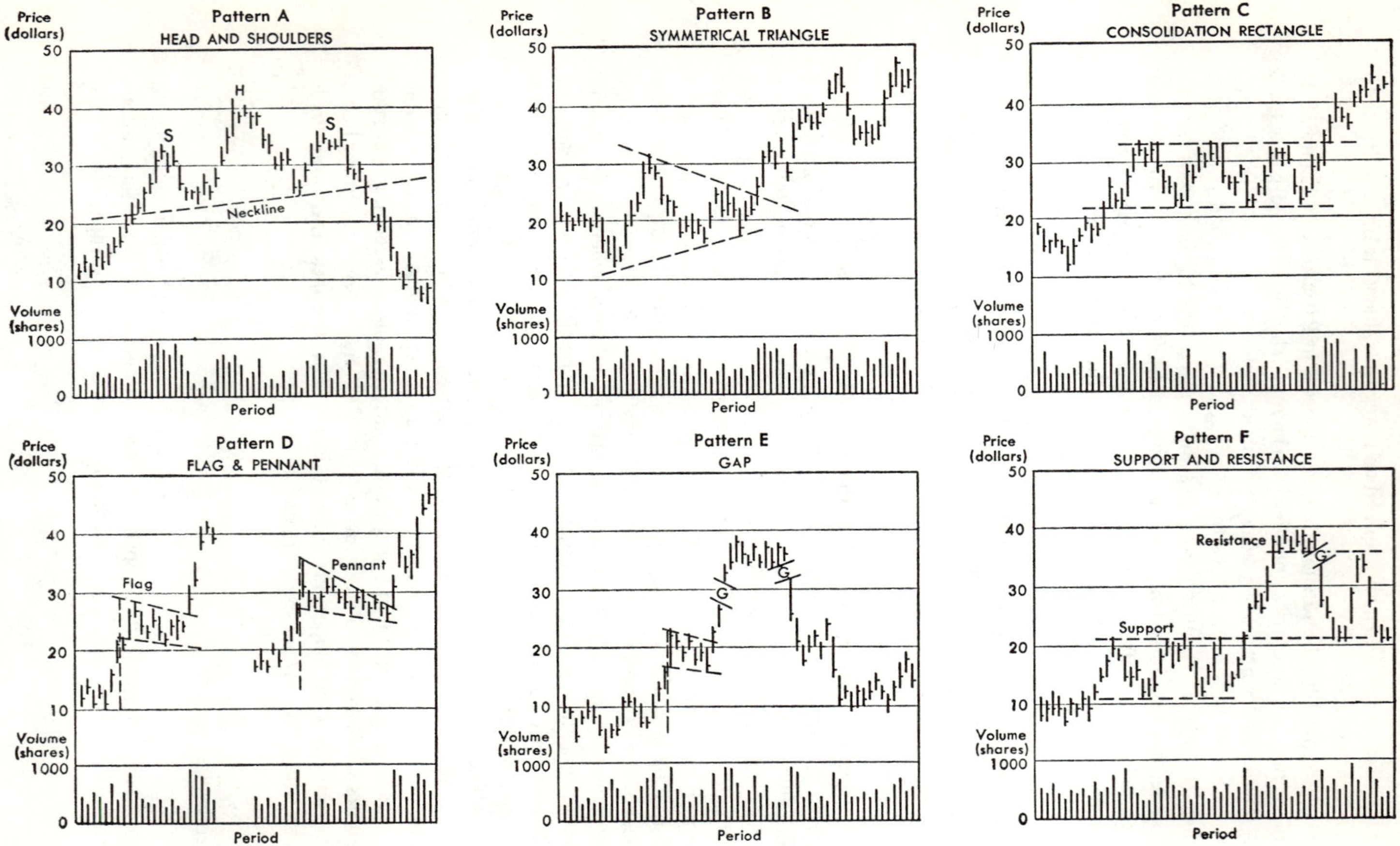

SOURCE: Sidney M. Robbins, ***Managing Securities*** (Cambridge, Mass: Houghton Mifflin, 1954), p. 502.

triangles, a rectangular area pattern may interrupt the continuity of a preceding trend or may signify the start of a reversal movement. The rectangle is alleged to represent a consolidation more often than a reversal formation. While the rectangle is developing, volume gradually dwindles; it then expands when the breakout occurs.

Flags and Pennants

Pattern D shows the formation commonly described as flags and pennants. These patterns appear after a swift upward move that follows a nearly straight line. Flags are short up-and-down price fluctuations that take the form of a compact parallelogram, usually sloping downward against the prevailing trend. Pennants are similar to flags, except that the main bounding lines converge to form a triangle rather than a parallelogram. While these patterns are developing—usually within a three-week period—the volume of turnover normally diminishes. Completion of the flag or pennant is revealed in a resurgence of the upward move on heavy volume. The pattern, with an upward tilt, may also interrupt a sharply downward price trend. Flags and pennants are considered among the important consolidation formations.

Gaps

Gaps occur when the lowest price at which a security sells during one day is above the highest price of the preceding day, or conversely, when the highest price of one day is below the lowest level of the previous day. A gap is closed when prices subsequently move through the area that was skipped. Technicians are not generally impressed with the commonly voiced contention that "gaps must be closed." Although they acknowledge the truth of the statement, they also point out that many years may elapse before a gap is closed and that this development is of little practical use.

There are various types of gaps, such as the common or area gap and the breakaway, runaway, and exhaustion gaps. Depending on their location, they may have little significance or may help to confirm the vigor and direction of indicated moves. Pattern E shows a runaway gap originating between the breakout and the termination of a swift upward or downward move. This gap, which is accompanied by intense volume, indicates generally that prices will rise as much beyond the gap level as they have already progressed from the preceding breakout point.

Support and Resistance Levels

Technicians use the principle of support and resistance levels both in interpreting the standard chart formations and in reaching independent trading conclusions. A support level is an indicated price range that will probably induce a buying surge, thus preventing the extension of a decline and possibly even contributing toward an upward move. A resistance level is a probable price ceiling which, when reached, brings on a wave of selling that not only limits the price advance but also may lead to a renewed decline.

Price fluctuations often meet support or resistance at levels which represent previous area formations. Thus, once a former top has been pierced, it may become the bottom of the following decline. The level at which a previous bottom was penetrated often becomes the top of a subsequent advance. Pattern F shows typical support and resistance zones.

Relative Strength Concept

The price performance of a particular stock can be compared with the price performance of the market as a whole as measured by one or more of the market indexes, or it may be compared with the price performance of stocks of companies in the same industry. For example, assume that over a six-month period the price of stock *X* fell from \$80 a share to \$72 a share, while the price of stock *Y* fell from \$20 a share to \$16 a share. Stock *X*'s price performance is better than stock *Y*'s, since it declined only 10 percent while stock *Y* declined 20 percent. If during the same period the market in general declined 15 percent, the relative strength concept would describe stock *X* as outperforming the market; stock *Y*'s performance would be considered weaker than that of the market. The relative strength concept assumes that relative trends, like actual trends, tend to persist over time. Therefore, a stock which has consistently outperformed the market is likely to continue to do so in the future.

Relative strength may be determined by calculating the ratio of a stock price to the Dow-Jones Industrial Average. A steady increase in the ratio would be a sign of strength; a steady decline in the ratio would be a sign of weakness. A more elaborate technique is to calculate a 200-day moving average for a group of stocks and then rank them according to their relative rate of growth in price, from highest to lowest.

Prior to the advent of the computer, the time required to calculate the relative strength of a large group of securities was prohibitive. With the computer, it is possible not only to calculate moving averages for all actively traded securities but also to rank them according to their relative price performance on a weekly basis.

In Table 26-1, the relative price performance of stock *A* was better than 95 percent of stocks generally in period 1. In period 2 the relative performance improved. However, in periods 4 through 6 its relative performance ranking declined, even though its market price increased.

TABLE 26-1

Relative Strength Ranking of Stock A

PERIOD	PRICE	RELATIVE PERFORMANCE PERCENTILE
1	30	95
2	36	96
3	32	90
4	37	92
5	41	83
6	42	72

According to the followers of the relative strength concept, the significant factor is first the change in the ranking and then a continuing decline. Presumably, holdings of stock *A* would be sold in period 6, even though its market price increased.

Point and Figure Charts

The point and figure chart is a highly specialized device used by market technicians for gauging the probable amplitude of a future move. In this type of chart, squares are filled with Xs for price increases and 0s for price decreases. Four things must be decided by the analyst: the value of each box, which may be a fraction of a point, 1 point, or a number of points; the frequency of observations; a rounding rule; and a reversal rule.

It is common to have each box represent 50 cents for stocks selling below \$20, \$1 for stocks selling from \$20 to \$100, and \$3 for stocks selling in excess of \$100. A few chartists concern themselves with every trade. This is extremely time consuming; therefore, charts are usually updated daily. In general, the technician focuses on the high and low of the period for which updating occurs. The common procedure is to round down for a high and up for a low (that is, if current entries are being made in an X column, round down; otherwise round up). Thus, with \$1 boxes, 69⅜ would be considered 69 if it was the period high and 70 if it was the period low. The usual reversal rule requires a 3-point change.*

Chart construction: an illustration. The construction of charts is best explained by an illustration. Consider the data in Table 26-2, where each box

*Change is measured after rounding. Thus, if the high was 49½, it would be represented by an X in the box representing 49. The price would then have to fall to 46 after rounding before the technician would move into a zero column. Since the technician is in an X column, a trade at 46⅞ would be treated as a trade at 46, and this would signal a reversal.

represents 1 point. Assume that just prior to April 2, prices had been drifting downward and that the low had been 42 (see column 2). The high of 45 on April 2 would thus represent a three-box reversal.* Therefore, in Figure 26-2, Xs are recorded in boxes 43-45 of the third column. On April 3, prices continued their rise to 48, and boxes 46-48 are filled in the same column. No matter how high prices rise, the same column is used.

TABLE 26-2

*Sample Data for Point and Figure Chart**

DATE	HIGH	LOW	ENTRIES	DATE	HIGH	LOW	ENTRIES
April 2	45.6	42.0	43 45 X	May 1	46.6	47.2	
3	48.4	45.5	46 48 X	2	50.5	47.0	48 50 X
4	48.6	48.2		3	51.0	46.0	51 X
5	48.4	48.2		4	53.7	45.2	52 53 X
6	47.6	46.0		7	53.0	48.7	52 49 O
9	48.4	46.3		8	51.2	50.7	
10	48.2	47.7		9	53.6	51.2	50 53 X
11	48.6	46.7		10	55.0	52.2	54 55 X
12	46.0	45.3	47 45 O				
13	44.1	43.4	44 O				
16	43.0	42.3	43 O				
17	43.3	42.3					
18	42.6	42.3					
19	43.5	42.6					
20	44.0	43.7					
23	44.0	42.2					
24	45.2	42.3					
25	46.0	44.2	44 46 X				
26	46.6	45.4					
27	46.2	46.2					
30	47.2	46.0	47 X				

*Decimals represent eighths.

At this point there can be no reversal until the stock trades at 45 or less. No new Xs will be recorded unless the stock trades for 49 or more. Neither of these prices was reached until April 12, when the stock traded at 45⅜. An 0 is therefore recorded in the 45 box. Similarly, 0s are entered in all boxes representing prices *between* 45 and the previous high of 48, but not including the 48 box itself. Columns of 0s always descend from one box below the one in which the previous high is recorded, and columns of Xs always ascend from one box above the one in which the previous low is recorded. This method of recording means that the minimum number of entries in any column is either three Xs or three 0s.

*The highs and lows referred to in this passage are the prices in Table 26-2 rounded in accordance with the convention noted in the preceding paragraph.

FIGURE 26-2

Point and Figure Chart

```
60

55            X
              X
            X X
            XOX
            XOX
50          XOX
            XO
          X X
          XOX
          XOX
45        XOX
          XOX
          XO



40
```

Continuing with Figure 26-3, we find that on April 13 and 16 successive new lows of 44 and 43 are reached and recorded. After this, new entries will be made only if the stock trades at 42 or less or 46 or more. Such trades did not occur until April 25, at which point a new ascending column begins at 44, and Xs are recorded through 46.

No reversal will now occur unless the stock trades at 43 or less. In the succeeding days the price actually rose, until it hit a new high of 53 on May 4. The very next trading day, however, the stock fell to less than 50, low enough to bring about a reversal. There was another reversal on May 9, and on May 10 the price was carried to 55, where we come to the end of our data.

Note that no entries were made from April 4 to April 11, from April 17 to April 24, from April 26 to April 27, and on May 1 and 8. Thus, there is no precise time dimension on Figure 26-2. A column can represent almost any length of time from one day on.

Interpretation. Essential to the interpretation of point and figure charts is the concept of the congested area. This is a series of reversals within roughly confined limits—that is, successive columns of Xs and 0s roughly bounded on both the upside and downside, such as in columns 2 to 7 in Figure 26-3. The more columns there are within the upper and lower bounds, the more intense the congestion is. A breakout is said to occur when these boundaries are penetrated, as in the eighth column, which rises above the old upper limit. Breakouts can be on either the upside or downside. Technicians consider an upside breakout, such as in the eighth column, evidence of relatively strong buyer interest and believe that purchases are appropriate at that time. They consider a downside breakout evidence of relatively strong selling interest; selling short is thus the indicated strategy.

FIGURE 26-3

Point and Figure Illustration of Congestion, Breakout, and Diagonal

```
60

55

                X
              X XO
    O      X  XOXO
50  O      XOXOXO
    O      XOXOXO
    OX X X XOXOXO
    OXOXOXOXOXO
    OXOXOXOXO
45  OXOXOXOX
    OXOXOXOX
    OXO O O
    O

40
```

Generally, a diagonal movement is expected after a breakout occurs. An upside breakout, for example, is expected to be followed by a succession of columns of Xs and Os with successively higher tops and bottoms, as in the last five columns of Figure 26-3. The diagonal following a downside breakout is a succession of columns with successively lower tops and bottoms. Trend lines are constructed by drawing a straight line touching three rising bottoms or three declining tops.

Point and figure chartists project the end of the diagonal movement by considering the width of the congested area. The vertical rise (drop) of the diagonal is expected to continue until it reaches the "target" area. To find this area, one must first count the number of columns in the congested area. In Figure 26-3 this number is eight. The walls, columns 1 and 8, should be included in the count. Next the count is multiplied by the number of points represented by each box in the chart (1). The product (8) is the number of squares vertically above (below) the top (bottom) of the congested area around which the next congested area will occur. Presumably, therefore, if Figure 26-3 were continued and the stock behaved in accordance with the above theory, the next congestion area should have an upper limit of 56 = 48 + 8. Unfortunately, price movements do not usually fall into quite so neat a pattern as in Figure 26-3.

Simulated Stock Charts

In his delightful book *A Random Walk Down Wall Street*, Burton G. Malkiel reports an experiment by his students, who simulated stock charts randomly by flipping coins. He asked his students to construct normal charts for a hypothetical stock initially selling at $50 per share. Price changes each day were determined by flipping a coin. If the toss was heads, the stock was assumed to close half a point higher than the previous day. If the coin came up tails, the price was assumed to be down half a point. The simulated stock charts generated in this fashion produced many of the trends and patterns used as a basis for technical analysis. Malkiel commented:

> . . . there were head-and-shoulders formations, triple tops and bottoms, and other more esoteric chart patterns. One of the charts showed a beautiful upward breakout from an inverted head and shoulders (a very bullish formation). I showed it to a chartist friend of mine who practically jumped out of his skin. "What is this company?" he exclaimed. "We've got to buy immediately. This pattern's a classic. There's no question the stock will be up 15 points next week."[3]

SUMMARY

Technical analysis involves the study of past market movements of a security or index in order to project future price performance. Analysis may be made either of the general market or of individual securities.

The primary objective of analyzing the general market may be to characterize individual trends, for which the Dow Theory is the traditional technique. Alternatively, the focus may be on anticipating turning points. For this purpose, various techniques have been developed that, by and large, are based on comparisons of statistical series that ostensibly measure the buying and selling power underlying market fluctuations.

Technicians also study individual securities to determine the direction and extent of future price changes by the configuration of price movements. Typical graphic patterns include heads and shoulders, triangles, rectangles, and flags and pennants. The point and figure chart is a specialized device to gauge the amplitude of a probable future move.

Technical analysis has attracted a wide following. Neither theory nor statistical research, however, provides support for this approach.

Questions and Exercises

The following discussion questions and numerical exercises are designed to furnish the reader with both a framework for reviewing the text and a means of testing his or her understanding of the material. In order to facilitate the integration of ideas, we have arranged these questions and exercises by subject matter rather than by chapters.

Instructors may use the discussion questions not only to stimulate classroom discussion but also, in many cases, as the theme for short essays. The problems are multipurpose: They are designed to help students to translate concepts into hard data and to provide them with a facsimile of experience. In many problems, for example, we require the students to examine actual data sources, such as annual reports and 10-Ks, instead of providing them with fabricated data sets. This means that the instructor can keep the exercises fresh and need not be concerned about the availability of solutions from prior semesters.

To strengthen the link between the classroom and Wall Street we have provided a number of discussion questions and problems that have been taken or adapted from examinations prepared for the Chartered Financial Analyst Candidate Study and Examination Program. These questions, which are preceded by an asterisk, have been reprinted with the permission of the Institute of Chartered Financial Analysts, which holds the copyright. In order to permit consistency with the text, the wording of the original questions was often modified. Accordingly, no identifying quotation marks have been used.

Introduction

1. What is the likelihood of getting rich by finding undervalued securities?

2. What is meant by the value of a security? What kind of information is necessary to determine this value?

3. What is meant by a portfolio of securities? What are the problems inherent in selecting individual securities compared with developing a portfolio of securities?

4. What skills does the individual need in selecting stocks? What skills does the professional analyst need in selecting these stocks?

5. How do the functions of a securities analyst who is employed by a brokerage firm differ from those employed by a life insurance company?

6. What are the major fields of knowledge for a securities analyst? What is the relative importance of theory, application, academic study, experience?

The Securities Markets
(Chapters 1-3)

1. How could the handling of an order affect its price? What is the function of the "trader" in a securities firm? What are the responsibilities of an institution in obtaining the best possible execution?

2. What are the overall purposes of each of the federal securities laws that have been enacted since 1933? In what ways does the SEC administer these measures and what have been the principal limitations impeding effective SEC administration? How has the SEC attempted to resolve these limitations and to extend investor protection in recent years?

3. What are the broad distinctions between the exchange, OTC, third, and fourth markets? What are the roles and the relative importance of the New York, American, and regional exchanges? Why has the NYSE been concerned about the third market? In what way has it sought to control the relationship between its members and the third market? What is the position of the third-market firms in respect to NYSE efforts to limit the third-market activities of its members? What action did the SEC take?

4. What are the characteristics of an auction market? How is an ordinary-sized transaction handled in the NYSE? What special measures has the NYSE devised to take care of big transactions? What is meant by a block transaction? Why has this method evolved in lieu of the special methods developed by the NYSE? How is a block transaction executed in the NYSE?

5. What is the difference between the broker and dealer functions of the specialist? To what extent is there a conflict in the conduct of these functions? What special responsibilities does the specialist have in carrying out the dealer function? In what way does the NYSE gauge the performance of the specialist? How will the central market affect the specialist?

6. How is a typical transaction executed in the OTC market? What are the roles played by market makers and retail brokers in these transactions? Why are bonds primarily traded in the OTC market?

7. What is a margin transaction? Why is it important to distinguish between initial and maintenance margins? How is a short sale consummated? What are the potential benefits and dangers of selling short? What kinds of orders may be placed? How may these orders be used?

8. Discuss:
The Meaning of a Central Market.
Problems Created by the Growth of Institutional Trading.
Developing Trading Rules for a Central Market.
Integrating Commercial Banks into the Central Market.
Foreign Access to the U.S. Securities Markets.
The Future of the Securities Industry.

9. In the legislative history of the Securities Acts Amendments of 1975, reference is made to "failsafe" powers, provisions which may only be used as regulatory powers of last resort. Summarize these powers and explain the reasons for their inclusion.

Comparing Investment Returns
(Chapters 4-5)

1. Compare dividends, interest, and capital gains as sources of income, covering such factors as level, stability, and predictability.

2. Discuss the pressures on a corporation to pay dividends and the restrictions that may limit or prevent payments.

3. Compare the meaning of the annual rate of return with that of the yield to maturity. How may the concept of yield to maturity be applied to stocks?

4. If a bond sells at a premium above par and is callable at par before maturity, is it more conservative to calculate the yield to call date or to maturity? If the same bond sells at a discount from par, which method is more conservative? If a bond sells at a premium but is also callable at a premium, which method is more conservative? Explain your conclusions.

5. Discuss the factors that might be considered in comparing the rates of return available through short-term U.S. government securities, savings banks, commercial banks, savings and loan associations, and credit unions.

6. How might changing economic circumstances and family responsibilities affect the kind of life insurance policy an individual purchases?

7. Select six corporations, one pair in each of three different fields of activity. Calculate the ratio of their dividend payments to earnings per share of common stock (dividend payout ratio) in the latest year for which information is available. Based upon a review of the backgrounds of these companies, explain the differences in their indicated dividend policies.

8. Calculate the annual rates of return for the same six common stocks. Rank these rates and account for the variations.

9. Select six bonds, one pair in each rating category of AAA, A, and BB. Calculate the annual rates of return for each of these bonds. Calculate the yields to maturity for each of the bonds, using bond tables and the approximate method. Explain the reasons for the differences in the annual rates of return and the yields to maturity.

Tax Considerations
(Chapter 6)

Taxes on Income

1. Discuss and contrast for tax purposes the concepts of realized income, unrealized income, and constructively received income. Give an example of each and illustrate income that is not constructively received.

2. Discuss the circumstances under which the cash dividends of a corporation may not be taxable.

3. Discuss the principles underlying the determination of whether a stock dividend is taxable.

Capital Gains or Losses

4. Contrast the adjustment in the cost basis of a stock as a result of the distribution of

(a) a nontaxable common stock dividend;

(b) a nontaxable preferred stock dividend.

5. Ms. A has owned for almost six months a stock which she is ready to sell. Discuss the circumstances which would lead her to liquidate immediately or to hold for a short while longer.

6. Mr. C has owned for over a year a stock which has declined substantially in value. Although he prefers to retain the stock because he thinks it will recover, he also wants to realize a loss for tax purposes. He therefore sells the stock and repurchases it a week later.

Under the same circumstances, Ms. D tries to achieve the objective by first doubling her holding and then selling her old stock ten days later.

Compare the two tax strategies. Can you suggest a third strategy?

7. There is considerable controversy regarding the justification for taxing the capital gains on securities. Discuss briefly your opinion on the subject.

8. Assume an individual pays a federal income tax of 40 percent and a state income tax of 15 percent. Calculate the net aftertax current yield of a

10 percent corporate bond, a 7 percent U.S. Treasury bond, and a 5 percent municipal bond.

9. Indicate the amounts that would be subject to federal income tax in the tax year 1976 in each of the following six cases:

(a) The semiannual interest on a 6 percent Treasury bond; interest is payable February 1, 1977.
(b) A 7 percent municipal bond, interest payable February 1 and August 1, sold on December 1, 1976, with a long-term profit of $100.
(c) An 8 percent corporate bond, interest payable February 1 and August 1, sold on December 1, 1976, with a long-term profit of $100.
(d) Interest of $100 accrued in 1976 on a Series E savings bond.
(e) A 90-day Treasury bill purchased for $900 on December 1, 1976.

Sources of Information
(Chapter 7)

1. Compare a company's latest annual report and one it issued five years previously. List the categories of information in the most recent report but not in the earlier one. Discuss the importance of this information and the probable reason for its inclusion.

2. In an article in the March 1975 issue of *Exchange* (p. 9) the following statement regarding the corporate chief executive is made: "In many cases, he cannot help revealing important information about his attitudes towards his company and its performance regardless of the choices of expression."[1]

Read the section of the annual report addressed to the shareowners and signed by the principal officer or officers of the same corporation over the past five years. In light of the information presented, provide an assessment of the character of the management.

3. Review the latest annual reports of three manufacturing companies for the same year. Rank each of the reports with respect to the following items: discussion of the products manufactured, description of technological achievements, summary of the problems encountered, information by product line, completeness of the financial statements, adequacy of footnotes, discussion of financial policies, management's analysis of operations, and historic financial summary. On the basis of these rankings, evaluate the relative merits of the reports.

4. It is important that the securities analyst check the statement of the independent accountant that appears in the annual report. What are the implications of the warning to "beware the three-paragraph audit"? What

kind of problems might require special comment in the accountant's statement? What is meant by "the red flag of questionable 'going-concern' value"?

5. Compare the annual report, 10-K, and prospectus of an established company that has recently had a public offering of securities. Discuss the extent to which information appears in one document but not another, and the comprehensiveness of the same information appearing in the different documents.

6. In an interview, John C. Burton, chief accountant of the SEC, made the following statement about the principal objectives of the disclosure regulations of the SEC: "I think the objective is to give investors more analytically-oriented information so that they can develop a better understanding in depth of what is going on, while at the same time putting upon management a responsibility to provide the average investor a textual analysis of what's going on."[2] Evaluate this statement in the light of the annual reports, 10-K reports, and prospectuses that you have examined.

Factors Affecting Securities Prices (Chapter 8)

1. Discuss the relationship between general business conditions and stock prices. Indicate two periods when the curves moved in different directions. Explain the reasons for these diverse movements.

2. Define "growth stock." What is the danger in attempting to select stocks on this basis? What opportunities for profit do growth stocks provide?

3. To what extent can a securities analyst detect undervalued securities and therefore outperform the general market?

4. Complete the following tables for five stocks representing companies in different industries:

TABLE 1

	MARKET PRICE			EARNINGS PER SHARE			PRICE/ EARNINGS RATIO	
NAME OF STOCK	JAN. 1 1967	JAN. 1 1969	CHANGE (%)	1966	1968	CHANGE (%)	JAN. 1 1967†	JAN. 1 1969‡

†Price at that time divided by 1966 earnings per share.
‡Price at that time divided by 1968 earnings per share.

TABLE 2

	MARKET PRICE			EARNINGS PER SHARE			PRICE/ EARNINGS RATIO	
NAME OF STOCK	JAN. 1 1973	JAN. 1 1975	CHANGE (%)	1972	1974	CHANGE (%)	JAN. 1 1973§	JAN. 1 1975‖

§Price at that time divided by 1972 earnings per share.

‖ Price at that time divided by 1974 earnings per share.

To what extent do the changes in earnings explain the changes in price? How do you account for the varying earnings and price changes of the different stocks? What conclusions may be drawn from the changes in the p/e ratios of the stocks? Explain both the similar and dissimilar reactions of the stocks during the two periods.

5. What is meant by the "pretty girl" approach in the selection of securities? To what extent is this a justifiable method?

The Nature and Risk Characteristics of Common Stock (Chapters 9-10)

Characteristics of Common Stock

1. Why is it impractical for a corporation to guarantee the dividend rate on its common stock?

2. What is meant by negotiability? Does a common stock certificate have the requisite characteristics of a negotiable instrument? Is a common stock certificate negotiable? Explain.

3. What is a beneficial owner? Discuss the advantages and disadvantages of leaving a stock in "street name"?

Risk

4. Explain why uncertainty leads to risk aversion (the drawing of a utility function will be helpful for this purpose).

5. Discuss the relationship between:

(a) the returns of an individual stock in a portfolio and the return of the total portfolio;

(b) the risk of an individual stock in a portfolio and the risk of the total portfolio.

Calculation and Significance of Beta

6. What is an investor-independent measure of risk, and why is it important to have one?

7. Discuss the difference between an optimal and an efficient portfolio.

8. If investors have homogeneous expectations, will they have the same portfolios? If not, how will they differ? Explain.

9. Describe the risk characteristics of a stock and the extent to which they could be eliminated through diversification. Various financial services publish estimates of beta (Value Line is a convenient one). Select ten stocks at random and compare the published beta for the latest and earliest years available. Discuss the reasons for the changes. Separate the ten stocks into two groups based on the percentage change that occurred in their beta's. How do you account for the differences between the two groups?

*10. You are director of research and a partner of a large investment consulting firm. Your chief investment officer has been approached several times, both by clients and by organizations offering services, proposing that beta analysis be used in the firm's investment management procedures. Certain questions exist in his mind as to whether such a practice can be expected to improve investment performance for the firm's clients, which are predominantly pension and profit-sharing funds. The investment officer has asked you to write a concise report with special emphasis on the following:

(a) How might beta analysis be used in performance measurement and portfolio management?

(b) What are the assumptions underlying the use of beta analysis to measure risk?

(c) How would you explain these assumptions?

*11. You are managing a $100 million pension fund portfolio and have received the following probability distribution for the expected one-year total return on the Standard & Poor's 500 Index.

MARKET PREDICTION	ONE-YEAR TOTAL RETURN, S&P 500	PROBABILITY
I	+20%	0.15
II	+10	0.30
III	+5	0.20
IV	−5	0.20
V	−10	0.10
VI	−20	0.05
		1.00

There are three possible portfolio strategies available, *A*, *B*, and *C*. Under each portfolio strategy is displayed the percentage return for each of the six market predictions.

MARKET PREDICTION	PORTFOLIO STRATEGY A	B	C
I	7%	50%	20%
II	7	30	12
III	7	10	10
IV	7	−10	4
V	7	−25	0
VI	7	−40	−8

(a) State the expected one-year total return for the Standard & Poor's 500 Index.

(b) Assuming that you desire to maximize return regardless of risk, select the proper strategy. Explain.

(c) Assuming that you are a "risk averter," select the proper strategy. Explain.

*12. Perform the following calculations:

(a) A general market index is likely to produce an annual average return of about 9 percent over a long period of time. Expected annual fluctuations range between +30 and −20 percent. Risk-free investment opportunities will average 5 percent. A fund wishes to strive for a return that is 11 percent "better than the market," over the long term. Calculate the average beta level for the portfolio that would be required to meet the 10 percent per year goal. Discuss your results.

(b) Assume a portfolio beta level of 1.5; a market index decline of 15 percent; and a risk-free rate of 4 percent. Calculate the expected return for a fund under these conditions. Discuss your results.

Evaluating the Quality of a Company's Earnings (Chapters 11-12)

1. Discuss the term "quality of earnings." Illustrate how such quality may be affected by different accounting practices with respect to long-term contracts, investment credit, depreciation, evaluation of accounts receivable, and capitalization of costs.

2. John C. Burton, chief accountant of the SEC, has stated that "the most significant inflation-related deficiencies in financial statements exist in the areas of inventories and productive facilities."[3] Discuss:

(a) The significance of these deficiencies to the analyst evaluating the financial statements of a company.

(b) The proposals that have been advanced to ameliorate the problem.

3. In 1974 many companies moved from the FIFO to the LIFO method of accounting. Fedders Corp. followed this policy and reduced its inventory at August 31, 1974 (its fiscal year) by $17.5 million and increased its net loss applicable to common stockholders by about the same amount. Throughout the fiscal year, the company had been paying regular quarterly dividends but took no action at its meeting on October 15, 1974. The announced reason in the annual report was that "the company is now restricted from paying dividends on its common stock by provisions of its long-term debt agreements." Discuss the merits of the decision of Fedders' management to shift from FIFO to LIFO in the light of economic conditions at that time, the popularity of the practice, and the company's own financial position.

4. In 1974 the per share earnings of Sterling Drug were $1.35, compared with $1.20 in 1973. Comment on the significance of this rise in the light of the method whereby the company accounted for its losses from foreign exchange as described in its annual report and 10-K.

5. A footnote on foreign exchange in Burroughs' 1974 annual report states: "The company translates long-term liabilities owed in foreign currencies at the rate of exchange in effect when the obligation was incurred."[4] Explain how differences in translation methods may affect reported earnings. What consideration would you give to a translation loss as compared to a conversion loss in analyzing the earnings of a company?

6. In an analysis of Republic Steel Corp., dated June 19, 1975, Becker Securities Corp. states:

> The conservative nature of Republic's accounting is most apparent in its policies of accruing for pension, expensing realistic sums for maintenance and depreciation, costing of raw material and inventories, providing ample operating reserves, reflecting interest expenses as incurred, and minimizing noncash earnings from nonoperating sources.

Discuss Republic's policies with respect to these items on the basis of information appearing in the annual reports and 10-Ks.

7. For the fiscal year ending March 31, 1974, Combustion Equipment Associates, Inc., reported earnings of $1.47 a share, compared with $1.14 the previous year. This increase was more than accounted for by $0.09 attributed to a lower tax rate, $0.14 by an increase in capitalized research and development costs, and $0.21 by a reduction of costs arising out of claims that the company filed against various governmental agencies for recovery of excess costs incurred by contract delays and changes. Comment on the significance of each of these factors in evaluating the company's earnings.

8. In discussing bank acquisitions, M. A. Schapiro & Sons, Inc. stated in its December 1974 *Bank Stock Quarterly* that "growth trends remain

realistic," in acquisitions accomplished under the "purchase method" of accounting, whereas "pooling can inflate the record" and therefore the gains under this method may be "illusory." Discuss the reasons underlying these comments. What are the implications to a securities analyst?

9. Determine the allowance for doubtful accounts as a percentage of notes and accounts receivable for pairs of companies in five different industries. Discuss the observed differences both from industry to industry and within the same industry.

Analysis of Financial Statements (Chapters 13-14)

1. The typical method of analyzing the financial statements of a company is through determining ratios between different items of the income statement and balance sheet. Discuss the advantages and limitations of this approach.

2. Indicate the capitalization changes that any company probably will and will not take into account when presenting a summary of earnings per share over time. What is the intent underlying the requirement to report "primary" and "fully diluted" earnings per share?

3. Discuss the various ways the capitalization of a company may affect the price of its common stock.

4. Below are various ratios, over a six-year period, from the financial statements of two companies, *A* and *B*, in the retail field.

	RATE OF RETURN ON INVESTED CAPITAL		PROFIT MARGIN		ACID-TEST RATIO	
YEAR	A	B	A	B	A	B
1975	6.1%	7.8%	6.5%	3.8%	0.8	2.7
1974	5.4	7.8	6.0	3.9	0.7	2.6
1973	10.8	8.9	9.5	4.0	1.0	3.4
1972	9.1	8.1	8.7	4.0	0.9	3.1
1971	8.2	8.2	8.5	3.8	3.9	2.9
1970	8.0	8.1	8.0	3.7	0.7	2.8

	OPERATING RATIO		CURRENT-ASSET RATIO		INVENTORY TURNOVER	
	A	B	A	B	A	B
1975	89.5%	95.9%	2.3	3.5	2.80	7.72
1974	90.0	95.8	2.1	3.3	2.55	7.80
1973	86.7	95.6	2.7	4.0	3.25	7.95
1972	87.3	95.7	2.5	3.7	3.05	7.36
1971	87.0	95.8	5.5	3.5	2.85	7.35
1970	88.2	96.0	2.3	3.4	2.70	7.30

	PLANT TURNOVER		DEBT/EQUITY RATIO		CAPITAL TURNOVER	
	A	B	A	B	A	B
1975	3.95	20.0	26.9%	3.9%	0.94	2.05
1974	3.85	19.5	27.0	3.8	0.90	2.00
1973	4.00	21.5	27.1	3.5	1.14	2.22
1972	3.05	17.0	30.5	4.9	1.05	2.02
1971	3.50	14.5	31.2	5.1	0.96	2.16
1970	3.87	12.9	23.5	5.4	1.00	2.19

(a) Group the ratios that measure earnings power, financial strength, and capital structure. Describe how each ratio is calculated.

(b) Interpret the fluctuations in the rates of return of the two companies. What are the principal factors contributing to the rate of return of each company? What are the implications of the differences?

(c) Explain the differences in both the level and fluctuations of the inventory turnover of the two companies.

5. Subtracting the operating ratio of *B* from 100 percent produces a figure that is close to the company's profit margin (in 1975, 100% – 95.9 = 4.1%, compared with a profit margin of 3.8%); for company *A*, the difference is consistently greater (in 1975, 100% –89.5% = 10.5%, compared with a profit margin of 6.5%). How would you explain this variation between the two companies?

6. What is the reason for the substantial differences in the plant turnover and debt/equity ratios of the two companies? If *A* and *B* are publicly held companies, to what extent would current reporting requirements help explain these differences? In 1971 the debt/equity ratio of company *A* experienced a sharp rise; in view of the changes in certain related ratios in the same year, explain what probably happened.

7. Evaluate the financial strength of the two companies.

8. Identify and define the major measures employed to gauge the tangible asset value of a stock. Calculate each of these measures for stocks of five companies as of the latest date for which statements are available. Compare the results with the prices of the stocks on that date, and interpret the significance of the differences between each of the measures of tangible value and the corresponding price of the stock. Summarize the importance of these measures in analyzing a stock.

9. Discuss the significance of the principal sources and application of funds for a corporation. Illustrate by reference to actual statements of sources and application of funds as published in corporate annual reports.

10. Compare the effective income tax rate and the federal statutory rate of five different companies as revealed in the footnotes to their latest

annual reports. Discuss the reasons assigned for these differences. What is the importance of these differences in analyzing securities?

Stock Appraisal (Chapters 15-17)

*1. Explain how changes in the value of the dollar may affect the profits of U.S. multinational companies.

*2. Indicate three ways in which a change in the quantity of money may influence the economy.

3. Discuss the advantages and shortcomings of common stock as a hedge against inflation.

*4. You are head of securities analysis in the trust department of a metropolitan bank. Top management has become very "quality minded" as a result of recent market swings and has asked you to give each stock on its approved list a quality rating (A, B, C, D) for the guidance of portfolio managers. List the major criteria you would use in assigning stocks to these classes and discuss two in detail.

*5. The XYZ Corp. has historically enjoyed a pre-interest pretax return on assets of 12 percent and an effective cost of borrowed funds of 6 percent. The company's financial leverage position (ratio of total long-term debt to total equity) is around 25 percent. Discuss the forces which would tend to work against attempts by the company to increase earnings per share and the price of the stock by raising its financial leverage to 40 percent.

*6. Rate of return on book value of common stock is often used as a measure of the profitability of earning power of a company. State the qualifications you would attach to the use of this measurement.

*7. Companies *A* and *B* are in the same industry. Company *A* has consistently distributed two-thirds of its earnings in dividends, while company *B* has distributed only one-third. Is this difference in payout ratios a significant factor in the evaluation of the company's stock? Discuss.

8. This exercise calls for the student to make forecasts regarding a company and its stock, measure the accuracy of the forecasts, and ascertain the reasons for the discrepancies that occur.

Select a company listed on the New York Stock Exchange. Obtain the annual reports for the last 6 years. Assume you are analyzing its stock at the time of the issuance of the annual report *prior to the latest one.*

(a) Based on the information in the first five reports, a study of the industry or industries in which the company is engaged, and an evaluation of the economy and the securities market, forecast the following information for the latest year (the information already will be available for that year, but the assumption is that you do not know it): total sales, operating expenses, nonoperating income, nonoperating expenses, net earnings before taxes, taxes, net earnings after taxes.

(b) Forecast for the latest year the net earnings after taxes directly by the models on pp. 356-357 of the text.

(c) Compare the forecasts of net earnings after taxes in (a) and (b) above with the actual results for the latest year. Analyze the reasons for the differences.

(d) Convert the forecast of net earnings after taxes to a per share basis. Forecast for the latest year dividends per share, the price/earnings ratio, and the price of the stock.

(e) Compare the forecasts of the p/e ratio and the price of the stock with actual results. Analyze the reasons for the differences. What conclusions can be drawn regarding the problems of forecasting the p/e ratio and the price of the stock?

9. It is a common practice to classify companies by industry. Pick five NYSE-listed companies at random. Place each in the industrial category you think most appropriate. Explain the basis of your classification. What difficulties did you experience in making these classifications?

10. Obtain IBM's annual reports for the past five years. For these years, prepare a table that shows separately—for the entire company, its domestic operations, and its foreign operations—the following information: total revenues and percentage changes; net earnings after taxes and percentage changes; total assets and percentage changes; net earnings after taxes divided by total assets (return on assets); net earnings after taxes divided by total revenues (profit margin); total revenues divided by total assets (turnover of assets). Analyze your findings, emphasizing especially the relative contribution of the domestic and foreign operations to the company's growth and profitability.

*11. Select an industry and compile the following information for the last ten years: output shipments in physical units, GNP in current dollars, Federal Reserve Board index of industrial production, implicit price deflator for total GNP, price index for the industry chosen, industry profits after taxes.

(a) Based on the data you have gathered, how would you characterize the growth of the industry relative to the national economy?

(b) How would you characterize the stability of the industry relative to the national economy?

*12. For a firm within the same industry as in question 11 prepare the following information: sales, profits after taxes, earnings per share, book value per share, long-term debt/equity ratio.

(a) How would you compare your company to its industry?

(b) What is the average price/earnings ratio for this industry? Find the estimated earnings per share for your company (use one published by a financial service). Accepting the appropriateness of the industry p/e ratio and based solely on the information you have been instructed to gather, what p/e ratio would you expect the market to assign to the common stock of the company you are examining? Support your reasoning.

13. Select a company and analyze the sources of its earnings growth. How sustainable is that growth? Discuss your conclusions with respect to the company's prospects.

14. Bring Figure 17-14 (Factors Contributing to Earnings per Share Growth for Two Companies, p. 408) up to date for Philadelphia Electric. Discuss the degree to which this additional information confirms or changes the discussion in the text regarding the company.

Analyzing Fixed-Income Securities (Chapters 18-22)

1. Describe and discuss the relative importance of the typical protective features provided for corporate bonds.

2. Discuss the importance of collateral in the evaluation of corporate bonds.

3. Assume that the general level of interest rates is about to fall because of an anticipated recession. As a fixed-income investor, explain the importance of considering maturity, coupon, quality rating, call price, and sinking fund.

*4. If you expected interest rates to drift upward for the next decade, would you prefer:

(a) a floating-rate note with an intermediate maturity and a coupon rate that could rise one percentage point above the Treasury bill rate (without a put);

(b) a short-term note or Treasury bill that could be rolled over as it matures;

(c) a fixed-rate bond with an intermediate maturity; or

(d) a fixed-rate bond with a long maturity?

Explain the reasons for your choice.

*5. In a period of high interest rates, discuss the probable relationship of yields on two bonds if the main difference between the issues is that one is callable starting immediately, while the other becomes callable after six years.

6. Define a yield curve. What is meant by riding the yield curve?

7. Describe the different types of opportunities for swapping bonds in order to benefit from yield differentials in issues of comparable quality.

8. In the calculation of fixed-charge coverage, explain the treatment of leases, proprietary reserves, nonrecurring profits and losses, equity in nonconsolidated subsidiaries, minority interest, and (in the case of public utilities) interest charged to construction (capitalized interest).

9. What is the difference between the interest coverage and fixed-charge coverage?

10. Define "capitalization ratio." What is its importance? How is it calculated? Analyze, on the basis of the 1973 financial statements, the Addressograph-Multigraph 9⅜s due 1995 and the Alabama Gas 7¼s due 1994. Do both bonds appear to justify their A ratings at that time? Identify and explain any factors that would suggest deterioration of the Addressograph-Multigraph issue.

Perform a similar analysis on the basis of the 1974 financial statements. Describe the factors that developed to explain the lowered rating for the Addressograph-Multigraph bonds.

11. With respect to preferred shares, describe and explain the importance of their basic features, common characteristics, and protective features.

12. Explain the reason for using the overall method of calculating fixed-charge coverage for bonds but the cumulative method for preferred stock.

13. In the calculation of the fixed-charge coverage for preferred stock, what is the problem in the treatment of federal taxes? How is this problem typically solved?

14. Evaluate the general merits of preferred stock as a high-grade investment. Why is such an issue ordinarily more attractive to corporate rather than individual investors in the United States?

15. Discuss the relative advantages and disadvantages of marketable vs. nonmarketable Treasury issues.

16. Compare the yields of the latest Treasury bills, short-term Treasury notes, medium-term Treasury notes and bonds, and long-term bonds. Explain the reasons for the differences.

17. Describe the different federal agencies with outstanding bonds that are guaranteed by the government. How do the yields of these bonds compare with the direct Treasury issues? Explain the difference.

18. Describe the federal agencies with outstanding bonds that are not guaranteed by the government. How do the yields of these bonds compare with the guaranteed issues? Do you think the difference is justified?

19. Describe international agencies with outstanding bonds. Discuss the relative quality and yields of the bonds issued by these agencies.

20. On Monday, September 22, 1975, the U.S. Treasury auctioned three-month bills at an average price of 98.386 and six-month bills at an average price of 96.550. Calculate the yield to maturity afforded by each type. Did the difference in maturity account for the difference in yield? Explain.

21. Why is a legal opinion important for municipal bonds? Is there also a legal opinion on corporate bonds? Explain the reason for any difference.

22. From what taxes is a municipal bond issued in your state and held by a resident of the state exempt? How important is this exemption in determining the return such an investor receives?

23. Deep-discount corporate bonds usually sell at a lower yield to maturity than corporate bonds of comparable quality and maturity that sell close to par. The opposite is true of municipal bonds. Explain.

24. What tests might an investor employ to gauge the quality of a municipal bond?

25. What regulatory changes did the Securities Acts Amendments of 1975 make in the area of municipal bonds? What is the importance of these changes? To what extent is regulation in the municipal area still less effective than in the corporate area?

26. Discuss the importance of the ratings assigned municipal bonds by the major rating agencies.

*27. Consider the Toledo Edison First 9s of 11/1/2000 and the Pacific Gas and Electric First 4¼s of 6/1/1995. For each, determine the current price, the call price at the first call date (if that date has passed the next call date), the yield to that call date, and the yield to maturity. (If either of these bonds has been called, substitute a comparable bond.) Calculate the yields by the approximate method and by means of a yield book. Explain any discrepancies. Discuss the price fluctuations of the two bonds if the interest rate on high-grade utility bonds:

(a) falls by 100 basis points.
(b) rises by 100 basis points.

28. A corporation has the following capitalization:

$50,000,000	7% first mortgage bonds due 2000
5,000,000	10% debentures due 1982
160,000	shares 6%, $50 par first preferred stock
900,000	shares 8%, $10 par second preferred stock
3,000,000	shares $10 par common stock

The corporation earns $8,000,000 before income taxes and pays taxes at a rate of 48 percent. Calculate by the method you think most appropriate the following (show all answers to two decimal places):

(a) the fixed-charge coverage of the first mortgage bonds;
(b) the fixed-charge coverage of the second mortgage bonds;
(c) the fixed-charge coverage of the first preferred stock;
(d) the fixed-charge coverage of the second preferred stock;
(e) the earnings per share of common stock based on shares outstanding.

Under present conditions, would you expect the first mortgage bonds to sell at par? Explain.

If the 10 percent debentures had been income bonds, what would be the fixed-charge coverage of the first mortgage bonds and the 10 percent income debentures?

Understanding Investment Companies (Chapter 23)

1. Define the following terms: face-amount certificate, dual-purpose funds, contractual plan, money-market funds, unit investment trust, sales load.

2. Compare the characteristics of open-end and closed-end investment companies. What is the primary distinguishing feature of an open-end company? Discuss the relative advantages of open-end and closed-end companies.

3. Describe the relationship between management companies and open-end investment companies. What major problem formerly limited the salability of a management company? How has this problem been resolved?

4. What is the typical method of reimbursing an investment adviser for managing an investment company? Do you think that the amount of reimbursement should be affected by performance? What is the nature of the regulation over the management fee that an investment adviser can charge?

5. What considerations should an individual take into account in determining whether to purchase the shares of an investment company?

6. Describe the different kinds of open-end investment companies that are available.

7. Why is it important for an individual to know the source of the dividends paid by an investment company?

8. If a sales charge of 8.5 percent is imposed on the public offering price of an investment company, what rate is paid on the net investment? How is this charge regulated?

9. Assume the rate of return is 10 percent on the market index and 6 percent on Treasury bills. What would be the expected rate of return on an unmanaged portfolio that had a volatility coefficient (beta) of 50 percent? What kind of an investment company would have such a volatility

coefficient? Discuss the advisability of measuring the performance of investment companies in this way.

Privileged Securities and Stock Options (Chapters 24-25)

1. Define "conversion parity" and "conversion premium." What is their importance in evaluating a convertible security?

2. What are the relative advantages to the investor of a bond with warrants attached, as compared with a convertible bond?

3. Define and discuss the importance of antidilution clauses in equity-linked securities.

4. Define and explain the significance of the following terms in option trading: underlying stock, striking price, expiration date, open-interest, writer, covered option, naked option, premium.

5. Discuss the special features that have been introduced to permit trading of options on exchanges.

6. Discuss the factors that determine the value of options.

7. On June 21 a company announces that it will distribute to stockholders of record as of July 1 the rights to buy at $26 per share, until November 1, one share of its common stock for every three now held. On July 1 the common stock sells at $30, and on September 15 at $29 per share. Calculate the value of the rights on both dates. Explain the calculations.

8. Discuss various strategies that may be employed by purchasers of options.

9. Discuss strategies that can be employed by writers of options.

10. Options are typically not exercised even when the striking price is below the market price of the underlying stock. Explain.

*11. Todd Hammer, a securities analyst in the trust investment department of National Bank, Inc., learns that corporation *X* has called for redemption of its $1.20 preferred stock on October 1, 1976, at par plus accrued dividends. Each preferred share is convertible into two common shares until June 20, 1976. A statistical analysis of *X*'s preferred stock is shown in the table on the following page.

Discuss the implications of (a) continuing to hold the preferred stock and (b) converting the preferred. Suppose Hammer decides he should replace the shares of *X* convertible preferred stock in accounts he manages with another convertible preferred stock. His search for a suitable replacement narrows down to the convertible preferred stocks of corporations *Y* and *Z*. *Y*'s $3.00 preferred stock is convertible share-for-share into common at any time until June 30, 1982, and is noncallable until 1980, when it becomes callable at $50 per share. *Z*'s $2.68 preferred stock is convertible into two common shares until June 30, 1976, and into 1.8 common shares thereafter until June 30, 1982. It is noncallable until 1977, when it becomes callable at $43 per share.

In his opinion, both corporations have equally good prospects. A statistical comparison of the two issues is shown in the table below.

Statistical Analysis of Convertible Preferred Stocks

	X	Y	Z
Current market price, preferred	30	50	44
Current market price, common	15	45½	20
Premium over conversion value	0	10%	10%†
			22%‡
Estimated earnings per share, common	$ .75	$4.50	$1.80
Preferred dividend	$1.20	$3.00	$2.68
Preferred yield	4.0%	6.0%	6.1%
Common dividend	$ .45	$2.50	$1.00
Common yield	3.0%	5.5%	5.0%
P/E ratio, common	20.0	10.1	11.1

†Based on conversion ratio of 2:1 until 6/30/76.
‡Based on conversion ratio of 1.8:1 after 6/30/76.

Select the better convertible preferred stock issue—that of *Y* or *Z*—to satisfy Mr. Hammer's request for a combination of capital appreciation and current income. Discuss fully.

12. A corporation has outstanding a $100 par preferred stock convertible into common stock at $25 per share. The common stock sells at $30 per share. For all practical purposes, what is the minimum price at which the preferred will sell at that time? Is there a maximum price? Explain.

13. The following table shows the relationships between the striking price of the option, closing price of the underlying common stock, and the price of January options for selected companies in the fall of 1975.

(1) COMPANY†	(2) STRIKING PRICE	(3) COMMON STOCK PRICE	(4) DIFFERENCE (3) − (2)	(5) JANUARY OPTION PRICE
Aluminum Co. of America (Alcoa)	45	45¾	¾	2⅛
Atlantic Refining	100	99½	−½	6⅞
Avon Products	35	35⅝	⅝	5
Dow Chemical	90	90½	½	6¼
Homestake Mining	35	35	0	4⅛

†All options traded on the CBOE.

The prices of all these options are substantially above their intrinsic value (the difference between the common stock price and the striking price). How do you account for this condition? Explain the differences in the prices of the options.

14. The following table shows information similar to that in question 12 for a different group of stocks.

(1) COMPANY†	(2) STRIKING PRICE	(3) COMMON STOCK PRICE	(4) DIFFERENCE (3) − (2)	(5) JANUARY OPTION PRICE
Deere‡	40	46⅞	6⅞	7½
Du Pont‡	100	116½	16½	18¾
International Mining	35	44¼	9¼	10½
Monsanto	60	72⅛	12⅛	12½
UAL	15	22⅝	7⅝	7⅝§

†Options, except for those indicated, are traded on CBOE.
‡Traded on American Exchange.
§February option.

The prices of all these options are very close to their intrinsic value as defined in question 13. How do you account for this condition? Explain the differences in the prices of the options.

Technical Analysis
(Chapter 26)

1. Evaluate the worth of technical market analysis to the investor in light of the doubts that have been raised about its validity and its continued use by some practitioners.

2. Discuss the major principles of the Dow Theory.

3. Explain the significance to a chartist of a decline in the ratio of average prices of low-priced stocks to average prices of high-priced stocks when securities prices are generally rising.

4. What is the principle underlying the methods employed by market technicians to anticipate turning points of established trends? Discuss the major methods employed for this purpose.

5. Distinguish between area and consolidation patterns that technicians identify in studying individual stocks. How are these formations used?

6. Define and explain the significance of break-outs, resistance levels, support, and reversals.

7. Identify and describe briefly the major formations used by technicians in studying individual securities.

8. What are the major features of point and figure charts?

NOTES

INTRODUCTION

1. Frank H. Knight, *Risk, Uncertainty and Profit* (New York: Harper Torchbooks, 1965). First published in 1921, in the Hart, Schaffner, & Marx series of prize essays on economics.

2. Solveig Jansson, "Is Preservation of Capital Making a Comeback?" *Institutional Investor* (April 1974): 55-59, 112.

3. Private sales of unregistered securities also may be arranged under specified conditions. In May 1974 the Securities and Exchange Commission issued Rule 146, establishing guidelines for private placements. In general, these guidelines require that the securities be sold to not more than 35 (those who buy $150,000 or more of the securities for cash are excluded from this number) "sophisticated" investors, who have access to similar information contained in a registration statement, and that there be no public advertisement of the sale. This rule is considered difficult to comply with.

4. "Adam Smith," *The Money Game* (New York: Random House, 1967), pp. 98-99.

5. Two early articles that illustrate these approaches appear in H. K. Wu and A. J. Zakon, *Elements of Investments* (New York: Holt, Rinehart and Winston, 1965). Illustrative of the first is Harry Markowitz, "Portfolio Selection," pp. 299-312; illustrative of the second is Geoffrey P. Clarkson and Allan H. Melzer, "Portfolio Selection: A Heuristic Approach," pp. 313-326.

6. As a result of a reorganization, the company is called Becker Securities Corporation. It is now a subsidiary of a holding company called Warburg Paribas Becker, Inc.

7. A. G. Becker & Co., "Polaroid Corporation," *Stock Market Comments*, April 15, 1974.

8. Benjamin Graham, David L. Dodd, and Sidney Cottle, *Security Analysis: Principles and Technique*, 4th ed. (New York: McGraw-Hill, 1962), pp. 404-415.

9. Wang Laboratories reached a high of 63 in 1972, fell to a low of 6⅜ in 1974, and was selling at about 15 in mid-1975. Graphic Sciences, after adjustments for stock dividends, reached a high of 121⅞ in 1968, fell to a low of 8¼ in 1970, and was selling at about 17 in early 1975 when the company was merged into Burroughs Corp.

CHAPTER 1

1. This last provision–limiting access to the services offered by a member–apparently is aimed at avoiding the type of situation that led to a famous Supreme Court decision. (See Silver v. New York Stock Exchange, 373 U.S. 341 [1963].) In that case, Silver was associated with two nonmember firms that had private wire connections with certain NYSE member firms and the ticker service from the exchange. Without divulging its reasons, the exchange ordered the wire connections severed and discontinued the ticker service. Silver sued for an injunction, antitrust damages, and certain other

additional grounds. While the Court ruled in favor of Silver, the decision was largely based on the failure of the exchange to notify Silver of the charges against him. The issue of the SEC's authority over NYSE rules was not resolved.

2. U.S. Congress, Senate, Committee on Banking, Housing and Urban Affairs, Subcommittee on Securities, *Securities Industry Study*, 93rd Cong., 1st sess., April 6, 1973, pp. 90-91; Securities and Exchange Commission, *Annual Report*, 1974, p. 163.

3. New York Stock Exchange, "The Exchange Market and the Public Interest." *Annual Report*, 1972, p. 14.

4. New York Stock Exchange, *1974 Fact Book*; ibid., *The Specialist: Role of the Specialist on the Floor of the New York Stock Exchange*, March 1975; *Wall Street Journal*, September 17, 1973, pp. 1, 19, and November 16, 1973, p. 24.

5. Securities and Exchange Commission, *Report of the Special Study of Securities Markets*, 88th Cong., 1st sess., H. Doc. 95, pt. 2, April 3, 1963, p. 241.

6. New York Stock Exchange, *Recommendations and Comments on Financial Reporting to Shareholders and Related Matters*, December 1972.

7. U.S. Congress, Senate, Subcommittee on Securities, *Securities Industry Study*, p. 91.

8. This description is based on a statement by Jerome Pustilnik, president of the Institutional Networks Corporation (Instinet), before the Securities and Exchange Commission, Hearings on Securities Market Structure and Regulations, November 22, 1971.

9. *Wall Street Journal*, May 5, 1975, p. 5.

10. New York Stock Exchange, *Margin*, November 24, 1972, p. 6; *Wall Street Journal*, January 3, 1974, p. 3.

CHAPTER 2

1. *Business Week*, September 22, 1973, p. 43.

2. U.S. Congress, Senate, Government Operations Committee, Intergovernmental Relations and Budgeting Subcommittees, *Disclosure of Corporate Ownership*.

3. Statement of Donald E. Weeden, chairman of the board of Weeden & Co., in the hearings before the U.S. Senate, Subcommittee on Securities of the Committee on Banking, Housing and Urban Affairs, 93d Cong., 2d sess., March 28, 1974, pp. 154-160.

4. Other factors also induced off-floor executions, including the evasion of certain New York taxes.

5. Securities and Exchange Commission, *Institutional Investor Study Report*, H. Doc. 92-64, 92nd Cong., 1st sess., 1971; Hans R. Stoll, "Parallel Trading: The Facts and Implications," Center for Research in Security Prices, Graduate School of Business, University of Chicago, May 1973.

6. James H. Lorie, *Public Policy for American Capital Markets*, Department of the Treasury, February 7, 1974, p. 13. Instinet has been discussed previously. AutEx, among other things, operates a multiterminal computer system to facilitate block trading of securities among brokers and financial institutions. A broker wishing to buy or sell a block of stock enters a message in a TV terminal connected by leased lines to a computer at AutEx headquarters. The information is processed and displayed on the screens of subscribers selected by the broker. Negotiations are then conducted by telephone, and the trade is completed on an exchange or in the OTC market. AutEx introduced a bond trading system in late 1971. In February 1972 the company went public.

7. Securities and Exchange Commission, *Institutional Investor Study Report of the Securities and Exchange Commission*, summary vol., p. 81.

8. New York Stock Exchange, *Maintaining Exchange Auction Markets in an Era of Competitive Commission Rates*, December 5, 1974.

9. See, for example, David L. Ratner, "The NYSE's Day of Judgment," *Wall Street Journal*, November 19, 1974, p. 26.

10. Securities and Exchange Commission, Securities Exchange Act of 1934, Release no. 11,395, May 2, 1975. This release announces the adoption of Rule 17a-20 and related form X-17A-20.

11. Securities and Exchange Commission, Release no. 9950, January 16, 1973.

12. U.S. Congress, House, Committee on Interstate and Foreign Commerce, *Legislative History of Securities Acts Amendments of 1975* (Washington, D.C.: Government Printing Office, 1975), p. 106.

13. Investment Company Institute v. Camp, 401, U.S. 617.

14. Securities and Exchange Commission, Securities Act of 1933, Release no. 5491, April 30, 1974.

15. John Thackray, "Why Foreigners are Buying into Wall Street Firms," *Institutional Investor* 8 (December 1974), p. 65.

16. This information is based primarily on a report issued by the New York Stock Exchange, *Recommendations on Access and Membership by Foreign-Controlled Broker-Dealers to the U.S. Securities Markets*, June 1974.

17. Advisory Committee on International Capital Markets, New York Stock Exchange, *Recommendations Regarding Foreign Access to the U.S. Securities Markets*, July 1973.

18. Securities and Exchange Commission, *Institutional Investor Study Report*, pt. 1, p. xxv.

19. Report by William McChesney Martin, Jr., to the New York Stock Exchange, August 5, 1971.

20. Securities and Exchange Commission, *Policy Statement on the Future Structure of the Securities Markets*, February 1972.

21. Securities and Exchange Commission, *Policy Statement*, March 1973.

22. For a detailed description of how a computerized central market might operate while preserving individual discretion, protecting its auction characteristics, and integrating the institutional and public segments, see Morris Mendelson, "From Automated Quotes to Automated Trading: Restructuring the Stock Market in the U.S.," New York University, *Institute of Finance Bulletin*, nos. 80-82 (1972).

23. *Wall Street Journal*, March 7, 1975, p. 20.

24. *Gordon* v. *New York Stock Exchange*, 498 F. 2d 1303 (c.a. 2, 1974). The decision has no immediate effect, since the commissions are fully negotiated, but it will be significant if the SEC ever elects to restore fixed rates.

25. U.S. Congress, House, Committee on Interstate and Foreign Commerce, *Securities Acts Amendments of 1975*, p. 100.

26. Securities and Exchange Commission, Securities Exchange Act of 1934 Release no. 11497, June 26, 1975.

CHAPTER 3

1. See Securities and Exchange Commission, Securities Act Release no 5362, February 2, 1973. The arguments in the debate on projections are summarized in David Herwitz, "Projections and Forecasts," in *Fourth Annual Institute in Securities Regulation*, Arthur Fleischer, Jr., Robert H. Mundheim, and J. Schupper, ed. (New York: Practising Law Institute, 1973), pp. 323-335.

2. Some of these efforts are examined in Victor Brudney, "Origins and Limited Applicability of the Reasonable Basis or Know Your Merchandise," ibid., pp. 239-269; Martin Lipton, "The Customer Suitability Doctrine," ibid., pp. 273-292.

3. See Stanley J. Friedman, "Conflict of Interest Problems Involving Investment Advisers and Broker-Dealers Serving Individual Accounts," ibid., pp. 295-321.

4. Recent developments in the law relating to insider trading are analyzed in Arthur Fleischer, Jr., Robert H. Mundheim, and John C. Murphy, "An Initial Inquiry into the Responsibility to Disclose Market Information," 121 *U. of Pa. L. Rev.* (1973): 800-860.

5. Securities and Exchange Commission, Securities and Exchange Act Release no. 9267, July 29, 1971 in [1970-71 Transfer Binder] CCH Fed. Sec. L. Rep. 78.163.

6. The *Georgetown Law Journal* has published a good series of articles on this

subject: See Donald E. Schwartz, "Federal Chartering of Corporations," 61 *Geo. L. J.* (1972): 71-149.

7. Almost all the states have securities laws (known as "blue sky laws") which govern the sale of securities within the state. The classic work on state securities regulation is Louis Loss and Edward M. Cowett, *Blue Sky Law* (Boston: Little, Brown, 1958). Unlike federal securities regulation, which endeavors to force full disclosure, many blue sky statutes permit state regulatory authorities to forbid the distribution of securities which do not meet a "fair, just and equitable" test.

8. For those interested in this subject the SEC publishes a helpful booklet, *The Work of the Securities and Exchange Commission*.

9. The process involved in the issuance of no-action letters is described and analyzed in William J. Lockhart, "SEC No-Action Letters: Informal Advice as a Discretionary Administrative Clearance," 37 *Law and Contemporary Problems* (1972): 95.

10. *The SEC Speaks* and the *Annual Institute on Securities Regulation* are published by the Practising Law Institute as edited transcripts.

11. See *Baird* v. *Franklin*, 141 F. 2d 238 (2d Cir. 1944), cert. denied, 323 U.S. 737.

12. In class actions the court determines how much the successful lawyer shall be paid out of the fund created for the benefit of the class. Awards ranging between 15 and 30 percent of the fund are usual.

13. There is a substantial literature on the merits of fostering private rights of action to enforce compliance with the standards of conduct developed under the federal securities laws. See, for example, Mordicai Rosenfeld, "The Impact of Class Actions on Corporate and Securities Law," *Duke Law Journal* 72 (February 1972): 1167.

14. *Securities Regulation and Transfer Report*, June 11, 1973.

15. *Escott* v. *BarChris Construction Corp*., 283 F. Supp. (S.D. N.Y. 1968).

16. The stimulating function of the BarChris case can be seen in "The BarChris Case: Prospectus Liability," 24 *Business Lawyer* (1969): 523-720.

17. *Silver* v. *New York Stock Exchange*, 373 U.S. 341 (1963).

18. Securities and Exchange Commission, *Annual Report*, 1971, pp. 1-2.

19. *Wall Street Journal*, May 30, 1973, p. 38.

20. *New York Times*, August 5, 1974.

21. Securities and Exchange Commission, *Study of Unsafe and Unsound Practices of Brokers and Dealers*, H. Doc. no. 92-231, 92nd Cong., 1st sess., December 1971.

22. Securities and Exchange Commission, Securities Exchange Act Release no. 9856, November 10, 1972.

23. Management Reports, Inc., *Securities Regulation and Transfer Report*, July 15, 1971.

CHAPTER 4

1. Standard & Poor's Corp., *Monthly Stocks Guide*.

2. The New York Stock Exchange has formulated rules to govern the extent to which prices of limit orders are automatically adjusted after the issue sells ex-dividend.

3. The financial services often summarize the principal dividend restrictions in corporate charters.

4. Probably the most noteworthy of these efforts was the controversial undistributed profits tax of 1936, which levied a graduated tax on earnings that a corporation did not disburse as dividends. The tax was bitterly criticized; it was reduced in 1938 and eliminated in 1939.

5. The current tax provides for a surtax of 27.5 percent on improperly accumulated surplus under $100,000 and 38.5 percent on the remainder. In the case of closely held firms, a prime consideration is the need to use liquid resources for genuine corporate purposes, e.g., payment of debt to outsiders, expansion to meet competition,

and so forth. A classic illustration of the application of the tax to a corporation with publicly held stock is the case of Trico Products. The fact that this company had to pay a penalty tax led to a stockholders' derivative suit against the directors that was eventually settled out of court.

6. For a theoretical discussion of this proposition, see John Lintner, "Distribution of Incomes of Corporations among Dividends, Retained Earnings, and Taxes," *American Economic Review* 46 (May 1956): 97.

7. In early 1971 the American Institute of Certified Public Accountants appointed a study group to inquire into the objectives of financial statements. In October 1973 the group submitted its report, which was intended as a "charter" for the new Financial Accounting Standards Board. Among its conclusions, the report recognized a new category of earnings–the unrealized gain or loss resulting from fluctuations in the value of a company's assets.

CHAPTER 5

1. *Wall Street Journal*, August 5, 1974, p. 17.
2. New York State Banking Department, *Report of the Superintendent's Advisory Committee on Financial Reform*, March 1974, p. 39.
3. *Wall Street Journal*, August 19, 1974, p. 22.
4. Securities and Exchange Commission, *Institutional Investor Study Report*, 92nd Cong., 1st sess., H. Doc. no. 92-64, pt. 1, March 10, 1971, p. 36.
5. Ibid., pp. 39-40.
6. Ibid., survey vol., p. 11.

CHAPTER 6

1. Many lower levels of government also impose taxes on personal property, including securities. These taxes are typically based on the market value of the securities at the end of the year. Sometimes securities of issuers that are native to the state are exempt from these taxes.

2. The Securities and Exchange Commission has adopted rules governing the capitalization of interest by companies that are not utilities. These rules prevent companies that have not capitalized interest previously from initiating such a policy; permit companies that have publicly disclosed such a policy to continue applying it on a consistent basis, but not to extend it to new types of assets; and require disclosure of the amount capitalized and the effect of the policy on net income, as compared with a policy of charging interest to expense as incurred. The commission intends to reconsider its position after the Financial Accounting Standards Board (FASB) comes out with new rules.

3. This allocation is made as follows: The aggregate value of the old and new preferred stock is determined at the time the preferred shares are received as a dividend; the percentage relationship each bears to the total is calculated; and these percentages are then applied to the cost price of the old stock. Assume, for example, that the cost of the old stock is $10,000. At the time the preferred stock dividend is received, the market value of the old shares is $12,000 and the fair market value of the new preferred issue is $3,000. The apportioned basis of the old stock is $8,000, calculated as follows: ($12,000/$15,000) × $10,000. The apportioned value of the new preferred stock is $2,000, calculated as follows: ($3,000/$15,000) × $10,000.

4. In at least one case, however, the commissioner of internal revenue permitted the recipient of taxable stock rights to count their market value at the time of receipt as taxable income and to include the difference between this amount and their sales proceeds as capital gains. When the recipient petitioned the Second Circuit Court of Appeals to have the full sales proceeds treated as capital gains, the court upheld the commissioner.

5. The allocation is made as follows: The aggregate value of the old stock and the new rights is determined when the new rights are issued; the percentage relationship each bears to the total is calculated; these percentages are applied to the cost price of the old stock. Assume the cost of the old stock is $10,000. At the time the rights are distributed, the market value of the shares is $12,000, while the fair market value of the rights is $500. The apportioned cost basis of the old stock is $9,600, calculated as follows: ($12,000/$12,500) × $10,000. The apportioned cost basis of the rights is $400, calculated as follows: ($500/$12,500) × $10,000.

6. The 1969 Tax Reform Act reduces the shelter value of capital gains. Thus, for married couples filing joint returns, capital gains in excess of $50,000 became subject to annually increasing maximum marginal tax rates, until in 1972 that maximum reached 35 percent.

7. Taxation is a regular subject of legislative consideration. Among current proposals is one for reducing capital gains according to how long an asset is held.

CHAPTER 7

1. *Wall Street Journal*, April 17, 1975, p. 24.

2. *Securities Regulation and Transfer Report*, September 24, 1973. The commission eventually rejected the petition, which it treated as if it had been addressed only to the content of the proxy material.

3. In line with its desire to simplify the registration procedure, the SEC permits issuance of an identifying statement containing limited information concerning the issuer, both for advertising purposes and as a screening device to locate persons interested in receiving a prospectus. The SEC also encourages use of an advance (the so-called "red herring") prospectus. Companies may insert the identifying statement in newspapers and magazines or send it through the mails, either before or after the effective date of the registration statement.

4. Nos. 5395, 5396, June 1, 1973.

5. Securities and Exchange Commission, Securities Act Release no. 5362, February 2, 1973.

6. Some of the sluggish accounts may not have been small. The 1973 annual report of Jamaica Water and Utilities, Inc., for example, states: "Specifically, the PSC [Public Service Commission] issued to the press statements that said JWS [a subsidiary of Jamaica Water] had $214,000 in cash and had over $800,000 in overdue payables, including large payables to the Consolidated Edison Company of New York."

7. *Wall Street Journal*, August 24, 1973, p. 5.

8. *Wall Street Journal*, September 24, 1974, p. 4; Securities and Exchange Commission, Securities Act Release no 5549, Dec. 19, 1974; Arthur Anderson & Co. *Executive News Briefs*, January 1975; ibid., February 1975.

9. Securities and Exchange Commission, Accounting Series Release no. 166, December 23, 1974, pp. 1-2.

10. *Wall Street Journal*, October 15, 1973, p. 31.

11. Lists of trade periodicals may be found in Ayer's *Directory of Newspapers and Periodicals* (Philadelphia, published annually). The New York Society of Security Analysts has published *A Guide to Industry Publications for Security Analysts* (1972).

12. Dun & Bradstreet reports probably are the main source of information on municipal securities. Moody's *Municipal & Government Manual* covers a broader area, but its data are not so detailed in current offerings as those published by Dun & Bradstreet itself.

13. *Wall Street Journal*, September 16, 1974, pp. 1, 20.

14. For a good description of the economic and statistical programs of the U.S. government see Office of Statistical Standards, *Statistical Services of the United States Government*, rev. ed. (Washington, D.C.: 1968).

15. A particularly useful guide to business facts and figures is the *Encyclopedia of Business Information Sources* (Detroit: Gale Research Co., 1970).

16. The Employment Act of 1946 established the Council of Economic Advisers to assist in the preparation of the president's annual economic report to Congress. The act also created the Joint Committee on the Economic Report, composed of members of both houses of Congress, to study matters relative to the report and make recommendations for legislative action. The council provides the mechanism for integrating the economic studies and conclusions of the departments and agencies of the government. In 1953 it was reorganized to centralize greater authority in its chairman.

17. U.S. Congress, Senate, Committee on Banking, Housing and Urban Affairs, Subcommittee on Securities, *Securities Industry Study*, 93d Cong., 1st sess., S. Doc. no. 93-13 (1973), p. 89. These estimates do not include trading in OTC stock outside of NASDAQ. There are some 20,000 securities traded solely in the OTC market, of which only about 15 percent go through NASDAQ, but these are by far the most active.

18. A booklet that may prove helpful to individuals inexperienced in reading financial news is Charles Norman Stabler, *How to Read the Financial News*, 10th ed. (New York: Harper & Row, 1965).

19. The equalizing figure is reported in the *Wall Street Journal* under the Dow-Jones averages.

CHAPTER 8

1. For a number of years, Avon's sales and earnings had grown at a 16-20 percent rate. In 1973 the earnings growth dropped to about 10 percent, and in 1974 earnings declined. Reflecting these changes and a generally falling market, the company's stock shrank to a low of 18⅝ in 1974. Moreover, several derivative suits were brought against officers who had sold substantial amounts of stock at prior high prices. In mid-1975 the stock was selling at 45 and had a price/earnings ratio of 24, based on the company's latest 12-month earnings.

2. For an alternative and more sophisticated proof, see William J. Baumol, *The Stock Market and Economic Efficiency* (New York: Fordham University Press, 1965), pp. 61-65.

3. John Maynard Keynes, *The General Theory of Employment, Interest, and Money* (New York: Harcourt, Brace, 1936), pp. 154-156.

4. In a study of 960 small companies going public from 1952 to 1962, the SEC found that only 34 percent were operating at a profit, while 37 percent had gone bankrupt, 24 percent were operating at a loss, and 5 percent had been merged with other companies.

5. *Securities Regulation and Transfer Report*, June 22, 1973, pp. 3-4. See p. 158 for statements from the prospectus of an unseasoned company.

6. This model simply states that the price of the stock is equal to the present value of an infinite stream of dividends discounted by the rate of return on equity required by the market k. If the current dividend, D_o, is expected to grow continuously at the annual rate g, the dividend at time t will be:

$$(1) \quad D_t = D_o e^{gt}$$

If dividends are paid continuously, the current market price of a share of stock, P_t, is expressed as:

$$(2) \quad P_o = \int_0^\infty D_t e^{-kt} dt$$

Combining equations (1) and (2):

$$(3) \quad P_o = D_o \int_0^\infty e^{-t(k-g)} dt = \frac{D_o}{k-g}.$$

Since date o is arbitrary,

$$(4) \quad P_t = D_t / (k-g).$$

See Myron J. Gordon and Eli Shapiro, "Capital Equipment Analysis: The Required Rate of Profit," *Management Science* 3 (October 1956): 102-110. It can also be shown that the model is applicable when an infinite stream of dividends is replaced by a combination of dividends and capital proceeds.

7. For an overall discussion of the efficient market hypothesis, see James H. Lorie and Mary T. Hamilton, *The Stock Market: Theories and Evidence* (Homewood, Ill.: Irwin, 1973), chap. 4.

8. Two early works that paved the way for a succession of later studies of the so-called "random walk" theory are M. F. M. Osborne, "Brownian Motion in the Stock Market," *Operations Research* 7 (March-April 1959): 145-173; and Harry V. Roberts, "Stock Market 'Patterns' and Financial Analysis: Methodological Suggestions," *Journal of Finance* 14 (March 1959): 1-10.

9. Typical studies include Arnold B. Moore, "Some Characteristics of Changes in Common Stock Prices," in *The Random Character of Stock Market Prices*, ed. Paul H. Cootner (Cambridge: 1964), pp. 139-161; Eugene F. Fama, "The Behavior of Stock-Market Prices," *Journal of Business* 38 (January 1965): 34-105.

10. See, for example, Sidney S. Alexander, "Price Movements in Speculative Markets: Trends or Random Walks," *Industrial Management Review* 2 (May 1961): 7-26; "Price Movements in Speculative Markets: Trends or Random Walks, No. 2," *Industrial Management Review* 5 (Spring 1964): 25-46.

11. See Paul A. Samuelson, "Proof that Properly Anticipated Prices Fluctuate Randomly," *Industrial Management Review* 6 (Spring 1965): 41-49; Benoit Mandelbrot, "Forecasts of Future Prices, Unbiased Markets, and Martingale Models," *Journal of Business* 39 (January 1966): 242-255 (Part Two, "Securities Prices: A Supplement").

12. Eugene F. Fama et al., "The Adjustment of Stock Prices to New Information," *International Economic Review* 10 (February 1969): 1-21; Myron S. Scholes, "The Market for Securities: Substitution versus Price Pressure and the Effects of Information on Share Prices," *Journal of Business* 45 (April 1972): 179-211; Ray Ball and Philip Brown, "An Empirical Evaluation of Accounting Income Numbers," *Journal of Accounting Research* 6 (Autumn 1968): 159-178.

13. Irwin Friend et al., "A Study of Mutual Funds," prepared for the Securities and Exchange Commission by the Securities Research Unit, Wharton School of Finance and Commerce (Washington, D.C.: Government Printing Office, 1962); William F. Sharpe, "Mutual Fund Performance," *Journal of Business* 39 (January 1966): 119-138; Michael C. Jensen, "Risk, the Pricing of Capital Assets, and the Evaluation of Investment Portfolios," *Journal of Business* 42 (April 1966): 167-247; Irwin Friend et al., *Mutual Funds and other Institutional Investors: A New Perspective* (New York: McGraw-Hill, 1970); J. Peter Williamson, "Measurement and Forecasting of Mutual Fund Performance: Choosing an Investment Strategy," *Financial Analysts Journal* 28 (November-December 1972): 78-84.

14. See Michael Edesess, "Resolved: the Capital Pricing Model Has Little Practical Value," unpublished paper (Chicago: Becker Securities Corporation, 1973).

CHAPTER 9

1. At one time, the Great Atlantic & Pacific Tea Co., the Parker Pen Co., and Talon, Inc., all had shares with limited voting power that were traded on the American Stock Exchange. Since then, all three enterprises have eliminated their nonvoting common stock; in each case, the stock was subsequently listed on the New York Stock Exchange. (Talon was acquired by Textron in 1968.)

The NYSE has made it a policy to delist a company which creates a class of nonvoting common stock. According to the rules of the exchange, "this does not apply to a non-voting class of stock which in the opinion of the Exchange has normal and appropriate preferences which entitle it to be regarded as a preferred stock." In carrying out this policy, for example, the NYSE delisted the shares of (W. A.) Shaeffer Pen in May 1957 after the company divided its common stock into class A (nonvoting) and class B (voting) shares. These issues continued on the Midwest Exchange's listing. In June 1965 the stockholders voted to restore voting rights to the class A shares; one year later the firm was acquired by Textron.

2. For a discussion of the "paper" problem and the general subject of facilitating transfers, leading to the elimination of the stock certificate, see Sidney Robbins, Walter Werner, et al., *Paper Crisis in the Securities Industry–Causes and Cures* (New York: Lybrand, Ross Brothers and Montgomery, 1969). An excellent treatment of street certificates appears in William L. Boyd, "Street-Name Stock Certificates: Their Relationship to Central Certificate Depositories," *Financial Analysts Journal* 26 (November-December 1970): 52-54, 88-95, 123-124.

3. Concavity is a mathematical concept. A function $f(x)$, such as $5x - .1x^2$, is said to be concave if for any two values of x which we may designate x_1 and x_2, and for $0 \leq \lambda \leq 1$

$f[\lambda x_1 + (1-\lambda)x_2] \geq \lambda f(x_1) + (1-\lambda)f(x_2)$. For example, if in $f(x) = 5x - .1x^2$ we let

$x_1 = 1$,
$x_2 = 5$, and
$\lambda = .1$, then
$f[\lambda x_1 + (1-\lambda)x_2] = f(4.6) = 20.88$, and
$\lambda f(x_1) + (1-\lambda)f(x_2) = .1f(1) + .9f(5) = 20.74$.

Since 20.88 is greater than 20.74, $5x - .1x^2$ is concave. Since the investor *always* chooses the third option, the concavity referred to is said to be "strict." When this is so, the "greater than" (>) sign rules.

4. Since the terminal value of the investment and the resulting consumption in period 2 are exactly equal, we use the two terms interchangeably. It would be more consistent to talk about consumption, but we periodically talk about the terminal value of the investment to remind the reader that this discussion is as pertinent to investment behavior and analysis as it is to consumption behavior.

5. Note that $C = U[\alpha X_1 + (1-\alpha)X_2]$ and $D = \alpha U(X_1) + (1-\alpha)U(X_2)$. Since $U(c_2)$ is concave, $U[\alpha X_1 + (1-\alpha)X_2] > \alpha U(X_1) + (1-\alpha)U(X_2)$ by definition.

6. I.e., $\alpha Y_1 + (1-\alpha)Y_2 = \bar{X}$. It should be noted that $X_1 - Y_1$ will equal $Y_2 - X_2$ only if $\alpha = .50$.

7. I.e., $\alpha U(Y_1) + (1-\alpha)U(Y_2) = G$.

8. Technically, this relationship is true only when the probability distribution of the rates of return is normal or when the utility function is quadratic–that is, some variant of $U = a + br + cr^2$, regardless of the nature of the probability distribution.

9. We have identified risk with the standard deviation of a portfolio's rate of return rather than with the standard deviation of a security's rate of return for good reason. In the above analysis h is the investor's total investment, his portfolio. It may consist of one or many assets; if it consists of many, we do not yet know anything of the impact of any one security on the standard deviation of expected utility of the portfolio.

10. See the second note on p. 219. While studies have shown that the historical standard deviation of a portfolio's rate of return is a reasonably good predictor of the future standard deviation, the historical standard deviation of a stock's rate of return is a much poorer predictor of its future standard deviation.

11. The degree to which variables move together or in opposite directions can be described by their correlation, a normalized measure of covariation. The covariation or covariance of two random variables X and Y is defined as the mean of the cross products $(X-\bar{X})(Y-\bar{Y})$ and is often written as σ_{XY}. Clearly, if X is measured in feet and Y is also, σ_{XY} is measured in square feet. The measure of correlation–that is, the correlation coefficient–is defined as $\sigma_{XY}/(\sigma_X \sigma_Y)$, and that clearly is just a number with no dimension. It is independent of the metric used. This ratio can only take on values between −1 and +1. It can be shown to be the percentage of variance in one of the variables that can be accounted for by the variance in the other. Variables which tend to move in opposite directions are said to be inversely correlated. Perfectly inverse correlations can be obtained by going long and short in the same stock. The expected return from going long and short simultaneously is zero minus the transaction costs.

Notes

CHAPTER 11

1. *Wall Street Journal*, February 12, 1975, p. 12.

2. See, for example, Securities and Exchange Commission, Accounting Series Release no. 147, October 5, 1973; ibid., no. 149, November 29, 1973; idem., Release no. 33-5427.

3. Securities and Exchange Commission, Accounting Series Release no. 159, August 14, 1974.

4. For a discussion of some basic accounting concepts, see Maurice Moonitz, *The Basic Postulates of Accounting*, Accounting Research Study no. 1 (New York: American Institute of Certified Public Accountants, 1961); Robert T. Sprouse and Maurice Moonitz, *A Tentative Set of Broad Accounting Principles for Business Enterprises*, Accounting Research Study no. 3 (New York: American Institute of Certified Public Accountants, 1962); Paul Grady, *Inventory of Generally Accepted Accounting Principles for Business Enterprises*, Accounting Research Study no. 7, (New York: American Institute of Certified Public Accountants, 1965); Accounting Principles Board, Statement no. 4, *Basic Concepts and Accounting Principles Underlying Financial Statements of Business Enterprises*, October 1970; John W. Kenley and George J. Staubus, *Objectives and Concepts of Financial Statements*, Accounting Research Study no. 3 (Melbourne: Accountancy Research Foundation, 1972); Financial Accounting Standards Board, "Conceptual Framework for Accounting and Reporting: Consideration of the Report of the Study Group on the Objectives of Financial Statements," discussion memorandum, June 6, 1974.

5. For income tax purposes, an affiliated group of companies may make consolidated returns. An affiliated group is one or more chains of includable corporations connected to a common parent corporation through stock ownership, when the parent corporation is an includable corporation. A parent corporation is includable if the requisite amount of stock "of each of the includable corporations (except the common parent corporation) is owned directly by one or more of the other includable corporations." The requisite amount of stock is 80 percent of the voting power of all classes of voting stock combined, and at least 80 percent of each class of nonvoting stock, not including nonvoting preferred (Internal Revenue Code, Sec. 1504[a]). See Bernard Wolfman, *Federal Income Taxation of Business Enterprises* (Boston: Little, Brown, 1969), pp. 861-862.

The Securities and Exchange Commission simply requires that a company not consolidate subsidiaries unless they are majority owned (Regulation S-X, Rule 4-02). In connection with the solicitation of proxies, the commission encourages the use of consolidated statements by requiring their inclusion in annual reports "if they are necessary to reflect adequately the financial position and results of operations of the issuer and its subsidiaries" (Securities Exchange Act, Rule 14a-3).

6. Boise Cascade Corp., *Annual Report*, 1972, p. 47; ibid., 1973, p. 51.

7. Accounting Principles Board, Opinion no. 18, *The Equity Method of Accounting for Investments in Common Stock*, March 1971. See also Peat, Marwick, Mitchell & Co., *The Equity Method of Accounting for Investments in Common Stock*, April 10, 1973.

To determine when financial statements or summarized financial information must be filed for unconsolidated subsidiaries, the SEC employs the notion of a "significant subsidiary." For this purpose, an asset, revenue, and subsequently added income test (Regulation S-X, Rule 1-02) are employed. Under the income test, a subsidiary is considered significant if "the parent's and its other subsidiaries' equity in the income before income taxes and extraordinary items of the subsidiary exceeds 10 percent of such income of the parent and its consolidated subsidiaries."

8. P. R. Mallory & Co., Inc., *Annual Report*, 1972, p. 23.

9. The 1972 annual report of Kaiser Industries noted that "the Corporation's equity in the undistributed earnings of unconsolidated companies is not represented by funds or property received by the Corporation and is not available to the Corporation for its separate corporate purposes" (p. 32).

10. See American Institute of Accounting, "Restatements and Revisions of Accounting Research Bulletins," *Accounting Research Bulletin*, no. 43 (1953), chap. 12, pars. 1-9, pp. 111-113.

11. Accounting Principles Board, Opinion no. 23, *Accounting for Income Taxes: Special Areas*, April 1972; no. 24, *Accounting for Income Taxes: Investments in Common Stock Accounted for by the Equity Method*.

12. Crown Cork & Seal Co., Inc., *Annual Report*, 1974, p. 10.

13. Black & Decker Manufacturing Co., *Annual Report*, 1974, p. 31.

14. Caterpillar Tractor Co., 10-K report, 1974, p. 26.

15. *Accounting Research Bulletin*, no. 43 (1953), chap. 12, calls for the current-noncurrent method, but under special circumstances permits inventory to be stated at the historical rate and long-term debt or capital stock to be restated at the new rate. Accounting Principles Board, Opinion no. 6 (October 1965), modifies chap. 12 by effectively permitting use of the monetary-nonmonetary method.

16. National Association of Accountants, "Management Accounting Problems in Foreign Operations," *NAA Research Report 36* (1960):16-17.

17. Leonard Lorensen, *Reporting Foreign Operations of U.S. Companies in U.S. Dollars*, Accounting Research Study no. 12 (New York: American Institute of Certified Public Accountants, 1972); Leonard Lorensen, "The Temporal Principle of Translation," *Journal of Accountancy* 134 (August 1972):48-54; Financial Accounting Standards Board, "Accounting for the Translation of Foreign Currency Transactions and Foreign Currency Financial Statements" exposure draft, December 31, 1974.

18. George C. Watt, "Unrealized Foreign Exchange Gains and Losses," *Management Accounting* (April 1968):31-38; Financial Accounting Standards Board, "An Analysis of Issues Related to Accounting for Foreign Currency Translation," discussion memorandum, February 21, 1974, p. iii.

19. Financial Accounting Standards Board, *Accounting for the Translation of Foreign Currency Transactions and Foreign Currency Financial Statements*, Statement of Financial Accounting Standards No. 8, October 1975.

20. *Accounting Research Bulletin*, no. 43 (1953), chap. 11, pars. 11-13. See also Peat, Marwick, Mitchell & Co., "Timing of Revenue Recognition: Problems Involving Transactions Which Are Not 'Closed' Exchanges or Where the Earning Process Is Not Complete," *Accounting Information Bulletin*, July 1, 1974.

21. Coenen & Co., *Quality of Earnings Report* 4, no. 14 (July 2, 1974):253.

22. In November 1974, two certified public accountants who audited National Student Marketing for Peat, Marwick, Mitchell & Co., the nation's largest accounting firm, were found guilty of knowingly making false and misleading statements in a 1969 proxy statement issued by the company. This was only the second time that auditors of a national accounting concern had been convicted of fraud. The first was in 1968, when three accountants from Lybrand, Ross Bros. & Montgomery (now called Coopers & Lybrand) were found guilty of fraud and conspiracy in the 1962 financial statements of Continental Vending Machine Corp. They were subsequently pardoned by President Nixon.

23. The resulting difference between taxes accrued and taxes actually payable is included as "deferred credits, principally income taxes related to installment sales." For the fiscal year ending January 31, 1974, this amount was $133,057,000, but for the fiscal year ending January 31, 1975, the amount was only $2 million. The reduction in deferred taxes reflects a deficiency arising from the IRS requirements, the application of the company's net operating loss, and changes in accounting policy.

24. In 1949 the AI[CP] A provided some initial guidance on the subject of leasing in an article entitled "Disclosure of Long-Term Leases in Financial Statements of Lessees," *Accounting Research Bulletin*, no. 38; this was followed, in 1962, by the publication of "Reporting of Leases in Financial Statements," *Accounting Research Study No. 4*. Thereafter, the APB, newly formed in 1959, issued four Opinions between September 1964 and June 1973 (nos. 5, 7, 27, and 31) concerned with leases. The AICPA supplemented them with three interpretations. The SEC contributed its bit to this accounting area by issuing a number of pronouncements on leases, including, in

1972 and 1973, three Accounting Series Releases (nos. 132, 141, and 147). Despite these extensive regulatory efforts, inconsistencies remained, and the FASB has been studying the leasing problem since 1973. In July 1974, it issued a *discussion memorandum*, entitled "An Analysis of Issues Related to Accounting for Leases," followed in August 1975 by an exposure draft, "Proposed Statement of Financial Accounting Standards for Leases."

25. See, for example, *Accounting Research Bulletin*, no. 43 (1953), chap. 8; Accounting Principles Board, Opinion no. 9, *Reporting the Results of Operations* (December 1966).

26. Accounting Principles Board, Opinion no. 30, *Reporting the Results of Operations* (June 1973); see also Peat, Marwick, Mitchell & Co., "Interpretation of APB no. 30: Reporting the Results of Operations," *Accounting Information Bulletin*, October 24, 1973.

27. Louis E. Levy, "Issues in Accounting: Unusual Events," *Exchange* (January 1974):8-11; Thomas J. Carroll, "The Accountants' Extraordinary Dilemma," *World* (Peat, Marwick, Mitchell & Co., Summer, 1974):14-20.

28. Pitney Bowes, Inc., *Annual Report*, 1973, pp. 3, 22.

29. Financial Accounting Standards Board, "Foreign Currency Transactions and Foreign Currency Financial Statements," pp. 26, 40-42.

30. See "Taxation," *Journal of Accountancy* 133 (February 1972):75-77.

CHAPTER 12

1. Storm Drilling & Marine, Inc. (formerly called Dearborn-Storm Corporation and prior to that Computer & Marine Corporation), *Annual Report*, year ended October 31, 1973. The company previously had a line of computerized equipment, on which it allowed 10 percent salvage value, but disposed of this segment of its activity. Subsequently, Odeco Drilling, Inc., a subsidiary of Ocean Drilling & Exploration Co., acquired the company.

2. Arthur Andersen & Co., *Executive Briefs*, September 1974; Financial Accounting Standards Board, "Financial Reporting in Units of General Purchasing Power," exposure draft, December 31, 1974; Peat, Marwick, Mitchell & Co., *Executive Newsletter*, June 1975.

3. First National City Bank, "Inventory Profits—More Unrealized than Real," *Monthly Economic Letter* (August 1974):6.

4. *Wall Street Journal*, October 7, 1974, p. 1.

5. Securities and Exchange Commission, Accounting Series Release no. 151, January 3, 1974.

6. AMF Inc., *Annual Report*, 1972, pp. 30-31.

7. Financial Accounting Standards Board, Statement no. 2, *Accounting for Research and Development Costs*, October 1974.

8. Accounting Principles Board, Opinion no. 16, *Business Combinations*, August 1970.

9. Accounting Principles Board, Opinion no. 17, *Intangible Assets*, August 1970.

10. *Wall Street Journal*, January 10, 1974, p. 1.

11. *Accounting Research Bulletin*, no. 43 (1953), chap. 6.

12. Financial Accounting Standards Board, Statement no. 5, *Accounting for Contingencies*, March 1975.

13. Eastman Kodak Co., *Annual Report*, 1974, p. 38.

14. Accounting Principles Board, Opinion no. 11, *Accounting for Income Taxes*, December 1967.

15. Scott Paper Co., *Annual Report*, 1972, p. 22.

16. Scott Paper Co., *Annual Report*, 1974, p. 22.

17. Quoted in Scott R. Schmedel, "Olivetti's Gamble: It Encounters Woes Trying to Revive Underwood," *Wall Street Journal*, January 29, 1962, p. 13.

18. American Institute of Certified Public Accountants, *Accounting Trends and Techniques* (New York, 1973), pp. 30, 33.

19. Comstat, *Annual Report*, 1974, p. 19.

20. International Telephone & Telegraph Corp., *Annual Report*, 1973, p. 29.

21. Securities and Exchange Commission, Accounting Series Release no. 163, November 14, 1974.

CHAPTER 13

1. See Financial Accounting Standards Board, "An Analysis of Issues Related to Financial Reporting for Segments of a Business Enterprise," discussion memorandum, May 22, 1974; "Financial Reporting for Segments of a Business Enterprise," exposure draft, September 30, 1975.

2. Two principal sources issued annually are Dun & Bradstreet, *Key Business Ratios in 125 Lines*, and Robert Morris Associates, *Statement Studies*. The latter covers 156 lines of business. Not to be overlooked is *Quarterly Financial Report for Manufacturing, Mining and Trade*, published by the Federal Trade Commission, which can be used as a basis for ratio analysis. For many industries, data can be found by checking the publications of the trade associations.

3. See Paul E. Dascher, "The Penn Central Revisited: A Predictable Situation," *Financial Analysts Journal* 28 (March-April 1972):61-64.

4. William Beaver, Paul Kettler, and Myron Scholes, "The Association Between Market Determined and Accounting Determined Risk Measures," *Accounting Review* 45 (October 1970):654-682.

5. In its first-quarter 1974 report, the Federal Trade Commission noted that merger movements and other forms of corporate diversification have rendered "whole company" classification less meaningful. Not uncommonly, large companies have been classified into industrial categories on the basis of 10 percent to 15 percent of their total activity.

6. Fixed expenses contribute to a positive intercept in a regression. By looking at ratios instead of regressions, an investor cannot tell to what extent a rise in the ratio was due to a decline in operations or to inadequate control over variable expenses.

7. The Tax Reduction Act of 1975 lowered the rate, for tax years ending in 1975, to 20 percent on the first $25,000 of income; the next $25,000 was taxed at 22 percent, with the current rate of 48 percent applied to income over $50,000. These reductions were intended to represent a one-time benefit but could be extended.

8. Securities and Exchange Commission, Accounting Release no. 142, March 15, 1973, p. 2.

CHAPTER 14

1. Peat, Marwick, Mitchell & Co., *Accounting Information Bulletin*, February 1, 1974.

2. The value of some stocks stems from their potential liquidating value; this is true of the shares of investment companies, whose assets consist of securities that may readily be sold.

3. These two ratios are probably the most widely used in measuring corporate liquidity. As the *New York Times* noted in an article on the subject (August 25, 1974), "In recent months analysts have spewed forth ratios as fast as automatic serving machines toss out tennis balls for practice shots." Among other ratios mentioned were net working capital to corporate sales, current assets minus inventory profits to current liabilities, earnings to interest payments due, and cash plus government and other securities as a percentage of total current liabilities. It is questionable whether this proliferation of ratios adds much to the liquidity picture.

4. See pp. 392-395 for an arithmetic illustration of the greater earnings fluctuations that flow from leverage. The effects of leverage can also be shown more formally. For simplicity, assume no taxes and let X, a random variable, represent net operating income (NOI = EBIT), with mean $\overline{X}$ and standard deviation σ. The earnings variation per dollar of NOI is $\sigma/\overline{X}$. This ratio, known as the coefficient of variation, permits the comparison of the variability of quantities when there are substantial differences in magnitude. Let F represent the interest bill. Then net income (NI) is $X - F$, and since the reduction of a random variable by a constant does not change its standard deviation, the standard deviations of NOI and NI are the same, σ. Earnings variation per dollar of NI is then $\sigma/(\overline{X}-F)>\sigma/\overline{X}$. Since *NI* is the income available for common stock and equals NOI for unleveraged firms, leveraging clearly increases risk.

5. See Franco Modigliani and M. H. Miller, "The Cost of Capital: Corporation Finance and the Theory of Investment," *American Economic Review* 48 (June 1958):261-297. This article, which initiated the controversy, has been followed by a host of other articles dealing with the subject.

6. Franco Modigliani and M. H. Miller, "Corporate Income Taxes and the Cost of Capital: A Correction," *American Economic Review* 53 (June 1963):433-443.

CHAPTER 15

1. Karl H. Borch, *The Economics of Uncertainty* (Princeton: Princeton University Press, 1968), p. 4.

2. Securities and Exchange Commission, *Statement on the Future Structure of the Securities Markets*, February 2, 1972.

3. See Securities Acts Amendments of 1975, Sec. 21 (2).

4. In 1970 some 50,000 companies were reputed to have stocks traded in the over-the-counter market. See Robert Metz, "Market Place," *New York Times*, July 31, 1970. p. 36. However, no accurate records of the number of companies traded in the OTC markets are kept. Although the number varies from year to year, the most important segment of the OTC market consists of companies listed on NASDAQ. The SEC reported that at the end of 1973 there were almost 3,000 issues in the system; see Securities and Exchange Commission, *Annual Report*, 1975, p. 158.

5. Henry A. Latané, O. Maurice Joy, and Charles P. Jones, "Quarterly Data, Sort-Rank Routines, and Security Evaluation," *Journal of Business* 43 (October 1970):427-438.

6. Charles P. Jones and Robert H. Litzenberger, "Quarterly Earnings Reports and Intermediate Stock Price Trends," *Journal of Finance* 25 (March 1970):143-148. The standard deviation about a trend line is a measure of the accuracy of estimates and therefore is called the standard error of estimate.

7. All the stocks mentioned in this section at one time were speculative favorites and produced substantial market gains. To indicate the risks involved, the following list shows the high point reached by each of these stocks in recent years and their approximate August 28, 1975 closing price. Franzia Brothers was acquired by Coca-Cola Bottling.

	Recent high point	*Approx. closing price (August 1975)*
Auto-Train Corporation	53⅜	6⅝
Levitz Furniture	60½	4⅝
Lion Country Safari	24½	⅝ (bid)
Steak and Ale Restaurant	50	19 (bid)

8. In this calculation, it was assumed that all stock splits and stock dividends occurred at the beginning of the year. Therefore, the actual amount of dividends received was somewhat smaller.

9. See *Wall Street Journal*, June 27, 1973, p. 1 for comments by some analysts.

10. Monetarists hold that the course of the economy is largely determined by the rate of change of the money supply, which, in turn, may be measured in various ways. The most common measure, labeled M_1, includes currency and demand deposits. Other measures of the money supply (thus far ranging through M_7) also have been identified, depending on the type of "near money" (time deposits with or without large certificates of deposit, deposits in savings institutions, etc.) included.

11. The National Bureau of Economic Research has undertaken a project, supported by a grant from the American Life Insurance Association, to study the effect of inflation on financial institutions and markets. The material on the general effect of inflation on common stocks is based primarily on Phillip Cagan, *Common Stock Values and Inflation: The Historical Record of Many Countries*, NBER Supplement Report, March 1974, and National Bureau of Economic Research, *Annual Report*, September 1974, which contains a report on a study by John Lintner, Thomas Piper, and Peter Fortune on the short-run effects of inflation on investments in common stocks (pp. 87-90).

12. *Time*, January 6, 1975, p. 26.

13. This discussion is largely based on Standard & Poor's Industry Survey, *Liquor*, October 7, 1971, and April 4, 1974.

14. Reynolds Metals, *Annual Report*, 1972, pp. 4-9. In 1973 these ratios improved and were in line with prior trends. In 1974 the ratios improved still more.

15. See, for example, John G. Cragg and Burton G. Malkiel, "The Consensus and Accuracy of Some Predictions of the Growth of Corporate Earnings," *Journal of Finance* 23 (March 1968):67-84; David Green, Jr., and Joel Segall, "The Predictive Power of First-Quarter Earnings Reports," *Journal of Business* 40 (January 1967):44-55; Philip Brown and Victor Niederhoffer, "The Predictive Content of Quarterly Earnings," *Journal of Business* 41 (October 1968):448-497; Green and Segall, "Brickbats and Straw-men: A Reply to Brown and Niederhoffer," ibid., 498-502.

16. After a flurry of activity relative to financial forecasting, interest has tended to abate. The accounting profession, the SEC, and academicians, however, are continuing to work in this area. For a discussion of the problems involved and possible approaches, see Eric N. Melgren and Robert K. Elliott, "Critical Issues in Forecasting," *World* (Peat, Marwick, Mitchell & Co., Winter 1975):12-18.

CHAPTER 16

1. This relationship was developed by Charles C. Holt, "The Influence of Growth Duration on Share Prices," *Journal of Finance* 17 (September 1962):465-467.

2. Since these two companies were of comparable risk, a comparison of this sort seemed reasonable.

3. Robert M. Baylis and Suresh L. Bhirud, "Growth Stock Analysis: A New Approach," *Financial Analysts Journal* 29 (July-August 1973):63-70.

4. *New York Times*, April 22, 1973, sec. 3, p. 1.

5. Oppenheimer Fund, internal memorandum, June 21, 1973.

6. For an interesting discussion of the two-tier market that existed in mid-1973, see Carol J. Loomis, "How the Terrible Two-Tier Market Came to Wall Street," *Fortune* (July 1973):82-89, 186-190.

7. The derivation and implications of β were discussed in Chapter 10.

8. The estimate of any coefficient b_i in an equation such as the above is just an estimate of the true value and is subject to error. It may turn out to be different from zero by chance. To test whether the nonzero value was indeed obtained by chance, statisticians calculate the ratio of the estimated value to its standard error, a figure that can be derived from the same basic data used to estimate the value of b_i. This ratio is known as the "t-statistic." Every statistics text includes a table that gives the probability of getting various values of t. The probability of getting a value of t as high as 32 by chance is infinitesimal. The probability of getting a figure as large as we got for b_2 or as

small as we got for b_3 by chance is less than 10 percent. In testing a theory, the hypothesis that the *b*-value is zero is not usually rejected unless the probability is less than 5 percent. In developing forecasting models, higher probabilities are often acceptable.

9. See James M. Warren and John P. Shelton, "A Simultaneous Equation Approach to Financial Planning," *Journal of Finance* 26 (December 1971), pp. 1123-1142.

10. Irwin Friend and Marshall Puckett, "Dividends and Stock Prices," *American Economic Review* 54 (September 1964):656-682.

11. Benjamin Graham, David L. Dodd, and Sidney Cottle, *Security Analysis: Principles and Technique*, 4th ed. (New York: McGraw-Hill 1962), pp. 517-518. The study did, however, cautiously suggest that investors might place higher valuations (but only moderately) on dividends than on retained earnings in nongrowth industries and that investors do the opposite for growth industries.

In Korea in mid-1973 a government-sponsored agency acted as the principal underwriter and established the prices at which new securities were issued. The agency discounted dividends and one-fourth of earnings by the rate of interest paid on bank deposits. It was the conclusion of the agency's analysts that investors were very conscious of the income received on stock. The analysts therefore followed the Graham-Dodd prescription that for stocks of this sort, distributed earnings were worth four times those retained. On the other hand, the experience of one of the authors in Brazil in 1971 was that dividends were substantially ignored in the evaluation of securities at that time.

12. See, for example, "Back to Basics–Slow Dividend Growth Weakens Stock Prices, Some Analysts Think," *Wall Street Journal*, June 27, 1973, p. 1.

13. American Motors, *Annual Report*, 1972, p. 28.

14. *Wall Street Journal*, June 29, 1973, p. 31.

15. For a theoretical discussion of the use of models in forecasting dividends, see John Lintner, *op. cit.* and John A. Brittain. *Corporate Dividend Policy* (Washington, D.C.: Brookings Institution, 1966).

CHAPTER 17

1. Fred E. Brown, "The Institutional Investor as a Shareholder," *Duke University School of Law Conference on Securities Regulation*, ed. R. H. Mundheim (New York: Commerce Clearing House, 1965), pp. 207-208. At the time of the address Mr. Brown was president of Tri-Continental Corporation, Broad Street Investing Corporation, National Investors Corporation, and Whitehall Fund, Inc.

2. *Business Week*, November 4, 1972, p. 70.

3. This discussion of foreign organizational development is based on Raymond Vernon, *Sovereignity at Bay* (New York: Basic Books, 1971), pp. 121-134, and John M. Stopford and Louis T. Wells, Jr., *Managing the Multinational Enterprise: Organization of the Firm and Ownership of the Subsidiaries* (New York: Basic Books, 1972), chaps. 1-6.

4. See American Institute of Management, *Manual of Excellent Managements*, (New York, 1970).

5. *Business Week*, November 11, 1972, p. 174.

6. *Business Week*, October 21, 1972, pp. 64-66.

7. Rensis Likert, "The Influence of Social Research on Corporate Responsibility," in William J. Baumol, Rensis Likert, Henry C. Wallich, and John J. McGowan, *A New Rationale for Corporate Social Policy*, Committee for Economic Development, Supplementary Paper, Number 31 (New York, 1970), pp. 20-38.

8. G. W. Murphy Industries, Inc., *Annual Report*, 1971, p. 2.

9. Address by G. Bradford Cook (then chairman of the Securities and Exchange Commission) to the SMU Graduate School of Business, summarized in *Securities Regulation and Transfer Report*, May 31, 1973.

10. *Securities Regulation and Transfer Report*, April 20, 1973.

11. Reed Tool Co., *Annual Report*, 1972, pp. 4, 6.

12. See *SEC Docket*, June 12, 1973, vol. 1, no. 18:2-3.

13. After its April 1973 meeting the Accounting Principles Board, which had exposed a proposed opinion several months previously, announced that it had decided to leave the matter to the FASB; see Financial Accounting Standards Board, "Proposed Statement of Financial Accounting Standards for Leases," August 1975.

14. Libby, McNeill & Libby, *Annual Report*, July 1, 1972, p. 2.

15. Harnischfeger Corp., *Annual Report*, 1971, p. 2.

16. These relationships can be derived mathematically; see Anthony J. Curley, "Conglomerate Earnings per Share," *The Accounting Review* 46 (July 1971):519-528. The illustration above has been drawn from that article.

CHAPTER 18

1. The interest equalization tax was a special levy on most foreign securities sold to U.S. residents. It was imposed in July 1963, to protect the weakening U.S. balance of payments, and was eliminated in January 1974. The first foreign borrower to tap the public debt market thereafter was the European Coal and Steel Community, an agency that represents nine nations that together ranked as the world's largest steel and third largest coal producer in 1973. The ECSC offered $100 million five-year notes. Subsequently, various other foreign borrowers made an appearance. In general, they found it necessary to pay higher rates to extract funds than those of domestic issues of comparable quality.

2. *Wall Street Journal*, September 5, 1974, p. 21.

3. For an excellent discussion of indexing, see Norman S. Poser, "A Banker's Primer on Indexing," *Bankers Magazine* 158 (Winter 1975):108-115.

4. Norman S. Poser, "Can You Use Price Adjustment and Gold Clauses in Loan Agreements?" *Securities Regulation and Transfer Report*, February 26, 1975.

5. Stocks may also be rated, but the meaning is different. For example, Standard & Poor's, in its *Stock Guide*, notes that "these scorings are not to be confused with bond quality ratings, which are arrived at by a necessarily altogether different approach."

6. *Wall Street Journal*, March 8, 1971, p. 19.

7. *Wall Street Journal*, February 1, 1973, p. 23.

8. *Wall Street Journal*, November 20, 1974, p. 37.

9. Salomon Brothers, *An Analytical Record of Yield and Yield Spreads* (New York, 1975), pp. 54-59; idem, *Bond Market Roundup* (Week Ending August 1, 1975).

10. Michael J. Press, "How Well Do the Experts Forecast Interest Rates?" *Federal Reserve Bank of Kansas City Monthly Review*, September-October 1973, pp. 3-13.

CHAPTER 19

1. "Taking a Second Look at Bond Management," *Institutional Investor* 8 (October 1974):27.

2. *Wall Street Journal*, September 17, 1974, p. 37.

3. This discussion is based on *Financial Accounting Standards Board*, "An Analysis of Issues Related to Accounting for Leases," discussion memorandum (July 2, 1974).

4. See page 417, where it is pointed out that trust indentures may require that the capital stock plus surplus must represent a minimum percentage of a corporation's total capitalization in order to permit full payment of dividends.

5. The commission has insisted on the insertion of this provision in corporate charters as a protective measure for preferred stockholders. It sets up an automatic dividend restriction on the common stock when the common stock equity is or becomes less than 25 percent of total capitalization and surplus.

6. Utility earnings, however, may be subject to special pressures. In 1974, for example, they were adversely affected by fuel shortages, skyrocketing supply prices,

tight money, and tardy rate increases. Accordingly, government regulators were exploring methods to ease the industry's economic plight through such measures as tax benefits, federally guaranteed debt issues, and relaxation of costly environmental controls.

7. The findings were published in a series of books; the one most relevant to this discussion is W. Braddock Hickman, *The Volume of Corporate Bond Financing since 1900* (Princeton: Princeton University Press for the National Bureau of Economic Research, 1953).

8. Railroads sometimes finance their purchases of equipment by means of the "New York" or conditional sale plan. This provides for the purchase of the equipment by the road on installment terms, with title remaining in the name of the manufacturer or an appointed trustee. Legal uncertainties have restricted the use of this method. Roads have occasionally purchased equipment by means of an ordinary bond secured by a chattel mortgage.

9. Since title passes by prearrangement, the Internal Revenue Service does not treat this type of agreement as a true lease. The lessee cannot deduct the entire annual payment to the trust company for tax purposes.

10. *Wall Street Journal*, January 5, 1971, p. 5.

11. During the real estate boom of the 1920s, specialized institutions in the real estate field, known as mortgage companies, were formed to service real estate and deal in mortgages. These organizations issued bonds backed by pledges of various properties, sometimes providing guaranties for the mortgages they sold, with disastrous consequences after the 1929 collapse. In addition, guaranties were made by independent surety companies, which also experienced big losses. During the real estate boom of the 1960s there was some revival of interest in this type of institution, but it did not make much headway.

12. The trust indentures of mortgage bonds may establish an order of priority for disbursement of the issuer's revenues that provides for calculating the accounting charge for depreciation after bond interest payments. It is desirable, however, to calculate the fixed-charge coverage of these bonds after an allowance for depreciation, which is an inescapable economic cost regardless of contractual agreements.

CHAPTER 20

1. First Boston Corp., *Handbook of Securities of the United States Government and Federal Agencies and Related Money Market Instruments*, 26th ed. (1974), biennial publication. We have derived much of the information in this chapter from this source. The average maturity in June 1975 is from *Treasury Bulletin* (July 1975), Table FD-4.

2. *Wall Street Journal*, September 17, 1974, p. 36.

3. *Wall Street Journal*, December 29, 1972, p. 2.

4. Federal Reserve Bank of Cleveland, "Securities of U.S. Government Agencies," *Economic Review* (October 1969):19-30.

5. The differential tax on interest income and capital gains affects the net yield to the investor. In discussing this result, Robichek and Niebuhr indicate that this factor may be substantial whenever current yields exceed coupon rates. See Alexander A. Robichek and W. David Niebuhr, "Tax-Induced Bias in Reported Treasury Yields," *Journal of Finance* 25 (December 1970):1081-1090.

6. *Wall Street Journal*, September 6, 1973, p. 1.

CHAPTER 21

1. This description is based on a special report in *Securities Regulation and Transfer Report*, October 31, 1974. The special report, in turn, contains a summary of a report of the Senate Committee on Banking and Finance which explains the origins, purposes, and operations of the proposed law to regulate the municipal field.

2. *Wall Street Journal*, June 24, 1974, p. 15.

3. During the depression period, 4,771 known defaults occurred of local governing bodies, including 206 obligations rated Aaa or Aa by Moody's. Perhaps because this memory lingers, several efforts have been launched to insure investors against losses on municipal bonds. The Municipal Bond Insurance Association—owned by Aetna Life & Casualty, the St. Paul Cos., Inc., Connecticut General Insurance Corp., and Crum & Forster Insurance Cos.—offers municipal bond guaranty insurance to municipalities seeking to sell obligations. MGIC Indemnity Corp., a subsidiary of MGIC Investment Corp., offers this form of insurance, as well as municipal bond coverage for individual portfolios.

4. George H. Hempel, *The Postwar Quality of State and Local Debt* (New York: Columbia University Press for the National Bureau of Economic Research, 1971), p. 21.

5. *Wall Street Journal*, July 8, 1974, p. 24.

6. *New York Times*, August 19, 1973, p. F-6. While holdings of municipal securities by the residual "household category" (which includes unincorporated businesses and personal trusts, as well as individual investors) have grown in dollar amount over the years, the percentage has declined from 44 percent of outstanding municipal securities in 1960 to 26 percent in 1973. Prior to 1960, individuals were the largest identifiable portion of investors in municipal securities, but since that year commercial banks have become the biggest purchasers (*Securities Regulation and Transfer Report*, October 31, 1974; based on the report of the Senate Committee on Banking and Finance).

7. In a three-year period, the SEC brought five injunctive actions, involving over 55 defendants, to halt fraudulent municipal securities trading practices. Included in these alleged practices were unconscionable markups, churning (excessive turnover in customer accounts), misrepresentation, disregard of suitability standards, and scandalously high-pressure sales techniques. In some instances, bonds were promoted as general obligations of the issuer when they were actually revenue bonds, sometimes in default (ibid.)

8. *New York Times*, December 20, 1973, p. 38.

9. *New York Times*, June 1, 1975, sec. 4, p. 6.

10. Standard & Poor's Corp., *The Fixed Income Investor*, November 3, 1973.

11. *Economic Report of the President* (February 1975), p. 331.

12. *Wall Street Journal*, January 15, 1971, p. 1.

13. *Wall Street Journal*, March 3, 1975, p. 7.

14. The New York State law governing investments of savings banks establishes a maximum ratio of overall debt to real property valuation of 12 percent for cities of not less than 10,000 inhabitants in states adjoining New York and for cities of not less than 30,000 inhabitants in other states. This restriction is waived for cities which have taxable real property with a tax valuation greater than $200 million, a population of at least 150,000, and unlimited taxing powers. See New York State Banking Law, par. 235 (5) (a), (b), (c), and (d).

15. U.S. Bureau of the Census, *Statistical Abstract: 1974*, p. 256.

16. New York State Banking Law, par. 235 (3).

17. Ibid., par. 235 (5)(a).

18. *Wall Street Journal*, February 28, 1975, p. 32; March 12, 1975, p. 29; March 21, 1975, p. 21; *New York Times*, March 2, 1975, sec. 4, p. 1.

19. Moody's *Municipal and Government Manual* (1974), p. 914.

20. Lebenthal & Co., Inc., *Municipal Bonds and the Industrial Investor*, June 6, 1974, p. 4.

21. See Moody's *Government Manual* for a description of the various laws under which local housing authority bonds have been issued.

CHAPTER 22

1. For a good, concise statement of the tax aspects of mergers that prevailed prior to the tax revisions of 1969, see George D. McCarthy, *Acquisitions and Mergers*

(New York: Ronald Press, 1963), chap. 9. For an updating of that chapter, see George D. McCarthy and Robert E. Healy. *Valuing a Company: Practices and Procedures* (New York: Ronald Press, 1971), chap. 8.

2. *Guttman* v. *Illinois Central Railroad Co.* 189F. 2d 927 (2d Cir. 1951), cert. den. 342 U.S. 867.

3. *Morris* v. *Standard Gas & Electric Co.* 63 Atlantic Reporter 2d 577 at 585 (Del Ch. 1949).

4. An innovation which appeared in 1974 in private placements was the creation of mutually redeemable preferred stock. This new instrument permits redemption by either the issuer or holder of the stock after an initial, and relatively short non-redemption period.

5. The tax rate is expressed as a decimal. In effect, this approach determines the earnings that must be realized to permit the company to pay taxes and still have enough left exactly to meet preferred dividends. Thus:

$$E - TE = D$$
$$E(1 - T) = D$$
$$E = D/(1 - T),$$

where E = earnings, D = preferred dividend requirements, and T = the tax rate.

CHAPTER 23

1. *Wall Street Journal*, January 31, 1973, pp. 1, 25; *Wiesenberger Management Results*, September 30, 1974.

2. U.S. Congress, Senate, Committee on Banking, Housing and Urban Affairs, Subcommittee on Securities, *Hearings on Institutional Membership on National Securities Exchanges*, 92nd Cong., 2nd sess., April 1972, pt. 1, pp. 108-109.

3. Investment Company Institute, *1972 Mutual Fund Fact Book*, p. 9.

4. *Wall Street Journal*, January 23, 1973, p. 3.

5. For a discussion of these restrictions and the problems they created, see Everett Mattlin, "The Trials and Tribulations of Mutual Fund Advertising," *Institutional Investor* 5 (March 1971):21-26, 63, 68-70.

6. Securities and Exchange Commission, Securities Act of 1933, Release no. 5248, "Adoption of Rule Changes Relating to Investment Company Advertising," May 9, 1972.

7. Securities and Exchange Commission, "Notice of Proposed Amendment of Rule 134 Relating to Investment Company Advertising and Proposed Rule 425B," Investment Company Act of 1940, Release no. 7632, January 1973; Securities Act of 1933, Release no. 5591, June 16, 1975.

8. A 1974 survey of mutual funds representing 75.4 percent of the industry's assets revealed a total of 1,282,949 fiduciary, business, and institutional accounts in force. Valued at $6.8 billion, they represented 25.1 percent of the assets of the reporting companies. A similar survey conducted in 1954 revealed a total of 35,821 accounts valued at $283.4 million and representing 10.5 percent of the assets of reporting companies (Investment Company Institute, *1975 Mutual Fund Fact Book*, p. 37).

9. Securities and Exchange Commission, *Institutional Investor Study Report*, summary vol., 92nd Cong., 1st sess., H. Doc. no. 92-64, pt. 8, 1971, p. 111.

10. Ibid., pt. 2, pp. 400-410. The description in the text is based on the SEC presentation.

11. A survey conducted by the Securities and Exchange Commission indicated that out of 103 companies included, 76 made no adjustment in their performance or that of the index for cash dividends. None seemed to follow the procedure established by the commission in Rule 205-1. See Securities and Exchange Commission, Investment Company Act Release no. 7130 (April 17, 1972).

12. *United States* v. *National Association of Securities Dealers*,–U.S.–, 45 L. Ed. 486 (1975).

13. Securities and Exchange Commission, *Applicability of the Commission's Policy Statement on the Future Structure of the Securities Market to Selection of Brokers and Payment of Commissions by Institutional Managers*, May 9, 1972.

14. *Moses* v. *Burgin*, 316 F. Supp. 31 (D.C. Mass. 1970); CCH Fed. Sec. L. Rep. 93,061 (1st Cir., 1971).

15. The investment advisory agreement between the Oppenheimer Management Corp. and the Oppenheimer funds, for example, provides that Oppenheimer & Co., Inc. may execute portfolio transactions for the funds except when a better price or execution has been determined to be obtainable through another broker. Brokerage charges on negotiated transactions executed by Oppenheimer & Co., Inc. for the funds may not be less favorable than its contemporaneous charges for the execution of similar transactions to its most favored unaffiliated customers.

16. For a discussion of the legal issues involved, see: "*Rosenfeld* v. *Black*," *Review of Securities Regulation*, October 21, 1971; "The *Rosenfeld* v. *Black* Muddle," *Securities Regulation and Transfer Report*, May 5, 1972.

CHAPTER 24

1. A small but interesting convertible security with an accelerating conversion schedule is the Newark Electronics convertible subordinated debenture 5¼s due 1982. This security is unusual for two reasons: first, it is convertible into the securities of another corporation, Premier Industrial Corp., which assumed the bonds under the terms of a merger; second, the debenture is convertible into a preferred stock. The terms of the conversion provided for converting the debenture into the $0.90 convertible Series A preferred shares of Premier Industrial Corp. at $11 a share to April 1, 1972, $12.50 to April 1, 1977, and $14 a share thereafter.

2. Eventually the offer was made at an indicated value of $1,290 per $1,000 bond; the acquisition ran into antitrust difficulties but was finally consumated.

3. This loss may not occur if the senior security has detachable warrants. In this case, the holder of a called senior security may still retain his warrants. At that time, their value is likely to approximate the difference between the market and redemption prices of the senior issue.

4. For a detailed discussion of this technique, see Edward O. Thorp and Sheen T. Kassouf, *Beat the Market: A Scientific Stock Market System* (New York: Random House, 1967).

5. The reason for adding 1 to the ratio between the old and the new stock may be clarified by the following explanation: The market price of the stock while it sells "cum-rights" is composed of its basic price plus the value of one right. To determine the value of one right, V (using the same symbols as in the text), the difference between the basic price of the stock ($M_o - V$) and the subscription price of the right, S, is divided by the number of shares needed to buy an additional share R. This equation may be originally stated and simplified as follows:

$$V = \frac{(M_o - V) - S}{R}$$

$$VR = M_o - V - S$$

$$VR + V = M_o - S$$

$$V(R + 1) = M_o - S$$

$$V = \frac{M_o - S}{R + 1}$$

6. Theoretically, the price should drop to $19.55, but since prices are given in ⅛ths, the price will go to $19.50.

7. The use of the term in this context is technical; it should not be confused with the warrant as an independent trading instrument distinct from a right, as previously discussed.

CHAPTER 25

1. Julie Connelly, "How Institutions Are Playing the Option Game," *Institutional Investor* 8 (February 1974):46.

2. *Securities Regulation Report*, September 24, 1973, pp. 5-6.

3. *Wall Street Journal*, March 5, 1973, p. 19.

4. Securities and Exchange Commission, Securities Exchange Act Release No. 10552, December 13, 1973.

5. The SEC has proposed Rule 9b-2, which would, among other things, establish special suitability requirements for option trading.

6. Norman S. Poser and William J. Brodsky "AMEX Options Regulation," *Review of Securities Regulation* 8 (March 5, 1975):959.

7. A stop order establishes an arbitrary price at which a position will be liquidated if the market moves past the price. An exchange official indicated that eliminating stop orders would end much of the heavy paper flow presently cluttering the floor (*Wall Street Journal*, October 24, 1974, p. 17).

8. Originally, trading continued until 2:00 P.M. of the second business day prior to the expiration date, which was 2:15 on the last business day of the expiration month. This time differentiation created a 2-day gap during which holders could not trade their "in money" options (market price above exercise price) and therefore were forced to exercise them. To encourage liquidation rather than exercise contracts, the 2-day gap was shortened. The expiration time was changed to 10:30 A.M. on the last Monday of the expiration month, and trading was permitted to continue until 2 P.M. of the preceding Friday. Finally, the OCC changed the expiration time to that given in the text (see p. 625).

9. This formula appears in a nontechnical context in Fischer Black, "Fact and Fantasy in the Use of Options," *Financial Analysts Journal* 31 (July-August 1975):36.

10. N. S. Poser and W. J. Brodsky, "AMEX Options Regulation," p. 960 n5.

11. Julie Connelly, "How Institutions Are Playing the Options Game," *Institutional Investor* 8 (February 1974):46.

12. The OTC dealer may be willing to redeem an option for a nominal premium as it approaches its expiration date, or the holder may purchase downside-out calls or upside-out puts, as described in the appendix to this chapter.

13. Investors may establish reservation prices when they sell short. For example, they must cover the short position when the price of the stock rises above 110 percent of the short-sale price. Even in these circumstances, however, they may find that when they attempt to cover, the price has risen still further. In lieu of this procedure, therefore, they might buy an upside-out put (see appendix to this chapter) rather than selling short. The premium for the option, however, is an offset to any profit realized in the short sale.

14. While investors are more interested in calls than in puts, writers (original sellers of puts and calls) prefer to write straddles (separable combinations of puts and calls; see appendix). A single long position suffices to cover the margin requirement for both the put and the call. It is generally believed that only one side of the straddle will be exercised. If the price of the stock rises, the call will be exercised. The writer will forgo the appreciation on his long position, but he will profit by the premium on the straddle. If the stock price falls, the put will be exercised. The writer will lose on both the long position and the put itself, but his losses will be offset by the premium. The actual loss may thus be less than if he had simply held the long position. Because of this preference of writers for straddles, the OTC premium for a put tends to be less than the premium for an OTC call on the same stock with comparable terms.

15. Firms specializing in this area employ computers to perform the calculations and provide indicated rates of return under varying assumptions.

16. The following two sections, on the taxation of holders and writers of options, are based on the Options Clearing Corporation prospectus for Exchange-Traded Options, January 6, 1975, pp. 31-32.

Notes

CHAPTER 26

1. Eugene F. Fama, "Efficient Capital Markets: A Review of Theory and Empirical Work," *Journal of Finance* 25 (May 1970):399.

2. Alan Seelenfreund, George G. C. Parker, and James C. Van Vorne, "Stock Price Behavior and Trading," *Journal of Financial and Quantitative Analysis* 3 (September 1968):3.

3. Burton G. Malkiel, *A Random Walk Down Wall Street* (New York: Norton, 1973), p. 120.

QUESTIONS AND EXERCISES

1. Mark J. Appleman, "Annual Reports Better This Year," *Exchange* 36 (March 1975):9.

2. "An Interview with John C. Burton," *Management Accounting* 56 (May 1975):21.

3. John C. Burton, "Accounting That Allows for Inflation," *Business Week*, November 30, 1974, p. 12.

4. Burroughs Corp., *Annual Report*, 1974, p. 46.

BIBLIOGRAPHY

Capital Market Theory

Baumol, William J. *The Stock Market and Economic Efficiency.* New York: Fordham University Press, 1965.

Blume, Marshall E., and Friend, Irwin. "A New Look at the Capital Asset Pricing Model." *Journal of Finance* 28 (March 1973):19.

Cooper, R. V. L. "Efficient Capital Markets and the Quantity Theory of Money." *Journal of Finance* 29 (June 1974):887.

Emery, John T. "Efficient Capital Markets and the Information Content of Accounting Numbers." *Journal of Financial and Quantitative Analysis* 9 (March 1974):139.

Fama, E. F. "Components of Investment Performance." *Journal of Finance* 27 (June 1972):551.

———. "Efficient Capital Markets: A Review of Theory and Empirical Work." *Journal of Finance* 25 (May 1970):383

Fama, E. F., and Laffler, A. B. "Information and Capital Markets." *Journal of Business* 44 (July 1971):289.

Fama, E. F., and MacBeth, J. D. "Risk, Return and Equilibrium: Empirical Tests." *Journal of Political Economy* 81 (May 1973):607.

Gonedes, Nicholas J. "Efficient Capital Markets and External Accounting." *Accounting Review* 47 (January 1972):11.

Jaffe, J. F., and Merville, L. J. "The Value of Risk Reducing Information." *Journal of Financial and Quantitative Analysis* 9 (November 1974):697.

Jensen, Michael C., ed. *Studies in the Theory of Capital Markets.* New York: Praeger, 1972.

Lorie, James, and Brealey, Richard, eds. *Modern Developments in Investment Management: A Book of Readings.* New York: Praeger, 1972.

Lorie, James H., and Hamilton, Mary T. *The Stock Market: Theories and Evidence.* Homewood, Ill.: Richard D. Irwin, 1973.

Merton, R. C., and Subrahmanyam, M. G. "The Optimality of a Competitive Stock Market." *Bell Journal of Economics and Management Science* 5 (Spring 1974): 145.

Mossin, Jan. *Theory of Financial Markets.* Englewood Cliffs, N.J.: Prentice-Hall, 1973.

Scholes, M. "The Market for Securities: Substitution versus Price Pressure and the Effects of Information on Share Prices." *Journal of Business* 45 (April 1972): 179.

Sharpe, William F. "Bonds vs. Stocks: Capital Market Theory." *Financial Analysts Journal* 29 (November-December 1973).

———. "Capital Asset Prices: A Theory of Market Equilibrium Under Conditions of Risk." *Journal of Finance* 19 (September 1964):425.

———. *Portfolio Theory and Capital Markets.* New York: McGraw-Hill, 1970.

Van Horne, James C. *The Function and Analysis of Capital Market Rates.* Englewood Cliffs, N.J.: Prentice-Hall, 1970.

Vasicek, O. A., and McQuown, J. A. "The Efficient Market Model." *Financial Analysts Journal* 28 (September-October 1971):71.

Walter, James E. "The Information Content of Stock Prices." *Business Economics* (Summer 1965):25.

Bibliography

Ethics

Malkiel, Burton G., and Quandt, Richard E. "Moral Issues in Investment Policy." *Harvard Business Review* 49 (March-April 1971):37.

Powers, Charles W., ed. *People/Profits: The Ethics of Investment*. New York: Council on Religion and International Affairs, 1972.

Simon, John G., Powers, Charles W., and Gunneman, Jon P. *The Ethical Investor: Universities and Corporate Responsibility*. New Haven: Yale University Press, 1972.

Foreign Investments

Hardy, C. Colburn. "An Easy Way to Invest in Foreign Companies." *The Exchange* 34 (February 1973):9.

Krefetz, Gerald, and Marossi, Ruth. *Investing Abroad*. New York: Harper & Row, 1965.

Litvak, Isaiah A., and Maule, Christopher I. *Foreign Investment*. New York: Praeger, 1970.

Nakamura, M. "Why Japanese Buy Eurobonds." *Euromoney* (August 1972):27.

Park, Y. S. *The Euro-bond Market: Function and Structure*. New York: Praeger, 1974.

Interest Rates

Conard, J. W. *The Behavior of Interest Rates: A Progress Report*. New York: Columbia University Press, 1966.

Fisher, Lawrence, and Weil, Roman L. "Coping with the Risk of Interest Rate Fluctuations: Returns to Bondholders from Naive and Optimal Strategies." *Journal of Business* 44 (October 1971):408.

Grossman, Herschel I. "Risk Aversion, Financial Intermediation, and the Term Structure of Interest Rates." *Journal of Finance* 22 (December 1967):611.

Guttentag, Jack M., ed. *Essays on Interest Rates*. Vol. 2. New York: Columbia University Press, 1971.

Guttentag, Jack M., and Cagan, P., eds. *Essays on Interest Rates*. Vol. 1. New York: Columbia University Press, 1969.

Homer, Sidney, and Leibowitz, Martin L. *Inside the Yield Book: New Tools for Bond Market Strategy*. Englewood Cliffs, N.J.: Prentice-Hall, 1972.

Malkiel, Burton G. *The Term Structure of Interest Rates: Expectations and Behavior Patterns*. Princeton: Princeton University Press, 1966.

Meiselman, David. *The Term Structure of Interest Rates*. Englewood Cliffs, N.J.: Prentice-Hall, 1962.

Nelson, C. R. *The Term Structure of Interst Rates*. New York: Basic Books, 1972.

Roll, R. *The Behavior of Interest Rates: An Application of the Efficient Market Model to U. S. Treasury Bills*. New York: Basic Books, 1970.

Soldofsky, Robert M., and Miller, Roger L. "Risk Premium Curves for Different Classes of Long-Term Securities, 1950-1966." *Journal of Finance* 24 (June 1969): 429.

Investment

Readings

Ball, Richard E., ed. *Readings in Investments*. Boston: Allyn and Bacon, 1965.

Elton, E. J., and Gruber, M. J., eds. *Security Evaluation and Portfolio Analysis*. Englewood Cliffs, N.J.: Prentice-Hall, 1972.

Fredrikson, E. Bruce, ed. *Frontiers of Investment Analysis*. Rev. ed. Scranton, Pa.: Intext Educational Publishers, 1971.

Institute of Chartered Financial Analysts. *C.F.A. 1973 Supplementary Readings in Financial Analysis*. Vol. 1. Homewood, Ill.: Richard D. Irwin, 1972.

———. *C.F.A. Readings in Financial Analysis.* 1st ed. Homewood, Ill.: Richard D. Irwin, 1966.

———. *C.F.A. Readings in Financial Analysis.* 2nd ed. Homewood, Ill.: Richard D. Irwin, 1970.

———. *Supplementary Readings.* Vols. 1-2. Homewood, Ill.: Richard D. Irwin, 1972, 1974.

Lishan, John M., and Crary, David T. *The Investment Process.* Scranton, Pa.: International Textbook, 1970.

West, David A. *Readings in Investment Analysis.* Scranton, Pa.: International Textbook, 1969.

Wu, Hsiu-Kwang, and Zakon, Alan J., eds. *Elements of Investments.* 2nd ed. New York: Holt, Rinehart and Winston, 1972.

Risk and return

Alder, Michael. "On the Risk-Return Trade Off in the Valuation of Assets." *Journal of Financial and Quantitative Analysis* 5 (December 1969):493.

Altman, E. I., and Schwartz, R. A. "Common Stock Price Volatility Measures and Patterns." *Journal of Financial and Quantitative Analysis* 5 (January 1970):603.

Arditti, Fred D. "Risk and the Required Return on Equity." *Journal of Finance* 22 (March 1967):19.

Arrow, Kenneth. *Essays in the Theory of Risk Bearing.* Chicago, Ill.: Markham, 1971.

Babcock, G. C. "A Note on Justifying Beta as a Measure of Risk." *Journal of Finance* 27 (June 1972):699.

Baesel, J. B. "On the Assessment of Risk: Some Further Considerations." *Journal of Finance* 29 (December 1974):1491.

Ball, R. J. "Risk, Return and Disequilibrium: An Application to Changes in Accounting Techniques." *Journal of Finance* 27 (May 1972):343.

Ben-Zion, U. "A Time Series Measure of Risk." *Journal of Economics and Business* 27 (Fall 1974):60.

Blume, M. E. "On the Assessment of Risk." *Journal of Finance* 26 (March 1971):1.

Borch, Karl. *The Economics of Uncertainty.* Princeton: Princeton University Press, 1968.

———. "The Rationale of the Mean-Standard Deviation Analysis: Comment." *American Economic Review* 64 (June 1974):428.

Brealey, Richard A. *An Introduction to Risk and Return from Common Stocks.* Cam-Bridge: MIT Press, 1969.

———. *Security Prices in a Competitive Market: More about Risk and Return from Common Stocks.* Cambridge: MIT Press, 1971.

Brenner, Menachem. "On the Stability of the Distribution of the Market Component in Stock Price Changes." *Journal of Financial and Quantitative Analysis* 9 (December 1974):945.

Conrad, Gordon R., and Plotkin, Irving H. "Risk/Return: U.S. Industry Patterns." *Harvard Business Review* 46 (March-April 1968):90.

Farrar, Donald E. *The Investment Decision under Uncertainty.* Englewood Cliffs, N.J.: Prentice-Hall, 1962.

Fisher, Lawrence. "Determinants of Risk Premiums on Corporate Bonds." *Journal of Political Economy* 67 (June 1959):217.

Fleming, R. M. "How Risky Is the Market?" *Journal of Business* 46 (July 1973):404.

Gonedes, Nicholas J. "Evidence on the Information Content of Accounting Numbers: Accounting-based and Market-based Estimates of Systematic Risk." *Journal of Financial and Quantitative Analysis* 9 (June 1974):407.

Jacob, N. L. "The Measurement of Market Similarity for Securities under Uncertainty." *Journal of Business* 43 (July 1970):328.

———. "The Measurement of Systematic Risk for Securities and Portfolios: Some Empirical Results." *Journal of Financial and Quantitative Analysis* 6 (March 1971):815.

Jaffe, Jeffrey F., and Merville, Larry J. "Stock Price Dependencies and Valuation of Risky Assets with Discontinuous Temporal Returns." *Journal of Finance* 29 (December 1974):1437.

———. "The Value of Risk-Reducing Information. *Journal of Financial and Quantitative Analysis* 9 (November 1974):697.

Joyce, J. M., and Vogel, R. C., "The Uncertainty in Risk: Is Variance Unambiguous?" *Journal of Finance* 25 (March 1970):127.

Kalymon, B. A. "Estimation Risk in the Portfolio Selection Model," *Journal of Financial and Quantitative Analysis* 6 (January 1971):559.

Kantor, M., "Market Sensitivities." *Financial Analysts Journal* 27 (January-February 1971):64.

Klemkosky, R. C., and Petty, J. W., "A Multivariate Analysis of Stock Price Variability." *Journal of Business Research* 1 (Summer 1973):1.

Knight, Frank. *Risk, Uncertainty and Profit*. Boston: Houghton Mifflin, 1921.

Levy, R. A. "On the Short Term Stationarity of Beta Coefficients." *Financial Analysts Journal* 27 (November-December 1971):55.

Melicher, Ronald W. "Financial Factors Which Influence Beta Variations within an Homogeneous Industry Environment." *Journal of Financial and Quantitative Analysis* 9 (March 1974):231.

Melicher, R. W., and Rush, D. F. "Systematic Risk, Financial Data, and Bond Rating Relationships in a Regulated Industry Environment." *Journal of Finance* 29 (May 1974):537.

Mlynarczyk, Francis A. "Beta, Alpha—or Omega?" *Institutional Investor* 6 (July 1972):93.

Mokkelbost, P. B. "Unsystematic Risk over Time." *Journal of Financial and Quantitative Analysis* 6 (March 1971):785.

Mumey, G. A., and Korkie, R. M. "Balance Sheet Additivity of Risk Measures." *Journal of Financial and Quantitative Analysis* 6 (September 1971):1123.

Officer, R. R. "The Variability of the Market Factor of the New York Stock Exchange." *Journal of Business* 46 (October 1973):434.

Parker, G. G. C., and Stewart, S. S. "Risk and Investment Performance." *Financial Analysts Journal* 30 (May-June 1974):49.

Pinches, George E., and Kinney, W. R., Jr. "The Measurement of the Volatility of Common Stock Prices." *Journal of Finance* 26 (March 1971):119.

Reints, W. W., and Vanderberg, P. A. "A Comment on the Risk Level Discriminatory Powers of the Wiesenberger Classifications." *Journal of Business* 46 (April 1973): 278.

Robichek, Alexander A. "Risk and the Value of Securities." *Journal of Financial and Quantitative Analysis* 4 (December 1969):513.

Robinson, R. S. "Measuring the Risk Dimension of Investment Performance." *Journal of Finance* 25 (May 1970):455.

Rosenberg, Barr, and McKibben, Walt. "The Prediction of Systematic and Specific Risk in Common Stocks." *Journal of Financial and Quantitative Analysis* 8 (March 1973):317.

Samuelson, Paul A. "General Proof that Diversification Pays." *Journal of Financial and Quantitative Analysis* 3 (March 1967):1.

Schilbred, C. M. "The Market Price of Risk." *Review of Economic Studies* 40 (April 1973):283.

Sharpe, W. F. "Mean-Absolute-Deviation Characteristic Lines for Securities and Portfolios." *Management Science* 18 (October 1971):B1.

Sharpe, W. F., and Cooper, Guy M. "Risk-Return Classes of New York Stock Exchange Common Stocks, 1931-1967." *Financial Analysts Journal* 28 (March-April 1972):B1.

Silver, J. B. "An Alternative to the Yield Spread as a Measure of Risk." *Journal of Finance* 28 (September 1973):933.

Soldofsky, Robert M. "Yield-Risk Performance Measurements." *Financial Analysts Journal* 24 (September-October 1968):130.

———. "Yield-Risk Performance of Convertible Securities." *Financial Analysts Journal* 27 (March-April 1971):61.

Vasicek, I. A. "A Note on Using Cross-Sectional Information in Bayesian Estimation of Security Betas." *Journal of Finance* 28 (December 1973):1233.

Welles, Chris. "The Beta Revolution: Learning to Live with Risk." *Institutional Investor* 5 (September 1971):21.

Zinbarg, Edward D. "Modern Approach to Investment Risk." *Financial Executive* 61 (February 1973):44.

Texts

Amling, Frederick. *Investments: An Introduction to Analysis and Management.* 2d ed. Englewood Cliffs, N.J.: Prentice-Hall, 1970.

Badger, Ralph E., Torgerson, Harold W., and Guthmann, Harry G. *Investment Principles and Practices.* 6th ed. Englewood Cliffs, N.J.: Prentice-Hall, 1969.

Barnes, L., ed. *Current Issues on the Frontiers of Financial Analysis.* Hempstead, N.Y.: Hofstra University, 1970.

Bellemore, Douglas H., and Richie, John C. *Investments.* Chicago: Southwestern, 1969.

Bernstein, Leopold A. *Financial Statement Analysis: Theory, Application and Interpretation.* Homewood, Ill.: Richard D. Irwin, 1974.

Bloomfield, E. D. *Portfolio Theory and Investment Decisions.* Canberra: Australian National University, 1973.

Bolten, Steven E. *Cases in Security Analysis and Portfolio Management.* New York: Holt, Rinehart and Winston, 1973.

———. *Security Analysis and Portfolio Management.* New York: Holt, Rinehart and Winston, 1972.

Bowyer, John W. *Investment Analysis and Management.* 4th ed. Homewood, Ill.: Richard D. Irwin, 1972.

Christy, George A., and Clendenin, John C. *Introduction to Investments.* 6th ed. New York: McGraw-Hill, 1974.

Cohen, Jerome B., Zinbarg, Edward D., and Zeikel, Arthur. *Investment Analysis and Portfolio Management.* Rev. ed. Homewood, Ill.: Richard D. Irwin, 1973.

D'Ambrosio, Charles A. *A Guide to Successful Investing.* Englewood Cliffs, N.J.: Prentice-Hall, 1970.

Dacey, Norman F. *Dacey on Mutual Funds.* New York: Crown, 1970.

Dougall, Herbert E. *Investments.* 9th ed. Englewood Cliffs: Prentice-Hall, 1973.

Fischer, Donald E., and Jordan, Ronald J. *Security Analysis and Portfolio Management.* Englewood Cliffs, N.J.: Prentice-Hall, 1975.

Foster, E. M. *Common Stock Investment.* Lexington, Mass.: Lexington Books, 1974.

Francis, Jack Clark. *Investments: Analysis and Management.* New York: McGraw-Hill, 1972.

Francis, Jack Clark, and Archer, Stephen H. *Portfolio Analysis.* Englewood Cliffs, N.J.: Prentice-Hall, 1971.

Graham, Benjamin, Dodd, David L., and Cottle, Sidney. *Security Analysis.* 4th ed. New York: McGraw-Hill, 1962.

Grodinsky, Julius. *Investments.* New York: Ronald Press, 1953.

Hayes, Douglas A. *Investments: Analysis and Management.* 2nd ed. New York: Macmillan, 1966.

Hirshleifer, Jack. *Investment, Interest, and Capital.* Englewood Cliffs, N.J.: Prentice-Hall, 1970.

Jessup, Paul F. *Competing for Stock Market Profits.* New York: Wiley, 1974.

Latané, Henry A., and Tuttle, Donald L. *Security Analysis and Portfolio Management.* New York: Ronald Press, 1970.

Levy, Haim, and Sarnat, Marshall. *Investment and Portfolio Analysis.* New York: Wiley, 1972.

Lishan, J. M., and Crary, D. T., eds. *The Investment Process.* Scranton, Pa.: International Textbook, 1970.

Markowitz, Harry M. *Portfolio Selection: Efficient Diversification of Investments.* New Haven: Cowles Foundation for Research in Economics, Yale University, 1959.
Sauvain, Harry C. *Investment Management.* 4th ed. Homewood, Ill.: Richard D. Irwin, 1973.
Shade, Philip A. *Common Stocks: A Plan for Intelligent Investing.* Homewood, Ill., Richard D. Irwin, 1971.
Smith, Keith. *Portfolio Management.* New York: Holt, Rinehart and Winston, 1971.
Smith, Keith V., and Eiteman, David K. *Essentials of Investing.* Homewood, Ill.: Richard D. Irwin, 1974.
Taylor, Basil, ed. *Investment Analysis and Portfolio Management.* New York: St. Martin's Press, 1970.
Valentine, Jerome L., and Mennis, Edmund A. *Quantitative Techniques for Financial Analysis.* Charlottesville, Va.: C.F.A. Research Foundation, 1970.
Vaughn, Donald E. *Survey of Investments.* 2d ed. Hinsdale, Ill.: Dryden Press, 1974.
Widicus, Wilbur W., and Stitzel, Thomas E. *Personal Investing.* Homewood, Ill.: Richard D. Irwin, 1971.
Williams, Edward E., and Findlay, M. Chapman. *Investment Analysis.* Englewood Cliffs, N.J.: Prentice-Hall, 1974.
Williams, John B. *The Theory of Investment Value.* Cambridge: Harvard University Press, 1938.
Williamson, J. Peter. *Investments: New Analytic Techniques.* New York: Praeger, 1970.

Investors

Individual

Baker, H. Kent, and Haslen, John A. "The Impact of Investor Socioeconomic Characteristics on Risk and Return Preference." *Journal of Business Research* 2 (October 1974):469.
Belfer, Nathan. "Construction of Private Investors' Portfolios." *Financial Analysts Journal* 21 (May-June 1965):101.
Bellemore, Douglas H. *The Strategic Investor.* New York: Simmons-Boardman, 1963.
Blume, Marshall E., Crockett, Jean, and Friend, Irwin. "Stockownership in the United States: Characteristics and Trends." *Survey of Current Business* 54 (November 1974):16.
Bolthouse, D. *Estate Planning for the Family.* New York: Delacorte Press, 1971.
Brandt, Catherine. *Woman's Money: How to Protect It and Increase It in the Stock Market.* Englewood Cliffs, N.J.: Parker, 1970.
Brosterman, Robert. *The Complete Estate Planning Guide.* New York: McGraw-Hill, 1964.
Buckley, Joseph C., and Schmidt, Henry. *The Retirement Handbook.* Harper & Row, 1971.
Cobleigh, Ira V. *Happiness Is a Stock that Doubles in a Year.* New York: Bernard Geis, 1969.
Eiteman, Wilford J. *Personal Finance and Investment.* Ann Arbor, Mich.: Masterco Press, 1952.
Fisher, Milton. *How to Make Money in the Over-the-Counter Market.* New York: William Morrow, 1970.
Goodzwaard, Maurice B., and Smith, Keith V. "How Trustmen View Their Objectives." *Institutional Investor* 6 (February 1972):40.
Graham, Benjamin. *The Intelligent Investor.* 4th ed. New York: Harper & Row, 1972.
Graham, Benjamin, and McGolrick, Charles. *The Interpretation of Financial Statements.* Rev. ed. New York: Harper & Row, 1964.
Jarvis, N. Leonard. *Under Thirty Guide to Wall Street.* New York: Cowles, 1970.
Keen, Geraldine. *Money and Art.* New York: Putnam, 1971.

Lebenthal & Co. *Municipal Bonds for the Individual Investor*. New York, 1950.

Loeb, Gerald M. *The Battle for Investment Survival*. New York: Simon and Schuster, 1965.

Margolius, Sidney. *The Innocent Investor and the Shaky Ground Floor*. New York: Trident Press, 1971.

Morris, William T. *How to Get Rich Slowly But Almost Surely*. Reston, Va.: Reston Publishing, 1973.

Price, Irving. *Buying Country Property*. New York: Harper & Row, 1971.

Rush, Richard. *Art as an Investment*. Englewood Cliffs, N.J.: Prentice-Hall, 1961.

———. *Antiques as an Investment*. Englewood Cliffs, N.J.: Prentice-Hall, 1968.

Samson, Earl A. Jr. "Total Financial Planning." *Trusts and Estates* (February 1971).

Springer, John L. *Financial Self-Defense*. New York: McGraw-Hill, 1969.

Washington, Lawrence. *How to Plan Your Financial Security*. New York: McGraw-Hill, 1949.

Institutional

Arditti, F. D. "Another Look at Mutual Fund Performance." *Journal of Financial and Quantitative Analysis* 6 (June 1971):909.

Atkins, Paul M. *Bank Bond Investment and Secondary Reserve Management*. Cambridge, Mass.: Bankers Publishing, 1940.

Bagehot, Walter. "Risk in Corporate Pension Funds." *Financial Analysts Journal* 28 (January-February 1972):80.

Bogle, J. C. "Mutual Fund Performance Evaluation." *Financial Analysts Journal* 26 (November-December 1970):25.

Brimmer, Andrew F. *Life Insurance Companies in the Capital Market*. East Lansing, Mich.: Michigan State University, 1962.

Carlson, R. S. "Aggregate Performance of Mutual Funds." *Journal of Financial and Quantitative Analysis* 5 (March 1970):1.

Dietz, Peter O. "Investment Goals: A Key to Measuring Performance of Pension Funds." *Financial Analysts Journal* 24 (March-April 1968):133.

———. *Pension Funds: Measuring Investment Performance*. New York: Graduate School of Business, Columbia University and The Free Press, 1966.

Dougall, Herbert E. *Capital Markets and Institutions*. Englewood Cliffs, N.J.: Prentice-Hall, 1965.

Ellis, Charles D. *Institutional Investing*, Homewood, Ill.: Dow Jones-Irwin, 1971.

Ford Foundation. Advisory Committee on Endowment Management. *Managing Educational Endowments*. New York: The Committee, 1972.

Friend, Irwin, Blume, Marshall, and Crockett, Jean. *Mutual Funds and Other Institutional Investors: A New Perspective*. New York: McGraw-Hill, 1970.

Gardner, E. B., ed. *Pension Fund Investment Management*. Homewood, Ill.: Richard D. Irwin, 1969.

Goldsmith, Raymond William. *Financial Institutions*. New York: Random House, 1968.

———. *Financial Structure and Development*. New Haven: Yale University Press, 1969.

Goldsmith, Raymond William, ed. *Institutional Investors and Corporate Stock: A Background Study*. New York: National Bureau of Economic Research, 1973.

Holland, Daniel M. *Private Pension Funds*. National Bureau of Economic Research, Occasional Paper no. 97. New York: Columbia University Press, 1966.

Investment Company Portfolio Management. C.F.A. Research Seminar no. 4. Homewood, Ill.: Richard D. Irwin, 1970.

Jacobs, Donald B. *Financial Institutions*. Homewood, Ill.: Richard D. Irwin, 1972.

Jensen, Michael. "The Performance of Mutual Funds in the Period 1945-69." *Journal of Finance* 23 (May 1968):389.

Klemkosky, Robert C. "Institutional Dominance of the NYSE." *Financial Executive*, 41 (November 1973):14.

Koontz, Harold. *Appraising Managers as Managers*. New York: McGraw-Hill, 1971.

Lintner, John V. *Mutual Savings Banks in the Savings and Mortgage Markets*. Cambridge: Harvard Univesity Press, 1948.

Lyon, Roger A. *Investment Portfolio Management in the Commercial Bank*. New Brunswick, N.J.: Rutgers University Press, 1960.

Mackin, John P. *Protecting Purchasing Power in Retirement: A Study of Public Employee Retirement Systems*. New York: Fleet Academic Editions, 1971.

McCahan, David, ed. *Investment of Life Insurance Funds*. Philadelphia: University of Pennsylvania Press, 1953.

Mills, H. D. "On the Measurement of Fund Performance." *Journal of Finance* 25 (December 1970):1125.

Polakoff, Murray E. *Financial Institutions and Markets*. Boston: Houghton Mifflin, 1970.

Pension Fund Investment Management. C.F.A. Research Seminar no. 3. Homewood, Ill.: Richard D. Irwin, 1969.

Rosenberg, Marvin. "Institutions and Market Liquidity." *Financial Analysts Journal* 30 (March-April 1974):53.

Securities and Exchange Commission. *Institutional Investor Study Report*, 92d Cong., 1st sess. H. Doc. no. 92-64. Washington, D.C., March 10, 1971.

________. *Public Policy Implications of Investment Company Growth*, Report of the Committee on Interstate and Foreign Commerce. 89th Cong., 2d sess., U. S. House of Representatives, 1966.

Sharpe, William F. "Mutual Fund Performance." *Journal of Business* 39 (January 1966): 119.

Silber, William L. *Portfolio Behavior of Financial Institutions:* New York: Holt, Rinehart and Winston, 1970.

Soldofsky, Robert M. *Institutional Holdings of Common Stock, 1900-2000*. Ann Arbor, Mich.: Bureau of Business Research, Graduate School of Business Administration, University of Michigan, 1971.

Treynor, Jack L. "Discussion: The Performance of Mutual Funds in the Period 1945-1964." *Journal of Finance* 23 (May 1968):418.

________. "How to Rate Management of Investment Funds." *Harvard Business Review* 43 (January-February 1965):63.

Treynor, Jack L., and Mazuy, K. K. "Can Mutual Funds Outguess the Market?" *Harvard Business Review* 44 (July-August 1966):131.

Tucker, J. Richard. *State and Local Pension Funds*. Washington, D.C.: Securities Industry Association, 1972.

U.S. Congress. Senate. Committee on Labor and Public Welfare. *Interim Report of Activities of the Private Welfare and Pension Plan Study, 1971*. 92d Cong., 1st sess., February 22, 1972.

University of Pennsylvania. Wharton School of Finance and Commerce. *A Study of Mutual Funds.* Washington, D.C.: Government Printing Office, 1963.

Voorheis, Frank L. *Bank Administered Pooled Equity Funds for Employee Benefit Plans*. East Lansing, Mich.: Bureau of Business and Economic Research, Michigan State University, 1967.

________. "Bank Trustees and Pension Performance." *Financial Analysts Journal* 28 (July-August 1972):60.

Walter, James E. *The Investment Process*. Boston: Harvard University Press, 1962.

Welles, Chris. "University Endowments: Revolution Comes to the Ivy Tower." *Institutional Investor* 1 (September 1967).

Williamson, J. Peter. *Performance Measurement and Investment Objectives for Educational Endowment Funds*. New York: Common Fund, 1972.

Market Analysis

Apilado, Vincent P., and Heathcotte, Bryan. "The Predictive Content of Some Leading Economic Indicators for Future Stock Prices." *Journal of Financial and Quantitative Analysis* 9 (March 1974):247.

Bonin, Joseph M., and Moses, Edward A. "Seasonal Variations in Prices of Individual Dow Jones Industrial Stocks." *Journal of Financial and Quantitative Analysis* 9 (December 1974):963.

Bowley, Arthur Lyon. *A New Index of Prices by Securities*. London: Royal Economic Society, 1931.

Carter, E. Eugene, and Cohen, Kalman. "Stock Averages, Stock Splits, and Bias." *Financial Analysts Journal* 23 (May-June 1967):77.

Cootner, P. H. "Stock Market Indexes: Fallacies and Illusions." *Commercial and Financial Chronicle* 23 (September 29, 1966):77.

Fanning, J. E. "A Four-Indicator System for Forecasting the Market." *Financial Analysts Journal* 27 (September-October 1971):49.

Fredman, A. J., and Choudhury, S. K. "Rates of Return on OTC, AMEX, and NYSE Common Stocks During the 1960's." *Marquette Business Review* 18 (Spring 1974):9.

Gup, Benton E. "A Note on Stock Market Indicators and Stock Prices." *Journal of Financial and Quantitative Analysis* 8 (September 1973):673.

Gupta, M. C. "Money Supply and Stock Prices: A Probabilistic Approach." *Journal of Financial and Quantitative Analysis* 9 (January 1974):57.

Hamburger, M. J., and Kochin, L. A. "Money and Stock Prices: The Channels of Influence." *Journal of Finance* 27 (May 1972):231.

Homa, K. E., and Jaffee, D. M. "The Supply of Money and Common Stock Prices." *Journal of Finance* 26 (December 1971):1045.

Kessel, R. A., and Alchian, A. A. "Effects of Inflation." *Journal of Political Economy* 70 (December 1962):521.

Klemkosky, Robert C. "The Bias in Composite Performance Measures." *Journal of Financial and Quantitative Analysis* 8 (June 1973):505.

Milne, Robert D. "The Dow-Jones Industrial Average Re-Examined." *Financial Analysts Journal* 22 (November-December 1966):83.

Nawrocki, David N., and Philippatos, George C. "The Information Inaccuracy of Stock Market Forecasts: Some New Evidence of Dependence on the New York Stock Exchange." *Journal of Financial and Quantitative Analysis* 8 (June 1973):445.

Niederhoffer, V. "The Analysis of World Events and Stock Prices." *Journal of Business* 44 (April 1971):193.

Palmer, M. "Money Supply, Portfolio Adjustments and Stock Prices." *Financial Analysts Journal* 26 (July-August 1970):19.

Rudolph, J. A. "The Money Supply and Common Stock Prices." *Financial Analysts Journal* 28 (March-April 1972):19.

Sprinkel, Beryl W. *Money and Markets: A Monetarist View*. Homewood, Ill.: Richard D. Irwin, 1971.

Portfolio Management

Baron, David P. "Information, Investment Behavior, and Efficient Portfolios" *Journal of Financial and Quantitative Analysis* 9 (September 1974):555.

Barry, C. B. "Portfolio Analysis under Uncertain Means, Variances, and Covariances." *Journal of Finance* 29 (May 1974):515.

Bierman, Harold. "Using Investment Portfolios to Change Risk." *Journal of Financial and Quantitative Analysis* 3 (December 1968):151.

Block, Frank E. "Elements of Portfolio Construction." *Financial Analysts Journal* 25 (May-June 1969):123.

Blume, M. E. "Portfolio Theory: A Step Toward Its Practical Application." *Journal of Business* 43 (April 1970):152.

Breen, William. "Monogeneous Risk Measures and the Construction of Composite Assets." *Journal of Financial and Quantitative Analysis* 3 (December 1968):405.

Brumelle, S. L. "When Does Diversification Between Two Investments Pay?" *Journal of Financial and Quantitative Analysis* 9 (June 1974):473.

Campanella, F. B. *The Measurement of Portfolio Risk Exposure: Use of the Beta Coefficient*, Lexington, Mass.: D. C. Heath, 1972.

Chen, A., Jen, F., and Zionts, S. "The Optimal Portfolio Revision Policy." *Journal of Business* 44 (January 1971):51.

Clarkson, G. P. E. *Portfolio Selection: A Simulation of Trust Investment*. Englewood Cliffs, N.J.: Prentice-Hall, 1962.

Cohen, Kalman J., and Pogue, Jerry A. "An Empirical Evaluation of Alternative Portfolio-Selection Models." *Journal of Business* 40 (April 1967):166.

Commission on Money and Credit, *Management Investment Companies*. Englewood Cliffs, N.J.: Prentice-Hall, 1962.

Cottle, C. Sidney, and Whitman, W. Tate. *Investment Timing: The Formula Plan Approach*. New York: McGraw-Hill, 1953.

Dickinson, H. O. "The Reliability of Estimation Procedures in Portfolio Analysis." *Journal of Financial and Quantitative Analysis* 9 (June 1974):447.

Dincc, Robert R. "Another View of Formula Planning." *Journal of Finance*, 19 (December 1964):678.

Elton, E. J., and Gruber, M. J. "Estimating the Dependence Structure of Share Prices: Implications for Portfolio Selection." *Journal of Finance* 28 (December 1973): 1203.

Evans, J. L. "An Analysis of Portfolio Maintenance Strategies." *Journal of Finance* 25 (June 1970):561.

Evans, John L., and Archer, Stephen H. "Diversification and the Reduction of Dispersion: An Empirical Analysis." *Journal of Finance* 23 (December 1968):761.

Farrell, J. L., Jr. "Analyzing Covariation of Returns to Determine Homogeneous Stock Groupings." *Journal of Business* 47 (April 1974):186.

Friend, Irwin, and Blume, Marshall. "Measurement of Portfolio Performance Under Uncertainty." *American Economic Review* 50 (September 1970):561.

Friend, Irwin, and Vickers, Douglas. "Portfolio Selection and Investment Performance." *Journal of Finance* 20 (September 1965):391.

Garand, J. J. "Fixed Income Portfolio Performance: A Discussion of the Issues." *Journal of Bank Research* 4 (Winter 1974):280.

Gaumnitz, Jack E. "Appraising Performance of Investment Portfolios." *Journal of Finance* 25 (June 1970):555.

Hakansson, Nils H. "On Optimal Myopic Portfolio Policies with and without Serial Correlation of Yields." *Journal of Business* 44 (July 1971):324.

Hodges, Stewart D., and Brealey, Richard A. "Using the Sharpe Model." *Investment Analyst* 27 (September 1970).

Jacob, Nancy L. "A Limited-Diversification Portfolio Selection Model for the Small Investor." *Journal of Finance* 28 (June 1973):847.

Jean, W. H. "More on Multidimensional Portfolio Analysis." *Journal of Financial and Quantitative Analysis* 8 (June 1973):475.

Jenkins, David. *How to Profit from Formula Plans in the Stock Market*. New York: Gosset & Dunlap, 1963.

Jensen, Michael. "Risk, Capital Assets, and the Evaluation of Investment Portfolios." *Journal of Business* 42 (April 1969):167.

Klevorick, A. K. "A Note on 'The Ordering of Portfolios in Terms of Mean and Variance.' " *Review of Economic Studies* 40 (April 1973):293.

Latané, Henry A., and Tuttle, Donald L. "Criteria for Portfolio Building." *Journal of Finance* 22 (September 1967):359.

Levy, Haim, and Sarnat, Marshall. "International Diversification of Investment Portfolios." *American Economic Review* 50 (September 1970):668.

Levy, Robert A. "The Principle of Portfolio Upgrading." *Industrial Management Review* 8 (Fall 1967):82.

Logue, Dennis E., and Simkowitz, Michael A. "The Interdependent Structure of Security Returns." *Journal of Financial and Quantitative Analysis* 8 (March 1973):259.

Lintner, John. "Security Prices, Risks, and Maximal Gains from Diversification." *Journal of Finance* 20 (December 1965):587.

Lyon, Roger A. *Investment Portfolio Management in the Commercial Bank*. New Brunswick, N.J.: Rutgers University Press, 1960.

Mao, J. C. T. "Essentials of Portfolio Diversification Strategy." *Journal of Finance* 25 (December 1970):1109.

Markowitz, Harry M. "Portfolio Selection." *Journal of Finance* 7 (March 1952):77.

———. *Portfolio Selection: Efficient Diversification of Investments.* New York: Wiley, 1959.

McEnally, R. W. "Some Portfolio-Relevant Risk Characteristics of Long-Term Marketable Securities." *Journal of Financial and Quantitative Analysis* 8 (September 1973):565.

Michaelsen, Jacob B., and Goshay, Robert C. "Portfolio Selection in Financial Intermediaries: A New Approach." *Journal of Financial and Quantitative Analysis* 2 (June 1967):166.

Mossin, Jan. "Optimal Multiperiod Portfolio Policies." *Journal of Business* 41 (April 1968):215.

Personal Trust Investment Management. C.F.A. Monograph Series, no. 2. Homewood, Ill.: Richard D. Irwin, 1968.

Pinches, G. E. and Simon, G. "An Analysis of Portfolio Accumulation Strategies Employing Low-Priced Common Stocks." *Journal of Financial and Quantitative Analysis* 7 (June 1972):1773.

Pogue, Gerald A. "An Intertemporal Model for Investment Management." *Journal of Bank Research* 1 (Spring 1970).

Richter, Marcel K. "Cardinal Utility Portfolio Selection and Taxation." *Review of Economic Studies* 42 (June 1960):152.

Robichek, Alexander A., Cohen, Richard A., and Pringle, John J. "Returns on Alternative Investment Media and Implications for Portfolio Construction." *Journal of Business* 45 (July 1972):427.

Sharpe, William F. "A Linear Programming Approximation for the General Portfolio Analysis Problem." *Journal of Financial and Quantitative Analysis* 6 (December 1971):1263.

———. "A Simplified Model for Portfolio Analysis." *Management Science* 9 (January 1963):277.

Smith, Keith V. "A Transition Model for Portfolio Revision." *Journal of Finance* 22 (September 1967):425.

Solnik, Bruno H. "Why Not Diversify Internationally?" *Financial Analysts Journal* 30 (July-August 1974):48.

Stone, Bernell K. "A Linear Programming Formulation of the General Portfolio Selection Problem." *Journal of Financial and Quantitative Analysis* 8 (September 1973):621.

———. *Risk, Return and Equilibrium: A General Single-Period Theory of Asset Selection and Capital-Market Equilibrium.* Cambridge: MIT Press, 1971.

Tomlinson, Lucile. *Practical Formulas for Successful Investing.* New York: Wilfred Funk, 1953.

Treynor, J. L., and Black, F. "How to Use Security Analysis to Improve Portfolio Selection." *Journal of Business* 46 (January 1973):66.

Wallingford, Buckner A. "A Survey and Comparison of Portfolio Selection Models." *Journal of Financial and Quantitative Analysis* 2 (June 1967):85.

Young, William E., and Trent, Robert H. "Geometric Mean Approximations of Individual Security and Portfolio Performance." *Journal of Financial and Quantitative Analysis* 4 (June 1969):179.

Securities Analysis

Convertibles

Baumol, W. J., Malkiel, B. G., and Quandt, R. E. "The Valuation of Convertible Securities." *Quarterly Journal of Economics* 80 (February 1966):48.

Frank, W. G., and Weygandt, J. T. "A Prediction Model for Convertible Debentures." *Journal of Accounting Research* 9 (Spring 1971):116.

Jennings, E. H. "An Estimate of Convertible Bond Premiums." *Journal of Financial and Quantitative Analysis* 9 (January 1974):33.

Vinson, Charles. "Pricing Practices in the Primary Convertible Bond Market." *Quarterly Review of Economics and Business* 10 (Summer 1970):47.

________. "Rates of Return on Convertibles." *Financial Analysts Journal* 26 (July-August 1970):110.

Walter, J. E., and Que, A. V. "The Valuation of Convertible Bonds." *Journal of Finance* 28 (June 1973):713.

Equities

Aber, J. W. *Beta Coefficients and Models of Security Returns*. Lexington, Mass.: Lexington Books, 1973.

Altman, Edward. "Financial Ratios, Discriminant Analysis and the Prediction of Corporate Bankruptcy." *Journal of Finance* 23 (September 1968):589.

Anderson, Corliss D. *Corporate Reporting for the Professional Investor*. Auburndale, Mass.: Financial Analysts Federation, 1962.

Babcock, G. C. "The Concept of Sustainable Growth." *Financial Analysts Journal* 26 (May-June 1970):108.

Backer, M. "Financial Reporting and Security Investment Decisions." *Financial Analysts Journal* 27 (March-April 1971):67.

Badger, Ralph Eastman. *The Complete Guide to Investment Analysis*. New York: McGraw-Hill, 1967.

Ball, R., and Watts, R. "Some Time Series Properties of Accounting Income." *Journal of Finance* 27 (June 1972):663.

Balog, James. "Market Reaction to Merger Announcements." *Financial Analysts Journal* 31 (January-February 1975):24.

Barnea, Amir, and Logue, Dennis E. "Evaluating the Forecasts of a Security Analyst." *Financial Management* 2 (Summer 1973):38.

Baumol, William J., Heim, Peggy, Malkiel, Burton G., and Quandt, Richard E. "Earnings, Retention, New Capital and the Growth of the Firm." *Review of Economics and Statistics* 50 (November 1970):343.

Baumol, William, and Malkiel, Burton. "The Firm's Optimal Debt-Equity Combination and the Cost of Capital." *Quarterly Journal of Economics* 81 (November 1967):581.

Baxter, Nevin. "Leverage, Risk of Ruin, and the Cost of Capital." *Journal of Finance* 22 (September 1967):395.

Baylis, Robert M., and Bhirud, Suresh L. "Growth Stock Analysis: A New Approach." *Financial Analysts Journal* 29 (July-August 1973):63.

Beaver, William. "The Information Content of Annual Earnings Announcements." *Empirical Research in Accounting: Selected Studies*. 1968 Supplement to *Journal of Accounting Research* 7:67.

Beaver, William H., and Dukes, Roland E. "Interperiod Tax Allocation and the Behavior of Security Prices." *Accounting Review*, 47 (April 1972):330.

Beidleman, C. R. "Limitations of Price-Earnings Ratios." *Financial Analysts Journal* 27 (September-October 1971):81.

Bell, F. W. "The Relation of the Structure of Common Stock Prices to Historical Expectational and Industrial Variables." *Journal of Finance* 29 (March 1974):187.

Beranek, William. *Common Stock Financing, Book Value, and Stock Rights: The Theory and the Evidence*. Madison: University of Wisconsin, 1961.

________. *The Effects of Leverage on the Market Value of Common Stock*. Madison: Bureau of Business Research and Service, University of Wisconsin, 1964.

Bernstein, Leopold A. "In Defense of Fundamental Analysis." *Financial Analysts Journal* 31 (January-February 1975):57.

Bernstein, P. L. "What Rates of Return Can You 'Reasonably' Expect?" *Journal of Finance* 28 (May 1973):273.

Bibliography

Bierman, H., Jr., Downes, D. H., and Hass, J. E. "Closed-Form Stock Price Models." *Journal of Financial and Quantitative Analysis* 7 (June 1972):1797.

Bierman, H., Jr., and Hass, J. "Normative Stock Models." *Journal of Financial and Quantitative Analysis* 6 (September 1971):1135.

Bing, R. A. "Survey of Practitioners' Stock Evaluation Methods." *Financial Analysts Journal* 27 (May-June 1971):55.

Blume, M. E. "Unbiased Estimators of Long Run Expected Rates of Return." *Journal of the American Statistical Association* 69 (September 1974):634.

Blume, M. E., and Husic, F. "Price, Beta, and Exchange Listing." *Journal of Finance* 28 (May 1973):283.

Branch, B. "Common Stock Performance and Inflation: An International Comparison." *Journal of Business* 47 (January 1974):48.

Brealey, R. A. *Security Prices in a Competitive Market: More About Risk and Return from Common Stocks*, Cambridge: MIT Press, 1971.

Brigham, Eugene F., and Gordon, Myron J. "Leverage, Dividend Policy, and the Cost of Capital." *Journal of Finance* 23 (March 1968):85.

Brigham, Eugene F., and Pappas, James L. "Rates of Return on Common Stocks." *Journal of Business* 42 (July 1969):302.

Briloff, Abraham. *Unaccountable Accounting*. New York: Harper & Row, 1972.

Brown, P., and Kennelly, J. W. "The Informational Content of Quarterly Earnings: an Extension and Some Further Evidence." *Journal of Business* 45 (July 1972):403.

Chung, Peter S. "An Investigation of the Firm Effects Influence in the Analysis of Earnings to Price Ratios of Industrial Common Stocks." *Journal of Financial and Quantitative Analysis* 9 (December 1974):1009.

Cohen, S., and Smyth, D. J. "Some Determinants of Price/Earnings Ratios of Industrial Common Stock." *Quarterly Review of Economics and Business* 13 (Winter 1973): 49.

Cottle, S., and Whitman, T. *Corporate Earning Power and Market Valuation, 1935-1955*. Durham, N.C.: Duke University Press, 1959.

Cragg, J. G. and Malkiel, B. G. "The Consensus and Accuracy of Some Predictions of the Growth of Corporate Earnings." *Journal of Finance* 23 (March 1968):67.

Crum, William L. *Corporate Size and Earning Power*. Cambridge: Harvard University Press, 1939.

Davis, E. G., Dunn, D. M., and Williams, W. H. "Ambiguities in the Cross-Section Analysis of Per Share Financial Data." *Journal of Finance* 28 (December 1973):1241.

Durand, David. "Growth Stocks and the Petersburg Paradox." *The Journal of Finance* 12 (September 1957):348.

Elliott, J. W. "Forecasting and Analysis of Corporate Financial Performance with an Econometric Model of the Firm." *Journal of Financial and Quantitative Analysis* 7 (March 1972):1499.

Elton, E. J., and Gruber, M. J. "Earnings Estimates and the Accuracy of Expectational Data." *Management Science* 18 (April 1972):B409.

Falk, H., and Ophir, T. "The Effect of Risk on the Use of Financial Statements by Investment Decision Makers: A Case Study." *Accounting Review* 48 (April 1973): 323.

Fama, Eugene, Fisher, Lawrence, Jensen, Michael, and Roll, Richard. "The Adjustment of Stock Market Prices to New Information." *International Economic Review* 10 (February 1969):1.

Fellner, William. *Probability and Profit*. Homewood, Ill.: Richard D. Irwin, 1965.

Fisher, Lawrence, and Lorie, James H. "Rates of Return on Investments in Common Stock: The Year-by-Year Record, 1926-1965." *Journal of Business* 41 (July 1968):291.

————. "Some Studies of Variability of Returns on Investments in Common Stocks." *Journal of Business* 43 (April 1970):99.

Foster, E. M. "Price-Earnings Ratio and Corporate Growth." *Financial Analysts Journal* 26 (January-February 1970):96.

________. "Price-Earnings Ratio and Corporate Growth: A Revision." *Financial Analysts Journal* 26 (July-August 1970):115.

Foster, G. "Stock Market Reaction to Estimates of Earnings per Share by Company Officials." *Journal of Accounting Research* 11 (Spring 1973):25.

Friend, Irwin, and Puckett, Marshall. "Dividends and Stock Prices." *American Economic Review* 54 (September 1964):656.

Furst, Richard W. "Does Listing Increase the Market Price of Common Stock?" *Journal of Business* 43 (April 1970):174.

Gonedes, N. J. "Evidence on the Information Content of Accounting Numbers: Accounting-Based and Market-Based Estimates of Systematic Risk." *Journal of Financial and Quantitative Analysis* 8 (June 1973):407.

Gonedes, N. J. "Some Evidence on Investor Actions and Accounting Messages." *Accounting Review* 46 (April 1971):320; (July 1971):535.

Goudzwaard, M. B. "Conglomerate Mergers, Convertibles, and Cash Dividends." *Quarterly Review of Economics and Business* 29 (Spring 1969):330.

Gunther, S. P. "Poolings, Purchases, Goodwill: A Review of APB Opinions 16 and 17." *New York Certified Public Accountant* (January 1971).

Haugen, R. A. "Expected Growth, Required Return, and the Variability of Stock Prices." *Journal of Financial and Quantitative Analysis* 5 (September 1970):297.

Heintz, J. A. "Price-Level Restated Financial Statements and Investment Decision Making." *Accounting Review* 48 (October 1973):679.

Helfert, Erich A. *Techniques of Financial Analysis*. 3d ed. Homewood, Ill.: Richard D. Irwin, 1972.

Holt, Charles C. "The Influence of Growth Duration of Share Prices." *Journal of Finance* 17 (September 1962):465.

Holt, Charles C., and Shelton, John P. "The Implication of the Capital Gains Tax for Investment Decisions." *Journal of Finance* 16 (December 1961):559.

Horwitz, B., and Young, A. "Extraordinary Gains and Losses and Security Prices." *Quarterly Review of Economics and Business* 14 (Winter 1974):101.

Jaffe, J. F. "Stock Price Dependencies and the Valuation of Risky Assets with Discontinuous Temporal Returns." *Journal of Finance* 28 (December 1974):1437.

Jaffee, D. M., Malkiel, B. G., and Quandt, R. E. "Predicting Common Stock Prices: Payoffs and Pitfalls." *Journal of Business Research* 3 (January 1974):1.

Jessup, Paul F., and Upson, Roger B. *Returns in Over-the-Counter Stock Markets*. Minneapolis: University of Minnesota Press, 1973.

Johnson, G. L., Reilly, F. K., and Smith, R. E. "Individual Common Stocks as Inflation Hedges." *Journal of Financial and Quantitative Analysis* 6 (June 1971):1015.

Jones, C. P., and Litzenberger, R. H. "Quarterly Earnings Reports and Intermediate Stock Price Trends." *Journal of Finance* 25 (March 1970):143.

Jordan, R. J. "An Empirical Investigation of the Adjustment of Stock Prices to New Quarterly Earnings Information." *Journal of Financial and Quantitative Analysis* 8 (September 1973):609.

Joy, O. M., and Jones, C. P. "Predictive Value of P/E Ratios." *Financial Analysts Journal* 26 (September-October 1970):61.

Kaplan, B. S., and Roll, R. "Investor Evaluation of Accounting Information: Some Empirical Evidence." *Journal of Business* 45 (April 1972):225.

King, Benjamin F. "Market and Industry Factors in Stock Price Behavior." *Journal of Business Security Prices* 39 (Supp., January 1966):139.

Kinney, W. J. "Predicting Earnings: Entity versus Subentity Data." *Journal of Accounting Research* 9 (Spring 1971):127.

Kochanek, R. F. "Segmental Financial Disclosure by Diversified Firms and Security Prices." *Accounting Review* 49 (April 1974):245.

Konrath, Larry F. "Accounting for Changing Price Levels." *Financial Analysts Journal* 30 (November-December 1974):50.

Latané, H. A. "Cross-Section Regularities in Returns on Investment in Common Stocks." *Journal of Business* 46 (October 1973):512.

Latané, H. A., Jones, C. P., and Rieke, R. D. "Quarterly Earnings Reports and Subsequent Holding Period Returns." *Journal of Business Research* 2 (April 1974):119.

Latané, H. A., Joy O. M., and Jones, C. P. "Quarterly Data, Sort-Rank Routines, and Security Evaluation." *Journal of Business* 43 (October 1970):427.

Lerner, E., and Auster, R. "Market Discounts Potential Dilution." *Financial Analysts Journal* 25 (July-August 1969):118.

Leveson, Sidney. "Have We Solved the Dilution Problem?" *Financial Analysts Journal* 24 (September-October 1968):69.

Litzenberger, R. H., Joy, O. M., and Jones, C. P. "Ordinal Predictions and the Selection of Common Stocks." *Journal of Financial and Quantitative Analysis* 6 (September 1971):1059.

McDonald, J. G., and Fisher, A. K. "New-Issue Stock Price Behavior." *Journal of Finance* 27 (March 1972):97.

McEnally, R. W. "An Evaluation of Some Costs and Consequences of Dividend-Oriented Investment Strategies." *Journal of Business Research* 2 (January 1974):59.

———. "An Investigation of the Extrapolative Determinants of Short-Run Earnings Expectations." *Journal of Financial and Quantitative Analysis* 6 (March 1971): 687.

———. "A Note on the Return Behavior of High Risk Common Stocks." *Journal of Finance* 29 (March 1974):199.

McIntyre, E. V. "Current-Cost Financial Statements and Common-Stock Investment Decisions." *Accounting Review* 48 (July 1973):575.

Mauriello, J. A. *Accounting for the Financial Analyst*. Rev. ed. Homewood, Ill.: Richard D. Irwin, 1971.

Mead, Edward Sherwood, and Grodinsky, Julius. *The Ebb and Flow of Investment Values*. New York: D. Appleton-Century, 1939.

Melicher, R. W. "Financial Factors Which Influence Beta Variations Within an Homogeneous Industry Environment." *Journal of Financial and Quantitative Analysis* 9 (March 1974):231.

Meyers, S. L. "A Re-examination of Market and Industry Factors in Stock Price Behavior." *Journal of Finance* 28 (June 1973):695.

———. "The Stationarity Problem in the Use of the Market Model of Security Price Behavior." *Accounting Review* 48 (April 1973):318.

Moor, R. E. "The Use of Economics in Investment Analysis." *Financial Analysts Journal* 27 (November-December 1971):63.

Nerlove, Marc. "Factors Affecting Differences Among Rates of Return on Investments in Individual Common Stocks." *Review of Economics and Statistics* 50 (August 1968):312.

Nichols, D. A. "A Note on Inflation and Common Stock Values." *Journal of Finance* 23 (September 1968):655.

Nicholson, S. F. "Price-Earnings Ratios." *Financial Analysts Journal* 26 (July-August 1970):43.

Niederhoffer, V. "The Predictive Content of First-Quarter Earnings Reports." *Journal of Business* 43 (January 1970):60.

Niederhoffer, V., and Regan, P. J. "Earnings Changes, Analysts' Forecasts and Stock Prices." *Financial Analysts Journal* 23 (May-June 1972):65.

O'Connor, M. C. "On the Usefulness of Financial Ratios to Investors in Common Stock." *Accounting Review* 48 (April 1973):339.

Oudet, Bruno A. "The Variation of the Return on Stocks in Periods of Inflation." *Journal of Financial and Quantitative Analysis* 8 (March 1973):247.

Parker, C. Reed. "The Trueblood Report." *Financial Analysts Journal* 31 (January-February 1975):32.

Paton, W. A. "Fancies and Fallacies in Business Finance." *Financial Executive* 42 (June 1974):76.

Pettit, R. Richardson, and Westerfield, Randolph. "Using the Capital Asset Pricing Model and the Market Model to Predict Security Returns." *Journal of Financial and Quantitative Analysis* 9 (September 1974):579.

Reilly, F. K. "Price Changes in NYSE, Amex, and OTC Stocks Compared." *Financial Analysts Journal* 27 (March-April 1971):54.

Robichek, A. A., and Bogue, M. C. "A Note on the Behavior of Expected Price/Earnings Ratios over Time." *Journal of Finance* 26 (June 1971):731.

Ross, Howard. *The Elusive Art of Accounting*. New York: Ronald Press, 1966.

Smith, David L. "The Performance of Merging Banks." *Journal of Business* 44 (April 1971):184.

Smith, K. V. "The Increasing Stream Hypothesis of Corporate Dividend Policy." *California Management Review* (Fall 1971).

Smith, R. E., Johnson, G. L., and Reilly, F. K. "A Year-by-Year Analysis of 'Real' Rates of Return on Common Stocks." *Quarterly Review of Economics and Business* 14 (Spring 1974):79.

Soldofsky, R. M., and Murphy, J. T. *Growth Yields on Common Stocks: Theory and Tables*. Iowa City: Bureau of Business and Economic Research, State University of Iowa, 1963.

Stern, Joel M. "Earnings Per Share Doesn't Count." *Financial Analysts Journal* 30 (July-August 1974):39.

Stewart, S. S., Jr. "A Behavioral Model for Predicting Stock Prices." *Journal of Business Research* 1 (Fall 1973):173.

Stitzel, T. E. "Investing in Intrastate Issues of Common Stock." *Journal of Financial and Quantitative Analysis* 4 (January 1970):697.

Treynor, Jack L. "The Trouble With Earnings." *Financial Analysts Journal* 28 (September-October 1972):41.

Tysseland, M. S. "Further Tests of the Validity of the Industry Approach to Investment Analysis." *Journal of Financial and Quantitative Analysis* 6 (March 1971):835.

Van Horne, James C., and Glassmire, William F. "The Impact of Unanticipated Changes in Inflation on the Value of Common Stock." *Journal of Finance* 27 (December 1972):1081.

Walsh, Cornelius F. "Does Listing Increase the Market Price of Common Stocks—Comment." *Journal of Business* 46 (October 1973):616.

Walter, James E. *Dividencd Policy in Enterprise Valuation*. Belmont, Calif.: Wadsworth, 1967.

________. "Dividend Policy: Its Influence on the Value of the Enterprise." *Journal of Finance* 18 (May 1963):280.

Warren, James M., and Shelton, John P. "A Simultaneous Equation Approach to Financial Planning." *Journal of Finance* 26 (December 1971):1123.

Wendt, Paul F. "Current Growth Stock Valuation Methods." *Financial Analysts Journal* 21 (March-April 1965):91.

Williamson, J. Peter. *Investments: New Analytic Techniques*. New York: Praeger, 1971.

Fixed-Income Securities

Ascher, L. W. "Selecting Bonds for Capital Gains." *Financial Analysts Journal* 27 (March-April 1971):74.

Atkinson, Thomas R., and Simpson, Elizabeth T. *Trends in Corporate Bond Quality*. New York: National Bureau of Economic Research, 1967.

Bildersee, John S. "Some Aspects of the Performance of Non-Convertible Preferred Stocks." *Journal of Finance* 28 (December 1973):1187.

Cohan, Avery B. *Yields on Corporate Debt Directly Placed*. New York: National Bureau of Economic Research, 1967.

Ederington, L. H. "The Yield Spread of New Issues of Corporate Bonds." *Journal of Finance* 29 (December 1974):1531.

Fraine, Harold G., and Mills, Robert H. "Effects of Defaults and Credit Deterioration on Yields of Corporate Bonds." *Journal of Finance* 16 (September 1961):423.

Hastie, K. L. "Determinants of Municipal Bond Yields." *Journal of Financial and Quantitative Analysis* 7 (June 1972):1729.

Hempel, George H. *The Postwar Quality of State and Local Debt*. New York: Columbia University Press for the National Bureau of Economic Research, 1971.

Hickman, W. Braddock. *Corporate Bond Quality and Investor Experience*. New York: National Bureau of Economic Research, 1958.

Hillhouse, A. M. *Municipal Bonds: A Century of Experience*. New York: Prentice-Hall, 1936.

Hoffland, D. C. "The Price-Rating Structure of the Municipal Bond Market." *Financial Analysts Journal* 28 (March-April 1972):65.

Hopewell, M. H., and Kaufman, G. G. "Bond Price Volatility and Term to Maturity: A Generalized Specification." *American Economic Review* 63 (September 1973): 749.

Horton, Joseph J., Jr. "Statistical Classification of Municipal Bonds." *Journal of Bank Research* (Autumn 1970).

Jantscher, Gerald R. *The Effects of Changes in Credit Rating on Municipal Borrowing Costs*. Washington, D.C.: Brookings Institution, 1970.

Jen, F., and Wert, J. "The Effect of Sinking Fund Provisions on Corporate Bond Yields." *Financial Analysts Journal* 23 (March-April 1967):126.

Johnson, Ramon. "Term Structures of Corporate Bond Yields as a Function of Risk of Default." *Journal of Finance* 22 (May 1967):313.

Norgaard, Richard L. "An Examination of the Yields of Corporate Bonds and Stocks." *Journal of Finance* 28 (September 1973):1275.

Pettway, Richard H., and Weintraub, Herbert J. "Profitable Bond Trading Among Bonds of the Same Risk Class and Maturity." *Financial Analysts Journal* 25 (November-December 1969):125.

Von Furstenberg, G. M. "The Equilibrium Spread Between Variable Rates and Fixed Rates on Long Term Financing Instruments." *Journal of Financial and Quantitative Analysis* 8 (December 1973):807.

West, R. R. "An Alternative Approach to Predicting Bond Ratings." *Journal of Accounting Research* 8 (Spring 1970):118.

————. "Bond Ratings, Bond Yields and Financial Regulation: Some Findings." *Journal of Law and Economics* 16 (April 1973):159.

Williamson, J. Peter. "Bond Switching and the Computer." *Financial Analysts Journal* 26 (July-August 1970):65.

Warrants and Options

Black, Fischer, "Fact and Fantasy in the Use of Options." *Financial Analysts Journal* 31 (July-August 1975):36.

Black, Fischer, and Scholes, Myron. "The Pricing of Options and Corporate Liabilities." *Journal of Political Economy* 81 (May-June 1973):637.

————. "The Valuation of Option Contracts and a Test of Market Efficiency." *Journal of Finance* 27 (May 1972):399.

Chen, Andrew H. Y. "A Model of Warrant Pricing in a Dynamic Market." *Journal of Finance* 25 (December 1970):1041.

Hausman, W. H., and White, W. L. "Theory of Option Strategy under Risk Aversion." *Journal of Financial and Quantitative Analysis* 3 (September 1968):343.

Hettenhouse, George, W., and Puglisi, Donald J. "Investor Experience with Put and Call Options." *Financial Analysts Journal* 31 (July-August 1975):53.

McGuigan, James R., and King, William R. "Security Option Strategy under Risk Aversion: An Analysis." *Journal of Financial and Quantitative Analysis* 8 (January 1973):1.

Malkiel, Burton G., and Quandt, Richard E. "Can Options Improve an Institution's Performance?" *Institutional Investor* 2 (November 1968):55.

————. *Strategies and Rational Decisions in the Securities Option Market*. Cambridge: MIT Press, 1969.

Merton, R. C. "Theory of Rational Option Pricing." *Bell Journal of Economics and Management Science* 4 (Spring 1973):141.

Miller, Jerry D. "Effects of Longevity on Values of Stock Purchase Warrants." *Financial Analysts Journal* 27 (November-December 1971):78.

Puglisi, D. J. "A Rationale for Option Buyer Behavior: Theory and Evidence." *Quarterly Review of Economics and Business* 14 (Spring 1974):55.

Reback, Robert. "Risk and Return in CBOE and AMEX Option Trading." *Financial Analysts Journal* 31 (July-August 1975):42.

Rush, D. F. "An Empirical Examination of Factors Which Influence Warrant Prices." *Journal of Finance* 28 (December 1973):1449.

Shelton, John P. "The Relation of the Price of a Warrant to the Price of Its Associated Stock." *Financial Analysts Journal* 23 (May-June 1967):143.

Stoll, H. R. "The Relationship between Put and Call Option Prices." *Journal of Finance* 24 (December 1969):801.

Van Horne, James C. "Warrant Valuation in Relation to Volatility and Opportunity Cost." *Industrial Management Review* (Spring 1969).

Securities Markets

Abbott, Howard Strickland. *A Treatise on the Law of Public Securities.* Chicago: Callaghan, 1913.

Atkins, Williard Earl. *The Regulation of the Security Markets.* Washington, D.C.: Brookings Institution, 1946.

Baker, G. "The Martin Report: Blueprint for Constructive Reform." *Financial Analysts Journal* 27 (November-December 1971):20.

Baruch, Hurd. *Wall Street: Security Risk.* Baltimore, Md.: Penguin Books, 1972.

Baxter, W. F. "NYSE Commission Rates: A Private Cartel Goes Public." *Stanford Law Review* 22 (April 1970):675.

Black, F. "Toward a Fully Automated Stock Exchange." *Financial Analysts Journal* 27 (July-August 1971):29; (November-December 1971):24.

Brooks, John. *The Go-Go Years.* New York: Weybright and Talley, 1973.

Cherrington, Homer Virgil. *The Investor and the Securities Act.* Washington, D.C.: American Council on Public Affairs, 1942.

Commerce Clearing House. *Federal Securities Law Reporter.* New York: Commerce Clearing House, 1933.

Davant, J. W. "The Martin Report: An Answer to the Critics." *Financial Analysts Journal* 27 (November-December 1971):14.

Demsetz, H. "The Cost of Transacting." *Quarterly Journal of Economics* 82 (February 1968):33.

Eiteman, Wilford J., Dice, Charles A., and Eiteman, David K. *The Stock Market.* 4th ed. New York: McGraw-Hill, 1966.

Eiteman, Wilford J., and Eiteman, Sylvia C. *Nine Leading Stock Exchanges.* Ann Arbor, Mich.: University of Michigan Press., 1968.

Farrar, D. E. "Toward a Central Market System: Wall Street's Slow Retreat into the Future." *Journal of Financial and Quantitative Analysis* 9 (November 1974):815.

________. "Wall Street's Proposed 'Great Leap Backward.' " *Financial Analysts Journal* 27 (September-October 1971):14.

Feuerstein, Donald M. "The Third and Fourth Markets." *Financial Analysts Journal* 28 (July-August 1972):57.

________. "Toward a National System of Securities Exchanges: The Third and Fourth Markets." *Financial Analysts Journal* 28 (July-August 1972):57.

Freund, W. C. "The Historical Role of the Individual Investor in the Corporate Equity Market." *Journal of Contemporary Business* 3 (Winter 1974):1.

________. "Issues Confronting the Stock Markets in a Period of Rising Institutionalization." *Journal of Financial and Quantitative Analysis* 7 (supp., March 1972): 1687.

Friend, Irwin. "Effect of Institutionalization of Savings on the Long-Term for the Securities Industry." *Journal of Financial and Quantitative Analysis* 7 (supp., March 1972):1691.

Friend, Irwin, and Blume, Marshall E. *The Consequences of Competitive Commissions on the New York Stock Exchange*. Philadelphia: Rodney White Center for Financial Research, Wharton School of Business, University of Pennsylvania, 1972.

Friend, Irwin, G. W., and Winn, W. J. *The Over-the-Counter Securities Markets*. New York: McGraw-Hill, 1958.

Friend, Irwin, Longstreet, James R., Mendelson, Morris, Miller, Ervin, and Hess, Arleigh. *Investment Banking and the New Issues Market*. New York: World, 1967.

Galbraith, John Kenneth. *The Great Crash*. Boston: Houghton-Mifflin, 1954.

Hazard, John W., and Christie, Milton. *The Investment Business*. New York: Harper & Row, 1964.

Henning, C. N., Pigott, William, and Scott, R. H. *Financial Markets and the Economy*. Englewood Cliffs, N.J.: Prentice-Hall, 1974.

James, Ralph and Estelle. "Disputed Role of the Stock Exchange Specialists." *Harvard Business Review* 40 (May-June 1962):133.

Jennings, Richard W. "The New York Stock Exchange and the Commission Rate Struggle." *Business Lawyer* (November 1965).

———. *Securities Regulation: Cases and Materials*. Brooklyn: Foundation Press, 1963.

Jones, L. D. "Some Contributions of the Institutional Investor Study." *Journal of Finance* 27 (May 1972):305.

Kraus, Alan, and Stoll, Hans. "Price Impacts of Block Trading on the New York Stock Exchange." *Journal of Finance* 27 (June 1972):569.

Leffler, George L., and Farwell, Loring C. *The Stock Market*. 3d ed. New York: Ronald Press, 1963.

Loll, Leo M., and Buckley, Julian G. *The Over-the-Counter Securities Markets*. 3d ed. Englewood Cliffs, N.J.: Prentice-Hall, 1967.

Loomis, Carol J. "How The Terrible Two-Tier Market Came to Wall Street." *Fortune* (July 1973).

Loss, Louis. *Securities Regulation*. Boston: Little, Brown, 1951.

Manne, Henry G., ed. *Economic Policy and the Regulation of Corporate Securities* Washington, D.C.: American Enterprise Institute, 1969.

Martin, William McChesney, Jr. *The Securities Markets: A Report with Recommendations*. Submitted to the Board of Governors of the New York Stock Exchange, August 5, 1971.

Massaro, Vincent G. "The Future of the Securities Industry." *Conference Board Record*, February 1972.

Mayer, Martin. *Wall Street: Men and Money*. New York: Collier Books, 1966.

McDonald, John G. "Pricing of Initial Equity Issues: The French Sealed Bid Auction." *Journal of Business* 47 (January 1974):37.

Mendelson, Morris. *From Automated Quotes to Automated Trading: Restructuring the Stock Market in the U.S.* Bulletin of the Institute of Finance, Graduate School of Business Administration, New York University, nos. 80-82, March 1972.

———. "The 'Martin Report' and Its Aftermath." *Bell Journal of Economics and Management Science* 4 (Spring 1973):250.

———. "Nostalgia versus the Computer: The Issue of Stock Market Reform." *Wharton Quarterly* (Fall 1971):32.

Murray, R. F. "Indirect Investment in the Securities Market and the Individual Investor." *Journal of Contemporary Business* 3 (Winter 1974):63.

Nadler, Marcus. *The Money Market and Its Institutions*. New York: Ronald Press, 1955.

New York Stock Exchange. *Crisis in the Securities Industry: A Chronology, 1967-1970*. New York: The Exchange, July 30, 1971.

Ney, Richard. *The Wall Street Gang*. New York: Praeger, 1974.

Petrillo, H. V., and Bullock, C. L. *Processing Securities Transactions*. New York: Ronald Press, 1969.

Regan, Donald T. *A View From the Street*. New York: New American Library, 1972.

Reilly, Frank K. "Evidence Regarding Segmented Stock Market." *Journal of Finance* 27 (June 1972):607.

Robbins, Sidney. *The Securities Markets: Operations and Issues*. New York: Free Press, 1966.

Robinson, Roland I. *Postwar Market for State and Local Government Securities*. Princeton: Princeton University Press, 1960.

Robinson, Roland I., and Wrightsman, Dwane. *Financial Markets: The Accumulation and Allocation of Wealth*. New York: McGraw-Hill, 1974.

Rolo, Charles J., and Nelson, George J. *The Anatomy of Wall Street*. New York: J. B. Lippincott, 1968.

Securities and Exchange Commission. *The Future Structure of the Securities Market*. Washington, D.C.: The Commission, February 2, 1972.

________. *Study of Unsafe and Unsound Practices of Brokers and Dealers*. H. Doc. 92-231. 92nd Cong., 1st sess., 1971.

________. *White Paper on the Structure of a Central Market System*. Washington, D.C.: The Commission, March 30, 1973.

Slaughter, William C., and Reilly, Frank K. "The Effect of Dual Markets on Common Stock Market Making." *Journal of Financial and Quantitative Analysis* 8 (March 1973):167.

Smidt, S. "The Changing Relative Roles of Individuals and Institutions in the Stock Market." *Journal of Contemporary Business* 3 (Winter 1974):13.

________. "Which Road to an Efficient Stock Market?" *Financial Analysts Journal* 27 (September-October 1971):8.

Smith, Adam [pseudo]. *The Money Game*. New York: Random House, 1967.

________. *Super Money*. New York: Random House, 1972.

Sobel, Robert. *The Big Board*. New York: The Free Press, 1965.

________. *The Money Manias*. New York: Weybright and Talley, 1974.

Stevenson, Richard A. "Odd-Lot Trading in the Stock Market and Its Market Impact: Comment." *Journal of Financial and Quantitative Analysis* 8 (June 1973):527.

Studness, C. M. "New York Stock Exchange Trading in Perspective." *Financial Analysts Journal* 24 (November-December 1968):26.

Tinic, S. M. E. "The Economics of Liquidity Services." *Quarterly Journal of Economics* 86 (February 1972):79.

Tinic, Seha, and West, Richard R. "Competition and the Pricing of Dealer Services in the Over-the-Counter Market." *Journal of Financial and Quantitative Analysis* 7 (June 1972):1707.

________. "Marketability of Common Stocks in Canada and the U.S.A.: A Comparison of Agent Versus Dealer Dominated Markets." *Journal of Finance* 29 (June 1974): 729.

U.S. Congress. House. Committee on Interstate and Foreign Commerce. *Legislative History of Securities Acts Amendments of 1975*. 94th Cong., 1st sess., 1975.

U.S. Congress. House. Committee on Interstate and Foreign Commerce. Subcommittee on Commerce and Finance. *Securities Industry Study: Report and Hearings*. 92d Cong., 1st and 2d sess., 1972.

U.S. Congress. Senate. Committee on Banking, Housing and Urban Affairs. Subcommittee on Securities. *Clearance and Settlement of Securities Transactions: Hearings*. 92d Cong., 2d sess., 1972.

________. *Fixed Rates and Institutional Membership: Hearings*. 93d Cong., 1st sess., 1973.

________. *Institutional Membership on National Securities Exchanges: Hearings*. 92d. Cong., 2d sess., 1972.

________. *National Securities Market System Act of 1973: Hearings*. 93d Cong., 1st sess., 1973.

———. *Regulation of Clearing Agencies and Transfer Agents: Hearings.* 93d Cong., 1st sess., 1973.

———. *Securities Act Amendments of 1975: Hearings.* 94th Cong., 1st sess., 1975.

———. *Security Industry Study: Report and Hearings.* 93d Cong., 1st sess., 1973.

———. *Stock Exchange Commission Rates: Hearings.* 92d. Cong., 2d sess., 1972.

U.S. Congress. Senate. Committee on Finance. *The Role of Institutional Investors in the Stock Market.* 93d Cong., 1st sess., 1973.

U.S. Congress. Senate. Committee on Finance. Subcommittee on Financial Markets. *Financial Markets: Hearings.* 93d Cong., 1st. sess., 1973.

Walter, James. E. *The Role of Regional Security Exchanges.* Berkeley: University of California Press, 1957.

Weeden, D. E. "Competition: Key to Market Structure." *Journal of Financial and Quantitative Analysis* 7 (supp., March 1972):1696.

Welles, Chris. "The Individual Investor and the Problem of Institutional Power." *Journal of Contemporary Business* 3 (Winter 1974):73.

———. "Should Money Management and Brokerage Be Separated?" *Institutional Investor* 4 (June 1971):21.

West, Richard R. "Institutional Trading and the Changing Stock Market." *Financial Analysts Journal* 27 (May-June 1971):17.

West, Richard R., and Tinic, Seha M. *The Economics of the Stock Market.* New York: Praeger, 1971.

———. "Institutionalization: Its Impact On the Provision of Marketability Services and the Individual Investor." *Journal of Contemporary Business* 3 (Winter 1974): 25.

———. "Minimum Commission Rates on New York Stock Exchange Transactions." *Bell Journal of Economics and Management Science* 2 (Autumn 1971):577.

Willet, Edward R. *Fundamentals of Securities Markets.* New York: Appleton-Century-Crofts, 1971.

Youngblood, C. E. "A Publicly Owned Stock Exchange?" *Financial Analysts Journal* 25 (November-December 1969):104A.

Technical Analysis

Alexander, Sidney S. "Price Movements in Speculative Markets: Trends or Random Walks." *Industrial Management Review* 2 (May 1961):7.

Barnes, A., and Downes, D. H. "A Reexamination of the Empirical Distribution of Stock Price Changes." *Journal of the American Statistical Association* 68 (June 1973): 348.

Bishop, George W. *Charles H. Dow and the Dow Theory.* New York: Appleton-Century-Crofts, 1960.

Black, F. "Implications of the Random Walk Hypothesis for Portfolio Management." *Financial Analysts Journal* 27 (March-April 1971):16.

Cheng, P. L., and Deets, H. K. "Portfolio Returns and the Random Walk Theory." *Journal of Finance* 26 (March 1971):11.

Cohen, A. W. *The Chartcraft Method of Point and Figure Trading.* New York: Chartcraft, 1966.

Cootner, Paul, ed. *The Random Character of Stock Market Prices*, Rev. ed. Cambridge: MIT Press, 1967.

Dines, James. *How the Average Investor Can Use Technical Analysis for Stock Profits.* New York: James Dines, 1972.

Drew, Garfield A. *New Methods for Profit in the Stock Market.* 4th ed. Wells, Vt.: Fraser, 1966.

Edwards, Robert D., and Magee, John. *Technical Analysis of Stock Trends.* 5th ed. Springfield, Mass.: John Magee, 1966.

Emery, John T. "The Information Content of Daily Market Indicators." *Journal of Financial and Quantitative Analysis* 8 (March 1973):183.

Emory, E. S. *When to Sell Stocks*. Homewood, Ill.: Dow Jones-Irwin, 1973.

Fama, Eugene F. "The Behavior of Stock Market Prices." *Journal of Business* 38 (January 1965):34.

________. "Efficient Capital Markets: A Review of Theory and Empirical Work." *Journal of Finance* 25 (May 1970):383.

________. "Random Walks in Stock Market Prices." *Financial Analysts Journal* 21 (September-October 1965):55.

Fama, Eugene F., and Blume, Marshall E. "Filter Rules and Stock Market Trading." *Journal of Business* 39 (January 1966):226.

Freeman, George K. "Advance-Decline Line: A Clue to the Underlying Strength or Weakness of the Market." *Barron's*, January 21, 1963.

Godfrey, Michael D., Granger, Clive W. J., and Morgenstern, Oscar. "The Random Walk Hypothesis of Stock Market Behavior." *Kyklos* 17 (January 1964):1.

Granville, Joseph E. *New Key to Stock Market Profits*. Englewood Cliffs, N.J.: Prentice-Hall, 1963.

________. *A Strategy of Daily Stock Market Timing for Maximum Profit*. Englewood Cliffs, N.J.: Prentice-Hall, 1960.

Granger, Clive W. J., and Morgenstern, Oscar. *Predictability of Stock Market Prices*. Lexington, Mass.: D. C. Heath, 1970.

Howrey, E. Philip. "Are Stock Prices Random or Predictable?" *Business Economics* 1 (Summer 1965):21.

Investors Intelligence, Inc. *Encyclopedia of Stock Market Techniques*. 2d ed., rev. Larchmont, N.Y., 1965.

James, F. E. "Monthly Moving Averages: An Effective Investment Tool?" *Journal of Financial and Quantitative Analysis* 3 (September 1968):315.

Jensen, Michael C., and Benington, George A. "Random Walks and Technical Theories: Some Additional Evidence." *Journal of Finance* 25 (May 1970):469.

Jiler, William L. *How Charts Can Help You in the Market*. New York: Commodity Research Publications Corp., 1961.

Kerrigan, Thomas J. "The Short Interest Ratio and Its Component Parts." *Financial Analysts Journal* 30 (November-December 1974):45.

Lerro, Anthony J., and Swayne, Charles B. *Selection of Securities: Technical Analysis of Stock Market Prices*. Braintree, Mass.: D. H. Mark, 1970.

Levy, Robert A. *The Relative Strength Concept of Common Stock Price Forecasting*. Larchmont, N.Y.: Investors Intelligence, 1968.

________. "Relative Strength as a Criterion for Investment Selection." *Journal of Finance* 22 (December 1967):595.

________. "The Predictive Significance of Five-Point Chart Patterns." *Journal of Business* 44 (July 1971):316.

Malkiel, Burton G. *A Random Walk Down Wall Street*. New York: Norton, 1973.

McQuown, J. A. "Technical and Fundamental Analysis and Capital Market Theory." *Journal of Bank Research* 4 (Spring 1973):8.

Nawrocki, David N., and Philappatos, George C. "The Information Inaccuracy of Stock Market Forecasts: Some New Evidence of Dependence on the New York Stock Exchange." *Journal of Financial and Quantitative Analysis* 9 (June 1974):445.

Neill, Humphrey B. *The Art of Contrary Thinking*. Caldwell, Ind.: Caxton Printers, 1967.

O'Connor, William P. *Techniques for Maximum Market Profits*. Englewood Cliffs, N.J.: Prentice-Hall, 1964.

Pinches, George E. "The Random Walk Hypothesis and Technical Analysis." *Financial Analysts Journal* 26 (March-April 1970):51.

Renshaw, E. F. and V. D. "Test of the Random Walk Hypothesis." *Financial Analysts Journal* 26 (September-October 1970):51.

Rhea, Robert. *The Dow Theory*. New York: Vail-Ballou Press, 1959.

Roberts, Harry V. "Stock Market Patterns and Financial Analysis: Methodological Suggestions." *Journal of Finance* 14 (March 1959):1.

Samuelson, Paul A. "Proof That Properly Anticipated Prices Fluctuate Randomly." *Industrial Management Review* 6 (Spring 1965):41.

Seligman, Daniel. "Playing the Market with Charts." *Fortune* 65 (February 1962):119.

———. "The Mystique of Point-and-Figure." *Fortune* 65 (March 1962):113.

Seneca, Joseph J. "Short Interest: Bearish or Bullish." *Journal of Finance* 22 (March 1967):67.

Staby, Ernest J. *Stock Market Trading*. New York: Cornerstone Library, 1970.

Weintraub, Robert E. "On Speculative Prices and Random Walks: A Denial." *Journal of Finance* 18 (March 1963):59.

Zieg, Kermit C. *Ticker Tape Trading*. Larchmont, N.Y.: Investors Intelligence, 1970.

Zinbarg, Edward D. "A Vote of No Confidence in the Confidence Index." *Institutional Investor* 1 (March 1967):37.

INDEX